MODERN
COMMERCIAL AIRCRAFT

MODERN
COMMERCIAL AIRCRAFT

Günter Endres

William Green • Gordon Swanborough • John Mowinski

PUBLISHED BY
SALAMANDER BOOKS LIMITED
LONDON

A SALAMANDER BOOK

Published by Salamander Books Limited
8 Blenheim Court
Brewery Road
London N7 9NT
United Kingdom

9 8 7 6 5 4 3 2 1

©Salamander Books Ltd. 1998

ISBN 1 84065 022 2

Printed in Italy

CREDITS

Editor:
Christopher Westhorp

Designers:
John Heritage and Mark Holt

Cutaway and three-view drawings:
Pilot Press Ltd, Mike Badrocke and Quadrant
Picture Library.

Diagram artwork:
Mike Badrocke © Salamander Books Ltd

Filmset:
SX DTP Ltd

Colour reproduction:
G. Canale & C. spa, Italy

AUTHOR AND EDITOR

Günter Endres started writing in the early
1970s, initially concentrating on historic airline
subjects before broadening out to encompass
commercial aviation as a whole. In the first 20
years this remained a hobby, while continuing
his profession in structural engineering, but in
1990 he joined the monthly trade journal
Interavia, as Business Reporter, then Market
Research Editor and finally Air Transport Editor.
After the sale of the magazine back to
Switzerland, he joined the freelance fraternity of
aviation journalists. He is presently News Editor
for *Jane's Airport Review* and Yearbook Editor of
Jane's Helicopter Markets and Systems, and is
working on three books for Airlife on the
McDonnell Douglas DC-10 and Airbus A300 and
A310. Several books have been written for Ian
Allan, among them *British Airways, McDonnell
Douglas DC-9/MD-80, British Aircraft
Manufacturers since 1908*, and three editions of
abc Airline Liveries. His articles have appeared in
most aviation journals, including *Flight
International, Air International, Aircraft Illustrated,
Air Pictorial, Regional Air, Commuter World,
Aviation News, Avmark* and *Aviation Strategy*,
and he prepares the airline sections in
Euromoney's *Airfinance Annual*.

CONTRIBUTORS

Brian Walters is a freelance writer and licensed pilot. He maintains a wide range of interests in aviation and often writes on technological subjects in other fields.

PRINCIPAL AUTHORS OF THE ORIGINAL (1987) EDITION

William Green entered aviation journalism more than 50 years ago with the *Air Training Corps Gazette* (now *Air Pictorial*) and has gained an international reputation for his many works of aviation reference, covering both aeronautical history and the current aviation scene. In 1971 he and Gordon Swanborough jointly created the monthly *Air International*, and they have also produced a number of books under joint authorship, including *Flying Colours* and *The Complete Book of Fighters*.

Gordon Swanborough has spent nearly all his working life as an aviation journalist and author. For 20 years he worked for the weekly magazine *The Aeroplane*, then in 1965 he became editor of *Flying Review International*, and in 1971 he joined forces with William Green to create *Air International*. As a team these two authors were also responsible for the production of the thrice-yearly, *Air Enthusiast*, and the annual *RAF Yearbook*.

John Mowinski has become an established contributor to a number of well known aviation journals, newspapers and books, writing on subjects ranging from aircraft manufacturers and operators to the development and application of high technology materials in the aerospace field.

CONTRIBUTORS

Roy Braybrook is a freelance aviation writer and consultant. He was formerly with Hawker Aircraft.

Ken Fulton contributes articles and newscolumns to aviation publications on both sides of the Atlantic.

Don Parry spent 33 years as a flight engineer with the RAF, BOAC and British Airways.

Bill Gunston, a former RAF pilot and instructor, is the former technical editor of the Flight International and author of numerous books on aviation topics.

Appreciation
This major update was to have been a joint effort by myself and my long-time friend and colleague John Cook. However, only days after we had formulated our plan and decided on a division of labour – over a pint of beer – John died suddenly.

I was abroad at the time and the news came like a bolt out of the blue. I know that John's experience and diligence would have made an immeasurable contribution to this book, but I hope my sole input would have met with his approval.

**This work is dedicated to
the memory of John.**

CONTENTS

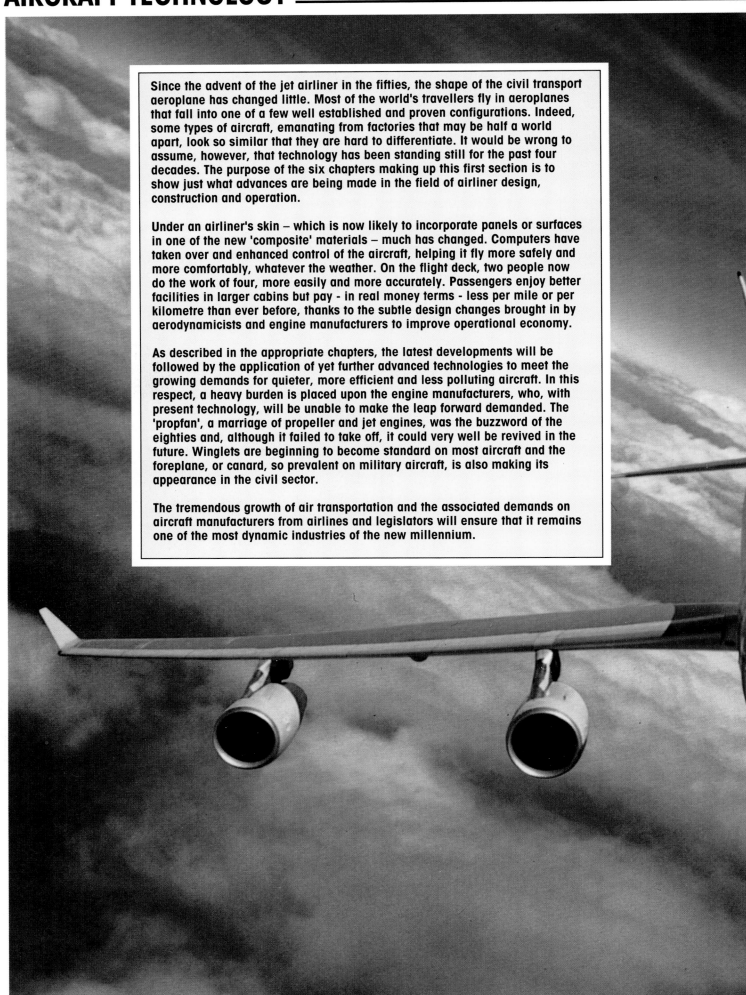

Since the advent of the jet airliner in the fifties, the shape of the civil transport aeroplane has changed little. Most of the world's travellers fly in aeroplanes that fall into one of a few well established and proven configurations. Indeed, some types of aircraft, emanating from factories that may be half a world apart, look so similar that they are hard to differentiate. It would be wrong to assume, however, that technology has been standing still for the past four decades. The purpose of the six chapters making up this first section is to show just what advances are being made in the field of airliner design, construction and operation.

Under an airliner's skin – which is now likely to incorporate panels or surfaces in one of the new 'composite' materials – much has changed. Computers have taken over and enhanced control of the aircraft, helping it fly more safely and more comfortably, whatever the weather. On the flight deck, two people now do the work of four, more easily and more accurately. Passengers enjoy better facilities in larger cabins but pay - in real money terms - less per mile or per kilometre than ever before, thanks to the subtle design changes brought in by aerodynamicists and engine manufacturers to improve operational economy.

As described in the appropriate chapters, the latest developments will be followed by the application of yet further advanced technologies to meet the growing demands for quieter, more efficient and less polluting aircraft. In this respect, a heavy burden is placed upon the engine manufacturers, who, with present technology, will be unable to make the leap forward demanded. The 'propfan', a marriage of propeller and jet engines, was the buzzword of the eighties and, although it failed to take off, it could very well be revived in the future. Winglets are beginning to become standard on most aircraft and the foreplane, or canard, so prevalent on military aircraft, is also making its appearance in the civil sector.

The tremendous growth of air transportation and the associated demands on aircraft manufacturers from airlines and legislators will ensure that it remains one of the most dynamic industries of the new millennium.

ANATOMY OF A FLIGHT

For the individuals who make up the crew of Flight 123 the day starts just like any other: relaxed breakfast; take the dog for a walk; deliver children to school or just quietly read the mail. Packing is done quickly and with little concern; it is all part of a long established pattern.

Depending upon how far away from the airport each one lives, their departure times are scattered, and cars, buses or trains finally deliver three flight deck crew members and 14 cabin crew members to the airport.

The aeroplane that is to take them – or, more specifically that they are to take – to New York is already airborne as they make their departures, inbound from Zürich at the end of a flight from Australia. It lands at about the time that the first crew member leaves home to begin a 75-minute journey. The incoming crew has handed over details of any mechanical problems or defects, and the engineering staff begins to ready the aircraft for its next flight.

In the airline's operations centre the flight planning staff has already interrogated the computer for flight plan details and these are being printed out to offer the most fuel-efficient operation, within the constraints of the available North Atlantic track systems. Approximate passenger figures are being assessed, to confirm the amount of freight that can also be accommodated in the large underfloor holds, which are a distinctive feature of the Boeing 747 that is operating the service.

Catering staff supervise the loading of the catering trays, food and beverages into metal containers that are then packed into easy-loading trucks, ready to be taken out to the aeroplane.

Although the complete crew will be operating as a well-trained team in a closely-knit environment for the next few hours, they see little of each other on arrival at the airport. Members of the cabin crew meet for a briefing under the supervision of the chief steward, and are apprised of the number of

The Route

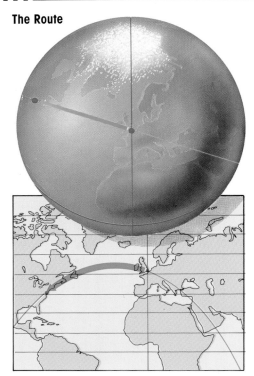

Above: Many passengers scanning their London to New York route map in the in-flight magazine must wonder why it seems to follow a curved path north over Canada. In fact, when viewed on the globe, the path can be seen to be a straight line between the two points. It is part of the 'great circle' route.

Below: Although it has only a single runway, London's Gatwick Airport manages to handle very large numbers of passengers by virtue of efficient terminal buildings and automatic 'people movers.' Regarded previously as a charter airport, Gatwick is now increasingly used by scheduled carriers.

passengers and any special requirements. These can vary from care for an invalid or handicapped passenger, through various forms of dietary requirements (six vegetarian and four kosher meals have been requested on this flight) to VIPs or the occasional show-biz personality, with the accompanying complications of press and public interest.

The three flight deck crew (captain, co-pilot and flight engineer) meet at the flight planning office. Often they are complete strangers to each other, and it is remarkable testimony to standardization and training procedures that within an hour of their first meeting, these total strangers can take a massive 362,880kg (800,000lb) aeroplane into the air with complete confidence in each other's abilities.

The flight plan is offered for the crew's inspection and a close look is taken at the meteorological reports. Today the weather looks good, with no problems greater than a little clear air turbulence (CAT) about half way across. The whole of the New York area is forecast to be fine and warm.

As the time for take-off approaches, the complete load figure has been decided by the control centre and this allows the final fuel figure to be calculated and approved by the captain. Already a provisional figure has been sent to the refuelling team which has started loading the many tons of fuel that will be needed to fly the aeroplane the 2,600 nautical miles (4,840km) or so across the Atlantic and to provide the reserves that may be called upon should something unforeseen extend the flight's destination.

At this point, the engineer heads out to the aircraft to begin his pre-flight checks. The two pilots attend to the remaining paperwork and the captain familiarizes himself with a quick read of a confidential file. This contains details of security procedures or related subjects, underlining the constant concern and care now taken by airlines to minimize the problems of international terrorism.

On arrival at the aircraft, the flight engineer ensures that the final fuel figure is acknowledged

Above: While the captain and his crew are responsible for conducting the aircraft from take-off to landing, a great deal of the necessary planning goes on on the ground. Airlines with fleets running into dozens or even hundreds of aircraft must maintain flight planning and operations centres such as this one to arrange each aircraft's daily schedule.

and he is briefed by the ground engineering supervisor about the state of the aircraft. Any defects or problems are invariably known as 'snags', and these are considered at this point; there is an established practice of allowing certain defects, which in no way affect flight safety, to be carried over, under the name of acceptable deferred defects (ADDs). Typically, these include parts of a galley, lighting or a broken seat arm which cannot be replaced in the time available before scheduled departure. Occasionally, a more complex ADD may be in the book and this has to be checked to ensure that the deficiency does not entail an operational limitation, which would then have to be allowed for.

The flight engineer now begins the short safety check, which is a method of ensuring that the aircraft is in a suitable condition to receive electrical and pneumatic power without the accidental operation of a system. He also checks out the three inertial navigation systems (INS) and inserts the co-ordinates of the present position (in this case the airport ramp), details of which are supplied in a manual. This is an important aspect of the preparation, for the INS equipment needs some time to run up and align in a process that cannot be commenced until the units receive the initial input from the flight engineer or pilot.

With the two pilots having now arrived on board, the co-pilot settles down to begin his own series of checks. All the pre-flight checks are divided between the co-pilot and flight engineer, while the captain ensures that all of the requested paperwork is in order, and then proceeds to load the three INS units with the waypoints as depicted on the flight plan: these are the pre-computed points along the aircraft's planned course that the INS will use to fly the aircraft accurately from London to New York.

The flight engineer leaves the flight deck to carry out an external check. Refuelling is almost complete, but it has been noticed that one of the tyres has a deep cut near the crown. It is quickly agreed that this has to be changed before take-off. The flight engineer makes a mental note to warn the co-pilot to leave the brakes alone until the job is finished – otherwise, brake plates are likely to be falling out of place and a real delay would ensue.

Returning to the flight deck, the flight engineer begins his own instrument panel check and assures

the captain that all pre-flight preparations are going well and to schedule.

During this time, members of the cabin crew are 'dressing' the aeroplane – putting out the magazines, supervising the loading of the food and amenities, and ensuring that all the equipment is working properly. This quickly reveals a problem: a hot cup in one of the rear galleys is not working. The chief steward heads to the flight deck to pass on the complaint. Along the way he is told by a stewardess that one of the lavatories does not flush. Passing these snags to the flight engineer, the chief steward

Above: The Boeing 777 is the most widely used of the new generation of twin-engined airliners which are regarded as perfectly safe to fly long non-stop sectors over water. The new 'big twins' are better suited to 'thinner' routes than the larger capacity Boeing 747.

Below: The captain (left) and first officer prepare for take-off in a Boeing 767, going through a carefully prepared and well-rehearsed sequence of pre-flight checks. Modern cockpit technology allows the largest of jetliners to be flown by a two-pilot crew, instead of the three or four once required.

makes the point that with a full passenger load there is a need for a full set of serviceable lavatories.

Perhaps the only bad thing about the Boeing 747 is the sheer size of the aeroplane. Crew members can lose a lot of weight running up and down stairs trying to find other staff. It can also take a lot of time, and in the 60 minutes of pre-flight preparation, time is at a premium. Fortunately, all airlines have a useful radio link with their respective control and maintenance departments, and this is usually known as company frequency. This is now used to call for a replacement hot cup and attention for the lavatory.

Meanwhile, the first passengers appear on board, and the cabin crew swings into its well-rehearsed routine of polite firmness and distant familiarity, which are the hallmarks of their trade.

Suddenly, in a flurry of activity, three airline ground staff appear on the flight deck – refueller, engineering supervisor and a young lady with the completed loadsheet. The signing of these documents represents the handing over of the aeroplane to the captain's control, and it is time to go. Pre-start checks proceed, many with a particular emphasis on the INS.

More recent models of the Boeing 747s and other later-generation airliners such as the Airbus family, are fitted with flight management systems (FMS) which have automated much of the flight planning and cruise control procedures. Indeed, new and more powerful FMS can handle such functions as communication, navigation and surveillance/air traffic management (CNS/ATM), which is revolutionising airliner navigation and control.

Begun in the early 1990s in the Asia/Pacific region and gradually introduced in other parts of the world since then, the Future Air Navigation System (FANS) enables airliners to make primary use of the satellite-based Global Positioning system (GPS) to provide highly accurate automatic position reports anywhere in the world. These advances are important steps along the road to complete automation on the flight deck and in the fullness of time doubtless most, if not all, airliners will be able to make better use of the skies by reducing both longitudinal and lateral separation to 30 nautical miles (nm) (55km).

READY TO GO

However, the Boeing 747 'Classic' operating this flight over the north Atlantic uses a lateral and longitudinal separation of 80nm (146km) and the co-pilot now obtains start-up clearance from the control tower together with the initial airways clearance, which will allow the aeroplane to go on its way. This is known as the standard instrument departure (SID) pattern and it is carefully reviewed by all crew members.

Start-up and taxi out are quickly done, as the cabin crew provide the cabin briefing on emergency procedures – a task that on some aircraft is now performed by means of a video presentation. Another ritual that often interests passengers is the call from the flight deck for all doors to 'automatic'. This is an operation which arms the door escape slide mechanisms. In the event of an incident requiring rapid evacuation of the cabin, simply opening the door will drive it out under the force of compressed gas and initiate inflation of the escape slide. It can be appreciated that it is also important to

Above: Airline catering using meals prepared prior to take-off, is now an advanced science.

Right: Most travellers today spend as much time at the airports as on the flight. This is Heathrow's Terminal 4.

return this system to manual after landing to prevent embarrassment!

As the 747 taxies out to the runway holding point, other checks are being made, including setting the wing flaps and ensuring that everything is ready for take-off. The height of the 747's flight deck above the ground means that judgement of ground speed is not always easy, and here the INS is useful in displaying an indication of ground speed to the pilot in the cockpit.

Among his pre-flight calculations, the co-pilot has

ates down the runway the co-pilot calls out the airspeed indications: V_1 the 'decision' speed, after which is it safer to continue take-off in the event of engine failure: V_R the 'rotation' speed at which the nosewheel is lifted to get the aircraft into its take-off attitude; and V_2 the lowest speed at which the aircraft can safely be lifted off the runway. Another flight is on its way.

As the climb progresses and the flaps are retracted, the automatic pilot is selected and the crew settles down to a six- or seven-hour stint of careful monitoring and closely co-ordinated procedures. As England's West Country slides past underneath, the co-pilot calls the oceanic air-traffic control (ATC) centre at Shannon to receive details of the clearance across the Atlantic. This should match the agreed track presented at London. There are times when this has not happened, because of congestion of the transatlantic airways, in which case there is a short period of intense flight deck activity as the new set of co-ordinates is accepted and placed into the computers.

Today, all is well and the operation settles down at the requested flight level, which is the current optimum for the weight of the aircraft. As fuel is burnt *en route*, the weight goes down and the aircraft will be climbed, in a series of steps, to ensure the most efficient use of fuel.

The workload on the flight deck is reduced at this point and if necessary one crew member at a time can take a few minutes rest away from the flight deck, or eat a meal. The two remaining crew members can still reach all the necessary controls to deal with any emergency that may arise. As the flight progresses and careful navigation checks are made, a reading of the figures for fuel consumed indicates that all is proceeding well, with even a suggestion that, by the time the aeroplane reaches New York, there will have been a slight saving in fuel over the original calculated figure. Perhaps it is a particularly clean aeroplane today.

As the flight continues, other vapour trails can be seen, all of them pointing roughly in the same direction, which is comforting! As each waypoint is reached, the co-pilot calls the applicable control centre to report the position and, if appropriate,

worked out a set of speeds to suit the prevailing conditions. These take account of variables such as aircraft weight, meteorological conditions (temperature, wind speed and direction, etc.), length of runway and airfield height. With the help of an individual graph for each runway and airfield, a set of figures can be derived. Known as V_R, V_1 and V_2, these signify critical aspects of the flight envelope during the take-off run, and are set on the airspeed indicator by means of small plastic cursors or 'bugs' for rapid visual identification.

Final take-off clearance is received from the airport control tower, and the aeroplane is carefully lined up at the end of the active runway. A last look around, and the captain pushes the thrust levers forward a small amount. The flight engineer carefully checks the response of the engines, notes all parameters and calls 'Engines stabilized'. Power is then increased and the flight engineer carefully adjusts the levers under the captain's hand to ensure that the maximum power settings for the prevailing conditions are not exceeded. As the aeroplane acceler-

Left: The control tower is an important and easily-recognised part of every airport. Although the control of aircraft along their designated routes is exercised chiefly from darkened radar rooms in control centres. The visual control room – this one is at Aberdeen – is concerned only with the aircraft's final approach, its take-off, and ground movements.

Above: Controllers in the London Air Traffic Control Centre look after the aircraft flying on the designated airways over most of England. This particular group is concerned with one of the Terminal Control Areas (TMAs), responsible for traffic around London's principal airports of Heathrow, Gatwick, Luton, Stansted and London City.

Right: The airways in the airspace over the UK, up to 7,467m (24,500ft), are divided between two Flight Information Regions, London and Scottish, and the aircraft flying in them are controlled from one of three centres (London, Manchester and Scottish) at any given time during their flight. The airways link Terminal Control Areas (TMAs) that block off all of the airspace around busy intersections and airports, the latter each having its own control zone extending from ground level to about 7,620m (25,000ft). The airways are normally 16km (10miles) wide and aircraft fly along them at carefully controlled intervals. Altitudes in 300m (1,000ft) steps are being used for aircraft flying in opposite directions.

Airways in UK Airspace

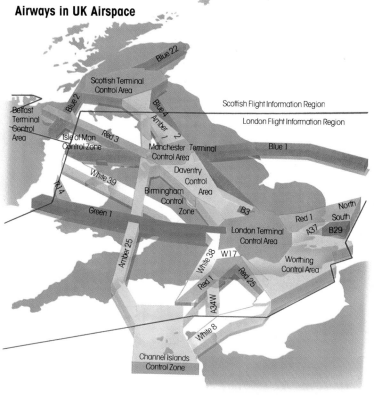

requests a change in height. The INS can carry up to nine waypoints at a time and about half way across the ocean the system has to be replenished with a new set of data to take the aeroplane on to New York. As was the case in London, this procedure is carefully checked. Radio contact over the ocean is by voice HF (high-frequency radio), although a VHF set is kept tuned to the emergency frequency and at least one crew member maintains a listening watch. This is always a requirement of ocean flying, but it is no less important to listen out for a message over sparsely populated land masses.

Back in the cabin, the passengers have by now been adequately fed and watered, served with duty-free requirements and are now given little choice but to watch the in-flight entertainment, or listen to one of the alternative audio entertainment channels. If they are flying with one of the more progressive airlines, they might be able to play blackjack or roulette, staking money by swiping their credit cards. To ensure they don't lose their shirt before the aircraft touches down, limits are put on stakes. Shopping is now also being added, but more usually it is one of the latest films keeping passengers entertained. To ensure that any film can be adequately viewed, it is usually necessary to pull down the cabin blinds; consequently, most passengers miss the awesome sight of the pack ice usually to be seen off Labrador.

As the North American land mass appears over the horizon, the crew begins to consider preparations for arrival at New York. *En-route* meteorological broadcasts have confirmed the good weather expectations, and the only concern now is the possibility of long air traffic delays. As Boston slips by, contact is established, on the company frequency, with New York and assurance is given that delays are minimal and a gate number is provided, this lat-

ter telling the crew where the aircraft will be parked on arrival.

Crew checks concerned with the arrival procedures are completed and a new set of performance figures compiled by the flight engineer, including details of the amount of diversion fuel available if for some reason it is not possible to land as planned at New York.

Clearance for descent is passed by the ATC and power is reduced as the 747 starts to nose down, some 30 minutes before the estimated time of arrival (ETA). The passengers barely notice any change in attitude, although a loud hiss of air as the engine bleed valves function often gives a clue to what is happening.

Most of the world's major airports offer a facility known as the automatic terminal information service (ATIS). This is a frequently updated recorded message giving details of local weather conditions, runway in use and any unusual conditions. ATIS takes some of the verbal work-load off the air traffic controllers, although the Americans tend to have a habit of recording the details at very high speed, which can be irritating to tired crew members attempting to copy the information in long hand.

Today's message is mercifully brief, and the crew settles down to a period of concentration. Check lists are read in order and a sharp look-out is maintained at all times, for this is a very busy area for aer-

ial activity. At regular intervals the ATC calls with a brief 'Traffic 12 o'clock – height unknown' message and scanning usually reveals a small light aeroplane well below the 747.

ARRIVAL

As the airport comes into view, it can be seen that our flight is but one of many arrivals, expertly threaded by ATC into a long line of aircraft curving across the sea. Chatter on the radio is now virtually constant as aircraft are sequenced into the final landing pattern. As the arrivals runway grows larger, other aircraft are to be seen taking-off from the parallel runway, creating a scene of carefully organized three-dimensional chess.

Final landing checks completed, the wheels are lowered and flaps and throttles adjusted. Although the weather is good, all on-board equipment, includ-

Below: Flying may still be a thrill for a few, but it is boring for many, and in-flight entertainment has become commonplace, with films, videos, music, shopping and gambling offered on long flights.

Right: The safe conduct of a flight calls for the interrogation of many aids, some on-board the aircraft and others ground-based. In the last few moments of a flight, visual cues from runway lights are vital.

ing the instrument landing system (ILS), is used to ensure adequate monitoring and to prevent the aircraft lining up with the wrong runway. The intensity of the whole operation is emphasized by the rapidity with which aircraft land and clear the runway as ATC gives clearance to the following aircraft.

Everything is now looking good: the radio altimeter is ticking off the feet in precise steps, all the needles are pointing in the right direction and all systems are prepared for landing. There is just one more aeroplane ahead, and as this touches down a large cloud of blue smoke marks the contact of rubber on concrete. It rolls along the runway, visibly slowing and aiming for the first high-speed turn off, but suddenly it appears to brake and slow down, coming to a stop just as it turns off, with the tail protruding over the active runway.

Instinctively, the crew of Flight 123 mentally pre-

pares for an overshoot and as ATC calls 'go around, airplane blown tyre on runway' the operation is carried out precisely, smoothly and in accordance with well rehearsed drills. Go-around power is applied and the nose raised, 'Flaps 20' (a 20-deg setting) are selected, and as the co-pilot notes and calls out 'Positive rate of climb' the gear is selected up.

The crew finds this development more irritating than inconvenient; it will add another 20 minutes or so to the flight time and use up the fuel that had been saved by careful procedures on the way across. ATC is equal to the situation and by a series of rapid instructions brings the 747 back into a slot that enables the crew once again to establish the aeroplane on the ILS and this time accomplish a successful landing.

As the runway is cleared the aircraft's auxiliary power unit (APU) is started, to provide power after engines are shut down, and the final set of checks is started to prepare the aeroplane for parking. The members of the cabin crew quickly pass around the cabin to hand out the various coats and belongings that have been stored in the wardrobes – pausing also to place all doors on 'manual' in response to a call from the flight deck on the PA system.

As the parking bay is approached, the crew carefully lines up the aeroplane with a set of lights, to ensure accurate placing, and carefully edges the aircraft into position. As the brakes are applied by the captain, the flight engineer switches all of the services over to the APU and shuts down the engines. The remainder of the check list is read out and the paperwork is completed. Any defects which have become apparent are written up and the total time since starting engines is carefully noted in the log. The flight deck is then tidied up and the crew leaves for the pre-arranged hotel.

Tomorrow, the whole process starts all over again – in reverse!

Above: The world-wide spread of air transportation has at times outpaced the provision of ground facilities, but modern aircraft – this is a Saab 340 – are designed and equipped to be able to fly safely into and out of small and simply-equipped airfields.

Below: Journey's end: with passengers disembarked through the air bridge, a Ryanair Boeing 737 is made ready for its flight to Dublin. The carefully controlled pilot duty hours permit the same crew to fly the return flight but on very long flights, relief crews must be carried.

Right: Only a few frequent flyers have avoided the misery of a lost bag but an automatic baggage sortation system, of the kind used at Brisbane International Airport, has helped to relieve passenger anxiety by improving the overall airline record.

THE FLIGHT DECK

To the untutored eye, the first sight of the flight deck of a large transport aircraft often suggests a rather confused mass of dials, indicators, switches, controls, warning lights and associated displays. There appears to be little order in their presentation, their positioning a result of someone's whim, and the controls apparently fitted in convenient spaces.

The truth is that the layout is based upon many years of careful development and the application of sound ergonomic principles in design, presentation, layout and operational requirements. This is necessary because any aircraft's cockpit or flight deck is a collection point for a vast amount of information. Detectors, sensors and receivers mounted throughout the airframe collate a great deal of data which are continually displayed for the benefit of the crew. To assist the process of assimilation, the information tends to be presented in 'blocks', each of which is concerned with a specific area or system.

Taking the flight deck of the Boeing 747-200 (still in widespread use today) as an example, the view is best described from the captain's seat which is always on the left. Until the 1980s, most large aircraft were operated by a crew of three but since then, new designs have continued a relentless drive towards two-pilot operation.

Immediately in front of the captain is a set of instruments which are duplicated on the co-pilot's side. These make up the modern version of what used to be called the blind flying panel. The basic philosophy remains the same, as this group of instruments gives the pilot the vital cues of heading, speed and attitude. The modern instruments use electronic techniques for additional refinements and selections, which allow different types of information to be 'called up' as required. The only instrument that seems to have escaped the electronic revolution is the vertical speed indicator (VSI), which provides an indication of the rate of climb or descent. An additional source of height information is available from a radio altimeter, which comes into its own in the final landing approach and during automatic landings.

Other indicators on this panel include automatic flight warnings, instrument warnings and computer selectors, emphasizing the considerable degree of automation inherent in modern aircraft.

The co-pilot's panel is virtually identical, with the addition of a large flying control position indicator, an air temperature gauge and hydraulic brake pressure indicator.

These two panels are separated by a large central panel containing the main engine parameter gauges. These indicate engine speeds, temperatures and fuel flows. A stand-by artificial horizon is mounted in this area, enabling the third crew member (flight engineer) to monitor all three attitude indicators. If either of the pilots' instruments becomes suspect, the faulty instrument can be quickly identified by reference to the stand-by.

This area also includes a central warning panel, covering all the primary systems. An incipient defect will illuminate one of these lights to attract the crew's attention. Flap indicators show the position of leading- and trailing-edge flaps, by a combination of twin needles and lights. The distinctive hallmark of many Boeing transports is the large handle for the landing gear selection, with the adjacent warning lights to monitor correct operation.

The 747 has a number of on-board computers, with the addition of a separate small computer which is fed with basic information to offer a read-out of engine power values for all aspects of the flight envelope. This read-out display is also mounted on the central panel, where it can be monitored easily, particularly during the climb, to ensure that maximum values are not accidentally exceeded.

Immediately above, mounted on the windscreen coaming, is the automatic pilot selection and control panel. The aircraft is usually fitted with a triple autopilot installation to enable fully automatic operations under very restricted visibility, right down to landing. All commands to the autopilots can be made through this panel, as well as the selection of associated navigation facilities. It is noteworthy that there is even a special mode for automatic flight in turbulence. To each side of this panel are radio navigation selectors to enable the correct frequency to be set up for navaids or the instrument landing system (ILS).

ENGINE CONTROLS

Between the two pilot's seats is the central console. Most prominent here is the set of four throttles, or thrust levers, which control the power output of the engines and enable reverse thrust to be selected on landing. Other control levers include the flap selector and the speed brake selector. Boeing has always been concerned about the need to ensure that both leading-edge and trailing-edge flaps are correctly sequenced in operation. To achieve this desirable situation, the flap selector lever operates a programmed controller during its movement to ensure that the flaps are always properly sequenced when being extended and retracted.

Also prominent in this area are the three inertial navigation system (INS) control and display units. The 747 was the first commercial aircraft to feature this system as a fully integrated element in the design. Earlier aircraft, like the Boeing 707 and

Above: Even when allowance is made for a telephoto lens, this Saab 340 has been brought in unusually close, providing a glimpse of the pilots' place of work from the outside. The aircraft captain always sits on the left side.

Below: The flight deck of the British Aerospace 146 was originally a mass of 'clock' type instruments but later models, including the Avro RJ development, feature the electronic displays seen here, to provide a much less cluttered cockpit.

Douglas DC-8, had been fitted with INS but these were add-on solutions which did not represent the best ergonomic answer.

Other navigation and communication system frequency selectors are also in the area in close proximity to all three crew members for ease of operation from any of the seats. This emphasizes the basic design philosophy and layout of all equipment, which enables complete integration of the crew members and ensures adequate monitoring of all flight deck functions.

Immediately to the rear of the pilot's seats and mounted on the right hand (starboard) side of the aeroplane, in three-crew layouts, is the flight engineer's position. This enables control to be exercised over aircraft systems such as the auxiliary power unit, electrics, hydraulics, fuel management, pneumatics, air conditioning and pressurisation.

Overhead, another wide panel carries additional selectors including the engine start units and the all important fire handles. In the event of an engine fire, a warning bell sounds and the relevant handle illuminates with an ominous red glow.

Also fitted to the roof structure are a number of circuit breaker (fuse) panels which protect the many electrical circuits. Other flight deck systems include oxygen, inter-communication and emergency equipment, the last comprising lifejackets and escape ropes to enable the crew to descend to the ground via a roof-mounted hatch.

This necessarily brief review of the layout of the flight deck is sufficient to indicate the considerable amount and disposition of instrumentation. For many years, the instruments have been based upon electro-mechanical technology, tending to take up a

Boeing 747-200 Flight Deck

Below: The flight deck of the Boeing 747-400 developed for two-crew operation and seen reproduced for a flight simulator, has been much simplified compared with the earlier 747-200 by the use of cathode ray tube (CRT) displays.

Above: The key to the 747-200's complex flight deck.

1 Essential services bus bar
2 Circuit breakers
3 Standby compass
4 Systems controls
5 Radio bus bar
6 APU and auxiliary power control panel
7 Electric power control panel
8 Autopilot mode selector
9 Cabin air control panel
10 Attitude director
11 Machmeter
12 Engine instruments
13 Fuel system panel
14 Weather radar scope
15 Landing gear selector
16 Flap position indicators
17 Engine instruments
18 Radar and communications
19 Throttles
20 Autopilot controls
21 Standby attitude director
22 Master warning panel
23 Captain's main flight instruments

Left: If they are to be operated safely alongside large aircraft and in an international airline environment, even small commuterliners must have fully-equipped flight decks. The BAe Jetstream 31 shows how it can be done.

Right: Moving up the size scale a little, from 19 seats to 30 seats, the Embraer Brasilia shows a layout strikingly similar to that of the Jetstream. Note, however, the modest use of electronic displays for primary flight information for the two pilots.

Below: The ATR 42, a product of Franco-Italian co-operation, represents a size increase from the other two types illustrated. The greater width of the fuselage and flight deck is obvious, but the instrument layout is similar.

great deal of panel space and often proving to be less reliable than desired.

Ergonomically, such a layout tends to be self-defeating, because at any one time the crew is interested in only about 10 per cent of the total displayed information. The remaining 90 per cent is not only unwanted but can be distracting, even confusing, as it can create ambiguity in the monitoring of the wanted data. So to ensure maximum operational efficiency, it became necessary to devise a series of drills and procedures to deal with all aspects of the operation and emergencies. These are then committed partially to memory and backed up by one crew member and monitored by another. However, the advent of today's more advanced two crew flight decks with increased levels of automation has eased their task considerably.

In general, transport aircraft are operated within carefully controlled parameters reflecting ambient conditions and relative to height, weight and air traffic control restrictions. These parameters are broken down into tables and graphs which are used by the crew to establish the correct flight profile for the prevailing conditions, all of which comes under the general heading of 'cruise control' procedures.

It can be appreciated that the crew is constantly in receipt of a considerable amount of information which can be processed for use in managing the progress of the flight. This is, of course, pure computational work and ideally suited to modern electronic computers. Computers are also free of the 'human' problems of workload, stress, emotion and fatigue, all of which can lead to the making of errors in calculations.

Perhaps the major watershed in air transport philosophy occurred during the oil crisis of the early 1970s. Until that time, the price of fuel had been of relatively little consequence among all the other factors in the equation of direct operating costs (DOCs). The massive increase in oil price, over a very short period, led to drastic rethinking about all aspects of commercial operations. This sparked off a strong move towards greater efficiency and cost awareness on the part of the airlines.

Coincidentally, the electronics revolution was also under way and digital techniques combined with miniaturization were offering new types of equipment which were light, compact, highly capable, extremely reliable, demanding of minimal power and relatively cheap to produce.

This computational potential offered the chance for a re-evaluation of the whole operation, and a programme of rationalization was undertaken to assess flight deck workload and composition, the intention being to develop a greater degree of automation and, as a consequence, to reduce the

manning levels, in an attempt to reduce costs and improve efficiency wherever possible.

Such thinking revived many of the older controversies about flight deck manning. Crew complement had become a very vexed question during the 1950s and early 1960s, leading to considerable industrial unrest as first, navigators, and then radio operators were displaced.

As the early piston engine transports grew into the mechanically complex multi-engined airliners of the 1940s, their operation required a number of highly specialized crew members on the flight deck. Apart from the basic job of flying the aeroplane, a long-range communications specialist was needed, and the continuous task of navigation also demanded a specialist crew member. Certain airlines made polar operations a normal part of their schedule, though it is less well known that such operations required the services of two navigators on the flight deck in order to handle the high work load occasioned by the vagaries of natural magnetic phenomenon at high latitudes.

In addition, the increasingly complex airframe systems and piston engines called for a flight engineer, with the result that by the end of World War II a new generation of airliners had appeared requiring five- and at times six-man crews. The pace of war had also accelerated the development of electronically-based systems, and it had already become apparent that long-range voice communications

could be conducted on automatically-tuned radio sets. This set the scene for the demise of the specialist radio operator as the pilots took over in-flight communications.

GLASS COCKPITS

As electronics became ever more dominant, the advent of the INS saw the demise of classical navigation and the flight crew complement stabilized, on the larger aircraft, at two pilots and a flight engineer. However, as computers have increasingly taken over more and more of the flight deck management role, it has been possible to reduce this to just two pilots, the 'glass' cockpit providing data as required.

This innovation has occurred as a consequence of the ability to translate many of the flight monitoring, cruise control, navigation and communications management tasks into computer software, which can then be stored and used to provide information on a 'call up' basis. Modern computers can store a vast amount of information, and can even 'prioritize' certain aspects. By use of suitable electronic display screens, this information can be presented to the pilot as and when it is required, all other extraneous data being withheld. The system can also be configured to display additional data such as weather radar pictures, check lists and airfield landing diagrams. In the event of a problem developing in a system, the pilot is warned of the situation and

the applicable drill is also displayed automatically. In this manner, the flight deck clutter is dramatically reduced, ambiguity is avoided and greater efficiency in information handling is achieved.

As might be expected of any major new development, the transition from a three-man crew using 'clock' type instruments, to a two-crew 'glass' cockpit configuration was not without its difficulties. Initially, reliability was not up to expectations and pilots occasionally faced with blank screens, understandably lacked confidence in the new displays, although these incidents did serve to show that back-up electro-mechanical instruments were clearly necessary.

Experienced crews tended to regard 'glass' cockpits with some suspicion, while younger pilots took to the new technology with equanimity. However, needless to say, both the equipment and crews settled down and electronics displays are now the rule rather than the exception. Indeed, some of the three-crew 747 'Classic' airliners have been upgraded with CRT displays and modified for two-crew operation.

Such has been the enthusiasm for the advanced flight decks, that airliners produced in the former Soviet Union are often fitted with Western avionics, because without them they would not be accepted in most export markets.

Despite these factors, the new types of flight deck are becoming increasingly common, both as initial

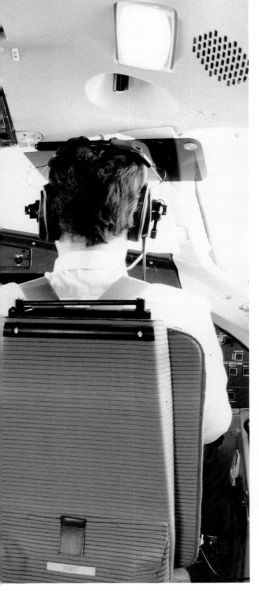

Left: Borrowing from military technology, some manufacturers offer a head-up display (HUD) in airliners such as this McDonnell Douglas MD-80. This provides the pilot with vital information while still looking straight ahead and is particularly useful when landing in conditions of poor visibility.

Below: The two-pilot flight deck of the Boeing 767 shows the uncluttered look obtained with so-called 'glass' electronic displays.

fit or as a retrofit. The Boeing 747 has undergone radical review and a long-range version, the 747-400, now has a fully computerized 'glass' flightdeck and a two-man crew.

Air transport has developed over some seven decades and has learned some hard lessons along the way. There is an innate conservatism that is not always in sympathy with every aspect of technical innovation. This is especially true when it is achieved by a large increase in the initial cost of ownership.

Intense competition between aircraft builders and engine companies has helped to drive down costs in all areas, including reducing fuel burn, as well as meeting the ever stricter environmental demands for quieter engines and cleaner operation with fewer noxious emissions.

Meanwhile innovation on the flight deck has also helped to reduce DOCs, two-crew operations cutting personnel costs, while the growing use of the satellite-based Future Air Navigation System (FANS) enables more direct routes to be flown. Sometimes hundreds of miles have been cut from routes which previously had to follow clearly determined 'air lanes'. However, perhaps the most controversial of all cost reduction campaigns has been the successful drive to offer long-range, trans-oceanic operations by twin-engined airliners.

Safety is always an emotive and difficult subject and many thousands of safe flights can be quickly forgotten in the face of a single, inevitably highly publicised disaster. Nevertheless, the controversy surrounding the question of long-range oceanic flights by twin-engined airliners soon died down and indeed, in some parts of the world, increasing use of small single-engined airliners is being made.

A320 DESIGN

To ensure maximum integrity within the limitations of the design, a number of additional back-up systems are applied and much reliance is placed upon the extremely high reliability of the modern jet engine. The one certainty, in the long term, is the increasing importance of the avionics equipment which will continue to expand in capability and offer very real advances in flight safety. The best example of this is to be found in the Airbus A320 which, when introduced into airline service in 1988, marked an important advance in flight deck design and procedures.

The full set of electronic flight instrumentation creates a clean uncluttered look, which in this case is enhanced even more by the absence of the large, traditional flying control column. Instead, there is a neat, unobtrusive sidestick controller mounted on a small ledge, adjacent to each pilot's seat, on the left- and right-hand sides of the cockpit. The layout is the

A320 Avionics

Right: The introduction of the Airbus A320 in 1988 marked a considerable advance in airliner design. This schematic shows the main elements incorporated in the A320's flight management and guidance systems (FMGS) and fly-by-wire (FBW) system originally developed by SFENA with Sperry and Bodenseewerk.

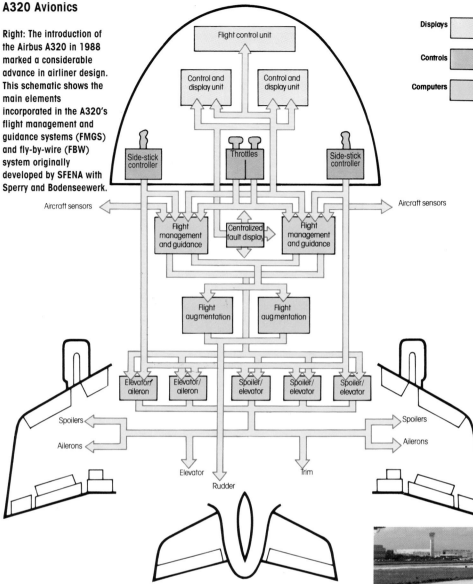

Below: The cockpit of the Airbus A330 is almost identical to that of the much smaller A320, the side-stick – borrowed from military practice, replacing the usual central control column – and six cathode ray tube displays enabling the pilots to switch from one to the other with ease.

Below: Adopted as standard in all Airbus airliners since the A320, side-stick controllers take the place of the usual central control column. This diagram shows how pilots' inputs are used – via flight computers – to command control surface movements.

Right: The cockpit of the MD-90 – shown here in a full-scale mock-up – presents an uncluttered look, thanks to the use of side-stick controllers and almost all 'glass' displays, using six identical colour cathode ray tubes. Each pilot has two CRTs for flight displays.

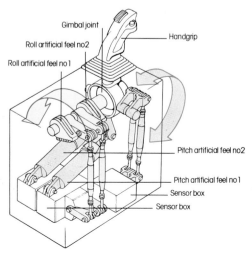

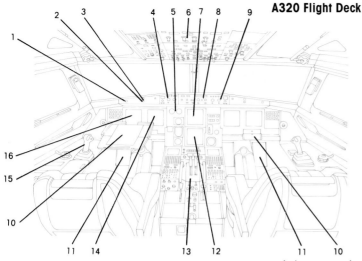

A320 Flight Deck

1 Autoland control
2 Master warning 'amber'
3 Master warning 'red'
4 EFIS controls, captain
5 Standby ASI, altimeter and attitude indicator 'clock' instruments
6 Systems control panels, fuel flow management
7 Engine and warning displays, part of electronic centralised aircraft monitoring (ECAM) system

8 Flight control unit, to dial in required heading, speed, altitude and vertical speed
9 EFIS controls, first officer
10 Slide-out table, shown stowed and in use (port)
11 Rudder pedals
12 Systems display, part of ECAM
13 Throttles
14 Navigation display CRT, one for each pilot
15 Side-stick controller, one each side 'handed' for captain and first officer
16 Primary flight display CRT, one for each pilot

most obvious external evidence of the revolutionary fly-by-wire system that offers precise, controlled and safe computer control of all flight conditions. The choice of this type of system also offers significant weight savings and reduction in mechanical parts. Instead, the main flying control surfaces are all signalled electrically under computer control. As the data banks have been supplied with all the speeds, attitudes and permissible manoeuvres of the flight envelope, the aircraft will never over-speed, over-stress or stall.

The design of the A320 and its systems provided a significant pointer to the future. Most aeroplanes are built to withstand greater strains than should be expected. This is to allow for the human element, which may impose too high a loading on the airframe through careless handling, or by accident. This need to 'over-engineer' the airframe inevitably increases its structural weight and thus reduces aerodynamic efficiency.

The advent of fly-by-wire and computer controlled flight envelopes offer the designer the opportunity to build an aeroplane that is stressed more efficiently, is lighter, and therefore more efficient – hence less expensive – to operate.

Inevitably, developments along these lines lead to arguments about the role of the pilot in future transport aeroplanes. Certainly it is within the scope of aeronautical engineering to build a totally automated aeroplane, but such a development is just as obviously socially unacceptable, at least within the next few decades. Space flight may be the forerunner in this application. Instead, the pilot is becoming a systems manager, supervising a highly automated process, but always ready to intervene if any aspect appears to become divergent.

Unfortunately, the human being is not a very efficient monitor over a long period and in a repetitive environment. In the early days of A320 operations, there were incidents and indeed accidents ascribed to an element of inattention, said to have been engendered by the atmosphere of the advanced flight decks.

Alas there was nothing new in this, for crew alertness has long been a problem in aviation although in the past, the problem was alleviated by a constant and often extremely variable workload and the presence of large crews. Today however, the pattern is of two-crew operation, long flights and considerable automation, yet although the technical abilities of the aircraft are undoubtedly greater than ever before, the pilots still remain the fallible, weak link in the control loop.

Industrial psychologists continue to agonize over such things, but it may be that computers will have the final answer, as it is not beyond the bounds of possibility for the crews to be kept under surveillance! Regular 'attention getter' actions may be instituted by the computer systems, to ensure a high level of pilot awareness. Typically, these could include exercises which have to be carried out at regular intervals, requiring an element of tactile, aural and physical co-ordination.

It seems that the aeroplane is approaching a point of extremely safe and efficient operation. Perhaps the real doubt about the future must be over the ability of the world-wide infrastructure – air traffic control, airfield facilities and en-route communications – to attain a similarly high standard. But that is another story.

THE CABIN AND ACCOMMODATION

When an airliner taxies to the passenger terminal at the end of a flight and the captain shuts down the engines, the aeroplane is rapidly surrounded by many different kinds of vehicle. So many, in fact, that it seems a wonder that they can all find room to perform their functions without getting in each other's way. That they can go about their tasks with unimpeded access to the aeroplane is a measure of the care which has been taken in the design of the airliner. Baggage and cargo trucks, water replenishment and lavatory trolleys, power and air-conditioning units, a special food truck with an elevating platform – these and other vehicles are driven on to the airport apron to ensure that the airliner is quickly made ready for the next leg of its journey.

Most passengers are unaware of the almost military precision necessary to speed the turnaround of an airliner after its arrival, but the key to the success of the operation has been established long before – in the drawing offices of the aircraft manufacturer. It is there that the shape and detail of the aircraft are determined, the final result always representing a compromise. For the designer must try to satisfy demands made by many individuals, including those who want to make sure that the airliner will be profitable, while others are more concerned with comfort or safety, or the ease with which the cabin crew can get on with their job.

Somewhere during the evolution of the design, these compromises have to be made. To achieve the maximum profit, the designer is asked to get as many seats into the cabin as possible – but the result may be so uncomfortable that passengers will prefer to travel on a different type of airliner. Or perhaps

757 Ground Servicing

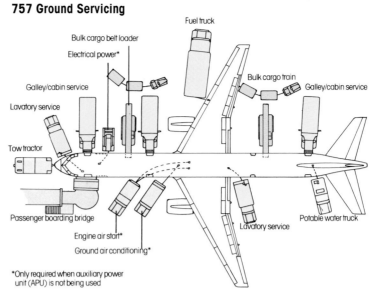

*Only required when auxiliary power unit (APU) is not being used

Left: When an airliner comes to rest on the airport apron, usually alongside an 'air bridge' as shown here, a swarm of vehicles arrives to undertake a variety of tasks related to the off-loading of passengers, baggage and waste, and preparation for the next flight.

Below: Providing seating on two decks is one way to increase passenger capacity without going for very long tubular cabins, but to date only the Boeing 747 has made use of this arrangement. This is the top deck of the 747-400.

Below: As airliners have grown steadily larger and passenger capacities have increased, wider cabins have been introduced, to allow twin-aisle arrangements that offer a welcome alternative to the 'long thin tube' look of large single-aisle aircraft. The spacious cabin of the Boeing 767, here, includes enlarged-capacity overhead baggage bins.

Right: The galley of the modern airliner – this is in the Boeing 767 – must be capable of holding ready-prepared meals and beverages for hundreds of passengers, and keeping them hot and appetizing for any time up to several hours after take-off.

Below: The galley requirements on commuter aircraft, such as this de Havilland Canada Dash 8, are much smaller than those on larger aircraft, not just because there are fewer passengers, but because only light snacks and hot drinks are needed on short flights.

the aeroplane will not be powerful enough to lift all the passengers and cargo that could be crammed into the available space on board.

The question of safety must always be paramount: are there, for example, enough emergency exits to ensure the swift evacuation of the cabin, if necessary? Maybe the demands of safety regulations are met, but if the seats are too tightly packed, there may not be enough room for the passengers and cabin crew to use the aisles at the same time.

The answer to every problem must always be a compromise, although advances in technology are constantly making such compromises easier. Indeed, flexibility is the trend nowadays: simple adjustments can be made to enable the configuration of the cabin to be changed quickly to account for different demands. Modules can now be produced to enable airlines to effect changes of this kind in what amounts to a matter of hours.

COMFORT AND SAFETY

Whilst conscious of the need for safety, most passengers have comfort and convenience uppermost in their minds as they climb aboard an airliner to begin their journey. However, someone, somewhere, has already made the compromises which have largely decided the issue. If the journey is to be a short one, perhaps of an hour's duration or less, it is probable that the airline will have decided that it need not install reclining seats in that particular cabin. If this is a holiday charter airliner about to embark on a slightly longer journey, it may have been judged that the passengers will not mind a little discomfort for the very low air fare which is part of the holiday 'package'.

A scheduled-service flight lasting about two hours, on the other hand, must offer a higher standard of comfort, with more space between the seats and more legroom. A really long journey, to the far side of the world, is tiring for even the most experienced passenger, so this demands that the airline provide the maximum level of comfort commensurate with profitability – compromise again.

More space for galleys is necessary for the really long-distance airliners, because passengers expect – and need – hot meals and plenty of refreshments. For the shorter 'commuter' journey, a cup of coffee and a packet of biscuits are all that most carriers offer – and few passengers expect more. So the level of comfort is largely determined by the length of the journey, and by the fare paid by the passenger. From the earliest days of commercial aviation, passengers have found themselves in some kind of tube because that is the best compromise that designers have been able to find. The long thin tube of Concorde is shaped that way so that it can achieve speeds in excess of Mach 2; the giant Boeing 747 flies subsonically, however, so the designer has been able to produce a three-deck airliner (with passengers on two decks and cargo at the bottom).

Many demands are made upon aircraft manufacturers to produce profitable airliners, so a generous underfloor baggage and cargo area is now essential. This enables airlines to boost their revenues by carrying freight in passenger aircraft, as well as the passengers' own baggage. Indeed, the Boeing 747 can accommodate more cargo in its belly than the all-cargo version of the earlier Boeing 707 could carry in the main cabin. Uniquely, Boeing's Jumbo can also carry as many as 69 passengers in an upper cabin located above the main passenger deck behind the cockpit, thus making the maximum use of the generous space available.

Aircraft designers are under pressure to get more out of their airliners, but new lightweight materials, combined with design ingenuity, ensure that more passengers and cargo can be carried in a given size of aircraft, without having to sacrifice comfort levels. Indeed, the advanced technology now being applied will ensure that standards of comfort will increase – sometimes in 'invisible' areas such as cabin air conditioning, or by ironing out bumps which can make a flight uncomfortable. In future, airliners will have gust-alleviation systems in which a computer, far out of sight of the cabin, will automatically respond to turbulence faster than the pilot could manage, activating control surfaces to smooth the passage of the aircraft. Computers are also being used at the design stage to determine the best position for the air-conditioning outlets to provide a draught-free circulation within the cabin. Both Airbus and Boeing have employed computer techniques in this way to determine the most comfortable flow of air. Boeing has also used computer modelling to discover the best method of removing cigarette smoke, devising a special ducting system just below the stowage bins on its new short-haul airliners. A growing number of airlines have made their flights completely 'no smoking' but virtually all of the remainder have separate areas in the cabin for smokers and non-smokers.

Another invisible aid to passenger comfort in the cabin is the pressurisation system. The early airliners did not have this facility, and therefore had to fly in the often turbulent weather at relatively low altitudes. By designing a strong pressure cabin, aircraft manufacturers ensure that airliners can fly 'above the weather' while protecting passengers from the discomforts of high-altitude flying.

Aspects of passenger comfort cover a multitude of subjects in a modern airliner, and the most basic element of all is perhaps the seat. Here, again, compromise is essential because seat manufacturers must provide designs which are as light as possible while being hard-wearing and comfortable, as well as conforming to safety standards in rigidity, etc. The earliest seats in pre-World War II airliners were simple wicker chairs that were not even securely fastened to the cabin floor, but seat design has now become a highly technical matter, with a reclining mechanism and carefully placed cushions combining to give maximum support to all of the body.

The size of the seat varies according to the class of travel (and therefore according to the fare paid). Real luxury is to be found in the exclusive atmosphere of the first class cabin where there is usually a gap (or 'pitch') of 96.5cm (38in) or more between seat rows, whereas a pitch of 76cm (30in) or so is all that economy-class passengers may expect. Business class is, as one might expect, somewhere in between, with a typical 86cm (34in) separation between seat rows. The latest convertible seats enable airlines to contract or expand seat width by the concertina principle to suit either business class or economy class passengers to match the passenger profile on a particular flight. Sleeperette seats or even beds on some airlines enable first-class passengers to get a good night's sleep, although this is not a new development, real beds (or rather bunks) having been provided in the early days of piston-engined airliners.

Convenient baggage bins (enclosed luggage racks above head level in the cabin) are an aspect of passenger comfort, too. The ability to stow hand baggage out of the way makes for an uncluttered floor and therefore more legroom, as well as greater safety. Considerable thought goes into the design of stowage bins and manufacturers vie with each other to provide just a little more space than the competition. A few airlines even boast of their ability to provide sufficient space for skis in their overhead baggage stowage facilities. Soviet aircraft offer a different solution to the hand baggage problem: the Il-86, for example, offers a 'below decks' baggage area

A320 Cabin Layouts

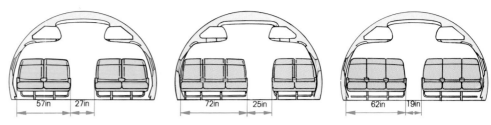

16 first (36in pitch) + 30 business (36in pitch) + 89 economy (32in pitch)

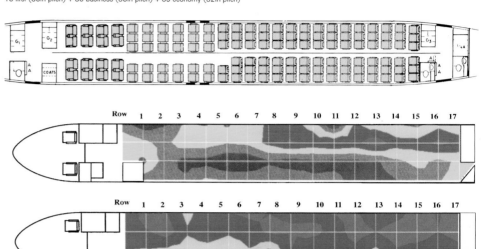

Top: Different seating layouts, depending on the route, can be installed in modern airliners.

Above: An Active Noise control system may be used in aircraft such as the Saab 2000. A series of tiny microphones measure cabin noise (red, orange and yellow), which is then counteracted by noise of opposite phase (green and blue) from loudspeakers.

Left: For really long journeys, and for first-class, some airlines provide seats big enough to sleep in. These are Air France 'sleeperettes'.

through which boarding passengers pass on their way to the main cabin. Thus, if a passenger has a bulky item that will not be needed on the journey, it can be placed on a shelf to be picked up again on arrival. Soviet designers have another unusual requirement to satisfy – that of providing wardrobe space for the winter coats of 150-300 passengers (depending on aircraft type). In some cases, this means rearranging cabin layouts between summer and winter, with the loss of up to six passenger seats in the latter case.

Air journeys can be boring – indeed most are, because there is little to be seen from 9,145m (30,000ft) or so, and even the majestic clouds lose their attraction after a while. So airlines have devised various ways of reducing the tedium and making the journey more comfortable. Food is one of the most obvious methods of keeping passengers from getting bored (especially on long journeys), the term being used to embrace liquid refreshment.

In the pioneer days of air transport, when airliners lumbered their way at low altitudes and slow speeds, passengers could expect little more than a sandwich prepared by the steward in a tiny kitchen. The main meals were taken on the ground in an hotel because the leisurely pace required frequent stops for servicing, a rest for the crew and an overnight stay for passengers and crew alike on longer journeys. Today, more and more airliners offer the opportunity for non-stop flights, even over very long distances. Just as transatlantic non-stop flights have long been taken for granted, so today services from London to Singapore, Johannesburg or San Francisco have quickly become routine. On these very long flights, it is necessary to serve every passenger with at least one main meal and perhaps several snacks, all of which have to be loaded on to the airliner before the journey begins. Cabin crews have to work hard to ensure that these are properly prepared before they are served, usually from a trol-

Comparative Cabin Dimensions

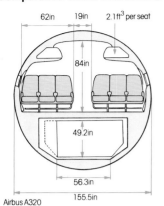

Airbus A320

Boeing 737/757

McDonnell Douglas MD-90

Above: Aircraft interior cabin designers go to great lengths to avoid giving passengers the impression of being overcrowded, but there is an ever-present pressure to maximize the payload within the 'envelope' of the given cabin diameter. These diagrams show a comparison between the Airbus A320 (left), the Boeing 737/757 and the MD-90 (right).

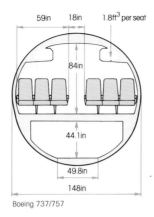

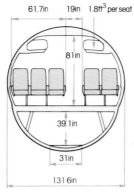

Left: First class passengers in such aircraft as this Kuwait Airways' A340 have access to their own video displays, allowing them to choose from a variety of films and games.

Below: Ceiling mounted monitors such as these on an Iberia McDonnell Douglas MD-87 are much easier to view than the large screens used on earlier airliners.

ley wheeled up and down the aisle from the galley. With the exception of first-class meals on some airliners, all food is prepared long before it is served, in an airport kitchen, each ingredient having been measured according to an airline manual so that all the portions are as near equal as possible.

The meals sometimes include lobster, caviar or some delicacy designed to convey an atmosphere of luxury – but the aim of providing an appetising hot course can fail because the meal has been reheated just a little too long. It is, nevertheless, a considerable achievement for any airline to provide hundreds of meals (often with a choice), several times during a long flight.

Modern technology has come a long way since the early airborne kitchens were introduced. Some wide-body airliners such as the DC-10 and TriStar have the option of underfloor galleys reached by a lift, so that a few crew members can prepare meals 'downstairs', while others serve them in the cabin from trolleys. Just as the latest technology is applied to the design of cabin seating and air conditioning, galleys also are being constantly developed with the objective of providing the lightest possible facility in the smallest possible space. Flexibility is the watchword in cabin design these days, so modular galleys are often produced to enable airlines to switch them around and take them off certain airliners, if for some reason they need to put in more seats for a particular journey or season.

IN-FLIGHT ENTERTAINMENT

Another method of relieving the tedium of long flights is to provide entertainment, in the form of films of taped music. This is not so new, either, for airborne musical entertainment was first provided on an aluminium piano in the great Zeppelin airships of the 1930s, and 16-mm film projectors were to be found on some airliners of the period too. On the giant Jumbos of today, however, there are many passengers who cannot see out of the windows, so film entertainment has come to be considered essential, although some airlines do provide cabin space for those who prefer to work or read. However, film systems that made use of large screens and projectors which retract into the ceiling, have largely given way to either television-type screens fixed at various points in the cabin, or more commonly to smaller monitors which can be stowed in the ceiling or in seat backs or arm-rests. Entertainment programmes for such systems sometimes include advertisements (just like home TV!) and the medium is often used to provide safety bulletins, in place of the demonstrations traditionally given by the cabin crews.

Some airlines use the cabin channels to advertise duty-free goods on board, or to promote their network of flights, while others – notably Virgin Atlantic – sometimes provide live entertainment by offering free transatlantic flights to 'buskers' and pop groups of an acceptable standard who perform *en route*. In-flight shopping and video games, as well as gaming of the casino variety have been added to the list of entertainments, while telephone and fax communications are available to passengers on many airlines.

Toilets, lavatories, powder rooms: call them what one will, the facilities are an essential aspect of comfort in an airliner cabin, and are an aspect which is not neglected in terms of modern technology. For example, the Boeing 747-400 and other modern airliners feature a vacuum waste disposal system and a modular design which will enable the location to be varied according to the demands of the individual airlines. The maximum use is made of the smallest possible space; mirrors and diffused lighting creating a comfortable atmosphere, while careful design ensures that practical needs (such as a nappy changing table) can be met.

Even the most experienced traveller cannot be unmindful of the hazards that may one day be encountered on an air journey. Yet despite the occasional tragic accident, safety standards continue to rise, year by year. The constraints placed upon the airliner design team put safety aspects at the top of their scale of priorities, and no one would have it otherwise. However, it must be acknowledged that compromises have to be made in this aspect of cabin design, too. For example, some experts insist that it is safer for passengers to be placed in rearward-facing seats than the more customary forward-facing layout, yet it is only some military operators who have adopted such a configuration in their transport aircraft. It is reasoned that in the event of a crash-landing, the sudden deceleration would force passengers into rearward-facing seats instead of out of them. However, airlines in general argue that passengers would not welcome such a seat layout, which would be considered unnatural, so designers have tended to concentrate on making seats safer in other ways. Seat manufacturers have produced new models in carbon-fibre laminates which are very light but also very strong. The authorities also lay down strict regulations regarding the strength of the method of anchoring seats to the floor.

Much thought and research has also gone into the development of safer cushions and seat coverings. Materials previously thought to be safe have actually proved to be dangerous in a fire because otherwise harmless gases given off by different components in a cabin have sometimes combined to produce a lethal mix. Good old-fashioned wool is

gaining popularity as one of the safest materials, and its natural flame resistance can be enhanced by special treatment with an additive; this has been tested by the authorities in seven major aircraft-producing countries and found to be safer than some man-made materials (which tend to melt easily).

Nowadays, the certification authorities demand that cabin seats must include 'fireblockers' which will inhibit the spread of burning materials. The polyurethane foam cushions used on most seats are highly inflammable, but if they are covered with such fireblocker materials, ignition can be delayed for vital seconds, or prevented altogether. In a trial carried out in the USA, it was estimated that the survival time in a cabin fitted with fireblocking covers

was increased by 40 seconds. Some companies have developed flame retardants for man-made materials such as polyester and nylon. Flamebar for example, has produced a solution which imparts self-extinguishing properties and eliminates flaming droplets, themselves often the source of secondary fires within the cabin of an aircraft.

Considerable research into the matter of cabin materials has been carried out in government establishments in various parts of the world, and gradually the right combinations have been found. Both Boeing and Airbus have played a pioneering role in the establishment of smoke and toxicity standards for cabin materials. Indeed, Airbus has tested over 20,000 samples of materials and has established its

Right: Satellite communications enable Emirates to provide its passengers with a fax service in addition to telephone links on its airliners.

Below: To enable cabin crews to get some rest on very long flights, Airbus devised this compartment which can be loaded on to the lower deck of the A340. Easily loaded like a freight container, the compartment minimises the use of valuable revenue-generating space in the main cabin.

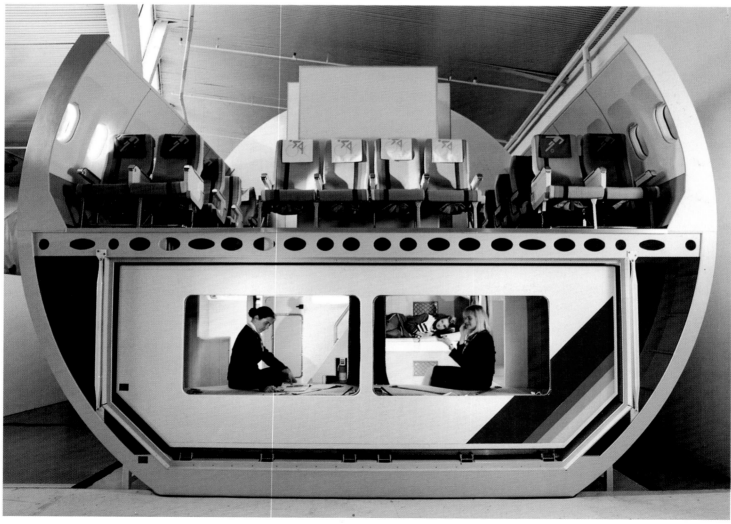

own specifications, which have been adopted as an aircraft industry standard. In fact, Airbus will not use some plastic materials in the cabin for although lightweight and strong, these give off smoke and gas at low ignition temperatures.

Many accidents which have claimed lives in the past have been deemed 'survivable' by present-day standards but for the emission of smoke and gases which have either prevented passengers from finding escape exits, or have hindered their movement because of their toxicity. To speed evacuation of a cabin in the event of fire, floor-mounted emergency lighting is now fitted to most airliners. This will help passengers to find the exits in dense cabin smoke conditions, and they are battery powered to ensure

Left: The Fire Service Training School at Tees-side Airport is a recognised leader in the field. As well as training fire crews from British airports, students from as far afield as Saudi Arabia and Hong Kong attend its courses.

Below: New technology is now as commonplace in the cabin, as elsewhere in a modern airliner. A feature of the Airbus A320, this panel with its keyboard allows cabin staff to control and monitor many of the cabin facilities from one spot.

their independence from the aircraft's power supply which may be severed in an accident.

Fires in aircraft lavatories have sometimes been the source of a subsequent disaster and a recent development involving an alloy with a low melting point has helped the design of an automatic fire-fighting system. This is set off when a certain temperature has been reached: the alloy melts and so triggers a piston which releases Halon gas into the overheated area.

It is rare for a pressurisation failure to occur in an airliner, but all modern aircraft are fitted with an emergency oxygen system in which masks drop out above the heads of passengers so that they can be quickly donned. As a further safety measure in the event of a sudden decompression at altitude, airliners are fitted with vents in the cabin to ensure that an explosive pressure does not build up. These and other measures have been developed in the light of earlier experience, and are examples of the way that designers quickly apply the latest safety techniques to modern airliners.

Inflatable escape chutes are another feature of airliner emergency equipment: they are designed to help passengers evacuate the cabin speedily in the event of an accident. In addition to carrying individual life jackets under each seat, airliners operating over major stretches of water are also equipped with large inflatable liferafts. Thus, in the unlikely event of an airliner ditching at sea, there are a number of emergency aids quickly available.

FUTURE DEVELOPMENTS

New developments in aircraft design will ensure that the airliners of tomorrow will be both safer and more comfortable even than those in current operation. For example, more airlines and manufacturers are taking steps to address problems sometimes encountered by disabled passengers. Airbus has devised a wheelchair which makes access to the cabin much easier. On the A320, a lavatory with a folding wall facilitates the entry of wheelchair or stretcher-borne passengers. When British Airways refurbished its 747 fleet, it included lavatories specifically designed for use by disabled passengers.

Airbus has developed a control panel which makes life easier for cabin crews. In the A320 a series of lights and buttons on a panel provides cabin attendants with a visual indication of the status of such items as lighting and water tank levels.

Bendix has introduced something called the Integrated Data Management System, which includes a Cabin Management Terminal. This enables cabin crews to maintain a direct electronic link with the ground, not by voice communication but by means of a keyboard. Items such as on-board sales reports, inventories, meal reports and crew time reports can be completed and transmitted before landing. In addition, special passenger requests, connecting flight information and reservations can be handled without involving the flight deck crew. The Data Management System includes a Duty-Free Terminal which can record sales, calculate currency exchanges and print customs documents. Other electronic gadgets of direct benefit mostly to business passengers, include on-board telephones and fax.

Despite the trend towards ever bigger aircraft (Airbus plans 600- or even 800-seat airliners), modern technology will be increasingly employed to ensure that safety standards as well as comfort levels, are constantly improved. The cabin of an airliner may look like a simple tube, but for the aircraft designer it is very much more complex. Passengers, however, remain largely unaware of such complexity – unless they glance at all those support vehicles which crowd around before take-off.

DESIGN AND MANUFACTURE

The art of successful commercial aircraft design can be defined as sizing the product correctly to meet current and future market demands, and using modern technologies in such areas as power plants, aerodynamics, structural materials, aircraft systems and manufacturing techniques in order to achieve a worthwhile reduction (e.g. 10 per cent) in direct operating costs (DOCs).

The overwhelming importance of economics in this field of design may simplify the decision-making process in comparison with that of combat aircraft, but the designer of airliners is nonetheless faced with some extremely difficult matters of judgement. For example, in selecting the power plant, one of the crucial factors is how the price of fuel is going to vary during the selling-life of the aircraft. In the mid-1970s, it was being forecast that fuel prices would continue to rise as oil reserves threatened to dry up during the 1990s, and that even by the mid-1980s fuel would account for 44 per cent of DOC. In the event, fuel prices stabilised (partly as a result of the fact that new oil reserves continue to be found), and associated costs now typically represent only some 20 per cent of DOC.

The stabilizing of fuel prices has had various ramification for the designer. Perhaps most importantly, since the choice of engines is the most fundamental decision in any aircraft design, it makes it considerably less easy to justify the adoption of a totally new power plant concept (such as the unducted propfan) aimed specifically at a major reduction in fuel consumption. In addition, the de-emphasizing of fuel costs causes the designer to pay greater attention to other aspects of DOC, notably maintenance costs. Aside from the mechanical engineering aspects, maintenance costs have benefited from a new generation of highly reliable avionics, automatic health-monitoring systems, and databus systems that replaced huge bundles of cables and connectors.

The basic shape of the airliner is the result of many different considerations, starting with the need to accommodate the predetermined number of passengers and quantity of cargo in a fuselage that will combine a largely constant cross-section for ease of manufacture with a cabin interior that appeals to the travelling public. The payload/range performance of the finished product dictates its take-off weight (for a given level of technology), which in turn determines the wing area required to achieve the desired approach speed and landing performance. For a given wing area, the span is selected to produce a reasonable compromise between lift-induced drag and structure weight.

ASPECT RATIO

Between the mid-1970s and mid-1980s, the high price of fuel encouraged the use of relatively high aspect ratios (i.e. a large wingspan in relation to mean chord) despite the higher wing weights produced, but this trend is now being reversed. Wing sweep and thickness/chord ratio are selected in combination, in order to achieve the chosen cruise speed or maximum operating Mach number for a reasonable structure weight. In the case of long-range aircraft, there is naturally a strong demand for the highest feasible cruising speed, because of the significant potential savings in block time. Advanced wing design also enables long range airliners such as the Airbus A340 and Boeing 777 to climb quickly to their optimum economical cruise levels.

Once the wing area has been chosen (and hence initial wing loading), take-off performance demands generally establish the thrust/weight ratio required, although the designer will check that this also provides the cruising altitude planned.

Right: Using a digital, three-dimensional computer software program called CATIA, parts and systems for the Boeing 777 can be viewed from any angle, thus ensuring that any misalignment can be corrected before releasing the final design.

Below: A loss-maker in its BAe 146 form, production of the four-engined airliner as the Avro RJ is much less labour-intensive and this has managed to save it from oblivion.

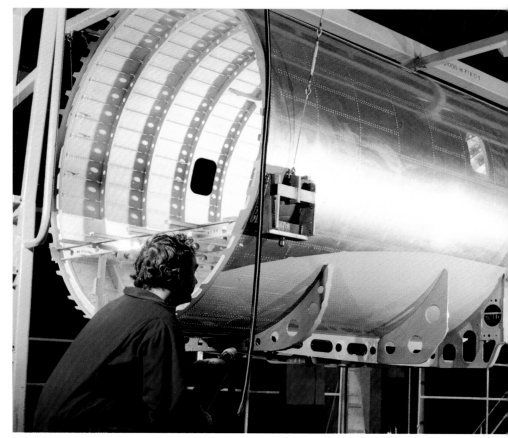

Below: From the earliest days, the three-engine layout has often been preferred, the Junkers 52 and Boeing 727 being classic examples. Russia has continued to produce trijets including the Yak-42.

Knowing the total thrust required, the designer can then select engines and consider how they should be mounted on the airframe. The greater the number of engines, the more capable the aircraft should be to survive a single engine failure, and thus the safer the passenger. However, increased engine reliability has led to twin-engined airliners being permitted to fly extended range (twin engine) operations (ETOPS) of up to 180 minutes. This means that regulations which specify the time that an aircraft should be able to reach an airfield in the event of one engine failing, have been relaxed. It is now commonplace for twin-engined airliners to fly long trans-oceanic sectors carrying over 300 passengers, without compromising safety.

At one time, there was a widely held view that three engines were better than two and more economical than four. It was reasoned that in the event of a single engine failure, the destination could be reached in safety, before ferrying the (empty) aircraft back to the operator's maintenance base with one engine inoperative. But trijets also have disadvantages, notably the difficulty in providing a satisfactory installation for the centreline engine. Various solutions have been tried but access for maintenance engineers is often difficult. The growing number of large long-range, twin-engined airliners is a result of more than just improved engine reliability. Duplicated sources of electrical power generation and many other refinements are necessary before the certification authorities will approve ETOPS.

To allow for an engine failure during take-off, twin engined aircraft are comparatively over-powered and consequently, long-range airliners powered by four less powerful (and less thirsty) engines are equally popular with airlines. However, the extra power of the big twins may enable them to climb more steeply and this can make for a smaller noise 'footprint' around airports than a four-engined aircraft.

In selecting a location for engines, economics favour hanging them on the wing, since wing weight

Left: The use of computer-aided design and manufacture enables Shorts in Northern Ireland to produce the centre fuselage of the Canadair Regional Jet for shipment to an assembly line in Canada where it fits other parts precisely.

Right: The aspect ratio that a designer chooses for the wing of any new airliner is based on a number of considerations. This diagram shows a variety of aspect ratios on aircraft of various configuration. The Saab 2000 (1), with a straight wing and turboprops, has an AR of 11.0, while that of the similarly configured ATR72 (2) is 12.0. Among the jets, the delta-winged Concorde (5) is in a class of its own with an AR of about 2.0; the high wing of the Avro RJ (3) has an AR of 8.9 and the Airbus A320 (4), at 9.4, is about typical today.

Comparative Aspect Ratio

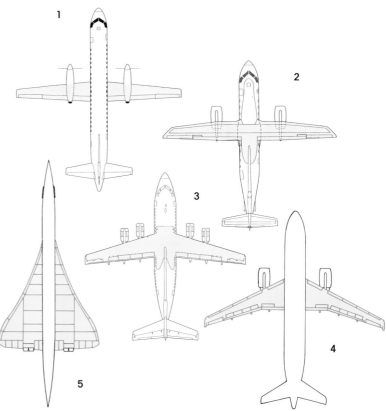

is primarily associated with providing bending strength to withstand lift loads, and since the weight of the engines subtracts from the lift-induced bending moments. The loads produced by the engines can furthermore be fed directly into the wing spars, whereas a rear fuselage mounting demands considerable strengthening in that area to diffuse thrust, weight and inertia loads into the structure. However, wing-mounted engines may well restrict the percentage of trailing edge available for flaps, or require much more complex flaps for the same lift coefficient to be achieved. It may also be noted that, when this type of arrangement originated with the Boeing 707, the (turbojet) engines were proportionally quite small and had little effect on the aircraft's stalling characteristics. Conversely, the turbofan engines of the twin-engined Boeing 757 are much larger in relation to the wing, so stalling characteristics had to be checked very carefully.

It may be argued that a rear-fuselage engine mounting minimizes not only cabin noise but also the yawing movement produced by engine failure and thus reduces the size of the vertical tail, although this is not to say that airliners with wing-mounted engines cannot deal even with outboard engine failures. One very real drawback associated with rear-mounted engines is that the designer is virtually obliged to use a high horizontal tail. Such a tailplane usually provides a long tail-arm, and it operates in clean air above the wing wake, but at high angles of attack it may be blanketed by the wing and possibly the engine nacelles. There is then a tendency to pitch up into a deep stall condition,

from which recovery may be impossible. As a result, it may be necessary to add a stick-shaker or even a stick-pusher in the aircraft's control system to ensure that such conditions are not encountered in the course of airline operations. Conversely, a low tail makes the aircraft increasingly stable as AOA (angle-of-attack, a measure of the aircraft's nose-up attitude in relation to the airflow) increases, but in normal flight operates in the wing wake, which may produce some buffeting and non-linearity of response.

Since the first jet-powered airliner (the de Havilland Comet) entered service in 1952, a wide variety of configuration has been used. Some concepts, such as the 'buried' engines in the wing roots of the Comet, have been ruled out (in that case because of difficulties in access and in re-engining) while the other ideas have become the norm, espe-

cially at the upper end of the weight range. Long-range aircraft have proportionally small payloads, hence there are the largest possible gains to be had from weight-saving and aerodynamic refinement. In this context, the Boeing 747's arrangement, with four engines mounted under the wing, reigns supreme, and it is difficult to visualize anyone today proposing a rear-engined configuration such as that of the Vickers VC-10 or Ilyushin Il-62.

By the same token, it is virtually certain that any large passenger-carrying airliner will have a low-set wing, since the wing carry-through structure then passes neatly through the underfloor freight area, with no interruption of the interior of the cabin. In smaller airliners with proportionally less of the fuselage cross-section devoted to freight, there are arguments in favour of a high wing, although this necessitates a bulge over the top line of the fuselage

Above: Near jet speeds can be attained by the turbo-prop Saab 2000 which combines powerful Allison engines with six-bladed Dowty propellers.

Left: The Boeing 737's low wing puts the engines very close to the ground and when larger engines were adopted for the 737-300, the intakes had to be flattened.

Engine Location

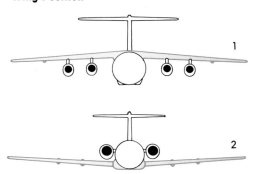

Above: Two, three or four engines, rear-mounted or on the wing — all layouts have been used. These are shown applied to the Embraer EMB-145 (1), Yakovlev Yak-42 (2), ATR42 (3), Airbus A330 (4), McDonnell Douglas MD-11 (5), and Boeing 747-400 (6).

Below: Just how different designs from the same job can be is shown by the Avro RJ (1) and the Fokker 100 (2), which are 100-seat airliners for short/medium ranges. Four engines and a high wing or two engines and a low wing do the same job for different customers.

Below: Providing for the carriage of freight is an important part of the civil transport designer's job today. The giant Antonov An-124 freighters accommodate loads which are both very large and heavy. Many passenger airliners can also be fitted with freight doors.

Tailplane Comparisons

Above: Tailplane position and configuration vary as much as wing and engine locations, and are related to the overall design. The diagrams show, top to bottom, the tail units of the Dornier 228 (1), Boeing 767 (2), ATR 42 (3), McDonnell Douglas MD-90 (4) and Beech 1900D (5).

mounted landing gear, which is more like that normally fitted to a military tactical transport. A more conventional aircraft such as the Boeing 737 was originally designed to operate from well-swept paved surfaces, hence it was perfectly acceptable to mount its engines below a low wing, although this does restrict the use of flaps. It is also noteworthy that in the case of the 737-300 with large CFM56 turbofans, the lower rim of the intake had to be flattened to increase separation from the ground.

One of the arguments used against high-wing aircraft is that this arrangement frequently leads to a long, stalky (engine nacelle-mounted) landing gear, which is not suited to rough surfaces. On the other hand, a high wing normally means a low floor line and easier access from the ground, which may be a significant factor at small airports. The ATR42, designed as a joint venture between Aerospatiale and Alenia, achieves a compromise by retracting the short undercarriage into fuselage sponsons, thus placing the aircraft systems at a convenient height for ground servicing since they are located in the belly of the aircraft, within easy reach of a man standing on the ground. While BAe argued that the low wing of its ATP turboprop airliner made it compatible with airport jetways and airbridges because it is slightly higher off the ground, the ATR42 and its larger derivative the ATR72, have sold in such numbers that special jetways have been developed for them. Despite the fact that it sits low on the ground, the ATR42 was stretched without being concerned about rotation considerations at take-off.

DESIGNING FOR FREIGHT

The carriage of freight is becoming an increasingly important factor in airliner design, due both to the growth in cargo traffic and to the need for operational flexibility. Boeing's first design in the evolutionary process that led to the highly successful 747 was actually a double-decked project, since this gave the highest number of passengers for a given cross-section. However, in the early 1960s, when jet fuel cost around 10 cents per US gallon, there was a

Wing Position

if the wing carry-through is not to restrict headroom in the cabin. In the case of the BAe 146/Avro RJ, it is argued that having a continuous upper surface to the wing generates four per cent more lift with eight per cent less drag at high AOA than in the case of the equivalent low wing. It is also argued by BAe that the high wing keeps the intakes well clear of the ground (and thus avoids debris ingestion) while permitting the use of relatively deep pylons that take the engine efflux well below the wing, allowing the use of a flap over almost 80 per cent of the trailing edge. It may be noted in this respect that the aircraft's tabbed Fowler flap was intended to give a lift coefficient of 3.38, and that a figure of 3.45 has been achieved.

The ability to operate from unpaved runways in undeveloped regions of the world was an important consideration in the design of the BAe 146, hence the high intakes and also the short fuselage-

widespread perception that Concorde and subsequent SSTs would win most of the long-haul passenger business. Boeing accordingly revised the 747 design to give it the best potential for cargo carrying.

Cargo considerations led Boeing to abandon the double-deck arrangement in favour of a single deck that was wide enough to take up to 10 seats abreast (US tourist class) or two freight containers 2.44m x 2.44m (8ft x 8ft) side-by-side. In establishing how the containers were to be loaded, the company looked at swing-noses and at visor-noses with the flight deck either below the cabin floor or above it. In the end it was decided to locate the cockpit above the main cabin, though this necessitated a long fairing behind the flight deck in order to achieve an acceptable drag at the design cruise speed. The associated space was initially used as a lounge for first-class passengers, and later as a cabin for up to 32 extra passengers. In the case of the stretched upper deck, since the 747-300 this second cabin has been extended by 7.1m (23ft 4in) to take up to 69 economy-class passengers. An incidental advantage of the stretched upper deck is that the increased fineness of the aerodynamic bulge improves optimum cruise speed from Mach 0.84 (for the standard airframe) to Mach 0.86.

Before leaving this basic matter of airliner configuration, it may be useful to mention an important change that is certain to occur before long. 'Super-Jumbos' will soon be built to accommodate as many as 1,000 passengers, both Airbus and Boeing having carried out design studies for future large aircraft. The latter initially considered a further stretch to the ubiquitous 747 but the prospects of a brand-new design from Airbus, the A3XX, with its promise of highly competitive operating costs, led to a less than enthusiastic welcome to Boeing's proposals.

American aircraft manufacturers have proved adept at improving original designs in such a way that airlines continue to order them in large numbers. McDonnell Douglas with its MD-80 and MD-90 series developed from the DC-9 is one such example but Boeing's 737 now being produced in third generation form, has amply demonstrated the wisdom of adding refinements to a popular airliner. However, having frequently applied this practice to the 747 originally designed in the 1960s, Boeing found that airlines preferred a completely new design. But why do they need such large aircraft? Quite simply because the relentless increase in passenger traffic suggests that larger aircraft offer a solution to traffic congestion, both in the skies and at airports.

ADVANCED TECHNOLOGIES

A wide range of enhancements is being introduced in order to improve the economics of current-generation airliners. One of the most important advances relates to the computer-aided design of wings that (for a given sweep angle) achieve unprecedented combinations of thickness/chord ratio and lift/drag ratio and high subsonic Mach number. Traditional aerofoils had triangular lift distributions with a peak suction far forward, associated with very high local velocities and a strong shock wave well forward on the section. Modern aerofoils produce a comparatively flat-top suction over most of the upper surface, with a weak shock well aft, and the undersurface is shaped to give positive lift toward the trailing edge. The whole chord is thus working effectively, and much higher efficiencies are produced. In addition, it is normal to take the maximum thickness forward at the wing root in order to give the wing the highest effective sweep back angle.

The comparatively thick sections made possible by this 'supercritical' approach to wing design benefit structure weight and allow increased aspect ratios to be used. Other possible aerodynamic refinements include the variable-camber (or 'mission-adaptive') wing, which changes its shape to match the flight regime. However, considerable work remains to be done on this. Already increasingly being fitted on airliners are winglets, which reduce induced drag without the bending moments produced by normal wingtip extensions. Winglets reduce the rotational flow around the wingtips and may generate a small forward thrust component.

A more radical form of drag reduction is the use of laminar flow control (LFC), which is conventionally achieved by sucking away the boundary air from the upper wing surface through a multiplicity of small holes. McDonnell Douglas has promoted the development of 'hybrid LFC', in which suction is used over only a small part of the wing chord, aft of which a large area of natural laminar flow is achieved by means of a favourable pressure gradient. Fuel gains of around 15 per cent have been predicted.

Trim drag can be reduced in various ways, including the use of inverse camber on the inboard sections of a swept wing. The CG should be as far aft as possible which has encouraged the use of the tailplane as a trim tank, although fuel pumping for CG adjustment was introduced with the Concorde. In time, most airliners may follow combat aircraft in adopting naturally unstable configurations (i.e. with the CG even farther aft), and relying on artificial stability and fly-by-wire (FBW) controls.

The use of FBW controls have other advantages, in saving weight and in making possible the use of gust alleviation systems, which may reduce structure weight. Initially, the tendency was to use FBW with mechanical reversionary systems, but in future these rods, cranks, pulleys and cables will eventually be eliminated in the interest of weight-saving. Other moves to reduce system weight include the use of fibre-optics in place of conventional cables, and new actuator concepts such as Boeing's projected electrostatic actuator, which would eliminate long runs of hydraulic piping.

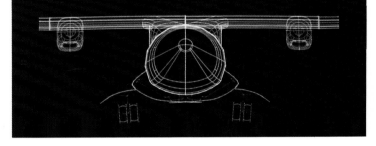

Right: Large drawing offices where draughtsmen prepare blueprints from which each individual item of an airliner is manufactured are becoming things of the past. The norm now is to use CAD (computer-aided design) techniques, as for this ATR 42.

Below: Wind tunnels are valuable design tools and the model of an Airbus A340-600 on test here has a new larger wing developed by British Aerospace.

Right: Airbus has pushed forward the frontiers of design with such innovations as fly-by-wire systems and side stick controls – both of which are featured on the A340.

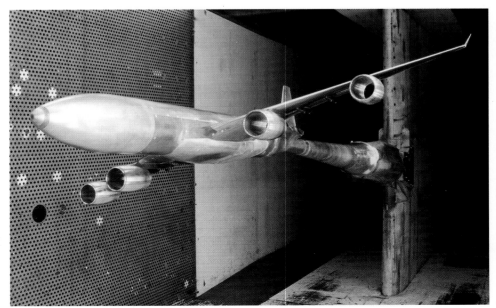

Above: Computers play a vital part in modern airliner technology, from design to operation. At the manufacturing stage computers aid precision machining, as shown here on a Boeing 757 wing.

Airframe materials are changing to reflect the emphasis on weight-saving. Composite materials are being used increasingly even for primary structures, achieving weight savings in the order of 20 per cent or more. Furthermore, carbon wheel brake assemblies provide major savings, while aluminium-lithium and other 'exotic' alloys offer significant weight reductions relative to conventional aluminium alloys.

Costs are also being reduced through improved manufacturing techniques. Computer-aided manufacturing (CAM) has made increased automation possible, in some cases approaching the levels achieved in car factories. Boeing and other manufacturers are making growing use of thermoplastic materials, allowing complex parts such as wing ribs to be formed as a single piece (rather than 20 or more pieces and up to 500 fasteners), with a cost saving of 30-40 per cent. New techniques such as superplastic forming and diffusion bonding promise to combine savings in both weight and cost. The airliner of the future may well change little in appearance, but the materials from which it is constructed and the manner in which its components are manufactured will certainly be different from those of today's aircraft.

ENGINE TECHNOLOGY

The airline engine of today has evolved along a long and difficult path, with many technical challenges on the way, since the pioneer commercial turbines of the early 1950s. Most of the engines in that period, (the de Havilland Ghost turbojet in the D.H. Comet, the Rolls-Royce Avon turbojet in the later Comets and the Sud-Aviation Caravelle, and the Pratt & Whitney JT3C turbojet in the Boeing 707 and Douglas DC-8) were adapted from military combat powerplants. The first real commercial power units, based on first-hand experience with turbine engines in airline operation and designed from the outset for passenger-carrying service, were the Rolls-Royce Tyne turboprop and Spey turbofan designed in the mid- to late 1950s.

From that time onwards, an increasing variety of fully-fledged commercial turbines began to emerge, with the big Pratt & Whitney JT9D turbofan developed in the late 1960s for the Boeing 747 representing perhaps the most dramatic single step forward. General Electric, which made a belated but highly successful entry into the airline market, did not entirely break with early practice, its CF6 series of big turbofans being initially derived from the TF39 powering the Lockheed C-5A, though this was in any case a purpose-built engine, for a military transport, not a combat aircraft.

What made these later-generation commercial engines so different from the predecessors were the differing performance and operating criteria applied to their design, compared with those for military engines. The airline operator wants low fuel

Right: Suited to propulsion at speeds of around Mach 0.6, the turboprop engine consists of a gas turbine driving a propeller via a gearbox. The large relatively low-moving prop slipstream provides the majority of the engine thrust.

Right: Simplest of the turbine powerplants, the turbojet expels its low mass flow exhaust gases rearwards at high speed to produce thrust. It is most suited to economic propulsion at supersonic speeds – as for the Concorde SST.

Right: Offering attractive fuel economy at Mach 0.85, the turbofan uses its fan to accelerate additional air around the outside of the engine (the bypass flow) to produce a larger, slower-moving exhaust mass for efficient high subsonic propulsion.

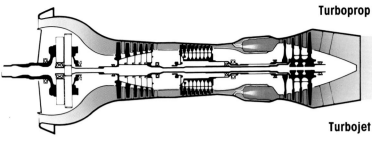

Turboprop

Turbojet

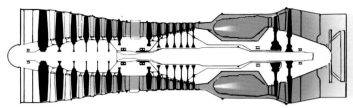

Turbofan

burn; high reliability, durability and maintainability; low noise and exhaust emissions; and competitive pricing. By contrast, the military combat engine tends to emphasize specific performance – that is, pounds (or kN) thrust per pound (kg) of engine weight and per square unit of frontal area, and pounds (kN) thrust per pound (kg) of air mass flow through the engine. Less stress is placed on specific fuel consumption (SFC) than is the case for an airline engine, and the various commercial criteria play a part, but less importantly.

The final outcome of this growing divergence between civil and military engines is that interchange in their roles has become limited to special cases only. Today, over 40 years since military engines powered many of the early turbine airliners, the cross-fertilization has changed direction: the P&W JT9D and PW2037, the GE CF6-50 – GE/Snecma CFM56 and the Rolls-Royce RB.211 – all developed in the first instance for commercial use, now each has at least one military transport application.

COMMERCIAL ENGINE TYPES

Since the introduction of the Vickers Viscount in the mid-1950s, powered by the Rolls-Royce Dart turboprop, airliner propulsion has undergone a radical

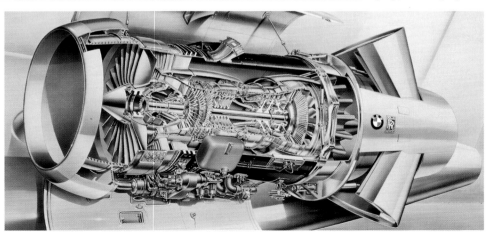

Above: One of the world's outstanding commercial turbine engines, the Rolls-Royce Dart civil turboprop was in production from 1953 (when the Dart Rda3-powered Viscount entered service with BEA) through to 1986, by which time over 7,000 units had been built. More than 110 million hours have been flown in service. One of the latest versions was the 2,330 ehp Dart Mk 552, shown here installed in a Fokker F27 Friendship.

Left: The product of a joint venture between BMW and Rolls-Royce, the BR710 is one of a family of two-stage turbine engines intended to power regional airliners and business jets. Featuring a high-intensity smokeless annular combustor, this turbofan belongs to the new-generation of environmentally friendly engines. The more powerful BR715 has been chosen for the MD-95 airliner.

series of changes of engine type. The turboprop was early relegated to mainly short-haul operations as the greater speed and glamour of the turbojet, and then the turbofan, displaced what came to be regarded as old-fashioned propeller propulsion. Fuel prices were considerably lower in the 1960s, so neither the better fuel economy of the turboprop nor its less noisy operation were enough to sustain it in the front line of airline propulsion. Conversely, it was the poor fuel economy of the turbojet, combined with its excessive exhaust noise, which resulted in its fairly rapid replacement by the quieter and more fuel efficient turbofan.

Today, the turbojet has been effectively eliminated from the commercial transport scene. At present, the major responsibility for airline propulsion rests with the turbofan. Rapidly rising fuel prices in the 1980s encouraged the development of the propfan – an entirely new form of propulsion which promised to bring important new levels of economy. The reason for the perceived breakthrough of the propfan into what otherwise appeared to be a stable and well-established market for the turbofan, can be found in the differing propulsion characteristics of the competing engine types.

Aside from the component and thermal efficiencies of the core engine (the main gas generating compressor, combustor and turbine), which are broadly comparable between one manufacturer and another, it is the basic configuration and propulsive efficiency of the overall powerplant system that influence an engine's position in the propulsion spectrum. A major parameter of configuration is bypass ratio (BPR), representing the ratio between the external mass of air accelerated and the air passing through the engine proper.

The highest BPR of all is in fact the piston engine/propeller combination, where the ratio can be as high as 200:1. Next in order is the turboprop, at between 70 and 100:1. In these two engine systems, the primary characteristic is their moderate acceleration of a relatively large mass of air through the propeller disc. In terms of propulsion efficiency, propeller engine combinations are suited to aircraft cruise speeds up to the equivalent of Mach 0.75. above this flight condition, the propeller begins to experience compressibility problems (its helical tip speed is considerably higher than the aircraft's forward speed), and its efficiency in accelerating air rearwards become increasingly impaired. Although advanced technology propellers have raised the limiting Mach number somewhat, this basic limitation to propeller propulsion remains.

The turbojet, where all the propulsive air passes through the engine core, is at the other end of the BPR scale, and has a ratio of zero. This means that regardless of the thermal efficiency of the core section, the fact that the turbojet accelerates a relatively small mass flow to a very high exhaust speed, the

Comparative Noise Footprints

Above: The diagram shows the benefit of a quieter, higher bypass ratio turbofan in the Boeing 737-300 compared with the earlier 727-200.

Below: The Pratt & Whitney JT9D pioneered the introduction of high bypass ratio turbofans offering high thrust, enhanced fuel economy and quieter operation. The PW4000 engine shown here represents the company's new generation of turbofans which today compete with such engines as the General Electric GE90 and Rolls-Royce Trent family.

Rolls-Royce/Snecma Olympus

Right: The world's only turbine engine in supersonic passenger-carrying service is the Olympus 593 turbojet with reheat developed by Snecma. As powerplant for the Anglo-French Concorde SST, the Olympus 593 produces an impressive 169kN (38,000lb) of thrust on take-off. Although a turbojet (the only one in civil use) the engine provides a competitive fuel economy at supersonic flight speeds.

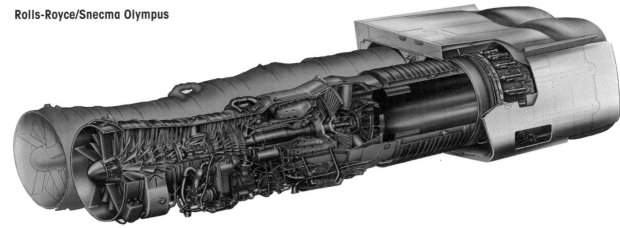

propulsive efficiency is low except at very high aircraft speeds. Hence the deliberate use of turbojets in the Concorde, and their virtual disappearance from subsonic areas of airline propulsion.

The turbofan was introduced specifically as a means of overcoming this fundamental limitation in the turbojet. While progressive improvements in component efficiency and higher compressor pressure ratios and turbine entry temperatures, tended to raise thermal efficiency more or less regardless of engine type, the turbofan concentrated on improving the propulsive efficiency by raising the BPR. As the fuel economy of an aero engine is the product of its thermal and propulsive efficiencies, this tactic offered potentially large benefits in the high subsonic speed regime.

The earliest airline turbofans, the Rolls-Royce Conway and Pratt & Whitney JT3D, had low BPRs in the range of 0.3:1 to 1.4:1. The benefits they offered over the Avon and JT3C turbojets were thus discernible but not dramatic. Even the next generation of purpose-built turbofans, the R-R Spey and P&W JT8D, still had BPRs of less than 1:1, although these engines have subsequently been refanned and, as the Tay and JT8D-200, have BPRs of about 2:1. The really big step forward was pioneered in 1960 by the P&W JT9D, which had a ratio of 5:1. This had a profound effect on fuel burn, corresponding to a 25 per cent reduction in SFC compared with other engines of the period. The GE CF6 and R-R RB.211 series of turbofans followed in the wake of the JT9D.

The second generation of bypass turbofans with BPRs of around 5:1 and 6:1 includes such engines as the Pratt & Whitney PW4000, the International Aero Engines V2500, the General Electric GE90, Rolls-Royce Trent and CFM International CFM56. Each has offered further improvements in SFC. The new Trent 500, 600 and 900 engines will have a BPR of 8:1. The reduction in cruise fuel consumption made available by the V2500 and later CFM56 models – both strongly contesting to power Airbus aircraft in particular – is around 20 to 25 per cent compared with previous turbofans.

In the early 1980s, when the price of crude oil reached about $25 per barrel, an airline's fuel bill represented as much as 30 per cent of the aircraft total operating costs. General Electric, which was seeking to contest Pratt & Whitney's dominance of the short/medium-haul market with the JT8D turbofan, decided that the propfan concept represented a viable means for achieving much higher BPRs and hence significantly lower fuel consumptions. In

Above: The Pratt & Whitney JT8D is the world's most successful commercial turbofan to date, with over 14,000 units built and production continuing of the re-fanned JT8D-200 series for the MD-80 aircraft family.

Below: The Rolls-Royce Trent is the most powerful engine in airline service in the world today, moving together with the GE90 and PW4000 engines towards an incredibly powerful 445kN (100,000lb) thrust level.

The Rolls-Royce Trent

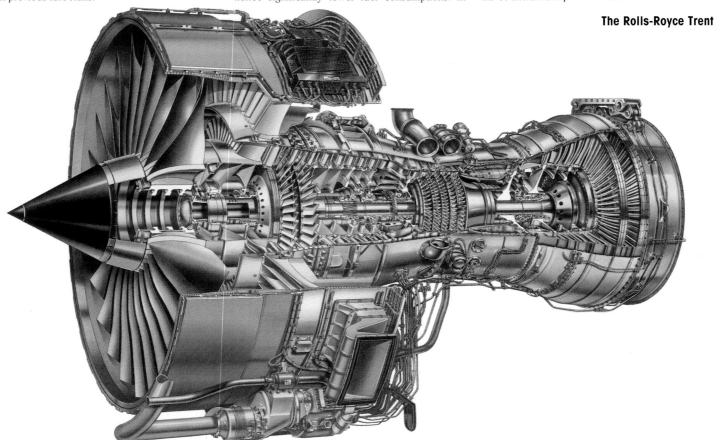

Comparative Engine Thrusts

Right: The contrasting configurations and sizes of turboprop, turbojet and turbofan engines – with three sizes of turbofan shown with differing magnitudes to bypass ratio (bpr). Top-to-bottom: Pratt & Whitney Canada PW124 turboprop of 70 to 100:1 bpr; Rolls-Royce/Snecma Olympus 593 reheated turbojet of zero bpr; Rolls-Royce RB211-524D4D turbofan of 4.4:1 bpr; Pratt & Whitney JT8D-219 turbofan of 1.77:1 bpr; and AlliedSignal ALF 502R-7 turbofan of 5.6:1 bpr. The length of the rectangle behind each engine is proportional to the unit's thrust output. The height of the rectangle indicates the relative diameter of the engine's slipstream or exhaust, which bears no direct relationship to the thrust of the engine. The colour represents the temperature of the slipstream, ranging from a cool blue for the turboprop, through mauve for the turbofans, to a hot red for the turbojet.

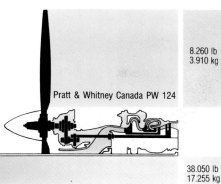
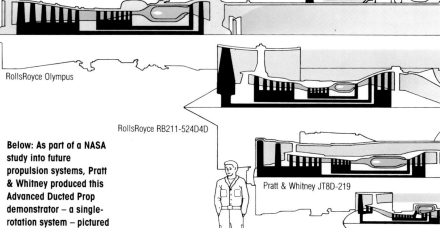

Pratt & Whitney Canada PW 124 — 8.260 lb 3.910 kg

RollsRoyce Olympus — 38.050 lb 17.255 kg

RollsRoyce RB211-524D4D — 58.000 lb 26.305 kg

Pratt & Whitney JT8D-219 — 21.000 lb 9.525 kg

AlliedSignal ALF 502R-7 — 7,000lb (3,180kg)

Below: As part of a NASA study into future propulsion systems, Pratt & Whitney produced this Advanced Ducted Prop demonstrator – a single-rotation system – pictured here being tested in the Ames Research Center's wind tunnel.

Below: Comparison of cruise performances (height/speed/sfc) of (1) Olympus 593 in Concorde; (2) JT8D-219 in McDonnell Douglas MD-80; (3) RB211-524D4D in Boeing 747; (4) ALF 502R-7 in BAe 146; and (5) PW124 in ATR 42.

Engine Cruise Performances

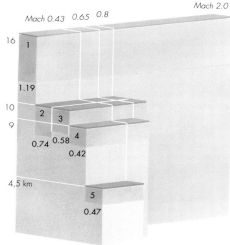

Mach 0.43 0.65 0.8 Mach 2.0
16 — 1
1.19
10 — 2 3
9
0.74 0.58 4
0.42
4,5 km
5
0.47

1984, development was started of the GE unducted fan (UDF) engine with a BPR of 35:1. Using thin, highly swept propfan blades designed to delay the onset of compressibility effects, the UDF was optimized for propulsion at a cruise Mach number of around 0.85, making it competitive with turbofan equipment.

General Electric vigorously promoted the propfan engine and its UDF was to have powered Boeing's proposed 150-seat 7J7, the prospect of this leading other engine manufactures to initiate their own projects. Estimated reductions in SFC compared with then current airline engines were an impressive 25 to 35 per cent. However, fuel prices began to fall as rapidly as they had been rising and with declining airline interest, it was no longer viable to invest a lot in the development of propfans. Interestingly, BMW R-R and MTU are looking into a geared ducted-fan with a high BPR for the next-generation aircraft.

THE TURBOFAN

Turbofans power the great majority of airline trans-

Propfan

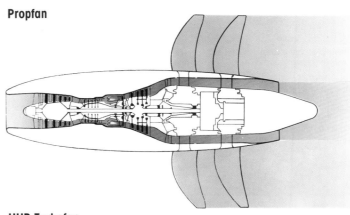

UHB Turbofan

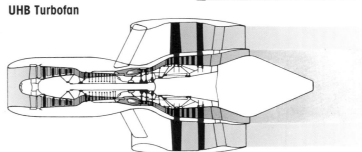

ports in service today and range from the 31kN (7,000lb) thrust AlliedSignal LF 507 in the Avro RJ regional airliner to the 400kN-plus (90,000lb) 'big fans' which power the Boeing 777 wide-body transport. The typical configuration is two-shaft, with a single-stage fan plus turbine on the low-pressure rotor, and the core section comprising an axial compressor (and combustor) plus turbine on the high-pressure rotor. An exception to this layout is the RB.211 which has three shafts, the compressor and HP turbine being split into intermediate and high-pressure rotors.

Other features of turbofans include the use of thrust reversers, normally of cascade or four-door type, acting on the fan slipstream which provides the major part of the engine's thrust; modular construction to avoid having to remove the entire engine in the event of a defect in one component; engine health or condition monitoring facilities on the combustor and main rotative assemblies to enable incipient failures to be detected; and increasingly more sophisticated engine control systems leading to fully automatic digital engine controls (FADECs).

THE PROPFAN

General Electric started ground testing its 111kN (25,000lb) thrust proof-of-concept UDF in 1986 and flight tests on a Boeing 727 began the following year. This engine, the lower-powered Allison/Pratt & Whitney Model 578-DX and Rolls-Royce design studies, were of similar concept in that they each featured aft-located open (or unducted) contra-rotating fans.

However, internally they differed quite markedly. GE's UDF had no reduction gearing between the LP turbine and the propfan, while the turbine itself was unusual in having intermeshed contra-rotating rotors. The Allison/P&W 578-DX was the most conventional of the three types in its layout, using the core engine to energise a power turbine driving a gearbox which in turn drove the fan.

Although all of these propfan layouts made use of 'pusher' propfans, the perception that they could be vulnerable to foreign object damage (FOD) meant that all proposed installations were to be rear-mounted, with the fans behind the fuselage aft pressure bulkhead. While some Rolls-Royce studies

Above: The Rolls-Royce ContraFan ultra high bypass turbofan study was at one time intended to power long-range transports, but development was abandoned.

Below: Pratt & Whitney and Allison teamed to produce a propfan engine which was the subject of flight tests on an MD-80. However, falling fuel prices put paid to further development

Top: Propfan – representative of small/medium size propfans, with two-spool gas generator and rear-located gearbox driving a contra-rotating open fan in pusher mode.

Above: UHB Turbofan – representative of ultra high bypass-ratio, high thrust turbofan engines equipped with a forward mounted gas generator and 'gearless' contra-rotating ducted fan.

considered the use of 'tractor' fans, only Russian and Ukrainian manufacturers have worked together to develop the concept to the point of series production.

After the price of crude oil peaked at around $34 per barrel in the mid-1980s, it fell to below $10 before the end of that decade, with the result that the expense of further research into propfans could no longer be justified. Airlines were simply not interested in buying a radical new type of engine, so work on the propfan stopped as abruptly as it had started. However, jet engines produced in Russia were not noted for their fuel economy so research there continued, even after the collapse of the former Soviet Union, with the result that in due course

the Antonov An-70 transport aircraft was powered by propfans.

Combining D-27 engines developed in the Ukraine by the Progress Design Bureau, driving SV-27 contra-rotating fans produced in Russia by the Aerosyla Design Bureau, the An-70 is the first production aircraft to make use of propfans.

THE TURBOPROP

To date, the most widely used configuration of turboprop has been the single-shaft layout as typified by the 1,500-2,240kW (2,000-3,000shp) R-R Dart and 2,985-3,730kW (4,000-5,000shp) Allison Model 501/T56. The former uses a centrifugal compressor and integral gearbox, and the latter an axial com-

Above: Computer-aided design was used extensively in the development of the Rolls-Royce Trent 800 for the Boeing 777.

Right: Pratt & Whitney PW 124 turboprop with Hamilton Standard six-bladed propeller on Viscount flying test bed.

Below: The outdoor engine noise test facility at Rolls-Royce Hucknall played an important part in the Trent's progress towards entry into airline service in the mid-1990s. The Trent 700 and 800 power the A330 and B777 respectively, with the Trent 900 being developed for the proposed A3XX.

pressor and strut-mounted gearbox. At the low/medium end of the power scale, two-shaft and three-shaft free turbine layouts are now in widespread service. The Pratt & Whitney Canada PT6A series with a compressor combining a single centrifugal and three axial stages, is particularly suited to commuter airliners, becoming a classic produced in thousands.

The turboprop has tended to be overshadowed by the turbofan and often prematurely written off as 'out of date' but new developments in propeller design have given this combination a new life. Engines such as the Allison Ae 2100 have given turboprop airliners such as the Saab 2000 and IPTN N-250 a cruise speed capability close to that of jets but at lower operating costs.

Clearly, the turboprop has established a niche at the lighter end of the regional airliner market, although its predominance has been challenged by turbofans which are increasingly being selected to power aircraft as small as 30-seaters. However, the new category of single-engined airliners – all powered by turboprops – will ensure a continued demand for this type of propulsion. The controversy over the ETOPS issue much debated in the 1980s, has been no less strong over the matter of carrying passengers in single turboprop aircraft but in both cases, the proven reliability of gas turbine engines decided the matter.

FUTURE DEVELOPMENTS

NASA, in reviewing future aeropropulsion opportunities, graded these as first, evolutionary; second, novel heat engine developments; and third, revolutionary concepts requiring radical changes in the structure of the aerospace industry. The stage applicable to today's commercial engines is 'evolutionary', and here NASA saw large rather than small gains in performance still to be won. The three main avenues of progress that can be exploited are via advanced aerodynamics, innovative design and new materials.

Advances in aerodynamics can be seen in the steady increase in compressor pressure ratios, with 40:1 being proposed with a similar number of stages as existing 30:1 ratio engines. Aerodynamics also form part of what Rolls-Royce calls aero-thermal technology, in particular concerning turbine blade cooling.

Innovative design is exemplified in GE's development of the short-lived UDF and the diversity of competitive designs which it inspired in the 1980s. However, to meet the demands of aircraft manufacturers, engine companies have produced new power units at both ends of the power scale. Larger airliners have demanded more powerful engines, yet the burgeoning number of small regional jets, has also encouraged advances in low powered turbofans.

While the use of composite materials and ceramics has been investigated, important advances have been made in the single crystal metal components which are both stronger and lighter. However, demands from airlines to cut costs, and from certification authorities for higher levels of reliability (if ETOPS is to be approved), have obliged engine manufacturers to achieve both. As a consequence maintenance costs have fallen, through such developments as the condition monitoring and performance analysis software system (COMPASS), allowing airlines to review engine data at any time.

While FADEC systems monitor engine functions, in future this information will be transmitted by satellite to a control centre so that engineers may be alerted to a problem before it happens. Continuous trend analysis will ensure early warning of faults which will result if corrective action is not taken.

FUTURE DEVELOPMENTS

Commercial aircraft come in different shapes and sizes, for contrasting purposes. It is clearly impossible to predict the future of giant passenger jets, heavy freighters, local-service turboprops and STOL utility machines for the so-called 'bush' market all in the same breath – to say nothing of helicopters and perhaps airships! This chapter, which looks as far ahead as one dare attempt, is concerned chiefly with the mass passenger market. Like most aircraft, big passenger carriers can be studied under four main subheadings: aerodynamics, structures, propulsion and systems.

Sixty years ago, the DC-3 era established the cantilever monoplane wing as the undisputed lifting surface for most airliners, and virtually all such wings have flaps to increase lift on take-off and increase drag on landing. With the coming of jets in the 1950s, wings became generally thinner: at least the ratio of thickness (measured from top to bottom) to chord (distance from leading edge to trailing edge) became significantly reduced, typically from around 17 per cent to barely half this value. To some degree this was accomplished by sweeping the wings back at an angle of about 35 deg. The trend seemed to be towards thinner wings and more sweepback, but – except for the special case of the Concorde SST – the reverse has happened.

AERODYNAMICS

Today's advanced jetliners have wings with greater thickness/chord ratio, typically around 12 per cent, and sweepback reduced to between 15 deg and 28 deg. On the other hand, aspect ratio (the slenderness in plan shape, defined as the square of the span divided by wing area) has never ceased to increase, from around 6 (6.96 for the Boeing 747) to 7.77 for the Boeing 757, 7.9 for the Boeing 767, 8.8 for the Airbus A310 and 9.39 for the A320. All this has been made possible by so-called 'supercritical' wing profiles, which enable wings to be relatively deeper at Mach numbers around 0.8-0.85 without any extra drag. In turn this reduces structure weight, leaves more room for fuel and has other advantages. Greater aspect ratio has a direct effect upon efficiency in cruising flight, so that range is increased for any given amount of fuel. There is no reason to doubt that, with improved materials, aspect ratios will reach 12 by 2000. Combined with improved engine cycle efficiency this will significantly improve the 'miles per gallon' figure.

This has already revolutionized the sector distances that can be flown economically by any given size of aeroplane. After World War II, a long-range airliner was one that could fly sectors longer than 1,000 statute miles (1,610km). To fly the Atlantic was virtually impossible until the late fifties when the Douglas DC-7C and Lockheed L-1649A, the last of the big piston-engined airliners, managed to eliminate tiresome refuelling stops. It could just be attempted, with totally uneconomic payload, by colossal aircraft such as the Bristol Brabazon. Today, heavy passenger and cargo loads can be

Below: Constant efforts by designers and engineers have resulted in many small but significant innovations such as the winglets on this McDonnell Douglas MD-11 which increases aspect ratio and reduces wingtip vortices. However, by no means all new airliners make use of them.

Above: The Airbus A340 long-range airliner looks conventional enough but it incorporates much of the technology introduced by the A320 in the late 1980s. Important features include advanced aerodynamic design, efficient manufacturing advances, structural ideas and systems.

Mission Adaptive Wing

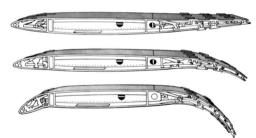

Left: Thanks to the pliability of new non-metallic materials that can be used in the airframe structure, Boeing has been able to develop this Mission Adaptive Wing, which can change its profile in flight without the usual drawbacks of gaps being opened up when slats or flaps are operated.

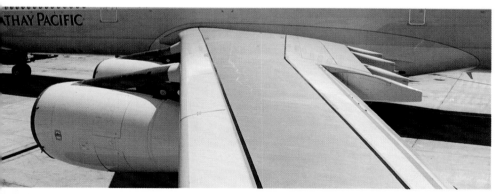

Above: Much of the wing of the Airbus A340 is covered with a plastic film with microscopic grooves that save fuel by reducing drag.

Left: Laminar flow control, as mentioned in this chapter, is a promising area for development. NASA has been using this JetStar to test wing sections with LFC.

flown over the North Atlantic by quite modest twin-engined machines. A sector of 1,000 statute miles (1,610km) is short range; medium-haul is around 3,000 statute miles (4,830km); and the long-haulers do upwards of 7,000 statute miles (11,270km) – a distance that was far beyond even the future plans of anyone designing aircraft 50 years ago.

It has often been stressed that the one thing aircraft have to offer is speed, and it has sometimes been assumed that it is natural to offer as high a speed as possible. Until about 1960 this was true. Piston-engined airliner designers sought more speed by every means possible but lost out to the turbo-prop, which in turn was almost swept away by the jet. Most designers have turned their attention to matters of safety and efficiency rather than speed. Today, not only has the propeller come back to the world's airports, but the jet has all the speed it needs and is being developed entirely along such fresh directions as greater reliability, reduced fuel burn, less noise, improved digital avionics and, above all, reduced costs.

From the aerodynamic point of view this means an all-round reduction in drag. Many former excrescences, such as wing fences, vortillons (underside fences) and vortex generators are being eliminated, while the winglet is being used increasingly. But a more fundamental goal is the attainment of laminar (non-turbulent) flow. The thin sheath of air surrounding today's airliners is almost always highly turbulent, and it gives rise to considerable drag. If this so-called boundary layer can be made laminar, drag can be reduced by more than half. Almost 50 years ago, engineers were working on ways of designing a laminar airliner, typically by sucking the boundary layer inside the aircraft through porous or finely perforated skins. This proved difficult to accomplish, and the slightest surface irregularity (such as a fly squashed against the leading edge on take-off) could cause severe turbulence.

Though not evident externally, future transports are certainly going to have cleverer wings than those flying today. The A330 and A340 heralded a new era in which the aerofoil section, or profile can be varied throughout each flight under computer control to achieve the highest lift/drag ratio at all times. These European aircraft simply use the trailing-edge flaps for this purpose, but the ideal solution is a fully variable profile, with no hinges or discontinuities, rivalling the variation in profile of a bird's wing. The Boeing Military Airplane Co. has fitted a crude form of such a wing, called a Mission Adaptive Wing (MAW) to an F-111, and it could be that by about 2010 the designers of airliners will be thinking in terms of refined MAWs as a matter of course.

Today the quest for laminar aircraft continues and by the turn of the century, perhaps the technical difficulties will have been overcome. Some designers have proposed radically new wing profiles, with little or no sweepback and it is theoretically possible to achieve 'natural' laminar flow, without expending energy on sucking and blowing. However, another means of smoothing airflow is the subject of an on-going trials by Airbus which has found that plastic film with microscopic grooves (called riblets) saves fuel by reducing drag. The same principle is to be found in dolphins and sharks which have similar grooves in their skin to help them to move more quickly through the water. The riblets on top of wings and fuselage work by reducing spanwise disturbances in the airflow, resulting in a reduction in fuel consumption by more than one per cent, equivalent to about one tonne of fuel on a 6,000nm (11,100km) flight. Trials have shown that the riblets do not become clogged by dust or insects and will last long enough to remain in service until the aircraft is due to be repainted. Meanwhile, more trials have been embarked upon to see if laminar flow can be successfully applied to tomorrow's airliners.

STRUCTURES

Turning to structures, it is a general rule that civil aircraft tend to introduce new technologies anything from three to 15 years later than do advanced combat aircraft, and on this basis the structure of the 21st century airliner is likely to be made chiefly of advanced composites. The latter can be thought of either as plastic materials reinforced by very strong fibres or, alternatively, as millions of fibres stuck together with glue, the latter usually being an epoxy resin, polyamide or other 'plastic'. In general, composites tend to be as strong as the strongest metal alloys, bulk for bulk, whilst weighing often less than half as much. The fibres are costly, but the costs of manufacturing each component are much less because there are so few separate parts, whereas in today's airliners there may be hundreds of parts all joined with rivets, bolts and welds. The move to the production of primary structures from composite materials primarily based on carbon fibre, began with the entire tail of the A320 but there is no reason to doubt that the next generation of transports will have most of the wings, fuselage and engine nacelles made of composites, leaving high-strength steel in the landing gears and other metal parts in a few highly stressed joints and, of course, the engines.

Composite Materials

- Primary structure and flight control surfaces
- Secondary structure

Left: The term 'composites' embraces a number of materials that are non-metallic, such as carbon fibre or glass-reinforced plastic (GRP). Fabric-like in their qualities before being 'set', they can be used for a large variety of aircraft parts.

Below: The turboprop Fairchild Dornier 328 is an example of the current generation of regional airliners which makes extensive use of composites.

Below: The decade of the eighties witnessed aircraft designers experimenting with many new ideas, made possible by such developments as non-metallic materials that offer great strength for low weight. The Beechcraft Starship is an example of unusual configuration featuring an airframe made almost entirely of composite materials. Few manufacturers, however, followed its example.

Above: Noseplanes, or canards, became popular on larger business aircraft in the mid-eighties, such as the Beechcraft Starship (shown below left) and the Piaggio Avanti (above) – the latter being unusual in having a tailplane also.

Left: At the height of interest in the propfan concept during the mid-eighties, several projects were planned, using this method of propulsion. The MPC 75 was one such design which was to have been a joint Sino-German venture.

Aluminium/lithium alloys were gradually introduced to jetliners, mainly by Boeing, from the early 1970s. However results have not met with expectations and even today, with several prolonged problems seemingly solved, these 'wonder metals' are no longer exciting. On the other hand, all bulk metals are made hundreds to thousands of times weaker than they could be because they are composed of astronomic numbers of strong crystals all jumbled together with very weak joints. If only a complete wing spar, for example, could be made from a single perfect crystal it could be made perhaps 99 per cent lighter than before without loss of strength. So far, a few small parts such as turbine blades can be made from single-crystal material, but there is not much hope of make a single-crystal metal aeroplane until well beyond 2000. For the present smaller gains must be sought from such improved manufacturing techniques as SPF/DB (superplastic forming and diffusion bonding), which in effect enables strong metals to be moulded like plastics into complex thin-walled shapes without joints.

Just as advanced materials technology can take up to 15 years to reach the civil sector, so too radical design developments are regarded with caution. On many combat aircraft, canards have replaced tailplanes and elevators which rotate the aircraft at take-off by forcing the tail down, in effect adding weight at the most crucial point of the flight. It has been found to be more sensible to use a canard surface which achieves the same objective by lifting the nose, effectively taking part of the weight off the wing. However, whereas the highly unstable canard configuration is good for fighters, it is not quite so suitable for airliners, although a canard with at least relaxed static stability is a distinct possibility for the future.

There is no reason to doubt that traffic will continue to grow, which means that the unit size of vehicles will grow with it. The Boeing 747-400 was widely perceived to have a little stretch left to enable as many as 700 passengers to be accommodated. This might have been achieved by extending the upper deck along the full length of the fuselage. Certainly at the start of the 747 project, Boeing looked carefully at twin-tube arrangements, either the traditional 'double bubble' with superimposed tubes comprising roughly equal upper and lower decks, or the radical parallel tube layout with left and right fuselages resulting in a cabin perhaps 12.2m (40ft) wide, with a row of pillars along the centreline to tie the upper and lower skins together against pressurisation forces measured in thousands of tonnes. Many other design teams have looked at this arrangement, which would result in a wide body like nothing yet seen outside the biggest passenger ship lounge. It seems unlikely that such a shape will be adopted, both Airbus and Boeing preferring double-deck configurations, largely because there is no obvious alternative. Certainly, the monster 1,000-seater will have two decks, despite the attractions of a near-circular fuselage with a floor 12.2m (40ft) wide.

It is perhaps worth noting that 50 years ago Northrop pioneered the all-wing aircraft which superficially seemed to be the most efficient shape possible. Certainly it seems attractive to eliminate the fuselage and tail, and bury the engines, but the fact remains that the most efficient transports ever built all have huge bodies and relatively small wings.

PROPULSION

Of all the subject headings considered, the most obvious revolution concerns that of propulsion. It is curious that, 50 years ago, the turbojet was thought applicable only to short-range aircraft, the turbofan (invented by Whittle in the 1930s) was ignored, and for long ranges the only answer was thought to be the compound diesel or advanced turboprop. Today the turbofan has made possible all the range needed: for example, Boeing 747s of Cathay Pacific can take off with a full load from Hong Kong on a hot day and fly to London with no need for an intermediate stop. Tomorrow's big laminar aircraft will do London to Sydney or Melbourne, and many travellers would say they would even welcome a stop in order to stretch their legs. Moves towards higher bypass ratios, notably by means of the propfan and unducted fan (UDF), which is discussed more fully in the chapter on engine technology, were aimed almost entirely at reducing fuel burn, not because of urgent need for greater range. Certainly there is no place in the world's airlines for the plain turbojet, but one can go too far in seeking higher propulsive efficiency. It would be possible to build a high-bypass engine with an overall pressure ratio of over 40 and a turbine entry temperature (TET) of 1,500°C (2,730°F). This might have an impressively low fuel consumption, provided one could tighten up the clearances and minimize air and gas leakage. Unfortunately it would also have a large number of extremely expensive blades, and its overall economics would probably look worse than a simpler engine with seemingly less-exciting design parameters. It cannot be too strongly emphasized that, certainly through 2000, airlines are looking to engine designers not so much for exciting performance as for absolute reliability and rock-bottom total costs over 25-year periods. Indeed, the world will continue to see a lot of the centrifugal compressor, which was derided by Whittle's critics 45 years ago as being completely passé!

As mentioned in the previous chapter, the introduction of UDF-type engines appeared to be only a matter of time during the 1980s but perhaps one reason for Boeing's enthusiasm for the new engine, may have been a desire to spoil the emerging market for the Airbus A320. Incorporating much in the way of advanced technology, the A320 was seen to pose a threat to Boeing's predominance in the smaller civil airliner market. In the event the fuel crisis went away, Boeing matching the Airbus 'high tech' with advanced models of the 737 and the propfan became yesterday's story. Instead, advances in engine design centred around the increasing use of digital controls, lower fuel burn, much reduced emissions and longer life. Indeed, such was the improvement in engine reliability and ease of maintenance, that their manufacturers lost a lot of business because of a reduced demand for spares! Boeing knows how to tempt airlines into delaying equipment purchase decisions and Airbus was doubtless relieved when the propfan died.

While General Electric, Pratt & Whitney and Rolls-Royce have remained in contention as engine suppliers for the larger airliners, even penetrating the hitherto closed market in Russia, they could only afford to do so by developing refinements to existing engines. Only General Electric developed the all-new GE90, while continuing production of the CF6 series. Rolls-Royce developed the Trent family from the RB.211 series, and Pratt & Whitney added to the PW4000 family.

In the longer term it may be necessary to find an alternative to today's fuels, though scare stories about petroleum running out have been current for a long time. Quite a bit of flying has been done on liquefied natural gas (LNG), which burns cleanly and presents no severe problem, but this too is a finite (and thus presumably dwindling) supply. Eventually, but probably not before at least 2020, there seems little alternative to LH_2 (liquid hydrogen). This is a super fuel in many ways, and NASA in the USA has run aircraft engines on it for 30 years, starting with a J65 whose British Sapphire ancestry gave it vaporizing burners which needed few changes. The problems are that this liquid is almost the coldest thing known, though the background of experience with Rocketdyne and Pratt & Whitney rocket engines (among others) is so great that transfer of the technology to the airlines would 'merely' be a matter of investing a few tens of billions of dollars. The low density of LH_2 means that airliners would swell enormously, either with gigantic tanks at front and rear of the passenger/cargo area or, alternatively, with huge fuel pods on the outer wings. The latter might be preferred, because passengers might not like being sandwiched between colossal tanks of liquid at –453°F (–253°C). Among planemakers, Lockheed-Martin has had most to say about hydrogen, and despite the enormous bulk of tankage needed, the possible aircraft appear entirely plausible.

Of course, for basic reasons of cycle efficiency the SST (supersonic transport) engine beats all the subsonic ones, chiefly because of the tremendous overall pressure ratios that are attainable. It is simplicity itself to sketch attractive 350-seat SSTs with much better economics than those of Concorde, but the investment would be daunting. It would be beyond the resources of a single company to produce a new SST and such a venture is likely to become an international project.

SYSTEMS

Systems can be discussed quite quickly, although this reality is one of the most exciting of all areas. The advent of the A320 ushered in the era of the advanced all-digital aircraft, with totally integrated data bus networks linking every functioning item. There is no fundamental problem in switching from wire looms to fibre optics (so-called FBL, fly-by-light), and this would enable networks so reduced in weight that a man could carry one large enough to handle billions of bits of data each second, enough for the on-board management and maintenance logging of the biggest and most complex airliner. Thus, tomorrow's captain, seated in his simple cockpit with just the odd TV-type screen, could instantly check the pressures in all the tyres, the location of each member of cabin crew, the status of every latch on every door or hatch, and the temperature and temperature trend in any chosen part of the aircraft. There could even be inbuilt crack-detection for every unduplicated part of primary structure!

In the long term designers clearly must get away from the idea that all the propulsion system has to do is push the aircraft forwards. The best way of integrating the burning of fuel into useful lift, as well as thrust, has for many years seemed to be upper-surface blowing (USB), pioneered by Boeing with the YC-14 and Antonov with the An-72 and An-74, although only the Antonovs entered production. There would be no difficulty in flying a short-haul 300-seater able to use a 305m (1,000ft) strip, with acceptable environmental qualities, but the market hardly seems likely to support the investment.

Below: Boeing is among several aircraft manufacturers which have carried out studies for a second-generation supersonic transport (SST) to succeed Concorde. Such an aircraft would be expected to carry at least 200 passengers over longer ranges.

Right: There seems little doubt that development of large airliners – such as this Boeing 777 – powered by only two engines will continue, although the giant 'super-jumbos' will have four engines. Future development must go hand in hand with advances in engine technology.

As for helicopters, it is difficult to foresee a future for this type of aircraft as an airliner, although proposals to fit them with short wings could result in higher speeds and lower operating costs. However, it has long been the dream of aircraft designers to develop an airliner which can operate to and from city centres and to such VTOL services, the tilt-wing or tilt-rotor may have the edge over the helicopter. As exemplified by the Bell/Boeing V-22 Osprey military transport, the tilt rotor can take-off and land vertically, becoming a turboprop airliner once airborne. The Osprey is judged to be only marginally economic as a passenger airliner, seating 28 to 30 passengers in a civil version, on 9,172kW (12,300shp). By 2010 it should be possible to have a next-generation 90-seater in scheduled service and a start is being made in the commercial sector with the 9-seat Bell Boeing 609. The cruise efficiency, in terms of ton-miles per pound of fuel, is better than double that of a helicopter, quite apart from the cruising speed of over 340kts (628km/h; 390mph). In terms of complexity, there is little to choose between the helicopter and the tilt-rotor or tilt-wing, so the operating costs of any VTOL is certain to be significantly higher than a conventional aircraft. Airlines are not clamouring for such unorthodox machines and seem content to operate STOL aircraft into airports such as London City.

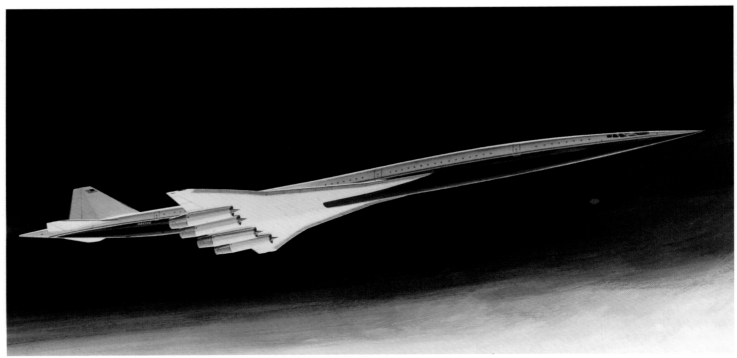

Above: It has long been the dream of aircraft designers to produce airliners which can operate into the centre of cities. The tilt-rotor concept developed by Bell/Boeing may help to realise this ambition.

Right: Relentless growth in air traffic has encouraged Airbus to develop a 'super-jumbo' with a capacity for as many as 854 passengers.

Right: This diagram shows how upper-surface blowing works. Air that is ejected at high velocity from the turbofan engine remains 'attached' to the curved upper wing surface – as found by Henri Coanda with his research into fluid flow – and provides lift when turned downwards.

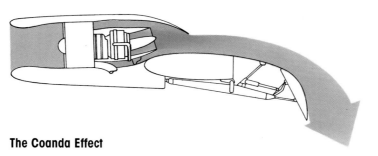

The Coanda Effect

In conclusion, there are many more unorthodox vehicles that one must consider when looking far ahead. One, very much a throwback to the distant past, is the airship. After lying dormant for 40 years, this suddenly attracted a lot of attention in the late 1960s, and various entrepreneurs tried to attract funds to build gigantic helium-filled ships made of carbon fibre, powered by highly efficient swivelling turboprops and able to hover over any factory in the world to pick up or set down standard 12.2m (40ft) containers. So far nothing so venturesome has been produced, although as in other fields of commercial aviation, the use of composite materials may yet lead to a resurgence in the use of the airship. Several companies are applying new technology to an old concept.

Another unorthodox vehicle is the semi-orbital aerospace plane, studies for which have been carried out both in the United States and Europe. This could fly 200 passengers to the other side of the globe in 90 minutes or so travelling in a low-Earth orbit and BAe's HOTOL vehicle proposed for this role would have been powered by a Rolls-Royce RB.545 powerplant. This would breathe air at lower altitudes but use liquid oxygen in cruising flight but sadly, the UK lacked the will (and the funds) to support such a venture.

The number of passengers travelling by air all over the world increases year by year. From time to time, the rate of growth is arrested, such as occurred in 1986 because of tension in the Middle East and the threat of terrorism, and in 1991 as a result of the Gulf War and the world economic recession. In 1997, the financial crisis in Asia threatened the world's biggest growth market. But the overall trend continues determinedly upwards – and air freight is increasing even more dramatically than passenger traffic.

Understandably, therefore, the design and production of aircraft for use by the world's airlines is an activity that attracts the attention of the world's aerospace manufacturing companies. Market surveys of the likely needs of the civil operators in the first 20 years of the new millennium indicates that many thousands of new aircraft will be bought, partly to account for new traffic, and partly to replace older types reaching the end of their design lives.

Gathered together in this section are descriptions, technical details and illustrations – in a consistent format to make possible direct comparisons – of the most important types of airliners in mainline service, as well as those older types still operated in large numbers. Thus, these types are the result of earlier market surveys, and their respective production totals give some indication of the success with which manufacturers judged the market and met the requirements.

These aircraft range from the largest wide-body jets to small piston-engined twins, from the slow to the supersonic, from designs that trace their origins back to before World War II, to those advanced new-technology types which entered service in the 1990s. At the larger end of the scale, the business is now dominated by just two manufacturers, Boeing in the US and Airbus in Europe. But there is no shortage of contenders for a share of the business in the smaller regional market, although some consolidation is also taking place. Because of the enormous cost involved in developing an entirely new type, more global partnerships are being formed to spread the risks.

Alas, two prolific companies, which shaped the history of aircraft development, have disappeared. McDonnell Douglas was taken over by Boeing in August 1997, and Fokker Aircraft was allowed to slip into bankruptcy in March 1996. Saab Aircraft has made known its intention to leave the regional aircraft business in the year 2000. A new era has begun.

Having celebrated 20 years of successful revenue service in the hands of British Airways and Air France in January 1996, the Concorde has a history that goes back to 1955. In that year, member companies of the British aerospace industry and government agencies undertook preliminary design work that led to the establishment in 1956 of a Supersonic Transport Aircraft Committee (STAC) to study the feasibility of an SST. Among the project studies looked at by STAC was the Bristol Type 198 – a design number covering several different aircraft configurations, of which the most favoured came to be a slender delta-winged layout with eight engines and able to operate across the North Atlantic at Mach 2.0. Through a process of continuous refinement, this evolved into the smaller Type 223, with four engines and 110 seats for a London to New York operation. While this work went on in the UK, a similar process was under way in France, leading by 1961 to evolution of a project called the Super Caravelle that was strikingly similar to the Bristol 223. At government behest, the British and French designers were merged into a single project, and a protocol of agreement was signed between the two governments on 29 November 1962. Principal airframe companies were BAC (which had absorbed Bristol) and Aérospatiale (incorporating Sud), and the engine companies were Rolls-Royce (which had meanwhile acquired the Bristol Siddeley engine company in which Concorde's Olympus engines originated) and

Aérospatiale/BAC Concorde Cutaway Drawing Key

1 Variable geometry drooping nose
2 Weather radar
3 Spring pot
4 Visor jack
5 'A'-frame
6 Visor uplock
7 Visor guide rails and carriage
8 Droop nose jacks
9 Droop nose guide rails
10 Droop nose hinge
11 Rudder pedals
12 Captain's seat
13 Instrument panel shroud
14 Forward pressure bulkhead
15 Retracting visor
16 Multi-layer windscreen
17 Windscreen fluid rain clearance and wipers
18 Second pilot's seat
19 Roof panel
20 Flight-deck air duct
21 Third crew member's seat
22 Control relay jacks
23 First supernumerary's seat
24 Second supernumerary's folding seat (optional)
25 Radio and electronics racks (Channel 2)
26 Radio and electronics racks (Channel 1)
27 Plug-type forward passenger door
28 Slide/life-raft pack stowage
29 Cabin staff tip-up seat

49 Nosewheel actuating jacks
50 Underfloor air-conditioning ducts
51 Nosewheel door actuator
52 Nosewheel secondary (aft) doors
53 Fuselage frame (single flange)
54 Machined window panel
55 Underfloor forward baggage compartment (237cu ft/6.72m³)
56 Fuel lines
57 Lattice ribs
58 No 9 (port forward) trim tank
59 Single-web spar
60 No 10 (port forward) trim tank
61 Middle passenger doors (port and starboard)
62 Cabin staff tip-up seat
63 Toilets
64 Emergency radio stowage
65 Provision for VHF3
66 Overhead baggage racks (with doors)
67 Cabin aft section
68 Fuselage frame
69 Tank vent gallery
70 No 1 forward collector tank
71 Lattice ribs
72 Engine-feed pumps
73 Accumulator
74 No 5 fuel tank
75 Trim transfer gallery

92 Spraymat leading-edge de-icing panels
93 Leading-edge anti-icing strip
94 Spar-box machined girder side pieces
95 No 7 fuel tank
96 No 7a fuel tank
97 Static dischargers
98 Elevon
99 Inter-elevon flexible joint
100 Combined secondary nozzles/reverser buckets
101 Nozzle-mounting spigots
102 Cabin air delivery/distribution
103 Inspection panels
104 Cold-air unit
105 Fuel-cooled heat exchanger
106 Fuel/hydraulic oil heat exchanger
107 Fire-suppression bottles
108 Main spar frame
109 Accumulator
110 No 3 aft collector tank
111 Control linkage
112 'Z'-section spot-welded stringers
113 Riser to distribution duct
114 Anti-surge bulkheads

136 Honeycomb intake nose section
137 Spraymat intake lip de-icing
138 Ramp motor and gearbox
139 Forward ramp
140 Aft ramp
141 Inlet flap
142 Spill door actuator
143 Intake duct
144 Tank vent gallery
145 Engine front support links
146 Engine-mounting transverse equalizers
147 Oil tank
148 Primary heat exchanger
149 Secondary heat exchanger
150 Heat-exchanger exhaust air
151 Rolls-Royce/SNECMA Olympus 593 Mk 610 Turbojet
152 Outer wing fixing (340 high-tensile steel bolts)
153 Engine main mounting

30 Forward galley units (port and starboard)
31 Toilets (2)
32 Coats (crew and passengers)
33 Twelve 26-man life-rafts
34 VHF1 antenna
35 Overhead baggage racks (with doors)
36 Cabin furnishing (heat and sound insulated)
37 Four-abreast one-class passenger accommodation
38 Seat rails
39 Metal-faced floor panels
40 Nosewheel well
41 Nosewheel main doors
42 Nosewheel leg
43 Shock absorber
44 Twin nosewheels
45 Torque links
46 Steering mechanism
47 Telescopic strut
48 Lateral bracing struts

76 Leading-edge machined ribs
77 Removable leading-edge sections
78 Expansion joints between sections
79 Contents unit
80 Inlet control valve
81 Transfer pumps
82 Flight-deck air duct
83 No 8 fuselage tank
84 Vapour seal above tank
85 Pressure-floor curved membranes
86 Pre-stretched integrally machined wing skin panels
87 No 8 wing tank
88 No 4 forward collector tank
89 No 10 starboard forward trim tank
90 No 9 starboard forward trim tank
91 Quick-lock removable inspection panels

115 No 6 (underfloor) fuel tank
116 Machined pressurised keel box
117 Fuselage frame
118 Double-flange frame/floor join
119 Machined pressure-floor support beams
120 Port undercarriage well
121 Mainwheel door
122 Fuselage/wing attachments
123 Main spar frame
124 Mainwheel retraction link
125 Mainwheel actuating jack
126 Cross beam
127 Forked link
128 Drag strut
129 Mainwheel leg
130 Shock absorber
131 Pitch dampers
132 Four-wheel main undercarriage
133 Bogie beam
134 Torque links
135 Intake boundary layer splitter

154 Power control unit mounting
155 No 5a fuel tank
156 Tank vent
157 Transfer pump
158 Port outer elevon control unit fairing
159 Static dischargers
160 Honeycomb elevon structure
161 Flexible joint
162 Port middle elevon control hinge/fairing
163 Power control unit twin output
164 Control rod linkage
165 Nacelle aft support link
166 Reverser-bucket actuating screw jack
167 Retractable silencer lobs ('spades')
168 Primary (inner) variable nozzle
169 Pneumatic nozzle actuators
170 Nozzle-mounting spigots
171 Port inner elevon control hinge/fairing

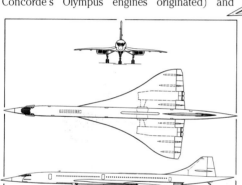

Above: Three-view drawing of the Anglo-French Concorde, the only supersonic aircraft in airline service. Its delta-wing shape and long streamlined body are unmistakable.

Right: British Airways, through innovative charter programmes including regular flights to Barbados and specialist round-the-world charters, has made a success of operating the small number of Concordes. The record for the flight from London to New York is under three hours.

172 Control rod linkage
173 Manual stand-by power control
174 Accumulator
175 Vent and pressurisation system
176 Forged wing/fuselage main
    frames
177 Ground-supply air-
    conditioning connection
178 Control mixing unit
179 Control rod (elevon) linkage

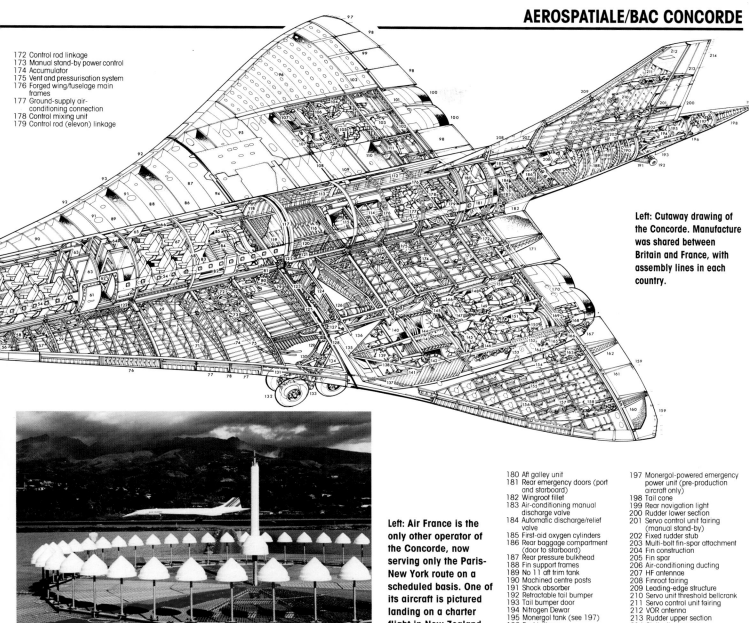

Left: Cutaway drawing of the Concorde. Manufacture was shared between Britain and France, with assembly lines in each country.

Left: Air France is the only other operator of the Concorde, now serving only the Paris-New York route on a scheduled basis. One of its aircraft is pictured landing on a charter flight in New Zealand.

180 Aft galley unit
181 Rear emergency doors (port and starboard)
182 Wingroot fillet
183 Air-conditioning manual discharge valve
184 Automatic discharge/relief valve
185 First-aid oxygen cylinders
186 Rear baggage compartment (door to starboard)
187 Rear pressure bulkhead
188 Fin support frames
189 No 11 aft trim tank
190 Machined centre posts
191 Shock absorber
192 Retractable tail bumper
193 Tail bumper door
194 Nitrogen Dewar
195 Monergol tank (see 197)
196 Fuel jettison

197 Monergol-powered emergency power unit (pre-production aircraft only)
198 Tail cone
199 Rear navigation light
200 Rudder lower section
201 Servo control unit fairing (manual stand-by)
202 Fixed rudder stub
203 Multi-bolt fin-spar attachment
204 Fin construction
205 Fin spar
206 Air-conditioning ducting
207 HF antennae
208 Finroot fairing
209 Leading-edge structure
210 Servo unit threshold bellcrank
211 Servo control unit fairing
212 VOR antenna
213 Rudder upper section
214 Static dischargers

SNECMA. The Concorde programme was handled in a number of stages, embracing the construction and testing of two prototypes, known as Concordes 001 and 002; two pre-production aircraft, originally known as Concordes 01 and 02 and subsequently as Concordes 101 and 102; and a production sequence commencing with Concorde 201. Production of an initial batch of 16 aircraft was authorised by the two governments and production of major airframe and engine components was divided between companies in the UK and France without duplication. Separate final assembly lines were set up at Toulouse and Filton, alternate aircraft being assembled in the UK and France. Concorde 001 made its first flight Toulouse on 2 March 1969, its first supersonic flight on 1 October 1969, and its first excursion to Mach 2 on 4 November 1970 (on its 102nd flight). Concorde 002 was the first to fly in the UK (at Filton) on 9 April 1969.

VARIANTS
Concordes 001 and 002 were slightly smaller than the production standard, which introduced lengthened front and rear fuselages, revised nose visors, changes to the wing geometry and uprated engines. These new features were progressively introduced on Concorde 101, first flown from Toulouse on 17 December 1971, and Concorde 102, flown at Filton on 10 January 1973. The more definitive production standard was represented by Concorde 201, flown at

Toulouse on 6 December 1973, and Concorde 202 flown at Filton on 13 February 1974. Production aircraft 203 to 216 flew alternately from the two assembly lines, the last two on 26 December 1978 and 20 April 1979 respectively.

SERVICE USE
Certification of the Concorde for full passenger carrying operations was obtained on 13 October 1975 in France and on 5 December 1975 in the UK, leading to introduction into service by British Airways and Air France simultaneously on 21 January 1976. The routes, respectively, were London to Bahrain and Paris to Rio de Janeiro (via Dakar). Services to Washington began on 24 May 1976 (extended in 1985 to Miami and New York in December 1977). BA flew a service from London to Singapore (via Bahrain) jointly with Singapore Airlines in 1979/80, and in the same period Braniff leased aircraft time from Air France and BA to extend the Washington services to Dallas/Fort Worth. For a time Air France flew scheduled services to Caracas and to Mexico via Washington; many other destinations around the world have been served under an extensive programme of charters. Twelve aircraft are flown by British Airways (7) and Air France (6), now operating only on the London-New York/Washington and Paris-New York schedules, and on extensive charter programmes. A British Airways-led life extension programme is designed to increase the airframe life

to 8,500 reference flights (from 6,700) – a reference flight is defined as one flight on a long-haul sector at a take off weight in excess of 170,000kg (375,000lb) – which should keep the youngest aircraft in service at least until the year 2014.

SPECIFICATION
(Aerospatiale/BAC Concorde)

Dimensions: Wingspan 25.56m (83ft 10¼in); length overall 62.10m (203ft 9in); height overall 11.4m (37ft 5in), wing area 358.25m² (3,856ft²).

Power Plant: Four Rolls-Royce Snecma Olympus 593 Mk610 turbojets, each rated at 169.3kN (38,05lb) static thrust.

Weights: Operating weight empty 78,700kg (173,500lb); max take-off 185,065kg (408,000lb); max landing 111,130kg (245,000lb); max payload 11,340kg (25,000lb).

Performance: Max cruising speed 1,176kt (2,179km/h); service ceiling 18,290m (60,000ft); take-off field length 3,415m (11,200ft); landing field length 2,225m (7,300ft); range with typical payload 3,360nm (6,225km).

Accommodation: Flight crew of two. Single-aisle cabin layout, seating typically 100 passengers, although a maximum of 144 is possible. Baggage/cargo compartments under the floor and in rear fuselage have a total volume of 19.74m³ (607ft³).

AERO INTERNATIONAL (REGIONAL) AI(R) ATR 42 FRANCE/ITALY

The Avions de Transport Regional (ATR) organisation was set up on 5 February 1982 under French law as a Groupement d'Intérêt Economique (GIE) to manage the programme of development, production and management of a regional airliner known as the ATR 42. The aircraft in question had been launched some three months earlier, on 29 October 1981, as a joint product of Aérospatiale in France and Aeritalia (now Alenia) in Italy, in continuation of a preliminary accord reached by the two companies in July 1980. Before that time, both companies had been studying the market for a regional airliner with 30-40 seats and had produced project designs under the designations Aérospatiale AS-35 and Aeritalia AIT 320. These projects were of generally similar configuration, and the ATR 42 was a continuation of the same theme, with a high wing, two turboprop engines, fuselage-side blisters for the main landing gear units, and a T-tail. Sizing of the aircraft was a matter for careful study, with 42 seats eventually adopted as the norm, a few more than in the earlier independent project designs (as their designations indicated). The division of labour between the two companies provides for Aérospatiale to manufacture the wing while Alenia produces the fuselage and tail unit. The Italian company is also responsible for the hydraulic, air-conditioning and pressurisation systems, while the French partner looks after the flight deck and cabin, the power plant, and the electrical and flight-control systems. Civil passenger versions of the ATR 42 are assembled and test flown at Toulouse; the ATM 42-F military cargo version and

any civil freighters with rear loading ramp are assembled at Naples. Flight testing of the ATR 42 began on 16 August 1984, the second development aircraft being flown on 31 October of that year and the first production ATR 42 on 30 April 1985.

VARIANTS
The designations ATR 42-100 and ATR 42-200 were at first applied to versions with gross weight of

Avions de Transport Régional ATR 42 Cutaway Drawing Key
1 Radome
2 Weather radar scanner
3 Scanner tracking mechanism
4 ILS glideslope aerial
5 Front pressure bulkhead
6 Pitot heads
7 Twin nosewheels, forward retracting
8 Nosewheel leg doors
9 Taxying lamps
10 Nose undercarriage wheel bay
11 Rudder pedals
12 Static ports
13 Instrument panel (Electronic Flight Instrument System)
14 Windscreen wipers
15 Instrument panel shroud
16 Windscreen panels
17 Overhead systems switch panels
18 Co-pilot's seat
19 Emergency equipment stowage
20 Centre control pedestal
21 Control column handwheel
22 Side console panel
23 Cockpit floor level
24 Underfloor control linkage
25 Pilot's flight bag stowage
26 Oxygen bottle
27 Angle of attack transmitter
28 Pilot's seat
29 Avionics equipment racks
30 Central Observer's folding seat
31 Electrical equipment racks
32 Cockpit roof escape hatch
33 Cockpit doorway
34 VHF aerial
35 Control cable runs
36 Baggage restraint net
37 Main cabin doorway
38 Forward baggage/cargo compartment
39 Baggage loading floor
40 External power socket
41 Baggage/cargo door, open
42 Door latch
43 Wing inspection light
44 Main cabin bulkhead (moveable to suit internal layout)
45 Four-abreast passenger seating, 46-seat layout (48 and 50-seat alternative configurations)
46 Emergency escape window hatch, port and starboard
47 Recirculating air fans
48 Floor beam construction
49 Underfloor conditioned air distribution ducting
50 Fuselage skin panel doubler/ propeller debris guard
51 Fuselage frame and stringer construction
52 Cabin wall trim panelling
53 ADF loop aerials
54 Fuselage skin panelling
55 Cabin wall soundproofing lining
56 Cabin roof lighting panels
57 Overhead stowage bins
58 Passenger service units
59 Cabin air distribution duct
60 Conditioned air delivery duct risers
61 Engine bleed air duct to conditioning plant
62 Wing/fuselage attachment main frames
63 Spar attachment joints
64 Wing centre section rib construction
65 Centre section dry bay
66 Control cable runs to engines
67 Wing leading edge fillet framing
68 Honeycomb leading edge fillet panels
69 Fuel pumps
70 Starboard wing integral fuel tank, total fuel capacity 1254 Imp gal (5,700l)

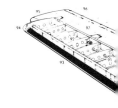

Right: A cutaway drawing of the ATR 42. This is representative of both the series 200 and 300, which differ in their operating weights.

Left: The ATR 42-500 is the latest and most powerful of the family, providing much enhanced performance.

14,900kg (32,848lb) and 15,750kg (34,722lb) respectively, the latter having a redesigned interior that allowed accommodation to be increased from 42 to 50 without any change in external dimensions. By the time production deliveries began, the ATR 42-200 had become the standard aircraft, with the ATR-42-300 available as a high gross weight option at 16,150kg (35,604lb), with a range of 890nm (1,650km) carrying the full passenger payload. Other designated variants of the basic aircraft include the ATR 42-F commercial freighter and the ATM 42 military freighter, the latter with a rear-loading ramp. The ATR 42-320 is identical except for optional PW 121 engines for improved hot-and-high performance. Further performance enhancements were incorporated in the ATR 42-400, which features PW121A engines with six-blade Hamilton Standard/Ratier-Figeac propellers. This version made its first flight on 12 July 1995. An uprated ATR 42-500 with more powerful 2,052kW (2,750shp) PW127E engines derated to 1,610kW (2,160shp) and a 'new look' interior flew before the -400, on 16 September 1994. Also available are the ATR 42 Cargo with a quick-change interior, the ATR 42F military/paramilitary freighter, the ATR 42 L with a

71 Detachable leading edge honeycomb panel
72 Engine bleed air ducting
73 Ventral exhaust nozzle
74 Starboard engine nacelle
75 Pratt & Whitney Canada PW120 turboprop engine
76 Engine accessory equipment gearbox
77 Digital engine controller
78 Particle separation intake air duct
79 Ventral oil cooler
80 Propeller reduction gearbox
81 Hamilton Standard four-bladed variable pitch, reversible propeller
82 Spinner
83 Propeller hub pitch change mechanism
84 Detachable engine cowling panels
85 Outer wing panel multi-bolt attachment joint
86 Outboard integral fuel tank
87 Fuel system piping
88 Pressure refuelling connection
89 Gravity fuel filler cap

90 Upper wing skin access panel
91 Aileron control linkage
92 Outer wing panel ribs
93 Leading edge pneumatic de-icing boot
94 Starboard navigation (red) and strobe (white) lights
95 Aileron horn balance
96 Static dischargers
97 Port aileron
98 Aileron tabs
99 Carbon-fibre aileron skin panelling
100 Starboard spoiler, open
101 Outboard double-slotted flap, down position
102 Flap hydraulic jack
103 Ventral flap hinge fairings
104 Flap slot closure panels
105 Inboard double-slotted flap segment, down position
106 Inboard flap jack
107 Wing root trailing edge fillet
108 Fillet honeycomb construction
109 Aileron central control linkage
110 Engine fire extinguisher bottles, port and starboard
111 Overhead stowage bins
112 Rear cabin seating
113 Curtained wardrobe
114 Galley unit
115 Passenger cabin rear bulkhead
116 Starboard side service/ emergency exit door
117 Rear baggage compartment door
118 Cabin attendant's control panel
119 Interphone

120 Cabin attendant's folding seat
121 Toilet compartment door
122 Starboard side rear baggage/ cargo compartment
123 Rear pressure bulkhead
124 Glass-fibre fin root fillet
125 Kevlar/Nomex honeycomb extended chord fin root section
126 Fin spar attachment joints
127 Elevator control rods
128 Three-spar tailfin construction
129 VOR aerial
130 Fin leading edge
131 Tailplane attachment joints
132 Starboard tailplane
133 Tailplane leading edge pneumatic de-icing boot
134 Starboard elevator
135 Rudder horn balance
136 Anti-collision light
137 Static dischargers
138 Rudder
139 Elevator hinge control
140 Elevator tab
141 Port elevator honeycomb construction
142 Elevator horn balance
143 Port tailplane construction
144 Leading edge nose ribs
145 Rudder honeycomb construction
146 Rudder tab
147 Tailcone transparency
148 Tail navigation and strobe lights (white)
149 Composite tailcone construction
150 Rudder hinge control
151 Tailcone vent
152 Autopilot controller
153 Tailcone rear bulkhead

154 Fin spar attachment main frames
155 Ventral access hatch
156 Crashproof cockpit voice and data recorders
157 Cabin pressurisation valves
158 Toilet compartment
159 Water tank
160 Wash basin
161 Folding handrail
162 Counterbalance spring
163 Rear passenger entry door/ airstairs
164 Entry lobby
165 Rear fuselage frame and stringer construction
166 Cabin window panels
167 Port inboard double-slotted flap
168 Honeycomb flap shroud panel
169 Inboard flap hydraulic jack
170 Flap vanes
171 Flap honeycomb core construction
172 Outboard double-slotted flap
173 Port spoiler
174 Spoiler hydraulic jack
175 Aileron spring tab
176 Port aileron rib construction
177 Aileron trim tab
178 Static dischargers
179 Aileron horn balance

180 Port navigation (red) and strobe (white) lights
181 Outer wing panel rib construction

182 Leading edge pneumatic de-icing boot
183 Fuel tank end rib
184 Fuel filler cap

185 Port wing integral fuel tank
186 Pneumatic de-icing valve
187 Port wing rib construction
188 Rear spar
189 Outer wing panel bolted joint
190 Front spar
191 Ventral engine exhaust nozzle
192 Port engine nacelle
193 Fireproof bulkhead
194 Sponson mounted hydraulic reservoirs and filters, port and starboard
195 Engine mounting frame bearer struts
196 Main engine mounting frame
197 Twin mainwheels, inward retracting
198 Levered suspension axle beam
199 Mainwheel doors
200 Shock absorber strut
201 Main undercarriage pivot fixing
202 Hydraulic retraction jack
203 Forward engine mounting/ gearbox support struts
204 Fuselage sponson mounted air conditioning plant, port and starboard
205 Oil cooler air intake
206 Engine air intake
207 Air conditioning system ram air intake
208 Port landing lamp
209 Fuselage sponson fairing

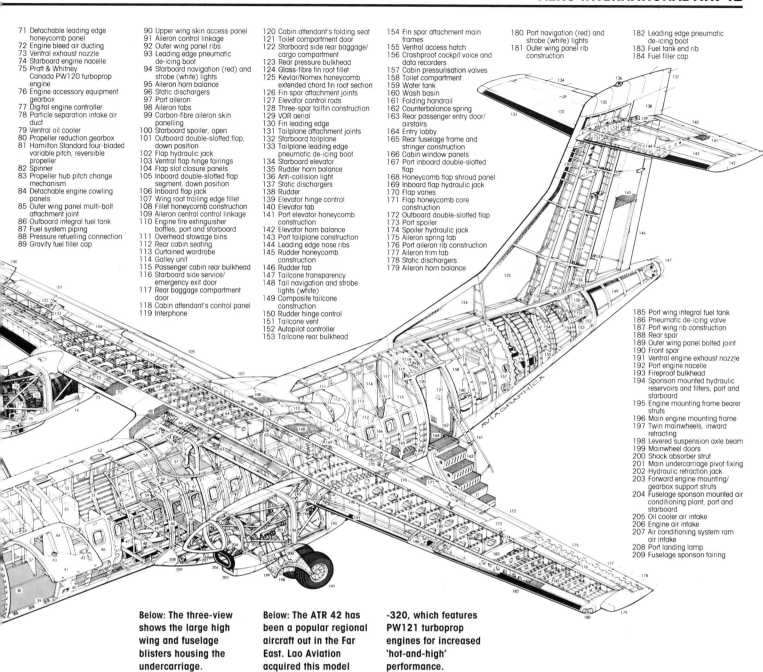

Below: The three-view shows the large high wing and fuselage blisters housing the undercarriage.

Below: The ATR 42 has been a popular regional aircraft out in the Far East. Lao Aviation acquired this model **-320, which features PW121 turboprop engines for increased 'hot-and-high' performance.**

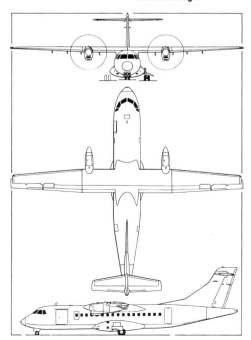

lateral cargo door, and the SAR 42, a surveillance and rescue version based on the ART 42-400 and fitted with a chin-mounted FLIR/TV camera, ventral radome and ESM antennae.

SERVICE USE

Simultaneous certification to JAR 25 by DGAC of France and Italy's RAI was granted for the ATR 42-200 and ATR 42-300 on 24 September 1985, followed by US FAR Part 25 on 25 October 1985. Deliveries began on 3 December 1985 to French regional Air Littoral, which began revenue service with the type on 9 December. Command Airways became the first US operator in March 1986. DGAC certification for the ATR 42-400 was received on 27 February 1996 and two were delivered to CSA Czech Airlines on 14 March 1996. The ATR 42-500 was certificated in July 1995 and first delivered to Air Dolomiti in October 1995. In November 1996, the ATR 42-500 received certification for 120 minutes ETOPS (Extended-range Twin-engine Operations). The Italian customs service ordered two SAR 42 in mid-1996 and took delivery in early 1997. At 31 January 1998 the ATR 42 order book totalled 340 aircraft of all versions, with 331 delivered.

AERO INTERNATIONAL (REGIONAL) AI(R) ATR 72 FRANCE/ITALY

The family concept of the ATR regional aircraft design was put into development soon after the ATR 42 entered flight testing. First announced at the 1985 Paris Air Show and officially launched on 15 January 1986, the ATR 72 was a stretched derivative with more power, greater wingspan and a longer fuselage for up to 74 passengers. Structurally similar to the ATR 42, the ATR 72 is distinguished by a fuselage stretched by 4.50m (14ft 9¼in) to 27.17m (89ft 1¾in) and a 2.48m (8ft 2¾in) greater wingspan of 27.05m (88ft 9in). Accommodation for up to 74 passengers in a high-density configuration is possible, and a second cabin attendant's seat is also provided. Three development aircraft were built and these made their first flights on 27 October 1988, 20 December 1988 and April 1989.

VARIANTS

The first version, still in production, is designated ATR 72-200. Powered by two PW124B turboprops, each rated at 1,611kW (2,160shp), it is available in both passenger configuration with 74 seats in a high-density layout, and for cargo, capable of carrying 13 small containers. More powerful 1,849kW (2,480shp) PW127 engines for better hot-and-high performance produced the ATR 72-210, which first flew in 1992. To keep ahead of requirements, AI(R) introduced the ATR 72-210A (previously referred to as the ATR 72-500) to the family portfolio in early 1997. This model features higher operating weights to accommodate new passenger regulations, increased range and improved airfield performance, and has the same powerful 2,052kW (2,750shp) PW127E engines and Hamilton Standard/Ratier-Figeac propellers fitted to the ATR 42-500. Cabin comfort also matches the ATR 42-500 in terms of appearance, comfort, low noise and vibration levels and overhead locker volume. Announced as long ago as April 1992 but yet to be put into production is the ATR 52C, a rear-loading civil/military cargo version of the ATR 72-210. The main difference, apart from the rear ramp-type door, is a 3.18m (10ft 5¼in) shorter fuselage. A proposed

stretch, designated ATR 82, has been shelved in favour of a jet development, now also cancelled.

SERVICE USE

French DGAC and US FAA certification was obtained on 25 September and 15 November 1989 respectively, with deliveries to Finnish airline Karair from 27 October 1989. The ATR 72-210 received French and US certification on 15 and 18 December 1992 respectively, and this improved type went into service that same month with American Eagle carrier Simmons Airlines. The ATR 72-210A was certificated on 14 January 1997. At 31 January 1998, a total of 222 ATR 72s of all versions had been ordered, of which 198 had been delivered.

Below: Charter carrier British World Airlines upgraded to the ATR 72 from the Viscount, to service its Shell contract in support of the North Sea oil business.

SPECIFICATION
ATR 72-200)

Dimensions: Wingspan 27.05m (88ft 9in); length overall 27.17m (89ft 1¾in); height overall 7.65m (25ft 1¼in), wing area 61.0m² (656.6ft²).
Power Plant: Two Pratt & Whitney Canada PW124B turboprops, rated at 1,611kW 2,160shp). Four-blade Hamilton Standard 14SF-11 propellers.
Weights: Operating weight empty 12,500kg (27,558lb); max take-off 21,500kg (47,400lb); max landing 21,350kg (47,068lb); max payload 7,200kg (15,873lb).
Performance: Max cruising speed 285kts (527km/h); service ceiling 2,680m (8,800ft); take-off field length 1,408m (4,620ft); landing field length 1,210m (3,970ft); max payload range 645nm (1,195km).
Accommodation: Flight crew of two. Two-abreast seating each side of the central aisle for 64 to 74 passengers. Typical baggage/cargo volume 10.6m³ (375ft³).

Right: Cutaway drawing of the Aero International ATR 72.

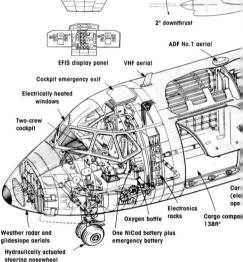

Gravity fuel

Refuel/defuel coupling feeds tanks total fuel 5,000kg

Propellor brakes on both engines; starboard may be run fully braked to perform as APU

Hamilton Standard 14SF fully feathering propellor

Engine air intake pneumatically de

2° downthrust

ADF No.1 aerial

EFIS display panel   VHF aerial

Cockpit emergency exit

Electrically heated windows

Two-crew cockpit

Weather radar and glideslope aerials

Hydraulically actuated steering nosewheel

Oxygen bottle

One NiCad battery plus emergency battery

Electronics racks

Cargo compartment 138ft³

Car (ele ope

50

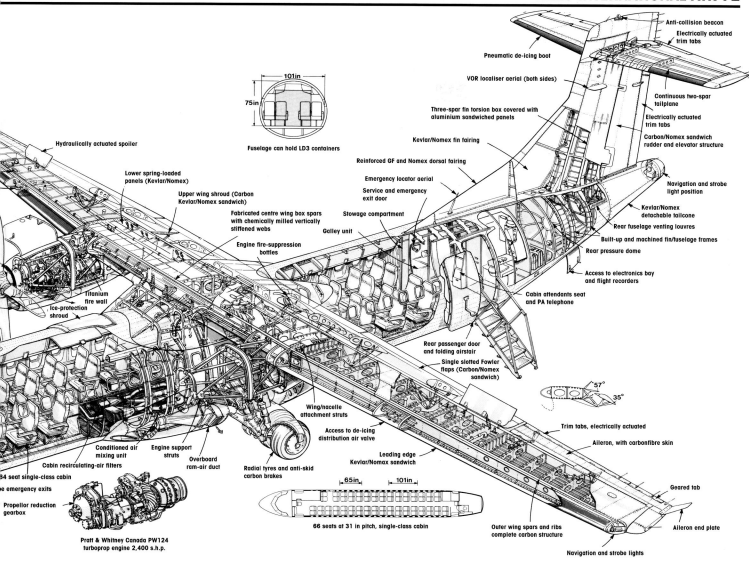

101in

75in

Fuselage can hold LD3 containers

Hydraulically actuated spoiler

Lower spring-loaded panels (Kevlar/Nomex)

Upper wing shroud (Carbon Kevlar/Nomex sandwich)

Fabricated centre wing box spars with chemically milled vertically stiffened webs

Engine fire-suppression bottles

Titanium fire wall

Ice-protection shroud

Conditioned air mixing unit

Cabin recirculating-air filters

Engine support struts

Overboard ram-air duct

64 seat single-class cabin

e emergency exits

Propellor reduction gearbox

Pratt & Whitney Canada PW124 turboprop engine 2,400 s.h.p.

Radial tyres and anti-skid carbon brakes

Wing/nacelle attachment struts

Access to de-icing distribution air valve

Leading edge Kevlar/Nomax sandwich

65in

101in

66 seats at 31 in pitch, single-class cabin

Reinforced GF and Nomex dorsal fairing

Emergency locator aerial

Service and emergency exit door

Stowage compartment

Galley unit

Three-spar fin torsion box covered with aluminium sandwiched panels

Kevlar/Nomex fin fairing

VOR localiser aerial (both sides)

Pneumatic de-icing boot

Anti-collision beacon

Electrically actuated trim tabs

Continuous two-spar tailplane

Electrically actuated trim tabs

Carbon/Nomex sandwich rudder and elevator structure

Navigation and strobe light position

Kevlar/Nomex detachable tailcone

Rear fuselage venting louvres

Built-up and machined fin/fuselage frames

Rear pressure dome

Access to electronics bay and flight recorders

Cabin attendants seat and PA telephone

Rear passenger door and folding airstair

Single slotted Fowler flaps (Carbon/Nomex sandwich)

57°

35°

Trim tabs, electrically actuated

Aileron, with carbonfibre skin

Geared tab

Aileron end plate

Outer wing spars and ribs complete carbon structure

Navigation and strobe lights

Above: The recent development of regional air services in the Asia/Pacific area has created a good market for the larger-capacity ATR 72, seen here in the earlier markings of Vietnam Airlines, which operates a fleet of six, carrying up to 74 passengers.

Right: The three-view of the ATR 72 shows its similarity to the ATR 42, but is 4.50m (14ft 9¼in) longer to permit a larger passenger load.

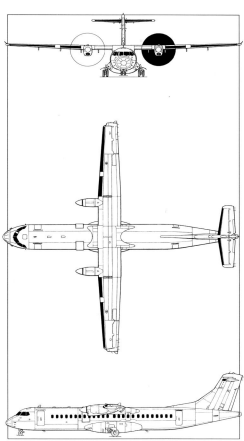

AERO INTERNATIONAL AI(R) AVRO RJ/BAe 146 UK

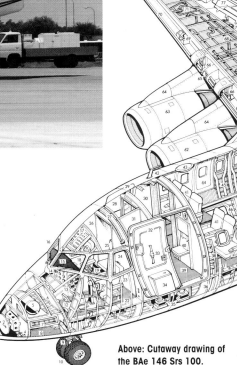

Above: Cutaway drawing of the BAe 146 Srs 100.

The history of the British Aerospace 146 goes back to the 1960s and to the design studies initiated by the then-independent de Havilland Aircraft company for a small turboprop engined feederliner designated D.H.123. This was a twin-engined, high-wing design, but further studies, which continued at Hatfield after de Havilland had been absorbed in the Hawker Siddeley Aviation company, favoured low-wing layouts with turbofan engines mounted on the rear fuselage. These studies culminated in the H.S. 144 project, but lack of a suitable engine led the designers in April 1971 to revert to a high-wing layout using four smaller turbofans, such as the Avco Lycoming ALF 502. In this form, as the H.S. 146, the project was formally launched on 29 August 1973, in partnership with the British government. But the economic recession of 1974–75 resulted in the termination of the programme in October 1974, when the H.S.146 reverted to project design status. In substantially the same form as originally planned, the aircraft was re-launched on 10 July 1978 by British Aerospace, into which HSA had meanwhile been nationalized, once again with government financial assistance, and an initial production batch was put in hand at Hatfied. From the start of development two fuselage lengths were planned for models identified as the Srs 100 and Srs 200, and construction, development and flight testing proceeded in parallel. The first Srs 100 flew on 3

Above: Air Botswana was one of only four African carriers to operate the BAe 146, the others served in Mali, South Africa and Zimbabwe. It now operates one 146-100 on regional services to neighbouring countries.

September 1981, followed by the first Srs 200 (the fourth airframe completed) on 1 August 1982. To revive the 146 family and at the same time eliminate particularly the engine reliability problems that dogged the 146 aircraft, British Aerospace developed the updated Avro RJ series, which approximates in size to the earlier type. Major changes include uprated FADEC-controlled LF507 engines, all-digital avionics and updated EFIS, digital flight guidance, and a new comfortable wide look 'Spaceliner' interior with overhead luggage bins. The first development aircraft, an RJ85, was flown at Hatfield on 23 March 1992, followed by the RJ100 on 13 May and the first RJ70 on 23 July. Drag improvements and weight savings were announced in September 1994. Final assembly is undertaken at Woodford.

VARIANTS

The initial variant was the BAe 146-100, with an overall length of 26.19m (85ft 11in), providing for 82 passengers at 840mm (33in) pitch, or up to a maximum of 93. This has the same power plant as the 146-200, but a maximum take-off weight of 38,102kg (84,000lb). The 146-200, developed in parallel with the 146-100, differs only in length of fuselage and operating weights, with associated structural and system changes. A freighter version of the 146-200 was developed, with an upward-hinged door in the rear fuselage port side. The 146-200 QT (Quiet Trader) first flew on 21 August 1986, and can accommodate six standard LD3 freight containers. In September 1984 BAe announced that it was launching a 146-300, featuring a further lengthening of the fuselage to increase the standard seating to 122 at 810mm (32in) pitch, or 130 a 740mm (29in) pitch. It first flew on 1 May 1987. The 146 Series was also built in QT Quiet Trader, QC Quick Change, and executive Statesman versions. The shortest fuselage version of the Avro RJ is the RJ70, which provides typical accommodation for 82 passengers, while up to 100 passengers can be accommodated in the 2.39m (7ft 10¼in) longer RJ85 which is the best-sell-

ing RJ model. Still further capacity increases have been achieved in the RJ100, which can carry 116 passengers in a fuselage stretched by another 2.44m (8ft 0in). All three are powered by the same 31.14kN (7,000lb) thrust AlliedSignal LF507 turbofan engines. A fourth model, the RJ115 with accommodation for 128 passengers is available, but has not yet found a buyer. In addition to passenger layouts, all versions can be built as freighters, designated QT Quiet Trader, as the QC Quick Change model, and as a Combi for the carriage of both passengers and freight.

SERVICE USE

Certification of the BAe 146-100 was achieved on 20 May 1983, and Dan-Air put the type into revenue service on 27 May. The Srs 200 was certificated in June 1983 in the UK and USA, allowing Air Wisconsin to become the first operator of the type on 27 June. Air Wisconsin also became the first operator of the 146-300, taking delivery on 28 December 1988, following certification on 6 September. UK CAA and US FAA certification of the RJ Series was completed on 1 October 1993 and 10 June 1994 respectively. The first aircraft, an RJ85, was delivered to Crossair on 23 April 1993, followed by the RJ100 to Turkish Airlines on 22 July 1993. US airline Business Express, operating as a Delta Connection carrier, took delivery of the first RJ70 on 11 September. A total of 209 BAe 146s were produced before being replaced by the Avro RJ, which had logged 140 orders and 100 deliveries at 31 January 1998.

SPECIFICATION
(Avro RJ85)

Dimensions: Wingspan 26.21m (86ft 0in); length overall 28.60m (93ft 10in); height overall 8.59m (28dr 2 in), wing area 77.29m² (832ft²).
Power Plant: Four AlliedSignal LF507 turbofans, each rated at 31.14kN (7,000lb).
Weights: Operating weight empty 24,267kg (53,500lb); max take off 43,998kg (97,000lb); max landing 38,555kg (85,000lb); max payload 11,566kg (25,500lb).
Performance: Max cruising speed 412kts (763km/h); take-off field length 1,385m (4,545ft); landing field length 1,189m (3,900ft); range with max fuel 1,600nm (2,963km); range with max payload 1,150nm (2,129km).
Accommodation: Flight crew of two. Maximum one-class layout for 112 passengers six-abreast. Underfloor baggage/cargo volume 18.83m³ (645ft³).

15 Instrument panel shroud
16 Windscreen panels
17 Overhead switch panel
18 First officer's seat
19 Centre control pedestal
20 Control column handwheel
21 Side console panel (area navigation system)
22 Cockpit floor level
23 Captain's seat
24 Direct vision window/flight deck emergency exit
25 Folding observer's seat
26 Flight deck bulkhead
27 Air conditioning ducting
28 Starboard galley unit
29 Forward service door
30 Main cabin divider
31 Port side forward toilet compartment
32 Forward entry door
33 Door latching handle
34 Escape chute stowage
35 Underfloor radio and electronics equipment bay
36 Machined doorway cut-out main frames
37 Nose section/forward fuselage skin joint strap

38 Door frame support structure
39 Entry vestibule
40 Cabin attendant's folding seat
41 Six-abreast passenger seating
42 VHF aerial
43 D/F loop aerial
44 Cabin wall trim panels
45 Air conditioning ducting
46 Forward cargo hold door
47 Forward underfloor cargo hold
48 Seat rail support structure
49 Fuselage keel construction
50 Pressurisation air control valve
51 Fuselage/front spar attachment main frame
52 Floor beam construction
53 Honeycomb sandwich floor panels
54 Centre fuselage frame and Redux-bonded stringer construction
55 Wing fuel tank vapour barrier sealing diaphragm
56 Wing spar carry-through structure
57 Centreline skin panel joint
58 Anti-collision light
59 Wing spar/fuselage frame attachment joint

60 Engine control cable and hydraulic pipe runs
61 Leading edge de-icing air ducts
62 Inboard engine nacelle
63 Outboard engine nacelle
64 Nacelle pylons
65 Starboard landing/taxying lamp
66 Wing spar/pylon attachment joints
67 Starboard wing integral fuel tank; total usable fuel capacity 2,540 Imp gal (11,547l)
68 Fuel system piping
69 Pressure refuelling connection
70 Outboard leading edge de-icing air duct
71 Fuel pump collector bay
72 Vent surge box
73 Starboard navigation light

74 Static dischargers
75 Starboard aileron
76 Aileron tabs
77 Roll control spoiler
78 Spoiler hydraulic jack and sequencing cam box

79 Flap slot behind roll spoiler
80 Starboard tabbed-Fowler flaps, down position
81 Lift spoilers
82 Spoiler hydraulic jacks
83 Flap drive hydraulic motor
84 Engine bleed air ducting
85 Flap pitch trim corrector
86 Cabin roof lighting panels
87 Overhead stowage bins
88 Passenger service units
89 Forward/rear fuselage skin joint strap
90 Wing root trailing edge fillet
91 Dorsal spine fairing
92 Hot air ducting
93 Rear cabin seating
94 Air system recirculation valve
95 Rear service door
96 Rear twin seats
97 Air conditioning system ram air intake
98 Leading edge de-icing air ducting
99 Fin front spar
100 Tailfin construction
101 Fin/tailplane attachment joints
102 De-icing air spill duct
103 Starboard tailplane
104 Starboard elevator
105 Elevator trim tab
106 Trim tab screw jack
107 Inboard servo tab
108 Elevator cable drive linkage
109 Port elevator rib construction
110 Static dischargers
111 Elevator horn balance
112 Fixed tailplane construction
113 Leading edge de-icing air duct
114 Rudder construction
115 Rudder hydraulic jacks
116 Yaw dampers and rudder trim jack
117 Split tailcone airbrake
118 Tail navigation lights
119 Port airbrake open position
120 Airbrake hydraulic jack
121 Garrett-AiResearch GTCP 36-100 auxiliary power unit (APU)
122 APU intake duct, exhaust to starboard
123 Fin root spar box

124 Sloping fin attachment frames
125 Air conditioning packs; port and starboard
126 Tail bumper
127 Rear pressure bulkhead
128 Aft toilet compartment
129 Rear entry doorway, aft hinging plug type door
130 VLF aerial
131 Rear underfloor cargo hold
132 Cabin window panels
133 Port tabbed-Fowler flap
134 Flap shroud ribs
135 Rear spar
136 Rear spar/fuselage attachment joint
137 Wing root rib
138 Front spar
139 Inboard engine pylon mounting rib
140 Chain driven flap screw jack
141 Flap drive shaft
142 Flap carriage track
143 Port flap, down position
144 Flap track fairings
145 Port lift spoilers
146 Roll spoiler
147 Cable driven aileron hinge control linkage
148 Port aileron construction
149 Aileron tabs
150 Static dischargers
151 Aileron horn balance
152 Wing tip fairing
153 Port navigation light
154 Wing fuel tank venting intake
155 Port wing integral fuel tank
156 Wing rib construction
157 Leading edge nose ribs
158 Leading edge de-icing air ducting
159 Engine pylon construction
160 Bleed-air system pre-cooler
161 Engine gas producer core (hot) exhaust duct
162 Fan air (cold) exhaust duct
163 Detachable engine cowlings
164 Avco Lycoming ALF 502R-3 turbofan engine
165 Oil tank
166 Engine accessory drive gearbox
167 Air intake, bleed air de-iced
168 Main engine mounting
169 Twin mainwheels
170 Port landing/taxying lamp
171 Main undercarriage door
172 Pivoted axle beam
173 Main undercarriage leg strut
174 Shock absorber strut
175 Undercarriage pivot fixing
176 Side breaker strut
177 Hydraulic retraction jack
178 Underfloor hydraulic equipment bay
179 Standby hydraulic generator
180 Port inboard engine nacelle

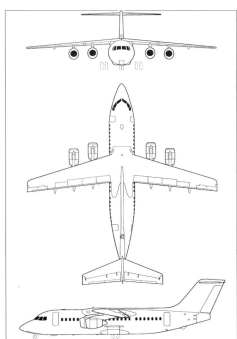

Left: Swissair-affiliated regional airline Crossair, was the first to take delivery of the RJ85 in April 1993. It has since enlarged its fleet with the bigger RJ100.

Above: The Avro RJ three-view reminds that the 146/RJ family is the only four-engined regional jet available. The four turbofans are attached on pylons to the anhedral wing.

The Jetstream was launched in 1965, at which time it was a product of Handley Page, designated the HP.137 and destined to be the last aircraft type produced by that company before its demise in 1969. Handley Page flew the first of several Jetstream prototypes on 18 August 1967, at which time the favoured engines were Turboméca Astazou XIV free-shaft turboprops; later prototypes represented the Jetstream Mk2 with Astazou XVIs and Jetstream Mk3 with Garrett TPE331s, which had been specified by the USAF when it ordered 11 Jetstream 3Ms as C-10As. Five prototypes and 35 production Jetstreams (with Astazou engines) had been completed when all work ceased at Radlett on 27 February 1970, and four more were completed from existing components under the initiative of Terravia Trading Service. Rights in the Jetstream were subsequently acquired by Scottish Aviation, which built 26 as navigation trainers for the RAF. In the USA some of the original HP built Jetstreams were modified by the Riley company, to have Pratt & Whitney Canada PTA6A-41 engines; others were brought up to Jetstream 200 standard with Astazou XVIs; and still more became Century III Jetstreams with TPE331 engines retrofitted by Volpar for Apollo Airways. Scottish Aviation was absorbed into British Aerospace upon the latter's formation and the Jetstream became part of the BAe civil aircraft product range, but it was not until December 1978 that the decision to launch an updated version of the Jetstream was announced, backed up in January 1981 with a full production commitment. In its reincarnation, the aircraft became the Jetstream 31, as a close relative of the Mk3 that Handley Page had built with Garrett TPE331 engines. These engines, and some structural changes, allowed the gross weight of the Mk3 to be increased to 6,577kg (14,500lb), compared with 5,670kg (12,500lb) for the earlier version, and this became the starting weight for the Jetstream 31. BAe introduced new advanced-technology propellers, a DC (in place of AC) electrical system, a revised air conditioning system, a changed hydraulic pump, a totally revised cockpit layout, and a range of new interior options. No significant changes were made to the external appearance or the structure of the Jetstream 31, the prototype of which (modified from Mk1) flew at Prestwick on 28 March 1980. A stretched adaptation for up to 29 passengers was announced on 24 May 1989 and launched on a risk-sharing basis with Field Aircraft, Pilatus Flugzeugwerke, ML Slingsby and Gulfstream Aerospace Technologies. Designated Jetstream 41, the new aircraft made its maiden flight on 25 September 1991. Four aircraft were used in the certification programme, with JAA approval awarded on 23 November 1992.

VARIANTS

The Jetstream 31 has benefited from some small increases in operating weights since being first produced, but there have been no important variations in production standard until the introduction of the Jetstream Super 31, also referred to as the Jetstream 32, which first flew on 13 April 1988. This version provided significant improvements in performance and passenger comfort, achieved with the introduction of more powerful 760kW (1,0020shp) Garrett (now AlliedSignal) TPE331-12 turboprop engines, a re-contoured interior providing greater cabin width at head height, and reduced noise and vibration. In basic airliner configuration, passenger capacity was 18/19, but Corporate and Executive Shuttle versions for 9/10 passengers were also produced. Other variants had the QC Quick Change and Special Role designation, intended for fast passenger/cargo conversion and for specialist application. One of these was a proposed Jetstream 31EZ for offshore

patrol in economic exclusion zones, fitted with a 360 degree scan radar, observation windows and searchlight. British Aerospace has completed a performance improvement package for the Super 31 for hot-and-high operations. This comprises flapless take-off flap setting and the fitting of aerodynamic devices to the engine nacelle/wing joint to reduce drag and enhance climb efficiency. Wingspan and fuselage were stretched by 2.44m (8ft 0in) and 4.88m (16ft 0in) respectively to produce the 29-seat Jetstream 41, powered by uprated 1,119kW (1500shp) TPE331-14 turboprop engines. Other changes include a Honeywell Primus II four-tube EFIS, inward-opening rear baggage door, lower mounted wing to clear cabin aisle, ventral baggage hold, increased fuel capacity in the wing and various aerodynamic improvements. The Jetstream 41 is available as a pure passenger aircraft with seating for 29 passengers; Corporate Shuttle for 8-14 passengers; and in Combi, Quick Change and Special Role variants similar to Jetstream 31. A package is available enabling an upgrade to J32EP (enhanced performance).

SPECIFICATION
(Jetstream 41)

Dimensions: Wingspan 18.42m (60ft.5in); length overall 19.25m (63ft 2in); height overall 5.74m (18ft 10in), wing area 32.59m² (350.8ft²).
Power Plant: Two AlliedSignal TPE331-14GR/HR turboprops, flat rated at 1,230kW (1,650shp). Five-blade McCauley metal propellers.
Weights: Operating weight empty 6,473kg (14,272lb); max take-off 10,886kg (24,000lb); max landing 10,569kg (23,300lb).
Performance: Max cruising speed 295kts (547km/h); rate of climb 11.2m/s (2,220ft/min); service ceiling 7,925m (26,000ft); take-off field length 1,523m (5,000ft); landing field length 1,280m (4,200ft); max payload range 775nm (1,434km).
Accommodation: Flight crew of two. Two-abreast seating on right hand side of the aisle and single row on left, for maximum 29 passengers. Rear and ventral baggage volume 6.16m³ (217.5ft³).

Below: The three-view shows the Jetstream 41, which is very similar to the smaller J31/32. The success of the former could not be repeated and production has ended.

SERVICE USE

The Jetstream 31 was certificated in the UK on 29 June 1982, using the prototype and the first production aircraft, which had flown on 18 March 1982. US certification was obtained on 30 November 1982. The first delivery was made on 15 December 1982 to Contactair in Stuttgart, followed on 30 December by the first to a UK operator, Peregrine Air Services. A Special Role Jetstream 31 was delivered to the Royal Saudi Air Force in November 1987 for navigator training. The Jetstream Super 31 was certificated in the UK on 6 September 1988 and by the FAA to Part 23 in the 19-seat commuter category on 7 October and went into service with Big Sky Airlines of the USA in October 1988. First deliveries of the Jetstream 41 were made to Loganair and Manx Airlines on 25 November 1992. FAA approval was given on 9 April 1993 and the first J41 for a US customer was handed over to Atlantic Coast Airlines in June 1993. AlliedSignal accepted the first Corporate Shuttle in Summer 1994. Production of the Jetstream 31 was completed in 1994 with the 381st aircraft and at the end of 1997 with the 106th Jetstream 41.

British Aerospace Jetstream 41 Cutaway Drawing Key

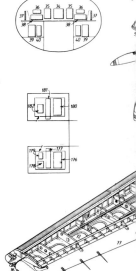

1 Glassfibre reinforced plastic (GRP) radome
2 Honeywell Primus 650 weather radar and glidescope antenna mounted on forward bulkhead
3 Windscreen wash-bottle
4 Nose bay
5 Inverter, also on stbd side
6 Windshield inverter/controllers; also stbd side
7 Nose wheel bay structure
8 Electric fan for avionics cooling
9 Pitot head (1 on port side, 2 on stbd side)
10 Total air temperature probe
11 Forward pressure bulkhead
12 Upward-opening nose-bay access door (stbd only shown)
13 Aluminium-alloy machined frames
14 Teleflex syneravia windscreen wipe and wash system
15 Triplex heated cockpit-window panels
16 Nose gear spade door (two), also two forward doors; in put position when undercarriage is down
17 AP Precision Hydraulics steerslide forward-retracting nose gear, actuated by a single double-acting, hydraulic jack. 2 landing lights and one taxi light and ground-crew jack box mounted on nose leg
18 Dunlop twin split-hub wheels with 17.5 x 6.25-6 tyres
19 Rudder pedals
20 Control columns
21 Two crew flight deck with fold-down jump seat
22 Electronic flight instrument display (EFIS)
23 AMI Industries crew seats
24 Avionics circuit-breaker panel
25 Side consoles
26 Angle-of-attack-vane
27 Electric circuit-breaker panel; also one on port side opposite
28 Folding back support for AMI industries jump seat; seat base folds down from port side
29 Overhead switch panels
30 VHF No 1 antenna
31 No 1 emergency lighting power supply
32 Flight control computer
33 Radio-altimeter transceiver No 1
34 Multifunction symbol generator
35 EFIS symbol generator
36 Communications unit
37 Junction panel
38 Navigation unit
39 Altitude and heading reference system
40 Digital air data computer
41 ATC No 2 antenna
42 Flux valve
43 Narco emergency locator transmitter antenna
44 VOR/LOC antenna
45 ADF No1 antenna
46 VHF No 2 antenna – below wingbox between ribs 1 & 2
47 Marker-beacon antenna
48 DME No 1 antenna; offset to port side of a/c centreline
49 Radio-altimeter RX 1 antenna; below fuselage
50 Radio-altimeter TX 1 antenna; below fuselage
51 ATC No 1 antenna; below fuselage
52 DME No 2 antenna; below fuselage
53 Stowage/wardrobe; max load 45.4kg
54 Main passenger door 1.42m x 0.73m door opens outwards and down and is suspended on links from the airstairs which is hinged to the fuselage
55 Jepson Burns passenger seats; nine single seats on port side and ten double seats on stbd side; sear pitch 0.75m

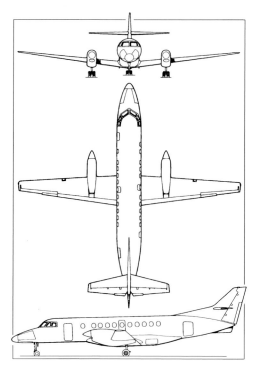

Above: In the USA the 18-seat Jetstream 31 was very popular, with most of the 381 aircraft produced serving with local commuter airlines.

Below: Cutaway of the Jetsream 41, the successor to the Jetstream 31 which was considerably successful. Production of both has now ceased.

Right: The larger, 29-seat Jetstream 41 is operated on regional routes in the UK, but has sold only slowly abroad.

115 Pen rib fairing
116 Rear main undercarriage door (two); also two forward doors, in up position when undercarriage is down
117 Main landing gear trunnion beams
118 AP Precision Hydraulics forward retracting main gear with Dunlop brakes and anti-skid control unit by Hydroarie
119 Dunlop twin wheels with 22 x 6.75-10 tyres
120 Outboard fuel cell Total fuel capacity -749 gal / 5,992lb (3,095 litres/2,725kb)
121 Inboard fuel cell Total fuel capacity – 749 gal / 5,992lb (3.095 litres/ 2,725 kg)
122 Vent tank, capacity 10 US gal/ 36 litres
123 Pipe from flush vent to vent tank
124 Siphon pipe
125 Gravity filter point
126 Pressurised refuelling point
127 Fuel and flow shut-off valves
128 Magnetic fuel-level indicators
129 Quality measuring probes
130 Dry bay under engine
131 BF Goodrich wing leading-edge de-icing boots

149 Support structure for baggage door
150 Baggage bay; capacity 4,81M³
151 Baggage-bay plug-type door 3.6mx1.32m; door opens inwards and tracks upwards assisted by Tensalor springs
152 Rear pressure bulkhead
153 Pressurisation outflow valve
154 Dorsal fin
155 Rudder control quadrani
156 Elevator control quadrani
157 Rudder/elevator lower control quadrant
158 Rudder and elevator trim quadrani
159 Vertical stabiliser of fabricated sheet-metal beams fastened to sheet-metal spars and skins
160 Horizontal stabiliser of conventional two-spar box construction, closed by upper and lower skins
161 Front and rear spade pick-ups for attachment of tailplane to fin

68 Wing built in two semi-spans and spliced at centre line; box structure consists of a front and rear spar joined by machined and fabricated ribs and closed by top and bottom wingskins
69 Front and rear spars integrally machined from artificially aged zinc-bearing alloy plate, integral spanwise crackstopper on each spar web
70 Bottom and top skins extended from toot to tip and are single-piece panels of clad naturally aged copper-bearing alloy which is chemically etched
71 'J' section stringers bonded to wing skins, manufactured from artificially aged zinc-bearing aluminium-alloy extrusions which are taper machined
72 Sheer carrying access panels in the lower wing skin between each of the twenty ribs
73 Wing leading-edge structure mounted on front spar via landing strips sandwiched between spar caps and skins. Comprises a stretch-formed, chemically etched skin supported by nose ribs and spanwise stiffeners

74 Trailing-edge shrouds; fabricated structure supported by riblets attached to the rear spar
75 Lower flap shroud articulates with flap movement
76 Wingtip housing strobe and navigation lights
77 Mass-balanced aileron; light alloy; supported by four hinges
78 Aileron trimtab – port side
79 Servo tab -stbd side
80 Push rod and cable linkage to aileron bell crank actuating mechanism
81 Aileron trim-tab actuation linkage
82 Lift-dump spoiler
83 Hydraulic actuator for spoiler
84 Flap; light-alloy construction hinging on four support brackets
85 Two-piece slat; mounted on the flap main body at our positions on inner slat and five positions on outer slat
86 Flap fairing
87 Flap driven on inboard end by hydraulic actuator
88 Interconnecting torque tube connected in board and of each flap by operating rod
89 McCauley five-bladed, constant-speed, variable-pitch 2.89m-diameter propellors; port side rotates clockwise and stbd side anti-clockwise when viewed from aft

56 Fuselage of aluminium alloy; rolled; rolled and stretched-formed skin panels supported by fabricated/machined frames and stringers. Z-section stringers are riveted to skin
57 Fuselage bottom boat frames are integrally machined from aluminium-alloy plate
58 Machine front spar frame
59 Machined rear spar frame
60 Castilion cockpit window frames
61 Type III over wing emergency exits (port & stbd); 0.99m x 0.5m
62 Flight-crew emergency exit; 3.6m x 0.47m
63 Type II emergency exit 1.21m x 0.5m
64 Wing-to-fuselage fairings manufactured by Slingsby
65 Forward lower fuselage fairing housing Normalair-Garrett environmental control system
66 Forward wing-to-fuselage pack up points
67 Aft wing-to-fuselage pick up points

90 Garrett TPE331-14GR/HR turboprop engines
91 Lucas Aerospace engine starter generator
92 Oil cooler
93 Upper engine support struts
94 Side engine support struts
95 Horsecollar
96 Engine isolators
97 Firewall
98 Aft upper struts
99 Diaphragm
100 Diaphragm
101 Hinge linkage allows jetpipe to be moved for access and maintenance
102 Heat shield
103 Heat-shield support structure
104 Upper front cowl
105 Lower intake cowl
106 Upper shear panel
107 Side cowl
108 Lower forward cowl
109 Forward jet-pipe cowl
110 Aft jet-pipe cowl
111 Rear side panel
112 EDAM fairing
113 Overwing interface
114 Aft end of nacelle articulates with flap (Singsby)

132 Seat-rail tracks
133 Lower cabin-air outlet ducting
134 Overwing light in fuselage to wing fairing
135 Access panels to hydraulics bay
136 Hydraulic fluid reservoir
137 Engine fire-extinguisher bottles
138 28V batteries, cone each side in aft fairing
139 Ventral baggage-bay; capacity 0.99m³
140 Ventral baggage-bay access door, both sides; 0.43m x 1.01m
141 Light in fairing for ventral baggage bay
142 Toilet servicing door/port side
143 Aft and forward fairings of glassfibre manufactured by Slingsby
144 Refreshment galley
145 Internal bulkheads
146 Toilet/cabin door (shown closed)
147 Toilet
148 Cabin attendantis seat, supported on bulkhead by two vertical V-shaped beams

162 Mass-balanced elevator with three hinges
163 Elevator trim tab
164 Elevator trim linkage
165 BF Goodrich de-icing boots on leading-edge of vertical and horizontal stabilisers
166 Rudder; sheet-metal construction
167 Rudder trim tab
168 Rubber trim tab linkage
169 Rudder control quadrani wheel
170 Tailcone
171 Anti-collision light
172 Position lights
173 Logo light in horizontal stabiliser
174 Electrically heated elevator horn
175 Static discharge wicks
176 Integrated engine computer (port)
177 Stall computer (port)
178 Audio warning unit
179 Syncro phaser
180 Integrated engine computer (stbd)
181 Stall computer (stbd)
182 PA amplifier

Product of a truly international programme of development and manufacture, the A300 was the first of the Airbus family of wide-body jet-liners that challenged long-held US primacy in the production of transport aircraft. Design activity began in 1965 as an Anglo-French initiative to develop a large-capacity transport for BEA and Air France; West German participation dates from 1967, with signature of a memorandum of understanding by the three governments on 26 September 1967. The initial tri-nation project was for 149,700kg (330,000lb) aircraft with two Rolls-Royce RB.207 engines, but this was scaled down after the British government withdrew on the grounds that a market could not be guaranteed, leaving Hawker Siddeley to maintain a British share on a privately-financed basis. The smaller A300B emerged in December 1968 with a 125,000kg (275,575lb) gross weight, two British or American engines each of about 200kN (45,000lb) thrust and accommodation for 252 passengers. Two prototypes were built in this configuration: under the designation A300B1, these two aircraft first flew on 28 October 1972 and 5 February 1973 at Toulouse with General Electric CF6-50A turbofans. These had a fuselage length 2.65m (8ft 8in) less than that of the production models, as described under the Variants heading below. Production of the A300 family is shared between the Airbus partners, comprising Aérospatiale in France, Daimler-Benz Aerospace (Dasa) in West Germany, British Aerospace in the UK and CASA in Spain, with Fokker in the Netherlands as an associate in the programme. All final assembly takes place in Toulouse, with major components ferried in from the other national production centres.

VARIANTS

Production began with the A300B2, later known as A300B2-100, with CF6-50C or C2 engines and first flown on 28 June 1983. The A300B2K (later A300B2-200) introduced wing-root leading-edge Krueger flaps for better field performance, and first flew 30 July 1976. Pratt & Whitney JT9D-59A engines were introduced on the A300B2-220 (and A300B2-320 with higher zero-fuel and landing weights), first flown 28 April 1979. The A300B4 (later A300B4-100 with CF6 engines, and A300B4-120 with JT9D engines) was introduced as a long-range version, with more fuel capacity and higher weights; the first flight of this variant was made on 26 December 1974. A higher-weight option, with structural strengthening, is the A300B4-200, which could also have more fuel in the rear cargo hold. A two-man forward-fac-

ing cockpit distinguishes the A300F4-200, first flown on 6 October 1981. A convertible freighter version is designated A300C4, based on the B4 with a forward side-loading door and reinforced floor, the first example flew in mid-1979. The A300-600 was launched in 1980 as an advanced version of the B-4, with a number of significant improvements including a rear fuselage of A310 profile, allowing two more seat rows in the cabin; a two-crew EFIS cockpit; use of composites and simplified systems for reduced structure weight; and advanced engines as quoted above, or the 249kN (56,000lb) thrust PW4156, 258kN (58,000lb) PW4158 or 236kN (53,000lb) RB.211-524D4A. The first A300-600 flew

Above: The world's largest freight company, Federal Express, has ordered a total of 36 of the A300-600F all-cargo version. Of these, 24 were in service at the beginning of 1998.

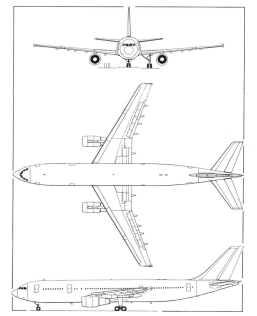

Left: The three-view drawing depicts the A300-600, introduced in 1987. It differs from earlier models through the introduction of more advanced engines, a two-crew 'glass' cockpit and, externally, the addition of winglets.

Below: Airbus competed well in the Asia/Pacific market and is continuing to make inroads. Private Indonesian carrier Sempati Air operates four of the type on high-density regional services.

SPECIFICATION
(Airbus A300-600R)

Dimensions: Wingspan 44.84m (147ffty 1in); length overall 54.08m (177ft 5in); height overall 16.53m (54ft 3in), wing area 260.0m² (2,798.6ft²).

Power Plant: Two General Electric CF6-80C2A5 rated at 273kN (61,500lb) each, or 262kN (59,000lb) Pratt & Whitney PW4158 turbofans. Other options available.

Weights: Operating weight empty 90,339kg (199,165lb); max take-off 171,700kg (378,535lb); max landing 140,000kg (308,645lb); max payload 39,735kg (87,600lb).

Performance: Max cruising speed 484kts (897km/h); service ceiling 12,200m (40,000ft) take-off field length 2,240m (7,350ft);landing field length 1,555m (5,100ft); range with typical payload 4,050nm (7,500km).

Accommodation: Flight crew of two. Twin-aisle cabin layout, seating typically 266 passengers in two classes, or up to 361 in 9-abreast high-density tourist configuration. Total baggage volume 24.98m³ (882ft³).

Airbus Industrie A300-600R Cutaway Drawing Key

1 Radome
2 Weather radar scanner
3 Scanner mounting and tracking mechanism
4 VOR localiser aerial
5 Front pressure bulkhead

6 Windscreen panels
7 Windscreen wipers
8 Instrument panel shroud
9 Control column
10 Rudder pedals
11 Cockpit floor level
12 ILS aerial
13 Pitot heads
14 Access ladder to lower deck
15 Captain's seat
16 Centre control pedestal
17 Direct vision opening side window panel
18 First officer's seat
19 Overhead systems switch panel
20 Maintenance side panel
21 Observer's seat
22 Folding fourth seat
23 Cockpit bulkhead
24 Air conditioning ducting
25 Crew wardrobe/locker
26 Nose undercarriage wheel bay
27 Hydraulic retraction jack
28 Taxying lamp
29 Twin nosewheels, forward retracting

30 Hydraulic steering jacks
31 Nosewheel leg doors
32 Nose undercarriage pivot fixing
33 Forward toilet compartment
34 Wash hand basin
35 Galley
36 Starboard entry/service door
37 Door mounted escape chute
38 Cabin attendant's folding seat
39 Curtained cabin divider
40 Forward main entry door
41 Door latch
42 Door surround structure
43 Underfloor avionics equipment racks
44 Runway turn-off light
45 Fuselage lower lobe frame and stringer construction
46 Floor beam construction
47 Cabin window panels
48 Forward freight hold door
49 Cabin wall trim panelling
50 Overhead stowage bins
51 Overhead stowage bins
52 Curtained cabin divider
53 First class passenger seating, 26 seats
54 Underfloor air system ducting

55 Door mounted escape chute
56 Main cabin entry door
57 Overhead stowage bins
58 Central galley unit
59 Starboard General Electric CF6-80 engine nacelle
60 Pratt & Whitney JT9D-7R4H1 or PW4156 alternative engine installation
61 Common nacelle pylon beam
62 Pylon attachment links
63 Pylon tail fairing
64 Starboard wing engine pylon
65 Tourist class passenger cabin seating, 241 seats (267 seats total in mixed class layout)
66 Air system distribution ducting
67 Conditioned air delivery ducting
68 LD3 baggage container; 12 in forward hold
69 Water tank
70 Slat drive shaft motor and gearbox
71 Wing spar centre-section carry through

72 Ventral air conditioning packs. 2
73 Wing centre box fuel tank
74 Three-spar wing centre-section construction
75 Centre-section floor beams
76 Front spar attachment main frame
77 Fuselage centre-section consruction
78 Starboard wing inboard main fuel tank. Standard fuel capacity 13,628 Imp Gal (62,000l)
79 Outer wing skin panel joint strap
80 Fuel system piping
81 Pressure refuelling connection
82 Refuelling valves
83 Fuel feed tank and pumps
84 Fuel tank dividing ribs
85 Leading-edge slat drive shaft
86 Three-segment leading-edge slats, open
87 Wing fence

88 Slat screw jacks
89 Outer wing panel integral fuel tank
90 Fuel vent tank
91 Starboard navigation light (green)
92 Wing tip fairing
93 Starboard winglet
94 Tail navigation and strobe lights (white)
95 Static dischargers
96 Fixed portion of trailing edge
97 One-piece single slotted Fowler-type flap, down position
98 Flap guide rails
99 Fuel jettison pipe
100 Outboard roll-control spoilers/lift dumpers (two)
101 Inboard airbrakes/lift dumpers (three)
102 Spoiler/airbrake hydraulic jacks
103 Flap screw jacks
104 Flap drive shaft
105 Starboard all-speed aileron
106 Aileron triplex hydraulic actuators

107 Wing root spoilers/lift dumpers (two)
108 Inboard flap segment
109 Cabin air system recirculation fan
110 Pressure floor above wheel bay
111 Rear spar attachment main frame
112 Starboard main undercarriage, retracted position
113 Undercarriage door jack
114 Equipment bay walkway
115 Undercarriage bay pressure bulkhead
116 Flap drive motor and gearbox
117 Hydraulic reservoir, triplex system
118 Eight-abreast tourist class passenger seating

119 Starboard Type 1 emergency exit door
120 Upper fuselage frame and stringer construction
121 Rear underfloor freight hold door
122 Freight/cargo compartment dividing bulkhead
123 Cabin wall insulating blankets
124 Cargo hold door
125 Cabin floor panelling
126 Seat mounting rails
127 Rear cabin air recirculation fan
128 ADF aerials
129 Fuselage skin panelling
130 Ceiling trim/lighting panels
131 Central overhead stowage bins
132 Rear galley
133 Fin root fairing
134 Fir spar attachment joints
135 Three-spar fin torsion box construction
136 Starboard trimming tailplane
137 Tailplane trim fuel tank, additional capacity 1,342 Imp Gal (6,100l)
138 Starboard elevator

139 Glassfibre reinforced fin leading-edge
140 Fin rib construction
141 Fin tip fairing
142 Static dischargers
143 Carbon fibre rudder skin panelling
144 Honeycomb core construction
145 Rudder triplex hydraulic actuators
146 APU equipment bay
147 Garrett GTCP331-250 auxiliary power unit (APU)
148 Tailcone fairing
149 APU exhaust duct
150 Port elevator construction
151 Elevator triplex hydraulic actuators
152 Static dischargers
153 Port tailplane rib construction

154 Leading-edge nose ribs
155 Port tailplane integral fuel tank
156 Tailplane pivot fixing
157 Moving tailplane sealing plate
158 Tailplane centre-section carry-through
159 Tailplane trim screw jack
160 Fin support structure
161 Rear pressure bulkhead
162 Rear toilet compartments (four)
163 Cabin attendant's folding seat
164 Rear entry door
165 Rear cabin seven-abreast passenger seating
166 Cabin side-wall frames
167 Underfloor bulk cargo hold, volume 610cu ft (17.3m³)
168 Cabin window panels
169 LD3 baggage containers, 10 in rear hold
170 Port Type-1 emergency exit door
171 Lower fuselage skin panelling
172 Wing root trailing-edge fillet
173 Port inboard single-slotted flap
174 Wing root spoilers/lift dumpers
175 Flap guide rail

176 Spoiler hydraulic jacks
177 Auxiliary spar
178 Main undercarriage side struts
179 Retractable ventral landing lamp, port and starboard
180 Hydraulic retraction jack
181 Main undercarriage pivot fixing
182 Inboard flap track mechanism
183 Aileron triplex hydraulic actuators
184 Port all-speed aileron construction
185 Port airbrakes/lift dumpers
186 Flap down position
187 Flap guide rails
188 Fuel jettison pipe
189 Flap track fairings
190 Roll control spoilers/lift dumpers
191 Fixed portion of trailing edge
192 Trailing-edge composite construction
193 Static dischargers
194 Tail navigation and strobe lights (white)
195 Port winglet
196 Wing tip fairing
197 Port navigation light (red)
198 Rear spar
199 Outer wing panel rib construction
200 Front spar
201 Port leading-edge slat segments
202 Slat screw jacks
203 Slat guide rails
204 Wing leading-edge de-icing air pipes
205 Telescopic de-icing air delivery ducts
206 Port wing integral fuel tank
207 Outer wing panel skin joint strap
208 Port main undercarriage four-wheel bogie
209 Main undercarriage leg strut
210 Nacelle pylon attachment joint
211 Engine pylon construction
212 Exhaust nozzle plug fairing
213 Core engine, hot stream, exhaust nozzle
214 Engine turbine section
215 Fan air, cold stream, exhaust duct
216 Reverser cascade, closed
217 Engine bleed air ducting
218 General Electric CF6-80C2-A1 turbofan
219 Engine fan blades
220 Noise attenuating intake lining
221 Intake cowling nose ring
222 Detachable engine cowling panels
223 Bleed air system pre-cooler
224 Inboard leading-edge slat
225 Bleed air delivery ducting
226 Inner wing panel three-spar construction
227 Inboard integral fuel tank
228 Inboard wing ribs
229 Wing root skin joint strap
230 Krueger flap actuator
231 Wing root Krueger flap, extended

Left: Shown in this cutaway drawing is the A300-600R, a long-range version which has a trimming fuel tank in the tailplane.

on 8 July 1983 with JT9D-7R4HI engines, and an A300-600 with CF6-80C2 engines flew on 20 March 1985. The A300-600R, first flown on 9 December 1987, differed in having small wingtip fences, a tailplane fuel tank with a computerised fuel trimming system, increased take-off weight and extended range capability. A small number of A300-600 Convertibles were also produced, whose main differences are a large forward upper deck cargo door, reinforced floor and a smoke detection system in the main cabin. Interest from Federal Express (FedEx) in a freighter version launched the A300-600F which first flew in December 1993. Many older models are also being converted for cargo use.

SERVICE USE

French and West German certification of the Airbus A300B2 was obtained on 15 March 1974, and service use began on 30 May 1974 with Air France. The first A300B2K was delivered to South African Airways on 23 November 1976. The Airbus A300B4 was certificated in France and West Germany on 26 March 1975, gained approval in the UYnited States on 30 June 1976, and entered service with Germanair on 1 June 1975. The A300B4-200FF was certificated on 8 January 1982 and entered service with Garuda. The convertible Airbus A300C4 entered service with Hapag-Lloyd at the end of 1979. The first Airbus A300-600 was delivered to

Saudi Arabian Airlines on 26 March 1984, and the first improved Airbus A300-600 to Thai Airways International in October 1985. Deliveries of the A300-600R to launch customer American Airlines began on 21 April 1988 and the first A300-600F freighter was delivered to FedEx on 27 April 1994. A large number of Airbus A300 B4s are now being converted for freight use with the installation of a forward freight door and strengthened floor. The first conversion (for Heavy Lift Cargo) was introduced at the 1997 Paris air show. At 1 January 1998, Airbus had orders for 488 A300s, of which 468 had been delivered, with 442 in airline service throughout the world.

Shortly after the A300 had been launched, Airbus Industrie began to investigate a number of possible future derivatives of the basic aircraft. These acquired designations from A300B5 onwards, and by 1974 interest was centred upon the B9, a fuselage-stretched variant; the B10, a fuselage shortened version; and the B11, with an enlarged wing and four engines. Of this trio, the B9 and B11 became the subject of further evolution under the TA9 and TA11 designations (now the A330 and A340), while the B10 was launched as the A310. Interest in a short/medium-range, medium-capacity transport crystallised in the mid-1970s as several European airlines indicated a need for such an aircraft for service from 1983 onwards. To achieve this timescale, Airbus made a marketing launch decision in July 1978, at which time 'pre-contracts' were obtained from Swissair, Lufthansa and Air France. The A310, as the A300B10 now became known, was not finally defined until the end of 1978, when the fuselage length was set at 13 frames less than the basic A300, but with some reprofiling of the rear fuselage to allow seating to extend farther aft. The wing was to remain structurally similar to that of the A300, but aerodynamically was completely new, taking advantage of extensive development work by British Aerospace at Hatfield. With government approval, British Aerospace (which had meanwhile absorbed the original Hawker Siddeley share in the A300) became a full partner in Airbus Industrie on 1 January 1979, with a 20 per cent share, and this is reflected in the work-sharing on the A310, with participation of Aérospatiale, Dasa, CASA and Fokker on a basis similar to that of the A300. The first A310 flew at Toulouse on 3 April and the second on 3 May 1983, both powered by JT9D-7R4 engines; the third aircraft, flown on 5 August 1982, had CF6-80A3 engines.

VARIANTS

Short and medium-range versions of the A310 were at first designated A310-100 and A310-200, at maximum take-off weights of 121,000kg (266,755lb) and 132,000kg (291,010lb) respectively. The former version was dropped, however, and the A310-200 was developed to have optional higher weights of 138,600kg (305,560lb) and 142,000kg (313,055lb) with a fuel capacity of 54,900l (12,077Imp.gal) in all versions. To extend the range of the basic aircraft, the A310-300 was developed with the tailplane trim tank to increase fuel capacity, and optional under floor tanks. The A310-300 is available at two weights as listed above, and has small wing tip fences, which also were retrospectively adopted for the A310-200. The first extended range A310-300, with JT9D-7R4E engines, flew on 8 July 1985 and the second, with CF6-80C2 engines, on 6 September 1985. Wingtip fences introduced as standard on A310-200 from Spring 1986. With the advances in power plants, a

SPECIFICATION
(Airbus A310-300)

Dimensions: Wingspan 43.89m (144ft 0in); length overall 46.66m (153ft 1in); height overall 15.80m (51ft 10in), wing area 219.0m^2 (2,357.3ft^2).
Power Plant: Two 262kN (59,000lb) General Electric CF6-80C2A8, or Pratt & Whitney PW4156A turbofans, each rated at 249kN (56,000lb). Other options available.
Weights: Operating weight empty 72,000kg (158,840lb); max take-off 164,000kg (361,550lb); max landing 124,000kg (273,375lb); max payload 32,117kg (70,805lb).
Performance: Max cruising speed 484kts (895km/h); service ceiling 12,200m (40,000ft); take-off field length 2,560m (8,400ft); landing field length 1,555m (5,100ft); range with typical payload 5,150nm (19,537km).
Accommodation: Flight crew of two. Twin-aisle cabin layout, seating typically 210-250 passengers in two class layout. Certificated for maximum of 280 passengers. Total cargo/baggage volume 102.1m^3 (3,605ft^3).

number of engines have been used, with current options for the A310-200 and -300 models being the 237kN (53,250lb) General Electric CF6-80C2A2 and the 231kN (52,000lb) Pratt & Whitney PW4152. A higher-gross weight version of the A310-300 has more powerful 262kN (59,000lb) CF6-80C2A8 and 249kN (56,000lb) PW4156A turbofans. Martinair Holland took delivery of the only example to date of a cargo-convertible A310-200C on 29 November 1984. Many used aircraft are now being converted to full freighter configuration under the designation A310-200/300F. A shorter range A310 Lite is on the drawing board and a military Multi-role Tanker Transport (MRTT) version is also projected. The latter would have a side cargo door and wing-mounted refuelling pods.

SERVICE USE

The A310-200 was certificated in France and West Germany on 11 March 1983, in the UK in January 1984 and in the USA early in 1985. First deliveries to Lufthansa and Swissair were made on 29 March 1983, and the first revenue services were flown on 12 and 21 April 1983 respectively. The A310-300 with JT9D engines gained French and West German certification on 5 December 1985, and service use by Swissair began on 16 December 1985 on routes linking Geneva and Zürich with points in Africa. Certification with alternative CF6-50C2 and PW4152 engines was granted in April 1986 and June 1987 respectively, and Wardair (Canada) received the first aircraft with additional centre tanks soon after certification in November 1987. Production ceased at the end of 1997 after delivery of 254 aircraft. These are operated by some 45 airlines.

**Airbus Industrie A 310
Cutaway Drawing Key**

1 Radome
2 Weather radar scanner
3 Radar scanner mounting
4 VOR localiser aerial
5 Front pressure bulkhead
6 Windscreen panels
7 Windscreen wipers
8 Instrument panel shroud
9 Control column
10 Rudder pedals
11 Cockpit floor level
12 ILS aerial
13 Pitot tubes
14 Access ladder to lower deck
15 Captain's seat
16 Centre control pedestal
17 Opening side window panels
18 First officer's seat
19 Overhead systems control panel
20 Maintenance side panel
21 Observer's seat
22 Folding fourth seat
23 Cockpit bulkhead
24 Air conditioning ducting
25 Crew wardrobe/locker
26 Nose undercarriage wheel bay
27 Hydraulic retraction jack
28 Taxying lamp
29 Steering jacks
30 Nosewheel doors
31 Forward toilet
32 Wash hand basin
33 Galley
34 Starboard entry/service door
35 Door mounted escape chute
36 Cabin attendant's folding seat
37 Hand baggage locker/wardrobe
38 Port main entry door
39 Door latch
40 Door surround structure
41 Radio and electronics racks
42 Runway turn-off lights
43 Fuselage frame and stringer construction
44 Floor beam construction
45 Forward freight hold
46 Freight hold door
47 Cabin wall trim panels
48 VHF communications aerial
49 Overhead stowage bins
50 Curtained cabin divider
51 First-class passenger compartment, 18 seats
52 Air system ducting
53 Cabin window panels
54 Overhead baggage lockers
55 Galley unit
56 Air system circulation fan
57 Tourist-class seating, 193 seats
58 Air conditioning supply ducting
59 Water tank
60 LD3 baggage container (eight in forward hold)
61 Slat drive shaft gearbox
62 Wing span centre section carry-through
63 Ventral air conditioning packs (two)

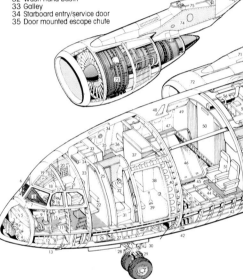

Left: Mexican holiday charter airline Aerocancun uses its A310-300 on flights to the United States and Latin America.

Right: China, once almost exclusively a Boeing customer, has warmed to Airbus and several models are now operated by the country's largest airlines. Xian-based China Northwest has three A310-200s.

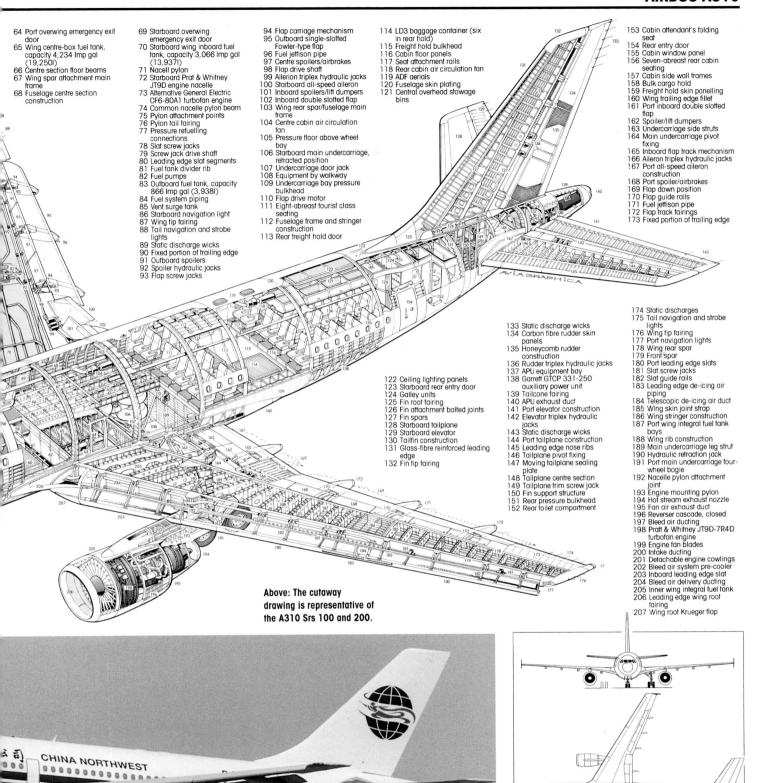

64 Port overwing emergency exit door
65 Wing centre-box fuel tank, capacity 4,234 Imp gal (19,250l)
66 Centre section floor beams
67 Wing spar attachment main frame
68 Fuselage centre section construction
69 Starboard overwing emergency exit door
70 Starboard wing inboard fuel tank, capacity 3,066 Imp gal (13,937l)
71 Nacell pylon
72 Starboard Pratt & Whitney JT9D engine nacelle
73 Alternative General Electric CF6-80A1 turbofan engine
74 Common nacelle pylon beam
75 Pylon attachment points
76 Pylon tail fairing
77 Pressure refuelling connections
78 Slat screw jacks
79 Screw jack drive shaft
80 Leading edge slat segments
81 Fuel tank divider rib
82 Fuel pumps
83 Outboard fuel tank, capacity 866 Imp gal (3,938l)
84 Fuel system piping
85 Vent surge tank
86 Starboard navigation light
87 Wing tip fairing
88 Tail navigation and strobe lights
89 Static discharge wicks
90 Fixed portion of trailing edge
91 Outboard spoilers
92 Spoiler hydraulic jacks
93 Flap screw jacks
94 Flap carriage mechanism
95 Outboard single-slotted Fowler-type flap
96 Fuel jettison pipe
97 Centre spoilers/airbrakes
98 Flap drive shaft
99 Aileron triplex hydraulic jacks
100 Starboard all-speed aileron
101 Inboard spoilers/lift dumpers
102 Inboard double slotted flap
103 Wing rear spar/fuselage main frame
104 Centre cabin air circulation fan
105 Pressure floor above wheel bay
106 Starboard main undercarriage, retracted position
107 Undercarriage door jack
108 Equipment by walkway
109 Undercarriage bay pressure bulkhead
110 Flap drive motor
111 Eight-abreast tourist class seating
112 Fuselage frame and stringer construction
113 Rear freight hold door
114 LD3 baggage container (six in rear hold)
115 Freight hold bulkhead
116 Cabin floor panels
117 Seat attachment rails
118 Rear cabin air circulation fan
119 ADF aerials
120 Fuselage skin plating
121 Central overhead stowage bins

122 Ceiling lighting panels
123 Starboard rear entry door
124 Galley units
125 Fin root fairing
126 Fin attachment bolted joints
127 Fin spars
128 Starboard tailplane
129 Starboard elevator
130 Tailfin construction
131 Glass-fibre reinforced leading edge
132 Fin tip fairing
133 Static discharge wicks
134 Carbon fibre rudder skin panels
135 Honeycomb rudder construction
136 Rudder triplex hydraulic jacks
137 APU equipment bay
138 Garrett GTCP 331-250 auxiliary power unit
139 Tailcone fairing
140 APU exhaust duct
141 Port elevator construction
142 Elevator triplex hydraulic jacks
143 Static discharge wicks
144 Port tailplane construction
145 Leading edge nose ribs
146 Tailplane pivot fixing
147 Moving tailplane sealing plate
148 Tailplane centre section
149 Tailplane trim screw jack
150 Fin support structure
151 Rear pressure bulkhead
152 Rear toilet compartment
153 Cabin attendant's folding seat
154 Rear entry door
155 Cabin window panel
156 Seven-abreast rear cabin seating
157 Cabin side wall frames
158 Bulk cargo hold
159 Freight hold skin panelling
160 Wing trailing edge fillet
161 Port inboard double slotted flap
162 Spoiler/lift dumpers
163 Undercarriage side struts
164 Main undercarriage pivot fixing
165 Inboard flap track mechanism
166 Aileron triplex hydraulic jacks
167 Port all-speed aileron construction
168 Port spoiler/airbrakes
169 Flap down position
170 Flap guide rails
171 Fuel jettison pipe
172 Flap track fairings
173 Fixed portion of trailing edge
174 Static discharges
175 Tail navigation and strobe lights
176 Wing tip fairing
177 Port navigation lights
178 Wing rear spar
179 Front spar
180 Port leading edge slats
181 Slat screw jacks
182 Slat guide rails
183 Leading edge de-icing air piping
184 Telescopic de-icing air duct
185 Wing skin joint strap
186 Wing stringer construction
187 Port wing integral fuel tank bays
188 Wing rib construction
189 Main undercarriage leg strut
190 Hydraulic retraction jack
191 Port main undercarriage four-wheel bogie
192 Nacelle pylon attachment joint
193 Engine mounting pylon
194 Hot stream exhaust nozzle
195 Fan air exhaust duct
196 Reverser cascade, closed
197 Bleed air ducting
198 Pratt & Whitney JT9D-7R4D turbofan engine
199 Engine fan blades
200 Intake ducting
201 Detachable engine cowlings
202 Bleed air system pre-cooler
203 Inboard leading edge slat
204 Bleed air delivery ducting
205 Inner wing integral fuel tank
206 Leading edge wing root fairing
207 Wing root Krueger flap

Above: The cutaway drawing is representative of the A310 Srs 100 and 200.

Above: Three-view drawing of the A310-300, which differs from the otherwise similar A310-200 mainly in having additional fuel and increased take-off weight.

**Airbus Industrie A320
Cutaway Drawing Key**

1 Radome
2 Weather radar scanner
3 Scanner tracking mechanism
4 VOR localiser aerial
5 Front pressure bulkhead
6 ILS glideslope aerial
7 Forward underfloor electronic
   equipment bay
8 Rudder pedals
9 Thomson-CSF Electronic Flight
   Instrument System (EFIS)
10 Instrument panel shroud
11 Windscreen wipers
12 Windscreen panels
13 Overhead systems switch
   panel
14 First-Officer's seat
15 Centre control pedestal
16 Circuit breaker panel
17 Observer's folding seat
18 Captain's seat
19 Direct vision opening side
   window panel
20 Sidestick controller (Fly-by-
   wire flight control system)
21 Artificial feel and sensor units
22 Crew wardrobe
23 Nose undercarriage wheel bay
24 Nosewheel doors
25 Twin nosewheels
26 Hydraulic steering jacks
27 Messier nose undercarriage
   leg strut
28 Nosewheel leg pivot fixing
29 Forward toilet compartment
30 Cockpit doorway
31 Galley unit
32 Starboard service door 32 ×
   72in (81 × 183cm)
33 Entry lobby
34 Cabin attendants' folding seats
   (2)
35 Door latch
36 Forward entry door 32 × 72in
   (81 × 183cm)
37 Door mounted escape chute

The 'decision in principle' to launch a short/medium-range jetliner in the 150-seat category was taken by Airbus Industrie in June 1981, and followed some 10 years of design activity in which all major European aircraft manufacturers had been either directly or indirectly involved, individually or in various collaborative groupings. Most directly a forerunner of the aircraft that became the A320 was the Aérospatiale AS200- actually a family of project designs that the French company studied in the mid-1970s. In 1977 Aérospatiale joined with British Aerospace, MBB and VFW-Fokker in the Joint European Transport (JET) study group, the objective of which was to provide a short/medium-range transport with 'a new order to quietness, fuel efficiency and operating economy'. The JET work was brought under Airbus Industrie direction when British Aerospace formally became an Airbus partner on 1 January 1979, and the studies continued under the SA (single-aisle) designation. The resulting SA-1, SA-2 and SA-3 had different fuselage lengths. The designation A320 was adopted early in 1981 as refinement of the design continued, while the optimum size remained under study. The aircraft was widely described as a '150-seater'. This being the typical, mixed-class capacity that was thought likely to be required by the airlines in the last decade of the present century. At the time of the marketing launch, however, there was still some interest in a somewhat larger capacity, so A320-100 and A320-200 projects were on offer with one-class accommodation at 32in (81cm) pitch, 154- and 172-seat capacities being provided by different fuselage lengths. Air France was the first to announce an intention to purchase the A320, in both these versions, but before Airbus was able to announce a full launch with the necessary financial backing on 2 March 1984, the decision had been made to concentrate on a single body size to accommodate 162 passengers, but still at two different weights, with different fuel capacities. The A320 made its maiden flight at Toulouse on 22 February 1987. Four aircraft were used in the development and certification programme culminating in JAA certification on 26 February 1988. The A320 was a wholly new design, the structure of which is based on well-proven principles used in the A300 and A310. Much use is made of the latest materials (including composites) and of advanced technology features in systems and equipment, with a quadruplex fly-by-wire control system, sidestick controllers for the two pilots, computerised control functions, an electronic flight instrument systems (EFIS) and electronic centralised aircraft monitor. Construction of the A320 is shared between the Airbus Industrie partners in the same way as those of the A300 and A310, with British

SPECIFICATION
(Airbus A320-200)

Dimensions: Wingspan 33.91m (111ft 3in); length overall 37.57m (123ft 3in); height overall 11.80m (38ft 8½in), wing area 122.4m² 1.317.5ft²).
Power Plant: Two 117.9kN (26,500lb) CFM International CFM56-5B4, or 111.2kN (25,500lb) IAE V2525-A5 turbofans. Other options available.
Weights: Operating weight empty 42,059kg (92,746lb); max take-off 77,000kg (U¡169,755lb); max landing 64,500kg (142,195lb); max payload 18,931kg (41,735lb)
Performance: Max cruising speed 487kts (900km/h); service ceiling 12,200m (40,000ft); take-off field length 2,286m (7,500ft); landing field length 1,442m (4,730ft); range with typical payload 2,900nm (5,370km).
Accommodation: Flight crew of two. Single-aisle cabin layout, seating typically 150 passengers in two class layout. Certificated for maximum of 179 passengers. Total cargo/baggage volume 38.76m³ (1,368.8ft³).

Above: Hong Kong-based Dragonair took delivery of its first A320 in February 1993. Its aircraft are fitted out either in a two-class layout with 12 Club and 144 economy seats, or in a 168-seat single-class configuration.

Right: An early cutaway drawing of the A320-200, showing the two engine options.

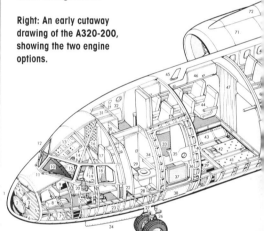

Aerospace (20 per cent of the work share) responsible for the wing, Aérospatiale (37.9 per cent) for the forward fuselage and nose; Daimler-Benz Aerospace Airbus (37.9 per cent) for the centre and rear fuselage, CASA (4.2 per cent) for rear fuselage panels and tailplane, and Belairbus for the wing leading edge.

VARIANTS

The two variants of the A320 are the A320-100 and A320-200, which have the same overall dimensions but different fuel capacities and operating weights. The A320-100, however, gave way to the A320-200 after the 20th aircraft, which is now the only production model, simply referred to as the A320. The A320-100 was powered by the 104.5kN (23,500lb) thrust CFM International CFM56-5A1, but a choice between the CFM56 and International Aero Engines (IAE) V2500 turbofans is available in the A320-200.

SERVICE USE

First deliveries of the A320-100 were made to Air France and British Caledonian (B.Cal) on 28 and 31 March 1988 respectively, although the B.Cal aircraft entered service with British Airways, following its take-over with effect from the next day. JAA certification for the CFM56-powered A320-200 was granted on 8 November 1988, and the first delivery was made to Ansett Australia 10 days later. Adria Airways took delivery of the first A320-200 with IAE V2500 engines on 18 May 1989. By 1 January 1998, orders stood at 905 of which 605 had been delivered.

38 Optional airstairs stowage
39 Underfloor avionics equipment racks
40 Door surround structure
41 Forward underfloor cargo hold, 490cu ft (13.87m³)
42 Mechanised cargo handling deck
43 Forward cargo hold door, 71.5 × 49in (182 × 125cm)
44 4-abreast first-class passenger seating at 36in pitch (12 passengers)
45 VHF communications aerial
46 Overhead stowage bins
47 Curtained cabin divider
48 Cabin wall trim panelling
49 6-abreast economy-class seating (138-passengers) alternative layout for 164 all-economy seats at 32in pitch

50 Overhead conditioned air delivery ducts
51 Cabin window panel
52 Cabin wall frames
53 Lower lobe frame and stringer construction
54 Wing root leading edge fillet
55 LD3-46 baggage/cargo container (3-forward, 4-aft)
56 Slat drive shaft gearbox
57 Conditioned air distribution ducting
58 Wing spar centre section carry-through
59 Fuselage keel assembly
60 Ventral air conditioning packs, port and starboard (Liebherr-Aerotechnik and ABG-Semca)
61 Port overwing emergency exit hatches, 20 × 40in (51 × 102cm)
62 Optional wing centre box fuel tank, capacity 1,767 Imp Gal (8,035l)
63 Wing front spar/fuselage main frame
64 Centre section floor beams
65 Starboard emergency exit hatches
66 Centre fuselage frame and stringer construction
67 Starboard wing integral fuel tank, normal total fuel capacity 3,499 Imp Gal (15,906l)
68 Wing tank dry bay
69 Inboard leading edge slat segment
70 Thrust reverser petal door (Rohr Industries)
71 Starboard CFM International CFM56-5 engine nacelle
72 Nacelle pylon

73 Outboard leading edge slat segments
74 Slat guide rails
75 Slat guide shaft and rotary actuators
76 Pressure refuelling connections
77 Fuel tank dividing ribs
78 Outboard vent surge tank
79 Starboard navigation lights
80 Wing tip fairing
81 Tail navigation and strobe lights
82 Starboard aileron
83 Aileron hydraulic actuators
84 Roll control and load alleviation spoilers
85 Spoiler hydraulic jacks
86 Flap rotary actuator and carriage mechanism
87 Starboard single-slotted Fowler-type flaps, down position
88 Roll control spoilers/speed brakes
89 Inboard flap segment
90 Inboard speed brake/lift dumper
91 Flap drive shaft and rotary actuator
92 Fuselage skin panelling
93 Cabin wall soundproofing linings
94 Pressure floor above wheel bay
95 Wing rear spar/fuselage main frame

96 Starboard main undercarriage, stowed position
97 Central flap drive motor and gearbox
98 Undercarriage bay pressure bulkhead
99 Floor beam construction
100 Composite cabin floor panelling
101 Seat mounting rails
102 Six-abreast passenger seating
103 ADF aerials
104 Rear cargo hold door, 71.5 × 49in (182 × 125cm)
105 Mechanised cargo handling deck
106 LD3-46 container
107 Rear underfloor cargo hold, 924cu ft (26.17m³)
108 Rear cabin seating
109 Overhead passenger service units
110 Overhead stowage bins
111 Cabin roof trim panels

112 Rear toilet compartments, port and starboard
113 Rear galley unit
114 Fin root fillet
115 Fin attachment bolted joints
116 3-spar fin box construction
117 Starboard trimming tailplane
118 Starboard elevator
119 All composite tailfin construction
120 Static dischargers
121 Rudder
122 Rudder composite construction
123 Hydraulic rudder actuators
124 Tailplane attachment main frame

125 APU equipment bay
126 Tailcone fairing
127 APU exhaust
128 Garrett GTP 36-300 Auxiliary Power Unit (APU)
129 Port elevator composite construction
130 Static dischargers

131 All composite trimming tailplane construction
132 Elevator hydraulic actuators
133 Tailplane pivot fixing
134 Tailplane sealing plate
135 Tailplane centre-section
136 Fin support structure (3-point)
137 Tailplane trim screw jack
138 Rear pressure bulkhead
139 Rear entry door, service door on starboard side 32 × 72in (81 × 183cm) each
140 Cabin attendant's folding seat
141 Rear cabin window panels
142 Underfloor bulk cargo hold
143 Outline of freight door (Possible freight or combi-version) 142 × 86in (361 × 218cm)
144 Fuselage lower lobe skin panelling
145 Wing root trailing edge fillet
146 Inboard flap segment
147 Composite flap shroud construction
148 Flap drive shaft
149 Main undercarriage wheel bay
150 Hydraulic retraction jack
151 Undercarriage leg side breaker strut
152 Main undercarriage pintle mounting

153 Dowty main undercarriage leg strut
154 Port speed brake/lift dumper
155 Flap track fairings
156 Outboard flap segment
157 Flap down position
158 Flap guide rails and carriages
159 Roll control spoilers/lift dumpers
160 Roll control/load alleviation spoilers
161 Aileron hydraulic actuators
162 Port aileron composite construction
163 Tail navigation and strobe lights
164 Port wing tip fairing
165 Static dischargers
166 Port navigation lights
167 Outboard vent surge fuel tank
168 Front spar
169 Port leading edge slat segments
170 Slat drive shaft and rotary actuators
171 Slat guide rails
172 Wing rib construction

173 Lower wing skin/stringer panel
174 Rear spar
175 Fuel tank access panels
176 Wing stringers
177 Leading edge de-icing air duct
178 Wing skin panelling
179 Slat rib construction
180 Twin mainwheels with carbon brakes
181 Port wing integral fuel tank
182 Nacelle pylon mounting ribs
183 Pylon attachment joint
184 Nacelle pylon construction
185 Vented exhaust tailcone
186 Core engine (hot stream) exhaust duct
187 Engine turbine section
188 Fan air (cold stream) exhaust duct
189 Petal type reverser doors (4), open
190 Reverser door jacks
191 Bleed air ducting
192 Main engine mounting
193 Engine oil tank
194 CFM International CFM56-5 turbofan engine
195 Full Authority Digital Engine Control (FADEC)
196 Engine fan blades
197 Air intake duct
198 Detachable engine cowling panels
199 Pylon forward fairing
200 Bleed air pre-cooler
201 Engine bleed air supply duct
202 Inboard wing ribs
203 Wing root rib attachment joint
204 Inboard leading edge slat segment
205 Slat guide rails
206 IAE V-2500 alternative engine
207 Engine accessory equipment

Left: The single-aisle A320 is operated in increasing numbers by several Chinese airlines, including Sichuan Airlines, which operates three from Chengdu, the capital of Sichuan province.

Right: The three-view depicts the A320 with CFM56 engines. Both the A320-100 and -200 are externally similar, although only the latter is now in production and also available with IAE V2500 turbofan engines.

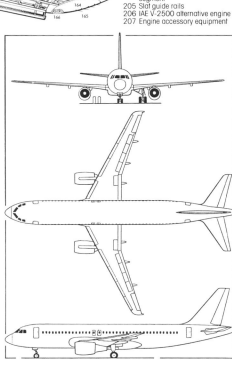

AIRBUS A319/A321 INTERNATIONAL

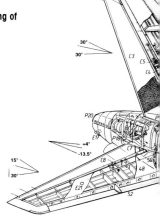

Right: Cutaway drawing of the Airbus A319.

The A321 stretched version of the single-aisle A320 was announced on 22 May 1989 and officially launched on 24 November. The A321 incorporates several airframe changes, the most noticeable being the insertion of a 4.27m (14ft 0in) fuselage plug forward of the wing and a 2.67m (8ft 9in) plug immediately aft, to provide 24 per cent more seating. Other changes include modified wing trailing-edges with double-slotted flaps, local structural reinforcement, uprated landing gear, repositioned and larger emergency exits, higher take-off weights, and more powerful CFMI or IAE engines. First Airbus aircraft assembled in Germany by Daimler-Benz Aerospace Airbus' plant at Hamburg. Front fuselage plug is produced by Alenia, rear fuselage by British Aerospace. First flight with V2500 lead engine took place on 11 March 1993 at Hamburg, followed by a CFM56-5B-powered model in May. Four aircraft were used in the certification programme, completed with JAA approval for the V2530-powered aircraft on 17 December 1993. The short-fuselage A319 was launched in June 1993 and made its first flight at Hamburg on 29 August 1995. Cross-crew qualification of all models in the A319/A320/A321 family is a significant advantage.

VARIANTS

The initial version produced was the A321-100, offering a choice of two standard engines, including the CFM International CFM56-5B1 and IAE V2530-A5 turbofans, both rated at 133.4kN (30,000lb) thrust, plus a more powerful option. An extended-range version, the A321-200, was launched in April 1995 and made its first flight in December 1996. It features further structural reinforcement, higher thrust versions of existing engines and additional centre fuel tank, and longer range. The elimination of seven A320 fuselage frames, reducing the overall length by 3.77m (12ft 4½in) to 33.80m (110ft 11in), resulted in the A319, which typically seats 124 passengers in a two-class layout, but is otherwise changed little. A corporate A319CJ is being offered for delivery in early 1999.

SERVICE USE

German flag-carrier Lufthansa accepted the first

SPECIFICATION
(Airbus A319)

Dimensions: Wingspan 34.09m (111ft 10in); length overall 33.80m (110ft 11in); height overall 11.80m (38ft 8½in), wing area 122.4m² (1.317.5ft²).
Power Plant: Two 97.9kN (22,000lb) CFM International CFM56-5A4 or IAE V2522-A5 turbofans. Higher 104.5kN (23,500lb) thrust options available.
Weights: Operating weight empty 40,149kg (88,513lb); max take-off 70,000kg (154,323lb); max landing 61,000kg (134,480lb); max payload 16,851kg (37,150lb).
Performance: Max cruising speed 487kts (900km/h); service ceiling 12,200m (40,000ft); take-off field length 1,829m (6,000ft); landing field length 1,356m (4,450ft); range with typical payload 2,650nm (4,907km).
Accommodation: Flight crew of two. Single-aisle cabin layout, seating typically 124 passengers in two class layout, going up to 148 in high-density.

SPECIFICATION
(Airbus A321-100)

Dimensions: Wingspan 34.09m (111ft 10in); length overall 44.51m (146ft 0in); height overall 11.81m (38ft 9in), wing area 122.4m² (1.317.5ft²).
Power Plant: Two 133.4kN (30,000lb) CFM International CFM56-5B1 or IAE V2530-A5 turbofans. Two 137.6kN (31,000lb) CFM56-5B2 engines optional.
Weights: Operating weight empty 47,966kg (105,745lb); max take-off 85,000kg (187,390lb); max landing 75,500kg (166,450lb); max payload 21,648kg (47,725lb).
Performance: Max cruising speed 487kts (900km/h); service ceiling 12,200m (40,000ft); take-off field length 2,345m (7,695ft); landing field length 1,587m (5,208ft); range with typical payload 2,300nm (4,260km).
Accommodation: Flight crew of two. Single-aisle cabin layout, seating typically 185 passengers in two class layout, or 200 in an all-economy arrangement. Total cargo/baggage volume 52.04m³ (1,838ft³).

A321-100 with V2530 engines on 27 January 1994. JAA certification with the A321-100 powered by the CFM56-5B2 was achieved on 15 February 1994 and the first of this model went into service with Alitalia at the end of March. Launch customer Aero Lloyd, a German holiday airline, put the A321-200 into service in Spring 1997 on its Mediterranean charters. The A319 with CFM56-5A engines received its initial certification on 10 April 1996 and made its service entry with Swissair on 8 May on its Zürich-Paris route. The first A319 powered by IAE V2500 engines made its maiden flight on 22 May. Launch customer United Airlines has ordered 28 aircraft. At 1 January 1998, total orders for the A321 stood at 219, with 76 delivered, while the A319 had logged 371 orders, with 65 delivered.

Below: German regional airline Eurowings put the A319 into service in Spring 1997. It has a total of four aircraft on order.

Airbus Industrie A319 Drawing Key

Structure and general
1 Upward hinging de-electric radome
2 Front pressure bulkhead
3 Two-crew cockpit, plus two supernumerary folding seats
4 Rearward-sliding side windows
5 Centre console, housing power levers, trim wheels and nac/comm panels
6 Forward toilet and washbasin
7 Forward galley
8 Passenger/service door, type (1.85 x 0.81): total four, incorporating single-lane escape chutes
9 Continuous extruded seat-rails
10 Adjustable furnishing bulkhead with curtains
11 First-class cabin, eight fully reclining seats at 0.91m pitch
12 Tourist-class cabin 116 seats at 810mm pitch
13 Toilets (two)
14 Rear galley, stowage for seven serving trolleys
15 Water tank (200 litres), glassfibre reinforced plastic (GFRP)
16 Cabin-wall insulation blankets
17 Cabin sidewall trim panels
18 Overhead passenger luggage stowage bins (2.1m long, 1.06m doors) incorporating built-in handrails
19 Passenger service panels
20 Separate forged and machined T-section window frames
21 Machined transverse floor beams supporting composite-sandwich floor panels
22 Main fuselage/wing frames, lower half built-up machined forging, top portion rolled
23 Rolled and notched fuselage frames
24 Rolled Z-section stringers riveted to chemically etched skin panels
25 Composite-material floor struts
26 Centre-boxes skin bracing struts

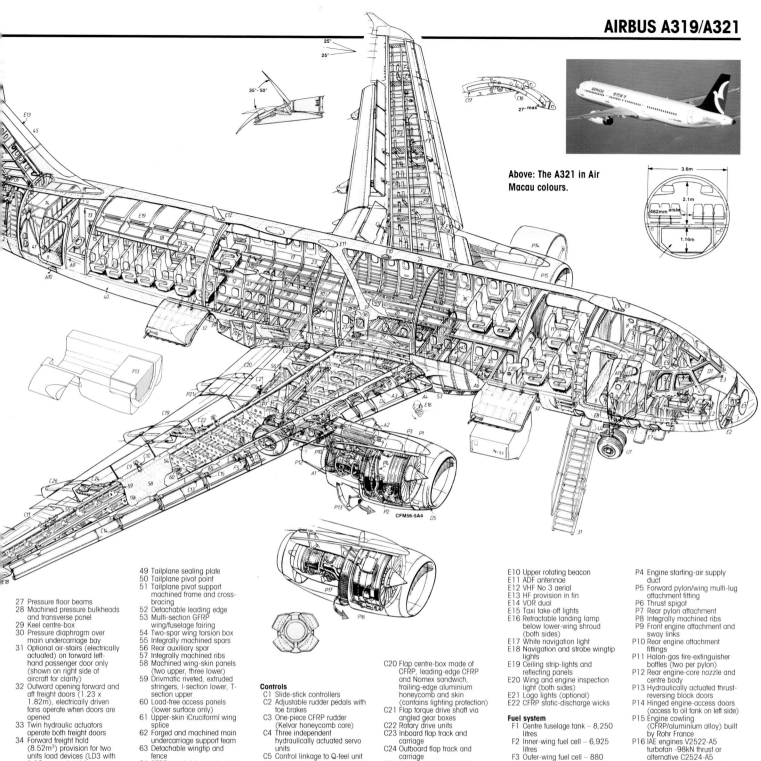

Above: The A321 in Air Macau colours.

25°
25°
35°- 50°
27° max

3.6m
2.1m
482mm aisle
1.16m

CFM56-5A4

27 Pressure floor beams
28 Machined pressure bulkheads and transverse panel
29 Keel centre-box
30 Pressure diaphragm over main undercarriage bay
31 Optional air-stairs (electrically actuated) on forward left-hand passenger door only (shown on right side of aircraft for clarity)
32 Outward opening forward and aft freight doors (1.23 x 1.82m), electrically driven fans operate when doors are opened
33 Twin hydraulic actuators operate both freight doors
34 Forward freight hold (8.52m³) provision for two units load devices (LD3 with 1.16m max height)
35 Forward and rear freight-hold freon-gas fire-extinguisher bottles
36 Overwing emergency exit (1.02 x 0.51m) on per side
37 Door and exit cut out surround doubler skin
38 Rear cargo compartment (19.12m³), provision for two full-width containers
39 Ball mat and power drive incorporated in door area and centre track
40 Aft cargo hold (19.12m³)
41 Rear pressure dome incorporating cabin-pressure safety valves (two)
42 Fin/fuselage attachment machined frames
43 Fin/fuselage attachment lugs (six)
44 Two-spar fin torsion-box with short centre-spar fabricated from carbonfibre reinforced plastic (CFRP)
45 Detachable leading edge with built-in erosion and static discharge strip
46 Fabricated integral stringer and skin panels (CFRP)
47 Trailing-edge fairings manufactured from plastic honeycomb material
48 Two piece tailplane joined on centreline (CFRP)

49 Tailplane sealing plate
50 Tailplane pivot point
51 Tailplane pivot support machined frame and cross-bracing
52 Detachable leading edge
53 Multi-section GFRP wing/fuselage fairing
54 Two-spar wing torsion box
55 Integrally machined spars
56 Rear auxiliary spar
57 Integrally machined ribs
58 Machined wing-skin panels (two upper, three lower)
59 Drivmatic riveted, extruded stringers, I-section lower, T-section upper
60 Load-free access panels (lower surface only)
61 Upper-skin ìCruciformì wing splice
62 Forged and machined main undercarriage support team
63 Detachable wingtip and fence
64 CFRP sandwich panels over main-undercarriage bay
65 Fixed leading edge, comprising machined ribs and diaphragm (Normex core access panels on upper and lower surface)

Air conditioning
A1 Engine bleed-air to environmental control system (ECS), bled from 5the and 9the stage intermediate-pressure (IP) and high-pressure (HP) compressors
A2 Engine-air pre-cooler
A3 Duct to air-conditioning pack, both sides
A4 Cooling-air ram intake to conditioning pack
A5 Air-conditioning mixing unit and silencer
A6 Air conditioning duct to forward fuselage
A7 Cabin main supply air-riser ducts
A8 Lower and upper air outlets
A9 Bleed-air duct from auxiliary power unit (APU) to air conditioners
A10 Cabin-pressure outflow control valve
A11 Electronic and electrical bay, cooling and venting ducts
A12 Outside-skin-cooling heat exchange

Controls
C1 Slide-stick controllers
C2 Adjustable rudder pedals with toe brakes
C3 One-piece CFRP rudder (Kelvar honeycomb core)
C4 Three independent hydraulically actuated servo units
C5 Control linkage to Q-feel unit and centring spring
C6 All-moving tailplane (hydraulically actuated by two servo motors, control linkage to valves driven by three electric motors)
C7 CFRP/Nomex honeycomb core elevator panels
C8 Twin, electrically signalled, hydraulic servo actuators control each elevator
C9 CFRP spoilers (five per side) inboard act as airbrakes/spoilers, outer three – roll/lift dump
C10 Hydraulic control jack (one per panel)
C11 All-speed CFRP aileron, operated by electrically signalled twin hydraulic servo jacks (aileron plus spoilers four and five act as load-alleviation function)
C12 Single hydraulic slat-actuator
C13 Slat torque drive shaft via angled gearboxes
C14 Five-section leading-edge slat (conventional built-up metal)
C15 Rotary-slat actuator (two per section)
C16 Titanium slat-track
C17 Track can incorporating condensation drains
C18 Single hydraulic flap-actuator
C19 Inboard and outboard Fowler-type single-slotted flaps

C20 Flap centre-box made of CFRP, leading-edge CFRP and Nomex sandwich, trailing-edge aluminium honeycomb and skin (contains lighting protection)
C21 Flap torque drive shaft via angled gear boxes
C22 Rotary drive units
C23 Inboard flap track and carriage
C24 Outboard flap track and carriage
C25 Flap track forward wing-attachment lugs, rear attachment on rear spar
C26 CFRP flap track fairings

Anti-icing
D1 Electrically heated windscreen, warm-air de-misted
D2 Bleed-air duct for slat anti-icing
D3 Bleed-air telescopic duct to ìpiccoloì tube (outboard only)
D4 Inboard leadingOedge ventilation, NACA intake below
D5 Engine-cowling intake anti-icing bleed-air duct

Electrics and electronics
E1 Weather radar
E2 Glideslope and dual localiser aerials
E3 Electrically driven windscreen wipers
E4 Pilotis overhead aircraft-systems panel
E5 Circuit-breaker panels
E6 Electrically heated pitot heads (3)
E7 Electrical compartment (both sides) housing two 23Ahr Ni-cad batteries
E8 Electronic and computer racks
E9 VHF no 1 aerial

E10 Upper rotating beacon
E11 ADF antennae
E12 VHF No 3 aerial
E13 HF provision in fin
E14 VOR dual
E15 Taxi take-off lights
E16 Retractable landing lamp below lower-wing shroud (both sides)
E17 White navigation light
E18 Navigation and strobe wingtip lights
E19 Ceiling strip-lights and reflecting panels
E20 Wing and engine inspection light (both sides)
E21 Logo lights (optional)
E22 CFRP static-discharge wicks

Fuel system
F1 Centre fuselage tank – 8,250 litres
F2 Inner-wing fuel cell – 6,925 litres
F3 Outer-wing fuel cell – 880 litres
F4 Surge tank
F5 Refuel/defuel coupling (RH standard, LH optional), refuelling panel in left rear-wing fairing -total fuel capacity 23,860 litres
F6 NACA intake and flame arrester
F7 Diffuser
F8 Fuel-tank vent lines
F9 Tank level-sensing capacitators – four per wing
F10 Engine feed pipe
F11 Fuel booster pumps (two per wing) situated between ribs one and two
F12 Wing dry bay
F13 Optional LD3-size additional centre tank container which fits in forward end of rear cargo compartment

Powerplant
P1 CFMI (General Electric/Snecma) CFM56-5A4 turbofan – 98kN thrust, alternative CFM56-5B5/B6 – 98/105kN thrust CFMs56-5A5-105kN thrust
P2 Full authority digital electronic engine control (FADEC) unit
P3 Engine-pylon services disconnect panel (both sides)

P4 Engine starting-air supply duct
P5 Forward pylon/wing multi-lug attachment fitting
P6 Thrust spigot
P7 Rear pylon attachment
P8 Integrally machined ribs
P9 Front engine attachment and sway links
P10 Rear engine attachment fittings
P11 Halon-gas fire-extinguisher bottles (two per pylon)
P12 Rear engine-core nozzle and centre body
P13 Hydraulically actuated thrust-reversing block doors
P14 Hinged engine-access doors (access to oil tank on left side)
P15 Engine cowling (CFRP/aluminium alloy) built by Rohr France
P16 IAE engines V2522-A5 turbofan -98kN thrust or alternative C2524-A5 turbofan – 105kN thrust
P17 Cascade-type thrust reverser and translating cowl
P18 AlliedSignal Garrett GTCP 36-300 auxiliary power unit (APU). Optional APU is the APIC APS3200
P19 Fire-extinguisher bottle
P20 APU exhaust
P21 Rear engine-pylon movable fairing

Undercarriage and hydraulics
U1 Messier-Bugatti forward-retracting, fully steering nose undercarriage
U2 Hydraulically actuated, electrically controlled, rack and pinon steering activator (+/-75 deg)
U3 Dowty Sideways-retracting main undercarriage
U4 Twin undercarriage main wheels incorporating increase energy multi-disc carbon brakes
U5 Breaker strut and down lock actuator
U6 Hydraulic retraction jack
U7 Main undercarriage-bay doors – CFRP/Nomex honeycomb core
U8 Hydraulic bay housing reservoirs and accumulators (three independent systems plus ram-air turbine)

AIRBUS A330 INTERNATIONAL

After studying a number of possible stretched versions and other derivatives of the basic A300 widebody twin-jet in the late 1970s to maintain its competitive position vis-a-vis the major US manufacturers, Airbus had narrowed down the choice to two designs. At the initial project stage, these were referred to as the A300B9 and A300B11. The latter grew into a four-engined long-range design and led to the TA11, later re-designated A340, which flew before the twin-engined model. Further into the study process, the medium-range large-capacity twin-engined A300B9 was renamed the TA9. As the 'TA' designation indicated, it was a twin-aisle design, based on the use of the basic A300 fuselage cross-section. As the project definition was firmed up and preliminary marketing efforts were initiated, the TA9 officially became the A330 in January 1986. Airbus offered a choice of General Electric CF6-80C2 and Pratt & Whitney PW4000-series turbofans and in 1987, Rolls-Royce engines became an option for the first time on an Airbus aircraft. Official launch, together with the A340, took place on 5 June 1987. Design features include an all-new wing with high-lift devices from root-to-tip on both leading and trailing edges to ensure optimum low-speed efficiency, A320-derived fly-by-wire control system, computer-managed fuel transfer system to control centre-of-gravity position and reduce drag, centralised maintenance system (CMS), and increased thrust versions of proven engines. Maximum use is made of advanced materials and processes, including composites, superplastic forming and diffusion bonding, and robotic assembly. The A330, together with the A340, is part of a unique manufacturing and operating concept, whereby two different but complementary types benefit from sub-stantially common structures, systems and assembly line, but serving different market sectors. The A330 has been optimised for high-density regional and extended-range international routes and can typically carry 335 passengers a distance of 4,500 nautical miles. First flight of the A330, powered by General Electric CF6 engines, was made from Toulouse on 2 November 1992, followed by a PW4168-engined aircraft on 14 October 1993. A 1,100-hour flight test programme with GE engines led to the first ever simultaneous European and US certification of an airliner on 21 October. The first Rolls-Royce Trent-powered aircraft flew on 31 January 1994. Certification with Pratt & Whitney engines was obtained on 2 June 1994 and with the Rolls-Royce Trent on 22 December 1994.

VARIANTS

The current basic production version is the A330-300, which has been certificated with a maximum take-off weight of 212,000kg (467,375lb). A longer-range, higher 218,000kg (480,603lb) weight model, previously designated A330-300X, is also available, as is a still higher gross weight version with strength-

ened wing and a take-off weight of 230,000kg (507,060lb). Range is increased by 700nm (1,300km) to 10,200km. On 24 November 1995, Airbus launched the short-fuselage, extended-range A330-200, formerly referred to as the A330M10, as a direct competitor to the Boeing 767-300ER. This differs in having a 10-frame reduction in fuselage length to 59.00m (193ft 6⅜in) and a maximum take-off weight of 230,000kg (507,060lb). It can carry 256 passengers in three classes a distance of 6,400nm (11,850km). First flight took place on 13 August 1997. All version are available with the three engine options. A proposed A300 Super Stretch, or A330-400, carrying additional passengers in a fully-furnished forward freight compartment, has been put on hold.

SERVICE USE

First deliveries of the A330-300 were made to launch customer Air Inter (now Air France Europe) on 30 December 1993 and the type entered service on 17 January 1994 with a flight from Paris Orly to Marseille. Aer Lingus flew the first service across the Atlantic in May 1994, after the GE-powered version was granted 120-minute ETOPS approval, since extended to A330s powered by Pratt & Whitney and Rolls-Royce. First orders for the new A330-200 came from ILFC and Korean Air in March and May 1996. First delivery of the CF6-80E1-engined A330-200, to ILFC for lease to Canada 3000, is planned for April 1998. PW4000s power the second aircraft, due to fly in January 1998, with delivery to Korean Air to follow after certification in May 1998. The Trent-engined version is due to enter flight testing in July 1998. At 1 January 1998, the A330 order book totalled 226, of which 64 had been delivered.

SPECIFICATION
(Airbus A330-300)

Dimensions: Wingspan 60.30m (197ft 10in); length overall 63.65m (208ft 10in); height overall 16.74m (54ft 11in), wing area 363.1m² (3,908.4ft²).
Power Plant: Two 300kN (67,500lb) st General Electric CF6-80E1A2 or 285kN (64,000lb) Pratt & Whitney PW4164 or 300kN (67,500lb) Rolls-Royce Trent 768 turbofans. Higher thrust versions are also available.
Weights: Operating weight empty 122,200kg (269,400lb); max take-off 217,000kg (478,400lb); max landing 179,000kg (394,625lb); max payload 46,800kg (103,175lb).
Performance: Max cruising speed 500kts (925km/h); service ceiling 12,500m (41,000ft); take-off field length 2,255m (7,400ft); landing field length 1,815m (5,955ft); range with typical payload 4,850nm (8,982km).
Accommodation: Flight crew of two. Twin-aisle cabin layout, seating typically 335 passengers in two class layout with six-abreast in economy, or 400 maximum high density.

Airbus Industrie A330-200 Drawing Key

1 Upward hinging di-electric radome
2 Front pressure bulkhead
3 Rearward sliging side windows (also serve as emergency exits)
4 Two crew cockpit
5 Observer seat (all crew seats fully adjustable)
6 Folding supernumerary seat
7 Machined frames, stringerless construction in hose section
8 Pilotis wardrobe and suitcase stowage
9 Forward toilets and washbasins for first class passengers (2)
10 Coat stowage
11 Forward gallery
12 Passenger/service doors, plug type (1.07 x 1.93m), total eight, incorporating slide rafts
13 Forward vestibule partition
14 First class cabin, reclining seats with electrically actuated movement controls (12 seats at 1.5m pitch)
15 Cabin divider
16 Cabin-attendant folding seats and p/a installation (both sides)
17 Double galley
18 Forward freight hold, capacity for 14 LD3 containers
19 Forward freight door (2.7 x 1.69m)
20 Business-class cabin (36 seats at 1m pitch)
21 Business class toilets and washbasins (2)
22 Economy-class cabin (205 seats at 812mm pitch)
23 Continuous seat rails
24 Toilets and washbasins (4) with special facilities for handicapped passengers
25 Machined floor beams supporting composite-sandwich floor panels
26 Rear gallery
27 Rear cabin vestibule and attendant folding seats
28 Upward-inclined (1.5 deg) rear cabin floor
29 Rear freight hold, capacity for 12 LD3 containers
30 Rear freight-hold door (2.7 x 1.68m) both doors hydraulically actuated, both holds fully fireproofed
31 Ball mat and power drive incorporated in door area and centre track
32 Inward-opening bulk cargo compartment door (0.95 x0.95m), capacity 19.7m³
33 Side, overhead and centre stowage bins (four-frame box) capacity 1m³
34 Cabin sidewall insulation blankets
35 Pressurised glassfibre reinforced plastic (GFRP) water tanks (2) 350 litres each
36 Waste water tanks (2) standard (700 litres) with optional third tank capacity is (1,050 litres), all toilets vacuum flushed
37 Rear pressure dome and doubler skin
38 Tailplane trim actuator attachment
39 Fin-to-fuselage attachment lugs (6)
40 Attachment fairing
41 Two-spar fin torsion box with short centre-spar carbonfibre reinforced plastic (CFRP), fin structure is 1.05m taller than that of A330-300
42 Skin panels (CFRP) with bonded stringers
43 Detachable leading edge with built-in erosion and static discharge strip (provision for HF aerial)
44 Removable tip, housing VOR dual aerial
45 Continuous two spar trimming tailplane (sealed for tankage)
46 Centre box machined light-alloy structure
47 Outer box and skin panels (CFRP)
48 Detachable leading edge and tips (composite construction)
49 Tailplane pivot-support machined frame and cross bracing
50 Removable aluminium tips contain lighting-protection system
51 Tailplane/fuselage sealing plate
52 Rolled unnotched frames
53 Extruded stringers hot bonded to chemically etched skin panels above windows, riveted below
54 Fuselage/wing main frames, lower half machined forgings, top portion rolled
55 Door-surround doubler skins
56 Separate drop forged and machined window frames (250 x 350mm)
57 Portal frames
58 Longitudinal curved diaphragms, (cabin floor connected to pressure floor by swinging iAî frames brackets for flexure)
59 Keel centre beam
60 Undercarriage bay rear pressure bulkhead (housing hydraulic bay)
61 Machined triangular panels (transmit torsion loads)
62 Multi-section CFRP wing/fuselage fairing
63 Centre-wingbox central spar
64 CFRP diagonal bracing struts
65 Cantilevered wing torsion box, comprising integrally machined front and rear spars plus inboard centre spar
66 Access panel towing box
67 Centre spar with machined web

68 Integrally machined ribs – several ribs strengthened from original A330-300 design
69 Integrally machined wing skin panels (four top and four bottom) – increased skin thickness compared with A330-300 design
70 Wing-shroud panels, composite with Nomex honeycomb core
71 Detachable combined winglet and tip
72 Drivematic-riveted extruded stringers (J-section upper surface, I section lower)
73 Access inspection panels (lower surface only)
74 Upper skin icruciformî wing splice itriformi wing splice lower surface
75 Undercarriage support beam behind rib six (machined forging)
76 Leading-edge iDî nose aluminium fixed structure supported by machined ribs (Nomex core access panels on lower surface)

Air conditioning
A1 Ram air in to environmental control system (ECS) pack (boot-strap system left and right)
A2 Primary and secondary heat exchangers
A3 Air cycle unit
A4 Condenser
A5 Water extractor
A6 Engine bleed air iinî
A7 Outlet to mixing unit
A8 Ram air outlet
A9 Cabin-air mixing unit (distributes air to cabin zones)
A10 Ground connector and emergency ram air iinî
A11 ECS bay ventilation manifold air iinî
A12 Piccolo tubes
A13 Engine bleed air to ECS, bled from high pressure compressor
A14 Engine precooler
A15 Air duct to air conditioning pack
A16 Air ducts to mid cabin
A17 Air riser duct to rear cabin
A18 Air-conditioning riser and distribution ducts to forward cabin
A19 Supply ducts to passenger individual overhead air outlets
A20 Forward cargo-hold air-conditioning and ventilation ducts (based on a suction system)
A21 Rear freight-hold ventilation ducts

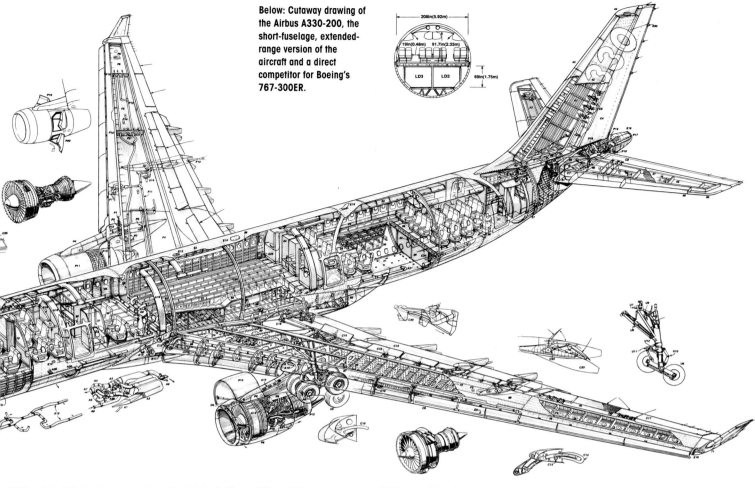

Below: Cutaway drawing of the Airbus A330-200, the short-fuselage, extended-range version of the aircraft and a direct competitor for Boeing's 767-300ER.

A22 Cockpit air-distribution ducts
A23 Cockpit sidewall and de-mist ducts
A24 Galley and toilet air-extraction and ventilation ducts
A25 Cabin sidewall plastic trim panels, air vents at floor level
A26 Forward cabin pressure outflow-valve
A27 Cabin pressure safety valve
A28 Re-heater

Controls
C1 Sidestick controller
C2 Adjustable rudder pedals with tow brakes
C3 Centre console housing power levers, trim wheels, and nav/comm panels
C4 One-piece CFRP rudder (Nomex honeycomb core). Larger rudder than that of A330-300 (increased chord of 6 per cent)
C5 Three independent, hydraulically actuated servo units – positioned diagonally
C6 Control linkage to iQi feel unit and centring spring
C7 Alt moving tailplane, hydraulically actuated by tow servo motors driving a fail safe ball screwjack, control linkage to valves driven by three electric motors
C8 CFRP/Nomex honeycomb core elevator panels actuated by three hydraulic servo units
C9 Seven-section leading edge slat (conventional built-up metal)
C10 Slat track (four for slat No 1 Two for slats for slat 2 to 7)
C11 Single hydraulic slat actuator with (2) independent motors
C1 Slat torque drive shaft via angled gearboxes
C1 Rotary slat actuator (two per section)
C14 Track cans, incorporating condensation drains
C15 CFRP spoiler panels (six per wing), also act as lift dumpers
C16 Hydraulic control jack (one per panel)
C17 CFRP ailerons (two per wing), each panel operated by one of two hydraulic jacks
C18 Two single-slotted Fowler type flaps per side, aluminium alloy – inboard, (CFRP) outboard
C19 Torque drive shaft via bevel gearboxes (driven by a single

hydraulic actuator), with (2) independent motors
C20 Inboard flap track (attached to fuselage side)
C21 Wing tracks and carriages (machined titanium) attached to built-up beams (four per wing)
C22 Rotary actuator (four per wing) moves flap via crank and tie-rod (electrically controlled by two computers)
C23 GFRP/Nomex honeycomb-filled flap track fairings (fixed and moveable)
C24 Pilotis emergency mechanical control cables to tailplane
C25 Manual pitch and roll control (spring loaded to neutral)
C26 Auto pilot disconnect or take-over switch
C27 Arm-rest incorporates height and pitch adjustment
C28 Memory position indicator

Anti-icing
D1 Electrically heated windscreen and cockpit window side panels (warm-air demisted)
D2 Bleed-air duct for slat anti-icing
D3 Telescopic duct to piccolo tube (outer four panels only)
D4 Engine-cowling valves anti-icing bleed air duct

Electrics and electronics
E1 Weather radar and dual localiser aerials
E2 Glideslope aerial (dual)
E3 Electrically driven windscreen wipers
E4 Fully shrouded instrument panel, incorporating six-tube electronic flight instrumentation
E5 Pilotis overhead aircraft systems panel
E6 Electrically heated pitot heads (three, both sides)
E7 In-flight access to avionics and electronic bay housing two 37Ah Ni-cad batteries
E8 Taxi/turn-off lights
E9 Electronic and computer racks (air-vented, electric fan cooled)
E10 High-angle-of-attack sensor (one left, two right, electrically heated)
E11 VHF No 1 data-radio aerial
E12 Engine and wing-scan lights
E13 Upper rotating beacon
E14 ADF aerials
E15 VHF No 3 data-radio aerial

E16 Logo light
E17 High-intensity landing light (both sides)
E18 Navigation and strobe lights
E19 Rear navigation light (white)
E20 GFRP static-discharge wicks
E21 One 115Kva integrated drive generator (IDG) on each engine

Fuel systems
F1 Refuel/defuel coupling (right wing only), total capacity 139,090 litres
F2 Overwing gravity fillers (both sides)
F3 Centre-wing tank – 41,560 litres
F4 Inner-wing tank (2) – 42,000 litres each (including collector tank)
F5 Outer-wing tank (2) – 3,650 litres each
F6 Vent and surge tank
F7 Tail-trimming tank – 6,230 litres (isolated during take-off and landing)
F8 Wing-root collector tank housing twin booster and standby pumps, jet pump cross-feed, check and non-return valves (both sides)
F9 Flush NACA-type fuel vent (non-icing)
F10 Tank end ribs
F11 Fuel transfer lines
F12 Vent lines
F13 Fuel jettison and overboard dump
F14 Tank capacitors
F15 Engine feed pipes

Powerplant
P1 Forward pylon/wing attachment (machined titanium forging)
P2 Double tail-safe attachment links and single spigot fitting
P3 Rear pylon attachment (dual triangular and single-link fitting)
P4 Two-spar pylon, integrally machined longerons and ribs, enclosed with machined titanium side panels
P5 Engine forward attachment fitting
P6 Engine rear attachment and sway links
P7 Freon gas fire-extinguisher bottles (two per pylon)
P8 General Electric CF6-80E1 two spool turbofan
P9 Engine-pylon services, disconnect panel (both sides)

P10 Core-mounted gearbox, accessories and engine-oil tank
P11 Engine cowlings (CFRP/aluminium-alloy), built by Rohr France
P12 Rear engine core nozzle and centre body
P13 Thrust-reverser translating cowl extended exposing fixed cascade panels (actuated by GE prime pneumatic system)
P14 Hinged engine-access doors and supports
P15 AlliedSignal RE331-350 auxiliary-power unit (APU) housed in self-contained titanium inner-skin and aluminium outer-skin compartment supplying engine starting air and driving a 115kVA generator
P16 Fire extinguisher bottle
P17 APU exhaust
P18 Generator air cooling outlet
P19 Four door target type thrust reverser
P20 Blocker doors hydraulically actuated (Trent installation)

Undercarriage and hydraulics
U1 Unpressurised nose-undercarriage bay housing forward-retracting, fully steerable Messier Dowty nose undercarriage (1,050 x 395mm R16 tyres)
U2 Dual steering actuators (range +/-75 deg)
U3 Drag strut
U4 Hydraulic reservoir accumulators and filters provide three independent systems 207 bar)
U5 Four-wheel twin-tandem rocking-type bogie main undercarriage (Dowty-Rotol)
U6 Wheels incorporate multi-disc carbon brake unit with 1,400 x 530mm R23 tyres
U7 Front torque on strut
U8 Hydraulic retraction jack
U9 Sidestay/breaker strut (hydraulically actuated)
U10 Torque links
U11 Articulating links
U12 Bogie pitch trimmer incorporated leg-shortening mechanism which prevents when opening
U13 Pre-opening and closing undercarriage doors (CFRP)
U14 Drop-down ram-air turbine (RAT) supplies emergency hydraulic power

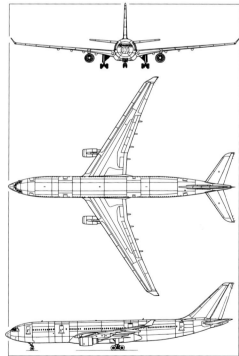

Above: The three-view drawing of the A330-300 shows its similarities to the A340-300, with which it shared joint development. The external dimensions are identical, but the A330 has only two engines.

AIRBUS A340 INTERNATIONAL

1 Upward hinging dielectric radome, covering weather radar and dual localiser aerials
2 Front pressure bulkhead
3 Glideslope aerial (dual)
4 Electrically heated windscreen, and side panels (warm-air demisted)
5 Rearward-sliding side windows (also serve as emergency exists)
6 Electrically driven windscreen wipers
7 Two-crew cockpit
8 Observer seat
9 Folding supernumerary seat
10 Fully shrouded instrument panel, incorporating six-tube electronic flight instrumentation
11 Pilot's overhead aircraft systems panel
12 Fully adjustable crew seats
13 Sidestick controller
14 Adjustable rudder pedals with ice-brakes
15 Centre console housing power levers, trim wheels, and nav/comm panels
16 Electrically heated pitot heads (three, both sides)
17 In flight access to avionic and electrical bay housing two 37 Ah Ni-Cad batteries
18 Machined frames, stringerless construction in nose section
19 Unpressurised nose undercarri8age bay
20 Forward-retracting, fully steering, nose undercarriage (1050mm x 395mm R16 tyres) (Messier -Bugatti)
21 Dual steering actuators (range +/-78 deg)
22 Taxi/take-off light
23 Drag strut
24 Electronic and computer racks (air-vented, electric-fan cooled)
25 High angle of attack sensor (one left, two right, electrically heated)
26 Pilot's wardrobe and suitcase stowage
27 Cockpit air-distribution ducts
28 Cockpit sidewall and demist ducts
29 Forward toilets and wash basins
30 Coal stowage
31 Galley and cocktail bar
32 Galley and toilet air-extraction ducts#33 Passenger/service doors, plug type (1.07m x 1.93m), total eight, incorporating slide rafts
34 Forward vestibule partition and curtains
35 First class-cabin, fully reclining sleeperette seats with leg rests (18 seats at 1,524mm (60in) pitch, electrically operated
36 Cabin divider and coat wardrobe
37 Business-class cabin (18 seats at 914mm (36in) pitch fully reclining
38 Wardrobe
39 Toilets and washbasins
40 Cabin-attendant folding seats and P/A installation (both sides)
41 Double galley
42 Forward freight hold capacity for 18 LD3 containers
43 Forward freight door (2.701m x 1.698m)
44 Forward cargo-hold air-conditioning and ventilation ducts (based on a suction system)
45 VHF 1 aerial
46 Engine and wing scan lights
47 Forward cabin pressure outflow valve
48 Air-conditioning riser and distribution ducts to forward cabin.
49 Supply ducts to passenger individual overhead air outlets
50 Air ducts to mid cabin
51 Air riser duct to rear cabin
52 Rear freight hold ventilation ducts
53 Economy class cabin (196 seats at 864mm (34in) pitch)
54 Continuous seat rails
55 Machined floor beams supporting composite sandwich floor panels
56 Toilets (five)
57 Rear galley units (all galleys cooled by chiller units)
58 Toilet and galley ventilation ducts
59 Rear-cabin vestibule and attendant folding seats
60 Coat wardrobe
61 Upward-inclined (1.5i) rear cabin floor
62 Rear freight hold, capacity for 14 LD3 containers
63 Rear freight-hold door (2.721m x 1.682m) both door hydraulically actuated, both holds fully fireproof.
64 Ball mat and power drive incorporated in door area and centre track
65 Bulk cargo compartment door (0.95m x 0.95m) capacity 9.68m³, inward opening
66 Side overhead and centre stowage bins (four-frame box 1.0m³
67 Cabin sidewall insulation blankets
68 Cabin sidewall plastic trim panels, air vents at floor level
69 GFRP water tanks, 350 litres each (pressurised)
70 Rear cabin pressure outflow valve
71 Waste water tanks (1,050 litres), all toilets vacuum flushed
72 Upper rotating beacon
73 ADF antennas
74 VHF 3 aerial
75 Rear pressure dome and doubler skin
76 Cabin pressure safety valves
77 Fin/fuselage attachment frames and vertical load path structure
78 Fin/fuselage attachment lugs (six)
79 Attachment fairing
80 Two-spar fin torsion box with short centre-spar (CFRP)
81 Integrally stiffened CFRP skin panels
82 Detachable leading edge with built-in erosion and static discharge strip (provision for HF aerial)
83 Removable tip, housing VOR dual aerial
84 One-piece CFRP rudder (Nomex honeycomb core)
85 Three independent, hydraulically actuated servo units
86 Control linkage to 'Q'-feel unit and centering spring
87 Continuous two spar trimming tailplane (sealed for tankage)

In the 1970s, Airbus began studying a number of possible stretched versions and other derivatives of the A300 twin-jet to build on its success in having broken the US manufacturers' monopoly of widebody aircraft. These studies eventually crystallised into two distinct, but parallel designs, initially referred to as the A300B9 and A300B11. The A300B9 grew into a twin-engined medium-range aircraft and led to the TA9, later re-designated A330, but it was the four-engined A300B11 which took priority in the development of the new widebody family. After first being redesignated TA11, TA standing for twin-aisle, the aircraft was given the next number in the Airbus sequence, namely A340, in January 1986. The A340 was jointly launched with the A330 on 5 June 1986. Using the same all-new wing, A320-derived fly-by-wire system, centre-of-gravity management system and advanced materials and manufacturing processes of the A330, the A340 diverged in the choice of power plant and engine-related systems. With four engines, a smaller turbofan was required and Airbus decided on using a higher thrust version of the CFM International CFM56 turbofan used in the A320/A321, with FADEC (Full Authority Digital Engine Control) as standard. No other suitable engine was available. Airbus had planned to power the A340 with the SuperFan, a ultra-high bypass development of the CFM56 or V2500 engines, but this came to nothing. Nevertheless, the choice of engine provides important commonality benefits with the single-aisle family. The A340, together with the A330, is also part of a unique concept, whereby two different but complementary types benefit from substantially common structures and systems, but serving different market sectors. The A340 has been optimised for medium-density long-range routes and typically carries 295 passengers a distance of over 7,000nm (13,000km). The A340-300 took off from Toulouse on its maiden flight on 25 October 1991, followed on 1 April 1992 by the shorter A340-200. Six aircraft (four A340-300 and two A340-200) were used in the flight test programme, which was concluded with the simultaneous certification of both versions by the European joint airworthiness authorities (JAA) on 22 December 1992. FAA certification was granted in May 1993.

VARIANTS

The first two versions to enter service were the A340-300 high-capacity model, intially powered by four 138.8kN (31,200lb) CFM56-5C2 engines and capable of transporting 295 three-class passengers, and the shorter-fuselage, but longer-range A340-200, with reduced three-class capacity of 263 passengers. The extended-range A340-300E, previously known as A340-400E and first flown on 25 August 1995, can carry a typical 295-passenger load over a distance of 7,150nm (13,242km) and is powered by higher

Above: Turkish Airlines now operates five A340-300s, having taken delivery of its first aircraft in July 1993. They are used on long-haul services, fitted out in three-classes.

151.2kN (34,000lb) thrust CFM56-5C4 engines. Three additional fuel tanks in the rear cargo hold, strengthened fuselage and wings of the A340-200 produced the A340-8000 growth version, first announced in November 1995, offering a range of over 8,000nm (15,000km) in a 253-seat three-class configuration. Further increases in range to 8,500nm (15,725km) are planned which would permit non-stop service between Europe and Australia. Launched in August 1997 were two further key projects to meet evolving market requirements, the A340-500 and A340-600, with a planned service entry at the turn of the century. The ultra-long range A340-500, previously referred to as A340-300Y, would be 3.2m (10ft 6in) longer than the A340-300 and carry 313 passengers over some 8,300nm (15,400km). The 'super stretch' A340-600, formerly A340-400Y, is projected to carry 382 passengers. The 249kN (56,000lb) Rolls-Royce Trent 500 has been selected as the initial power plant.

SERVICE USE

The A340-300 and A340-200 entered service in March 1993 with Air France and Lufthansa respectively. Singapore Airlines took delivery of the first high gross weight A340-300E on 17 April 1996 and the Sultan of Brunei received the first A340-8000, configured in a VVIP arrangement, in 1997. A total of 204 firm orders had been placed for the A340 by 1 June 1997, with 126 delivered.

SPECIFICATION
(Airbus A340-300)

Dimensions: Wingspan 60.30m (197ft 10in); length overall 63.65m (208ft 10in); height overall 16.74m (54ft 11in), wing area 363.1m² (3,908.4ft²).
Power Plant: Four CFM International CFM56-5C engines at various thrust levels, including 138.8kN (31,200lb) each in -5C2, 114.6kN (32,500lb) in -5C3 and 151.2kN (34,000lb) in -5C4.
Weights: Operating weight empty 129,806kg (286,175lb); max take-off 275,000kg (606,275lb); max landing 190,000kg (418,875lb); max payload 48,194kg (106,250lb).
Performance: Max cruising speed 494kts (914km/h); service ceiling 12,500m (41,000ft); take-off field length 2,790m (9,150ft); landing field length 1,855m (6,090ft); range with typical payload 7,300nm (13,520km).
Accommodation: Flight crew of two. Twin-aisle cabin layout, seating typically 335 passengers in two class layout with eight-abreast in economy, or 440 maximum high density.

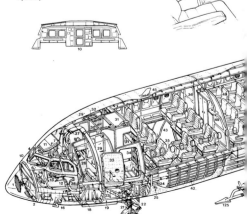

88 Centre box, machined light-alloy structure
89 Outer box and skin panels (CFRP)
90 Detachable leading edge and tips (composite construction)
91 Tailplane pivot-support machined frame and cross-bracing
92 All-moving tailplane (hydraulically actuated by two servo motors driving a fail-safe ball screwjack, control linkage to valves driven by three electric motors
93 CFRP/Nomex-honeycomb-core elevator panels (actuated by three hydraulic servo units)
94 Removable aluminium tips contain lighting protection system
95 Logo light
96 Tailplane/fuselage sealing plate
97 Garrett/ZF/BKT/Turbomeca auxiliary power unit (APU) housed in self-contained titanium inner-skin and aluminium outer-skin compartment, supplying engine starting air and driving a 115kVA generator
98 Fire extinguisher bottle
99 APU exhaust
100 Generator cooling air outlet
101 Air duct to air conditioning packs
102 Rolled unnotched frames
103 Extruded stringers hot bonded to chemically etched skin panels above windows, riveted below
104 Fuselage/wing main frames, lower half machined forgings, top portion rolled
105 Door-surround doubler skin
106 Separate drop forged and machined window frames (250mm x 350mm)
107 Wing centre section, sealed for tankage
108 Undercarriage bay (unpressurised)
109 Portal frames
110 Longitudinal curved diaphragms (cabin floor connected to pressure floor by swinging A brackets (allows for flexure)
111 Keel centre beam (provides housing for centre undercarriage and doors)

112 Rear pressure bulkhead (hydraulic bay)
113 Hydraulic reservoir, accumulators and filters provide three independent systems (207bar) (3,000lb/in)
114 Machined triangular panels (transmits torsion loads)
115 Ram air in to environmental control system (ECS) pack (boot strap system)
116 Primary and secondary heat exchangers
117 Turbine
118 Reheater
119 Water extractor
120 Engine bleed air iinî
121 Outlet to mixing unit
122 Air outlet
123 Cabin-air mixing unit (distributes air to cabin zones)
124 Ground connector and emergency ram air iinî
125 ECS by-ventilation manifold air 'in'
126 Piccolo tubes
127 Multi-section CFRP wing/fuselage fairing
128 High-intensity landing lamp (both sides)
129 Centre wingbox centre spar
130 CFRP diagonal bracing struts
131 Cantilevered wing torsion box, comprising integrally machined front and rea spar plus inboard centre spar.
132 Access panel to wing box
133 Centre spar, machined web and separate boom angles
134 Integrally machined ribs
135 Integrally machined wing skin panels (four top and four bottom)
136 Wing shroud panels, composite with Nomex honeycomb core
137 Detachable combined winglet and tip
138 Drivmatic-rivetted extruded stringers (J-section upper surface, I section lower)
139 Load-free access inspection panels (lower surface only)
140 Upper-skin 'Cruciform' wing splice, 'triform' wing splice lower surface
141 Undercarriage support beam behind rib six (machined forging)
142 Leading-edge 'D'- nose aluminium fixed structure supported by machined ribs (Nomex core access panels on lower surface)
143 Seven-section leading-edge slat (conventional built-up metal)

144 Titanium slat tracts (four for slat No1, two for slats No 2 to 7)
145 Single hydraulic slat actuator
146 Slat torque drive shaft via angled gearboxes
147 Rotary slat actuator (two per section)
148 Track cans, incorporating condensation drains
149 Bleed-air duct for slat anti-icing
150 Telescopic duct to ipiccoloî tube (outer four panels only)
151 CFRP spoiler panels only)
151 CFRP spoiler panels (six per wing), also act as lift -dumpers
152 Hydraulic control jack (one per panel)
153 CFRP ailerons (two per wing) each operating by one of two hydraulic jacks
154 Two single-slotted Fowler-type flaps per side (aluminium)
155 Torque diveshaft via bevel gearboxes (driven by a single hydraulic actuator)
156 Inboard flap track (attached to fuselage side)
157 Wing tracks and carriages (machined titanium) attached to built-up beams (four per aircraft)
158 Rotary actuator (four per wing), moves flap via crank and tie-rod (electrically controlled by two computers)
159 GRP/Nomex honeycomb-filled flap track fairings (fixed and movable)
160 Forward pylon/wing attachment (machined titanium forging)
162 Double fail-safe attachment links and single spigot fitting
162 Rear pylon attachment (dual tri-angular and single link fitting)
163 Two-spar pylon, integrally machined longerons and ribs enclosed with machined titanium side panels
164 Front engine attachment fitting
165 Rear engine attachment and sway links
166 Freon gas fire-extinguisher bottles (two per pylon)
167 General Electric/Snecma CFM56-5C2 two-spool turbofan 151.1Kn (31,200lb thrust), FADEC controlled
168 Engine-pylon service disconnect panel (both sides)
169 Fan mounted gearbox, accessories and engine oil tank (20 litres)

170 Engine bleed air to ECS, bled from high pressure compressor 5th and 9th stage
171 Engine precooler
172 Engine-cowling intake anti-icing bleed-air duct.
173 Engine cowlings (CFRP/aluminium-alloy, built by Rohr France)
174 Rear engine core nozzle and centrebody
175 Four-door target-type thrust reverser
176 Blocker doors (hydraulically actuated)
177 Hinged engine access doors and supports
178 Oil-tank access panel
179 Centreline undercarriage incorporating twin wheels, without brakes (Dowty Canada)
180 Hydraulic retraction jack
181 Diagonal bracing strut
182 Hydraulically actuated breaker strut and downlock
183 Main undercarriage incorporating a four-wheel, twin-tandem docking-type bogie (Dowty-Rotol)
184 Wheels incorporate multi-disc carbon brake units with 1,400mm x 530mm R23 tyres (ABS or Goodrich)
185 Front trunnion support
186 Hydraulic retraction jack
187 Sidestay/breaker strut (hydraulically actuated)
188 Torque links
189 Articulating links
190 Bogie pitch trimmer (main undercarriage incorporates leg-shortening mechanism, prevents wheel overlap)
191 Pre-opening and closing main undercarriage doors (CFRP)
192 Centre wing tank (41,468 litres)
193 Inner tank (40,231 litres)
194 Outer tank (3,797 litres)
195 Vent and surge tank
196 Tank end ribs
197 Over wing gravity fillers (both sides)
198 Tail trimming tank (5476 litres)
199 Refuel/defuel coupling (both sides), total capacity 135,000 litres
200 Collector tank in wing root housing twin booster pumps, jet pumps and check valves
201 Fuel transfer lines
202 Vent lines
203 Fuel jettison and overboard dump
204 Engine feed pipes
205 Tank capacitators
206 Flush NACA type-fuel vent (non-icing)

207 Drop-down ram air turbine (RAT) supplies emergency hydraulic power
208 Navigation and strobe lights
209 Rear navigation light (white)
210 GFRP static-discharge wicks
211 Pilotis emergency mechanical control cables to tailplane
212 Manual pitch and roll control (spring loaded to neutral)
213 Autopilot disconnect or take over switch
214 Arm-rest incorporates height and pitch adjustment
215 Memory position indicator

Above: Three-view drawing of the A340-300, powered by four CFM56 turbofan engines. In line with all the latest Airbus aircraft, the A340 is distinguished by its winglets.

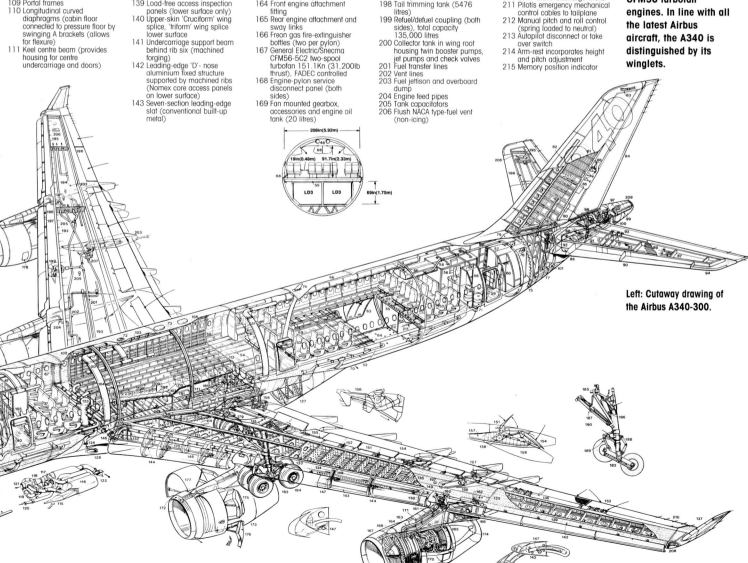

Left: Cutaway drawing of the Airbus A340-300.

AIRTECH (CASA/IPTN) CN-235 SPAIN/INDONESIA

Left: Binter Mediterraneo and Binter Canarias, both part of Spanish flag-carrier Iberia, are two of only four airlines using the high-wing turboprop transport. Binter Canarias serves the Canary Islands, while Binter Mediterraneo links southern Spain with the Balearics.

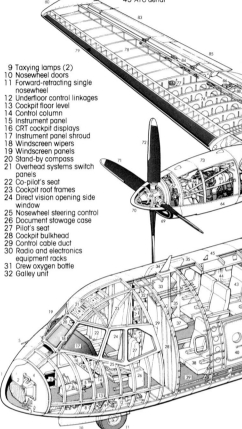

Airtech CN-235 Cutaway Drawing Key

1 Radome
2 Weather radar scanner
3 ILS glideslope aerial
4 Front pressure bulkhead
5 Pitot tube, port and starboard
6 Radar transmitter and receiver
7 Rudder pedals
8 Nosewheel bay
9 Taxying lamps (2)
10 Nosewheel doors
11 Forward-retracting single nosewheel
12 Underfloor control linkages
13 Cockpit floor level
14 Control column
15 Instrument panel
16 CRT cockpit displays
17 Instrument panel shroud
18 Windscreen wipers
19 Windscreen panels
20 Stand-by compass
21 Overhead systems switch panels
22 Co-pilot's seat
23 Cockpit roof frames
24 Direct vision opening side window
25 Nosewheel steering control
26 Document stowage case
27 Pilot's seat
28 Cockpit bulkhead
29 Control cable duct
30 Radio and electronics equipment racks
31 Crew oxygen bottle
32 Galley unit
33 Toilet compartment
34 VHF aerial
35 Starboard side forward entry door and airstairs
36 Control cable runs
37 Cabin attendant's folding seat
38 Front passenger-seat row
39 Passenger cabin floor panelling
40 Emergency exit hatch
41 Seat mounting rails
42 Cabin window panels
43 Four-abreast passenger seating (39-seat layout)
44 Cabin wall trim panels
45 ATC aerial

etails of the CN-235 were made public in June 1981, when Construcciones Aeronauticas SA (CASA) in Spain and P T Nurtanio in Indonesia (now IPTN) announced their intention to develop and produce the aircraft on an equally-shared basis for both commercial and military applications. Subsequently, a company known as Aircraft Technology Industries (Airtech) was set up in Madrid to handle the programme. With accommodation for up to 44 passengers or 48 troops, the short-range CN-235 entered what appeared to be an overcrowded marketplace for aircraft of approximately the same capacity, but it differed noticeable from its several competitors in being designed as much for military use as commercial application, as indicated in particular by the provision of a large rear ventral loading and supply dropping ramp/door, and the retractable tandem wheel main landing gear units suitable for rough field operations. The size of the cabin in the circular cross-section fuselage was such as to offer a high degree of comfort in commuter airline layouts; at the same time, the military aspects of the design made the aircraft potentially useful also for mixed traffic and quick-change operations or as a pure commercial freighter able to carry, for example, 18 passengers and two LD3 containers, or four standard LD3s or five LD2s. The agreement between CASA and Nurtanio provided for each company to be responsible for 50 per cent of the development and production of the CN-235, without duplication of manufacturing effort but with final assembly lines at the CASA works in Madrid and those of IPTN (previously Nurtanio) at the Husein Sastranegara Air Force Base at Bandung in Indonesia. So far as manufacture is concerned, CASA is responsible for the forward and centre portions of the fuselage, the wing centre section and inboard flaps. IPTN produces the rear fuselage section, outer wings complete with flaps and ailerons, and the entire tail unit. Preliminary design activities concerned with the CN-235 began in January 1980, with manufacture of two prototypes commencing in May 1981 and final assembly starting in 1983. Simultaneously, the two prototypes were rolled out on 10 September 1983, one in Madrid and the other at Bandung. First to fly was the CASA-assembled aircraft on 11 November 1983, the Indonesian following on 30 December of the same year. Spain and Indonesian certification was obtained 20 June 1986 and deliveries began on 15 December from Indonesian production and on 4 February 1987 from CASA. A total of 50 aircraft are being assembled under licence by Tusa Aerospace Industries (TAI) to fulfil a Turkish order. The first Turkish-assembled aircraft flew on 24 September 1992, with deliveries starting on 13 November that same year. The CN-235 is certificated to FAR Parts 25 and 36 and to the European JAR 25. FAA certification was grated on 3 December 1986.

SPECIFICATION
(CN-235-100)

Dimensions: Wingspan 25.81m (84ft 8in); length overall 21.40m (70ft 2½in); height overall 8.18m (26ft 10in), wing area 59.10m² (636ft²).
Power Plant: Two General Electric CT9-7C turboprops each flat rate at 1,305kW (1,750shp). Four-blade Hamilton Standard 14RF-21 propellers.
Weights: Operating weight empty 9,800kg (21,605lb); max take-off 15,100kg (33,289lb); max landing 14,900kg (32,849lb); max payload 4,000kg (8,818lb).
Performance: Max cruising speed 228kts (422km/h); rate of climb 9.65m/s (1,900ft/min); service ceiling 6,860m (22,500ft); take-off field length 1,290m (4,235ft); landing field length 772m (2,530ft); range with max fuel 810nm (1,501km); range with typical payload 2,350nm (4,352km).
Accommodation: Crew of two on flight deck plus one cabin attendant. Commuter configuration for 44 passengers in four-abreast seating with central aisle. Baggage compartment volume 7.0m³ (247.2ft³).

VARIANTS
Initial production version, of which 15 were built in each location, was the CN-235-10 with General Electric CT7-7A engines. This was replaced in 1988 by the CN-235-100/110, incorporating 1,305kW (1,750shp) CT7-9C engines in composite nacelles and a number of systems improvements. The designation –100 distinguishes Spanish-built models from the Indonesian –110 production. Structural reinforcements, higher operating weights and increased range produced the CN-235-200/220. Civil versions are available in passenger, cargo or quick-change (QC) passenger/cargo configurations. Military aircraft are the CN-235M transport, CN-235-330 Phoenix, and the CN-235 MP Persuader and CN-235 MPA for maritime patrol missions. A CN-235 AEW airborne early warning aircraft is proposed. Civil and military versions have the same overall dimensions. Stretched C-295 development is due to fly in March 1998.

SERVICE USE
Of the many CN-235 originally entered into the order book, only 24 are in airline service today. Many of the initial options taken out by Spanish and Indonesian operators, including Aviaco, Bouraq, Deraya, Dirgantara and Mandala, never materialised and the only commercial operators are Merpati Nusantara, which put the type into service on 1 March 1988 and has 14 Series 10 in service and another 16 Series 210 on order; Spanish regional airlines Binter Canarias and Binter Mediterraneo with eight; and Argentinian airline Inter Austral with two. The aircraft has achieved greater success in the military market.

Below: The three-view shows the CN-235 configuration as initially certificated, with small ventral fins. The rear ramp/door makes freight particularly suitable.

Above: The cutaway of the CN-235 gives an indication of the passenger seating in the civil version and shows provision for an optional baggage container on the ramp.

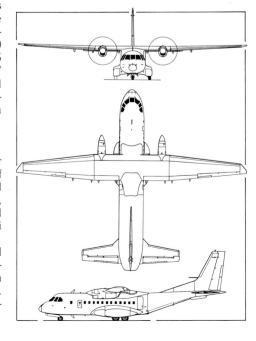

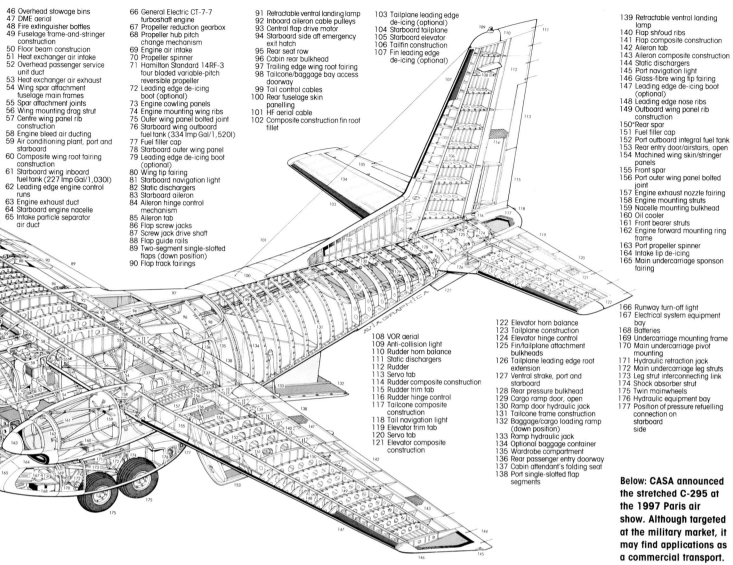

46 Overhead stowage bins
47 DME aerial
48 Fire extinguisher bottles
49 Fuselage frame-and-stringer construction
50 Floor beam construcion
51 Heat exchanger air intake
52 Overhead passenger service unit duct
53 Heat exchanger air exhaust
54 Wing spar attachment fuselage main frames
55 Spar attachment joints
56 Wing mounting drag strut
57 Centre wing panel rib construction
58 Engine bleed air ducting
59 Air conditioning plant, port and starboard
60 Composite wing root fairing construction
61 Starboard wing inboard fuel tank (227 Imp Gal/1,030l)
62 Leading edge engine control runs
63 Engine exhaust duct
64 Starboard engine nacelle
65 Intake particle separator air duct

66 General Electric CT-7-7 turboshaft engine
67 Propeller reduction gearbox
68 Propeller hub pitch change mechanism
69 Engine air intake
70 Propeller spinner
71 Hamilton Standard 14RF-3 four bladed variable-pitch reversible propeller
72 Leading edge de-icing boot (optional)
73 Engine cowling panels
74 Engine mounting wing ribs
75 Outer wing panel bolted joint
76 Starboard wing outboard fuel tank (334 Imp Gal/1,520l)
77 Fuel filler cap
78 Starboard outer wing panel
79 Leading edge de-icing boot (optional)
80 Wing tip fairing
81 Starboard navigation light
82 Static dischargers
83 Starboard aileron
84 Aileron hinge control mechanism
85 Aileron tab
86 Flap screw jacks
87 Screw jack drive shaft
88 Flap guide rails
89 Two-segment single-slotted flaps (down position)
90 Flap track fairings

91 Retractable ventral landing lamp
92 Inboard aileron cable pulleys
93 Central flap drive motor
94 Starboard side aft emergency exit hatch
95 Rear seat row
96 Cabin rear bulkhead
97 Trailing edge wing root fairing
98 Tailcone/baggage bay access doorway
99 Tail control cables
100 Rear fuselage skin panelling
101 HF aerial cable
102 Composite construction fin root fillet

103 Tailplane leading edge de-icing (optional)
104 Starboard tailplane
105 Starboard elevator
106 Tailfin construction
107 Fin leading edge de-icing (optional)

108 VOR aerial
109 Anti-collision light
110 Rudder horn balance
111 Static dischargers
112 Rudder
113 Servo tab
114 Rudder composite construction
115 Rudder trim tab
116 Rudder hinge control
117 Tailcone composite construction
118 Tail navigation light
119 Elevator trim tab
120 Servo tab
121 Elevator composite construction

122 Elevator horn balance
123 Tailplane construction
124 Elevator hinge control
125 Fin/tailplane attachment bulkheads
126 Tailplane leading edge root extension
127 Ventral strake, port and starboard
128 Rear pressure bulkhead
129 Cargo ramp door, open
130 Ramp door hydraulic jack
131 Tailcone frame construction
132 Baggage/cargo loading ramp (down position)
133 Ramp hydraulic jack
134 Optional baggage container
135 Wardrobe compartment
136 Rear passenger entry doorway
137 Cabin attendant's folding seat
138 Port single-slotted flap segments

139 Retractable ventral landing lamp
140 Flap shfroud ribs
141 Flap composite construction
142 Aileron tab
143 Aileron composite construction
144 Static dischargers
145 Port navigation light
146 Glass-fibre wing tip fairing
147 Leading edge de-icing boot (optional)
148 Leading edge nose ribs
149 Outboard wing panel rib construction
150 Rear spar
151 Fuel filler cap
152 Port outboard integral fuel tank
153 Rear entry door/airstairs, open
154 Machined wing skin/stringer panels
155 Front spar
156 Port outer wing panel bolted joint
157 Engine exhaust nozzle fairing
158 Engine mounting struts
159 Nacelle mounting bulkhead
160 Oil cooler
161 Front bearer struts
162 Engine forward mounting ring frame
163 Port propeller spinner
164 Intake lip de-icing
165 Main undercarriage sponson fairing
166 Runway turn-off light
167 Electrical system equipment bay
168 Batteries
169 Undercarriage mounting frame
170 Main undercarriage pivot mounting
171 Hydraulic retraction jack
172 Main undercarriage leg struts
173 Leg strut interconnecting link
174 Shock absorber strut
175 Twin mainwheels
176 Hydraulic equipment bay
177 Position of pressure refuelling connection on starboard side

Below: CASA announced the stretched C-295 at the 1997 Paris air show. Although targeted at the military market, it may find applications as a commercial transport.

ANTONOV AN-24/26/30/32 UKRAINE (CHINA)

The design bureau headed by the late Oleg K. Antonov began the development in 1958 of a twin-turboprop transport intended to replace the large numbers of piston-engined twins (such as the Lisunov Li-2 and the Ilyushin Il-12 and Il-14) used on internal routes in the Soviet Union. First flown in April 1960, the An-24 (NATO reporting name 'Coke') is a conventional high-wing monoplane seating 44/52 passengers. A second prototype and five pre-production airframes were built, two of the latter being for static and fatigue testing, and flight testing and certification were completed during 1963, by which time full production had been initiated. One of the first generation of turbine-engine transports for civil use developed in the Soviet Union, the An-24 became one of the most widely exported of Soviet post-war transports.

VARIANTS
The standard 50-seat production version of the Antonov transport was designated An-24V (often

appearing in cyrillic characters on the side of the aircraft as AH-24B) and was powered by (1,902kW) 2,550shp AI-24 engines. It was followed in production by the An-24V Seriiny II (Series 2) which had improved AI-24A engines (with water injection), increased chord on the wing centre section, and larger flaps . For aircraft operating in 'hot and high' conditions, 2,103kW (2,820shp) AI-24T engines could be fitted. The designation An-24T referred to a specialised all-freight variant which incorporated a

loading door in the rear of the cabin floor, hinged to open upwards into the rear fuselage. To allow both the AN-24V and An-24T to carry bigger payloads out of 'difficult' airfields, an optional installation was an RU19-300 auxiliary turbojet in the starboard engine nacelle in the An-24RV and An-24RT versions. Developed in 1971 the An-24P was a special fire fighting version, with provision to drop firefighters and equipment by parachute. Primarily intended for military duties, the An-26 was based on the An-24RT

SPECIFICATION
(Antonov An-24V)

Dimensions: Wingspan 29.20m (95ft 9½in); length overall 23.53m (77ft 2½in); height overall 8.32m (27ft 3½in), wing area 74.98m² (807ft²).
Power Plant: Two Ivchenko AI-24A turboprops, each rated at 1,902kW(2,550shp). An-24RV has auxiliary turbojet in starboard nacelle, rated at 8.82kN (1,984lb) thrust.
Weights: Operating weight empty 13,300kg (29,321lb); max take off 21,000kg (46,296lb); max landing 21,000kg (46,296lb); max payload 5,500kg (122,125lb).
Performance: Max cruising speed 243kts (450km/h); rate of climb 8.0m/s (1,575ft/min); service ceiling 8,400m (27,560ft); take-off field length 1,720m (5,645ft); landing field length 1,590m (5,215ft); range with max fuel 2,293nm (2,400mn); range with typical payload 296nm (550mn).
Accommodation: Flight crew of two plus one cabin attendant. Standard layout for 52 passengers in paired seats four-abreast with central aisle. Rear baggage hold 2.8m³ (99ft³).

ANTONOV AN-124 UKRAINE

The An-124 was first reported to be under development in the late 1970s, when the designation was thought to be an An-40, later changed to An-400. The definitive designation of An-124 emerged on May 1985 when an example of this very large transport made an appearance at the Paris air show. The first flight of the prototype had been made on 26 December 1982, and production examples were reported to be in service by January 1986. Loads carried by the An-124 range from the largest tanks to complete SS-20 nuclear missile systems, and from earth movers to oil well equipment; it is therefore of value in major civil engineering schemes and is now used to transport heavy and outsize equipment across the world. The An-124 is of conventional aerodynamic design but makes extensive use of composite materials in its structure, representing some 1,500m² (16,150sq ft) of surface area and saving 1,800kg (3,970lb) of weight. The floor of the main hold is fabricated from titanium, and the flight control system is completely fly-by-wire. A 24 wheel landing gear (10 main wheels on each side of the fuselage and four nose wheels) helps to spread the weight of the An-124, which is the largest production aircraft in the world, and allow it to operate from unprepared fields, hard-packed snow and ice-covered swampland, although not necessarily at its maximum weights. The An-124 has large front and rear loading access equipped with fold-down

hydraulic ramps for roll-roll-on/roll-off capability. Its cavernous cargo hold is fitted with two overhead cranes, each with a 10-tonne lifting capacity. Two further optional cranes can increase lifting capacity to 37 tonnes. NATO reporting name is 'Condor'.

VARIANTS
Basic model is the An-124, used largely by Aeroflot and the military. On 20 December 1992, the aircraft was certificated by AviaRegistr of Interstate Aviation Committee of CIS for commercial operations as the An-124-100, with restricted take-off weight and payload. A prototype An-124-100M was completed in late 1995, equipped with Western avionics, reducing crew to four. Crew is further reduced to three in EFIS-equipped An-124-102. A firefighting water-bomber, capable of dropping 200 tonnes of retardant, is under consideration as the An-124FFR.

IN SERVICE
The An-124 entered service in January 1986 in Aeroflot markings. First foreign operator was UK airline Air Foyle, which began operations in September 1989 in a joint venture with the Antonov Design Bureau, followed by another joint venture between HeavyLift Cargo Airlines (UK) and Volga-Dnepr of Russia. Around 80 aircraft are believed to have been built to date. They can be seen wherever there is a need for outsize cargo.

SPECIFICATION
(Antonov An-124-100)

Dimensions: Wingspan 73.30m (240ft 5¾in); length overall 69.10m (226ft 8½in); height overall 21.08m (69ft 2in), wing area 628.0m² (6,760ft²)
Power Plant: Four ZMKB Progress (Lotarev) D-18T turbofans, each rated at 229kN (15,590lb).
Weights: Operating weight empty 175,000kg (385,800lb); max take-off 392,000kg (864,200lb); max landing 330,000kg (727,513lb); max payload 120,000kg (264,550lb).
Performance: Max cruising speed 467kts (865km/h); service ceiling 12,200m (40,000ft); take-off field length 3,000m (9,840ft); landing field length 900m (2,955ft); range with max fuel 8,900nm (16,500km); range with max payload 2,430nm (4,500km).
Accommodation: Six or seven flight crew plus 10-12 technician and load masters. Cabin for up to 88 passengers, Cargo volume 1,000m³ (35,315ft³).

Right: Antonov's giant An-124 Ruslan is the largest commercial freighter in service. Its ability to operate from an unprepared airfield **in remote locations, makes it sough-after for the carriage of large and heavy pieces of equipment and machinery.**

and, first seen in public in 1969, incorporated a completely new rear fuselage with a 'beaver tail' and a unique rear door which could either hinge down conventionally as a loading ramp or slide forward under the fuselage to provide a clear exit for parachuting. Many variants were produced. A specialised version of the An-24 for aerial survey duties is designated An-30, and appeared in 1973. This differs from the An-24 primarily in having a raised cockpit and a more bulbous, largely transparent nose to give the navigator a wide field of view. In May 1977 details became known as another derivative of the basic aircraft, designated An-32 and in effect a hot-and-high versions of the An-26, produced also in a higher payload An-32B version and the An-32P Firekiller. With the same rear fuselage and loading ramp arrangements as the latter, and also intended primarily for military use as a personnel or supplies transport, the An-32 is powered by AI-20M engines of more powerful 3,128kW (4,195shp) or, for even better field performance, 3,863kW (5,180shp) AI-20DM turboprops. In China, a version of the An-24 was put into production at the State Aircraft Factory in Xian, and is known as the Y-7 or Yun-7. After nine pre-production examples had been built, the first full production Y-7 flew early in 1984, and production is continuing. The Y-7 has Chinese-built WJ5A-1 turboprops based on the AI-24A, each rated at 2,162kW (2,900shp). An upgrade with Western avionics systems and winglets produced the Y7-100, while further improvements, including Pratt & Whitney engines were incorporated in the Y7-200A convertible passenger/cargo model and the stretched Y7-200B. Chinese derivatives of the An-26 include the Y7H military cargo transport and the civil Y7H-500, the latter certificated on 15 June 1994.

SERVICE USE

The An-24 entered service with Aeroflot in September 1963 on the routes between Moscow, Voronezh and Saratov. It became widely used in the Soviet Union, and was also exported (for airline use) to some 14 other airlines, including most of those of the Soviet bloc nations. Production ended in the Soviet Union in 1978, with about 1,360 reported to have been built. CAAC in China was one of the airlines which acquired An-24s in the early 1970s, and in 1984 CAAC began to put into service the locally-built Y-7 versions. Approximately 1,400 An-26 were built between 1968 and 1985, before being superseded on the line by the An-32, which remains in production. Although the An-24/26/30/32 Series is no longer in frontline use, around 1,500 remain in service across the world.

ANTONOV AN-124

BEECHCRAFT 1900 USA

Having stopped production of the Beechcraft 99 in 1975, and thus separated itself from the developing market for small commuterliners and regional airliners, Beech Aircraft announced in 1979 its intention to develop one or more new types of aircraft suitable for this portion of the market. Design studies were already in hand for a pressurised aircraft in the 30/40-seat category but to provide a more immediate entry into the regional airliner market place, variants of the Super King Air 200 were projected. One such, known as the Model 1300 used the same airframe as its progenitor with a cabin arranged to seat 13 passengers (hence the designation), whilst the Model 1900 was to have a lengthened fuselage (for 19 passengers) and uprated engines, With indication of airline interest, development of the Model 1900 was continued and in 1981 work began on three flying prototypes, a static test airframe and a fuselage for pressure-cycle testing. The first two flying prototypes made their maiden flights on 3 September and 30 November 1982. The third, after being used for function and reliability testing, equipment certification and demonstration, was refurbished for customer delivery. Before the first flight of the prototype, testing of the PT6A-65 engine began in a Super King Air flying test bed on 30 April 1981. Based as it is on the Super King Air 200, the Model 1900 had the same fuselage cross section, the parallel section of the fuselage being lengthened by some 14ft (4.27m). Most other major components, including the wing centre section and the tail unit, are dimensionally similar to those of the Super King Air, but strengthened structurally where necessary to permit operations at higher weights. The PT6A-65B engines are flat-rated in order to provide constant power in elevated ambient temperatures. An unusual feature of the Beechcraft 1900 is its use of auxiliary horizontal fixed tail surfaces, known to Beech as stabilons, on each side of the rear fuselage just forward of the tailplane, which is mounted atop the fin. Small 'taillet' vertical fins are also mounted beneath each

tailplane half, near the tips. A 'wet' wing was also developed for the Model 1900, with integral tankage replacing the five bladder tanks in the original design, increasing fuel capacity by some 60 per cent and maximum range by an impressive 85 per cent. Beech revisited the 13-seat development of the Super King Air and in January 1988 announced the go-ahead for the Model 1300 for long thin routes. Deliveries began on 30 September that same year. A new development of the Model 1900 with stand-up headroom and a 28.5 per cent increase in cabin volume was announced at the US Regional Airlines Association (RAA) meeting in 1989. Known as the Model 1900D, it first flew on 1 March 1990 and

received its FAA certification to FAR Pt 23 Amendment 34 in March 1991.

VARIANTS
The basic 19-seat commuterliner was given the designation 1900C. It is powered by two Pratt & Whitney PT6A-65B turboprops each rated at 820kW (1,100shp) and incorporates a passenger door forward and upward hinged cargo-loading door in the port side of the rear fuselage. Accommodation is provided in two single seat rows each side of a central aisle. The Model 1900 Exec-Liner has a standard passenger door in this position and seats from 12-18 passengers. All doors are fitted with integral airstairs. From September 1987, the USAF took delivery of six 1900C aircraft, designated C-12J, for Air National Guard mission support. The Model 1900D replaced the 1900 Series on the production line from November 1991. Main differences are more powerful PT6A-67D turboprops each flat rated at 954kW (1,279shp), a flat floor with stand-up headroom, winglets for better hot-and-high performance, and twin ventral strakes for improved directional stability.

IN SERVICE
The Model 1900 was certificated under FAR Part 41C regulations on 22 November 1983, which included single-pilot approval under FAR 135 Appendix A. The first Model 1900C entered service with Bar Harbor Airlines in February 1984, and the first 1900 Exec-Liner was delivered to the General Telephone Company of Illinois in July 1985. A total of 248 1900C, mostly to US commuter/regional airlines, were sold before being replaced by the Model 1900D. Following the initial delivery to Mesa Airlines, which ordered a large number of the stand-up 1900D, this latest model is steadily making inroads in the export market and a total of nearly 300 had been delivered by 1 January 1998. It is also available in executive configuration, the first of which was delivered in April 1995.

SPECIFICATION
(Beech 1900D)

Dimensions: Wingspan 17.67m (57ft 11¾in); length overall 17.63m (57ft 10in); height overall 4.72m (15ft 6in), wing area 28.80m² (310ft²).
Power Plant: Two Pratt & Whitney Canada PT6A-67D turboprops, each flat rated at 954kW (1,279shp). Four-blade Hartzell composite propellers.
Weights: Operating weight empty 4,815kg (10,615lb); max take-off 7,688kg (16,950lb); max landing 7,530kg (16,600lb).
Performance: Max cruising speed 276kts (511km/h); rate of climb 13.3m/s (2,625ft/min); service ceiling 10,058m (33,000ft); take-off field length 1,140m (3,740ft); landing field length 844m (2,770ft); typical range with reserves 1,500nm (2,778km).
Accommodation: Crew of one or two on flight deck. Commuter seating for 19 passengers in single seat rows each side of a central aisle. Baggage volume 6.34m³ (223.9ft³).

Below: Holiday Airlines was one of several US commuter airlines operating the 1900C from the beginning in February 1983. This model had the normal cabin height which, at 1.45m (4ft 9in) was not a stand-up cabin and gave rise to the 1900D's development.

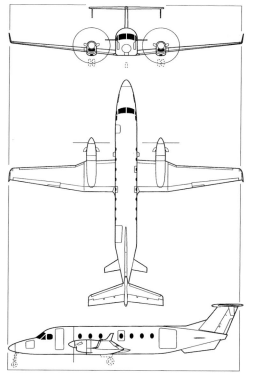

Above: The three-view drawing of the Beech 1900D shows the overgrown fuselage to provide increased headroom for the passenger. Note the ventral strakes on the T-tail, added to improve stability.

Above: Morocco's first regional carrier, Regional Air Lines, took delivery of four Beech 1900Ds in Spring 1997. The new airline links its base at Casablanca with the cities of Agadir, Fes, Marrakech, Rabat and Tangier.

Below: Canadian airline Central Mountain Air, based at Smithers, British Columbia, has operated Beechcraft since its foundation in 1987. It has now upgraded to the 1900D, providing regional business-class service.

BEECHCRAFT KING AIR/SUPER KING AIR USA

The King Air family was derived from the Queen Air, which itself entered production in 1958 as the largest of the Beechcraft twins. The King Air provided the basis for development of the Beechcraft 1900 Airliner, but variants of the smaller King Air are also used as third-level airliners and as air taxis by a number of operators in various parts of the world. Development of the King Air began with a installation of PT6A turboprops in a Queen Air airframe, leading to construction of a true King Air prototype which first flew on 20 January 2964. Initial deliveries of the Model 90, with PT6A-6 engines began later in 1964, this model being superseded by the A90 and B90 with slightly more powerful PT6A-20s and the C90 and C90-1 with PT6A-21s and cabin improvements. The C90A introduced 'pitot' cowlings with reduced-area intakes to increase ram-air flow to the engines. The improved C90B became the standard production model from 1991. A C90SE (Special Edition) was first delivered in October 1994. The King Air 100, introduced in 1969, featured more powerful PT6A-28 engines, a lengthened cabin to provide up to 13 seats in airline commuter configuration, and reduced wing span. The A100 had a series of refinements and the B100 switched to 536kW (715shp) Garrett TPE331-6-252B engines. The E90 combined the airframe of the C90 with PT6A-28 engines of the A100 and the F90, which appeared in 1979, combined the basic Model 90 fuselage with the short span wings of the Model 100 and the T-tail of the Super King Air 200. The F90-1 features PT6A-135 engines and 'pitot' intake as on the C90A-1. The larger Super King Air family has a distinctive T-tail configuration. The Super King Air 200, powered by twin Pratt & Whitney PT6A-41 turboprops, received certification to FAR Part 25 on 14 December 1973. It was replaced by the B200 in March 1981, which was generally similar except for the installation of higher

SPECIFICATION
(Beech Super King Air B200)

Dimensions: Wingspan 16.61m (54ft 6in); length overall 13.34m (43ft 9in); height overall 4.57m (15ft 0in), wing area 28.15m² (303ft²).
Power Plant: Two Pratt & Whitney Canada PT6A-42 turboprops, each flat rated at 634kW (850shp). Four-blade Hartzell propellers.
Weights: Operating weight empty 3,675kg (8,102lb); max take-off 5,670kg (12,500lb); max landing 5,670kg (12,500lb).
Performance: Max cruising speed 289kts (536km/h); rate of climb 12.45m/s (2,450ft/min); service ceiling 10,670m (35,000ft); take-off field length 786m (2,580ft); landing field length 632m (2,075ft); typical range with reserves 1,190nm (2,204km).
Accommodation: Crew of one or two on flight deck. Typical seating 7-9 passengers. Baggage volume at rear of cabin 1.51m³ (53.5ft³).

performance PT6A-42 turboprops. The B200C differed in having a 1.32m x 1.32m (4ft 4in x 4ft 4in) cargo door. Wingtip tanks of the maritime patrol B200T and the cargo door are combined in the B200CT. A special edition B200SE, certificated in October 1995, has improved avionics and three-blade propellers. Further improvements led to the Super King Air 300 with 783kW (1,050shp) PT6A-60A engines, introduced in January 1984, and the 300LW (Light Weight) development for the European market in 1988. The 'stretched' Model 350 replaced the 300 in Spring 1990. It has a fuselage lengthened by 0.86m (2ft 10in) to provide accommodation for up to 12 passengers, but retains the power plant of the Model 300. The 350C has a cargo door and built-in airstairs passenger access, and Special Missions and ELINT versions are also available. The B200 Super King Air has been popular with commuter airlines.

Below: The Beechcraft King Air 100 and smaller King Air variants have the general layout shown in this three-view drawing. The Super King Air differs markedly in having a T-tail.

Right: Norwegian commuter and business airline Air Stord operates a fleet of King Air 100s and Super King Air 200s on scheduled and charter services from its island base at Stord.

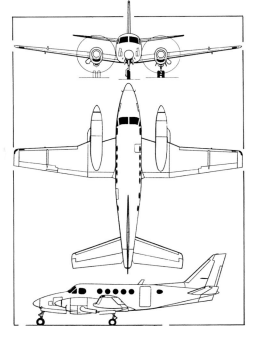

BOEING 707/720 USA

The first of the company's jetliners and first US jet transport to enter service, the Boeing 707 had its origins in the design studies conducted by the company in the late 1940s and early 1950s for a new tanker for the USAF as a successor to the C-97/KC-97 family. From a number of turboprop and turbojet designs studied, Boeing selected its Model 367-80 for prototype construction and this aircraft, which later became best known simply as the 'Dash 80', made its first flight on 15 July 1954 at Renton, powered by four Pratt & Whitney JT3C turbojets. The

Model 367-80 successfully demonstrated its potential to the USAF, which subsequently purchased many hundred KC-135A tankers and related reconnaisance and special-purpose variants, similar in size and configuration to the prototype. For airline use, however, Boeing decided that the cross-section of the fuselage should be increased so that more comfortable six-abreast seating could be provided and the new commercial project became identified as the Model 707. With 57.85kN (13,000lb) JT3C-6 engines, the Model 707 was offered in 'short-body'

and 'long-body' versions, and the latter was chosen by Pan American when it placed a launch order on 13 October 1955 (more than three years after the de Havilland Comet had become the world's first jet airliner in service). The first two Boeing 707s, used for certification, were flown on 20 December 1957 and 3 February 1958, and Boeing adopted a series of designation suffixes by which the first number of a three-numerical group indicated the model variant and the second and third numbers served as a means of identifying the particular customer.

SPECIFICATION
(Boeing 707-320C)

Dimensions: Wingspan 44.42m (145ft 9in); length overall 46.61m (151ft 11in); height overall 12.93m (42ft 5in), wing area 283.4m2 (3,050ft2).
Power Plant: Four Pratt & Whitney JT3D-7 turbofans, each rated at 84.55kN (19,000lb) st.
Weights: Operating weight empty 66,406kg (146,400lb); max take-off 151,315kg (333,600lb); max landing 112,037kg (247,000lb); max payload 23,856kg (52,593lb).
Performance: Max cruising speed 525kts (973km/h); rate of climb 20.3m/s (4,000ft/min); service ceiling 11,885m (39,000ft); take-off field length 3,055m (10,020ft); landing field length 1,950m (6,400ft); range with max fuel 5,000nm (9,270km); range with typical payload 3,150nm (5,840km).
Accommodation: Flight crew of three. Maximum one-class layout for 189 passengers six-abreast. Underfloor baggage/cargo volume 48.15m3 (1,700ft3). Upper deck cargo volume 161.2m3 (5,693ft3).

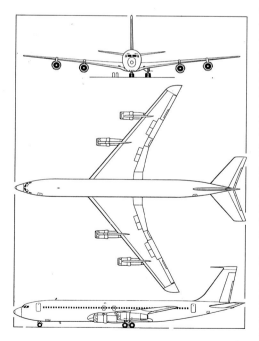

Left: The Boeing 707 was once found in all the major airlines' fleets. It opened up long-distance jet travel in the 1960s, but has now been relegated to the carriage of cargo.

Above: Three-view drawing of the 707-320B fitted with hush-kits to comply with noise regulations. The stricter requirements to come will severely limit the use of the 707.

VARIANTS

Most early orders were for the so-called 'long-body' variant of the Boeing 707-120; only Qantas ordered the 'short-body' version of the -120 (this being the Model 707-138, with 38 referring to the customer, Qantas). With the same fuselage length as the 'long-body -120, the Model 707-220 introduced 70.30kN (15,800lb) JT4A-3 or 5 engines for hot-and-high performance but was specified only by Braniff, the first flight being made on 11 June 1959. These same engines – or the 74.76kN (16,800lb) JT4A-9 or 77.88kN (17,500lb) JT4A-11 – were then adopted for the third model, the Model 707-320. This was the intercontinental versions of the aircraft, whereas the -120 was the transcontinental model, and it has the fuselage lengthened enough to accommodate up top 189 passengers, and a larger wing to cope with the higher weights. The first Model 707-320 flew on 11 January 1959, and was followed on 20 May 1959 by the first Model 707-420, which featured 73.4kN (16,500lb) Rolls-Royce Conway 505 engines. In 1957 Boeing offered a short/medium-range version of the basic aircraft as the Model 720, featuring a fuselage 0.51m (1ft 8in) longer than that of the short-body Model 707-120 used by Qantas, a lightened structure, lower fuel capacity 53.40kN (12,000lb) JT3C-7 engines and extended chord on the inboard wing leading edges. The Model 720 first flew on 23 November 1959. In 1960 Boeing introduced versions of the Models 707 and 720 with the newly-developed JT3D turbofan engines, identified by 'B' designation suffix. The Model 707-120B, with the aerodynamic refinements of the Model 720, first flew on 22 June 1960, and the first Model 720B flew on the 6 October 1960. The turbofan-engined Model 707-320B, which

first flew on 31 January 1962, also had new low-drag wing tips with a span increase of 1.0m (3ft 3½in), slotted leading-edge flaps and improved trailing-edge flaps. The passenger/cargo convertible version, with side-loading cargo door, was designated Model 707-320C and flew on 19 February 1963. One Model 707 was flown (starting on 27 November 1979) with CFM56 turbofans, but a proposed retrofit programme for these engines did not proceed, and variants, some with lengthened fuselages, designated up to Model 707-820, also remained in the project stage.

SERVICE USE

The first model of the Boeing 707 was certificated on 23 September 1958 and revenue service was inaugurated by Pan American on 26 October across the North Atlantic. Key dates for other variants were: Model 707-220 certificated on 5 November 1958 and first service by Braniff on 20 December 1959; Model 707-320 certificated on 15 July 1959 and first service by Pan American on 10 October 1959; Model 707-420 certificated on 12 February 1960 and first service by BOAC in May 1960; Model 720 certificated on 30 June 1960 and first service by United on 5 July 1960; Model 707-120B certificated on 1 March 1961 and Model 720B on 3 March 1961, first service by American Airlines on 12 March 1961; and Model 707-320B certificated on 31 May 1961 and first service by Pan American in June 1963. Boeing built a total of 917 Model 707s (excluding airframes for the E-3 and E-6 military programmes), made up of 63 -120, 78 -120B, five -220, 60 -320, 174 -320B, 337 -320C, 37 -420, 65 -720 and 89 -720B variants. Some 125 remain in service, most converted for cargo use.

BOEING 727-100/200 USA

1 Radome
2 Radar dish
3 Radar scanner mounting
4 Pressure bulkhead
5 Windscreen panels
6 Instrument panel shroud
7 Back of instrument panel
8 Rudder pedals
9 Radar transmitter and receiver
10 Pitot tube
11 Cockpit floor control ducting
12 Control column
13 Pilot's seat
14 Cockpit eyebrow windows
15 Co-pilot's seat
16 Engineer's control panel
17 Flight engineer's seat
18 Cockpit door
19 Observer's seat
20 Nosewheel bay
21 Nosewheel doors
22 Twin nosewheels
23 Retractable airstairs (optional)
24 Handrail
25 Escape chute pack
26 Front entry door
27 Front toilet
28 Galley
29 Starboard galley service door
30 Cabin bulkhead
31 Closet
32 Window frame panel
33 Radio and electronics bay
34 First class passenger cabin, 18 seats in mixed layout
35 Cabin roof construction
36 Seat rails
37 Cabin floor beams
38 Cargo door
39 Anti-collision light
40 Air conditioning supply ducting
41 Forward cargo hold
42 Cargo hold floor
43 Baggage pallet container
44 Tourist class passenger cabin, 119 seats in mixed layout
45 Communications antenna
46 Fuselage frame and stringer construction

The Model 727 was the second member of the Boeing jet family to appear, design work on a 'junior partner' for the Boeing 707/720 series having begun a full two years before the first Model 707 entered service. Many possible configurations were studied before Boeing decided to adopt the tri-jet arrangement with one engine in the rear fuselage and the other two on the sides of the rear fuselage in pods. By the autumn of 1959 the design had been frozen, based on three Allison-built Rolls-Royce Speys (which had also been specified for the Hawker Siddeley Trident, launched in 1958 with a near-identical layout). By the time a launch decision was made on 5 December 1960, however, with orders for 40 aircraft each placed by Eastern and United Air Lines, Pratt & Whitney JT8D engines had been chosen, and these were destined to be used, in progressively more powerful versions, in every Model 727 built. The new airliner was designed to have as much commonality as possible with the Model 707, and this applied in particular to the entire upper lobe of the fuselage (from the cabin floor up), thus permitting closely-similar cabin layouts and fitments to be used. At the time of its launch, the Model 727 had the most advanced aerodynamics of any commercial aircraft, with greater wing sweep back than was then and is now common, and a combination of high-lift devices on the leading and trailing edges to ensure reasonable field performance. The first flight of the Model 727 was made on 9 February 1963, the second aircraft following on 12 March 1963.

VARIANTS

The original Model 727 production aircraft had an overall length of 40.59m (133ft 2in) and were later designated Model 727-100; engine options were the 62.3kN (14,000lb) JT8D-1 or 7, and the 64.6kN (14,500lb) JT8D-9, and maximum take-off weight went from 68,965kg (152,000lb) to 72,595kg (160,000lb). A convertible passenger/cargo version with side-loading freight door flew as the Model 727C (later Model 727-100C) on 30 December 1965. The 'stretched' Model 727-220 flew on 27 July 1967 and became the standard aircraft, initially with JT8D-7 engines and 76,680kg (169,000lb) maximum take-off weight but later with engine and weight options as listed above. Introducing a number of refinements, improved cabin and greater fuel capacity, the Advanced 727 first flew on 3 March 1972, with JT8D-15 engines and a 83,660kg (191,000lb) gross weight. A pure freighter, with cabin windows blanked off, was the final Model 727 variant to appear, in 1983, and was known as the Model 727-200F, with a maximum payload (for the Federal Express 'small package' operation) of 26,650kg (58,750lb). Many have now been fitted with hush-kits in order to comply with stricter noise regulations.

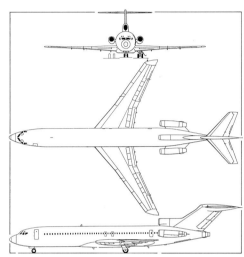

SPECIFICATION
(Boeing 727-200)

Dimensions: Wingspan 32.93m (108ft 0in); length overall 46.69m (103ft 2in); height overall 10.36m (34ft 0in), wing area 157.9m² (1,700ft²).
Power Plant: Three Pratt & Whitney JT8D turbofans, each rated at 64.52kN (14,500lb) (JT8D-9A) or 66.75kN (15,000lb) (-11) or 68.98kN (15,500lb) (-15) or 71.2kN (16,000lb) (-17) or 73.0kN (16,400lb) (-17R).
Weights: Operating weight empty 46,164kg (101,773lb); max take-off basic 83,820kg (184,800lb); max landing 70,081kg (154,500lb); max payload 18,598kg (41,000lb).
Performance: Max cruising speed 530kts (983km/h); initial cruise altitude 10,060m (33,000ft); take-off field length 3,035m (9,950ft) landing field length 1,495m (4,900ft); range with max fuel 2,400nm (4,449km); range with max payload 2,140nm (3,967km).
Accommodation: Flight crew of three. Basic two-class layout for 135 passengers, with maximum six-abreast tourist configuration for 189 passengers.

Above: Although the use of the Boeing 727 tri-jet is being limited by toughening noise regulations, some airlines, like UK charter operator Sabre Airways' 727-200, have been fitted with hush-kits.

Left: Most of the 1,832 727s produced were of the -200 version shown in this three-view drawing. The -100 has a shorter fuselage and the new-built -200Fs have no windows.

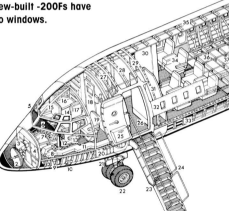

Right: Many Boeing 727s have found their way to corporate owners, equipped with high-quality furnishings and equipment. This 727-100 was photographed at London's Stansted Airport.

SERVICE USE

FAA Type Approval of the Model 727-100 was obtained on 24 December 1963, and the first revenue services were flown by Eastern on 1 February and by United Airlines on 6 February 1964. The first operator outside the USA was Lufthansa which introduced the type into service on 16 April 1964. Lufthansa later also acquired the quick-change (QC) version and large numbers of the bigger 727-200. The Model 727C was certificated on 13 January 1966 and entered service with Northwest on 23 April 1966. Boeing obtained certification of the Model 727-200 on 29 November 1967, and Northwest flew the first service on 14 December, while All Nippon

Airways was the first to fly the Advanced 727 in July 1972 following certification on 14 June. The first Model 727 with automatic thrust reverse on its Pratt & Whitney JT8D-17R engines flew with Hughes Airwest on 27 May 1976, and Federal Express took delivery of the last Model 727 built, on 18 September 1984, bringing total production to 1,832 of all variants. These consisted of 408 Srs 100 (including one test aircraft not delivered to customer), 164 Srs 100C and QC (Quick Change), 1, 245 Srs 200 and 15 Srs 200F. Some 1,300 Boeing 727s remain in service, including 400 Model 100s and 900 Model 200s, more than half of these are serving with airlines in the Americas.

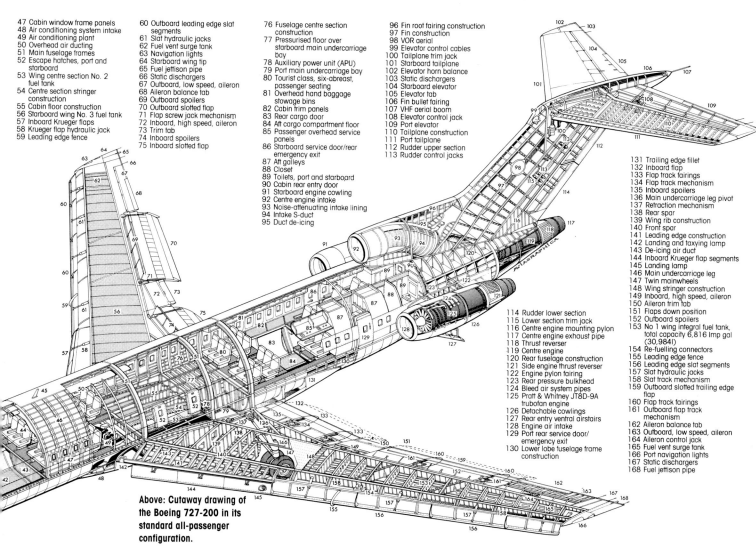

47 Cabin window frame panels
48 Air conditioning system intake
49 Air conditioning plant
50 Overhead air ducting
51 Main fuselage frames
52 Escape hatches, port and starboard
53 Wing centre section No. 2 fuel tank
54 Centre section stringer construction
55 Cabin floor construction
56 Starboard wing No. 3 fuel tank
57 Inboard Krueger flaps
58 Krueger flap hydraulic jack
59 Leading edge fence

60 Outboard leading edge slat segments
61 Slat hydraulic jacks
62 Fuel vent surge tank
63 Navigation lights
64 Starboard wing tip
65 Fuel jettison pipe
66 Static dischargers
67 Outboard, low speed, aileron
68 Aileron balance tab
69 Outboard spoilers
70 Outboard slotted flap
71 Flap screw jack mechanism
72 Inboard, high speed, aileron
73 Trim tab
74 Inboard spoilers
75 Inboard slotted flap

76 Fuselage centre section construction
77 Pressurised floor over starboard main undercarriage bay
78 Auxiliary power unit (APU)
79 Port main undercarriage bay
80 Tourist class, six-abreast, passenger seating
81 Overhead hand baggage stowage bins
82 Cabin trim panels
83 Rear cargo door
84 Aft cargo compartment floor
85 Passenger overhead service panels
86 Starboard service door/rear emergency exit
87 Aft galleys
88 Closet
89 Toilets, port and starboard
90 Cabin rear entry door
91 Starboard engine cowling
92 Centre engine intake
93 Noise-attenuating intake lining
94 Intake S-duct
95 Duct de-icing

96 Fin root fairing construction
97 Fin construction
98 VOR aerial
99 Elevator control cables
100 Tailplane trim jack
101 Starboard tailplane
102 Elevator horn balance
103 Static dischargers
104 Starboard elevator
105 Elevator tab
106 Fin bullet fairing
107 VHF aerial boom
108 Elevator control jack
109 Port elevator
110 Tailplane construction
111 Port tailplane
112 Rudder upper section
113 Rudder control jacks

114 Rudder lower section
115 Lower section trim jack
116 Centre engine mounting pylon
117 Centre engine exhaust pipe
118 Thrust reverser
119 Centre engine
120 Rear fuselage construction
121 Side engine thrust reverser
122 Engine pylon fairing
123 Rear pressure bulkhead
124 Bleed air system pipes
125 Pratt & Whitney JT8D-9A trubofan engine
126 Detachable cowlings
127 Rear entry ventral airstairs
128 Engine air intake
129 Port rear service door/emergency exit
130 Lower lobe fuselage frame construction

131 Trailing edge fillet
132 Inboard flap
133 Flap track fairings
134 Flap track mechanism
135 Inboard spoilers
136 Main undercarriage leg pivot
137 Retraction mechanism
138 Rear spar
139 Wing rib construction
140 Front spar
141 Leading edge construction
142 Landing and taxying lamp
143 De-icing air duct
144 Inboard Krueger flap segments
145 Landing lamp
146 Main undercarriage leg
147 Twin mainwheels
148 Wing stringer construction
149 Inboard, high speed, aileron
150 Aileron trim tab
151 Flaps down position
152 Outboard spoilers
153 No 1 wing integral fuel tank, total capacity 6,816 Imp gal (30,984l)
154 Re-fuelling connectors
155 Leading edge fence
156 Leading edge slat segments
157 Slat hydraulic jacks
158 Slat track mechanism
159 Outboard slotted trailing edge flap
160 Flap track fairings
161 Outboard flap track mechanism
162 Aileron balance tab
163 Outboard, low speed, aileron
164 Aileron control jack
165 Fuel vent surge tank
166 Port navigation lights
167 Static dischargers
168 Fuel jettison pipe

Above: Cutaway drawing of the Boeing 727-200 in its standard all-passenger configuration.

BOEING 737-100/200 USA

The model 737 is the 'baby' of the Boeing jetliner family and the third of the series of commercial jet transports to appear from the Seattle company. Even though it started late, the family became Boeing's most successful aircraft. Boeing announced its intention to develop a twin jet with 80-100 seats in November 1964, by which time two other new types in a similar category, the BAC One-Eleven and the Douglas DC-9, were already well advanced. By contrast with its two rear-engined competitors, however, the Boeing design featured a more conventional layout with underwing engines and a low tailplane position; for commonality with the Models 707 and 727, Boeing also chose to use the same basic cabin cross-section (from the floor up), allowing comfortable six-abreast seating and interchangeability for passenger facilities, galley equipment, etc, for airlines using more than one of the Boeing jetliner types. Named Model 737 to continue the Boeing family of designations that had begun with the Model 707, the new type won a launch order from Lufthansa on 19 February 1965 – the first time that a non-US airline had been in the position of ordering a new American airliner that was not already in production for at least one major US operator. As launched, the Model 737 was sized for 100 seats and powered by 62.3kN (14,000lb) Pratt & Whitney JT8D-1 engines. Design work on the 737 began on 11 May 1964 and the first flight, by a company-owned prototype, was made on 9 April 1967.

VARIANTS

Only 30 aircraft were built in the original Model 737-100 configuration, this version quickly being superseded by the Model 737-200, with a fuselage 'stretch' of 1.82m (6ft) to allow basic accommodation for 119 and, eventually, a maximum of 130. United Airlines was the first to order this variant, and the fifth example of the Model 737 to fly, on 8 August 1967, was the first stretched Model 737-200. A passenger/cargo convertible version, with a forward side door similar to that of the Model 727-200C, was flown in August 1968 and designated Model 737-200C. Aircraft from no.135 onwards introduced a series of modifications to the thrust reversers (switching from clamshell to target type) and wing flaps, and another series of changes to the leading edge and trailing-edge devices, nacelle mountings and other items led to the introduction of the Advanced 737, whose first flight was made on 15 April 1971. The Model 737-200 first appeared at a maximum take-off weight of 43,999kg (97,000lb), but this has been progressively increased. As noise regulations at airports became more stringent, Boeing introduced in 1973 a Quiet Nacelle modification, and an optional gravel runway kit was offered, including deflection shields on the main and nosewheel legs, fuselage abrasion protection, flaps protection, blow-away

jets beneath the engine intakes and other special features. Several schemes for stretching the Boeing 737 were studied during the late 1970s, eventually leading to the launch of the Model 737-300 as described separately. Several Model 737s have been sold as corporate or executive transports and the designation 77-32 is used for aircraft in this role.

SPECIFICATION
(Boeing 737-200)

Dimensions: Wingspan 28.35m (93ft0in); length overall 30.53m (100ft 2 in); height overall 11.28m (37ft 0in), wing area 102.0m² (1,098ft²).
Power Plant: Two Pratt & Whitney JT8D turbofans, each rated at 62.2kN(14,000lb) JT8D-7 or 64.52kN (14,500lb) (-9) or 68.98kN (15,500lb) (-15/15A) or 71.2kN (16,000lb) (-17/17A) or 73.0kN (16,400lb) (-17R).
Weights: Operating weight empty 27,310kg (60,201lb); max take-off standard 52,391kg (115,500lb); max landing 46,720kg (103,000lb); max payload 15,781kg (34,790lb).
Performance: Max cruising speed 488kts (905km/h); take-off field length 1,830m (6,000ft); landing field length 1,350m (4,430ft); range with standard fuel and 115 passengers 1,855nm (3,439km).
Accommodation: Flight crew of two. Basic arrangements for 115 passengers six-abreast, or 130 in high-density configuration. Underfloor cargo/baggage hold volume 24.78m³ (875ft³).

SERVICE USE

The Boeing 737-100 was certificated on 15 December 1967, and this variant entered service with Lufthansa on 10 February 1968. Type Approval for the Model 737-200 followed quickly, on 21 December 1967, and United operated the first services on 28 April 1968. Wien Consolidated was the first operator of the Model 737-200C towards the end of 1968, after certification in October. The Advanced 737-200 gained its Type Approval on 3 May 1971, allowing All Nippon Airways to become the first operator of this model in June 1971; the first example with a 'wide look' interior was operated by Air Algerie in January 1972, and Eastern Provincial Airways was the first to receive the Quiet Nacelle modification in October 1973. Total production of the Boeing 737 amounted to 30 Model 100, 219 Model 200 and 865 Model 200 Advanced totalling 1,114 aircraft. Some 950 remain in service today with a wide spectrum of the world's airlines.

Right: Cutaway drawing of the Boeing 737-200 showing some optional features – such as the gravel deflector on the nose gear and the vortex dissipator situated underneath the engine air intakes.

Right:The 737-200, which has largely been replaced in first line service with major airlines by later models, has found a niche with low-fare operators across the United States. This -200 belonging to New Jersey-based Eastwind was photographed at Baltimore Washington International Airport.

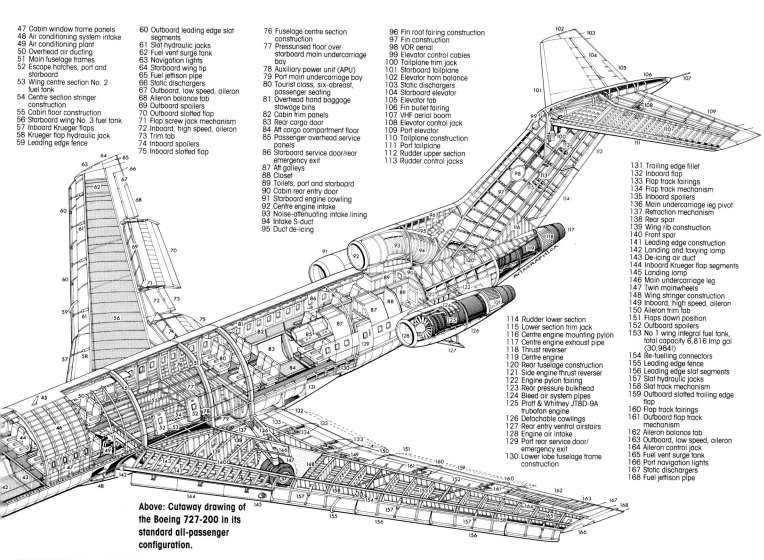

47 Cabin window frame panels
48 Air conditioning system intake
49 Air conditioning plant
50 Overhead air ducting
51 Main fuselage frames
52 Escape hatches, port and starboard
53 Wing centre section No. 2 fuel tank
54 Centre section stringer construction
55 Cabin floor construction
56 Starboard wing No. 3 fuel tank
57 Inboard Krueger flaps
58 Krueger flap hydraulic jack
59 Leading edge fence

60 Outboard leading edge slat segments
61 Slat hydraulic jacks
62 Fuel vent surge tank
63 Navigation lights
64 Starboard wing tip
65 Fuel jettison pipe
66 Static dischargers
67 Outboard, low speed, aileron
68 Aileron balance tab
69 Outboard spoilers
70 Outboard slotted flap
71 Flap screw jack mechanism
72 Inboard, high speed, aileron
73 Trim tab
74 Inboard spoilers
75 Inboard slotted flap

76 Fuselage centre section construction
77 Pressurised floor over starboard main undercarriage bay
78 Auxiliary power unit (APU)
79 Port main undercarriage bay
80 Tourist class, six-abreast, passenger seating
81 Overhead hand baggage stowage bins
82 Cabin trim panels
83 Rear cargo door
84 Aft cargo compartment floor
85 Passenger overhead service panels
86 Starboard service door/rear emergency exit
87 Aft galleys
88 Closet
89 Toilets, port and starboard
90 Cabin rear entry door
91 Starboard engine cowling
92 Centre engine intake
93 Noise-attenuating intake lining
94 Intake S-duct
95 Duct de-icing

96 Fin root fairing construction
97 Fin construction
98 VOR aerial
99 Elevator control cables
100 Tailplane trim jack
101 Starboard tailplane
102 Elevator horn balance
103 Static dischargers
104 Starboard elevator
105 Elevator tab
106 Fin bullet fairing
107 VHF aerial boom
108 Elevator control jack
109 Port elevator
110 Tailplane construction
111 Port tailplane
112 Rudder upper section
113 Rudder control jacks

114 Rudder lower section
115 Lower section trim jack
116 Centre engine mounting pylon
117 Centre engine exhaust pipe
118 Thrust reverser
119 Centre engine
120 Rear fuselage construction
121 Side engine thrust reverser
122 Engine pylon fairing
123 Rear pressure bulkhead
124 Bleed air system pipes
125 Pratt & Whitney JT8D-9A trubofan engine
126 Detachable cowlings
127 Rear entry ventral airstairs
128 Engine air intake
129 Port rear service door/ emergency exit
130 Lower lobe fuselage frame construction

131 Trailing edge fillet
132 Inboard flap
133 Flap track fairings
134 Flap track mechanism
135 Inboard spoilers
136 Main undercarriage leg pivot
137 Retraction mechanism
138 Rear spar
139 Wing rib construction
140 Front spar
141 Leading edge construction
142 Landing and taxying lamp
143 De-icing air duct
144 Inboard Krueger flap segments
145 Landing lamp
146 Main undercarriage leg
147 Twin mainwheels
148 Wing stringer construction
149 Inboard, high speed, aileron
150 Aileron trim tab
151 Flaps down position
152 Outboard spoilers
153 No 1 wing integral fuel tank, total capacity 6,816 Imp gal (30,984l)
154 Re-fuelling connectors
155 Leading edge fence
156 Leading edge slat segments
157 Slat hydraulic jacks
158 Slat track mechanism
159 Outboard slotted trailing edge flap
160 Flap track fairings
161 Outboard flap track mechanism
162 Aileron balance tab
163 Outboard, low speed, aileron
164 Aileron control jack
165 Fuel vent surge tank
166 Port navigation lights
167 Static dischargers
168 Fuel jettison pipe

Above: Cutaway drawing of the Boeing 727-200 in its standard all-passenger configuration.

BOEING 737-100/200 USA

The model 737 is the 'baby' of the Boeing jetliner family and the third of the series of commercial jet transports to appear from the Seattle company. Even though it started late, the family became Boeing's most successful aircraft. Boeing announced its intention to develop a twin jet with 80-100 seats in November 1964, by which time two other new types in a similar category, the BAC One-Eleven and the Douglas DC-9, were already well advanced. By contrast with its two rear-engined competitors, however, the Boeing design featured a more conventional layout with underwing engines and a low tailplane position; for commonality with the Models 707 and 727, Boeing also chose to use the same basic cabin cross-section (from the floor up), allowing comfortable six-abreast seating and interchangeability for passenger facilities, galley equipment, etc, for airlines using more than one of the Boeing jetliner types. Named Model 737 to continue the Boeing family of designations that had begun with the Model 707, the new type won a launch order from Lufthansa on 19 February 1965 – the first time that a non-US airline had been in the position of ordering a new American airliner that was not already in production for at least one major US operator. As launched, the Model 737 was sized for 100 seats and powered by 62.3kN (14,000lb) Pratt & Whitney JT8D-1 engines. Design work on the 737 began on 11 May 1964 and the first flight, by a company-owned prototype, was made on 9 April 1967.

VARIANTS

Only 30 aircraft were built in the original Model 737-100 configuration, this version quickly being superseded by the Model 737-200, with a fuselage 'stretch' of 1.82m (6ft) to allow basic accommodation for 119 and, eventually, a maximum of 130. United Airlines was the first to order this variant, and the fifth example of the Model 737 to fly, on 8 August 1967, was the first stretched Model 737-200. A passenger/cargo convertible version, with a forward side door similar to that of the Model 727-200C, was flown in August 1968 and designated Model 737-200C. Aircraft from no.135 onwards introduced a series of modifications to the thrust reversers (switching from clamshell to target type) and wing flaps, and another series of changes to the leading edge and trailing-edge devices, nacelle mountings and other items led to the introduction of the Advanced 737, whose first flight was made on 15 April 1971. The Model 737-200 first appeared at a maximum take-off weight of 43,999kg (97,000lb), but this has been progressively increased. As noise regulations at airports became more stringent, Boeing introduced in 1973 a Quiet Nacelle modification, and an optional gravel runway kit was offered, including deflection shields on the main and nosewheel legs, fuselage abrasion protection, flaps protection, blow-away

jets beneath the engine intakes and other special features. Several schemes for stretching the Boeing 737 were studied during the late 1970s, eventually leading to the launch of the Model 737-300 as described separately. Several Model 737s have been sold as corporate or executive transports and the designation 77-32 is used for aircraft in this role.

SERVICE USE

The Boeing 737-100 was certificated on 15 December 1967, and this variant entered service with Lufthansa on 10 February 1968. Type Approval for the Model 737-200 followed quickly, on 21 December 1967, and United operated the first services on 28 April 1968. Wien Consolidated was the first operator of the Model 737-200C towards the end of 1968, after certification in October. The Advanced 737-200 gained its Type Approval on 3 May 1971, allowing All Nippon Airways to become the first operator of this model in June 1971; the first example with a 'wide look' interior was operated by Air Algerie in January 1972, and Eastern Provincial Airways was the first to receive the Quiet Nacelle modification in October 1973. Total production of the Boeing 737 amounted to 30 Model 100, 219 Model 200 and 865 Model 200 Advanced totalling 1,114 aircraft. Some 950 remain in service today with a wide spectrum of the world's airlines.

Right: Cutaway drawing of the Boeing 737-200 showing some optional features – such as the gravel deflector on the nose gear and the vortex dissipator situated underneath the engine air intakes.

SPECIFICATION
(Boeing 737-200)

Dimensions: Wingspan 28.35m (93ft 0in); length overall 30.53m (100ft 2 in); height overall 11.28m (37ft 0in), wing area 102.0m² (1,098ft²).
Power Plant: Two Pratt & Whitney JT8D turbofans, each rated at 62.2kN (14,000lb) JT8D-7 or 64.52kN (14,500lb) (-9) or 68.98kN (15,500lb) (-15/15A) or 71.2kN (16,000lb) (-17/17A) or 73.0kN (16,400lb) (-17R).
Weights: Operating weight empty 27,310kg (60,201lb); max take-off standard 52,391kg (115,500lb); max landing 46,720kg (103,000lb); max payload 15,781kg (34,790lb).
Performance: Max cruising speed 488kts (905km/h); take-off field length 1,830m (6,000ft); landing field length 1,350m (4,430ft); range with standard fuel and 115 passengers 1,855nm (3,439km).
Accommodation: Flight crew of two. Basic arrangements for 115 passengers six-abreast, or 130 in high-density configuration. Underfloor cargo/baggage hold volume 24.78m³ (875ft³).

Right: The 737-200, which has largely been replaced in first line service with major airlines by later models, has found a niche with low-fare operators across the United States. This -200 belonging to New Jersey-based Eastwind was photographed at Baltimore Washington International Airport.

Left: TAP Air Portugal was one of many European airlines to use the 737-200 on its short-haul scheduled services. These are now gradually being replaced by single-aisle Airbus types.

Right: Three-view drawing of the 737-200, which has been replaced by later models. The original 737-100, of which only 30 were built, is 1.82m (6ft) shorter.

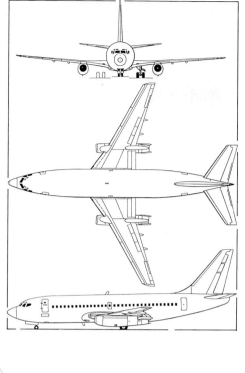

Above: There are few areas of the world where the 737 has not been seen regularly. Egyptair, a prolific Boeing user, had a fleet of 737-200s; one is seen here at Cairo.

88 Rudder balance
89 Static dischargers
90 Rudder
91 Fibre glass honeycomb construction
92 Rudder stand-by actuator
93 Rudder dual-tandem actuator
94 Elevator actuator torque-tube

116 Mainwheel well
117 Forged undercarriage mounting
118 Triple-slotted flaps
119 Undercarriage side strut
120 Fuselage frame attachment
121 Wingroot/fuselage fairing
122 Air-conditioning conduits
123 Coolant air fan
124 Primary heat exchanger
125 Fuselage/front spar attachment
126 Water separator
127 Crew air (port)/passenger cabin air (starboard) ducts
128 Ram air intake
129 Intake scoop
130 Taxi/landing lights
131 Leading-edge Krueger/flap (inboard section)
132 Pre-cooler air
133 Inboard wing ribs
134 Undercarriage drag strut
135 Twin mainwheels
136 Engine pylon nacelle strut
137 Vortex dissipator
138 Inlet centre body/starter
139 Fan
140 Pratt & Whitney JT8D-9 turbofan

Boeing 737-200 Cutaway Drawing Key

1 Hinged nose cone
2 Search radar
3 Glideslope aerial
4 Forward pressure bulkhead
5 Instrument panel shroud
6 Windscreen sections
7 Sliding side windows
8 Eyebrow windows
9 First officer's seat
10 Overhead panel
11 Centre console
12 Captain's seat
13 Flight kit stowage
14 Circuit breaker panel
15 Nose gear deflector housing
16 Twin nosewheels
17 Nosewheel doors
18 Nose gear gravel deflector
19 Steering cylinders
20 Lock
21 Drag strut
22 Fixed side windows
23 Second observer's seat (optional)
24 First observer's seat (stowable)
25 Wall circuit breaker panel
26 Dome light

27 Flight deck door
28 Forward galley
29 Service door (starboard) 30in by 65in (76 by 165cm)
30 Coat closet
31 Forward toilet
32 Forward entry door (port), 34in by 72in (86 by 183cm)
33 Airstairs stowage (deployed through hatch)
34 Electrical/electronics bay
35 Underfloor forward freight hold
36 Cabin windows
37 Fourteen-seat first-class cabin configuration (38in/96.5cm seat pitch)
38 Inter-class bulkhead
39 Engine air intakes
40 Air-conditioning pre-cooler
41 Integral wing fuel tank (Tank No 2)
42 Dry bay
43 Overwing filler
44 Leading-edge slats (extended)
45 Vent surge tank
46 Starboard navigation light (flashing)
47 Starboard navigation light (white)
48 Starboard aileron

49 Aileron balance tab
50 Triple-slotted flaps (extended)
51 Ground spoiler/lift dumper (outer)
52 Wing spoilers (two segments)
53 Ground spoiler/lift dumper (inner)
54 Triple-slotted flap (inner section)
55 Tailpipe shroud
56 Aft wing/nacelle fairing
57 Thrust reverser doors (closed)
58 VHF communications antenna
59 HF communications antenna (optional)
60 Starboard escape hatch frame surround
61 Forged alloy fuselage main frames (three off)
62 Rolled alloy intermediate frames
63 Floor level (air-conditioning outflow)
64 Centre-section fuel bladder cells (three off)

65 Fuel pump
66 Centre-section floor beams
67 Port escape hatch frame
68 Hydraulics service bay (starboard mainwheel well)
69 Pressure-bearing floor structure
70 Insulation blankets
71 Overhead air distribution duct
72 Flat cabin ceiling sections
73 Passenger conditioned air ducts and outlets
74 Overhead in-flight luggage stowage bins
75 Aerial
76 Tourist-class 88-seat cabin configuration (34in/86cm seat pitch)
77 Aft bulkhead
78 Aft service door (starboard) 30in by 65in (76 by 165cm)
79 Aft galley
80 Aft forward spar/pressure bulkhead attachment
81 Starboard tailplane
82 Starboard tailplane
83 Starboard elevator
84 Fin front spar
85 Fin structure
86 Fin skinning
87 VOR/ILS antennae

95 Tail cone
96 APU exhaust outlet
97 Port elevator tab
98 Port elevator
99 Port horizontal tailplane (variable incidence)
100 Tailplane ribs
101 APU exhaust pipe
102 APU package
103 Forged-beam tailplane centre-section
104 Fin rear spar terminal fittings
105 Variable-incidence screw-jack fitment
106 Air-conditioning
107 Collapsible airstairs (attached to door)
108 Aft pressure dome bulkhead
109 Aft galley
110 Aft toilet
111 Aft entry door (port) (lowered, deploying airstairs)
112 Door surround frame
113 Fuselage skinning
114 Aft underfloor freight hold
115 Wingroot fillet

141 Oil tank
142 High-pressure section
143 Forward wing box-spar
144 Outer wing ribs
145 Aft wing/nacelle fairing
146 Thrust-reverser doors (extended)
147 Thrust-reverser actuator fairing
148 Flap tracks
149 Wing integral fuel tank (Tank No 1)
150 Leading-edge slats
151 Krueger flap anti-icing pipes (telescopic)
152 Flap hydraulic rams
153 Retractable taxi/landing lights
154 Aft wing-box spar
155 Port aileron balance tab
156 Vent surge tank
157 Fuel vent outlet
158 Port aileron
159 Port navigation light (white)
160 Port navigation light (flashing)

BOEING 737-300/400/500 USA

Development of a stretched version of the Boeing 737 began in 1979, when market studies began to show the need for what Boeing was later to describe as 'a longer-bodied version of the popular 737 twinjet, designed to burn less fuel per passenger and provide reduced noise levels for the short-haul markets of 1985 and beyond'. As has been the case with many programmes to 'stretch' an existing aircraft, the exact degree of lengthening that was desirable remained open to question for some time, as airline reactions were studied and launch customers sought. By early 1980, the Model 737-300 designation had been adopted for the proposal and, when details were published by Boeing in the course of the Farnborough Air Show later that year, a stretch of 2.13m (84in) was indicated, compared with earlier studies that provided for a lengthening of only 1.02m (40in). However much the aircraft was lengthened, engines more advanced and more powerful than the JT8Ds used in the Model 737-200 were needed, with fuel efficiency and low noise levels the two most important characteristics. As plans for the Model 737-300 were confirmed it became clear that the CFM56 was the only suitable engine which could be developed with a suitable thrust and in the required time-frame. The latter, based on launch orders announced in March 1981 from USAir and Southwest Airlines, was established with an entry into service date of late 1984. By the time of the launch, the fuselage had grown again, by a further 0.51m (20in), with a 1.12m (44in) plug head of the wing and a 1.52m (60in) plug aft of it. This allowed the maximum seating to be increased to 149 and gave the Model 737-300 some 21 more seats than the Model 737-200 in a comparable all-tourist layout. Apart from (and to some extent because of) the higher weights at which the Model 737-300 was to operate, some airframe modifications were made, including wing tip extensions that added 230mm (9in) to each tip, some changes to the leading-edge slots, revised trailing-edge 'flipper' flaps and flap track fairings, an addition to the dorsal fin area, and a lengthened nosewheel leg to provide adequate ground clearance for the engines. To fit the larger-diameter CFM56 engines under the wings, their accessory drives were located on the sides of the engines, resulting in a somewhat unusual flat-bottomed nacelle shape. The first Model 737-300, destined for delivery eventually to USAir, flew at Seattle on 24 February 1984.

VARIANTS

The Model 737-300 is available at two maximum weights, the higher weight being required when the optional fuel tanks are carried in the aft cargo bay. Uprated CFM56-3B2 engines are available for operation in hot-and-high conditions. Corporate/executive versions of the stretched aircraft carry the designation 77-33. Soon after launching the Model 300, Boeing was considering both a lengthened and shortened version, initially known as the 737-300L and 737-100L(Lite) respectively, later given the designations 737-400 and 737-500. Details of the 737-400 were announced in June 1986 and the first aircraft made its maiden flight on 19 February 1988, receiving FAA certification on 2 September. The new model was stretched 3.05m (10ft 0in) by means of two 'plugs', forward and aft of the wing, providing up to 170 passengers in an all-tourist layout. Other changes were a tail bumper, strengthened outer wings and landing gear and additional emergency exits. Power plant was either the 97.86kN (22,000lb) thrust CFM56-3B-2 as used on the 737-300, or the 104.5kN (23,500lb) CFM56-3C. A high gross weight version with a ramp weight of 68,265kg (150,500lb) was rolled out on 23 December 1988. Combining the advanced technology of both the -300 and -400 models, but with a fuselage shortened to 29.95m (101ft 9in), almost the same size as the 737-200, the 737-500 was first announced on 20 May 1987 and made its maiden flight on 30 June 1989. It is powered by CFM56-3C1 turbofan engines of 88.97kN (20,000lb) thrust, or derated to 82.29kN (18,500lb) according to gross weight.

SERVICE USE

FAA certification of the Model 737-300 was obtained on 14 November 1984, and Boeing began delivering the new variant on the 28th day of that month, when USAir accepted its first aircraft, followed two days later by Southwest Airlines. The latter operator flew the first revenue service on 7 December 1984, with USAir following on 18 December. The first delivery to a non-US customer was made to Orion Airways in the UK on 29 January 1985, with service entry on 22 February, and Pakistan International Airlines took delivery of the first Model 737-300 with the uprated -3B2 engines on 31 May 1985, for first service on 1 July. First delivery of the 737-400 was made to launch customer Piedmont Airlines on 15 September 1988 and the higher gross weight version followed on 21 March 1989. Southwest Airlines accepted the first 737-500 on 28 February 1990, 16 days after FAA certification. Launch customer Braathens SAFE of Norway received its first aircraft on 7 March 1990. By 1 January 1998, a total of 1,122 Model 300, 483 Model 400 and 383 Model 500 had been ordered, with deliveries amounting to 1,032, 442 and 354 respectively.

SPECIFICATION
(Boeing 737-300)

Dimensions: Wingspan 28.88M (94ft 9in); length overall 33.40m (109ft 7in); height overall 11.13m (36ft 6in), wing area 105.4m² (1,135ft²).
Power Plant: Two CFM International CFM56-3C-1 turbofans each rated at either 89.0kN (20,000lb) or 97.9kN (22,000lb).
Weights: Operating weight empty basic 32,704kg (72,100lb); max take-off basic 56,470kg (124,500lb); max landing 51,720kg (114,000lb).
Performance: Max cruising speed 491kts (908km/h); initial cruise altitude 10,195m (33,450ft); take-off field length 2,286m (7,500ft); landing field length 1,433m (4,700ft); range with typical payload 2,270nm (4,204km).
Accommodation: Crew of two. Typical mixed-class layout for 128 passengers, with maximum of 149 six-abreast. Underfloor baggage/cargo volume 30.24m³ (1,068ft³).

Above: Lufthansa operated all first generation 737s including this 737-400.

Right: The Boeing 737-300 differs from the 737-200 in having a lengthened fuselage and more powerful CFM International CFM56 engines.

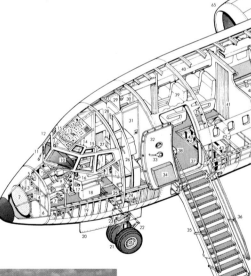

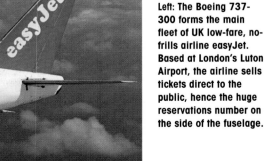

Left: The Boeing 737-300 forms the main fleet of UK low-fare, no-frills airline easyJet. Based at London's Luton Airport, the airline sells tickets direct to the public, hence the huge reservations number on the side of the fuselage.

Boeing 737-300 Cutaway Drawing Key

1 Radome
2 Weather radar scanner
3 Scanner tracking mechanism
4 Lightning conductor strips
5 ILS glideslope aerial
6 Front pressure bulkhead
7 Rudder pedals
8 Control column
9 Instrument panel
10 Instrument panel shroud
11 Windscreen wipers
12 Windscreen panels
13 Overhead systems switch panel
14 Co-pilot's seat
15 Cockpit eyebrow windows
16 Pilot's seat
17 Nosewheel steering control
18 Flight bag stowage
19 Nose undercarriage wheel bay
20 Nosewheel doors
21 Twin nosewheels
22 Torque scissor links
23 Nosewheel steering jacks
24 Nose undercarriage pivot fixing
25 Pitot heads (2)
26 Crew wardrobe
27 Observer's folding seat
28 Cockpit doorway
29 Forward galley unit
30 Starboard side service door
31 Toilet compartment
32 Forward entry door, open
33 Door latch
34 Escape chute stowage
35 Retractable airstairs
36 Folding handrail
37 Entry lobby
38 Cabin attendant's folding seat
39 First-class cabin, four-abreast seating (eight-passengers)
40 Overhead stowage bins
41 Curtained cabin divider
42 Passenger emergency oxygen bottles
43 Underfloor avionics equipment bay
44 Cabin window panels
45 Seat rail support structure
46 Lower VHF aerial
47 Forward underfloor freight/baggage hold, capacity 425cu ft (12.03m³)
48 Forward freight hold door
49 Overhead air conditioning distribution ducting
50 Tourist class cabin, six-abreast seating (114 to 120 passengers)
51 Air system ducting
52 Wing inspection light
53 Conditioned air riser
54 Wing root leading edge fillet
55 Ventral air conditioning intake
56 Landing and taxying lamps
57 Wing panel/fuselage bolted root joint
58 Ventral air conditioning pack, port and starboard
59 Centre section fuel tanks
60 Floor beam construction
61 Front spar/fuselage main frame
62 Anti-collision light
63 Starboard nacelle pylon
64 Starboard engine nacelle
65 Engine air intake
66 Hinged cowling panels
67 Pressure refuelling connection
68 Starboard wing integral fuel tank. Total system capacity 4,422 Imp gal (20,104l)
69 Fuel venting channels
70 Overwing fuel filler cap
71 Vortex generators
72 Leading-edge slat segments, open
73 Slat drive shaft
74 Screw jacks
75 Guide rails
76 Vent surge tank
77 Wing tip fairing
78 Starboard navigation light (green) and strobe light (white)
79 Tail navigation light (white)
80 Starboard aileron
81 Aileron hinge control
82 Aileron tab
83 Outboard triple-slotted Fowler-type flap, down position
84 Flap guide rails
85 Screw jacks
86 Flap track fairings
87 Outboard (flight) spoilers, open
88 Spoiler hydraulic jacks
89 Nacelle tail fairing
90 Inboard flap screw jack
91 Inboard (ground) spoiler, open
92 Fuselage skin panelling
93 Upper VHF aerial
94 Centre fuselage frame and stringer construction
95 Emergency exit window hatches, port and starboard
96 Pressure floor above starboard wheel bay
97 Cabin soundproofing lining
98 Rear spar/fuselage main frame
99 Overhead stowage bins
100 Passenger service units
101 Cabin roof lighting panels
102 Rear freight hold door
103 Cockpit voice recorder
104 Cabin wall trim panelling
105 Cabin roof frames
106 Rear cabin tourist class seating
107 Starboard side rear galley unit
108 Fin root fillet construction
109 Fin spar attachment joints
110 Optional flush HF aerial
111 Starboard tailplane
112 Starboard elevator mass balance
113 Fin rib construction
114 VOR aerial
115 Fin tip aerial fairing
116 Rudder mass balance
117 Static dischargers
118 Rudder
119 Honeycomb rudder panel construction
120 Rudder hydraulic actuators
121 Tailcone
122 Rear position light (white)
123 Elevator tab
124 Port elevator honeycomb construction
125 Elevator mass balance
126 Static dischargers
127 Port tailplane construction
128 APU exhaust duct
129 Elevator hinge control
130 Trimming tailplane pivot fixing
131 Garrett GTCP85-129(C) Auxiliary Power Unit (APU)
132 Fin/tailplane support main frame
133 Tailplane trim screw jack
134 APU intake duct
135 Rear pressure dome
136 Rear toilet compartments, port and starboard
137 Rear entry and service doors, port and starboard
138 Cabin attendant's folding seat
139 Wardrobe/closet
140 Rear cabin window panels
141 Rear underfloor freight/baggage hold, capacity 643cu ft (18.21m³)
142 Rear fuselage frame and stringer construction
143 DME aerial
144 Wing root trailing-edge fillet
145 ADF sense aerial
146 Central flap drive hydraulic motor
147 Port main undercarriage wheel bay
148 Main undercarriage mounting beam
149 Hydraulic retraction jack
150 Spoiler hydraulic jack
151 Inboard (ground) spoiler
152 Inboard triple-slotted Fowler-type flap
153 Flap guide rails and screw jacks
154 Flap down position
155 Flap thrust gate segments
156 Nacelle tail fairing
157 Outboard triple-slotted Fowler-type flap
158 Outboard flap screw jacks and guide rails
159 Outboard four-segment (flight) spoilers
160 Flap track fairings
161 Flap down position
162 Aileron tab
163 Port aileron
164 Fixed portion of trailing-edge
165 Static dischargers
166 Tail navigation light (white)
167 Port navigation light (red) and strobe light (white)
168 Leading-edge slat segments, open
169 Slat screw jacks
170 Guide rails
171 Telescopic de-icing air ducts
172 Front spar
173 Port wing integral fuel tank
174 Wing rib construction
175 Rear spar
176 Wing stringers
177 Wing skin panelling
178 Engine pylon mounting ribs
179 Twin mainwheels
180 Main undercarriage leg strut
181 Undercarriage leg pivot mounting
182 Inboard wing rib construction
183 Engine bleed air ducting
184 Krueger flap jacks
185 Inboard two-segment Krueger flaps, open
186 Nacelle strake
187 Nacelle pylon construction
188 Intake lip de-icing air duct
189 Port engine air intake
190 CFM International CFM56-3 turbofan engine
191 Engine fan casing
192 Laterally mounted accessory equipment gearbox
193 Thrust reverser cascades
194 Engine turbine section
195 Fan air (cold stream) exhaust duct
196 Core engine (hot stream) exhaust duct
197 Tailcone fairing
198 Cowling open position to expose reverser cascades

Below: Braathens SAFE in Norway paints one aircraft each summer in a special colourscheme.

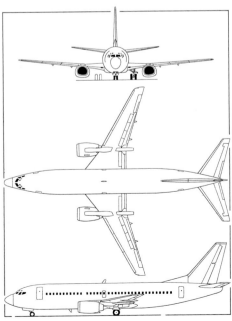

Right: This three-view shows the 737-300. The 737-400 is longer and the 737-500 shorter.

BOEING 737-600/700/800 USA

PROVISIONAL SPECIFICATION
(Boeing 737-700)

Dimensions: Wingspan 34.31m (112ft 7in);
length overall 33.63m (110ft 4in); height overall
12.50m (41ft 2in).
Power Plant: Two CFM International CFM56-7B24
turbofans each rated at 106.8kN (24,000lb).
Weights: Operating weight empty 37,584kg
(82.860lb); max take-off 69,399kg
(153,000lb); max landing 58,059kg
(128000lb).
Performance: Cruise speed Mach 0.781; initial
cruising altitude 11,490m (337,700ft); take-off
field length 2,042m (6,700ft); landing field length
1,356m (4,450ft); range with typical payload
3,245nm (6,009km).
Accommodation: Crew of two. Typical mixed-
class layout for 128 passengers, with maximum
of 150 six-abreast. Overhead baggage volume
7.02m³ (248ft³).

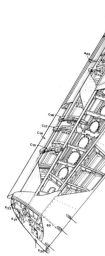

In 1991 Boeing began working with more than 30 airlines to develop a new-generation derivative family of its highly-successful twin-engine 737 airliner. The new 737-X was to be offered in three sizes, approximately matching the 737-300, -400 and -500 models. Boeing stressed that the earlier versions would continue to be produced alongside the new models, for as long as customers demanded. After narrowing down design parameters, Boeing's board of directors authorised the offering for sale of the 737-X on 29 June 1993, with full launch into production following an order for 63 Model 737-700 (32 converted from options for the 737-300), plus 63 new options, from Southwest Airlines on 18 November 1993. Boeing's decision to proceed was also strongly influenced by the inroads made into the market by the more advanced Airbus A320, which was itself being expanded into a three-member family. Key design features of the new 737s are a modified wing, enlarged in area by 25 per cent through increased chord and a 4.88m (16ft 0in) extension of the wingspan, larger tail surfaces, increased tankage to provide US transcontinental range, and new quieter, cleaner and more fuel-efficient CFM International CFM56-7B (previously CFM56-3XS) turbofans with full authority digital engine control (FADEC). The CFM56-7B combines the core of the CFM56-5 with the improved low pressure compressor of the CFM56-3. It will have a 10 per cent higher thrust capability than the -3C which powers the existing 737s. A new advanced flight deck, similar in many respects to those of Boeing's other new airliners, will emulate their electronic flight instrumentation system (EFIS) and primary flight display – navigation display (PFD-ND). These improvements will provide greater range (approximately 900nm further), higher speeds and altitude, reduced fuel burn, as well as lower noise signatures and emission levels, while maintaining commonality with earlier 737s. The first of the three models, the 737-700, was rolled out on 8 December 1996 and took off on its maiden flight from Seattle on 9 February 1997. The flight-test programme, to be concluded in 1998, will involve 10 aircraft, including four 737-700, three 737-800 and three 737-600. The 737-800 flew in July 1997, followed by the smallest member, the 737-600, on 22 January 1998.

VARIANTS

The first model is the 737-700, which uses the fuselage of the 737-300, but is 0.23m (9in) longer due to an increased tail span. Wingspan is 5.45m (17ft 10in) greater at 34.31m (112ft 7in). It seats between 128 and 149 passengers and is powered by two wing-mounted CFM56-7B24 turbofans, each rated at 106.8kN (24,000lb) static thrust. Roughly equivalent to the 737-400, the new 737-800 is stretched to carry

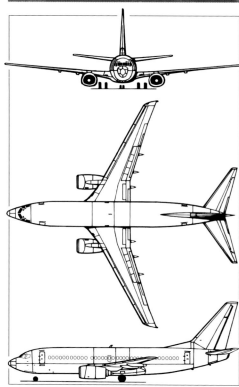

Above: The new-generation 737 family is set to continue the success story of this twin-engined aircraft, with 742 orders, bringing the 737 total to 3,884 units.

Left: This three-view drawing shows the first of the new-generation models to fly, the 737-700, which in general appearance is similar to the earlier 737-300.

from 160 to 189 passengers and will have more powerful 116.5kN (26,200lb) thrust CFM56-7B26 engines to take account of the heavier weight. The 737-600 is the smallest variant, similar in size to the 737-500, providing seating for 108 to 132 passengers. It will be powered by the CFM56-7B22 engine, rated at 97.9kN (22,000lb). Boeing is also producing a business jet derivative, combining the fuselage of the -700 with the strengthened wings and landing gear of the -800, and a still longer 737-900.

IN SERVICE

The Boeing 737-700 was the first to enter service with launch customer Southwest Airlines in October 1997. The first European delivery was made to Maersk Air of Denmark. Following expected certification of the 737-800 in early 1998, German airline Hapag-Lloyd, the first customer for this model with an order for 16 aircraft signed in September 1994, will put the type on its Mediterranean charter flights. First flight of the 737-600 took place on 22 January 1998, with certification in July. Launch customer Scandinavian Airlines System (SAS) will receive the first aircraft soon after. At 1 January 1998, Boeing had orders for 742 of the new-generation twins, including 122 for the 737-600, 321 for the 737-700 and 299 for the 737-800.

Boeing 737-700 Drawing Key

Structure and general
1 Upward-hinging de-electric radome
2 Front pressure bulkhead
3 Rearward sliding window (both sides)
4 Two-crew flight deck
5 Fully adjustable crew-seats plus fold-away seat (captain's seat removed for clarity)
6 Shrouded instrument panel with EFIS displays
7 Document and flight-manual stowage (both sides)
8 Forward galley
9 Forward foiled
10 Cabin attendants twin fold down seats (redesigned entry way)
11 Modular panel and public address telephone
12 Nose undercarriage – unpressurised bay
13 Fold away airstair (electrically actuated)
14 Forward passenger – entry/emergency door 864mm x 1.83m with inflatable escape slide/raft (counterbalanced)
15 Forward service/emergency door 762mm x 1.62m (with slide/raft)
16 First-class cabin with eight fully reclining seats (914mm pitch)
17 Cabin divider (movable via seat rails)
18 Forward passenger-cabin with 120 seats at 812mm pitch
19 Forward cargo hold door 889mm x 1.22m (electrically actuated)
20 Forward cargo-hold (117m³ volume)
21 Built-up machined wing-to-fuselage main frames
22 Notchless built-up rolled fuselage frames
23 Fuselage double-bubble cusp joint
24 Longitudinal 'top-hat' stingers supporting chemically etched skin panels
25 Type III overwing emergency exits each side -508 x 965mm
26 Skin doubler panels
27 Longitudinal floor beams (machined and built up)
28 Continuous seat track (aluminium/titanium) combining three-position seat locks
29 Separate forged and machined window frames
30 Wing centre-section carry-through structure (sealed for tankage)
31 Cabin pressure floor above main undercarriage bay
32 Pressure bulkhead (rear of undercarriage bay)
33 Aluminium skin bonded to PVC core floor panels
34 Rear passenger-cabin
35 Rear cargo-door (838mm x 1.22m)
36 Rear cargo-hold (181m³ volume)
37 Overhead stowage bins, 2.03m long (doors 1.01m long) with moulded integral hand-rails
38 Cabin-sealed insulation blankets
39 Existing type 737 PVC wall panels
40 Rear passenger-entry door 762mm x 1.83m, with inflatable slide/raft
41 Rear service-door 762mm x 1.65m, with inflatable slide/raft
42 Rear cabin-attendantsi vestibule
43 Two rear toilets and hand basins
44 Waste water, vacuum-system storage tank
45 Potable-water storage tank, glass-reinforced plastic (GFRP) – 181 litres capacity – 2895 litres optional
46 Overflow outlet
47 Transverse galley unit
48 Rear pressure dome
49 Dorsal fin (GFRP)
50 two-spar modified fin box (60ft³ root extension)
51 Detachable leading edge and tip
52 Fin/fuselage multiple-attachment lugs

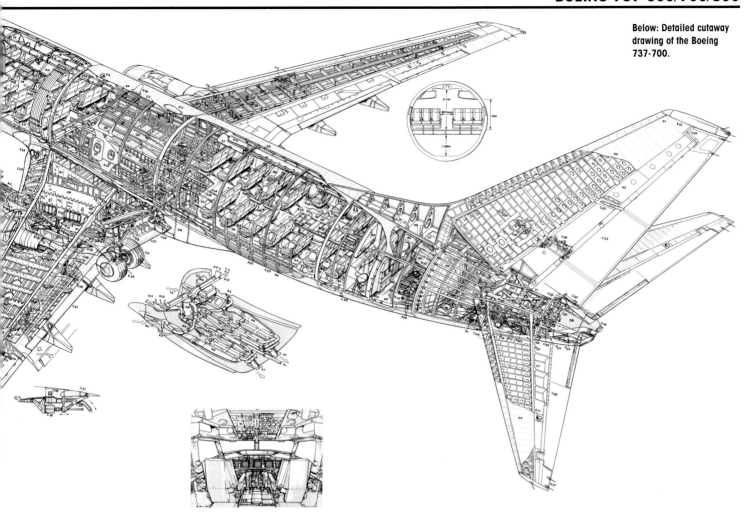

Below: Detailed cutaway drawing of the Boeing 737-700.

53 Composite rear-fin panels
54 Two-spar trimming tailplane (838mm tip extension)
55 Centre section itrussi structure
56 Fulcrum pivot/attachment multi-bolt fitting
57 Trailing-edge panels (GFRP)
58 Tailcone (GFRP)
59 Two-spar cantilevered wing structure (2.72m semi-span increase)
60 Machined built-up web and chord extrusion caps
61 Machined ribs
62 Extruded/machined stringers riveted to top and bottom chemically milled skin panels (sealed for tankage)
63 Tank-access panels (lower surface)
64 Fixed-wing leading edge machined multiple ribs covered with GFRP skin panels
65 Detachable raked wing-tip
66 Wing secondary structure (glassfibre and GFRP)
67 Wing root/fuselage multi-bolt joint strap and load-path machined fittings
68 Main-undercarriage support beam and lugs (titanium)
69 Redesigned wing/fuselage and flaps fairing (GFRP)
70 Centreline video-entertainment system (total of four monitors – optional)
71 Vortex generators (both sides)
72 Closet

Air conditioning/anti-icing systems

A1 Control engine bleed-air to environmental control system (ECS) packs, bled from 5th and 9th stage of high-pressure (HP) compressor via regulating valve
A2 Engine pre-cooler
A3 To ECS (both sides)
A4 Cross-over ducts to mixing manifold
A5 Ram-air in to heat exchanger (NACA ducts below aircraft belly)
A6 Air-cycle machine (three wheel, boot-strap systems)
A7 Exhaust-air outlet
A8 Mixing and distribution manifold
A9 Re-circulation air filter
A10 Recirculation fan
A11 Cabin air, sidewall riser ducts (both sides)
A12 Cooling air riser ducts to gasper air system
A13 Ducts to electronic equipment and flight deck systems
A14 Electronic-equipment distribution ducts (double push-pull system via fans)
A15 Overhead air distribution to forward and rear cabins
A16 Diffuser outlets
A17 Cockpit air distribution ducts, side windows and windshield de-mist
A18 Gasper air-system to individual overhead passenger service units (PSUs)
A19 PSUs telescope units to match seat pitch
A20 PSU housing oxygen generators, cylinder and drop down oxygen masks
A21 Air-supply duct from auxiliary power unit (APU) supplying engine start air and air to ECS
A22 Thermally heated slats (air exits through lower surface)
A23 Telescopic tube to piccolo duct
A24 Thermally anti-iced engine-inlet duct
A25 Thermally heated cargo holds
A26 Cabin air exits at floor-level venting louvres
A27 Cabin pressure-relief valves (two) also via one at forward cabin
A28 Rear outflow valve (maintains safe, comfortable, environment)

Flying controls

C1 Control column wheels with trim and autopilot in/out switches (incorporating stick shaker)
C2 Adjustable rudder pedals with the toe brakes
C3 Centre console with trim wheels, flap stabiliser and trim cut-out switches
C4 Control cables pass through floor beams via fairleads
C5 Aileron cable quadrants and power control units (PCUs), In the even of hydraulic failure, the system reverts to manual
C6 Aileron panel (GFRP)
C7 Aileron cable quadrant and push-pull rod
C8 Aileron balance tab
C9 Spoiler mixer unit
C10 Flight-spoiler panels (four per whing) curved GFRP, also act as speed brakes
C11 Ground spoiler panels (lift dumpers) two per wing – hydraulically actuated
C12 Spoiler actuators stroked off via cables from aileron circuit
C1 Inboard leading-edge Kruegar flap (hydraulically actuated
C14 Leading-edge slat (four sections per wing)
C15 Ballscrew-type hydraulic actuators (two per section)
C16 Guide rails (two per section) retract into receptacles in fuel tanks
C17 Slat support guides
C18 Flap drive unit and torque shaft (hydraulically driven with electric motor back-up
C19 Flap ballscrew bevel gearbox (total four)
C20 Flap track and carriage (inboard shown)
C21 Main flap and rear flap, forming double-slotted Flower-type flaps (inboard and outboard)
C22 Flap transmission and torque limiter
C23 One-piece rudder panel (GFRP)
C24 Rudder 'Q' feel pitot head
C25 Balance weights
C26 Control quadrants
C27 Input push-pull rod
C28 Dual hydraulic power control unit and yaw-damper system combined with electric trim actuator
C29 Elevator one-piece panel (GFRP)
C30 Cabin Input quadrant (left and right side)
C31 Twin hydraulic power control units
C32 Output torque unit
C33 Balance tab control rods (both sides)
C34 Moveable horizontal trimming tailplane
C35 Stabiliser screw-jack (electrically actuated)
C36 Screw-jack nut support structure

Fuel system

F1 Centre tanks – capacity 16,232 litres
F2 Main tank – left and right each 4,902 litres
F3 Pressure refuel/defuel manifold and contents panel under wing leading-edge total capacity 26,036 litres
F4 Surge tank
F5 Tank-end ribs
F6 Fuel venting channels
F7 Tank cross over pipes
F8 Boost and fuel-feed pumps situated on rear face of the rear spar (can be removed without draining tanks)
F9 Engine feed pipe
F10 Tank capacitance units (total of 32)
F11 Fuel measuring sticks (total of 16)

Electrics and electronics

E1 Two speed electrical windscreen wipers
E2 Weather radar and glideslope antenna
E3 Electrically heated pitot head (both sides, total of three)
E4 Five 203 x 203mm liquid-crystal displays (LCDs) plus one on centre console
E5 Overhead electrical-systems panel
E6 Main avionic equipment and electrical bay and battery stowage -28v 36ahr
E7 Traffic-alert/collision-avoidance system (TCAS)
E8 ATC antenna
E9 Upper anti-collision rotating beacon
E10 VHF antenna
E11 ADF antenna
E12 VOR/LOC antenna
E13 Overhead cabin-lighting panels
E14 Wing and nacelle inspection light
E15 External floodlight, illumination doors and overwing (both sides)
E16 Rear anti-collision light (white)
E17 Logo light
E18 High intensity landing and runway turn-off lamps (retractable lamps below body fairing)
E19 Taxiing nose wheel light
E20 Wing tip position lights (white)
E21 Anti-collision wing strobe lights (white)
E22 Navigation lights
E23 Passenger overhead reading lights in PSUs
E24 Emergency floor lighting strip
E25 Cargo bays fully illuminated
E26 90kva constant frequency generator on each engine and APU
E27 Static-discharge wicks – glassfibre
E28 Aircraft-to-ground static discharge wire
E29 Cockpit voice recorder (automatically erases, leaving the last 120min in memory), situated in rear freight hold
E30 Flight data recorder (records the last 26h)
E31 Circuit-breaker panels behind pilots seats

Powerplant and APU

P1 General Electric/Snecma CFM56-7 turbofan engine (FADEC controlled)
P2 Engine gearbox (oil tank on opposite side)
P3 Air starter
P4 EEC alternator
P5 Engine core exhaust nozzle (2.5 tilt down)
P6 Engine inlet tip stainless steel (flattened off at lower edge)
P7 Fan thrust-reverser translating cowl
P8 Thrust reverser cascades
P9 Thrust-reverser hydraulic actuators
P10 Pylon structure box
P11 Pylon to wing attachment fitting
P12 Rear pylon attachment lugs (retained by fuse-bolts)
P13 Pylon to wing diagonal thrust strut
P14 Aluminium pylon fairing, inconel in hot areas
P15 Nacelle chine
P16 Nacelle to wing fairing
P17 Allied Signal 131-9(B) APU FADEC controlled, mounted in shroudless compartment to improve access
P18 Titanium torque box firewall
P19 Oil tank and contents sightglass
P20 Oil cooler (eductor cooled)
P21 Ram-air intake (NACA duct on right side)
P22 APU compartment, eductor air cooled
P23 Eductor exhaust
P24 APU exhaust (silencer optional)

Safety and fire suppression

S1 APU compartment fire-bottle
S2 Fire bottle in each toilet (situated in waste bin)
S3 Engine fire-suppression bottles – Halon (two)
S4 Both cargo hold sealed with fire-resistant liners
S5 Cockpit side windows can be used as emergency exits

Undercarriage and hydraulics

U1 Forward-retracting, fully steering, nose undercarriage (+/-78 deg via tiller and +/-78 deg via rudder pedals)
U2 Retraction hydraulic jack
U3 Upper and lower drag brace strut
U4 Sideways-retracting main undercarriage incorporating twin multi-disc, anti-skid, steel brakes with fuse plus
U5 Trunnion mountings (spherical mounting on rear spar
U6 Retraction hydraulic jack and walking beam
U7 Nitrogen and oil main shock strut
U8 Side strut
U9 Reaction link
U10 Three independent hydraulic redundancy systems. System 'A'and 'B' reservoirs (207 bar)
U11 Standby reservoir (all three filled from single point service connection)
U12 Hydraulic fluid cooler/heat exchanger situated in wing tank, (fuel cooler)
U13 Undercarriage leg doors.

BOEING 747-100/200/SP USA

Boeing's development of its fourth individual jetliner design, and the largest built to date, began in the early 1960s as a by-product, in the first instance, of the work done on a large military logistics transport, the CH-X. When Lockheed won the military order with the C-5A Galaxy, Boeing studied civil alternatives of its military project, with 'double-bubble' fuselage arrangements and a mid-wing layout, but eventually adopted a more orthodox Model 707-type configuration, though at much larger scale. The design that became the Model 747 then evolved around the concept of a single main deck, wide enough over most of its length for 10-abreast seating with two aisles, whilst the flight deck was at a higher level, with a small passenger cabin in the fuselage behind it and reached by a spiral staircase from the main deck. By 1965, the basic concept of this very large jetliner, with seating for up to 500 passengers, had been settled and the all-new Pratt & Whitney JT9D turbofan chosen to power it. The launch order, from Pan American, came on 14 April 1966, and the production go-ahead was given in July after orders were placed by Lufthansa and JAL. The first flight was made on 9 February 1969 at Everett, Washington, where Boeing established a completely new production facility for the massive new transport, which soon became known as the Jumbo Jet. Subsequently evolution of the design has produced a number of variants as set out below, most of which have retained the same external dimensions and shapes of the original. The Model 747-300 with a longer upper deck, the Model 747-400 with the same upper deck plus an extended wing and winglets, and possible further stretches of the basic Model 747, are described separately.

VARIANTS

The original Boeing 747 was introduced with JT9D-1 or -3 engines at 193.6kN (43,500lb) and a certificated gross weight of 322,140kg (710,000lb). Other engines used were the JT9D-3A, -3W, -7 and -7W, and higher gross weights were approved in due course. These early variants all became the Model 747-100 when the designation Model 747-200B was adopted for a version first flown on 11 October 1970 with the increased weight, more fuel and uprated engines. A reduced gross weight, shorter-range version introduced in 1973 as the Model 747SR later became the Model 747-100B and in used primarily in Japan. Versions of the Model 747-200 were developed as pure freighters (Model 747F) or convertible passenger/freighter (Model 747C) with upward-hinged nose for straight-in freight loading; the first Model 747F flew on 30 November 1971, and the first Model 747C on 23 March 1973. A version with a large side-loading freight door aft of the wing appeared in 1974 as the Model 747 Combi, sometimes combined with the nose-loading door. All the foregoing Model 747 variants are dimensionally similar, but the Model 747SP (Special Performance), first flown on 4 July 1975, has a fuselage shortened by 14.6m (48ft) for a typical mixed-class accommodation of 288, and a taller fin and rudder, together with other less obvious changes. Retaining the full tankage of the basic aircraft, the Model 747SP achieves a full payload range of 5,750nm (10,660km). There have been a number of increases in the maximum permitted weights of the basic Model 747-200, hand-in-hand with the introduction of more powerful engines, including the options quoted above. Other engine variants applicable have included the JT9D-7J, -7Q, -7AW and 7O, the CF6-50D, -50E and -45AZ and the RB.211-524B2 and -524C2.

SERVICE USE

The Model 747 was originally certificated on 30 December 1969, and Pan American put the 'jumbo' into service on the North Atlantic on 21 January 1970. The Model 747-200B was certificated on 23 December 1970 and entered service with KLM early in 1971. Type Approval of the Model 747F was obtained on 7 March 1972 and service use by Lufthansa began on 19 April 1972; and the Model 747C convertible with nose-loading door entered service with World Airways after certification on 24 April 1973, while Sabena was first to operate the Model 747 Combi in 1974. The 'lightweight' Model 747SR entered service with Japan Air Lines on 9 October 1973, and the short-body Model 747SP with Pan American in May 1976. Boeing built 643 of these 747 models, including 205 -100, 393 -200 and 45 SPS.

SPECIFICATION
(Boeing 747-200B)

Dimensions: Wingspan 59.64m (195ft 8in); length overall 70.66m (231ft 10in); height overall 19.33m (63ft 5in), wing area 511m² (5,500ft²).
Power Plant: Four General Electric CF6-50E2 turbofans, each rated at 233.5kN (52,500lb) or Pratt & Whitney JT9D-7R4G2 at 243.5kN (54,750lb) or Rolls-Royce RB211-524D4 at 236.25kN (53,110lb).
Weights: (P&W engines) Operating weight empty 169,961kg (374,400lb); max take-off 377,840kg (833.000lb); max landing 285,765kg (630,000lb); max payload 68,855kg (151,800lb).
Performance: Max cruising speed 507kts (940km/h); cruise ceiling 13,715m (45,000ft); take-off field length 3,170m (10m400ft); landing field length 2,120m (6,950ft); range with max fuel 7,100nm (13,135km); range with max payload 6,150nm (11,380km).
Accommodation: Flight crew of three. Typical mixed-class layout for 452 passengers, with maximum of 516 ten-abreast, all with twin aisles. Underfloor baggage/cargo volume 147.0m³ (5,190ft³).

Left: The early Boeing 747s, now often referred to as the 'Classic', have shown themselves to be particularly suited to the carriage of cargo, and many were produced both as pure freighters and as passenger/cargo combis. Europe's major all-cargo operator Cargolux flies an all 747 fleet including these 747-200Cs.

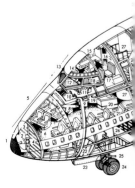

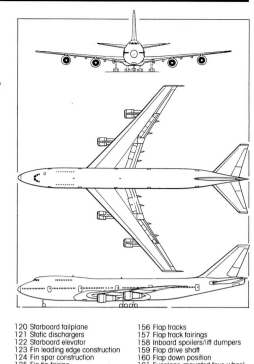

Left: The 'dumpy' 747SP (Special Performance) was built at the behest of Pan American World Airways to provide non-stop range between New York and Tokyo. Only 45 were built, as the improvements of the larger models soon provided similar performance. Syrianair was one of the few airlines to purchase it.

Right: The three-view drawing depicts the 747-200B, the most numerous of the early models. The -100 is externally similar; the SP has the same wing but a shorter fuselage.

Boeing 747-200 Combi Cutaway Drawing Key

1 Radome
2 Weather radar scanner
3 Forward pressure bulkhead
4 Radar scanner mounting
5 Nose visor cargo door
6 First class passenger cabin
7 Typically, 32 seats in forward cabin
8 Nose visor hydraulic jack
9 Visor hinge fixing
10 Rudder pedals
11 Control column
12 Instrument panel shroud
13 Curved windscreen panels
14 Co-pilot's seat
15 Flight engineer's control panel
16 Cockpit doorway
17 Observers' seats (2)
18 Captain's seat
19 Cockpit floor level
20 First class bar unit
21 Window panel
22 Nose undercarriage wheel bay
23 Nosewheel doors
24 Twin nosewheels, forward retracting
25 Steering hydraulics jacks
26 Underfloor avionics equipment racks

27 Circular staircase between decks
28 Upper deck crew door, port and starboard
29 Cockpit air conditioning
30 First class galley
31 First class toilet
32 Plug-type forward cabin door, No. 1
33 First class passenger seating
34 Cabin dividing bulkhead
35 Upper deck window panel
36 Upper deck toilet
37 Anti-collision light
38 Cabin roof construction
39 Upper deck galley
40 Upper deck passenger seating, up to 32 seats
41 Air conditioning supply ducts
42 Forward fuselage frame construction
43 Baggage pallet containers
44 Forward underfloor freight compartment
45 Air conditioning system ram air intake
46 Wing root fairing
47 Ventral air conditioning plant, port and starboard
48 No. 2 passenger door, port and starboard
49 Lower deck forward galley
50 Upper deck galley
51 Meal trolley elevator
52 Communications aerial
53 Forward tourist-class cabin, typically 141 seats
54 Fuselage frame and stringer construction
55 Cabin floor beam construction
56 Centre-wing section skin/ stringer panel
57 Fresh water tanks
58 Wing spar bulkhead
59 Wing centre-section fuel tank, capacity 14,154 Imp gal (64,345l)

60 Front spar attachment fuselage main frame
61 Air conditioning cross-feed ducts
62 Air distribution duct
63 Risers to distribution ducts
64 Wing centre spar attachment main frame
65 Satellite navigation aerial
66 Fuselage skin panelling
67 Starboard wing inboard fuel tank, capacity 10,240 Imp gal (46,555l)
68 Fuel pumps
69 Engine bleed air supply duct
70 Krueger flap operating jacks
71 Inboard Krueger flap
72 Starboard inner engine nacelle
73 Inboard engine pylon
74 Leading edge Krueger flap segments
75 Krueger flap drive shaft
76 Ventral refuelling panel
77 Krueger flap motors
78 Starboard wing outboard fuel tank, capacity 3,680 Imp gal (16,730l)
79 Starboard outer engine nacelle
80 Outboard engine pylon
81 Outboard Krueger flap segments
82 Krueger flap drive mechanism
83 Extended range fuel tank, capacity 666 Imp gal (3,028l)
84 Surge tank
85 Wing tip fairing
86 Starboard navigation light
87 VHF aerial boom
88 Fuel vent
89 Static dischargers
90 Outboard, low-speed, aileron
91 Outboard spoilers
92 Outboard slotted flaps
93 Flap drive mechanism

94 Inboard, high-speed, aileron
95 Trailing edge beam
96 Inboard spoilers/lift dumpers
97 Inboard slotted flap
98 Flap screw jack
99 Centre fuselage construction
100 Pressure floor above starboard wheel bay
101 Wing-mounted main undercarriage wheel bay
102 Central flap drive motors
103 Undercarriage mounting beam
104 No. 3 passenger door, port and starboard
105 Fuselage-mounted main undercarriage wheel bay
106 Hydraulic retraction jack
107 Wheel bay pressure bulkhead
108 Cargo net
109 Rear underfloor freight hold
110 Freight and baggage container, LD-1
111 Cargo loading deck
112 Roller conveyor floor tracks
113 Cabin wall trim panelling
114 Rear cabin air supply duct
115 Control cable runs

116 Rear fuselage frame and stringer construction
117 Upper deck freight containers, M1
118 Rear toilet compartments
119 Fin root fairing

120 Starboard tailplane
121 Static dischargers
122 Starboard elevator
123 Fin leading edge construction
124 Fin spar construction
125 Fin tip fairing
126 VOR aerial
127 Static dischargers
128 Upper rudder segment
129 Lower rudder segment
130 Rudder hydraulic jacks
131 Tailcone fairing
132 APU exhaust
133 Auxiliary Power Unit (APU)

134 Port elevator inner segment
135 Elevator outer segment
136 Static dischargers
137 Tailplane construction
138 Elevator hydraulic jacks
139 Tailplane sealing plate
140 Tailcone frame construction
141 Fin attachment joint
142 Tailplane centre section
143 Trimming tailplane screw jack
144 APU air duct
145 No. 5 passenger door, port and starboard
146 Stowage lockers, port and starboard
147 Rear fuselage window panel
148 Side loading cargo door, open
149 Cargo doorway 10ft (3.05m) x 11ft 2in (3.4m)
150 No. 4 passenger door, port and starboard

151 Fuselage lower lobe frame and stringer construction
152 Trailing edge wing root fillet
153 Fuselage mounted main undercarriage pivot fixing
154 Trailing edge beam
155 Port inboard slotted flap

156 Flap tracks
157 Flap track fairings
158 Inboard spoilers/lift dumpers
159 Flap drive shaft
160 Flap down position
161 Fuselage-mounted four-wheel main undercarriage bogie
162 Wing spar and rib construction
163 Wing root bolted attachment joint
164 Front spar
165 Engine bleed air supply duct
166 Leading-edge ribs
167 Landing/taxying lamps
168 Inboard Krueger flap
169 Krueger flap motor and drive
170 Wing-mounted main undercarriage leg strut
171 Four-wheel main undercarriage bogie
172 Mainwheel leg side brace
173 Wing-mounted undercarriage hydraulic retraction jack
174 Wing skin panelling
175 Wing stringer construction
176 Inboard engine mounting rib
177 Pylon attachment strut
178 Inboard engine pylon
179 Pylon construction
180 Detachable engine cowling panels
181 Engine air intake
182 General Electric CF6-50 turbofan engine
183 Engine accessory equipment gearbox

184 Fan air, cold-stream, exhaust duct
185 Engine turbine section
186 Core engine, hot-stream, exhaust nozzle
187 Port wing integral fuel tankage
188 Inboard, high-speed aileron
189 Aileron hydraulic actuator
190 Outboard slotted flap
191 Flap track fairing
192 Outboard flap, down position
193 Outboard spoilers
194 Flap tracks
195 Flap track mounting beams
196 Wing spar and rib construction
197 Leading air rib construction
198 Krueger flap segments
199 Krueger flap hinge mechanism
200 Outboard engine mounting rib
201 Port outer engine pylon
202 Outer engine cowling panels
203 Thrust reverser cascades
204 Thrust reverser cowling door, open

205 Door operating jacks
206 Outboard Krueger flap segments
207 Krueger flap hinge mechanism
208 Outer wing panel construction
209 Aileron hydraulic actuators
210 Outboard, low-speed, aileron
211 Static dischargers
212 Fuel vent
213 Wing tip fairing
214 Port navigation light
215 VHF aerial boom

Above: A cutaway of the 747-200 Combi with freight door behind the wing.

BOEING 747-300/400 USA

Having launched the Model 747 in 1966, Boeing soon turned its attention to the possibility of 'stretching' the basic aircraft in a number of possible ways. Increasing engine power, fuel capacity and operating weights enhanced the aircraft's economics and broadened its operational spectrum, but plans to increase the passenger-carrying ability matured more slowly. It was not until 1980 that a modest stretch proposal emerged in which the upper passenger deck, behind the flight deck, was extended aft by 7.11m (23ft 4in) effectively doubling the 'upstairs' seating area. This proposed new variant was identified at first as the Model 747SUD (stretched upper deck), later as the Model 747EUD (extended upper deck) and finally as the Model 747-300. The importance of the upper deck seating area as a revenue earner for the airlines is indicated by its progressive development, since initial certification of the Model 747 allowed only eight fare-paying passengers to be carried in that cabin. First, a smoke barrier increased the limit to 16; then a straight staircase in place of the original spiral allowing seating to increase to 24; then the addition of a second type emergency exit/door made it possible to seat 32 (special staircase) or 45 (straight staircase), and finally extending the upper deck fairing aft made the cabin large enough for 69 seats in the Model 747-300 and later models. The first -300 flew on 5 October 1982, with JT9D-7R4G2 engines, and the second on 10 December 1982 with CF6-50E2 engines. As a further development of the stretched upper deck aircraft, Boeing launched the model 747-400 in July 1985 on the back of an order for 10 aircraft placed by Northwest Airlines. The 747-400 differs greatly from the -300 in incorporating extensive changes to the structure and systems, an advanced two-crew flight deck, extended wing tips plus winglets that increase the wingspan to 64.44m (211ft 5in), and a choice of advanced technology lean burn engines, including the 252.4kN (56,750lb) thrust PW5056, 257.7kN (57,900lb) CF6-80C2B1F, 258.1kN (58,000lb) RB.211-524G and 269.7kN (60,600lb) RB.211-524H. Other options are available. The 747-400 first flew on 29 April 1988, obtaining certification (with Pratt & Whitney engines) on 10 January 1989. In May 1990, Boeing decided to market only the Model 400, the last of the earlier 'Classic' types, a 747-200F, being delivered to Nippon Cargo Air Lines on 19 November 1991.

VARIANTS

The Model 747-300 was available with engine and gross weight options similar to those of the Model 747-200. The Model 747-300 Combi has a rear side freight door and provision for mixed passenger/freight loads and the Model 747-300SR is a short-range variant designed, like the SR version of the Model 747-100, to operate at lower weights in order to achieve a higher ratio of flights to flight hours. At least one Model 747-300 has been completed in VIP configuration for a Middle East head of state and carried the designation Model 77-43 in line with Boeing practice for its corporate aircraft. The

SPECIFICATION
(Boeing 747-400)

Dimensions: Wingspan 66.44m (211ft 5in); length overall 70.66m (231ft 10in); height overall 19.41m (63ft 8in), wing area 524.9m^2 (5,650ft^2).
Power Plant: Four General Electric CF6-80C2B1F, each rated at 252kN (56,750lb) or Pratt & Whitney PW4056 also rated at 252kN (56,750lb) or Rolls-Royce RC211-524G/H rated at 258kN (58,000lb).
Weights: (P&W engines) Operating weight empty 180,958kg (399,000lb); max take-off 362,875kg (800,000lb); max landing 260,360kg (574,000lb) max payload 62,690kg (138,206lb).
Performance: Max cruising speed 507kts (938km/h); initial cruise altitude 10,030m (32,900ft); take-off field length 3,322m (10,900ft); landing field length 2,072m (6,800ft); range with max fuel 8,400nm (15,540km); range with max payload 7,125nm (13,180km).
Accommodation: Two flight crew with seats for two observers. Typical three-class layout for 421 passengers.

basic passenger 747-400 was followed by the 747-400M Combi passenger/freight version, certificated on 1 September 1989. Demand for a high-density configuration on Japan's domestic trunk routes produced the 747-400 Domestic, which was certificated for 568 passengers on 10 October 1991. An all-freighter, the 747-400F, flew on 7 May 1993. It differs from the other variants in retaining the short upper deck of the Model 200, and has a strengthened floor and cargo loading facilities. Maximum cargo payload is 113,000kg (249,120lb). Boeing is considering five possible derivatives of the 747, with various combinations for up to 500 passengers and ranges to 8,300nm (15,400km). Four proposals are stretches of the basic 747-400 fuselage, and one is the 747-400LRX, which matches the -200 body with the wing and strengthened undercarriage of the -400 Freighter, giving an extra 600nm (1,110km) range. It could be in service by December 2001.

SERVICE USE

The model 747-300 was certificated on 7 March 1963 and entered service with Swissair on 28 March, with JT9D engines. The first operator with CF6-50E2 engines was UTA, starting on 1 April 1983, and the first with RB.211-524D4 engines was Qantas, starting on 25 November 1984. Northwest Airlines received its first 747-400 on 29 January 1989 and put the type into service on 9 February. The 747-400F freighter entered service with Luxembourg-based Cargolux in November 1993. Since ending production after 81 of the 747-300 had been built, Boeing has received 534 orders for the 747-400, of which 373 had been delivered by the end of 1996.

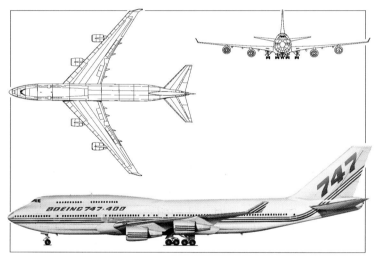

Left: The three-view drawing of the 747-400 shows the long upper deck and the model's distinctive winglets, the only 747 to have succumbed to this general trend. The -400 is now the most successful of all 747s, having won more than half of orders placed.

Right: Cutaway of the Boeing 747-400.

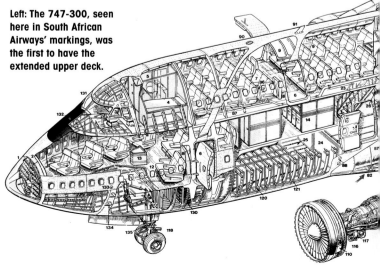

Left: The 747-300, seen here in South African Airways' markings, was the first to have the extended upper deck.

Boeing 747-400 Drawing Key

1 Sideways-hinging radome, housing weather radar, localiser and glideslope aerials
2 Front pressure bulkhead
3 Two-crew flightdeck plus two observers seats
4 Crew rest bunks
5 Toilets (two)
6 Passenger entry door 42in x 76in (plug type, containing escape chutes, total 12)
7 Upper deck, business class shown, 52 seats at 38in pitch or 69 seats at 34in-pitch economy class (max)
8 Cabin attendantis folding seat
9 New contoured ceiling and sidewall panels
10 Gallery unit
11 coat stowage
12 First-class section, 34 fully reclining seats at 62in pitch
13 Bar unit
14 Gallery units (total eight)
15 Centre-line toilets (total ten)
16 Sidewall, toilets (two shown, total five). Vacuum-flush odourless system
17 Economy cabin, 302 seats at 33 in pitch (life vests under seats)
18 Waste tanks (two each side, 85 US gal), single-point service panel below aircraft
19 Outer overhead stowage bins 10.9ft[3] per 60in long)
20 Centre overhead stowage bins (5.7ft[3] per 40 in long), reduced-angle opening
21 Life raft and escape rope stowage over each door
22 Overhead cabin-crew rest area (four bunks and four seats), one of three versions, access via stairs
23 Stairs to upper deck
24 Forward containerised belly hold, capacity 2,800ft
25 Cargo floor ball transfer panel (powered floor optional)
26 Forward and rear cargo hold Freon-gas fire extinguishers

27 Water tanks
28 Rear containerised freight hold (2,340ft[3])
29 All bulk cargo hold (845ft[3])
30 Bulk cargo hold door (44in x 47in Inward-opening)
31 Cargo hold doors (104in x 68in), electrically powered
32 Rear pressure dome
33 Two-spar, multi-rib/stringer fin torsion box
34 Removable light-alloy leading edge and glass fibre tip (provision for HF aerials)
35 Two-piece rudder, dual hydraulic actuators lower hall, triple hydraulic actuators upper hall
36 Continuous two-spar tailplane torsion box
37 Milti-rib and stringer, spilt skin tailplane panels. Thiokol-sealed for tankage
38 Long-range fuel tank (3,3000 US gal)
39 Surge and vent tank
40 Hydraulically actuated tailplane drive unit (electrically driven autopilot trim change drive)
41 Two-piece elevator (hydraulically actuated)
42 Pratt & Whitney Canada PW901A auxiliary power unit (APU)
43 API air inlet
44 APU exhaust, elector cooled
45 APU housed in titanium fireproof compartment
46 Freon gas bottle fire extinguisher
47 Cooling-air inlet for accessories
48 APU air delivery duct
49 Wing torsion box, two spars continuous root to tip, with centre spar from root to outer pylon
50 Four-panel wing skins (top and bottom), rear panel continuous
51 Extruded channel-section stringers (Thiokol-sealed for tankage)
52 Multi-plate web/riveted stiffened ribs

53 Wing extension, 6gt
54 6ft-high winglet, carbonfibre front and rear spar covered with carbonfibre epoxy honey-comb sandwich skin panels
55 Aluminium leading edge
56 Detachable glassfibre laminate tip
57 Recontoured wing/fuselage fairing
58 Kruger flap, three sections, forms underside of wing when retracted (pneumatically actuated)
59 Leading-edge flap, 11 sections each side (pneumatically actuated, electrically actuated standby)
60 Inner high-speed aileron (hydraulically actuated)
61 Outer low-speed aileron (hydraulically actuated)
62 Triple-slotted Fowler-type flaps
63 Flap tracks and carriges (hydraulically actuated torque-tube drive via angled gearboxes, and ball screwjacks)
64 Spoiler/speedbrake panels (hydraulically actuated)
65 Elevator and rudder cables run from the control columns to the rear quadrants and feel units via pulleys
66 Main flap aluminium honeyplate skin panels, light-alloy ribs and spars; leading-alloy slat similar, with glassfibre honeycomb leading edge; trailing flap has glassfibre trailing edge.
67 Wing/fuselage mainframes, built-up forged and machined light alloy
68 Wing main undercarriage support beam (titanium)
69 Glassfibre flap track shroud
70 Engine support pylon hung from strengthened chordwise ribs
71 Front and rear engine attachment lugs., interchangeable with the three engine alternatives.
72 Pylon/wing upper attachment link

73 Diagonal brace/thrust strut attached at the rear end to the centre and rear wing spars
74 Engine-driven hydraulic pump; air-driven pump with electric standby supplies four separate and independent hydraulic systems (one per engine)
75 System reservoir (32-371/2 gal/min, 3,000lb delivery)
76 Air tapped from engine 8th and 15th stages to air conditioning packs
77 Pre-cooler and air exhaust
78 Engine fire bottles (Freon gas)
79 Hot-air duct to engine intake anti-icing
80 Hot air delivery duct to leading-edge de-icing spray tube; from outboard of inner pylon to the tip
81 Main distribution manifold
82 Ram-air lini to air-conditioning packs (three beneath centre section)
83 Plenum chamber for conditioned air delivery
84 Riser ducts to overhead cabin distribution ducts
85 Cabin zone delivery ducts via recirculating booster fans
86 Cabin riser ducts to overhead individual passenger units
87 Ducts forward to flightdeck
88 Cabin outflow valves (two)
89 Cabin pressure-relief valves, in bulk cargo hold, air dumped overhead below aircraft (two)
90 Upper rotating beacon
91 VHF No 2 aerial (No 1 and No 3 beneath aircraft)
92 Standard pressure fuelling/defuelling coupling
93 Over wing filler caps (four places)
94 Centre wing tank 26,990 US gal capacity
95 Inboard main tank 34,600 US gal total
96 Outboard main tank 8,840 US gal total
97 Reserve tank 1,000 US gal total

98 Two AC-driven booster pumps per main tank
99 Vent manifold, also in top wingskin stringers
100 Dry bay
101 Vent surge tank
102 Jettison/fuelling/defuelling manifold
103 Jettison nozzles
104 Vent outlet (Naca vent underwing)
105 Tank contents probes (63 total each aircraft)
106 Fuel feed/crossfeed manifold to engines via valves
107 Pratt & Whitney PW4000 two spool high-bypass turbofan engine, 56,000lb-thrust at seal level
108 75kva generator (90kva optional off each engine)
109 Engine oil tank
110 Electronic engine control (EEC) box
111 Hinged cowl panels confaining support strut
112 Thrust-reverser translating cowl extended exposing fixed cascade panels (hydraulically actuated)
113 Acoustically treated engine inlet and case linings
114 Rolls-Royce RB.211-524CG, three-spool high-bypass turbofan engine, 58,000lb thrust at sea level, incorporating 24 wide-chord fan blades.
115 Integrated exhaust-mixing nozzle
116 General Electric CF6-80C2 two-spool high-bypass two-speed turbofan engine, 57,900lb-thrust at sea level
117 Accessory gear box
118 Fully steering hydraulically actuated forward retracting nose undercarriage (retracts into unpressurised nose wheel bay)

119 Keel centre box carry through structure
120 Built-up, un-notched fuselage frames appropriate to subassembly panels (skin locally stiffened by bonded doublers)
121 Rolled alloy stringers
122 Wing main and body main undercarriage, low profile 22in tyres and wheels with multi-carbon anti-skid brakes, redesigned to take new take-off weight of 853,000lb, and landing weight of 574,000lb
123 Retraction jack
124 Breaker strut
125 Breaker-strut actuator
126 Oleo-pneumatic suspension system interlinked with main undercarriage
127 Pressure-bearing cabin floor over unpressurised undercarriage bay
128 Aluminium skin boned to PVC-core floor panels
129 Cabin floor-level rapid venting panels
130 Electrical and avionics service bay (aft of nose undercarriage bay)
131 Electrically heated, optically-ground curved windscreen panels
132 Outside temperature probes
133 Angle-of-attack vane (both sides)
135 Pitot head (two both sides, electrically heated)
135 Runway/turn-off and taxi lights
136 Wing inspection light
137 Overwing emergency egress lamps
138 Landing lamps
139 Navigation and strobe light, (white lights on tailplane)
140 Glassfibre static discharge wicks

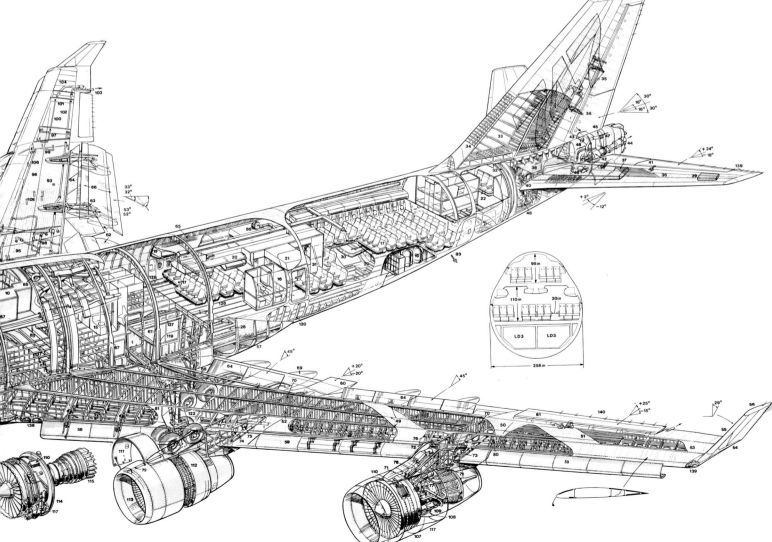

BOEING 757-200/300 USA

The Boeing 757, launched in mid-1978, is essentially a 'big brother' for the Model 727 which, up to the mid-1980s, retained its position as the best-seller among the Western world's jetliners. During the 1970s Boeing devoted much time and effort to studying possible stretches of the Model 727, with particular attention to the advantages to be gained from the use of more modern engines. In the end, the Model 757 emerged as a wholly new design. Although attempts were made to retain commonality with the Model 727, the switch from a configuration using three rear-mounted engines to one with a pair of engines in underwing pods made this difficult, and with a new wing and a low-mounted tailplane the Model 757 retained little of the Model 727 other than the same basic fuselage cross section, which was therefore similar to that also used in the Models 707 and 737. Even the original intention of using a flight deck with Model 727 features was eventually abandoned in favour of achieving the best possible commonality with the Boeing 767, and as finally built, the Model 757 had more in common with the latter than the former, to the extent that it is possible for pilots to obtain a single flight rating that allows them to fly either the Model 757 or the Model 767. Of the several advanced high bypass ratio turbofans under development, the RB.211-535 was chosen as one of the most suitable for the Model 757, with the General Electric CF-32C1 rated at 73.7kN (36,500lb) as an alternative. Until the launch of the new aircraft, the first Boeing aircraft to be launched with a foreign engine, on 31 August 1978, two alternative fuselage lengths were on offer, as the Model 757-100 and Model 757-200; the two launch customers, British Airways and Eastern Air Lines, both chose the -200 with Rolls-Royce engines, and the -100 was eventually dropped as an option. Also dropped, by General Electric's decision not to proceed with its development, was the CF6-32 engine option, after Pratt & Whitney had entered the market with the PW2000 family, and a version of the latter has become the alternative to the RB.211 in the Model 757. Flight testing began on 19 February 1982 at the Boeing factory at Renton, with four more aircraft used in the flight development programme. The first flight with PW2037 engines was made on 14 March 1984.

VARIANTS

The Model 757 is available at two different gross weights, and with several different engine options from Rolls-Royce and Pratt & Whitney. In 1985, the first sale was made of a freighter version, designated Model 757PF (package freighter), with a large cargo door in the forward fuselage port side, a single crew entry door and no cabin windows. The same large loading door is used in the Model 757 Combi which retains the standard features for passenger-carrying and can be used to accommodate mixed cargo/passenger loads in varying combinations. The designation Model 77-52 is used to identify corporate/executive versions of the 757. ETOPS (extended twin-engine operations) were certified with Rolls-Royce RB.211-535E4 engines in December 1986. In 1992, Pemco Aeroplex developed a 757-200F freighter version by converting existing passenger models. This is available in all-cargo, combi and quick-change configurations. An extended-range version providing a 600nm (1,110km) increase in maximum range has been given the suffix ER. The 757-300 'stretch' was launched at the 1996 Farnborough air show, following receipt of an order for 12 aircraft from German charter airline Condor. The -300 is 7.1m (23ft 3½in) longer than the standard -200 and will be able to accommodate some 20 per cent more passengers, bringing maximum capacity close to 300. Some

strengthening of the wing and landing gear and a retractable tail-skid is required.

SERVICE USE

Following its certification by the FAA on 21 December 1982 and the CAA (in the UK) on 14 January 1983, Boeing 757 deliveries to Eastern Air Lines began on 22 December 1982 and to British Airways on 25 January 1983. These two airlines started revenue service with the type on 1 January and 9 February 1983 respectively. The Model 757 with PW2037 engines was certificated in October 1984, and deliveries to Delta Air Lines began on 5 November that year, with the first service flown on 28 November. The first Model 757 with the uprated RB.211-535E4 engines was delivered to Eastern on 10 October 1984. United Parcel Service (UPS) acquired its first 757-200PF on 17 September 1987, while the first extended-range passenger model, suffixed ER, was delivered to Royal Brunei Airlines on 6 May 1986. Boeing had received orders for 915 of the Model 757 by 1 January 1998, including 901 757-200s of which 782 had been delivered to airlines worldwide.

SPECIFICATION
(Boeing 757-200)

Dimensions: Wingspan 38.05m (124ft 10in); length overall 47.32m (155ft 3in); height overall 134.56m (44ft 6 in), wing area 185.2m² (1,994ft²).
Power Plant: Two Pratt & Whitney PW2037 turbofans rated at 178.4kN (40,100lb) or PW2040 rated at 185.5kN (41,700lb) or Rolls-Royce 535C rated at 166.4kN (37,400lb) or 535E4 rated at 178.4kN (40,100lb).
Weights: (with R-R 535E4 engines) Operating weight empty 57,108kg (126,060lb); max take-off 99,790kg (22,000lb); max landing 89,810kg (198,000lb); max payload 24,830kg (54,740lb).
Performance: Max cruising speed 505kts (935km/h); initial cruising altitude 11,880m (38,970ft); take-off field length 2,225m (7,300ft); landing field length 1,494m (4,900ft); range with max fuel 4,270nm (7,900km); range with max payload nm (7,060km).
Accommodation: Flight crew of two with provision for an observer. Mixed-class arrangements mainly six-abreast ranging from 178 to a maximum tourist layout for 239 passengers. Underfloor cargo volume 50.7m³ (1,790ft³).

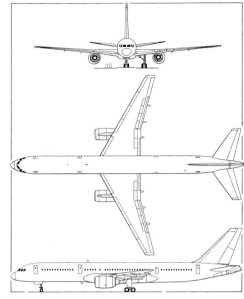

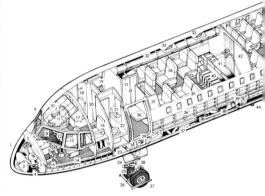

Above: Three-view drawing of the 757-200. The designation derives from the fuselage lengths initially projected, but the shorter -100 was not produced. The new 757-300 has a stretch of more than 7m (23ft).

Below: Cutaway drawing of the Boeing 757-200 in its standard form. Shown in this drawing are the Rolls-Royce RB.211-535 engines that have been specified for more than half of all 757s; others have PW2037 turbofans.

88

**Boeing 757-200
Cutaway Drawing Key**

1 Radome
2 Weather radar scanner
3 VOR localiser aerial
4 ILS glideslope aerials
5 Front pressure bulkhead
6 Rudder pedals
7 Windscreen wipers
8 Instrument panel shroud
9 Windscreen panels
10 Cockpit roof systems control panels
11 First officer's seat
12 Centre console
13 Captain's seat
14 Cockpit floor level
15 Crew baggage locker
16 Observer's seat
17 Optional second observer's seat
18 Coat locker
19 Forward galley
20 Cockpit door
21 Wash basin
22 Forward toilet compartment
23 Nose undercarriage wheel bay
24 Nosewheel leg doors
25 Steering jacks
26 Spray deflector
27 Twin nosewheels
28 Taxying and runway turn-off lamps
29 Forward entry door
30 Cabin attendants' folding seats
31 Closets, port and starboard
32 Overhead stowage bins
33 DABS aerials
34 First-class cabin four-abreast seating, 16 seats
35 Cabin window panels
36 Fuselage frame and stringer construction
37 Underfloor radio and electronics compartment
38 Negative pressure relief valves
39 Electronics cooling air ducting
40 Radio racks
41 Forward freight door
42 Curtained cabin divider
43 Tourist-class six-abreast seating, 162 seats
44 Ventral VHF aerial
45 Underfloor freight hold
46 Passenger entry door, port and starboard
47 Door mounted escape chutes
48 Upper VHF aerial
49 Overhead air conditioning distribution ducting
50 LD-W cargo container, (seven in forward hold)
51 Graphite composite wing root fillet
52 Landing lamp
53 Air system recirculating fan
54 Air distribution manifold
55 Conditioned air risers
56 Wing spar centre-section carry-through
57 Front spar/fuselage main frame
58 Ventral air conditioning plant, port and starboard
59 Centre section fuel tank
60 Floor beam construction
61 Centre fuselage construction
62 Starboard wing integral fuel tank; total system capacity 9,060 Imp gal (41,185l)
63 Dry bay
64 Bleed air system pre-cooler
65 Thrust reverser cascade doors, open
66 Starboard engine nacelle
67 Nacelle pylon
68 Fuel venting channels
69 Fuel system piping
70 Pressure refuelling connections
71 Leading edge slat segments, open
72 Slat drive shaft
73 Guide rails
74 Overwing fuel filler cap
75 Vent surge tank
76 Starboard navigation light (green) and strobe light (white)
77 Tail navigation strobe light (white)
78 Starboard aileron
79 Aileron hydraulic jacks
80 Spoiler sequencing control mechanism
81 Outboard double-slotted flaps, down
82 Flap guide rails
83 Screw jacks
84 Outboard spoilers, open
85 Spoiler hydraulic jacks
86 Inboard flap outer single-slotted segment
87 Inboard spoilers
96 Port overhead stowage bins, passenger service units beneath
97 Mid-section toilet compartments (two port, one starboard)
98 Emergency exit doors, port and starboard
121 Port elevator
122 Elevator hydraulic jacks
123 Honeycomb panel construction
124 Static dischargers
125 Tailplane construction
126 Fin 'logo' light
127 Tailplane sealing plate
128 Fin support frame
129 Tailplane centre-section
130 Tailplane trim control jack
131 Rear pressure bulkhead
132 Aft galley
133 Rear entry door, port and starboard
134 Underfloor freight hold
135 LD-W cargo containers, (six in rear hold)
136 Ventral VHF aerial
137 Roller tray cargo handling floor
138 Graphite composite wing root fillet
139 Port inboard double slotted flap
140 Main undercarriage mounting beam
141 Undercarriage leg side strut
142 Hydraulic retraction jack
143 Inboard spoilers
144 Flap hinge linkage
145 Inboard flap single slotted outer segment

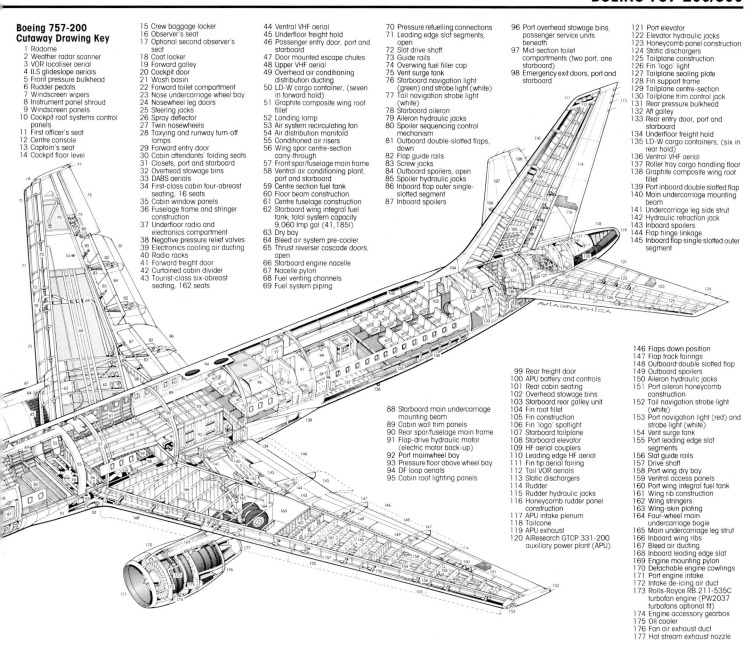

88 Starboard main undercarriage mounting beam
89 Cabin wall trim panels
90 Rear spar/fuselage main frame
91 Flap-drive hydraulic motor (electric motor back-up)
92 Port mainwheel bay
93 Pressure floor above wheel bay
94 DF loop aerials
95 Cabin roof lighting panels

99 Rear freight door
100 APU battery and controls
101 Rear cabin seating
102 Overhead stowage bins
103 Starboard rear galley unit
104 Fin root fillet
105 Fin construction
106 Fin 'logo' spotlight
107 Starboard tailplane
108 Starboard elevator
109 HF aerial couplers
110 Leading edge HF aerial
111 Fin tip aerial fairing
112 Tail VOR aerials
113 Static dischargers
114 Rudder
115 Rudder hydraulic jacks
116 Honeycomb rudder panel construction
117 APU intake plenum
118 Tailcone
119 APU exhaust
120 AiResearch GTCP 331-200 auxiliary power plant (APU)

146 Flaps down position
147 Flap track fairings
148 Outboard double slotted flap
149 Outboard spoilers
150 Aileron hydraulic jacks
151 Port aileron honeycomb construction
152 Tail navigation strobe light (white)
153 Port navigation light (red) and strobe light (white)
154 Vent surge tank
155 Port leading edge slat segments
156 Slat guide rails
157 Drive shaft
158 Port wing dry bay
159 Ventral access panels
160 Port wing integral fuel tank
161 Wing rib construction
162 Wing stringers
163 Wing-skin plating
164 Four-wheel main undercarriage bogie
165 Main undercarriage leg strut
166 Inboard wing ribs
167 Bleed air ducting
168 Inboard leading edge slat
169 Engine mounting pylon
170 Detachable engine cowlings
171 Port engine intake
172 Intake de-icing air duct
173 Rolls-Royce RB.211-535C turbofan engine (PW2037 turbofans optional fit)
174 Engine accessory gearbox
175 Oil cooler
176 Fan air exhaust duct
177 Hot stream exhaust nozzle

Left: The Boeing 757 is available with a choice of power plants, including the Pratt & Whitney PW2037 and Rolls-Royce 535C engines. This Caledonian Airways aircraft, operated on lease from British Airways, is fitted out with Rolls-Royce engines.

Right: The 757-200 has been the major medium-range, single-aisle aircraft on the European charter scene, carrying holiday makers from northern Europe as far as the Canary Islands and to Funchal on Madeira, where this 757-200 of German airline LTU Süd was photographed.

BOEING 767-200/300 USA

Boeing conducted many studies during the early and mid seventies with a view to providing a new medium-range aircraft of large capacity, in order to maintain its competitive position vis-à-vis Airbus Industrie, which was at the same time projecting an aircraft of similar size. For much of the time, the project was known as the 7X7, and its precise size and overall configuration remained uncertain until the first airline orders were obtained. As finally launched, the Boeing 767 was a twin-aisle aircraft, breaking away from the constant cabin cross section used by Boeing for the 707/727/737/757 narrow-body series and having a fuselage that was 1.24m (4ft 1in) wider. This allowed an eight-abreast layout with two aisles (2+4+2) and no passenger more than one seat away from an aisle. Initially, Boeing planned to use a three-man flight deck, with a two-pilot arrangement offered later as an option, but airline preference led to adoption of the two-man flight deck as standard before deliveries began, although this called for modification of a number of aircraft already completed. Much use was made in the design of advanced materials, including new alloys as well as composites, and the avionics included an advanced digital flight management system with electronic flight instrument systems (EFIS) – one of the first to be applied as standard to a commercial transport. Two variants of the basic aircraft were planned at first as the 767-100 and 767-200 with different fuselage lengths, but all early orders were for the larger capacity version and the 767-100 was not continued. The Boeing-owned 767-200 prototype made its first flight at Everett, Washington, on 26 September 1981 with Pratt & Whitney engines, followed by three in United Airlines configuration. The fifth aircraft was the first with General Electric engines, in Delta Air Lines configuration, and was flown on 19 February 1982. A stretched model, the 767-300 was announced in February 1983. Using the same basic airframe as the 767-200ER, the 767-300 incorporates fuselage plugs fore and aft of the wing, with lengths of 3.07m (10ft 1in) and 3.35m (11ft 0in) respectively, providing seating for up to 290 passengers. It also has strengthened main and nose gear legs and some thickening of wing skins. The 767-300 made its first flight on 30 January 1986, powered by the JT9D-7R4D rated at 213.5kN (48,000lb).

VARIANTS

The basic variant is the 767-200 at a max take-off weight of 136,078kg (300,000lb). A medium-range variant operates at 142,991kg (315,000lb). The extended-range 757-200ER with additional wing centre-section tanks and a gross weight of 156,490kg (345,000lb) made its first flight on 6 March 1984. The basic 737-300 is offered with the same take-off weight and engine options as the 767-200ER, but includes heavier models, including a 159,211kg (351,000lb) high gross weight variant. Additional fuel capacity with enlarged wing centre-section

SPECIFICATION
(Boeing 767-300)

Dimensions: Wingspan 47.57m (156ft 1in), length overall 54.94m (180ft 3in); height overall 15.85m (52ft 0in), wing area 283,3² (3,050ft²).
Power Plant: Two General Electric CF6-80C2B2F or Pratt & Whitney PW4050 turbofans, each rated at 222.5kN (50,000lb).
Weights: Operating weight empty 86,955kg (191,700lb); max take-off 159,210kg (351,000lb); max landing 136,080kg (300,000lb); max payload 37,470kg (82,605lb).
Performance: Max cruising speed 492kts (910km/h); initial cruise altitude 11,250m (36,910ft); take-off field length 2,652m (8,700ft); landing field length 1,646m (5,400ft); range with typical payload 4,250nm (7,860km).
Accommodation: Flight crew of two. Typical mixed-class configuration seats 250 passengers, with maximum 328 in 8-abreast tourist layout. Hold volume 114.10m³ (4,030ft³).

tanks and higher weights up to 181,437kg (400,000lb) resulted in the 767-300ER, certificated in December 1987. A specialised 767-300PF package freighter was launched with a UPS order in January 1993, followed later that year by the 767-300F, which differed in having cargo loading and an enhanced environmental system. Engine options for all 767 models include the CF6-80A and JT9D-7RD4 both rated at 213.5kN (48,000lb), and the CF6-80A2 and JT9D-7R4E and -7R4E4 rated at 222.4kN (50,000lb). Other GE and P&W variants, as well as the Rolls-Royce RB211-524G and H are available for specific versions. The 767-400ER is basically a derivative of the 767-300ER with a 6.43m (21ft 1in) fuselage stretch, new main landing gear, and extended wingspan and canted winglets to improve performance; first delivery is scheduled for mid-2000.

SERVICE USE

Initial certification of the 767-200 by the FAA was obtained on 30 July 1982 (JT9D-7R4D engine) and on 30 September 1982 (CF6-80A engines). First customer delivery with CF6-80A engines, to Delta, was on 25 October 1982 and first service flown 15 December. First 767-200ER, with JT9D-7RE4 engines, was delivered to Ethiopian Airlines on 18 May 1984 and entered service 6 June. First delivery with JT9D-7R4E4 engines (-200 ER) was made to CAAC, 8 October 1985. Japan Airlines placed the first order for the 767-300 on 29 September 1983 and put the type into service on domestic routes on 20 October 1986, following certification on 22 September. The 767-300ER entered service with launch customer American Airlines in February 1988. Both freighter variants are now in service, the 767-300PF with UPS since October 1995 and the 767-300F with Korean airline Asiana since August 1996. At 1 January 1998, Boeing's order book stood at 822 (229 for the 767-200, 437 for the 767-300 and 156 for the -400ER).

Boeing 767-200 Cutaway Drawing Key

1 Radome
2 Radar scanner dish
3 VOR localiser aerial
4 Front pressure bulkhead
5 ILS glideslope aerials
6 Windscreen wipers
7 Windscreen panels
8 Instrument panel shroud
9 Rudder pedals
10 Nose undercarriage wheel bay
11 Cockpit air conditioning duct
12 Captain's seat
13 Opening cockpit side window
14 Centre console
15 First officer's seat
16 Cockpit roof systems control panels
17 Flight engineer's station
18 Observer's seat
19 Pitot tubes
20 Angle of attack probe
21 Nose undercarriage steering jacks
22 Twin nosewheels
23 Nosewheel doors
24 Waste system vacuum tank
25 Forward toilet compartment
26 Crew wardrobe
27 Forward galley
28 Starboard overhead sliding door
29 Entry lobby
30 Cabin divider
31 Port entry door
32 Door control handle
33 Escape chute stowage
34 Underfloor electronics racks
35 Electronics cooling air system
36 Skin heat exchanger
37 Fuselage frame and stringer construction
38 Cabin window panel
39 Six-abreast first class seating compartment (18 seats)
40 Overhead stowage bins
41 Curtained cabin divider
42 Sidewall trim panels
43 Negative pressure relief valves
44 Forward freight door
45 Forward underfloor freight hold
46 LD-2 cargo containers, 12 in forward hold
47 Centre electronics rack
48 Anti-collision light
49 Cabin roof frames
50 VHF aerial
51 Seven-abreast tourist class seating (193 seats)
52 Conditioned air riser
53 Air conditioning distribution manifolds
54 Wing spar centre section carry through
55 Floor beam construction
56 Overhead air conditioning ducting
57 Front spar/fuselage main frame
58 Starboard emergency exit window
59 Starboard wing integral fuel tank; total system capacity 12,955 Imp gal (58,895l)
60 Thrust reverser cascade door, open
61 Starboard engine nacelle
62 Nacelle pylon
63 Fixed portion of leading edge
64 Leading edge slat segments, open
65 Slat drive shaft
66 Rotary actuators
67 Fuel system piping
68 Fuel venting channels
69 Vent surge tank
70 Starboard navigation light (green)
71 Anti-collision light (red)
72 Tail navigation strobe light (white)
73 Static dischargers
74 Starboard outer aileron
75 Aileron hydraulic jacks

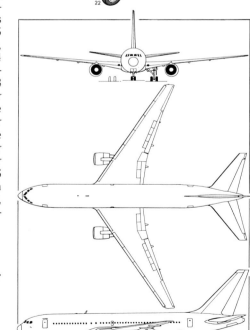

Left: Malév Hungarian Airlines was the second Central European carrier to introduce the Boeing 767 (the first was LOT of Poland), which reflected the general trend of replacing old Soviet aircraft with modern western equipment. Malév operates two Boeing 767-200s on its long-haul North American flights to New York.

Above: Three-view of the 767-300, which differs from the basic -200 variant externally only in its increased overall length (by 6.42m/21ft).

Right: Spanair, one of Spain's largest scheduled and charter carriers, operates two 767-300ER on long-haul services.

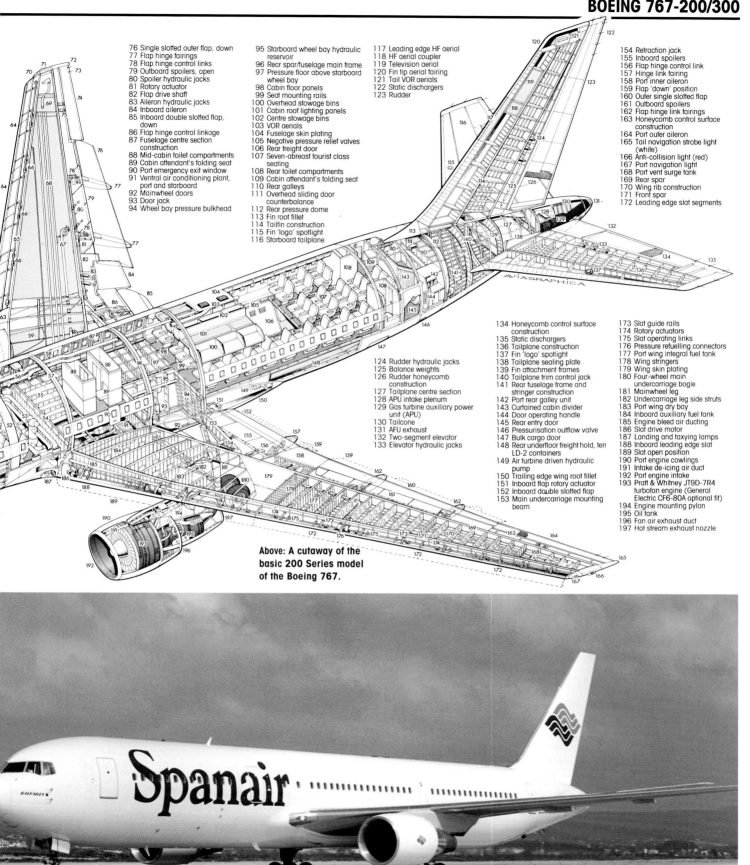

76 Single slotted outer flap, down
77 Flap hinge fairings
78 Flap hinge control links
79 Outboard spoilers, open
80 Spoiler hydraulic jacks
81 Rotary actuator
82 Flap drive shaft
83 Aileron hydraulic jacks
84 Inboard aileron
85 Inboard double slotted flap, down
86 Flap hinge control linkage
87 Fuselage centre section construction
88 Mid-cabin toilet compartments
89 Cabin attendant's folding seat
90 Port emergency exit window
91 Ventral air conditioning plant, port and starboard
92 Mainwheel doors
93 Door jack
94 Wheel bay pressure bulkhead

95 Starboard wheel bay hydraulic reservoir
96 Rear spar/fuselage main frame
97 Pressure floor above starboard wheel bay
98 Cabin floor panels
99 Seat mounting rails
100 Overhead stowage bins
101 Cabin roof lighting panels
102 Centre stowage bins
103 VOR aerials
104 Fuselage skin plating
105 Negative pressure relief valves
106 Rear freight door
107 Seven-abreast tourist class seating
108 Rear toilet compartments
109 Cabin attendant's folding seat
110 Rear galleys
111 Overhead sliding door counterbalance
112 Rear pressure dome
113 Fin root fillet
114 Tailfin construction
115 Fin 'logo' spotlight
116 Starboard tailplane

117 Leading edge HF aerial
118 HF aerial coupler
119 Television aerial
120 Fin tip aerial fairing
121 Tail VOR aerials
122 Static dischargers
123 Rudder

124 Rudder hydraulic jacks
125 Balance weights
126 Rudder honeycomb construction
127 Tailplane centre section
128 APU intake plenum
129 Gas turbine auxiliary power unit (APU)
130 Tailcone
131 AFU exhaust
132 Two-segment elevator
133 Elevator hydraulic jacks

134 Honeycomb control surface construction
135 Static dischargers
136 Tailplane construction
137 Fin 'logo' spotlight
138 Tailplane sealing plate
139 Fin attachment frames
140 Tailplane trim control jack
141 Rear fuselage frame and stringer construction
142 Port rear galley unit
143 Curtained cabin divider
144 Door operating handle
145 Rear entry door
146 Pressurisation outflow valve
147 Bulk cargo door
148 Rear underfloor freight hold, ten LD-2 containers
149 Air turbine driven hydraulic pump
150 Trailing edge wing root fillet
151 Inboard flap rotary actuator
152 Inboard double slotted flap
153 Main undercarriage mounting beam

154 Retraction jack
155 Inboard spoilers
156 Flap hinge control link
157 Hinge link fairing
158 Port inner aileron
159 Flap 'down' position
160 Outer single slotted flap
161 Outboard spoilers
162 Flap hinge link fairings
163 Honeycomb control surface construction
164 Port outer aileron
165 Tail navigation strobe light (white)
166 Anti-collision light (red)
167 Port navigation light
168 Port vent surge tank
169 Rear spar
170 Wing rib construction
171 Front spar
172 Leading edge slat segments

173 Slat guide rails
174 Rotary actuators
175 Slat operating links
176 Pressure refuelling connectors
177 Port wing integral fuel tank
178 Wing stringers
179 Wing skin plating
180 Four-wheel main undercarriage bogie
181 Mainwheel leg
182 Undercarriage leg side struts
183 Port wing dry bay
184 Inboard auxiliary fuel tank
185 Engine bleed air ducting
186 Slat drive motor
187 Landing and taxying lamps
188 Inboard leading edge slat
189 Slat open position
190 Port engine cowlings
191 Intake de-icing air duct
192 Port engine intake
193 Pratt & Whitney JT9D-7R4 turbofan engine (General Electric CF6-80A optional fit)
194 Engine mounting pylon
195 Oil tank
196 Fan air exhaust duct
197 Hot stream exhaust nozzle

Above: A cutaway of the basic 200 Series model of the Boeing 767.

BOEING 777-200/300 USA

Responding to airline interest in an aircraft with a capacity between the 767-300 and 747-400, Boeing began an intensive market study in winter 1986 which culminated in an authorisation by the board of directors on 8 December 1989 to offer airlines a new aircraft, then known as the 767-X. At the same time, Boeing set up a New Airplane Division in Renton, Washington, to oversee its development. The design was shaped by the input from several airlines and the competition from the McDonnell Douglas MD-11 and the Airbus A330/340 family of long-range widebody aircraft, and included initial 'A-Market' and longer-range 'B-Market' models. Orders and options for 68 aircraft (34+34) from United Airlines on 15 October 1990 led to the formal launch of the 777 two weeks later. All Nippon Airways became the second launch customer on 19 December with a firm order for 15 aircraft and options for 10 more. Boeing and Japanese airframe manufacturers signed an agreement, on 21 May 1991, for a risk-share programme covering about 20 per cent of the structure. As offered to the airlines, the A-Market model envisaged 375/400 passengers in a twin-aisle, two-class layout with a standard take-off weight of 229,520kg (506,000lb) and a range of 4,050 nm (7,500km), plus two heavier and longer-range options. The B-Market 777 was available with weights of up to 267,620kg (590,000lb) and a range to 6,600nm (12,250km). The 777 is the first Boeing aircraft to feature a fly-by-wire system and other design features include award-winning 'cool' six-across flat panel displays visible in all lighting conditions and from all angles, and new lightweight structural materials. A long-span, large area new technology wing with increased thickness was developed for improved operating performance, including take-off, climb rate, fast high altitude cruise and payload/range. The three major engine manufacturers all developed large new fuel-efficient and quiet high bypass ratio turbofan engines capable of eventually developing thrusts of 445kN (100,000lb). The entirely new 777 is undoubtedly a product of the computer age. It was the first jet airliner to be 100 per cent digitally defined and pre-assembled using a powerful Dassault/IBM CATIA CAD/CAM (computer-aided design and computer-aided manufacturing) system and made extensive use of finite element analysis, so that virtually no paper drawings were made. Another innovation was the design/build approach which brought together all design and manufacturing disciplines and airlines at an early stage in the design to minimise any in-service surprises. The first 777 was rolled out of the Boeing factory on 9 April 1994 and made its maiden flight at Seattle on 12 June 1994. It was joined in the flight-test programme by eight other 777s, including two powered by GE90 engines (first flight 2 February 1995) and two with Rolls-Royce Trent 800 engines. The first Rolls-Royce-powered aircraft took to the skies on 26 May 1995. Four days later, the 777 became the first aircraft ever to earn FAA approval for extended-range twin-engine operations (ETOPS) at service entry.

VARIANTS

The 777-200 is the basic medium-range aircraft capable of carrying 375 passengers a distance of up to 4,785nm (8,850km). It is available with three different take-off weights from 229,520kg (506,000lb) to 242,670kg (535,000lb). Longer ranges to 7,335 nm (13,584km) are offered in the 777-200IGW (increased gross weight, now the -200ER), with 286,897kg (632,500lb). The 777-300 'stretch' was launched on 26 June 1995 on the strength of 31 commitments by four airlines announced at the Paris air show a few days before. The fuselage will be stretched by 10.13m (33ft 3in) to increase passenger capacity to 451 in a two-class layout and up to 550 in an all-economy configuration, and will be strengthened together with the inboard wing and landing gear. Customers have a choice of three engine types which can be installed on all 777 models. These are the General Electric GE90, Pratt & Whitney PW4074/77 and Rolls-Royce Trent 800, rated between 329.17kN (74,000lb) and 423kN (95,050lb). All three are in operation. A proposed 777-100X 'shrink' appears to have been put aside in favour of same size ultra long-range derivatives, dubbed the 777-200X and 777-300X. The 777-200X would have an increased weight of 326,590kg (720,000lb) and carry more fuel to give it a range of between 8,500 and 9,000nm (15.725-16,650km), while the 777-300X would weigh around 317,518kg (700,000lb).

IN SERVICE

Following simultaneous FAA and JAA certification with Pratt & Whitney engines on 19 April 1995, launch customer United Airlines officially took delivery on 17 May. The first 777 revenue service was flown on 7 June between London and Washington, DC. British Airways received the first 777-200IGW on 6 February 1997 and initiated revenue services three days later on the London-Boston route. Inaugural service of the 777-300 by Cathay Pacific Airways is planned for May 1998 following the first flight on 16 October 1997. Firm orders stood at 364 (310 Model 200 and 54 Model 300) at 1 January 1998, of which 59 Model 200 had been delivered.

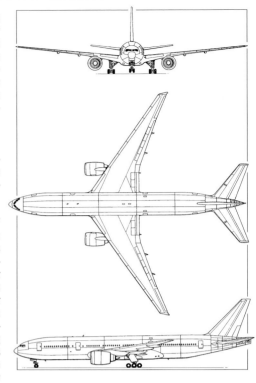

Above: The Boeing 777-200 shown in this three-view drawing is available in basic form and as the increased gross weight version, 777-200ER. Both models look identical.

Boeing 777-300 Cutaway Drawing Key

1 Glass fibre radome
2 Weather radar scanner
3 Dual ILS glideslope antennae
4 Front pressure bulkhead
5 Rudder pedals
6 Fully-shrouded instrument panel, six-tube EFIS displays
7 Windscreen wipers
8 Windscreen panels, electrically heated
9 Overhead system switch panel
10 Dual observers' seats
11 Two-crew cockpit, Captain and First Officer
12 Crew wardrobe/stowage locker

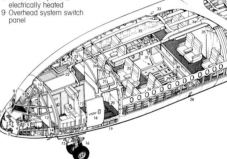

SPECIFICATION
(Boeing 777-200)

Dimensions: Wingspan 60.93m (199ft 11in); length overall 63.73m (209ft 1in); height overall 18.51m (60ft 9in), wing area 427.8m² (4,605ft²).
Power Plant: Two General Electric GE90-85B turbofans, each rated at 377kN (84,700lb) or Pratt & Whitney PW4077 or Rolls-Royce Trent 877 both rated at 342kN (76,850lb)
Weights: Operating weight empty 141,340kg (311,600lb); max take-off 247,210kg (545,000lb); max landing 201,850kg (445,000lb); max payload 29,050kg (64,050lb).
Performance: Max cruising speed 499kts (923km/h); service ceiling 13,135m (43,100ft); take-off field length 2,135m (7,000ft); landing field length 1,585m (5,200ft); range with typical payload 7,260nm (13,430km).
Accommodation: Flight crew of two. Twin-aisle cabin layout, seating typically 375-400 passengers in two classes, or up to 440 in 10-abreast tourist configuration.

13 Nose undercarriage wheel bay
14 Dual pilot heads and incidence probe
15 Nose wheel hydraulic steering jacks
16 Twin nose wheels, forward retracting
17 Forward toilet compartments, first class and crew
18 Forward entry door
19 Under floor electrical and avionics equipment bay
20 Entry lobby
21 Stowage bin, above all doors
22 Forward galley, first class
23 Starboard service/emergency exit door
24 Curtained cabin divider
25 First-class passenger seating, six-abreast, 30 seats
26 Cabin window panels
27 Fuselage frame and stringer structure
28 Pressure relief outflow valves
29 Forward under floor cargo hold
30 LD3 baggage containers, 24 in forward hold
31 Outward opening cargo door
32 Cabin wall trim panelling
33 ATC antenna
34 Forward cabin conditioned air distribution ducting
35 Mid-cabin dividing bulkhead
36 Anti-collision beacon (red)
37 VHF antenna
38 Central galley unit, business class
39 Side wall toilet compartment, port and starboard
40 Forward cabin door/emergency exit
41 Wing/nacelle inspection light
42 Conditioned air riser ducts to overhead distribution
43 Business-class passenger seating, seven abreast, 364 seats
44 Forward fuselage 5.3m (17 ft 6in) stretch section, ten frames longer than -200 aircraft
45 Cabin wall insulation blankets
46 Carbon-fibre composite floor beams
47 Conditioned air distribution manifold
48 Forward wing spar to fuselage attachment main frame
49 Wing centre section carry through structure
50 Centre section integral fuel tankage
51 Mid-cabin doorway/emergency exit additional to -200
52 Machined floor beams above wing centre section
53 Centre fuselage frame and stringer structure
54 SATCOM No 1 high gain antenna
55 Starboard wing integral fuel tank
56 Nacelle pylon rear mounting strut
57 Pylon-mounted hydraulic reservoir, triple system
58 Inboard leading edge slat segment
59 Gap-sealing Kruger flap
60 Thrust reverser cascades, open
61 Starboard engine nacelle
62 Nacelle pylon, short version for GE and P&W engines
63 Wing tank dry bay
64 Wing stringers
65 Skin panelling
66 Fuel venting channels
67 Vent surge tank
68 Leading edge slat drive shaft and gearboxes
69 Roller-mounted slat guide rails with geared arc track
70 Outboard six-segment leading edge slats
71 Starboard navigation (green) and strobe (white) lights
72 Rear position light (white)
73 Starboard aileron
74 Aileron dual hydraulic actuators
75 Fuel jettison
76 Starboard outer spoiler panels
77 Flap hinge control linkage, screw-jack operated
78 Outboard single-slotted flap
79 No 11 (and No 4 port) spoiler panels limited travel
80 Inboard drooping aileron (flaperon)
81 Flap drive torque shaft
82 Screw-jack right-angle gearbox
83 Inboard flap hinge control linkage
84 Inboard spoiler panels
85 Inboard double-slotted flap segment
86 ADF antennae
87 Rear wing spar to fuselage attachment main frame
88 Pressure floor above wheel bay
89 Main wheel bay door hydraulic jack
90 Port main undercarriage wheel bay
91 Flap drive motor
92 Central hydraulic reservoir
93 Engine fire suppression bottles
94 Tourist-class nine-abreast passenger seating, 135-seats in mid cabin
95 ATC mode antenna
96 Rear fuselage 4.8m (15ft 9in) stretch section, eight frames longer than -200 aircraft
97 Overhead baggage lockers
98 Cabin wall trim/lighting panels
99 Passenger service units
100 Rear cabin conditioned air distribution ducting
101 Tourist-class cabin divider and toilet compartments
102 Optional No 2 SATCOM high-gain antenna
103 Rear cargo door
104 Rear under floor cargo hold
105 LD3 baggage containers, 20 in rear hold
106 Rear tourist-class cabin seating, 118 passengers
107 Fuselage skin panelling
108 Fin root fillet
109 Aluminium alloy leading edge skin
110 Glass fibre leading edge structure
111 Toughened carbon-fibre reinforced plastic (CFRP) two-spar fin torsion box structure
112 HF antenna coupler
113 Starboard trimming tailplane
114 Starboard elevator
115 TV low-band antenna
116 TV high-band antenna
117 Glass fibre fin tip fairing
118 VOR localiser antenna
119 Static dischargers
120 Rudder
121 CFRP rudder structure
122 Rudder triple hydraulic actuators
123 Rudder trim tab
124 Auxiliary Power Unit (APU) air intake, open
125 Allied Signal GTCP331-500 APU
126 Rear strobe light (white)
127 APU exhaust
128 Port elevator
129 Elevator CFRP structure
130 Static dischargers
131 Port trimming tailplane
132 CFRP two-spar tailplane torsion box structure
133 Optional fin logo lights
134 Glass fibre reinforced plastic (GFRP) leading edge structure with aluminium alloy leading edge skin
135 Tailplane pivot mountings
136 Hinge aperture sealing plate
137 Spar box centreline joint
138 Tailplane trim screw jack and hydraulic motor
139 Rear pressure dome
140 Rear cabin galley unit
141 Cockpit voice and flight recorder stowage
142 Central and side wall toilet compartments
143 Rear cabin doorway/emergency exit, port and starboard
144 Rear fuselage pressurisation outflow valve
145 Under floor potable and waste water tanks
146 Rear bulk cargo hold
147 Rear cabin window panels
148 Tourist-class section -mid-cabin door emergency exit, port and starboard
149 Composite wing root trailing edge fillet
150 Hydraulic system air-driven auxiliary pumps
151 Port inboard double-slotted flap
152 Inboard spoiler panels (2)
153 Flap inboard guide rail
154 Titanium main undercarriage support beam
155 Pre-closing main wheel bay doors
156 Main undercarriage leg pivot mounting
157 Spoiler hydraulic jacks
158 Port flaperon
159 Flap CFRP structure
160 Port outboard spoiler panels (5)
161 Flap hinge fairings
162 Outboard single-slotted flap
163 Port fuel jettison
164 Aileron CFRP structure
165 Port outboard aileron
166 Static dischargers
167 Rear position light (white)
168 Wingtip fairing
169 Port strobe light (white)
170 Port navigation light (red)
171 Port leading edge slat segments
172 leading edge slat rib structure
173 Wing panel access manholes
174 Bottom wing/skin stringer panel
175 Two-spar wing torsion box structure
176 Wing ribs
177 Port wing integral fuel tankage
178 Leading edge slat guide rail mounting ribs
179 Pressure refuelling/defuelling connections, starboard fitting optional
180 Slat de-icing air duct
181 Six-wheel main undercarriage bogie
182 Steerable rear pair of wheels
183 Main undercarriage leg strut
184 Hydraulic retraction jack
185 Side breaker strut
186 Ventral air conditioning pack, port and starboard
187 Engine bleed air ducting to air conditioning system
188 Landing and runway turn-off lights
189 Composite wing leading edge root fairing
190 Conditioning system heat exchanger air intake
191 Leading edge slat drive motor
192 Inboard leading edge slat segment
193 Nacelle pylon attachment fitting
194 Port nacelle pylon, long version for RR Trent engine
195 Nacelle strake
196 CFRP engine cowlings
197 Intake lip bleed air de-icing
198 Rolls-Royce Trent 800 turbofan engine
199 Accessory equipment gearbox
200 Fan casing
201 FADEC controller
202 Forward engine mounting
203 Engine bleed air pre-cooler
204 Thrust strut
205 Exhaust turbine section
206 Rear engine mounting
207 Core engine (hot stream) exhaust nozzle
208 Fan air (cold stream) exhaust duct
209 Thrust reverser cascades and blocker doors
210 Oil cooler
211 Hinged side cowling panels
212 Pratt & Whitney PW 4090 alternative engine
213 Core engine-mounted accessory equipment gearbox and oil tank
214 General Electric GE 90-100B alternative engine
215 Engine mounting pad and thrust struts

Left: The high-capacity Boeing 777 is Boeing's first commercial aircraft with fly-by-wire controls and digitally defined and pre-assembled using a powerful computer system.

Right: All Nippon Airways was a partner in the development of the Boeing 777 as ;aunch customer in the 'Working Together' programme.

BOMBARDIER CANADAIR REGIONAL JET CANADA

When Canadair designed the CL-600 Challenger business jet, the aircraft was given a wide fuselage cross-section which made it suitable for use as a commuter airliner, and soon after Bombardier had acquired Canadair in 1986, design studies were begun to stretch the Challenger into a 50-seat regional jet. An advanced design phase was initiated on 16 November 1987 and substantially compeleted by December the following year. Main elements of the design include a 3.25m (10ft 8in) fuselage extension forward of the wing and a 2.84m (9ft 4in) insertion aft, which more than doubled the Challenger's 19-seat capacity to 50 seats; additional emergency exits overwing and opposite second passenger door; drop-down air stair; modified tailplane leading-edges; and a 15 per cent increase in wing area to meet the more stringent field length requirements. The CRJ wing also differed in having a strengthened box and modified outboard leading-edges and inboard spoilers, plus new 'fly-by-wire' flight spoilers and outboard 'spoilerons'. The 38.83kN (8,729lb) thrust General Electric CF34-3A1 turbofan engine of the Challenger 601-3A was retained in the CRJ. The go-ahead for the Regional Jet programme was announced on 31 March 1989, at which point a total of 62 commitments had been received. The prototype was rolled out on 6 May 1991 and the 1 hour 25 minute maiden flight took place four days later. The test programme was joined by two more aircraft in August and November, but one of these was lost in a spinning accident in July 1993.

VARIANTS

The Series 100 is the initial production version with a maximum take-off weight of 21,523kg (47,450lb), while the 100ER has a higher weight of 23,133kg (51,000lb) and an additional 2,582 litres (681.3 US gallons) of fuel for increased range. Certificated in 1994, the Series 100LR (for long range) offered further increases in maximum take-off weight to 23,995kg (52,900lb) for European operators and 24,040kg (53,000lb) for the North American market, extending the range to 2,005nm (3,710km). Product improvements, including Cat IIIa landing capability with HGS, installation of overwater equipment, seat-back telephones, enhanced field performance and more became available on new aircraft in 1996/1997, some of which can be retrofitted. Canadair also produced the Series 200 and Series 200B hot-and-high version, both fitted with improved CF34-3B1 turbofans. Corporate Jetliner is an executive version, typically seating 18-30 passengers, and capable of cruising at 458kts (850km/h) and flying non-stop in excess of 2,000nm (3,700km), and the Canadair Special Edition (SE) has a 3,000nm (5,550km) trans-Atlantic capability and state-of-the art avionics. In January 1997, Canadair announced the go-ahead of the CRJ-X, now known as the Series 700, a stretched derivative with a 4.72m (15ft 6in) longer fuselage to accommodate 70 passengers, a slight increase in wingspan, and more powerful 58.14kN (13,070lb) CF34-8C1 engines. The Series 700 will be available in two versions, the 70-seat 'A' model and the 78-seat 'B' model. Certification and initial deliveries are scheduled for the fourth quarter of the year 2000.

SERVICE USE

On completion of a 1,400 hour flight test and certification programme, the Regional Jet received Transport Canada type approval on 31 July 1992, but European JAA certification was delayed until 15 January 1993, primarily by a newly introduced passenger impact safety requirement, from which the manufacturer had to request a temporary exemption. US FAA approval was obtained on 21 January 1993. In the meantime, Lufthansa CityLine had received its first aircraft on 19 October 1992 and, operating on the Canadian register under Transport Canada certification, had inaugurated revenue service on 1 November 1992 on routes from Berlin to Cologne/Bonn, Stuttgart and Stockholm. The first 100ER went into service with Lauda Air in Spring 1994. First delivery of the Corporate Jetliner was made to Xerox in June 1993, and Saudi Arabian company TAG Aeronautics is the first customer for the SE. At 1 January 1998, the order book had passed the 300 mark, with 351 firm commitments, of which 204 had been delivered. Those 204 aircraft had accumulated 975,000 flying hours.

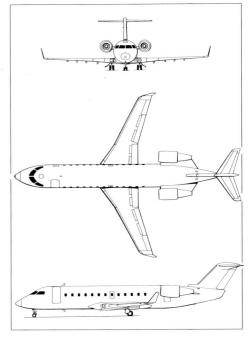

Above: This three-view drawing shows its Challenger business jet origins, differing largely by having two fuselage plugs added.

Canadair Regional Jet Cutaway Drawing Key

1 Radome
2 Weather radar scanner
3 ILS glidescope aerial
4 Emergency air-driven generator (Sundstrand)

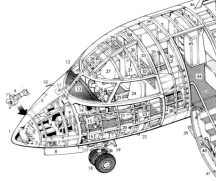

Right: French regional airline Brit Air became the launch customer for the stretched 70-seat CRJ-700, when it ordered four aircraft in January 1997. It will feature a fuselage stretch, enlarged wing and empennage and more powerful turbofan engines. First flight is scheduled for first quarter of 1999.

Left: Bombardier Regional Aircraft reached a significant milestone on 24 October 1997, when it delivered the 200th Canadair Regional Jet. The CRJ-200 was handed over to Lufthansa CityLine, the original launch customer for the type which has placed firm orders for 32 aircraft.

SPECIFICATION
(CRJ Series 200ER)

Dimensions: Wingspan 21.21m (69ft 7in); length overall 27.77m (87ft 10in); height overall 6.22m (20ft 5in), wing area 54.54m^2 (587.1ft^2).
Power Plant: Two 41.0kN (9,220lb) General Electric CF34-3B1 turbofans.
Weights: Operating weight empty 13,740kg (30,292lb); max take-off 23,133kg (51,000lb); max landing 21,319kg (47,000lb); max payload 6,217kg (13,708lb).
Performance: Max cruising speed 464kts (859km/h); service ceiling 12,500m (41,000ft); take-off field length 1,527m (5,010ft); landing field length 1,423m (4,670ft); range with max payload 1,645nm (3,046km).
Accommodation: Flight crew of two. Seating for up to 52 passengers, four-abreast , two seats each side of central aisle. Total baggage volume 13.64m^3 (483ft^3).

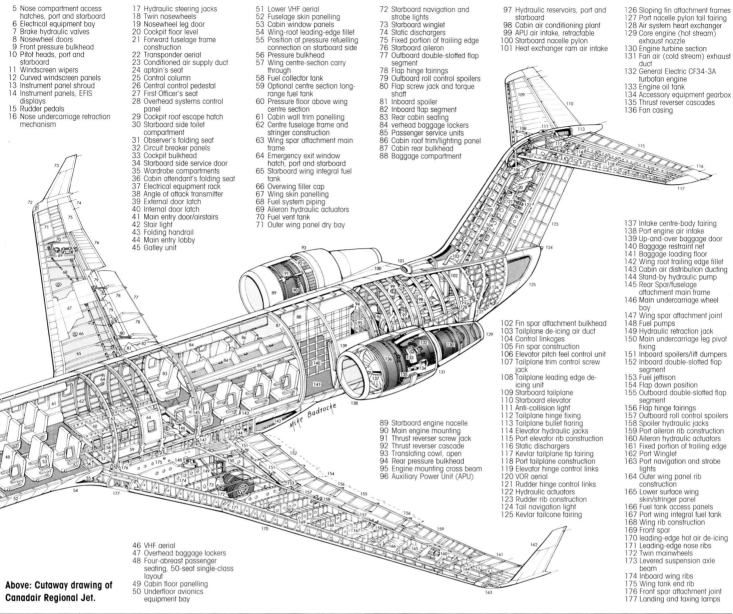

5 Nose compartment access hatches, port and starboard
6 Electrical equipment bay
7 Brake hydraulic valves
8 Nosewheel doors
9 Front pressure bulkhead
10 Pitot heads, port and starboard
11 Windscreen wipers
12 Curved windscreen panels
13 Instrument panel shroud
14 Instrument panels, EFIS displays
15 Rudder pedals
16 Nose undercarriage retraction mechanism
17 Hydraulic steering jacks
18 Twin nosewheels
19 Nosewheel leg door
20 Cockpit floor level
21 Forward fuselage frame construction
22 Transponder aerial
23 Conditioned air supply duct
24 Captain's seat
25 Control column
26 Central control pedestal
27 First Officer's seat
28 Overhead systems control panel
29 Cockpit roof escape hatch
30 Starboard side toilet compartment
31 Observer's folding seat
32 Circuit breaker panels
33 Cockpit bulkhead
34 Starboard side service door
35 Wardrobe compartments
36 Cabin attendant's folding seat
37 Electrical equipment rack
38 Angle of attack transmitter
39 External door latch
40 Internal door latch
41 Main entry door/airstairs
42 Stair light
43 Folding handrail
44 Main entry lobby
45 Galley unit

46 VHF aerial
47 Overhead baggage lockers
48 Four-abreast passenger seating, 50-seat single-class layout
49 Cabin floor panelling
50 Underfloor avionics equipment bay

51 Lower VHF aerial
52 Fuselage skin panelling
53 Cabin window panels
54 Wing-root leading-edge fillet
55 Position of pressure refuelling connection on starboard side
56 Pressure bulkhead
57 Wing centre-section carry through
58 Fuel collector tank
59 Optional centre section long-range fuel tank
60 Pressure floor above wing centre section
61 Cabin wall trim panelling
62 Centre fuselage frame and stringer construction
63 Wing spar attachment main frame
64 Emergency exit window hatch, port and starboard
65 Starboard wing integral fuel tank
66 Overwing filler cap
67 Wing skin panelling
68 Fuel system piping
69 Aileron hydraulic actuators
70 Fuel vent tank
71 Outer wing panel dry bay

72 Starboard navigation and strobe lights
73 Starboard winglet
74 Static dischargers
75 Fixed portion of trailing edge
76 Starboard aileron
77 Outboard double-slotted flap segment
78 Flap hinge fairings
79 Outboard roll control spoilers
80 Flap screw jack and torque shaft
81 Inboard spoiler
82 Inboard flap segment
83 Rear cabin seating
84 verhead baggage lockers
85 Passenger service units
86 Cabin roof trim/lighting panel
87 Cabin rear bulkhead
88 Baggage compartment

89 Starboard engine nacelle
90 Main engine mounting
91 Thrust reverser screw jack
92 Thrust reverser cascade
93 Translating cowl, open
94 Rear pressure bulkhead
95 Engine mounting cross beam
96 Auxiliary Power Unit (APU)

97 Hydraulic reservoirs, port and starboard
98 Cabin air conditioning plant
99 APU air intake, retractable
100 Starboard nacelle pylon
101 Heat exchanger ram air intake

102 Fin spar attachment bulkhead
103 Tailplane de-icing air duct
104 Control linkages
105 Fin spar construction
106 Elevator pitch feel control unit
107 Tailplane trim control screw jack
108 Tailplane leading edge de-icing unit
109 Starboard tailplane
110 Starboard elevator
111 Anti-collision light
112 Tailplane hinge fixing
113 Tailplane bullet fairing
114 Elevator hydraulic jacks
115 Port elevator rib construction
116 Static dischargers
117 Kevlar tailplane tip fairing
118 Port tailplane construction
119 Elevator hinge control links
120 VOR aerial
121 Rudder hinge control links
122 Hydraulic actuators
123 Rudder rib construction
124 Tail navigation light
125 Kevlar tailcone fairing

126 Sloping fin attachment frames
127 Port nacelle pylon tail fairing
128 Air system heart exchanger
129 Core engine (hot stream)
130 Engine turbine section
131 Fan air (cold stream) exhaust duct
132 General Electric CF34-3A turbofan engine
133 Engine oil tank
134 Accessory equipment gearbox
135 Thrust reverser cascades
136 Fan casing

137 Intake centre-body fairing
138 Port engine air intake
139 Up-and-over baggage door
140 Baggage restraint net
141 Baggage loading floor
142 Wing root trailing edge fillet
143 Cabin air distribution ducting
144 Stand-by hydraulic pump
145 Rear Spar/fuselage attachment main frame
146 Main undercarriage wheel bay
147 Wing spar attachment joint
148 Fuel pumps
149 Hydraulic retraction jack
150 Main undercarriage leg pivot fixing
151 Inboard spoilers/lift dumpers
152 Inboard double-slotted flap segment
153 Fuel jettison
154 Flap down position
155 Outboard double-slotted flap segment
156 Flap hinge fairings
157 Outboard roll control spoilers
158 Spoiler hydraulic jacks
159 Port aileron rib construction
160 Aileron hydraulic actuators
161 Fixed portion of trailing edge
162 Port Winglet
163 Port navigation and strobe lights
164 Outer wing panel rib construction
165 Lower surface wing skin/stringer panel
166 Fuel tank access panels
167 Port wing integral fuel tank
168 Wing rib construction
169 Front spar
170 leading-edge hot air de-icing
171 Leading-edge nose ribs
172 Twin mainwheels
173 Levered suspension axle beam
174 Inboard wing ribs
175 Wing tank end rib
176 Front spar attachment joint
177 Landing and taxing lamps

Above: Cutaway drawing of Canadair Regional Jet.

BOMBARDIER (de Havilland Canada) DHC-8 CANADA

As interest in commuter aircraft with a capacity of 30-40 seats grew at the end of the 1970s, de Havilland Aircraft of Canada chose this portion of the airline market for its project to follow the Dash 7. The DHC-8, or Dash 8, that resulted from this decision neatly filled the gap between the 19-seat Twin Otter and the 50-seat Dash 7, but it also came into competition with the new aircraft of similar capacity being developed in a similar timescale by CASA/Nurtanio, Embraer, Shorts and Saab-Fairchild. In keeping with DHC policy and experience, the Dash 8 was designed to have particularly good field performance, and its configuration was that of a scaled-down Dash 7, with a high wing, a T-tail, a two-element rudder, and powerful single-slotted flaps supplemented by roll control spoilers. Once again, with the Dash 8, de Havilland designers avoided the use of movable leading-edge devices as a means of achieving high lift for good field performance, believing that such devices were prone to damage in the type of operations for which the aircraft was designed. To power the Dash 8, the company selected the newest engine type offered by Pratt & Whitney Canada, a turboprop developed under the PT7 designation but put into production as the PW100 family. Under a new P&W designating procedure, the individual variants of this basic engine were identified as to their power by the last two digits in the designation: thus the 2,000shp (1,41kW) model for the initial production version of the Dash 8 became the PW120, and the uprated engine for later variants is the PW123. The decision to launch the Dash 8 was reached during 1980. Four pre-production aircraft were assigned to the test flying and certification programme, the first of these flying on 20 June 1983. The second followed on 26 October 1983, the third in November 1983 and the fourth (the first to be fitted with definitive PW120 engines) in early 1984.

VARIANTS

The initial version was the 36-seat DHC-8-100, or Dash 8 Series 100, available with a choice of 1,491kW (2,000shp) Pratt & Whitney Canada PW120A or PW121 engines. A restyled interior with 63.5mm (2.5in) more headroom was incorporated from 1990 in the Series 100A, and the Series 100B, introduced from 1992, provides PW121 engines as standard for enhanced airfield and climb performance. A projected Series 200 with higher operating weights was first overtaken by the Series 300, but re-launched on 16 March 1992 in the Series 200A, which has the same airframe as the 100A/B, but more commonality with the Series 300. The Series 200A has 1,603kW (2,150shp) PW123C engines to

Above: De Havilland Canada achieved a light and spacious appearance in the interior of the Dash 8, shown here in its Series 100 form. The seat pitch in this 36-seat layout is 79cm (31in), which is quite adequate for the stages normally flown.

give a 30kt (56km/h) increase in speed; while the Series 200B with PW123D engines offers full power for better hot-and-high performance. The Series 300 was the second model, put in hand in mid-1985, and continued after Boeing had acquired DHC in January 1986. It differs from the 100A in having extended wingtips, two fuselage extensions totalling 3.43m (11ft 3in) to bring passenger capacity to 56, and larger cabin facilities, such as galleys and baggage compartments. Introduced in 1990 was the Series 300A with improved payload/range, followed in 1992 by the Series 300B, which introduced the optional higher gross weight and 1,864kW (2,500shp) PW123B engines of the 300A as standard. Further increase in operational performance in high ambient temperatures was achieved with the Series 300E, added in 1994. Redesigned interior and Noise and Vibration Suppression (NVS) system became standard from latter half of 1996; aircraft with NVS are suffixed with the letter Q. Multi-mission military derivatives are known as DHC-8 Dash 8M. A further stretch was launched in June 1995 in the Series 400, which made its first flight on 31 January 1998. Major changes include a 6.83m (22ft 5in) longer fuselage to accommodate up to 78 passengers; revised control surfaces, new avionics and baggage and service doors. Power plant will be two 3,602kW (4,830shp) PW150 turboprops with FADEC.

SERVICE USE

The Dash 8 was certificated in Canada to the standards of FAR Pts 25 and 36, and SFAR No. 27, on 28 September 1984, shortly followed by FAA approval in the USA. Deliveries began on 23 October 1984, the

Right: Cutaway drawing of the Dash 8 Series 100, which follows de Havilland Canada practice in its structural design. Notably, the Dash 8 does not rely upon leading-edge flaps to achieve its short take-off and landing capability.

second production aircraft going to NorOntair, and this company put the type into revenue service on 19 December 1984. The Series 300 first flew on 15 May 1987 and received Canadian DoT approval on 14 February 1989, followed by the FAA on 8 June. Canadian airline Time Air took delivery of the first aircraft on 27 February 1989. First Series 200 was delivered to launch customer National Jet Systems in Australia in January 1996. Initial deliveries of the Series 400 is scheduled for 1999. At 1 January 1998, orders for the Dash 8 stood at 554, including 297 Series 100, 79 Series 200, 136 Series 300 and 32 Series 400. A total of 481 had been delivered.

Left: SA Express was set up after domestic deregulation in South Africa, by a Canadian consortium and African National Congresss officials, to take over some thinner routes from the national carrier South African Airways. It acquired a fleet of 12 DHC-8-300E variants, which provide increased hot-and-high performance necessary in Africa.

De Havilland Canada Dash 8 Cutaway Drawing Key

1 Radome
2 Weather radar scanner
3 Radar mounting bulkhead
4 ILS glideslope aerial
5 Nose compartment access doors
6 Taxying lamp
7 Radar transmitter receiver
8 Transformer rectifier units
9 Oxygen bottle
10 Electrical distribution box
11 Battery
12 Nosewheel bay
13 Nose undercarriage leg doors
14 Nosewheel forks
15 Twin nosewheels

16 Ground power socket
17 Front pressure bulkhead
18 Rudder pedals
19 Instrument panel
20 Windscreen wipers
21 Instrument panel shroud
22 Windscreen panels
23 Overhead switch panel
24 Co-pilot's seat
25 Folding observer's seat
26 Control column handwheel
27 Pilot's seat
28 Safety harness
29 Document case
30 Cockpit floor level
31 Underfloor control runs and air conditioning ducting
32 Control system access panels
33 Pitot head
34 Circuit breaker panel
35 Curved cockpit side window panels
36 Fire extinguisher
37 Cockpit rear bulkhead
38 Control cable runs
39 Electrical distribution panel

SPECIFICATION
(de Havilland Canada DHC-8 Series 300B)

Dimensions: Wingspan 27.43m (90ft 0in); length overall 25.68m (84ft 3in); height overall 7.49m (24ft 7in), wing area 56.21m² (605ft²).
Power Plant: Two 1,864kW (2,500shp) Pratt & Whitney Canada PW123B turboprops with Hamilton Standard four-blade reversible-pitch fully-feathering metal propellers.
Weights: Operating weight empty 11,677kg (25,743lb); max take-off 19,504kg (43,000lb); max landing 19,050kg (42,000lb); max payload 6,240kg (13,757lb).
Performance: Max cruising speed 285kts (528km/h); max rate of climb 9.15m/s (1,800ft/min); service ceiling 7,620m (25,000ft); take-off field length 1,177m (3,865ft); landing field length 1,042m (3,420ft); range with typical payload 700nm (1,297km).
Accommodation: Flight crew of two and seating for up to 56 passengers, four-abreast with central aisle. Baggage compartment volume 7.93m³ (280ft³).

40 Cockpit roof escape hatch
41 Starboard side toilet compartment
42 VHF aerial
43 Starboard side service door/emergency exit
44 Buffet/drinks unit
45 Main cabin doorway
46 Wardrobe compartment
47 Cabin attendant's folding seat
48 Interphone
49 External inspection light
50 Radio and electronics racks
51 Airstairs external handle
52 Passenger entry door/airstairs
53 Folding handrail
54 Entry lobby
55 Four-abreast passenger seating, 36 seats
56 Cabin wall trim panels
57 Fuselage frame and stringer construction
58 Floor beam construction
59 Cabin window panels
60 Navigation system electronics equipment
61 Underfloor air conditioning ducting

62 External floodlights
63 Main cabin honeycomb floor panels
64 Seat mounting rails
65 Emergency exit window panels, port and starboard
66 Overhead stowage bins
67 Wing attachment fuselage main frames
68 Centre wing panel rib construction
69 De-icing control valve
70 Kevlar honeycomb wing root fairing
71 Engine bleed air ducting
72 Engine control runs
73 Starboard main undercarriage leg struts
74 Starboard engine nacelle
75 Pratt & Whitney Aircraft of Canada PW120 turboprop engine
76 Engine accessory equipment
77 Propeller reduction gearbox
78 Engine air intake
79 Hamilton Standard four-bladed variable pitch reversible propeller
80 Spinner
81 Propeller hub pitch change mechanism
82 Engine accessory equipment access panels
83 Twin landing lamps
84 Outer wing panel joint rib

85 Starboard wing integral fuel tank; total fuel capacity 720 Imp gal (3,271l)
86 Leading-edge stall strip
87 Wing access panels
88 Fuel filler cap
89 Pneumatic leading edge de-icing boot
90 Starboard navigation light
91 Wing tip fairing
92 Static dischargers
93 Starboard aileron
94 Aileron trim tab
95 Aileron spring tab
96 Aileron hinge control
97 Outboard differential roll control spoilers, open
98 Flap track fairings
99 Flap single slotted flap, down position
100 Flap guide rail
101 Outboard ground spoiler/lift dumper, open
102 Flap screw jack
103 Starboard engine exhaust duct
104 Exhaust shroud
105 Pressure refuelling connection
106 Main undercarriage wheel bay
107 Inboard ground spoiler/lift dumper, open
108 Inboard flap segment
109 Trailing-edge wing root fairing
110 Control cable linkages
111 Flap hydraulic motor
112 Fire extinguisher bottles
113 Port inboard ground spoiler
114 Flap screw jack housing

115 Flap drive shaft
116 Port inboard single-slotted flap segment
117 Overhead passenger service units
118 Rear seat row
119 Cabin rear bulkhead
120 Up-and-over baggage/cargo door, open
121 Bleed air supply duct to air conditioning
122 Fin root fillet
123 Heat exchanger flush air intake
124 Emergency location transmitter
125 Emergency location transmitter aerial
126 Fin leading edge flush HF aerial
127 Tailfin construction
128 Rudder hydraulic actuators

129 Fin skin panels
130 Elevator cable pulley
131 Elevator control rods
132 Tailplane centre section attachment
133 Upper position light
134 Anti-collision light
135 Tailplane pneumatic leading edge de-icing boot
136 Starboard tailplane
137 Starboard elevator
138 Elevator trim tabs
139 Elevator spring tabs
140 Port elevator rib construction
141 Static dischargers
142 Elevator horn balance
143 Tailplane construction
144 Two segment rudder construction

145 Fore rudder
146 Trailing rudder
147 Lower position light
148 Heat exchanger exhaust duct
149 Tailcone
150 Ventral access hatch

151 Sloping fin attachment frames
152 Flight data and cockpit voice recorders
153 Rear fuselage frame and stringer construction
154 Air conditioning plant
155 Rear pressure bulkhead
156 Baggage restraint net
157 Baggage/cargo bay floor
158 Baggage door guards
159 Port nacelle tail fairing
160 Exhaust duct shroud
161 Port engine exhaust pipe
162 Port outer ground spoiler
163 Honeycomb trailing edge shroud panels
164 Port outer single slotted flap
165 Flap down position
166 Flap rib construction
167 Port roll control spoilers
168 Aileron hinge control
169 Aileron spring tab
170 Port aileron rib construction
171 Static dischargers
172 Aileron mass balance
173 Glass-fibre wing tip fairing
174 Port navigation and strobe lights
175 Leading edge de-icing
176 Leading edge honeycomb skin panels
177 Rear spar
178 Fuel filler cap
179 Wing rib construction
180 Port wing integral fuel tank
181 Front spar
182 Pneumatic de-icing valves
183 Leading edge stall strip
184 Hydraulic equipment bay
185 Outer wing panel joint rib
186 Main undercarriage upper yoke
187 Mainwheel leg doors
188 Main undercarriage faired leg strut
189 Twin mainwheels
190 Hydraulic brake pipes
191 Faired forward V-strut
192 Main leg breaker strut
193 Twin landing lamps
194 Undercarriage mounting frame
195 Engine oil cooler
196 Engine bay firewall
197 Intake snow and debris ejector
198 Wing inspection lamp
199 Engine bearer struts
200 Intake duct
201 Forward engine mounting ring frame
202 Port propeller spinner
203 Intake lip de-icing

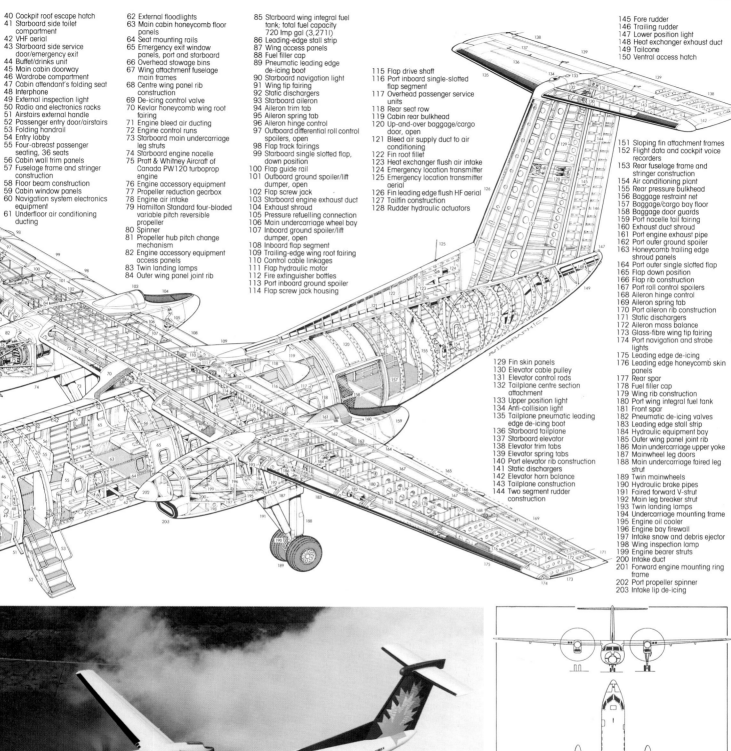

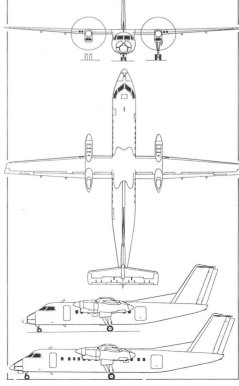

Above: The DHC-8-400 represents the final practicable stretch for the type and will enter service in 1999 with a 6.83m (22ft 5in) extension compared to the Series 300, **Right: This three-view drawing clearly shows the Dash 8's Challenger business jet origins, .** The Dash 8 differs largely by having had two fuselage plugs added to it.

BRITISH AEROSPACE (Hawker Siddeley) 748 UK

Seeking to diversify its product line as it was aware that orders for military aircraft, upon which it was then heavily dependent, were likely to dwindle, the Avro company began to explore commercial aircraft designs in the late 1950s. Efforts soon after World War II to enter the civil aircraft market with the Tudor had not been successful, and by the mid-1950s all Avro's design and production activity related to defence contracts. Following the 1957 decision to re-enter the commercial field, attention was focused upon the small short-haul turboprop category of aircraft, as a replacement for such piston twins as the Douglas DC-3 and Vickers Viking, and as a competitor for the Fokker F27, by then already in flight test. Early studies under the Avro 748 designation were for a 20-seat, high-wing, twin-engined aircraft with a gross weight of only 8,165kg (18,000lb), but analysis of airline reaction to this proposal, and of other market studies, led to the development of a new low-wing design with a gross weight of 14,968kg (33,000lb), two Rolls-Royce Darts and 36 seats. Features of this design, which was launched into prototype construction in January 1959, included a high-aspect-ratio wing with a novel type of single slotted flap to enhance field performance, and the use of fail-safe principles in structural design. Known at first as the Avro 748, this aircraft later became the H.S.748 when Avro was absorbed into the Hawker Siddeley Group, and then as the British Aerospace 748 after HSA's nationalization. The 748 remained in production from 1961 to 1986, and provided the basis for development of the British Aerospace ATP, which then succeeded it. The two prototypes entered flight testing on 24 June 1960 and 10 April 1961 respectively.

VARIANTS
The prototype and first production batch, to Srs 1 standard, had 1,402kW (1,880shp) Rolls-Royce RDa6 Dart Mk 514 engines. The Srs 2, first flown 6 November 1961, introduced 1,570kW (2,105shp RDa7 Dart Mk 531 engines and was superseded in 1967 by the Srs 2A with uprated Darts, usually the 1,700kW (2,280shp) Mk 535-2 (originally designated Mk 532-2S), but some with the Mk 534-2 (originally Mk 532-2L) and nine special-purpose aircraft with RDa8 variants. The Srs 2C, first flown 31 December 1871, was a Srs 2A fitted with large freight door in rear port fuselage side. The Srs 2B introduced a number of refinements and improvements, including a 1.22m (4ft) span increase with new wingtips, modified tail surfaces and Dart Mk 536-2 engines, plus a hush-kit option; the first production Srs 2B flew on 22 June 1979. The final variant was the BAe Super 748, similar to the Srs 2B but with a new flight deck, Dart Mk 552 engines with hush kit and automatic water-methanol injection options, new cabin interior design, and a number of other improvements. The Super 748 first flew on 30 July 1984. Military variants of the 748 were also produced, either similar to the Srs 2B but cleared to operate at higher weights, or with a new rear fuselage incorporating clamshell doors and a loading ramp; in the latter form, the type was named Andover. The actual name Coastguarder was applied to a variant equipped for maritime patrol and surveillance and first flown on 18 February 1977.

SPECIFICATION
(British Aerospace Super 748)

Dimensions: Wingspan 31.23m (102ft 5½in); length overall 20.42m (67ft 0in); height overall 7.57m (24ft 10in), wing area 77.0m² (828.9ft²).
Power Plant: Two 1,700kW (2,280shp) Rolls-Royce Dart Mk 552-2 turboprops with Dowty Rotol four-blade constant-speed fully-feathering metal propellers.
Weights: Operating weight empty 12,327kg (27,176lb); max take-off 21,092kg (46,500lb); max landing 19,504kg (43,000lb); max payload 5,136kg (11,323lb).
Performance: Max cruising speed 244kts (452km/h); max rate of climb 7.2m/s (1,420ft/min); service ceiling 7,620m (25,000ft); take-off field length 1,134m (3,720ft); landing field length 1,036m (3,400ft); range with max payload 926nm (1,715km).
Accommodation: Flight crew of two and seating for up to 58 passengers, four-abreast with central aisle. Cargo/baggage compartment volume 9.54m³ (337ft³).

SERVICE USE
The 748 Srs 1 was certificated on 7 December 1961 and entered service with Skyways in 1962. The Srs 2 was certificated in October 1962 and entered service with BKS Air Transport. Deliveries of the Srs 2B began in January 1980 to Air Madagascar. Deliveries of the Super 748 in 1984, to LIAT. The last delivery was made to Makung Airlines in 1989 bringing total production to 379, including 31 rear-loading Andover C.Mk.1 for the Royal Air Force, and 89 licence-built in India.

BRITISH AEROSPACE ATP/JETSTREAM 61 UK

SPECIFICATION
(British Aerospace ATP)

Dimensions: Wingspan 30.63m (100ft 6in); length overall 26.00m (85ft 4in); height overall 7.59m (24ft 11in), wing area 78.32m² (843ft²).
Power Plant: Two 2,051kW (2,750shp) Pratt & Whitney Canada PW127D turboprops with BAe/Hamilton Standard slow-truning propellers with six light composite blades.
Weights: Operating weight empty 14,242kg (31,400lb); max take-off 23,678kg (52,200lb); max landing 23,133kg (51,000lb); max payload 7,167kg (15,800lb).
Performance: Max cruising speed 271kts (502km/h); take-off field length 1,345m (4,410ft); landing field length 1,164m (3,818ft); range with max payload 619nm (1,146km).
Accommodation: Flight crew of two and seating for up to 68 passengers, four-abreast with central aisle. Cargo/baggage compartment volume 13.75m³ (485.6ft³).

The idea of stretching the original Avro/Hawker Siddeley 748 feederliner dates back at least to 1961 when an Avro 748E was projected, with a 1.83m (6ft) fuselage extension and the uprated 2,709kW (2,400shp) RDa 10 Dart engines. Market forecasts for this project indicated that it was premature and it did not proceed beyond the paper stage. Twenty years or so were to elapse, in fact, before the need for an enlarged derivative of the 748 could be clearly demonstrated, and it was not until 1980 that serious work on such a possibility was resumed at the Manchester works of what had by then become British Aerospace. Although conceived in essence as a stretched and modernised 748, the new aircraft became known as the Advanced Turboprop, shortened to ATP, in preference to BAe 846, its official type number in the drawing office. Several possible stretches of the 748

fuselage were considered, and were evaluated alongside a wholly new aircraft. The 'middle-course' that emerged as the best way to go forward was to aim for a capacity of 60-70 seats and to combine the best features of the Super 748 with new fuel-efficient engines. The 'marketing launch' was announced in September 1982 on this basis, the ATP being designed to use PW124 engines on the basic 748 wing, with a lengthened version of the 748 fuselage (retaining the same cross-section) and a swept-back fin and rudder, adopted to give the aircraft a more modern appearance. By the time the full launch decision was made, on 1 March 1984, the original concept of 'minimum change' from the 748 had been modified to one of 'maximum change', in order to give operators the most modern systems and equipment available in the second half of the 1980s. This included a wholly new, variable frequency AC electrical system; a new environmental control system; a revised hydraulic system; carbon brakes; a completely new avionics suite based on a digital data bus; and an advanced flight deck. The latter incorporates a Smiths electronic flight instrument system (EFIS) with four cathode ray tube displays (two for each pilot) and a Bendix multi-function display (located centrally between the pilots). First flight of the prototype took place on 6 August 1986, followed by the first production model on 20 February 1987. JAR 25 certification was obtained in March 1988, and FAR 25 in August 1988.

VARIANTS
The basic ATP is certificated in accordance with the US FAR Pt25 and the equivalent Joint Airworthiness Requirements (JAR25) in Europe. The latter permits a higher engine operating temperature than FAR Pt25 allows in the emergency power reserve case. Production of the ATP ceased in 1993, but on 26 April the company announced an improved version, the Jetstream 61, to restimulate the market, but this proved ultimately unsuccessful. The Jetstream 61, certificated on 16 June 1995, had more powerful PW127D engines, increased weights and a new interior, including extra wide seats. Two further new

Left: British Airways was an early operator of the Advanced Turboprop (ATP). Including franchise airlines, 20 are operated in British Airways markings.

Right: Attempts by British Aerospace to restimulate a sluggish market with the Jetstream 61 proved misguided and also put paid to plans for shorter and stretched designs.

Left: Thirty-five years after its entry into service, less than one-third of British Aerospace 748s remain active. In the 1980s, British Airways used a large number of 748-2A and -2B models on its Highlands and Islands services in Scotland, where it was affectionately known as 'Budgie'.

Below: Three-view drawing of the 747 Series 2B showing the optional freight door in the rear port side of the fuselage.

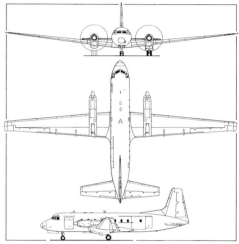

BRITISH AEROSPACE ATP/JETSREAM 61

derivatives were proposed, the shorter Jetstream 51 and the longer Jetstream 71, but neither plan went beyond the project definition phase.

SERVICE USE

The first revenue service with the ATP was flown by British Midland Airways on 9 August 1988. Total production amounted to 64 aircraft.

Below: The three-view of the ATP shows its similarities to, and differences, from, the British Aerospace 748.

The same-section fuselage is longer, and the fin and rudder are swept back to streamline appearance.

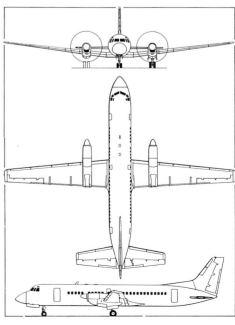

BRITISH AEROSPACE (BAC) ONE-ELEVEN UK

The One-Eleven had its origins in a design known as the Hunting H,107, projected in the mid-1950s by Hunting Aircraft Ltd as a 48-seat (four-abreast) short-range jet transport. Proposed engines in the period 1956-59, when wind-tunnel testing and mock-up construction continued, were the Bristol Siddeley Orpheus turbojet, and the BS.61 or BS.75 turbofans, but after Hunting had been acquired by British Aircraft Corporation (BAC) in 1960, the design was enlarged to provide five-abreast seating for about 65 passengers, and Rolls-Royce Speys were adopted. In this form, the aircraft became the BAC One-Eleven and a decision to put the type into production was taken in March 1961. A prototype/company demonstrator first flew on 20 August 1963, with Spey Mk 505 engines, 33,340kg (73,500lb) gross weight and a maximum of 79 seats. The One-Eleven design followed the fashion of its day in having rear-mounted engines and a T-tail, a configuration that led to the loss of the prototype on 22 October 1963 after it entered a deep stall during high angle of attack investigation. This revealed a hitherto unsuspected characteristic of the layout, calling for the development of protective systems and causing a delay in certification and production. After building more than 200 One-Elevens in the variants described, British Aerospace (into which BAC had meanwhile merged) concluded in 1979 an agreement with the National Centre of the Romania Aircraft Industry (CNIAR), providing for the latter to establish a One-Eleven production line in Romania. This deal provided for BAe to supply three complete aircraft and 22 kits from the UK production line, the latter in progressively less complete stages of construction, for final assembly in a plant in Bucharest. The first aircraft assembled by Romania flew at Bucharest on 18 September 1982 and deliveries of

SPECIFICATION
(BAC One-Eleven Series 500)

Dimensions: Wingspan 28.50m (93ft 6in); length overall 32.61m (107ft 0in); height overall 7.47m (24ft 6in), wing area 95.78m² (1,031ft²).
Power Plant: Two 55.85kN (12,250lb) thrust Rolls-Royce Spey Mk 512DW turbofans.
Weights: Operating weight empty 24,758kg (54,582lb); max take-off 47,400kg (104,500lb); max landing 39,462kg (87,000lb); max payload 11,983kg (26,418lb).
Performance: Max cruising speed 470kts (871km/h); intial rate of climb 11.6m/s (2,280ft/min); service ceiling 10,670m (35,000ft); take-off field length 2,225m (7,300ft); range with typical payload 1,480nm (2,744km).
Accommodation: Flight crew of two. Seating for up to 119 single-class passengers, five-abreast with single aisle. Total baggage volume fore and aft 14.44m³ (510ft³).

components from the UK under this agreement ended in 1986.

VARIANTS
The first production version of the One-Eleven was designated Srs 200, with 46kN (10,330lb) RB.168-25 Spey Mk 506 engines and a maximum weight of 35,833kg (79,000lb). The Srs 300 was generally similar but had 50.7kN (11,400lb) Spey Mk 511 engines, increased fuel in centre section tank and structural modification for a gross weight of 39,462kg (87,000lb). The Srs 400, first flown on 13 July 1965, was based on the Srs 300 but optimized for US operators. A stretched version, the Srs 500, was developed primarily to meet BEA requirements, and used the Srs 300/400 airframe with a fuselage lengthened by 4.1m (13ft 6in) and span increased by 1.52m (5ft) at the wingtips. More powerful engines matched the higher weights of this version. The Srs 500 prototype (a converted Srs 400) flew on 30 June 1967. To provide improved field performance and the ability to operate from unprepared surfaces, the wings and power plant of the Srs 500 were combined with the fuselage of the Srs 400 to produce the Srs 475, flown in prototype form on 27 August 1970 and in production guise on 5 April 1971. The Srs 670 flew as a prototype only, and had some aerody-

CESSNA CARAVAN USA

Cessna launched the Model 208 as a brand-new design in 1981, aimed at providing a light general utility aircraft for passengers or cargo-carrying, and suitable for adaptation to a variety of other roles. These could include, according to Cessna, such activities as parachuting of supplies or personnel, firefighting, photographic duties, agricultural spraying, casualty evacuation, border patrol and so on. Named Caravan I, the Model 208 prototype first flew on 9 December 1982, and the first production aircraft was rolled out in August 1984. FAA type approval was obtained on 23 October 1984, and in March 1986 certification of a float-equipped version was completed, using Wipline floats.

VARIANTS
Model 208 Caravan I is the basic utility version for passengers and cargo, powered by a single 447kW (600shp) Pratt & Whitney Canada PT6A-114 turbo-prop with 3-bladed propeller. Also produced as the Caravan Amphibian with floats and tailplane finlets, and as the Cargomaster freighter for Federal Express, with increased take-off weight of 3,629kg (8,000lb), Bendix/King avionics, underfuselage composite cargo pannier, a 152mm (6in) vertical extension of tailfin, and no windows or rear starboard door. Federal Express also commissioned the stretched 208B as the Super Cargomaster, which made its first flight on 3 March 1986. Apart from a 1.22m (4ft) longer fuselage and the corresponding increase in cargo volume, the PT6A-114 engine was replaced from 1991 by the more powerful 503kW (675shp) -114A. The same engine powers the quick-change Grand Caravan, the largest model capable of carrying up to 14 passengers. The

U-27A is a military utility/special missions derivative based on the 208 Caravan I.

SERVICE USE
Federal Express was the first customer for both the 208A Cargomaster, delivered following certification in October 1984, and the 208B Super Cargomaster, which joined the fleet from 31 October 1986. Brasil Central, already a prolific user of the Caravan I on commuter operations in Brazil, took delivery of the first Grand Caravan in Spring 1996. At 1 January 1998, 923 Caravans were in service in 54 countries. Some 400 operate in the freight role, while another 320 are passenger/freight combi models.

SPECIFICATION
(Cessna Grand Caravan)

Dimensions: Wingspan 15.88m (52ft 1in); length overall 12.67m (41ft 7in); height overall 4.52m (14ft 10in), wing area 25.96m² (279.4ft²).
Power Plant: One 503kW (675shp) Pratt & Whitney Canada PT6A-114A turboprops with McCauley three-blade constant-speed reversible-pitch and feathering metal propeller.
Weights: Operating weight empty 2,064kg (4,550lb); max take-off 3,969kg (8,750lb); max landing 3,856kg (8,500lb); max payload 1,921kg (4,235lb).
Performance: Max cruising speed 184kts (341km/h); max rate of climb 4.7m/s (925ft/min); service ceiling 6,950m (28,800ft); take-off field length 428m (1,405ft); landing field length 279m (915ft); range with typical payload 960nm (1,776km).
Accommodation: Flight crew of one or two. Seating for up to 14 passengers.

namic refinements to the wing to improve the field performance in line with Japanese requirements. Romanian production versions of the Srs 475 and 500 were designated Srs 495 and 560 respectively. A forward side freight-loading door was developed for Srs 475 aircraft in military service.

SERVICE USE

The One-Eleven 200 was certificated on 6 April 1965 and entered service with the first customer, British United, on 9 April, followed on 25 April by the first services by Braniff in the USA, where FAA certifica-tion was obtained on 20 April. The Srs 400 was approved in the US on 22 November 1965 and by ARB on 10 December 1965, American Airlines being the first user. The Srs 500 was certificated at the initial BEA gross weight on 18 August 1968, but entered revenue service on 17 November. The Srs 475 was certificated in July 1975 and the first example was delivered to Faucett in Peru during the same month. Production of the One-Eleven totalled 230 in the UK, made up of 56 Srs 200, nine Srs 300, 69 Srs 400, nine Srs 475 and 87 Srs 500 aircraft. Nine were built by Romaero in Romania. Some 100 remain in service.

Below Left: In recent years, the One-Eleven has become a popular entry-level jet for low-cost airlines in Europe. This Series 500 is operated by AB Airlines between London and Shannon. Some are being fitted with hush-kits to meet forthcoming noise regulations.

Below: Three-view drawing of the One-Eleven Series 500 with engine hush-kits (to meet new, more stringent regulations), which was the last and longest of the family and was designed to specifications provided by British European Airways (BEA).

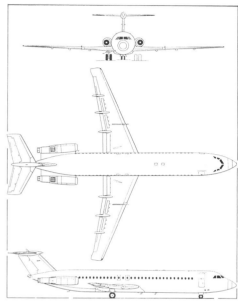

CESSNA CARAVAN

Left: The rugged and versatile single-engine Grand Caravan is operated in a multitude of roles, which tend towards the carriage of cargo. Several airlines in more remote regions, like Costa Rica's SANSA, use the 14-seat aircraft on air taxi and commuter routes.

Below: The single-engine Cessna Caravan is a highly versatile aircraft being used on a multitude of missions, including passengers and cargo. The three-view drawing shows the original Caravan I, which is shorter than the largest model, the Grand Caravan.

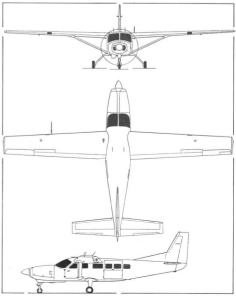

DE HAVILLAND CANADA DHC-6 TWIN OTTER CANADA

The de Havilland Aircraft of Canada Ltd has had a variety of owners since its foundation in 1928 as a subsidiary of the then-independent de Havilland Aircraft company in the UK. The latter eventually became part of the Hawker Siddeley Group, which transferred ownership of the Canadian subsidiary to Canada's federal government in 1974. At the end of January 1986, DHC, as the Canadian company was frequently known, was purchased by The Boeing Co. and operated as a subsidiary of Boeing of Canada Ltd, until being acquired by Bombardier and the Province of Ontario on 22 January 1992. Now wholly-owned by Bombardier. Despite these changes of ownership, the DHC product policy has changed little over the years, with the emphasis upon light transport aircraft with STOL capabilities. After successfully developing the DHC-2 Beaver for Canadian 'bush' type operations, and the large but generally similar DHC-3

Otter, the company gained twin-engined experience with the DHC-4 Caribou and DHC-5 Buffalo, both of which were intended primarily for military operations. DHC began in January 1964 to design a twin-engined derivative of the Otter. Appropriately named the Twin Otter, this DHC-6 project was intended specifically for the commercial operator, especially in the role of commuter airliner with short-field capabilities. The design objective was to use as much of the Otter as possible, and the DHC-6 emerged with the same basic fuselage cross-section as its single-engined forebear, and the same basic wing section though of longer span. The cabin length was extended, and new nose and tail assemblies were introduced. Fixed tricycle landing gear was adopted, and following experience with the Caribou and Buffalo, STOL performance was achieved solely by aerodynamic means, using double-slotted full-span trailing-edge flaps, the outboard portions of which also operated differentially as ailerons. In November 1964, DHC put in hand the construction of an initial batch of five Twin Otters, and the first of these flew at the Downsview, Ontario, plant on 20 May 1965.

VARIANTS
The first three Twin Otters were powered by 432kW (579shp) PT6A-6 turboprops, after which a switch was made to the similarly-rated but improved PTA6A-20 as the definitive power plant. Retrospectively, this initial production version became known as the Twin Otters Srs 100, superseded after 115 aircraft had been built by the Twin Otter Srs 200. The latter differed in having a lengthened nose fairing with increased baggage capacity. Production of the Srs 200 also totalled 115, after which the Twin Otter Srs 300 became the standard production model, with uprated PT6A-27 engines and increased maximum take-off weight, with corresponding benefit to the payload/range performance. During 1974 six aircraft with the designation

Above: The vast majority of the Twin Otters were sold in Canada and the United States. Air Inuit, owned by the indigenous Inuit people in Quebec, uses its Twin Otter 300s in the Ungava and Hudson coast regions.

Twin Otter Srs 300S were used for the Airtransit experiment conducted by Air Canada for the Canadian government. This was an evaluation of the practicability of using suitably adapted aircraft to operate to and from city-centre STOLports which – in this case at Montreal and Ottawa – comprised 610m (2,000ft) paved strips 30m (100ft) wide. The 11-passenger Twin Otter Srs 300S was equipped with upper wing spoilers to facilitate steep approach angles; high-capacity brakes and an anti-skid braking system; emergency brakes; improved fire protection for the engines; a sophisticated instrument flight rules (IFR) avionics package; and other changes. Float and combination wheel/ski landing gear were available for the Twin Otter, and a ventral pod was also developed, with a capacity of up to 272kg (600lb) of baggage or freight. Military derivatives of the basic type are designated DHC-6-300M or -300MR.

SERVICE USE
The Twin Otter was first certificated (to FAR 23 Pt 135 standards) in May 1966, allowing customer deliveries to start in July to US company Floair. Deliveries of the Srs 200 began in April 1968 and of the Srs 300 in the spring of 1969. Production totalled 842, including 115 each of Series 100 and 200 and 512 series 300, with the last aircraft delivered in December 1988. Many remain in service. The majority of all variants has been delivered for commercial use, in the designed role of third-level airliner, but about 70 were sold for military use in a dozen countries and others have been specially equipped for such tasks as photographic and geological surveys, firefighting and oil-spill dispersal.

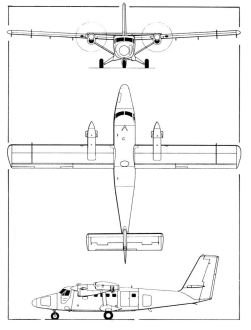

Above: Three-view drawing of the de Havilland Canada DHC-6 Twin Otter 300 STOL aircraft. The Series 200

Twin Otter is identical in appearance, while the Series 100 variant can be distinguished by its shorter nose.

Below: Cutaway drawing of the Twin Otter Series 300, the standard production version of the aircraft since 1969.

Above: Scenic Airlines operates the Twin Otter 300 on sightseeing flights over and through the Grand Canyon. Its

17 aircraft have been remodelled with large square windows for improved view and are known as Vista Liners.

DHC-6 Twin Otter Cutaway Drawing Key

1 Lightning protection rod – not used when weather radar is fitted
2 Weather radar (customer option)
3 Baggage compartment – forward
4 Forward baggage compartment door
5 Avionics equipment
6 Instrument panel – pilot and co-pilot
7 Control columns – pilot and co-pilot
8 Engine power and propeller levers
9 Door to passenger cabin
10 Pulleys and cables – elevator and rudder tabs
11 Engine and propeller control cables
12 Airflow duct
13 Oil cooler
14 Air intake deflector

15 Hartzell constant speed, reverse pitch, fully feathering propeller
16 Pratt & Whitney Canada PT6A-27 turboprop
17 Engine exhaust nozzles
18 Engine air inlet
19 Engine oil tank filler
20 ADF loop antenna (two places, customer option)
21 Engine and propeller control cables
22 Engine and propeller control pulleys
23 Aileron control quadrant
24 Flap/elevator trim interconnect screw jack
25 Wing flap actuator and control quadrants
26 VHF antenna (two places, customer option)
27 ADF sense antenna (two places, customer option)
28 Wing/fuselage attachment – forward
29 Wing/fuselage attachment – aft

30 Cabin door – right
31 Door to aft baggage compartment
32 Baggage compartment – aft
33 Passenger oxygen cylinder – customer option
34 Pulleys and cables – elevator and rudder trim tabs
35 Aft baggage compartment extension
36 HF antenna – customer option
37 Rudder control pulleys
38 Elevator control quadrant
39 Elevator control rod
40 Elevator torque tube
41 VOR/ILS antenna (customer option)
42 Anti-collision light and lightning protection horn
43 Rudder
44 Rudder attachment point
45 Rudder trim tab
46 Rudder trim tab screw jack
47 Rudder trim cables
48 Rudder geared tab

49 Elevator/flap interconnect trim tab
50 Elevator trim tab
51 Elevator trim tab screw jack
52 Elevator attachment point
53 Elevator
54 Rudder lever
55 Rudder geared tab geabox
56 Rudder control pulleys
57 Tail bumper
58 Rudder and elevator cables
59 No. 1 and No. 2 static inverters
60 Aft baggage compartment door
61 Oxygen recharging point – (customer option)
62 Rudder and elevator pulleys
63 28-volt battery
64 Air conditioning unit – (customer option)
65 Cabin door – left

66 Airstair door
67 Wing flap bellcrank – intermediate
68 Wing flaps – fore and trailing
69 Wing flap push-pull rod
70 Aileron geared tab
71 Wing flap bellcrank – outboard
72 Adjustable push-pull rod-wing flap

73 Aileron control pulley
74 Aileron push-pull rod
75 Aileron
76 Aileron trim tab actuator
77 Aileron trim tab – left wing only
78 Position light and lightning protection horn
79 Position light visual indicator
80 Long range fuel pressure pump and transfer valve (customer option)

81 Long range fuel tank (customer option)
82 Wing front spar
83 Wing fence
84 Reinforced upper skin
85 Aileron pulleys
86 Aileron cables
87 Lift transducer – left wing only
88 Engine power control pulleys
89 Landing light – both wings
90 Main landing gear leg
91 Main landing gear shock absorber
92 Wing strut attachment point at fuselage
93 Engine power and propeller control cables
94 Hinged leading edge
95 Emergency door – both sides
96 Engine attachment point – 3 places
97 Engine air intake
98 Fuel cells – 315 Imp gallons (1,432l) usable fuel, or with long range tanks 392 Imp gallons (1,782l)
99 Interconnecting fuel vent lines
100 Fuel filler
101 Pulleys and cables – aileron control
102 Hydraulic reservoir and recharging panel
103 Aileron trim console
104 Centre pedestal
105 Rudder pedals
106 Taxi light (customer option)
107 Nosewheel leg
108 Nosewheel torque links
109 Nosewheel steering actuator
110 Crew oxygen cylinder
111 Glideslope antenna (customer option)

DE HAVILLAND CANADA DHC-7 (DASH 7) CANADA

In pursuance of its policy of specialising in the production of small/medium-capacity transport aircraft with STOL capability, de Havilland Aircraft of Canada conducted an extensive market survey of short-haul transport requirements in the early 1970s. Based on the results of this survey, design definition was finalised for a STOL aircraft in the 50-seat category and, with the backing of the Canadian government, prototype construction was put in hand in late 1972. The DHC-7, or Dash 7 as it soon became known, was de Havilland's first four-engined aircraft, but its configuration followed earlier practice, with a high-wing, T-tail layout and an aerodynamic high-lift system. The latter made use of double-slotted flaps over some 80 per cent of the wing span, operating in the slipstream from the propellers. The flaps operate mechanically for take-off and hydraulically for landing, and are supplemented by two outboard spoilers in each wing that can be operated symmetrically or, to supplement the ailerons, differentially. Pratt & Whitney Canada worked with DHC to develop a new variant of the PTA6 turboprop, matched to new slow-running five-blade propellers to achieve the lowest possible noise levels. Special attention was given to the aircraft's noise characteristics and the noise 'footprint', since it was expected that the type would be applicable to planned intercity services using close-in downtown airports or STOLports. Such operations developed less rapidly than DHC anticipated, however, and sales of the Dash 7 suffered accordingly;

many regional airlines requiring an aircraft of Dash 7 size have continued (for commercial or regulatory reasons) to use out-of-town airports where STOL performance and ultra-low noise levels are less significant than the lower first costs and operating costs offered by the Dash 7's principal competitors. The Dash 7 development programme made use of four airframes: one for static testing, one fatigue test specimen, and two for flight test and certification, which made their first flights at Downsview on 27 March and 26 June 1975.

VARIANTS

The basic production model was the Dash 7 Srs 100. An all-cargo or mixed passenger/cargo variant was designated Dash 7 Srs 101 and incorporates a large forward freight door in the port side of the fuselage. The Dash 7 Srs 150 has an increased take-off weight of 21,319kg (47,000lb) and provision for an extra 4,145l (1,094 US gallons) of fuel in the wings. With this extra fuel, the maximum range of the Srs 150 was increased to 2,525 naut mls (4,679km). The all-cargo or mixed passenger/cargo version of the Srs 150 is designated Dash 7 Srs 151 and, like the Srs 101, can carry up to five standard pallets in the all-cargo role. A specialised ice reconnaissance version, the Dash 7 IR Ranger, was produced for the Canadian Department of the Environment. Projected developments of the type included the Dash 7 Srs 200 with 981kW (1,230shp) PT6A-55 engines and the same weights as the Srs 150, and the Dash 7 Srs 300 with

SPECIFICATION
(de Havilland Canada DHC-7 Series 100)

Dimensions: Wingspan 28.35m (93ft 0in); length overall 24.54m (80ft 6in); height overall 7.98m (26ft 2in), wing area 79.9m² (860ft²).
Power Plant: Four 835kW (1,120shp) Pratt & Whitney Canada PT6A-50 turboprops with Hamilton Standard four-blade reversible-pitch constant-speed feathering propellers.
Weights: Operating weight empty 12,560kg (27,690lb); max take-off 19,958kg (44,000lb); max landing 19,958kg (44,000lb); max payload 5,130kg (11,310lb).
Performance: Max cruising speed 213kts (427km/h); rate of climb 6.2m/s (1,220ft/min); service ceiling 6,400m (21,000ft); take-off field length 685m (2,250ft); landing field length 660m (2,160ft); range with typical payload 1,170nm (2,168km).
Accommodation: Two pilots and seating for up to 54 passengers, four-abreast with central aisle. Baggage volume in rear compartment 6.8m³ (240ft³).

the fuselage stretched to increase the maximum seating to about 70. The advent of such aircraft as the British Aerospace ATP and the ATR72, combined with the reduced opportunities for STOL operations, led DHC to suspend development, however, and after the company had been acquired in 1986 by Boeing, attention focused on stretched versions of the Dash 8. Production ended in December 1988

DOUGLAS DC-3 USA

SPECIFICATION
(Douglas DC-3)

Dimensions: Wingspan 28.96m (95ft 0in); length overall 19.66m (64ft 6in); height overall 5.16m (16ft 11½in), wing area 91.69m² (987ft²).
Power Plant: Two 895kW (1,200shp) Pratt & Whitney R-1830-92 Twin Wasp air-cooled radial piston engines with Hamilton Standard Hydromatic three-blade constant-speed feathering propellers.
Weights: Operating weight empty 8,030kg (17,720lb); max take-off 11,430kg (25,200lb); max payload 2,994kg (6,600lb).
Performance: Max cruising speed 187kts (346km/h); initial rate of climb 5.4m/s (1,070ft/min); service ceiling 6,675m (21,900ft); range with max payload 305nm (563km).
Accommodation: Flight crew of two. Seating for up to 32 passengers, four-abreast with central aisle. Baggage compartment volume 3.48m³ (123ft³).

A product of the 1930s, the DC-3 soldiers on with an unequalled record of world-wide service to airlines and military operators over more than half a century. Evolution of this ubiquitous twin began in 1932, primarily to meet a TWA requirement for an aircraft to compete with the Boeing 247 that had newly entered service with United Air Lines. Responding to that requirement, Douglas – under the guiding influence of the company's founder, Donald Douglas, Snr – produced the DC-1, a twin-engined low-wing monoplane of similar configuration to the Boeing 247, with a retractable landing gear and a number of 'state-of-the-art' technical innovations. First flown on 1 July 1933, the DC-1 entered production in slightly developed form as the DC-2, which first flew on 11 May 1934. TWA's successful operation of DC-2s led American Airlines to ask Douglas to produce a further improved and somewhat enlarged version,

which emerged as the DC-3 (or DST, for Douglas Sleeper Transport) to fly on 17 December 1935 – the 27th anniversary of the Wright brothers' first successful powered flight in 1908. Compared with the DC-2, the DC-3 had a wider fuselage, larger wing and tail areas, and increased power and weights. It was intended to seat 24 passengers or carry 16 sleeping berths – hence the DST appellation. Up to the time that the USA became involved in World War II some 430 examples of the DC-3 had been built for civil use, including almost 100 for export; after the war ended in 1945, another 28 were delivered to the commercial market. Wartime requirements, however, saw the production of about 10,200 of the Douglas twin-engined transports for military use – mostly under the USAAF designation C-47 Skytrain or the RAF name Dakota. Post-war, substantial numbers of these ex-military machines reached the airlines, often being known as C-47s or Dakotas rather than DC-3s. Indeed, in the period from 1945 to the mid-1960s, these aircraft became the true workhorses of the world's airline industry, and few companies operating in that period did not have at least one example in the fleet at some time, while not a few built their business exclusively on the revenues generated by a Dakota or two.

VARIANTS

Initial production versions of the DC-3 were powered by 686kW (920hp) Wright GR-1820-G5 Cyclone engines, but 746kW (1,000hp) Pratt & Whitney R-1830 Twin Wasps were soon offered as alternatives in the DST-A and DC-3A, while 820kW (1,100hp) Wright Cyclone G-102s distinguished the DC-3B. Production for and use by the military accounted for numerous other variants (and several different USAAF and USN designations, including C-53, C-117 and R4D). After World War II several schemes were developed, by Douglas and other companies, to improve the performance and standard of passenger comfort. This led to the appearance of some modified airframes in Super DC-3 guise. Several

other schemes have involved the replacement of the original piston engines with turboprops of various types, including one three-engined variant. In the Soviet Union, the DC-3 was built under a pre-war licensing agreement, with the designation Lisunov Li-2; these had Shvetsov M-62R or M-36R engines and numerous differences from the US version.

SERVICE USE

The DC-3 obtained its first civil airworthiness certificate on 21 May 1936 and entered service with American Airlines on 25 June 1936. From total production (excluding Soviet versions) of 10,926, several thousand have seen airline use since 1945. Numbers are now declining steadily but some 300 were still in active service, primarily in Latin America, in 1998.

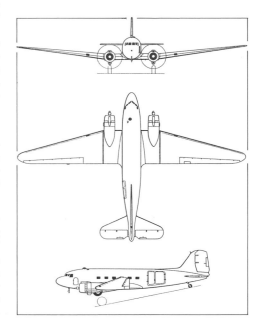

after the 111th customer delivery.

SERVICE USE

Canadian certification of the Dash 7 was obtained (to FAR Pt 25 standards) on 2 May 1977, based on the flight test and development of the two prototypes. The first production aircraft flew on 30 May 1977 and the second production aircraft entered service with Rocky Mountain Airways in the USA on 3 February 1978. Srs 150 aircraft became available for commercial use in 1986, after the first Dash 7IR had been completed for the Canadian Department of the Environment. In 1998, some 70 DHC-7s remained in service with some 25 operators, most of them located in the Middle East, Australasia and North and South America.

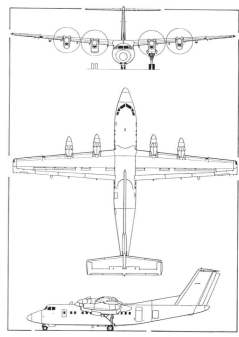

Left: The DHC-7's superb STOL performance was perfect for Norwegian airline Wideroe's needs.

Above: Three-view drawing of the DHC-7 Dash 7 in its basic Series 100 form.

DOUGLAS DC-3

Right: This South Coast Airways DC-3C, now flown on sightseeing and corporate hospitality flights, started life in July 1943 with the USAAF.

Left: Three-view drawing of the Douglas DC-8-73.

Below: The UK has always been a major user of the DC-3. Air Atlantique still has eight in service on charter and aerial survey work.

DOUGLAS DC-8 USA

The decision to launch development of a four-jet medium/long range jetliner was taken by Douglas Aircraft Company in June 1955, almost a year after Boeing had flown its Dash 80 prototype from which the Model 707 family emerged. As the DC-8, the new aircraft was the first Douglas commercial jet and a successor for the DC-7C. It also closely resembled the Boeing 707 in overall configuration, although with slightly less sweepback on the wing. Subject of a launch order from Pan American on 13 October 1955, the DC-8 quickly attracted further orders from US and foreign airlines, and 142 were on order by the time the prototype made its first flight on 30 May 1958. Powered by JT3C turbojets, the prototype represented the medium-range domestic version; other variants were already in production, as detailed below under the Variants heading.

VARIANTS

Subsequent to its introduction, the initial version of the DC-8 was designated the DC-8 Srs 10, distinguishing it from the long-range DC-8 Srs 30 which, with JT3C engines, first flew on 21 February 1959. For airlines requiring enhanced take-off performance in the domestic variant, the DC-8 Srs 20 had the JT4A engines, but operated at the lower Srs 10 weights, and was first flown on 29 November 1958 (being the second DC-8 to fly). As an alternative to the Pratt & Whitney JT4As, Douglas offered to fit Rolls-Royce Conways in the DC-8 Srs 40, first flown on 23 July 1959. During the DC-8's production life, several different versions of the JT4A were fitted in the airliner, with ratings ranging from 66.75kN (15,500lb) to 77.9kN (17,500lb), and the intercontinental Srs 30 and Srs 40 featured extended wing tips and the so-called 'four per cent' wing, the leading edge being modified to increase chord by this amount. The advent of a turbofan adaptation of the JT-3C in the form of the JT-3D led to the appearance of the DC-8 Srs 50, first flown on 20 December 1960, and this was also the basis for the Jet Trader (DC-8 Srs 55) with a side-loading freight door, reinforced

floor and cargo-handling provisions, first flown on 29 October 1962. Up to this point, all DC-8 variants had the same fuselage length, but in April 1965 three new variants were launched, introducing two new fuselage lengths. Known generically as the Sixty Series, these comprised the DC-8 Srs 61 first flown on 14 March 1966, the DC-8 Srs 63 first flown on 10 April 1967 with the same 11.18m (3ft 8in) fuselage stretch but a number of aerodynamic improvements, and the DC-8 Srs 62 with only a 2.03m (6ft 8in) stretch but the same aerodynamic changes, including an

SPECIFICATION
(Douglas DC-8-73)

Dimensions: Wingspan 45.20m (148ft 5in); length overall 57.12m (187ft 5in); height overall 13.11m (43ft 0in), wing area 271.9m² (2,927ft²).
Power Plant: Four CFM International CFM56-2-C5 turbofans, each rated at 97.9kN (22,000lb) or 106.8kN (24,000lb) static thrust.
Weights: Operating weight empty 75,500kg (166,500lb); max take-off 161,025kg (355,000lb); max landing 117,000kg (258,000lb); max payload 29,257kg (64,500lb).
Performance: Max cruising speed 479kts (887km/h); service ceiling 10,000m (32,800ft); take-off field length 3,050m (10,000ft); range with max payload 4,830nm (8,950km).
Accommodation: Flight crew of three. Seating for up to 269 passengers, six-abreast with central aisle. Underfloor cargo/baggage volume 70.80m³ (2,500ft³).

Below: Ivory Coast based multi-national carrier Air Afrique was the only African airline to purchase new DC-8s for its passenger services. This DC-8-50 was its first to be delivered in October 1963.

Right: Cutaway drawing of the DC-8 Series 71. The airframe is structurally unchanged from the 61 in most respects other than the new powerplant, but some systems updating was also part of the conversion programme.

McDonnell Douglas/ Cammacorp DC-8-Super 71 Cutaway Drawing Key

1 Radome
2 Weather radar scanner
3 Air conditioning system ram air intake
4 Pitot tubes
5 Air conditioning units, port and starboard
6 Front pressure bulkhead
7 Rudder pedals
8 Instrument panel
9 Windscreen rain dispersal air ducts
10 Windscreen panels
11 Overhead systems switch panels
12 Co-pilot's seat
13 Cockpit eyebrow window
14 Pilot's seat
15 Cockpit floor level
16 Air system heat exchanger exhausts
17 Nosewheel doors, closed after cycling of undercarriage
18 Landing/taxiing lamps
19 Nosewheel steering jacks
20 Twin nosewheels, forward retracting
21 Nosewheel leg door
22 Nose undercarriage leg pivot point
23 Navigator's station
24 Supernumary crew seat
25 Flight engineer's station
26 Engineer's instrument panels
27 Cockpit bulkhead
28 Avionics equipment racks
29 Forward entry door, open
30 Cabin attendant's folding seat
31 Toilet compartments (2)

32 Wardrobes (2)
33 Forward cabin seating
34 Galley unit
35 VHF aerial
36 Starboard side service door/ emergency exit

37 Outline of freight door (Super 71CF variant) 85in by 140in (216cm by 356cm)
38 Cabin window panels
39 Fuselage lower lobe frame construction
40 Underfloor freight compartment, volume 1,290cu ft (36.53m³)
41 Floor beam construction
42 Starboard side freight door, 54in by 63in (137cm by 160cm)
43 Cabin wall trim panelling
44 Seat mounting rails
45 Main cabin floor panelling
46 Six-abreast passenger seating, 251-seat single class layout
47 Forward cabin emergency exit doors, port and starboard
48 Cabin air distribution ducting
49 Bulk cargo door, 36in by 44in . (91cm by 112cm)
50 Cabin wall soundproof lining
51 Optional auxiliary power unit (APU) installation, port and starboard
52 Fuselage skin panelling
53 Fuselage frame and stringer construction
54 Wing inspection light
55 APU exhaust
56 Runway turn-off lamp
57 Forward cargo bay pressure bulkhead
58 Recirculated air ducting
59 Wing attachment fuselage main frames
60 Wing root joint strap

61 Overwing emergency exit hatches, port and starboard
62 Wing centre section construction
63 Pressure floor above wing carry-through
64 Fuselage centre section construction
65 Fuel system piping
66 Variable leading edge slot operating mechanism

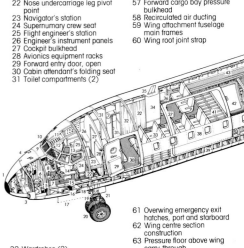

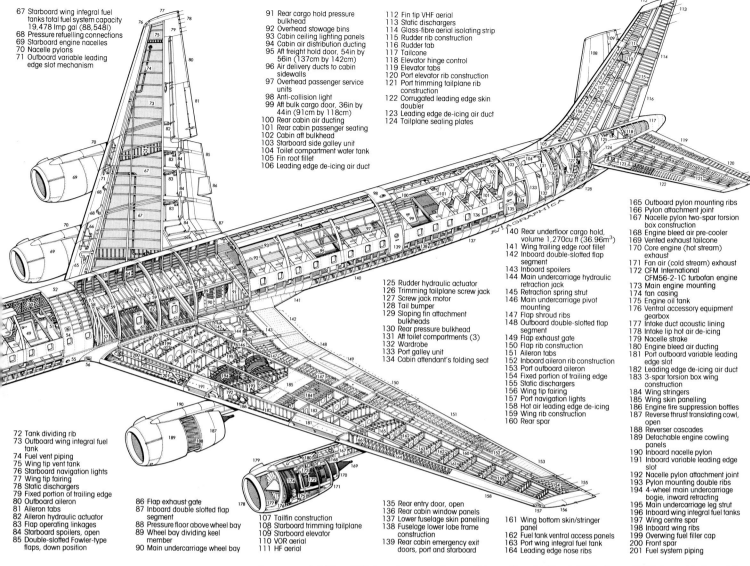

67 Starboard wing integral fuel tanks total fuel system capacity 19,478 Imp gal (88,548l)
68 Pressure refuelling connections
69 Starboard engine nacelles
70 Nacelle pylons
71 Outboard variable leading edge slot mechanism

72 Tank dividing rib
73 Outboard wing integral fuel tank
74 Fuel vent piping
75 Wing tip vent tank
76 Starboard navigation lights
77 Wing tip fairing
78 Static dischargers
79 Fixed portion of trailing edge
80 Outboard aileron
81 Aileron tabs
82 Aileron hydraulic actuator
83 Flap operating linkages
84 Starboard spoilers, open
85 Double-slotted Fowler-type flaps, down position
86 Flap exhaust gate
87 Inboard double slotted flap segment
88 Pressure floor above wheel bay
89 Wheel bay dividing keel member
90 Main undercarriage wheel bay

91 Rear cargo hold pressure bulkhead
92 Overhead stowage bins
93 Cabin ceiling lighting panels
94 Cabin air distribution ducting
95 Aft freight hold door, 54in by 56in (137cm by 142cm)
96 Air delivery ducts to cabin sidewalls
97 Overhead passenger service units
98 Anti-collision light
99 Aft bulk cargo door, 36in by 44in (91cm by 118cm)
100 Rear cabin air ducting
101 Rear cabin passenger seating
102 Cabin aft bulkhead
103 Starboard side galley unit
104 Toilet compartment water tank
105 Fin root fillet
106 Leading edge de-icing air duct

107 Tailfin construction
108 Starboard trimming tailplane
109 Starboard elevator
110 VOR aerial
111 HF aerial
112 Fin tip VHF aerial
113 Static dischargers
114 Glass-fibre aerial isolating strip
115 Rudder rib construction
116 Rudder tab
117 Tailcone
118 Elevator hinge control
119 Elevator tabs
120 Port elevator rib construction
121 Port trimming tailplane rib construction
122 Corrugated leading edge skin doubler
123 Leading edge de-icing air duct
124 Tailplane sealing plates

125 Rudder hydraulic actuator
126 Trimming tailplane screw jack
127 Screw jack motor
128 Tail bumper
129 Sloping fin attachment bulkheads
130 Rear pressure bulkhead
131 Aft toilet compartments (3)
132 Wardrobe
133 Port galley unit
134 Cabin attendant's folding seat
135 Rear entry door, open
136 Rear cabin window panels
137 Lower fuselage skin panelling
138 Fuselage lower lobe frame construction
139 Rear cabin emergency exit doors, port and starboard
140 Rear underfloor cargo hold, volume 1,270cu ft (36.96m³)
141 Wing trailing edge root fillet
142 Inboard double-slotted flap segment
143 Inboard spoilers
144 Main undercarriage hydraulic retraction jack
145 Retraction spring strut
146 Main undercarriage pivot mounting
147 Flap shroud ribs
148 Outboard double-slotted flap segment
149 Flap exhaust gate
150 Flap rib construction
151 Aileron tabs
152 Inboard aileron rib construction
153 Port outboard aileron
154 Fixed portion of trailing edge
155 Static dischargers
156 Wing tip fairing
157 Port navigation lights
158 Hot air leading edge de-icing
159 Wing rib construction
160 Rear spar

161 Wing bottom skin/stringer panel
162 Fuel tank ventral access panels
163 Port wing integral fuel tank
164 Leading edge nose ribs
165 Outboard pylon mounting ribs
166 Pylon attachment joint
167 Nacelle pylon two-spar torsion box construction
168 Engine bleed air pre-cooler
169 Vented exhaust tailcone
170 Core engine (hot stream) exhaust
171 Fan air (cold stream) exhaust
172 CFM International CFM56-2-1C turbofan engine
173 Main engine mounting
174 Fan casing
175 Engine oil tank
176 Ventral accessory equipment gearbox
177 Intake duct acoustic lining
178 Intake lip hot air de-icing
179 Nacelle strake
180 Engine bleed air ducting
181 Port outboard variable leading edge slot
182 Leading edge de-icing air duct
183 3-spar torsion box wing construction
184 Wing stringers
185 Wing skin panelling
186 Engine fire suppression bottles
187 Reverse thrust translating cowl, open
188 Reverser cascades
189 Detachable engine cowling panels
190 Inboard nacelle pylon
191 Inboard variable leading edge slot
192 Nacelle pylon attachment joint
193 Pylon mounting double ribs
194 4-wheel main undercarriage bogie, inward retracting
195 Main undercarriage leg strut
196 Inboard wing integral fuel tanks
197 Wing centre spar
198 Inboard wing ribs
199 Overwing fuel filler cap
200 Front spar
201 Fuel system piping

increase of 1.83m (6ft) in wingspan. Convertible (CF) and all-freight (AF) versions of all three were later offered. In 1979, the Cammacorp company launched a conversion programme to fit CFM56 turbofans to the Sixty Series aircraft, with substantial benefit to economics. The first conversion flew on 15 August 1981 and the designations DC-8 Srs 71, 72 and 73 were adopted for the converted aircraft.

SERVICE USE
The DC-8 Srs 10 was certificated on 31 August 1959, and United Air Lines and Delta Air Lines flew the first revenue services on 18 September. The DC-8 Srs 30 was certificated on 1 February 1960 and was in service with KLM and Pan American on transatlantic services in April. Certification of the DC-8 Srs 40 on 24 March 1960 allowed TCA (now Air Canada) to put this version into operation in April. The DC-8 Srs 50 was certificated on 10 October 1961, and the DC-8 Srs 55 Jet Trader on 29 January 1963. Certification dates for the Sixty Series were 2 September 1966, 27 April 1967 and 30 June 1967, and entry into service dates were 25 February, 22 May and 27 July respectively. The DC-8 Super 71, 72 and 73 were certificated in April, June and September 1982. Production of the DC-8 totalled 556 and ended in May 1972, including 263 of the Super Sixty series, of which 110 had been converted to Super Seventy series when the Cammacorp programme came to an end in March 1986. Some 250 DC-8s, almost exclusively cargo aircraft, remained service in 1998.

Above: Three-view drawing of the Douglas DC-8-73. The Series 71, 72 and 73, are stretched Series 60 DC-8s, retrofitted by Cammacorp with CFM56 turbofans, and some aerodynamic improvements.

Right: After the DC-8 was withdrawn from mainline passenger service, the stretched and re-engined DC-8-70 Series became sought after for the carriage of cargo. Long-established Southern Air Transport operates four DC-8-73F.

EMBRAER EMB-110 BANDEIRANTE BRAZIL

The EMB-110 Bandeirante (pioneer) has played a key role in the successful foundation of a Brazilian aircraft industry of international status and the development of regional air services in this huge country. Development of the Bandeirante began in the late 1960s at the Institute of Research and Development under the direction of French engineer Max Holste, and to meet a specific requirement of the Brazilian air force for a multi-role transport/trainer. Three prototypes were built by the IRD, making their first flights on 26 October 1968, 19 October 1969 and 26 June 1970 respectively, these aircraft being slightly smaller than the later production type and having circular 'port hole' type windows and PT6A-20 engines. To handle production of the aircraft, primarily for the Brazilian air force in the first instance, Embraer (Empresa Brasilièra de Aeronáutica SA) was founded in August 1969, and from the new facilities set up near São Paulo, the first production Bandeirante flew on 9 August 1972 with PT6A-27 engines, slightly lengthened fuselage with 'square' windows and redesigned nacelles. A domestic requirement for a version of the Bandeirante rapidly emerged, and Embraer set about meeting this need as soon as the initial demands of the air force had been met. This gave the company, which was still a largely unknown quantity outside Brazil, an opportunity to build up its experience of civil operations and the confidence subsequently to launch into the export business, in which it has enjoyed substantial success.

VARIANTS

After production of the EMB-110, EMB-110A and EMB-110B versions for the Brazilian Air Force, the first version of the Bandeirante intended specifically

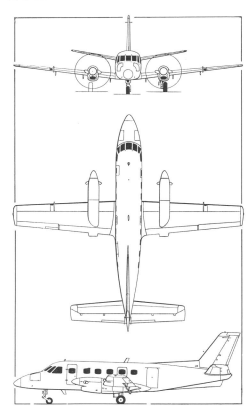

Above: Three-view drawing of the Embraer EMB-110P1A variant, showing the dihedral tailplane that distinguishes it from the other models that have been manufactured.

SPECIFICATION
(Embraer EMB-110P2/41 Bandeirante)

Dimensions: Wingspan 15.32m (50ft 3in); length overall 15.10m (49ft 6½in); height overall 4.92m (16ft 2in), wing area 29.1m² (313.2ft²).
Power Plant: Two 559kW (750shp) Pratt & Whitney Canada PT6A-34turboprops with Hartzell three-blade reversible-pitch autofeathering metal propellers.
Weights: Operating weight empty 3,833kg (8,450lb); max take-off 5,900kg (13,007lb); max landing 5,700kg (12,566lb); max payload 1,561kg (3,443lb).
Performance: Max cruising speed 248kts (459km/h); max rate of climb 9.4m/s (1,787ft/min); service ceiling 6,860m (22,500ft); take-off field length 431m (1,414ft); landing field length 565m (1,854ft); range with typical payload 1,060nm (1,964km).
Accommodation: Two pilots and seating for 19 passengers, two-abreast with single aisle. Total cargo/baggage volume front and rear 2.0m³ (70.6ft³).

for commercial use, as a 15-passenger feeder-liner operated by Brazilian third-level airlines, was the EMB-110C. It was followed by the EMB-110P, developed more specifically for export markets, with PT6A-27 engines and accommodation for up to 18 passengers; the maximum weight of this version was 5,600kg (12,345lb). After a lengthened version of the Bandeirante had been developed for military use as a cargo carrier (the EMB-110K1) with a 0.85m (2ft 9½in) fuselage plug and upward-opening freight-loading door aft of the wing, this same longer fuselage was adopted for the EMB-110P1 and EMB-120P2 commercial versions, the former

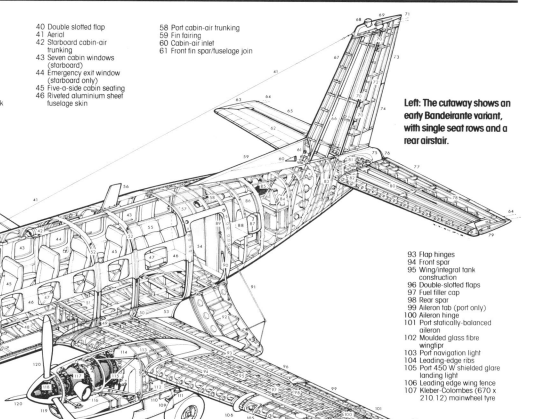

Embraer EMB-110 Bandeirante Cutaway Drawing Key

1 Nose cone
2 Radar array (Bendix RDR-1200 or RCA AVQ-47)
3 Nosewheel well
4 Nosewheel doors (close after activation)
5 Pitot probe

19 Second pilot's seat
20 Clear vision panel
21 Pilot's adjustable seat
22 Control column
23 Rudder pedals
24 ADF antenna
25 Forward/centre fuselage join
26 Port cloaks/stores
27 Aerial mast
28 Starboard equipment rack

40 Double slotted flap
41 Aerial
42 Starboard cabin-air trunking
43 Seven cabin windows (starboard)
44 Emergency exit window (starboard only)
45 Five-a-side cabin seating
46 Riveted aluminium sheet fuselage skin

58 Port cabin-air trunking
59 Fin fairing
60 Cabin-air inlet
61 Front fin spar/fuselage join

Left: The cutaway shows an early Bandeirante variant, with single seat rows and a rear airstair.

93 Flap hinges
94 Front spar
95 Wing/integral tank construction
96 Double-slotted flaps
97 Fuel filler cap
98 Rear spar
99 Aileron tab (port only)
100 Aileron hinge
101 Port statically-balanced aileron
102 Moulded glass fibre wingtip
103 Port navigation light
104 Leading-edge ribs
105 Port 450 W shielded glare landing light
106 Leading edge wing fence
107 Kleber-Colombes (670 x 210.12) mainwheel tyre

6 250W taxi light
7 Nosewheel fork
8 Goodyear 6.50 x 8 nosewheel tyre
9 Nosewheel oleo (by ERAM)
10 Nosewheel oleo flap
11 External power socket
12 Avionics bay
13 Avionics bay access doors (upward hinged)
14 Bulkhead
15 Plexiglass windscreen side panels
16 13-mm stressed acrylic windscreen centre panels
17 Instrument panel shroud
18 Variable speed wipers

29 Starboard nacelle
30 Spinner
31 Hartzell HC-B3TN-3C/T10178H-8R constant speed propeller
32 Leading-edge wing fence
33 Starboard 450 W shielded glare landing light
34 Riveted aluminium sheet wing skin
35 Starboard navigation light
36 Aileron static dischargers
37 Starboard statically-balanced aileron
38 Fuel filler cap
39 Two wing integral fuel tanks each side (total capacity 370 Imp gal/1,690l)

47 Five cabin windows (port)
48 Floor support structure (stressed for cargo)
49 Front spar/fuselage steel join
50 Rear spar/fuselage steel join
51 Centre box structure
52 Main fuselage frames
53 Wingroot fairing
54 Entry door with integral steps
55 Three-place bench seat (C-95: optional cargo space)
56 Dorsal antenna
57 Cabin rear bulkhead (cargo compartment)

62 Starboard tailplane
63 Elevator balance
64 Elevator static dischargers
65 Starboard elevator
66 All-metal cantilever fin
67 Fin leading-edge
68 Anti-collision beacon
69 Rudder balance
70 Rudder hinges
71 Rudder static dischargers
72 Rudder structure
73 Rudder tab (upper)
74 Rudder tab (lower)
75 Tail cone
76 Rear navigation light
77 Elevator tab
78 Port elevator
79 Elevator balance

80 All-metal cantilever tailplane
81 Tailplane centre-section structure
82 Tailplane/fuselage join
83 Angled fuselage frames
84 Air trunking
85 Aircycle air-conditioning plant
86 Aft cabin bulkhead
87 Aft window (port and starboard)
88 Rear single seat (C-95: optional cargo space)
89 Entry door frame
90 Door actuating cylinder
91 Handrails
92 Entry steps

108 Mainwheel door (closes after activation)
109 Mainwheel fork
110 Mainwheel oleo flap
111 Mainwheel oleo leg (by ERAM)
112 Mainwheel well
113 Nacelle structure
114 Firewall
115 Engine bearers
116 Exhaust trunk
117 Pratt & Whitney (Canada) PT6A-27 turboprop
118 Propeller auto-feather/reverse pitch
119 Air intake
120 Hartzell three-blade propeller

Left: Although the Bandeirante was developed specifically to open up the interior of Brazil, it has seen prolific use in the UK, including extensive night postal service for the Royal Mail; shown here is an improved EMB-110P1A.

Below: Based on the outskirts of Paris, Aigle Azur was one of the many French third-level airlines which found the 18-seat aircraft comfortable and economical to operate. This EMB-110P1 was operates cross-Channel from Rouen to London.

being for mixed or all-cargo operations with the same door as the K1 and quick-change facilities, and the latter being a dedicated airliner with up to 21 seats. The EMB-110P2, which became the major civil variant, first flew on 3 May 1977, and in 1981 was joined by the EMB-110P2/41, which was certificated at a maximum take-off weight of 5,900kg (13,010lb), an increase of 230kg (510lb), in accordance with the provisions of the US SFAR Pt 41 regulations. The EMB-110P1/41 was the equivalent quick-change version. In 1983, after 438 Bandeirantes had been deliv-

ered, a series of changes was introduced to improve passenger comfort and handling; the most obvious external change concerned the tailplane which acquired 10 degrees of dihedral. The commercial versions previously described, but with these new features, were then designated EMB-110PA, EMB-110P2 and EMB-110P2A-41. The designation EMB-110E(J) applied to a seven-seat corporate transport version of the Bandeirante, and the EMB-110S1 was a geophysical survey version, with provision for wing-tip tanks similar to those developed for the EMB-111, a maritime patrol version. Embraer projected in the early 1980s a pressurised version of the Bandeirante, the EMB-110P3, but it was discontinued before a prototype had flown.

SERVICE USE

The original EMB-110 military transport version was certificated to FAR Pt 23 standards, providing a basis for the subsequent approval of individual variants. The civil EMB-110C entered airline service on 16 April 1973, with Transbrasil, and the EMB-110P entered service with TABA, also in Brazil, early in 1976. The first EMB-110P1/41 was delivered to Provincetown-Boston Airlines in the USA during the spring of 1981, and this operator was also the first to receive the EMB-110P1A variant, in December 1983. When production ended in 1995, a total of 494 aircraft had been built, with the last being delivered to the Brazilian Air Force.

EMBRAER EMB-120 BRASILIA BRAZIL

Very soon after the Bandeirante had been established in production by the newly-founded Embraer organization at Sao José dos Campos near Sao Paulo, a series of related projects was drawn up under EMB-12X designations. These grew out of a wish to produce a pressurised version of the Bandeirante, and the three projects shared a common fuselage diameter with different lengths; the smallest was the EMB-121 Xingu, which made use of the Bandeirante's wing (with slightly reduced span) and was intended as a business transport. Production of the Xingu eventually proceeded (about 100 being built), but neither the EMB-120 Araguaia nor the EMB-123 Tapajos were developed in the form projected in 1975, with 20 and 10 seats respectively, a 'Xingu-diameter' fuselage and a new supercritical wing with tip tanks. The concept of a pressurised regional airliner somewhat larger than the Bandeirante continued to interest the Brazilian design team, however, and by 1979 market surveys had convinced the company that its next step should be to develop a regional airliner in the 30-seat category. Development was launched officially in September 1979. The EMB-120 designation was retained for the new project, which was named Brasilia in due course, and which retained the same overall configuration as the earlier Araguaia: it was thus a twin-engined low-wing monoplane with a circular-section fuselage and a T-tail. To power the Brasilia, Embraer turned once again to Pratt & Whitney in Canada, selecting that company's new turboprop that was then being developed as the PT7A-1 and would enter production as the PW100 series. In the 1,119kW (1,500shp) version originally selected for the Brasilia, this engine was designated PW115 and began flight tests on 27 February 1982 in the nose of Pratt & Whitney's Vickers Viscount testbed in a representative Brasilia nacelle. Metal was cut for the first aircraft on 6 May 1981. Six airframes were put in hand for the development, test and certification of the Brasilia: of these, three were the flying prototypes. First flights were made by these three aircraft on 27 July 1983, 21 December 1983 and 9 May 1984.

VARIANTS

Initial production models of the basic EMB-120 had 1.118kW (1,500shp) PW115 engines and a maximum take-off weight of 10,800kg (23,810lb), replaced at an early stage with higher output PW115s of 1,193kW (1,600shp). The more powerful 1,342kW (1,800shp) PW118 was introduced in 1986 in the EMB-120RT (Reduced Take-off) to provide

SPECIFICATION
(Embraer EMB-120ER Advanced)

Dimensions: Wingspan 19.78m (64ft 10¾in); length overall 20.00m (65ft 7½in); height overall 6.35m (20ft 10in), wing area 39.43m² (424.4ft²).
Power Plant: Two 1,342kW (1,800shp) Pratt & Whitney Canada PW118 or PW118A turboprops with Hamilton Standard four-blade reversible-pitch fully-feathering propellers with aluminium spars and glassfibre blades.
Weights: Operating weight empty 7,580kg (16,711lb); max take-off 11,990kg (26,433lb); max landing 11,700kg (25,794lb); max payload 3,320kg (7,319lb).
Performance: Max cruising speed 298kts (552km/h); max rate of climb 10.2m/s (2,000ft/min); service ceiling 9,145m (30,000ft); take-off field length 1,560m (5,118ft); landing field length 1,380m (4,528ft); range with typical payload 800nm (1,480km).
Accommodation: Two pilots and seating for up to 30 passengers, three-abreast with single aisle. Total baggage volume in rear compartment 6.4m³ (226ft³).

Embraer EMB-120 Brasilia Cutaway Drawing Key

1 Radome
2 Weather radar scanner
3 ILS glideslope aerial
4 Radar mounting bulkhead
5 Nose compartment construction
6 Avionics equipment bay
7 Access doors from wheel bay
8 Nose undercarriage wheel bay
9 Cooling air scoop
10 Radio and electronics racks
11 Nosewheel hydraulic retraction jack
12 Nosewheel leg doors
13 Nose undercarriage leg strut
14 Twin nosewheels
15 Torque scissor links
16 Hydraulic steering jacks
17 Taxiing lamps (2)
18 Battery
19 Cooling air outlet grille
20 Front pressure bulkhead
21 Windscreen wipers
22 Curved windscreen panels
23 Instrument panel shroud
24 Instrument panel CRT displays
25 Angle of attack vane
26 Rudder pedals
27 Ground power supply socket
28 Pitot tube
29 Temperature probe
30 Underfloor control linkages
31 Cockpit floor level
32 Nosewheel steering control
33 'Rams-horn' control column
34 Co-pilot's seat
35 Overhead systems switch panel
36 Cockpit roof framing
37 Cockpit/passenger cabin doorway
38 Cockpit rear bulkhead
39 Pilot's seat
40 Safety harness
41 Opening side window panel
42 Cabin attendant's folding seat
43 Entry lobby
44 Main entry door (open)
45 Integral airstairs
46 Folding handrail
47 Fuselage frame-and-stringer construction
48 Fuselage skin panelling
49 Cabin window panels
50 Forward cabin seating (30-seat layout)
51 VHF aerial

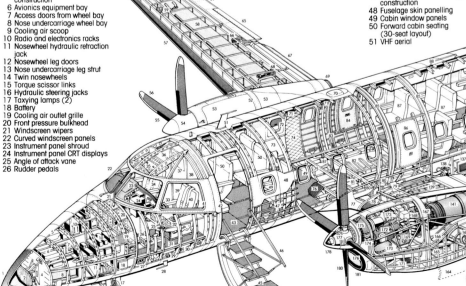

better field performance at a higher 11,500kg (25,353lb) weight, and this variant was also available from later that year in hot-and-high specification with PW118As. Since 1994, the standard production version is the EMB-120ER Advanced, previously referred to as EMB-120X. In addition to increased range through higher T-O weight, the ER also incorporates aerodynamic improvements, including new leading-edges for all flying surfaces, and re-designed cockpit and cabin features to increase comfort levels. The Brasilia has also been produced in all-cargo, Combi and QC (Quick-Change) versions; and the Brazilian Air Force has ordered two military derivatives, the EMB-120SA for airborne early warning (AEW) and EMB-120RS for remote sensing.

SERVICE USE

The Brasilia was certificated by the Brazilian CTA on 16 May 1985, followed by FAA approval (to FAR Pt 25) on July 9. British certification was confirmed in April 1986. The second prototype was the subject of a formal handover to the first customer, Atlantic Southeast Airlines of Atlanta, Georgia, on 1 June 1985 during the Paris air show, but this was for crew training purposes only and the first production aircraft for ASA went into service in October. Two early-standard aircraft were delivered to DLT in Germany in the same month, and in 1986 the first 18-seat corporate version of the Brasilia was handed over to United Technologies Corporation. The first EMB-120QC was handed over to Total Linhas Aéreas of Brazil on 14 May 1993, while the first two production EMB-120ER went to Great Lakes Aviation in December 1994. At 1 January 1998, the Brasilia had logged 331 orders, of which 330 had been delivered. Orders have slowed and production is likely to end when the ERJ 135 jet comes into service in 1999.

Left: Although most operate in the Americas, several airlines in Europe have chosen the Brasilia over local aircraft. Dutch airline Air Excel Commuter flies two.

Above: Pantanal Linhas Aereas is one of several Brazilian regional airlines to operate the 30-seat Embraer Brasilia, alongside the smaller Bandeirante aircraft.

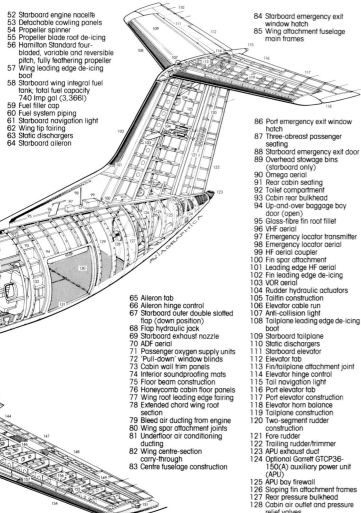

52 Starboard engine nacelle
53 Detachable cowling panels
54 Propeller spinner
55 Propeller blade root de-icing
56 Hamilton Standard four-bladed, variable and reversible pitch, fully feathering propeller
57 Wing leading edge de-icing boot
58 Starboard wing integral fuel tank; total fuel capacity 740 Imp gal (3,366l)
59 Fuel filler cap
60 Fuel system piping
61 Starboard navigation light
62 Wing tip fairing
63 Static dischargers
64 Starboard aileron
65 Aileron tab
66 Aileron hinge control
67 Starboard outer double slotted flap (down position)
68 Flap hydraulic jack
69 Starboard exhaust nozzle
70 ADF aerial
71 Passenger oxygen supply units
72 'Pull-down' window blinds
73 Cabin wall trim panels
74 Interior soundproofing mats
75 Floor beam construction
76 Honeycomb cabin floor panels
77 Wing root leading edge fairing
78 Extended chord wing root section
79 Bleed air ducting from engine
80 Wing spar attachment joints
81 Underfloor air conditioning ducting
82 Wing centre-section carry-through
83 Centre fuselage construction

84 Starboard emergency exit window hatch
85 Wing attachment fuselage main frames
86 Port emergency exit window hatch
87 Three-abreast passenger seating
88 Starboard emergency exit door
89 Overhead stowage bins (starboard only)
90 Omega aerial
91 Rear cabin seating
92 Toilet compartment
93 Cabin rear bulkhead
94 Up-and-over baggage bay door (open)
95 Glass-fibre fin root fillet
96 VHF aerial
97 Emergency locator transmitter
98 Emergency locator aerial
99 HF aerial coupler
100 Fin spar attachment
101 Leading edge HF aerial
102 Fin leading edge de-icing
103 VOR aerial
104 Rudder hydraulic actuators
105 Tailfin construction
106 Elevator cable run
107 Anti-collision light
108 Tailplane leading edge de-icing boot
109 Starboard tailplane
110 Static dischargers
111 Starboard elevator
112 Elevator tab
113 Fin/tailplane attachment joint
114 Elevator hinge control
115 Tail navigation light
116 Port elevator tab
117 Port elevator construction
118 Elevator horn balance
119 Tailplane construction
120 Two-segment rudder construction
121 Fore rudder
122 Trailing rudder/trimmer
123 APU exhaust duct
124 Optional Garrett GTCP36-150(A) auxiliary power unit (APU)
125 APU bay firewall
126 Sloping fin attachment frames
127 Rear pressure bulkhead
128 Cabin air outlet and pressure relief valves

129 Baggage compartment
130 Baggage loading floor
131 Baggage loading doorway
132 Galley unit
133 Overhead passenger service units
134 Air conditioning delivery ducts
135 Floor level ventilating air ducts
136 Trailing edge root fillet
137 Heat exchanger
138 Port air conditioning plant
139 Port wing inboard integral fuel tank
140 Inboard double-slotted flap
141 Jet pipe
142 Exhaust nozzle
143 Nacelle 'Flapette'
144 Port outer double-slotted flap
145 Flap hydraulic jack
146 Honeycomb flap shroud panel
147 Flap rib construction
148 Aileron tab
149 Port aileron rib construction
150 Static dischargers
151 Compass flux valve
152 Glass-fibre wing tip fairing
153 Port navigation light
154 Leading edge de-icing boot
155 Fuel filler cap
156 Wing rib construction
157 Leading edge honeycomb construction
158 Port wing outboard integral fuel tank
159 Three-spar wing torsion box assembly
160 Main undercarriage pivot fixing
161 Landing lamp (port and starboard)
162 Main undercarriage leg strut
163 Twin mainwheels
164 Mainwheel doors (closed after cycling of undercarriage leg)
165 Mainwheel bay
166 Engine nacelle construction
167 Main engine mounting ring frame
168 Pratt & Whitney Canada PW115 turboprop
169 Engine integral oil tank
170 Particle separator intake air duct
171 Oil cooler
172 Electronic engine control units
173 Engine accessory equipment
174 Gearbox mounting
175 Propeller reduction gearbox
176 Engine air intake
177 Propeller hub pitch change mechanism
178 Port propeller spinner
179 Port Hamilton Standard 4-bladed propeller
180 Propeller blade root de-icing
181 Engine intake lip de-icing system

Above: InterBrasil Star received the 300th Brasilia in September 1995. It operates three EMB-120ER versions in a quick-change (cargo–passengers) configuration.

Below: Three-view of the EMB-120 Brasilia, retaining the basic shape for all models, but developed with higher take-off weights, more powerful engines and better aerodynamics.

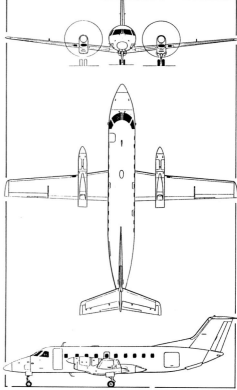

EMBRAER RJ145 BRAZIL

Having established its position in the commuter market with the Bandeirante and Brasilia, Embraer studied a number of projects to enable it to keep a foothold in the market by introducing a new type at the appropriate time. A joint development with Shorts, agreed in May 1984, was stillborn, but the CBA-123 of 1986, which involved Fabrica Militar de Aviones (FMA) of Argentina went a great deal further. Using a new supercritical wing, the design was unusual in having two pusher turboprops located high on the rear fuselage. First flight was planned for March 1990. However, the general clamour for jet aircraft persuaded Embraer to change direction. Original development plans for a twin-jet regional aircraft were revealed at the Paris air show on 12 June 1989, which showed a low-risk 50-seat Brasilia development with wing-mounted turbofan engines, but the programme was put in abeyance by company cutbacks in Autumn 1990. The following years were spent on a substantial re-design of the wing, landing gear and engine installation, with the latter moved to the rear of the fuselage in October 1991. Extensive wind-tunnel testing confirmed, and in some cases

exceeded, performance predictions, and the first metal for the RJ 145, as it was now known, was cut in September 1993. Assembly of the prototype began in October 1994, and this made its first flight on 11 August 1995, ahead of the official roll-out. Three pre-series aircraft were flown on 17 November 1995 and on 14 February and 2 April 1996. The RJ145 programme is being financed by Embraer (34 per cent); four major risk sharing partners comprising C&D Interiors (USA), Enaer (Chile) Gamesa (Spain) and Sonaca (Belgium); some 70 risk-sharing suppliers (10 per cent); and Brazilian development funding institutions (23 per cent).

VARIANTS

Basic initial production version is the RJ 145, which was certificated in 1996 by the Brazilian DCA to FAR/JAR 25, FAR Pt.36, ICAO Annex 16 and FAR Pt.121. FAA certification followed in December 1996 and the European type approval was given by the JAA on 15 May 1997. Also available are the RJ145ER (Extended Range), RJ145EU, RJ145EP, RJ145MR and RJ145LR (long-range) models with increased take-off weight and payload/range performance. Both models are powered by the Allison AE 3007A turbofan. Five aircraft are to be fitted with the Ericsson Erieye airborne-early-warning and control systems for use by the Brazilian Government on its SIVAM surveillance programme. The company has launched a shortened 37-seat derivative, the EMB-135, using a derated AE3007, and is planning a stretched EMB-170 for 70 passengers. The EMB-170 would have a wider fuselage, 610mm (2ft) wing-root extensions and leading-edge slats, and a 45kN (10,000lb) thrust growth version of the Allison AE3007.

SERVICE USE

At 1 January 1998, sales of the RJ 145 stood at 171 firm and 228 options. Thirty-seven had been delivered, starting with US launch customer Continental Express. The first European customers were Regional Airlines of France and Portugese jet operator Portugalia, both of which took delivery of their aircraft in May 1997.

SPECIFICATION
(Embraer RJ 145ER)

Dimensions: Wingspan 20.04m (65ft 9in); length overall 29.87 m (98ft 0in); height overall 6.75m (22ft 1¾in), wing area 51.18m² (550.9ft²).
Power Plant: Two 31.3kN (7,040lb) Rolls-Royce Allison AE 3007A turbofans with FADEC.
Weights: Operating weight empty 11,585kg (25,540lb); max take-off 20,600kg (45,415lb); max landing 18,700kg (41,226lb); max payload 5,515kg (12,158lb).
Performance: Max cruising speed 410kts (760km/h); max rate of climb 12.1m/s (2,380ft/min); service ceiling 11,275m (37,000ft); take-off field length 1,500m (4,925ft); landing field length 1,290m (4,235ft); range with max payload 1,200nm (2,222km).
Accommodation: Flight crew of two. Seating for 50 passengers, three-abreast with single aisle. Total baggage volume 14.75m³ (520.9ft³).

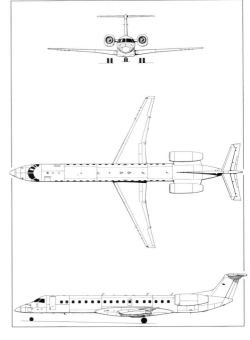

Above: The Embraer RJ145 went through a number of engine metamorphoses before it was decided to settle on the rear-mounted jet engines.

Right: Launch customer Continental Express has has 50 Embraer RJ145 on firm order, with another 200 options. It has been in service since April 1997.

Embraer RJ 145 Cutaway Drawing Key

Structure and general
1 Upward hinging composite nosecone
2 Machined nose-undercarriage support
3 Machined and etched pressure-bulkhead
4 Instrument panel
5 Panel shroud
6 Co-pilot's seat
7 Rearward sliding side emergency window
8 Centre console
9 Pilot's fully adjustable seat
10 Cockpit oxygen supply
11 Wardrobe/baggage compartment
12 Fire extinguisher
13 Attendant's seat (folding type)
14 Main door incorporating fully folding airstair

15 Stowage compartment
16 Service/emergency door
17 Galley
18 Single class adjustable cabin seat
19 Skin joint/doubler panel
20 Typical built-up fuselage frame
21 Under floor construction incorporating seat tracks

Below: Portuguese regional airline company Portugalia has ordered six Embraer RJ145s to supplement its larger Fokker 100s. The RJ145 entered service with Portugalia in June 1997 and achieves a daily utilisation of seven hours. Portugalia was one of the very first European customers for this particular aircraft.

Right: The Embraer RJ145 has gone through a number of metamorphoses during its development, beginning with pusher turboprop engines, followed by turbofans positioned on the wings, before it was finally decided to settle on the rear-mounted jet engines we see on the aircraft today.

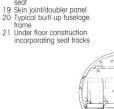

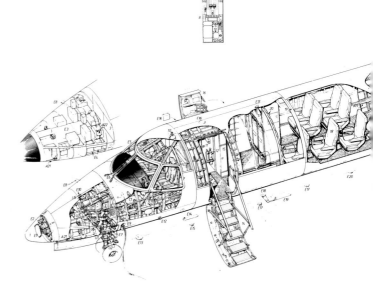

22 Cabin side-seat tracks
23 Cabin insulation
24 Machined wing pick-ups
25 Centre stub-wing assembly
26 Emergency door
27 Internal doubler
28 Three-section wing leading-edge assembly
29 Wing to fuselage fairing
30 Wing inspection panels
31 Machined forward and rear spar
32 Machined wing skin and integral stringers
33 Main landing gear bay
34 Aft stub-wing assembly incorporating main-gear well and machined ski for abnormal landing protection
35 Cabin side panel
36 Window blind
37 Overhead luggage bin

48 Avionics rear rack
49 Aft pressure bulkhead
50 Sloping frames providing vertical fin mounting points
51 Auxiliary power unit (APU) mounting frame
52 Three-spar vertical fin assembly
53 Two-spar continuous taper variable incidence tailplane
54 Static discharge wicks

Air-conditioning and anti-icing
A1 Bleed air from APU
A2 Fin leading-edge anti-icing duct
A3 Tailplane leading-edge piccolo tube
A4 Bleed air-to-air turbine starter
A5 Engine bleed air
A6 Bleed air inter-cooler
A7 Nacelle air inlet anti-icing

A14 PHE exhaust
A15 Re-circulation fans
A16 Noise attenuators
A17 Distribution inter-connector duct
A18 Under floor heating vents
A20 Air-to-cockpit heating ducts
A21 NACA air inlet for forward avionics bay
A22 Cooling exhaust duct

Controls
C1 Adjustable rudder pedals
C2 Control yoke
C3 Aileron control pulleys
C4 Aileron control cable fair leads
C5 Aileron bell-crank
C6 Hydraulic actuator
C7 Neutral recovery unit
C8 Aileron hinges
C9 All-speed aileron

C10 Rudder/elevator control runs
C11 Rudder power control unit
C12 Rudder hydraulic actuators
C13 Dual rudder (trailing rudder automatically deflected for trim)
C14 Tailplane pitch – dual screw-jack actuators
C15 Elevator control linkage
C16 Spring tab
C17 Servo tab
C18 Mass balance
C19 Flap track guide slots
C20 Screw-jack actuator
C21 Screw-jack actuator shaft
C22 Actuator flexible drive shaft
C23 Flap central-guide track
C24 Double slotted fixed-vane flap
C25 Flap track aerodynamic fairing
C26 Flap vane spacer
C27 Flap guide roller
C28 Speed-break spoiler
C29 Ground spoiler
C30 Flexible shaft-drive unit
C31 Leading-edge vortex generators

Avionics and electrical
E1 Honeywell Primus 1000 weather radar
E2 Glide-slope antenna
E3 Forward avionics bay
E4 Batteries 28V 400Ah

E5 Electrically heated windscreen
E6 Electrically operated windscreen wipers
E7 Undercarriage landing lights
E8 Hearted pitot heads
E9 Ground receptacle point
E10 MLS antennae
E11 Angle-of-attack vane
E12 Total air-temperature probe
E13 TACAS II antenna
E14 MB2 antenna
E15 DME 1 antenna
E16 GPS unit and antenna
E17 TDR antennae
E18 VHF II antenna
E19 MB IU antenna
E20 ME II antenna
E21 VHF I antenna
E22 Red anti-collision beacon

E34 Flitephone antenna
E35 HF ANTENNA
E36 Omega antenna
E37 VOR/LOC antenna
E38 Optional logo-light

Fuel system
F1 Wing fuel cell – 2,590 litres
F2 Vent surge tank with NACA inlet below wing
F3 Fuel tank end rib
F4 Fuel float valve
F5 Fuel-vent valve
F6 Re-fuelling pilot valve
F7 Fuel-vent line
F8 Fuel-tank gravity filler point
F9 Pressure refuelling-defuelling in starboard fuselage fairing
F10 Collector tank

Powerplant
P1 Allison AE 30007 high by-pass turbofan – 31-3kN (FADEC installed in fuselage)
P2 Engine forward-pylon mount

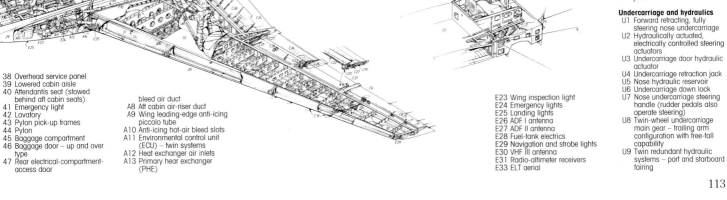

38 Overhead service panel
39 Lowered cabin aisle
40 Attendantis seat (stowed behind aft cabin seats)
41 Emergency light
42 Lavatory
43 Pylon pick-up frames
44 Pylon
45 Baggage compartment
46 Baggage door – up and over type
47 Rear electrical-compartment-access door

bleed air duct
A8 Aft cabin air-riser duct
A9 Wing leading-edge anti-icing piccolo tube
A10 Anti-icing hot-air bleed slots
A11 Environmental control unit (ECU) – twin systems
A12 Heat exchanger air inlets
A13 Primary hear exchanger (PHE)

E23 Wing inspection light
E24 Emergency lights
E25 Landing lights
E26 ADF I antenna
E27 ADF II antenna
E28 Fuel-tank electrics
E29 Navigation and strobe lights
E30 VHF III antenna
E31 Radio-altimeter receivers
E33 ELT aerial

P3 Engine rear-pylon mount
P4 Exhaust mixer
P5 Inert after body exhaust fairing
P6 Upper fixed cowling
P7 Engine noise-suppression zone
P8 Hinged lower cowling
P9 Engine/APU extinguisher bottles
P10 Engine-mounted generator cooling inlet ducts
P11 APU cooling vent
P12 APU air inlet
P13 APU exhaust
P14 APIC, APS-500 APU – 18.5kW
P15 Engine fire extinguisher pipes
P16 Thrust reverser
P17 Primary door lock (two off)
P18 Door lock latches
P19 Thrust reverser door actuation jack

Undercarriage and hydraulics
U1 Forward retracting, fully steering nose undercarriage
U2 Hydraulically actuated, electrically controlled steering actuators
U3 Undercarriage door hydraulic actuator
U4 Undercarriage retraction jack
U5 Nose hydraulic reservoir
U6 Undercarriage down lock
U7 Nose undercarriage steering handle (rudder pedals also operate steering)
U8 Twin-wheel undercarriage main gear – trailing arm configuration with free-fall capability
U9 Twin redundant hydraulic systems – port and starboard fairing

FAIRCHILD (SWEARINGEN) METRO USA

The Metro has its origins with the company formed by Ed Swearingen, which used the Beechcraft Queen Air as the basis of a family of business aircraft known as the Merlin I, II and IIB. By continuous refinement and development, Swearingen eventually replaced all major components of the Queen Air to produce the Metro, a 19-seat commuter transport, with a parallel version for the corporate market known as the Merlin III. The Metro first flew on 26 August 1969 and production was well under way by the time the Swearingen company was taken over in November 1971, by the Fairchild Industries Corporation. As Fairchild Swearingen, the company continued to produce the Metro at its San Antonio plant, and to develop new variants. The Swearingen name was later dropped, the Texas branch of Fairchild Industries then becoming the Fairchild Aircraft Corporation.

VARIANTS

The original SA-226TC Metro was followed in 1974 by the Metro II, which introduced some internal

SPECIFICATION
(Fairchild Metro 23)

Dimensions: Wingspan 17.37m (57ft 0in); length overall 18.10m (59ft 5in); height overall 5.08m (16ft 8in), wing area 28.71m² (309ft²).
Power Plant: Two 776kW (1,000shp) AlliedSignal TPE331-11U-612G turboprops with McCauley four-blade reversible-pitch fully-feathering metal propellers.
Weights: Operating weight empty 4,300kg (9,480lb); max take-off 7,484kg (16,500lb); max landing 7,110kg (15,675lb); max payload 2,277kg (5,020lb).
Performance: Max cruising speed 290kts (537km/h); max rate of climb 13.7m/s (2,700ft/min); service ceiling 7,620m (25,000ft); take-off field length 1,341m (4,400ft); landing field length 1,273m (4,175ft); range with typical payload 540nm (1,000km).
Accommodation: One or two pilots and seating for up to 20 passengers, two-abreast with single aisle. Total cargo/baggage volume front and rear 5.05m³ (178.5ft³).

changes, 'square' cabin windows and the optional installation of a small rocket unit in the tail to improve take-off performance in hot-and-high conditions as encountered in many areas where the Metro was likely to operate. Like the initial model, the Metro II was restricted to a gross weight of 5,670kg (12,500lb) to comply with US regulations for commuter airliners. When this restriction was lifted, by Special Federal Aviation Regulation (SFAR) 41, Fairchild introduced in 1980 the Metro IIA at a gross weight of 5,941kg (13,100lb), and followed this with further improvements in the SA-227AC Metro III at 6,350kg (14,000lb). Structural changes and uprated engines made the increased operating weights possible, and the standard aircraft was subsequently approved for 6,577kg (14,500lb), with an option at 7,257kg (16,000lb). Other changes distinguishing the Metro III from the Metro II included an extension of 3.05m (10ft) in wing span, with conical cambered wing tips to reduce drag; new landing gear doors; more streamlined nacelle cowlings; and Dowty Rotol four-blade propellers. Large loading doors in

Fairchild Metro II Cutaway Drawing Key

1 Radome
2 Weather radar scanner
3 Oxygen bottle
4 Radio and electronics equipment
5 Nosewheel door
6 Baggage restraint net
7 Baggage doors, forward opening
8 Fuselage nose construction
9 Nose baggage hold
10 Landing and taxi lamp
11 Nosewheel leg
12 Twin nosewheels
13 Torque scissors
14 Pitot tube
15 Cockpit pressure bulkhead
16 Windscreen panels
17 Instrument panel shroud
18 Curved centre panel
19 Windscreen wipers
20 Rudder pedals
21 Control column
22 Co-pilot's seat
23 Cockpit roof construction
24 Cockpit bulkhead
25 Electrical panels
26 Pilot's seat
27 Pilot's side control panel
28 Passenger door
29 Airstairs
30 Handrails
31 Entry doorway
32 Cabin centre aisle floor
33 Air conditioning duct louvre
34 Forward fuselage frame construction
35 Starboard engine cowlings
36 Engine intake
37 Hartzell three-bladed constant-speed reversing and feathering propeller
38 Propeller de-icing boot
39 Leading edge de-icing
40 Starboard wing fuel tank, capacity 270 Imp gal (1,226l)
41 Starboard navigation light
42 Fuel filler cap
43 Starboard aileron
44 Static dischargers
45 Starboard flap
46 Tailpipe exhaust duct
47 Fuselage frames
48 Cabin interior trim panels
49 Passenger seats
50 Window side panel
51 Cabin floor construction
52 Seat rails
53 Air trunking
54 Cabin windows
55 Starboard emergency escape hatches
56 Main fuselage frames
57 Centre box construction
58 Port emergency escape hatch
59 Starboard seating, 10 passengers

Right: Cutaway drawing of the Fairchild Metro II, one of the earliest and now most successful of the 19-seaters.

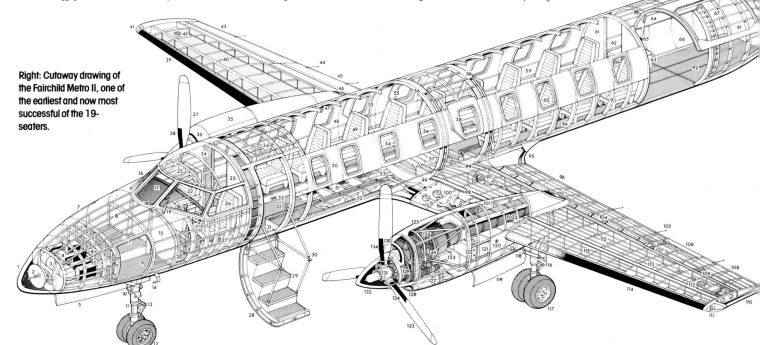

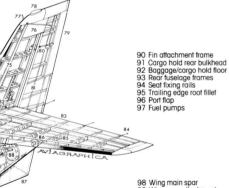

90 Fin attachment frame
91 Cargo hold rear bulkhead
92 Baggage/cargo hold floor
93 Rear fuselage frames
94 Seat fixing rails
95 Trailing edge root fillet
96 Port flap
97 Fuel pumps

98 Wing main spar
99 Wing spar attachment
100 Air conditioning plant
101 Engine cowling construction
102 Tailpipe
103 Engine exhaust duct
104 Double slotted flap
construction
105 Static dischargers
106 Aileron trim tab
107 Trim tab hinge control
108 Port aileron
109 Aileron hinge control
110 Port wing-tip
111 Port navigation light
112 Fuel tank filler cap
113 Wing rib construction
114 Leading edge de-icing
115 Port wing fuel tank, 270 Imp
gal (1,226l)
116 Main undercarriage leg
117 Twin mainwheels
118 Retraction strut
119 Mainwheel door
120 Leading edge ice inspection
light
121 Main undercarriage wheel bay
122 Hydraulic system reservoir
123 Engine oil tank, capacity
3.3 Imp gal (15l)
124 Engine bearers
125 Detachable engine cowlings
126 Garrett AiResearch TPE
331-3UW-303G turboprop
127 Oil cooler
128 Oil cooler intake
129 Propeller gearbox
130 Engine intake
131 Propeller reversing and
feathering hub mechanism
132 Spinner
133 Hartzell three-bladed propeller
134 Propeller blade de-icing boots

60 Port seating, nine passengers
61 Cabin rear bulkhead
62 Toilet compartment door
63 Toilet
64 Rear cargo door
65 Door actuator
66 Rear cargo and baggage
compartment
67 Fuselage frame and stringer
construction
68 Fin root fillet
69 Tailplane electric trim jacks
70 Starboard tailplane
71 Leading edge de-icing
72 Elevator horn balance
73 Starboard elevator
74 Static dischargers
75 Fin construction
76 Rudder balance
77 Antenna
78 Anti-collision light
79 Rudder trim tab
80 Trim tab control jack
81 Rudder construction
82 Elevator hinge control
83 Port elevator
84 Static dischargers
85 Tailplane construction
86 Tail navigation light
87 Ventral fin
88 Rudder hinge control
89 Tailplane control cables

Left: The Fairchild Metro III was first introduced into service 1980 but remains in service in large numbers, today, providing feeder services to the large airport hubs. The particular aircraft depicted is flown by Mesaba Airlines, operating as a feeder carrier, for Northwest Airlink.

Above: The sale of the Metro 23 to China's Hainan Airlines was a considerable scoop for Fairchild, having sold only a handful in the Far East. Hainan Airlines utilises the aircraft on services within the large island of Hainan.

Below: Three-view drawing of the Fairchild Metro III, showing the large freight door for loading cargo, which is an obvious feature of the passenger versions as well as the freight-carrying Expediter 23 version.

the rear fuselage, a reinforced cabin floor, reduced empty weight and the high weight option allow an all-cargo version of the Metro, known as the Expediter, to carry a cargo payload of 2,268kg (5,000lb). For operators wishing to standardise on the Pratt & Whitney PT6A engine, Fairchild developed the Metro IIIA with 746kW (1,000shp) PT6A-45Rs, first flown on 31 December 1981. Current production model is the high-gross weight Metro 23, certificated in June 1990 to FAR Pt 23 commuter category, which incorporates many of the improvements of the C-26A and C-26B transport versions built for the US National Guard, and is also available as the Expediter 23, which has a rear cargo door and a payload of 2,495kg (5,500lb). It replaced the Expediter I from 1991. Each Metro variant was accompanied by respective Merlin corporate versions, and a number of special missions aircraft. Studies have been undertaken into a Tall Cabin Metro with a 'stand-up' cabin.

SERVICE USE
The Metro entered service in early 1971, the first major commuter airline operator being Air Wisconsin. The Metro III was certificated to SFAR 41 standard (the first to be so approved by the FAA) on 23 June 1980. First customer was Crossair, which put the type into service in spring 1981, and the Expediter was first operated by SAT-Air on behalf of United Parcel Service. The Metro 23 began commercial operations in 1991. Total Metro/Merlin orders at 1 January 1998 amounted to 1,022 aircraft.

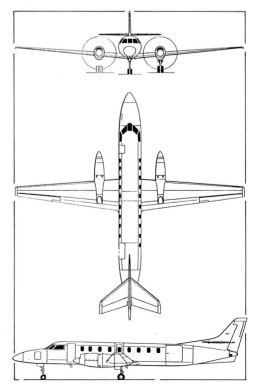

FAIRCHILD DORNIER 228 GERMANY/INDIA

Development of the Dornier 228 began with the work the company undertook, under a government-funded research contract, to evolve a 'new technology wing' (*Tragflügels Neuer Technologie*, or TNT). An example of this wing, featuring the Do A-5 supercritical section and unusual planform with raked tips, flew for the first time on a converted Do 28D-2 Skyservant on 14 June 1979. Associated with the TNT wing was a new power plant installation, two Garrett TPE331-5 turboprops in conventional wing nacelles replacing the Skyservant's sponson-mounted piston engines. To take full advantage of the performance and economic gains possible with the TNT, Dornier designed a new fuselage to provide an aircraft able to fulfil a range of missions, among which commuter passenger operations were to be the most important. Although some of the structural philosophy of the Skyservant was retained, the aircraft was completely new, a fact that the original designation (Do 28E) did little to emphasize. In 1989, Dornier redesignated its range of light transport aircraft and the new type, then still underdevelopment, became the Dornier 228. Two versions, with different fuselage lengths, had already been proposed as the Do 28E-1 and do 28E-2: to carry 15 or 19 passengers respectively, these became the Dornier 228-100 and 228-200, and work on the pair proceeded in parallel. The new fuselage, in the shorter of its two forms, was some 3.5m (12ft) longer than that of the Dornier 128-2 (as the Do 28D-2 had meanwhile become), whilst the 228-200's fuselage was 1.52m (5ft) longer than that of the 228-100. The prototypes made their first flights on 28 March and 9 May 1981 respectively. On 29 November 1983, Dornier concluded a licence agreement with Hindustan Aeronautics Ltd providing for the construction of up to 150 Dornier 228s in India to meet local military and commercial requirements, and the first aircraft assembled in India (using components supplied by Dornier) was flown at Kanpur on 31 January 1986.

VARIANTS

The Dornier 228-100 and 228-200 differ from each other in fuselage length, providing 15 and 19 passengers respectively. The Dornier 228-100 has the same take-off and landing weights as the 228-200, but can carry approximately 136kg (300lb) more payload, and has more than twice the range of the 228-200 with maximum passenger payload. In 1984, Dornier introduced the 228-101 and 228-201, which differed from earlier models in having a reinforced floor and new mainwheel tyres to permit higher operating weights and greater range. Available from Autumn 1987 was the 228-202, designed to offer further increases in payload/range performance. Current production model is the 228-212, certificated in August 1989, which introduced among several innovations, greater engine power in the 579kW (776shp) AlliedSignal (Garrett) TPE331-5-252D or TPE331-10 turboprops, stronger landing gear, carbon brakes, two strakes under the rear fuselage to improve short-field performance and new avionics. Dornier 228 also produced in troop, paratroop, ambulance, cargo, maritime patrol, maritime pollution surveillance and fisheries patrol and photogrammetry/geological survey versions. Plans to transfer production to Harbin Aircraft Manufacturing Company in China in an effort to restimulate the market appear to have foundered.

SERVICE USE

The Dornier 228-100 was certificated in West Germany, in accordance with FAR Pt 23 requirements, on 18 December 1981 and deliveries began in February 1982 to the first commercial operator, Norving Flyservice in Norway. The 228-200 was certificated on 6 September 1982. British and US certification was obtained on 17 April and 11 May 1984 respectively. Deliveries from the Hindustan Aeronautics assembly line at Kanpur began on 22 March 1986, when the Indian domestic airline Vayudoot received the first of a batch of five Indian-built examples. At 1 January 1998, total orders for the 228 amounted to 236 aircraft.

SPECIFICATION
(Dornier 228-212)

Dimensions: Wingspan 16.97m (55ft 8in); length overall 16.56m (54ft 4in); height overall 4.86m (15ft 11½in), wing area 32.00m² (344.3ft²).
Power Plant: Two 579kW (776shp) AlliedSignal TPE331-5-252D or TPE331-10 turboprops with Hartzell four-blade reversible-pitch fully-feathering metal propellers.
Weights: Operating weight empty 3,739kg (8,243lb); max take-off 6,400kg (14,110lb); max landing 6,100kg (13,448lb); max payload 2,201kg (4,852lb).
Performance: Max cruising speed 223kts (413km/h); max rate of climb 9.5m/s (1,870ft/min); service ceiling 8,535m (28,000ft); take-off field length 671m (2,200ft); landing field length 450m (1,480ft); range with typical payload 560nm (1,038km).
Accommodation: One or two pilots and seating for up to 19 passengers, two-abreast with single aisle. Total baggage volume front and rear 3.49m³ (123.2ft³).

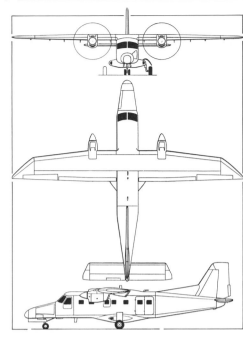

Above: This three-view drawing shows the short-fuselage Series 100 version of the Dornier 228. Note the planform of the supercritical new technology wing which is quite distinctive.

Right: The success of the 228-200 with Air Guadeloupe has encouraged the airline to increase its fleet to five of the type, which fly its main schedules to points in the Leeward Islands and Cayenne.

Dornier 228-200 Cutaway Drawing Key
1 Glassfibre radome
2 Weather radar scanner (optional)
3 Radar mounting bulkhead
4 Nosewheel doors, closed after cycling of undercarriage
5 Ground power socket
6 Battery
7 Pitot heads
8 Nose compartment construction
9 Forward baggage compartment, 31.4cu ft (0.89m³)
10 Nose undercarriage pivot fixing
11 Nosewheel leg strut
12 Twin nosewheels, forward retracting
13 Torque scissor links
14 Hydraulic retraction jack
15 Baggage door
16 Baggage loading floor
17 Cockpit front bulkhead
18 Rudder pedals
19 Instrument panel
20 Instrument panel shroud
21 Stand-by compass
22 Windscreen wipers
23 Curved windscreen panels
24 Overhead systems switch panels
25 Folding sun visors
26 Co-pilot's seat
27 Centre control pedestal
28 Control column
29 Cockpit floor level
30 Underfloor control linkages
31 Boarding step
32 Lower VHF aerial
33 Pilot's seat mounting
34 Crew entry door
35 External door latch
36 Safety harness
37 Pilot's seat
38 Electrical equipment racks
39 Cockpit rear bulkhead
40 Radio and avionics equipment racks
41 Curtained doorway to main cabin
42 Fuselage skin panelling
43 Cabin wall trim panelling
44 Cabin roof frames
45 Forward passenger seats, 19-seat layout

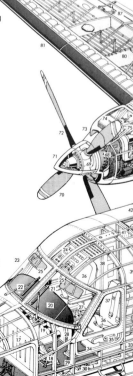

Left: The Dornier 228's excellent short field performance opened up the market in many of the islands of the Caribbean and the South Pacific. Air Moorea utilises a Dornier 228 on its inter-island flight services linking Tahiti's Faa'a International Airport with the Society Islands.

Right: Cutaway drawing of the Dornier 228-200, which is designed for a long structure life combined with ease of maintenance and for operations independent of ground equipment.

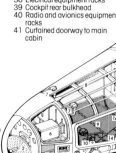

46 Cabin window panel
47 Forward fuselage frame and stringer construction
48 Seat mounting rails
49 Underfloor control runs
50 Floor beam construction
51 Hydraulic equipment module
52 Port emergency exit window panel
53 Wing spar attachment fuselage
54 Wing joint frame drag member
55 Passenger cabin ceiling lighting and trim panels
56 Front spar attachment light
57 Wing panel centre section construction

58 Front spar
59 Wing mounting main ribs
60 Cabin heater
61 Heater air intake
62 Kevlar composite leading-edge fillet
63 Starboard inboard main fuel tank. Total fuel capacity 525 Imp Gal (2,386l)
64 Fuel tank access panels
65 Leading-edge engine control runs
66 Starboard engine nacelle
67 Garrett TPE331-5-252D turboprop
68 Propeller reduction gearbox
69 Propeller hub pitch change mechanism
70 Hartzell four-bladed constant speed, fully feathering and reversible propeller
71 Spinner
72 Propeller blade root de-icing (optional)
73 Oil cooler air intake
74 Oil radiator
75 Engine accessory equipment

76 Main engine bearers
77 Wing skin panelling
78 Outer wing panel skin joint strap
79 Fuel filler cap
80 Outer wing panel integral fuel tank
81 Leading-edge de-icing boot (optional)
82 Raked wing-tip fairing
83 Starboard navigation light
84 Static dischargers
85 Aileron external hinge
86 Aileron mass balance weight
87 Aileron hinge control
88 Starboard drooping aileron
89 Aileron Kevlar skin panelling
90 Starboard single-slotted Fowler-type flap
91 Flap hinge fittings

92 Trailing-edge hinged links
93 Central flap drive motor
94 Wing rear spar
95 Kevlar composite flap shroud panel
96 Starboard rear emergency exit window hatch
97 Anti-collision light
98 Upper VHF aerial
99 Trailing-edge fairing corrugated skin panel

132 Tailplane rib construction
133 Trimming tailplane spar pivot joint
134 Tailplane control access panel
135 Fin spar attachment main frame
136 Tail control run
137 Rear fuselage frame and stringer construction
138 Baggage compartment door
139 Baggage loading floor
140 Freight door, closed
141 Two-segment passenger and freight doorway
142 Rear three-abreast seat row
143 External door latches
144 Folding handrail
145 Passenger door/airstairs, open
146 Port single-slotted flap
147 Flap rib construction

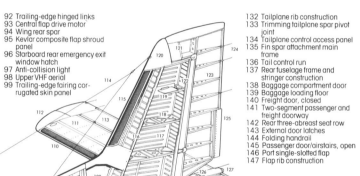

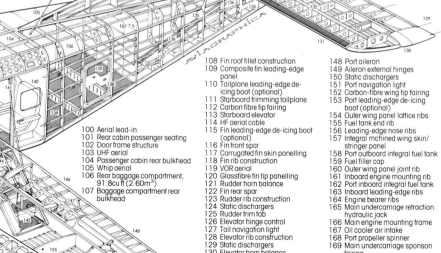

108 Fin root fillet construction
109 Composite fin leading-edge panel
110 Tailplane leading-edge de-icing boot (optional)
111 Starboard trimming tailplane
112 Carbon fibre tip fairing
113 Starboard elevator
114 HF aerial cable
115 Fin leading-edge de-icing boot (optional)
116 Fin front spar
117 Corrugated fin skin panelling
118 Fin rib construction
119 VOR aerial
120 Glassfibre fin tip panelling
121 Rudder horn balance
122 Fin rear spar
123 Rudder rib construction
124 Static dischargers
125 Rudder trim tab
126 Elevator hinge control
127 Tail navigation light
128 Elevator rib construction
129 Static dischargers
130 Elevator horn balance
131 Leading edge de-icing boot

100 Aerial lead-in
101 Rear cabin passenger seating
102 Door frame structure
103 UHF aerial
104 Passenger cabin rear bulkhead
105 Whip aerial
106 Rear baggage compartment, 91.8cu ft (2.60m³)
107 Baggage compartment rear bulkhead

148 Port aileron
149 Aileron external hinges
150 Static dischargers
151 Port navigation light
152 Carbon-fibre wing tip fairing
153 Port leading-edge de-icing boot (optional)
154 Outer wing panel lattice ribs
155 Fuel tank end rib
156 Leading-edge nose ribs
157 Integral mchined wing skin/stringer panel
158 Port outboard integral fuel tank
159 Fuel filler cap
160 Outer wing panel joint rib
161 Inboard engine mounting rib
162 Port inboard integral fuel tank
163 Inboard leading-edge ribs
164 Engine bearer ribs
165 Main undercarriage retraction hydraulic jack
166 Main engine mounting frame
167 Oil cooler air intake
168 Port propeller spinner
169 Main undercarriage sponson fairing
170 Engine air intake
171 Intake lip de-icing (optional)
172 Port engine nacelle
173 Landing/taxying lamps
174 Main undercarriage leg pivot fixing
175 Torque scissor links
176 Port mainwheel, inward retracting
177 Composite mainwheel leg door

117

FAIRCHILD DORNIER 328 GERMANY/USA

In late 1986, the Dornier Board approved development of a 30-seat growth version of the 228, but a lack of clear market definition halted the programme until 3 August 1988, when Dornier decided to resume work. The Model 328 was intended to offer comparable performance to its earlier utility aircraft, including the capability to operate from short and unprepared landing strips, while offering a stand-up cabin and airline-style comfort with seats wider than a typical Boeing 727/737 configuration. Noise levels were also pegged at 78dB for 75 per cent of the cabin. Dornier combined the basic TNT supercritical wing of the 228 with a new enlarged and pressurised circular fuselage, developed from the Federal Ministry of Research and Technology's NRT (*Neue Rumpf-Technologien*) programme, and a new-design T-tail. A new flap system with ground and flight spoilers was also introduced. Extensive use was made of composite materials, including the entire rear fuselage and tail unit, making up some 23 per cent of the structural weight. On 28 October 1988, Dornier selected the Pratt & Whitney Canada PW119 turboprop to power the new aircraft, which made its first flight on 6 December 1991, Two more development aircraft flew on 4 June and 20 October 1992, followed by the first production aircraft on 23 January 1993. The Dornier 328 obtained 14-country European certification to JAA 25 on 15 October 1993. The 328 is being built in an international risk-sharing partnership, which includes Aermacchi of Italy, Daewoo Heavy Industries of South Korea, and the UK's Westland Aerostructures. Final assembly takes place at Dornier's main plant at Oberpfaffenhofen in southern Germany.

VARIANTS

The initial production 328-100, with a maximum take-off weight of 13,440kg (29,630lb), has been replaced by the 328-110, whose improvements are being progressively incorporated into existing aircraft. External changes and performance enhancements of the 328-110 include enlarged dorsal fin and reconfigured and repositioned ventral fin, an increase in take-off weight by 350kg to 13,990kg (30,842lb) and range by 270 nautical miles to

SPECIFICATION
(Fairchild-Dornier 328-110)

Dimensions: Wingspan 20.98m (68ft 10in); length overall 21.28m (69ft 9¾in); height overall 7.24m (23ft 9in), wing area 40.0m² (430.6ft²).
Power Plant: Two 1,626kW (2,180shp) Pratt & Whitney Canada PW119B turboprops with Hartzell 6-B composite propellers.
Weights: Operating weight empty 8,920kg (19,665lb); max take-off 13,990kg (30,842 lb); max landing 13,230kg (29,167lb); max payload 3,690kg (8,135lb).
Performance: Max cruising speed 335kts (620km/h); service ceiling 7,620m (25,000ft); take-off field length 1,090m (3,570ft); landing field length 1,165m (3,825ft); range with max payload 900nm (1,666km).
Accommodation: Flight crew of two. Seating for 33 passengers, three-abreast with single aisle. Total baggage volume 6.30m³ (222.5ft³).

1,000nm (1,850km). Further improvements are offered in the 328-120 through an improvement performance kit (IPK), with the main elements being increased thermodynamic power of its PW119C engines; greater propeller diameter, optional ground spoilers and enlarged dorsal and ventral fins. Take-off field length is reduced to 800m (2,625ft). A 48-seat 328 Stretch was being studied to meet a requirement by 328 launch customer Horizon Air, but has now been abandoned in favour of a jet programme. In addition, for markets where greater capacity is required, it is planned to introduce a four-abreast 328-200 for 37-39 passengers within the existing airframe. These would be available also in corresponding 328-210 and 328-220 configurations. Initial designation of 328-300 for a 30-seat jet version and 328-700 for a stretched 50-seat derivative, have been changed to 328 JET and 428 JET respectively. The 328 JET is to be powered by two 27kN (6,000lb) Pratt & Whitney Canada PW306 turbofans and will be sized for 32-34 passengers. The prototype first flew on 2 January 1998 and the type is expected to enter service in early 1999. The stretched 428 JET would follow on a year later. A hydrogen-powered 328 testbed is expected to fly in

Right: Cutaway drawing of the Dornier 328-110

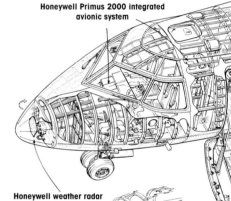

Refuel pane

Six-bladed Hartzell, fully feathering and reversible pitch propeller-hydraulically actuated, electrically de-iced (foam filled carbon fibre construction) (3.6m diameter)

Engine downthrust 1.5 deg

Instrument panel EFIS displays

Honeywell Primus 2000 integrated avionic system

Honeywell weather radar

Passenger door/ai

Air distribution equipment below cabin floor

Left: A large early order from Alaska Air carrier Horizon Air for 20 aircraft failed to stimulate the market and sales of the 328 have remained low. Improved performance and a reduction in the high acquisition cost have failed to reverse its fortunes.

Right: This Tyrolean Fairchild Dornier 328 ambulance airliner operates from Innesbruck, Austria. It has a cruising speed of 340 knots and a range of 1700 nautical miles. When fully loaded it can carry 4 intensive care or up to 12 non-intensive care patients.

1998, with possible service introduction by 2005.

SERVICE USE

Swiss regional, Air Engiadina, received the first 328-100 on 21 October 1993, following European JAA certification six days earlier. FAA type approval was granted on 10 November, after which Horizon Air accepted its first aircraft. German LBA and FAA certification of the 328-110 came a year later, on 4 November 1994, followed in May 1995 by the 328-120. First customer for the latter was Formosa Airlines of Taiwan. The first application on any aircraft type of the Lockheed Martin APALS (autonomous precision approach and landing system) – fitted to Lone Star Airlines' four 328-110 – led to Cat I certification at non-precision airports. At January 1998, the manufacturer had logged 104 sales of the 328, and 17 of the 328 JET.

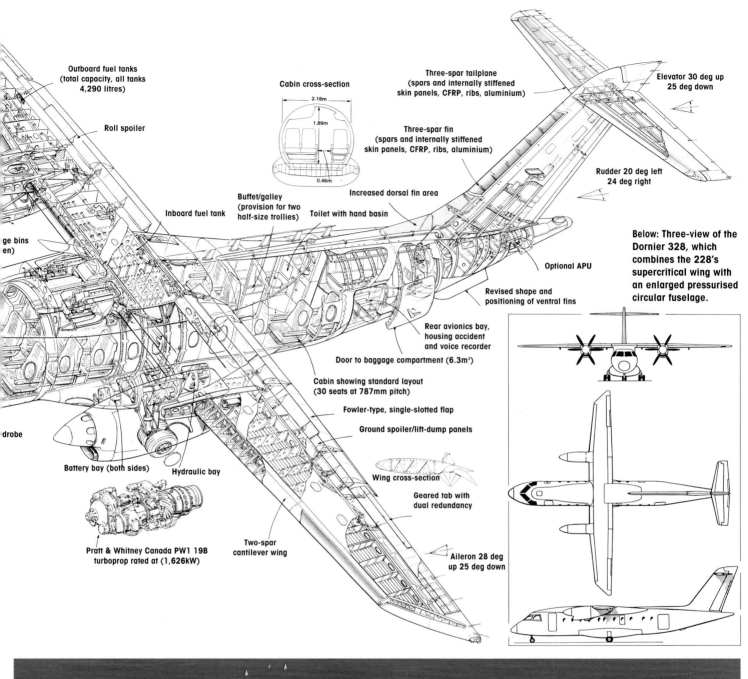

Outboard fuel tanks
(total capacity, all tanks
4,290 litres)

Roll spoiler

Cabin cross-section

2.18m

1.89m

0.46m

Three-spar tailplane
(spars and internally stiffened
skin panels, CFRP, ribs, aluminium)

Elevator 30 deg up
25 deg down

Three-spar fin
(spars and internally stiffened
skin panels, CFRP, ribs, aluminium)

Rudder 20 deg left
24 deg right

ge bins
en)

Inboard fuel tank

Buffet/galley
(provision for two
half-size trolleys)

Toilet with hand basin

Increased dorsal fin area

Optional APU

Below: Three-view of the
Dornier 328, which
combines the 228's
supercritical wing with
an enlarged pressurised
circular fuselage.

Revised shape and
positioning of ventral fins

Rear avionics bay,
housing accident
and voice recorder

Door to baggage compartment (6.3m³)

drobe

Cabin showing standard layout
(30 seats at 787mm pitch)

Fowler-type, single-slotted flap

Ground spoiler/lift-dump panels

Battery bay (both sides)

Hydraulic bay

Wing cross-section

Geared tab with
dual redundancy

Pratt & Whitney Canada PW1 19B
turboprop rated at (1,626kW)

Two-spar
cantilever wing

Aileron 28 deg
up 25 deg down

FOKKER F27 FRIENDSHIP THE NETHERLANDS

Europe's best-selling turboprop transport emerged as Fokker's first post-war commercial aircraft, designed at the beginning of the 1950s to provide airlines with a 'DC-3 replacement'. Among several project studies, the P.275 of August 1950 became the basis for further development, taking shape by the end of 1952 as a high-wing monoplane with a pressurised circular-section fuselage, two Rolls-Royce Dart turboprops and accommodation for up to 40 passengers. The full payload range was to be only 260 naut mls (482km), restricting the aircraft to the short-haul market, and attention was given to providing good field performance. With Netherlands government backing, two prototypes of the F27, as the project became known, were launched in 1953, and these made their first flights on 24 November 1955 and 29 January 1957 respectively, the second having a lengthened fuselage to increase basic seating from 32 to 36. Increases in fuel capacity were made later to give the F27 greater operational flexibility. Production of the F27, for which the name Friendship was later adopted, was initiated both by Fokker in the Netherlands and, under licence agreements, by Fairchild in the USA. The first production aircraft flew at Schiphol, Amsterdam, on 23 March 1958 and at Hagerstown, Maryland, USA, on 12 April 1958, and a Fairchild-built example became the first to operate revenue services by the type.

VARIANTS

The first Fokker production variant was the F27 Mk 100 with Dart Mk 511 (RDa6) engines, matched by the Fairchild F27. The F27 Mk 200, first flown on 20 September 1962, and F27A introduced uprated Dart RDa7 engines; associated with these engines were progressive increases in gross weight. The F27 Mk 300 Combiplane and F27B had RDa6 engines and a side-loading freight door in the forward fuselage for mixed passenger/freight operations. The F27 Mk 400 (and similar F27M Troopship) first flown on 24 April 1965, combined the freight door and freight floor with RDa7 engines, while the Mk 600, flown on 28 November 1968, was similar but lacked the former's special all-metal watertight freight door. The Mk 600 was a true quick-change version, its roller floor enabling rapid reconfiguration of the interior. In addition to the Mk 400 Troopship other military versions were also built, including a maritime patrol aircraft. All these were suffixed with the letter M. Fairchild's F27F was an F27A with Dart Mk.529s for corporate users, while the F27J and F27M had Dart Mk 532-7 and Mk 532-7N engines respectively. In all, Fairchild built 128 of its F27 variants, ending in 1970. Fairchild also developed a stretched-fuselage variant, the FH-227, with a 1.83m (6ft) plug, and built several subvariants with different weights and Dart ratings. The first FH-227 flew on 27 January 1966 and production totalled 79. Fokker's stretched F27 Mk

SPECIFICATION
(Fokker F27-500 Friendship)

Dimensions: Wingspan 29.00m (95ft 1¾in); length overall 25.06m (82ft 2¼in); height overall 8.71m (28ft 7¼in), wing area 70.0m² (753.5ft²).
Power Plant: Two 1,648kW (2,210shp) Rolls-Royce Dart Mk 552 turboprops with Dowty Rotol constant-speed four-blade propellers.
Weights: Operating weight empty 12,701kg (28,000lb); max take-off 20,820kg (45,900lb); max landing 19,731kg (43,500lb); max payload 5,896kg (13,000lb).
Performance: Normal cruising speed 259kts (480km/h); max rate of climb 7.5m/s (1,480ft/min); service ceiling 8,990m (29,500ft); take-off field length 988m (3,240ft); landing field length 1,003m (3,290ft); range with typical payload 935nm (1,741km).
Accommodation: Two flight crew and seating for up to 60 passengers, four-abreast with central aisle. Total cargo/baggage volume front and rear 8.41m³ (297ft³).

500, in the project stage for several years, flew on 15 November 1967, and remained in production, with the F27 Mk 200, through 1986. By the time production of these variants was phased out in favour of the Fokker 50, sales of the F27 had totalled 579 from the Dutch production line. The last was delivered in 1987.

FOKKER F28 FELLOWSHIP THE NETHERLANDS

Plans to develop a short/medium-haul jet transport partner for its F27 turboprop twin were made by Fokker at the beginning of the 1960s, the first details of this F28 Fellowship being published in April 1962. Projected to carry about 50 passengers over 1,000 naut mls (1,850km), the F28 was at first studied with Bristol Siddeley BS.75 engines, but the eventual selection was a lightened and simplified version of the Rolls-Royce Spey, known at first as the Spey Junior. In configuration, the F28 was similar to the BAC One-Eleven and Douglas DC-9, with a moderately swept wing, engines mounted on the sides of the rear fuselage and a T-tail, but it was smaller than either of those types, although the basic capacity of the initial version grew to 60 and eventually to 65. To help establish production of the F28, Fokker concluded risk-sharing agreements with several companies, including Shorts in the UK (for the wings), and HFB and VFW (later MBB) in West Germany for fuselage sub-assemblies. Three prototypes of the F28 were built, making their first flights on 9 May, 3 August and 20 October 1967 respectively, and production went ahead on the basis of a launch order placed by LTU, a German inclusive-tour charter operator, in November 1965. The first production F28, the fourth aircraft completed, flew on 21 May 1968.

VARIANTS

The initial production version of the F28 became known as the F28 Mk 1000 after a stretched-fuselage variant was introduced as the F28 Mk 2000 in 1970. The Mk 1000 is basically a 65-seater (one-class) aircraft, the gross weight of which was initially 28,123kg (62,000lb), but subject to subsequent increases. With a side-loading freight door and provision for mixed passenger/freight loads, the designation is F28 Mk 1000C. The F28 Mk 2000 has a 2.21m (7ft 3in) longer fuselage and seats up to 79 passengers in a one-class arrangement. It first flew on 28 April 1971. In 1972, Fokker introduced the F28 Mk 5000 (short fuselage) and F28 Mk 6000 (long fuselage), whose new features were an increase of 1.57m (6ft 11½in) in wing span, with leading-edge

slats added, and improved Spey Mk 555-15H engines with additional noise reduction features. A Mk 6000 prototype flew on 27 September 1973, but the take-off performance bestowed by the flaps proved to be an unwanted luxury for most airlines and the F28 Mk 3000 (short fuselage) and F28 Mk 4000 (long fuselage) became the preferred versions, with the extra span and new engines, but without the slats. Interior redesign also took the maximum seating up to 85 in the Mk 4000, which first flew on 20 October 1976.

SERVICE USE

The F28 Mk 1000 was certificated by the Dutch authorities on 24 February 1969 and entered service with LTU immediately after. The first F28 Mk 2000 went to Nigeria Airways in October 1972, two months after certification. The F238 Mk 6000 was certificated on 27 September 1973, but was not produced. The F28 Mk 4000 entered service with Linjeflyg of Sweden late in 1976, and the first operator of the F28 Mk 3000 was Garuda in Indonesia. Sales of the F28 totalled 241 by the end of 1986, when production ended. Of these 160 remained in service in January 1998.

SPECIFICATION
(Fokker F28-4000 Fellowship)

Dimensions: Wingspan 25.07m (82ft 3in); length overall 29.61m (97ft 1¾in); height overall 8.47m (27ft 9½in), wing area 79.0m² (850ft²).
Power Plant: Two 44kN (9,900lb) Rolls-Royce Spey Mk 555-15P turbofans.
Weights: Operating weight empty 17,645kg (38,900lb); max take-off 33,110kg (73,000lb); max landing 31,524kg (69,500lb); max payload 10,478kg (23,100lb).
Performance: Max cruising speed 455kts (843km/h); service ceiling 10,675m (35,000ft); take-off field length 1,585m (5,200ft); landing field length 1,065m (3,495ft); range with typical payload 1,025nm (1,900km).
Accommodation: Flight crew of two. Seating for up to 85 passengers, five-abreast with single aisle. Total cargo/baggage volume forward and rear 15.84m³ (559.5ft³).

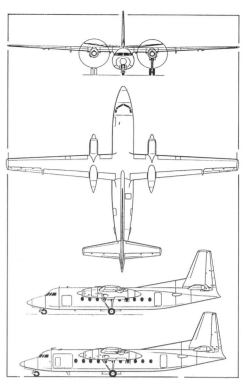

SERVICE USE

The Fairchild F27 was certificated on 16 July 1958 and entered service on 27 November 1958 with West Coast Airlines. The first Fokker-built F27 entered service with Aer Lingus in December 1958. The Fairchild F27B was certificated 25 October 1958 and first entered service with Northern Consolidated. The F27F was certificated on 24 February 1961, and F27J on 3 August 1965 and the F27M on 12 June 1969. At 1 January 1998, some 290 of all versions remained in service, primarily in Asia, Australasia and North America.

Above: The 50-seat Fokker F27 Friendship was in production for nearly 30 years and has served in large numbers in all parts of the world. Some 20 still serve in the United Kingdom, including this Jersey European Airways Mk.500, although now with a new owner.

Right: Three-view drawing of the F27 Mk.200, plus a lower side-view of the longer Mk.500, showing the larger port side door forward of the wing.

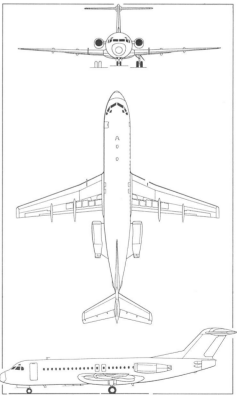

Left: Iran's government-owned regional airline Iran Asseman has been operating the twin-jet Fokker F28 since 1981 on government flights and scheduled domestic services. It operates the F28-4000, fitted out for 85 passengers, and the smaller F28-1000 for 65 passengers.

Above: Three-view drawing of the F28 Mk.4000, which was the final production version and was built with the shorter Mk.3000 until 1986.

FOKKER 50/60 THE NETHERLANDS

The Fokker 50 was announced on 24 November 1983 on the occasion of a celebration in Amsterdam of the 25th anniversary of airline service with the F27 Friendship, which the Fokker 50 was designed to succeed. After prolonged studies of possible stretched derivatives of the F27, Fokker concluded that the size of the aircraft was about right for that portion of the regional airline market it sought to fill. Nevertheless, and despite an ongoing programme of product improvement since the F27 had first appeared in 1957, there was much room to introduce the benefits of new technology in the structure and system of the basic aircraft, and this was the keynote of Fokker's approach to the design of the Fokker 50. The most obvious change is in respect of the power plant, a switch being made from the Rolls-Royce Dart of the F27 family to the more modern Pratt & Whitney Canada PW124 with significant gains in fuel economy. Less obvious but more extensive changes have been made under the skin, to the extent that 80 per cent of the Fokker 50's component parts are new or modified by comparison with those of the F27. Thus, apart from the engines with their new nacelles and six-blade propellers, the Fokker 50 has a hydraulic instead of pneumatic system for landing gear and flap operation; a new Hamilton Standard air-conditioning system with a Garrett digital cabin pressure-control system; and Sundstrand integrated drive generators on each engine to supply the electric system. The F27's much-appreciated (by passengers) large cabin windows have given way to a larger number of smaller windows, in the interest of great flexibility of cabin layout, and the cabin itself is wholly redesigned, with large overhead stowage bins and the main passenger access door at the front instead of the rear, with the F27's forward baggage/cargo loading door deleted. The flight deck was also extensively redesigned, with an all-new avionics fit including a Honeywell electronic flight instrument system (EFIS) with cathode ray tube (CRT) displays for primary flight and navigation information. A small airframe change is made with the addition of the wingtips or 'Foklets' (a variation of the larger winglets that serve a similar purpose) and extensive use is made throughout the airframe of carbon, aramid and glass fibre composites. Flight development of the Fokker 50 began on 28 December 1985, using an F27 airframe with the new power plants; a second prototype flown on 30 April 1986 had more representative Fokker 50 systems. Both aircraft made use of F27 fuselages, and the first true Fokker 50 flew on 13 February 1987.

VARIANTS

The basic Fokker 50, with 1,864kW (2,500shp) Pratt & Whitney Canada PW125B turboprops, was certificated to JAR 25 by the Dutch RLD on 15 May 1987. It was made available in four-door and three-door configurations, providing dedicated access for ground handling services. Maximum capacity is 58 passengers. The installation of more powerful PW127Bs, each rated at 2,050kW (2,750shp), produced the Fokker 50 High Performance, offering better airfield performance, especially in hot-and-high locations. The Fokker 50 Utility is based on the standard three-door model, with an additional 1.65 × 1.30m (5ft 5in × 4ft 3¼in) multi-purpose door and heavy-duty floor. There were also a number of special missions variants for military and government use. Stretched Fokker 60 and Fokker 60 Utility models for 60 passengers were launched in February 1994 and ordered by the Royal Netherlands Air Force. First flight was made on 2 November 1995.

SERVICE USE

German regional DLT, now Lufthansa CityLine, took delivery of the first Fokker 50 on 7 August 1987. FAA type approval to FAR Pt.25 was achieved on 16 February 1989, but no aircraft were delivered new to a US customer. Dutch RLD approval for the Fokker 50 High Performance was won in early 1993, prior to first customer delivery to Avianca Colombia on 2 April 1993. When production ended in 1996 following Fokker's bankruptcy, a total of 232 Fokker 50/60s had been built.

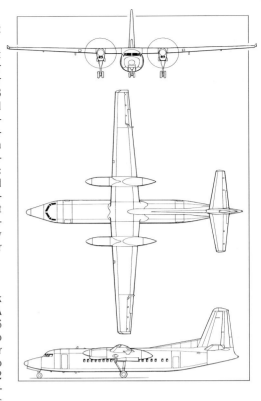

Right: Cutaway drawing of the Fokker 50.

SPECIFICATION
(Fokker 50 High Performance)

Dimensions: Wingspan 29.00m (95ft 1¾in); length overall 25.25m (82ft 10in); height overall 8.32m (27ft 3½in), wing area 70.0m² (753.5ft²).
Power Plant: Two 2,050kW (2,750shp) Pratt & Whitney Canada PW127B turboprops with Dowty propellers with six composite blades.
Weights: Operating weight empty 12,520kg (27,602lb); max take-off 20,820kg (45,900lb); max landing 19,730kg (43,500lb); max payload 6,080kg (13,404lb).
Performance: Typical cruising speed 282kts (512km/h); service ceiling 7,620m (25,000ft); take-off field length 890m (2,920ft); landing field length 1,017m (3,340ft); range with max payload 1,535nm (2,843km).
Accommodation: Flight crew of two. Seating for up to 58 passengers, four-abreast with central aisle. Total baggage volume 10.42m³ (368.2ft³).

Above: The modern Fokker 50 has helped many airlines establish a niche presence on secondary routes. Air Nostrum operates in the liberalised Spanish domestic market.

Overwing fil

Dowty Rotol ARA-D
12ft dia composite propellors

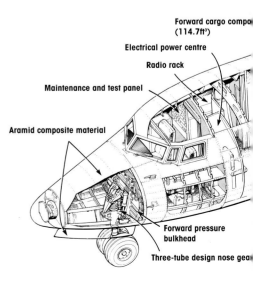

Forward cargo compa
(114.7ft³)

Electrical power centre

Radio rack

Maintenance and test panel

Aramid composite material

Forward pressure bulkhead

Three-tube design nose gea

Left: Three-view of the Fokker 50, which clearly shows its F27 Friendship ancestry, although it underwent considerable changes. Note the 'Foklet' wingtips.

Right: Nakanihon Airline Service (NAL) operates its 56-seat Fokker 50s on scheduled services in Japan from Nagoya to Toyama, Yonago, Fukushima and the holiday resort of Hakodate. The size and comfort of the aircraft allows for an orderly transfer of international passengers at Nagoya.

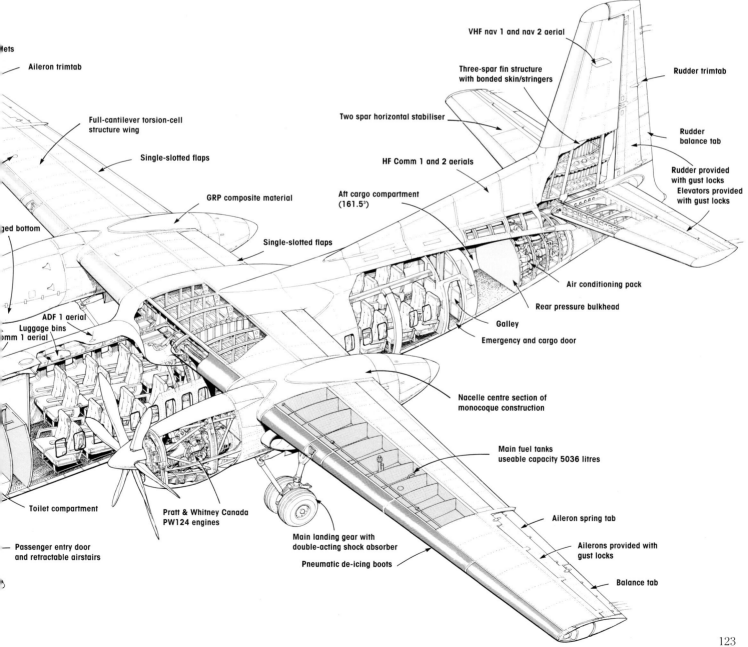

lets

Aileron trimtab

Full-cantilever torsion-cell structure wing

Single-slotted flaps

GRP composite material

ged bottom

ADF 1 aerial

Luggage bins

mm 1 aerial

Toilet compartment

Passenger entry door and retractable airstairs

Single-slotted flaps

Pratt & Whitney Canada PW124 engines

Main landing gear with double-acting shock absorber

Pneumatic de-icing boots

VHF nav 1 and nav 2 aerial

Three-spar fin structure with bonded skin/stringers

Two spar horizontal stabiliser

HF Comm 1 and 2 aerials

Aft cargo compartment (161.5³)

Rudder trimtab

Rudder balance tab

Rudder provided with gust locks

Elevators provided with gust locks

Air conditioning pack

Rear pressure bulkhead

Galley

Emergency and cargo door

Nacelle centre section of monocoque construction

Main fuel tanks useable capacity 5036 litres

Aileron spring tab

Ailerons provided with gust locks

Balance tab

FOKKER 70/100 THE NETHERLANDS

In its search for a programme to maintain its share of the regional airliner market through the 1990s, Fokker evaluated a number of possible derivative versions of its F28. These included projects variously identified as the Super F28, the F29 and (in collaboration with McDonnell Douglas) the MDF-100. Finally, on 24 November 1983, the company announced that it was going ahead with a derivative known as the Fokker 100, with backing from the Netherlands government; the designation was chosen to reflect the basic seating capacity (actually 107), in the same way that the improved F27 – announced simultaneously – was renamed the Fokker 50. To achieve the Fokker 100, the original F28 Mk 4000 fuselage was extended by 5.74m (18ft 10in) in two 'plugs', one ahead of and one behind the wing. Although Fokker studied, through extensive wind tunnel testing, the potential of completely new wing aerofoil sections, the final decision favoured retention of the basic F28 wing box unchanged. However, aerodynamic efficiency was improved by changes at the leading and trailing edges, with increased leading-edge chord resulting in the F28's prominent leading-edge 'kink' being virtually eliminated. The changes in the aerofoil brought about by the new leading edge resulted, according to Fokker, in a 30 per cent improvement in aerodynamics efficiency, an increase in the high-speed buffet limit and a reduction in drag at both high and low speeds. New trailing-edge flaps were adopted, and the landing gear was strengthened for the higher operating weights. Wing span was increased, at the tips, by 3.0m (9ft 9½in), and tailplane span by 1.4m (4ft 7in). Considerable use is made of composites in the structure, for such items as the nosecone, wing/fuselage fairings, cabin floor panels, etc. Cabin redesign gives the Fokker 100 a new look, and on the flight deck, digital electronics have been introduced to provide a state-of-the-art presentation and equipment fit, with a four-screen electronic flight instrument system (EFIS). The digital autoflight control system provides for Cat II operation, with operators having the option to upgrade to Cat III if an autothrottle is fitted. The two Fokker 100 prototypes flew on 30 November 1986 and 25 February 1987. Authorisation for a shortened version for up to 79 passengers was given by the Board in November 1992 and formally launched as the Fokker 70 in June 1993, on the back of 15 firm orders. The second Fokker 100 prototype was modified to Fokker 70 configuration by removing two fuselage plugs (one forward of the wing and one aft), reducing the overall length by 4.62m (15ft 2in). The Fokker 70 retained the same Rolls-Royce Tay Mk 620 turbofans installed on the basic Fokker 100 and made its first flight on 2 April 1993. Final assembly of the first production aircraft, built alongside the Fokker 100, started in February 1994 and was completed with the first flight on 12 July. Plans for a stretched 137-seat Fokker 130 were abandoned.

VARIANTS

The basic Fokker 70 for airline use has typical accommodation for 79 passengers in five-abreast seating. A VIP/corporate shuttle version with customised interior and optional belly tanks, the Fokker Executive Jet 70, was the first to be delivered. Additional range capability was incorporated in the Fokker Executive Jet 70ER, extending range to 3,237nm (6,000km). The standard Fokker 100, in a typical airline configuration for 107 passengers, was produced with optional intermediate take-off weight of 44,450kg (98,000lb) and high take-off weight of 45,810kg (101,000lb), higher thrust Tay Mk.650 engines, larger capacity air conditioning system, and forward toilet. Complementing the executive line of the Fokker 70, the Fokker 100 was also avail-

able in Executive Jet 100 and Executive Jet 100ER customised versions, but none of these were ever delivered.

SERVICE USE

The larger Fokker 100 was the first to be certificated, receiving RLD type approval to JAR 25 on 20 November 1987. First customer was Swissair, which took delivery on 29 February 1988. Eleven days after simultaneous RLD and FAA certification on 14 October 1994, the Ford Motor Company accepted

the first Fokker 70, an Executive Jet 70 model. The first airline version went to Sempati Air Transport on 9 March 1995, while the Kenyan Government received an Executive Jet 70ER on 15 December 1995. When the Dutch manufacturer went into receivership in February 1996, it was agreed that outstanding orders would be completed, but this was only partially carried out. Final production (unless Fokker is re-activated, which looked unlikely in 1998), amounted to 282 Fokker 100s and 77 Fokker 70s.

SPECIFICATION
(Fokker 70)

Dimensions: Wingspan 28.08m (92ft 1½in); length overall 30.91m (101ft 4¾in); height overall 8.51m (27ft 10½in), wing area 93.5m² (1006.4ft²).
Power Plant: Two 61.6kN (13,850lb) Rolls-Royce Tay Mk.620 turbofans.
Weights: Operating weight empty 22,784kg (50,230lb); max take-off 41,730kg (92,000lb); max landing 36,740kg (81,000lb); max payload 10,780kg (23,766lb).
Performance: Max cruising speed 462kts (856km/h); service ceiling 10,670m (35,000ff); take-off field length 1,665m (5,465ft); landing field length 1,274m (4,180ff); range with max payload 2,015nm (3,731km).
Accommodation: Flight crew of two. Seating for up to 80 passengers, five-abreast with single aisle. Total cargo/baggage volume 21.57m³ (761.9ft³).

SPECIFICATION
(Fokker 100)

Dimensions: Wingspan 28.08m (92ft 1½in); length overall 35.53m (116ft 6¾in); height overall 8.51m (27ft 10½in), wing area 93.50m² (1,006.4ft²).
Power Plant: Two 61.6kN (13,850lb) Rolls-Royce Tay Mk.620 or 67.2kN (15,100lb) Tay Mk.650 turbofans.
Weights: Operating weight empty 24,747kg (54,558lb); max take-off 45,810kg (101,000lb); max landing 39,915kg (88,000 lb); max payload 12,013kg (26,486lb).
Performance: Max cruising speed 462kts (856km/h); service ceiling 10,670m (35,000ft); take-off field length 1,825m (5,990ft); landing field length 1,350m (4,420ft); range with max payload 1,680nm (3,111km).
Accommodation: Flight crew of two. Seating for up to 109 passengers, five-abreast with single aisle. Total baggage volume 24.87m³ (878.4ft³).

Left: The Fokker 100 has been the backbone of many fleets, including that of Portugalia.

Fokker 100 Cutaway Drawing Key

1 Radome, Aramid Fibre Reinforced Plastic (AFRP)
2 Weather radar scanner
3 Scanner mounting and tracking mechanism
4 LS glideslope aerials
5 Retractable approach and taxing lamps
6 Heat exchanger ram air intake
7 Front pressure bulkhead
8 Rudder pedals
9 Control column, digital automatic flight control and augmentation system (AFCAS)
10 Cathode ray tube electronic flight instrumentation system (EFIS)
11 Instrument panel shroud
12 Windscreen wipers
13 Windscreen panels
14 Overhead systems switch panel
15 Circuit breaker panel
16 First Officer's seat
17 Centre console panel
18 Captain's seat
19 Nosewheel steering tiller
20 Side console stowage lockers
21 ockpit floor level
22 Underfloor air conditioning plant
23 Nosewheel doors
24 Dowty-Rotol nose undercarriage strut
25 Twin nosewheels, forward retracting
26 Hydraulic nosewheel steering jack
27 Pitot head
28 Conditioned air delivery duct
29 Carry-on baggage locker
30 Cockpit rear bulkhead
31 Cockpit doorway
32 Starboard service door/emergency exit
33 Twin galley units

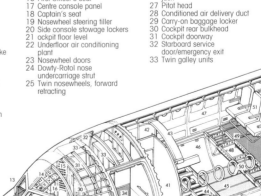

34 Entry lobby
35 Cabin attendant's folding seat
36 Main entry doorway
37 Door actuator
38 Main entry door/airstairs, open
39 Folding handrail
40 Door latch and control panel
41 Stowage locker/wardrobe
42 Starboard wardrobe
43 Air delivery ducting

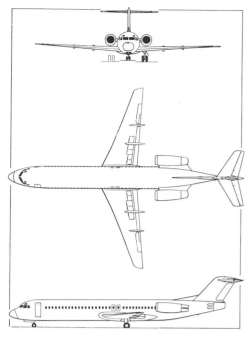

Above: Three-view of the Fokker 100, which has a lengthened F28 fuselage and Rolls-Royce Tay engines. The Fokker 70's fuselage is shorter by 4.62m (15ft 2in).

Right: The Kenyan Government was the first to acquire the Fokker 70ER (extended range) version, which is being used on VIP transport. It is flown by the Kenyan Air Force.

44 Underfloor avionics equipment racks, Sperry Advanced Flight Management System (AFMS)
45 Forward underfloor cargo hold capacity 346 cu ft (9,8m³)
46 Cargo hold forward door
47 Cabin wall trim panelling
48 Floor beam construction
49 Seat mounting rails
50 Main cabin windows
51 Five-abreast passenger seating, 107 seat standard layout

52 Upper VHF aerial
53 Cargo hold rear door, optional increased area door
54 Carbon-fibre and glass-fibre composite floor panels
55 Lower VHF aerial
56 Lower lobe fuselage skin panelling
57 Wing inspection light
58 Cargo hold movable, powered bulkhead, optional mechanical cargo handling system
59 Underfloor air ducting
60 Cabin air valve
61 Wing spar centre-section carry-through
62 Cabin wall soundproofing linings

63 Centre fuselage frame and stringer construction
64 Wing centre-section torsion box construction
65 Centre-section fuel tanks
66 Port emergency exit window hatches
67 Pressure floor above wheel bay
68 Front spar/fuselage main frame

69 Starboard emergency exit window hatches
70 Starboard wing integral fuel tank, total fuel capacity, 2,868 Imp gal (3,445 US gal/13,040 l)
71 Leading-edge wing fence
72 Hot air leading-edge de-icing
73 Fuel filler cap
74 Fuel venting piping
75 Outer wing panel dry bay
76 Starboard navigation (green) and strobe (white) lights

77 Wing-tip fairing
78 Static dischargers
79 Ventral, retractable landing lamp
80 Starboard aileron
81 Inboard aileron balances
82 Aileron servo tab
83 Aileron hydraulic actuator
84 Flap tracks
85 Flap drive shaft and screw jacks
86 Starboard lift dumpers, open
87 Outboard double-slotted flap segment, down position
88 Flap vane articulating linkage
89 Flap track fairings
90 Inboard double slotted flap segment
91 Rear spar/fuselage main frame
92 Mid-cabin passenger seating
93 Overhead stowage bins
94 ADF loop aerials
95 Cabin roof trim/lighting panels

96 Passenger service units
97 Rear cargo hold door
98 Overhead stowage bins
99 Starboard engine intake
100 Hinged cowling panels
101 Starboard engine nacelle graphite-epoxy cowling panels
102 Aft passenger seat row
103 Cabin rear bulkhead
104 Wardrobe, port and starboard
105 Forward engine mounting bulkhead
106 Toilet compartment, port and starboard
107 Cabin attendants' folding seats (2)
108 Rear engine mounting/pressure bulkhead

109 Auxiliary Power Unit (APU) bay
110 Engine bleed air ducting
111 Rear fuselage hydraulic equipment bay
112 Fin root fillet
113 Thrust reverser clamshell doors, open
114 Fin root fillet AFRP construction
115 Tailplane de-icing air ducting
116 Rudder hydraulic actuator
117 Four-spar fin torsion box construction
118 Fin leading-edge ribs
119 Trimming tailplane pivot fixing
120 Anti-collision light
121 Starboard trimming tailplane
122 Starboard elevator
123 Elevator hinge control and hydraulic actuators
124 Tailcone fairing
125 Tail navigation light
126 Starboard elevator
127 Static dischargers
128 Tailplane tip fairing
129 Port trimming tailplane rib construction
130 Hot air leading-edge de-icing
131 Rudder
132 Carbon-fibre composite rudder construction
133 Port airbrake panel, open position
134 Airbrake panel construction
135 Hinge fairings
136 Airbrake hydraulic jack
137 Sloping fin mounting bulkhead
138 Tail bumper
139 Nacelle pylon fairing
140 Port thrust reverser clamshell door
141 Door actuator housing
142 Engine exhaust nozzle
143 Multi-lobe exhaust duct mixer/silencer
144 Carbon-fibre engine by-pass ducting
145 Fore and aft engine mounting beams

146 Rolls-Royce Tay Mk620-15 turbofan engine
147 Ventral accessory equipment gearbox
148 Acoustically lined intake duct
149 Intake lip hot air de-icing
150 Rear underfloor cargo hold capacity 260 cu ft (7,36m³)
151 Door surround structure
152 Optional rear service door
153 AFRP wing root fillet construction
154 Inboard flap track
155 Flap hydraulic motor and interconnecting shaft
156 Undercarriage wheel bay
157 Mainwheel leg side stay and hydraulic retraction jack
158 Main undercarriage leg pivot fixing
159 Inboard lift dumper panels
160 Port inboard double slotted flap segment
161 Flap track fairings
162 Flap down position
163 Outboard double slotted flap segment
164 Flap carbon-fibre composite construction
165 Outboard lift dumper
166 Flap shroud ribs
167 Port aileron hydraulic actuator
168 Servo tab
169 Carbon-fibre composite aileron construction
170 Port aileron
171 Static dischargers
172 Retractable landing lamp
173 Wing-tip fairing
174 Port navigation (red) and strobe (white) lights
175 Outer wing panel rib construction
176 Corrugated inner skin de-icing air ducts
177 Port wing integral fuel tank
178 Lower wing skin stringer panel
179 Ventral access hatches
180 Wing lattice rib construction
181 Leading-edge rib construction
182 Corrugated inner skin/stringer panel
183 Wing skin panelling
184 Twin mainwheels
185 Port leading-edge wing fence
186 Dowty-Rotol main undercarriage leg strut
187 Position of pressure refuelling connection in starboard wing
188 Fuel pumps
189 Multi-bolt wing root joint strap
190 Spar attachment joints
191 Leading-edge de-icing air duct

Mike Badrocke

HARBIN Y-12 PEOPLE'S REPUBLIC OF CHINA

The Y-12 (Y indicates 'Yunshuji' or Transport aircraft, and the designation is sometimes rendered as Yun-12) is a product of the Harbin aircraft factory in Heilongjiang province, one of the major centres of aerospace activity in China. Known as the Harbin Aircraft Manufacturing Corporation (HAMC), the factory was set up in 1952, and for six years was concerned only with aircraft repair. It then progressed to the licence production of Soviet aircraft, building the Mil Mi-4 helicopter (as the Z-5) and the Ilyushin Il-28 light bomber (as the H-5) before building the 7-seat twin-engined Y-11 utility aircraft, the first modern aircraft of wholly-Chinese design and construction. From the Y-11, with which it shared the configuration but little else, the Y-12 was developed. The first of three prototypes flew on 14 July 1982. Picking the Pratt & Whitney PT6A to power the Y-12, Harbin adopted such new features (compared with the Y-11) as a NASA GAW supercritical aerofoil section, bonded construction in place of rivets, and integral rather than bag fuel tanks. Two prototypes and a static test airframe (at first known as Y-11T1 but then as Y-12 I) were followed by three Y-12 II (originally Y-11T2) development aircraft, used to obtain certification in compliance with US FAR Pt 23 and Pt 135 standards. The first of the Y-12 II flew on 16 August 1984 and received domestic certification in December 1985. Under an agreement between Harbin and the Hong Kong Aircraft Engineering Co. (HAECO), the latter installed Western avionics and interior in the sixth Y-12 to help 'westernise' the aircraft for export. UK certification was received on 20 June 1990.

VARIANTS

The initial production version was the Y-12 (I), powered by twin PT6A-11 engines, but this was soon replaced by the upgraded Y-12 (II), which differs primarily in having uprated 462kW (620shp) PT6A-27s and a smaller vertical fin. Leading-edge slats have also been deleted. The Y-12 (II) remains in production but is expected to be replaced by the Y-12 (IV), which made its first flight on 30 August 1993 and received domestic approval on 3 July 1994. FAA certification to FAR Pt 23 followed on 26 March 1995. The Y-12 (IV) incorporates a number of changes to improve performance and make the aircraft more attractive to non-Asian customers, particularly North America. Changes include modifications to wing tips, control surface actuation, main landing gear and brakes, and remodelled seating for up to 19 passengers. The PT6A-27 has been retained, but in uprated form producing 507kW (680shp). Maximum take-off weights and payload are increased to 5,670kg (12,500lb) and 1,984kg (4,374lb) respectively. Installation of EFIS, TCAS, GWPS and flight data recorder is being considered. Stretched and pressurised versions are also on the drawing board. The Y-12 (IV) will also be assembled in Canada under an agreement signed with Canadian Aerospace Group (CAG). The aircraft, to be marketed as the Twin Panda, will receive Western instrumentation, interiors, wheels and brakes.

SERVICE USE

The Y-12 first entered service with local airlines, but is now also operated by airlines in Fiji, Nepal, Laos, Nepal and Sri Lanka, and several non-airline customers in Asia-Pacific and Africa. Production exceeds 100 aircraft.

SPECIFICATION
(Harbin Y-12 (II))

Dimensions: Wingspan 17.23m (56ft 6½in); length overall 14.86m (48ft 9in); height overall 5.57m (18ft 3½in), wing area 34.27m² (368.9ft²).
Power Plant: Two 462kW (620shp) Pratt & Whitney Canada PT6A-27 turboprops with Hartzell three-blade constant-speed reversible-pitch propellers.
Weights: Max take-off 5,300kg (11,684lb); max landing 5,300kg (11,684lb); max payload 1,700kg (3,748lb).
Performance: Max cruising speed 157kts (292km/h); max rate of climb 8.1m/s (1,594ft/min); service ceiling 7,000m (22,960ft); take-off field length 425m (1,395ft); landing field length 340m (1,120ft); range with typical payload 723nm (1,340km).
Accommodation: Flight crew of two and seating for 17 passengers, three-abreast with single aisle. Baggage compartment volume front and rear 2.66m³ (93.95ft³).

IPTN N-250 INDONESIA

The first fully indigenous aircraft design project of Indonesia's fledgling aerospace industry was announced at the Paris air show on 15 June 1989 by Indonesia's technology minister and IPTN's president director Prof Dr Ing B J Habibie. Indonesia's most ambitious programme to date, while of conventional high-wing configuration and non-swept T-tailplane, nevertheless features latest technology, including fully-powered fly-by-wire controls, electronic flight instrumentation system (EFIS) and engine indication and crew alerting system (EICAS) with six CRT colour displays. The sixth CRT is for an optional global positioning system (GPS). The structure includes 10 per cent composites, primarily for control surfaces. Allison AE 2100C turboprops with low-noise six-bladed propellers were chosen in July 1990. Prototype construction began in 1992, but it soon became evident that for a 50-seater, the aircraft would be overweight and plans were made the following year to stretch the airframe to provide a 64-68 passenger capacity. The prototype rolled out in the original configuration on 10 November 1994 and made its maiden flight on 10 August 1995. Four more development aircraft and two static/fatigue test airframes participated in the certification programme, with the first N-250-100 flown on 13 December 1996. Domestic certification and FAA/IAA approval delayed to 1998, with first customer deliveries expected towards the end of the year.

VARIANTS

The initial production version is the N-250-100 with a fuselage 1.525m (5ft 0in) longer than the prototype and shorter engine nacelles. It is to be made available in passenger, cargo and combi models. Based on the short fuselage prototype for 50/54 passengers, the N-250-50 will have a lower-mounted wing box, to reduce weight and drag, and a larger diameter to increase cabin and baggage volume. An AEW version is under consideration for the future, with a planned in-service date of 2004. The N-270 is a stretched and uprated derivative of the N250-100 optimised for the US market, and is to be assembled at a new plant in Mobile, Alabama, by American Regional Aircraft Industry (AMRAI), owned 40 per cent by IPTN. Principal changes include the same AE 2100C engines uprated to 2,983kW (4,000shp), six additional fuselage frames to produce a 3.05m (10ft 0in) stretch to accommodate typically 70 passengers, higher gross weight and additional cargo and baggage compartments. First flight is scheduled for late 1998, with initial deliveries in the latter part of 1999. IPTN also wants to extend further the market for the N250 with plans to set up a European production line in Germany.

SERVICE USE

At 1 January 1998, orders and options, mostly from Indonesian airlines, totalled 213 aircraft, just 46 short of the company's stated break-even figure. IPTN expects to sell at least 400 to local carriers. First

SPECIFICATION
(IPTN N-250-100)

Dimensions: Wingspan 28.00m (91ft 10¼in); length overall 28.15m (92ft 4½in); height overall 8.78m (28ft 9¾in), wing area 65.00m² (699.7ft²).
Power Plant: Two 2,386kW (3,200shp) Allison AE 2100C turboprops, with Dowty six-blade propellers.
Weights: Operating weight empty 15,700kg (34,612lb); max take-off 24,800kg (54,674lb); max landing 24,600kg (54,233lb); max payload 6,200kg (13,668lb).
Performance: Max cruising speed 330kts (611km/h); max rate of climb 10.0m/s (1,968ft/min); service ceiling 7,620m (25,000ft); take-off field length 1,220m (4,000ft); landing field length 1,220m (4,000ft); range with max payload 686nm (1,270km).
Accommodation: Flight crew of two. Seating for up to 68 passengers, four-abreast with central aisle. Total baggage volume 11.65m³ (411.4ft³).

Below: Three-view of the Y-12(II) in its production form, with a larger dorsal fin than the prototype.

Right: The latest Y-12(IV) version, seen here at Zhuhai, has been improved and 'westernised'.

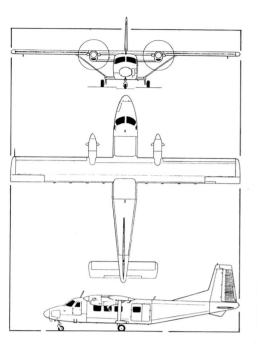

Left: The N-250, shown here on its Paris debut in June 1997, is the embodiment of the bold ambitions of Indonesia's technology minister to develop an aircraft manufacturing industry in his country. But while the aircraft will find a role with Indonesia's domestic operators, the trend towards jet aircraft may limit its appeal elsewhere in the world.

ILYUSHIN IL-62 RUSSIA

The Il-62 was first unveiled in September 1962 and made its first flight in January 1963, having been developed to provide Aeroflot with a long-range jet transport comparable in comfort and performance to the equipment already in service with Western airlines. Soviet design bureaux matched Western products in most categories of airliner, both turboprop and turbojet, with the notable exception of a four-jet design featuring podded engines on the wing, as exemplified by the Boeing 707/Douglas DC-8/Convair 880 generation. Instead, when the first Soviet four-jet design was developed by the Ilyushin bureau, a rear-engined, high-tail layout was chosen, closely matching the configuration of the Vickers VC-10. In common with Western designs of similar layout, the Il-62 required lengthy flight development to overcome the tendency of this type to enter a deep stall from which recovery was impossible. An additional complication resulted from the tardy development of an engine suitable for the Il-62, the first example(s) of which flew with 73.6kN (16,535lb) Lyulka AL-7 turbojets. The 103kN (23,150lb) Kuznetsov NK-8-4 turbofans were introduced later in the programme, which involved two prototypes and three pre-production aircraft. The Il-62 has the NATO reporting name 'Classic'.

VARIANTS

The Il-62 entered production with NK-8-4 turbofans, and was normally furnished to accommodate 168

passengers in a single-class layout, although up to 186 could be carried. This version had cascade-type thrust-reversers on the outer engines only. By 1971 Ilyushin had produced the Il-62M, in which Soloviev D-30KU engines replaced the Kuznetsov engines. The improved specific fuel consumption of this new engine was combined with increased fuel capacity (through the introduction of a tank in the fin) to give the Il-62M considerably better payload/range performance, thus overcoming one of the failings of the original version. A number of internal changes were made, with a revised layout of the flight deck, new avionics to allow routine operation in Cat II conditions (with provision to extend to Cat III), and a change in the wing spoiler control system to permit the spoilers to be used differentially for better roll control. A further variant appeared in 1978 as the Il-62MK, with the same engines as the Il-62M, but with structural, landing gear and control system changes to permit operation at the higher take-off and landing weights of 167,000kg (368,170lb) and 110,000kg (242,500lb) respectively. Maximum accommodation increased to 195, with an interior redesign featuring a 'widebody' look and enclosed overhead baggage lockers. Clamshell-type thrust reversers were used on the D-30KU engines.

SERVICE USE

The Il-62 entered service with Aeroflot on 15 September 1967, on the Moscow-Montreal route,

SPECIFICATION
(Ilyushin Il-62M)

Dimensions: Wingspan 43.20m (141ft 9in); length overall 53.12m (174ft 3½in); height overall 12.35m (40ft 6¼in), wing area 279.5m² (3,009ft²).
Power Plant: Four 107.9kN (24,250lb) Soloviev D-30KU turbofans.
Weights: Operating weight empty 71,600kg (157,520lb); max take-off 165,000kg (363,760lb); max landing 105,000kg (231,483lb); max payload 23,000kg (50,706lb)
Performance: Max cruising speed 496kts (920km/h); take-off field length 3,300m (10,830ft); landing field length 2,500m (8,200ft); range with max payload 4,210nm (7,800km).
Accommodation: Flight crew of four or five. Seating for up to 186 passengers, six-abreast with central aisle. Total cargo/baggage volume 48.0m³ (1,695ft³).

after a period of proving flights within the Soviet Union. It replaced the Tu-114 on the Moscow-New York route in July 1968 and subsequently became standard equipment on most of Aeroflot's long-distance routes, internationally and domestically. The Il-62M entered service on the Moscow-Havana route in 1974. Production of the Il-62 in all versions is thought to have exceeded 250, of which about 150

ILYUSHIN IL-76 RUSSIA

The design of the Il-76 began in the late 1960s to provide a heavy transport for both military and civil use, primarily as a replacement for the Antonov An-12. Key design requirements were the ability to accommodate and lift specific items of military equipment and civil engineering hardware, but also included a rough-field capability and facilities for operation in extreme climatic conditions as encountered in Siberia and elsewhere. The prototype Il-76 first flew on 25 March 1971, and was demonstrated at that year's Paris air show. It was joined by two more prototypes and three static test airframes. Series production started in 1975 and continues at the Chkalov Plant in Tashkent, Uzbekistan. The NATO reporting name for the Il-76 is 'Candid'.

VARIANTS

The original unarmed Il-76 military version was followed by the Il-76T for civil use, featuring an additional fuel tank in the wing centre-section and higher operating weights. Further increases in fuel

capacity and weights, strengthened wings and centre-fuselage, as well as improved Aviadvigatel (Soloviev) D-30KP-1 turbofans produced the generally unarmed Il-76TD. The Il-76M and Il-76MD are armed military variants with rear gun turret, based on the -T and -TD models respectively. First flight of the stretched and modernised military Il-76MF, powered by 156.9kN (35,275lb) PS-90AN turbofans, was made on 1 August 1995, and this model is also being offered in civilianised Il-76TF configuration. The Il-76 was also produced in many other specialised military versions, and a new version with CFM56 turbofans is under development.

SERVICE USE

Many Il-76s were used by Aeroflot and are now in service with its successor airlines in the cargo role and can be seen all over the world. Luton-based Air Foyle operates the type in Western Europe. It is believed that total production has exceeded the 1,000 mark, although many of these were built for military purposes.

Below: Ilyushin's Il-76 also found its way to many of the Soviet Union's strongest allies, including Syria, whose national airline operates it mainly on government flights. It can carry 50 tonnes of cargo, loaded through the rear clamshell doors, or passengers in specially built 30-seat modules.

Below: This three-view shows the IL-76 in its military guise, with an armed not faired turret.

Right: The IL-76 typically has a seven-man crew plus provision for a navigator in the nose.

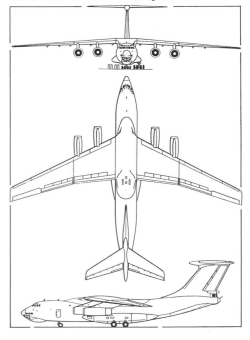

SPECIFICATION
(Ilyushin Il-76T)

Dimensions: Wingspan 50.50m (165ft 8in); length overall 46.59m (152ft 10in); height overall 14.76m (48ft 5in), wing area 300.0m² (3,229.2ft²).
Power Plant: Four 117.7kN (26,455lb) Aviadvigatel D-30KP turbofans.
Weights: Operating weight empty 89,000kg (196,211lb); max take-off 170,000kg (374,785lb); max landing 140,000kg (308,640lb); max payload 40,000kg (88,185lb).
Performance: Max cruising speed 432kts (800km/h); service ceiling 15,500m (50,850ft); take-off field length 850m (2,790ft); landing field length 450m (1,475ft); range with max payload 3,600nm (6,660km).
Accommodation: Flight crew of five. Cabin volume 235.5m³ (8,310ft³) for cargo. Also available passenger modules for 30 passengers each.

have been for Aeroflot, with the balance going to nations in the Soviet sphere of influence, for airline use by CAAC (China), Interflug (East Germany), Balkan Bulgarian, LOT (Poland), Tarom (Romania), CSA (Czechoslovakia), Cubana, LA Mozambique and Choson Minhang (North Vietnam). Around 160 were still in service in 1998, the vast majority in Russia and other CIS countries.

Below: Like many other commercial aircraft types produced in the old Soviet Union, the Ilyushin Il-62 enabled the USSR's satellite states to maintain their air connections with headquarters in Moscow. Cubana is the largest user left outside what is now Russia, still operating a dozen of the improved Ilyushin Il-62Ms on its long-haul flights.

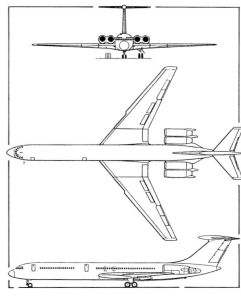

Above: A three-view drawing of the Il-62M, which was the principal version of this four-jet transport produced in the 1970s and 1980s. New Soloviev engines and various internal changes now distinguish it from the original Il-62 production version.

ILYUSHIN IL-76

ILYUSHIN IL-86 RUSSIA

SPECIFICATION
(Ilyushin Il-86)

Dimensions: Wingspan 48.06m (157ft 8¼in); length overall 59.54m (195ft 4in); height overall 15.81m (50ft 10½in), wing area 320.0m² (3,444ft²).
Power Plant: Four 127.5kN (28,660lb) Kutznetsov NK-86 turbofans.
Weights: Max take-off 206,000kg (454,150lb); max landing 175,000kg (385,810lb); max payload 42,000kg (92,593lb).
Performance: Max cruising speed 512kts (950km/h); service ceiling 11,000m (36,090ft); take-off field length 2,600m (8,530ft); landing field length 1,980m (6,500ft); range with max payload 1,945nm (3,600km).
Accommodation: Flight crew of three. Seating for up to 300 passengers, nine-abreast with twin aisles.

Intended as a successor to the Ilyushin Il-62 and developed in response to the Boeing 747 to give Aeroflot a chance to compete effectively on long-haul routes, the Il-86 was the first to provide a 'wide-body' cabin and the first to have its engines in wing-mounted pods, all previous Soviet jet transports either having their engines rear-mounted on the fuselage or buried in the wing roots. Even so, it is interesting to record that the first published illustration of the Il-86 design showed a rear-engined configuration. The Il-86 design dates back to the early 1970s, the first of two prototypes having made its initial flight from a Moscow airfield on 22 December 1976. To power the Soviet 'airbus', the Kuznetsov bureau developed a new engine, the NK-86, although it is believed that Soloviev turbofans

were in view from the outset, and these have now been adopted in the Il-96 derivative. Flight development of the Il-86 appears to have proceeded relatively smoothly, and the third aircraft, described as the first production example, flew on 24 October 1977 at Voronezh, where the final assembly line was set up. A substantial contribution to Il-86 production was made by the Polish aircraft industry, which manufactured the fin and tailplane, engine pylons and wing slats at the PZL Mielec plant. One of the interesting features of the Il-86, and related to the limited support facilities available at many airports served by Aeroflot, is that entry to the cabin is by way of airstairs incorporated in three doors at ground level in the lower fuselage. From the lower deck vestibules, where heavy winter overcoats can

be stowed, stairs lead up to the main cabin, making the aircraft independent of airport loading stairs. The type has the NATO reporting name 'Camber'.

VARIANTS
After going into production, the Il-86 underwent routine improvement and updating, in the course of which the gross weight was increased to a maximum permitted 208,000kg (458,560lb). As early as

Below: The Soviet Union's first wide-body passenger aircraft was intended to replace the Il-62 on long-haul flights but proved **seriously deficient in range and had limited international exposure. Few are seen abroad; AJT serves within Russia and the CIS.**

ILYUSHIN IL-114 RUSSIA

SPECIFICATION
(Ilyushin Il-114)

Dimensions: Wingspan 30.00m (98ft 5¼in); length overall 26.88m (88ft 2in); height overall 9.32m (30ft 7in), wing area 81.9m2 (881.6ft2).
Power Plant: Two 1,839kW (2,466shp) Klimov TV7-117 turboprops, with six-blade SV-34 CFRP propellers.
Weights: Operating weight empty 15,000kg (33,070lb); max take-off 22,700kg (50,045lb); max payload 6,500kg (14,330lb).
Performance: Normal cruising speed 270kts (500km/h); service ceiling 7,200m (23,625ft); take-off field length 1,550m (5,085ft); landing field length 1,300m (4,265ft); range with max payload 540nm (1,000km).
Accommodation: Flight crew of two. Seating for up to 64 passengers, four-abreast, two seats each side of central aisle.

Designed as a successor to the Antonov An-24 on Aeroflot routes with ranges of up to 540nm (1,000km), the basic design parameters and configuration was established as long ago as 1986. Equipped to operate in weather minima down to ICAO Cat II standard, the Il-114 is a conventional pressurised low-wing monoplane with swept fin and rudder and slight dihedral on the wing centre-section. Extensive use is made of composite materials and advanced metal alloys, including titanium, making up about 10 per cent of structural weight. In configuration, it has a striking resemblance to the British Aerospace ATP, also typically seating 64 passengers. Two 1,839kW (2,466shp) Klimov TV7-117 turboprop engines drive low-noise six-bladed CFRP propellers. The Il-114 has built-in airstairs and can operate from unpaved airfields with little ground

support. The prototype first flew at the Zhukovsky flight test centre on 29 March 1990. Two more flying prototypes and two for static tests were used in the certification programme which was completed in 1993. The first production aircraft flew on 7 August 1992 at Tashkent in Uzbekistan, where the aircraft is built. Some components are produced by Polish, Romanian and Bulgarian aerospace companies.

VARIANTS
The basic production version is the Il-114 with the Klimov TV7-117 turboprops and a maximum take-off weight of 22,700kg (50,045lb). With higher-rated TV7M-117 engines, increased take-off weight and 500kg (1,102lb) more payload, the aircraft is known as the Il-114M. The Il-114PC export version with Pratt & Whitney Canada PW127C turboprops, new avionics and improved systems, which made its maiden flight in 1996. Also being offered are the Il-114P maritime patrol version, and the Il-114T Cargo model, featuring a maximum take-off weight of 23,500kg (51,808lb) and a 3.31m × 1.78m (10ft 10in × 5ft 10in) cargo door in the rear fuselage. The Il-114T was developed specifically for Uzbekistan Airways. First flight of production aircraft took place on 14 September 1996. The Il-114FK is a military reconnaissance/cartographic version with a glazed nose, small undernose radome, large observation blister below flight deck windows and container for side-looking airborne radar (SLAR) on portside. Cabin windows have been deleted. A stretch for 70-75 passengers is planned.

SERVICE USE
First delivery made to Uzbekistan Airways. Other orders placed by a number of other CIS airlines, but no details are available.

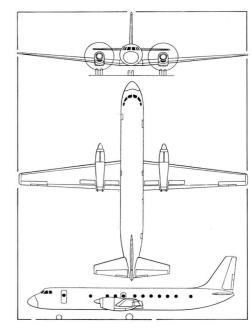

Above: The three-view drawing of the Ilyushin Il-114 shows its similarities with the British Aerospace ATP, which has the same capacity.

Right: The Il-114T freighter demonstrated at the Paris air show in 1997. In its circular fuselage it can carry up to 6,500kg (14,300lb) of cargo a distance of some 1,000km (620 miles). The propellers are carbon-fibre reinforced plastic.

1981 reports were appearing that a longer-range derivative of the Il-86 was under development, and by 1986 this was known to have been redesignated Il-96. Production terminated after 103 civil examples had been built, including the two prototypes. Re-engining with CFM56 engines is being considered to increase its range, which had always been insufficient for intercontinental routes, but it is unlikely to proceed, given the shortage of cash among the CIS airlines.

SERVICE USE

The Il-86 entered service on 26 December 1980, operating between Moscow and Tashkent. Many other domestic destinations were added to the Il-86 network during 1981, and the first international service, between Moscow and East Berlin, was flown on 3 July 1981. Some 90 remain in service, all in Russia and other CIS countries, with the exception of three flown by China Xinjiang Airlines. The two largest users are Aeroflot and Vnukovo Airlines.

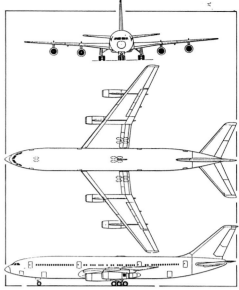

Left: Aeroflot initially operated virtually all of the 100 Il-86s built, but these have now been dispersed among the new airlines which emerged from the old Aeroflot directorates. Only 19 remain in the fleet of Aeroflot Russian International Airlines (ARIA). Two are shown here at Tashkent.

Above: The three-view depicts the only version of the Il-86 to have actually been built. It was the Soviet Union's first wide-body aircraft. The passengers enter the aircraft at the lower deck level, where a flight of stairs leads them through to the main cabin accommodation.

ILYUSHIN IL-114

ILYUSHIN Il-96 RUSSIA

The Il-96 (also known as the Il-96-300 in its basic 300-seat form) is an obvious derivative of the Il-86, although described as an almost wholly new design. Compared with its predecessor, the Il-96 has a shorter fuselage, though of the same cross-section, and a new supercritical wing of greater span and area but reduced sweepback (30 deg), with the addition of large winglets at the tips. Fuel capacity is almost double that of the Il-86, giving the type a substantially increased range capability. Structurally, the Il-96 makes use of newer materials to reduce weight, and systems have been modernised, with the introduction of a triplex fly-by-wire control system and 'glass' cockpit featuring six displays (three for each pilot) for presentation of all performance and system status information. Equipment is of a standard to allow operation in Cat III weather minima, but modernisation has not been taken so far as to allow two-crew operation and a flight engineer's position is retained on the flight deck. Accommodation for 300 passengers is provided on an upper deck, with the lower deck reserved for cargo and baggage. The first of five prototypes flew on 28 September 1988. A further two airframes were built for static and fatigue testing. Production was started in 1991 and a total of nine aircraft were flying by the time the new type received certification on 29 December 1992.

VARIANTS

The initial production version is designated Il-96-300, alluding to its maximum passenger capacity, although a more normal mixed configuration provides for 235 passengers. It is powered by four Aviadvigatel PS-90A turbofans each generating 156.9kN (35,275lb) static thrust and has a take-off weight of 216,000kg and typical range of 4,860nm (9,000km). A westernised version with 164.6kN (37,000lb) Pratt & Whitney PW2337 turbofans and Rockwell Collins digital avionics, for Cat IIIb fully automatic landing capability, was first projected as the Il-96-350, but this was changed to Il-96M in 1990. A prototype, designated Il-96MO first flew on 6 April 1996. The Il-96M has a fuselage lengthened to 63.94m (209ft 9in) to provide accommodation for up to 386 passengers, and an increased take-off weight of 270,000kg (595,238lb). A cargo version, the Il-96T, has a 4.85m x 2.87m (15ft 11in x 9ft 5in) cargo door on the port side forward of the wing, and a maximum payload of 92,000kg (202,820lb). It first flew on 16 May 1997 and was expected to receive certification at the end of the year. The Il-96MK is a projected development with high bypass-ratio ducted engines, while a proposed twin-engined derivative of the Il-96M/T is known as the Il-98.

SERVICE USE

Aeroflot took delivery of the first IL-96-300 aircraft in early 1993, operating a small number until supplemented by the first IL-96M, due to enter service at the end of 1997.

Below: The Il-96T freighter has no windows fitted. This new version will be flown by Aeroflot-Aria and may have export potential.

SPECIFICATION
(Ilyushin Il-96M)

Dimensions: Wingspan 60.11m (197ft 2½in); length overall 63.94m (209ft 9in); height overall 15.72m (51ft 7in), wing area 391.6m² (4,215ft²).
Power Plant: Four 156.9kN (35,275lb) Aviadvigatel PS-90A turbofans.
Weights: Operating weight empty 132,400kg (257,940lb); max take-off 270,000kg (595,238lb); max landing 175,000kg (385,810lb); max payload 58,000kg (127,866lb).
Performance: Max cruising speed 469kts (870km/h); service ceiling 11,000m (36,090ft); take-off field length 3,350m (11,000ft); landing field length 2,250m (7,385ft); range with max payload 6,195nm (11,482km).
Accommodation: Flight crew of two. Seating for up to 386 passengers, nine-abreast with twin aisles.

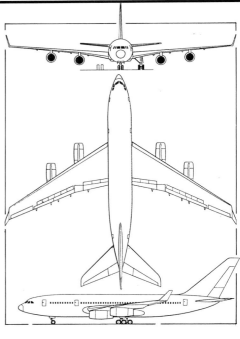

**Ilyushin Il-96-300
Cutaway Drawing Key**

1 Radome
2 Weather radar scanner
3 Scanner mounting and tracking mechanism
4 Front pressure bulkhead
5 Retractable landing lamp, port and starboard
6 Rudder pedals
7 Control column
8 Instrument panel, electronic flight instrumentation system (EFIS)
9 Instrument panel shroud
10 Windscreen panels
11 Overhead systems switch panel
12 Engineering and maintenance panel
13 First officer's seat
14 Flight engineer's seat
15 Captain's seat
16 Side console panel
17 Underfloor avionics equipment racks
18 Observer's seat
19 Crew wardrobe
20 Cabin attendant's seat
21 Cockpit doorway
22 Toilet compartments, port and starboard
23 Starboard service door/emergency exit
24 Entry vestibule
25 Wardrobe
26 No1 forward entry door
27 Door mounted escape chute
28 Nose undercarriage leg strut
29 Hydraulic steering jacks
30 Twin nosewheels, forward retracting
31 Fuselage lower lobe frame and stringer construction
32 Main cabin floor level
33 Cabin window panel
34 Ball-mat cargo handling floor
35 Forward cargo door 5.8 ft by 6 ft (1.78 m by 1.825m)
36 Film screen
37 Cabin wall trim panelling
38 Forward underfloor cargo hold, capacity 1,307 cu ft (37.0m³)
39 ABK 1.5 (LD-3 equivalent) container, six in forward hold
40 First class passenger cabin, 22 seats, six abreast
41 Cabin attendants' seats (total 12)
42 Curtained cabin bulkhead
43 Buffet stall
44 Starboard service door/emergency exit
45 Cabin attendants' work area
46 Forward cabin conditioned air delivery duct
47 Wardrobe
48 No 2 centre cabin entry door
49 Water tanks
50 Leading-edge wing root fillet
51 Underfloor galley
52 Food cart elevators
53 Business class passenger cabin, 40 seats, eight-abreast
54 Wing centre section carry through structure
55 Centre section long range fuel tankage provision (stretched version)
56 Floor beam construction
57 Wing spar attachment fuselage main frames
58 Centre fuselage frames and stringer construction
59 Starboard wing integral fuel tank; total maximum fuel capacity 33,572 Imp gal (152 620 l) for long-range stretched version
60 Fuel collector box and pump housing
61 Leading-edge slat drive shaft
62 Slat screw jacks
63 Inboard slat segments

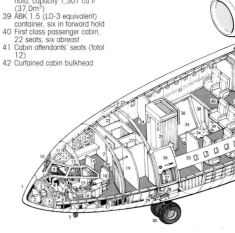

Left: This three-view shows the similarities, and differences, from the Il-86 which it has replaced. The fuselage has the same cross-section and length, but the wing is all-new, with greater chord and winglets.

Right: The Ilyushin Il-96M, powered by four Pratt & Whitney PW2337 turbofans, each generating a static thrust of 164.6kN (37,000lb), goes through its paces at the 1997 Paris air show.

64 Starboard engine nacelles
65 Nacelle pylons
66 Fuel system piping
67 Outboard leading-edge slat segments
68 Starboard navigation (green) and strobe (white) lights
69 Winglet
70 Starboard outboard ride control and load alleviation aileron
71 Outboard spoiler/airbrake segments (four)
72 Outboard single slotted flap segment
73 Inner spoiler segments (two)
74 Flap drive shaft and screw jacks
75 Starboard aileron
76 Triplex hydraulic actuators
77 Inboard double slotted flap segment
78 Flap track and carriage
79 Inboard airbrakes/lift dumpers
80 Pressure floor above wheel bay
81 Starboard main undercarriage wheel bay
82 Centre undercarriage wheel bay
83 Hydraulic retraction jack
84 Centre undercarriage leg pivot fixing
85 Flap drive motor and gearbox

86 Tourist-class passenger cabin 173 seats, nine-abreast (alternative layout for 300 all-tourist class passengers)
87 ADF aerials
88 Cabin roof trim/lighting panels
89 Rear cargo hold door (size as item 35)
90 Rear cabin conditioned air delivery duct
91 ABK 1.5 containers, 10 in rear hold
92 Cabin floor beams
93 Rear cabin seat rows
94 Wardrobe
95 Cabin attendants' stowage compartment
96 Cabin attendant's folding seat
97 Rear vestibule area
98 Fin root fillet
99 Tailfin attachment joints
100 Three-spar fin torsion box construction
101 Starboard tailplane
102 Starboard elevator
103 Fin leading edge
104 Fin rib construction
105 Anti-collision light
106 Communications aerial panel

107 Two-segment rudder
108 Rudder rib construction
109 Rubber hydraulic actuators
110 Auxiliary power unit (APU)
111 APU exhaust
112 Elevator rib construction
113 Port two-segment elevator
114 Tailplane tip fairing
115 Starboard trimming tailplane
116 Tailplane rib construction
117 Three-spar tailplane torsion box construction
118 Tailplane pivot fixing
119 Sealing plate
120 Tailplane centre-section carry-through structure

121 Tailplane trim control screw jack
122 Aft pressure bulkhead
123 Rear cabin toilet compartments (six)
124 No 3 rear cabin door, port and starboard
125 Underfloor bulk cargo hold capacity 530 cu ft (15,0m³)
126 Rear underfloor cargo hold

capacity 2,260 cu ft (64,0m³)
127 Overhead stowage bins
128 Passenger service units
129 Wing root trailing-edge fillet
130 Undercarriage bay pressure bulkhead
131 Centre undercarriage four wheel bogie
132 Auxiliary rear spar
133 Port main undercarriage pivot fixing
134 Hydraulic retraction jack
135 Port inboard lift dumpers
136 Inboard double slotted flap segment
137 Aileron hydraulic actuators
138 Port aileron
139 Flap down position
140 Outer single slotted flap segment
141 Port outboard spoilers/lift dumpers
142 Flap tracks and carriages
143 Flap track fairings

144 Port ride3 control and loan alleviation aileron
145 Winglet
146 Port navigation (red) and strobe (white) lights
147 Leading-edge slat segments
148 Outer wing panel joint rib
149 Lower wing skin/stringer panel
150 Port wing rib construction
151 Port wing integral fuel tank
152 Nacelle pylon attachment joint
153 Port outer nacelle pylon
154 Thrust reverser cowling, open
155 Thrust reverser cascades
156 Detachable engine cowling panels
157 Acoustically lined intake-duct
158 Port outer engine nacelle
159 Intermediate slat segments
160 Two-spar wing torsion box construction
161 Wing stringers
162 Wing skin panelling
163 Nacelle pylon drag strut
164 Engine exhaust nozzle

165 Multi lobe exhaust duct mixer
166 Thrust reverser blocker door
167 Soloview PS-90A (D-90A) turbofan engine
168 Ventral engine accessory equipment gearbox
169 Engine compressor face
170 Cowling intake nose ring, hot air de-iced
171 Starboard inner engine nacelle
172 Nacelle pylon construction
173 Port main undercarriage four wheel bogie
174 Main undercarriage leg strut
175 Side breaker strut
176 Inboard wing rib construction
177 Inboard slat segments
178 Engine bleed air ducting
179 Ventral air conditioning pack, port and starboard
180 Wing root rib attachment joint
181 Air conditioning system heat exchanger ram air intake

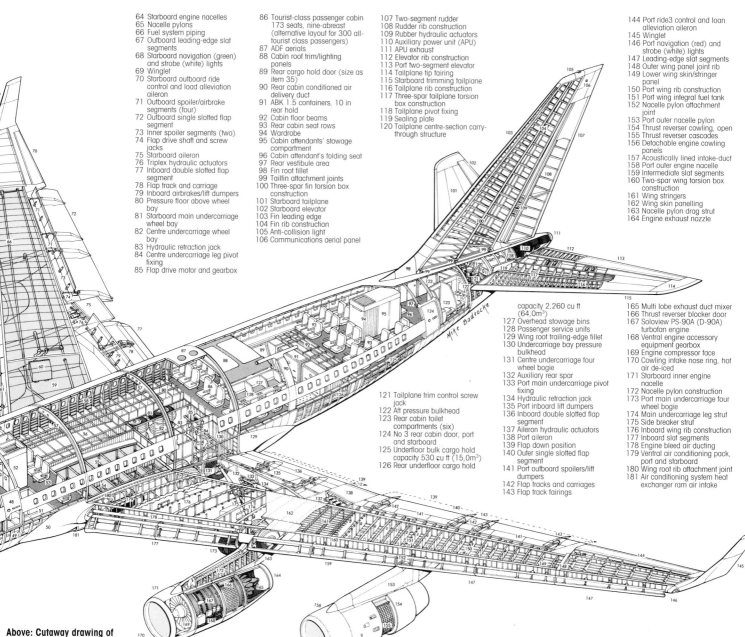

Above: Cutaway drawing of the Ilyushin Il-96-300.

LET L-410 TURBOLET CZECH REPUBLIC

SPECIFICATION
(Let L-410UVP-E)

Dimensions: Wingspan 19.98m (65ft 6½in);
length overall 14.43m (47ft 4in); height overall
5.83m (19ft 1½in), wing area 35.18m²
(378.7ft²).
Power Plant: Two 559kW (750shp) Motorlet
Walter M 601E turboprops, driving Avia V 510
five-blade constant-speed reversible-pitch metal
propellers.
Weights: Operating weight empty 3,985kg
(8,785lb); max take-off 6,400kg (14,110lb);
max landing 6,200kg (13,668lb); max payload
1,615kg (3,560lb).
Performance: Max cruising speed 168kts
(311km/h); max rate of climb 7.4m/s
(1,455ft/min); service ceiling 7,050m
(23,125ft); take-off field length 445m (1,460ft);
landing field length 240m (787ft); range with
max payload 294nm (546km).
Accommodation: Flight crew of one or two.
Seating for 19 passengers, two seats on one side
of the aisle, one on the other. Total baggage
volume front and rear 1.37m³ (48.4ft³).

After some years of licence-production of Soviet types, the Let Kunovice works began in 1966 the design and development of a small twin-engined light transport intended to meet the needs of East European nations in general (including the Soviet Union) as well as Czechoslovakia in particular. A high wing monoplane of conventional appearance, this aircraft emerged as the XL-410 in 1969, making its first flight on 16 April 1969. New turboprop engines under development by Motorlet at the Walter works were not ready, so prototypes and early production aircraft were fitted with imported Pratt & Whitney engines.

Above: Estonian regional airline ELK operates two Let L-410UVP-E aircraft on scheduled and charter services across the Baltic. Note the prominent external tip tanks.

VARIANTS
The initial production version of the Turbolet, as the aircraft came to be known, was the L-410A, with 533kW (715shp) PT6A-27 engines. Thirty-one were built, including four prototypes, one of which later became L-410AB when test flown with Hartzell four-blade (in place of the original three-blade) propellers. One L-410AF was built (for Hungary) with a revised, glazed nose compartment and was equipped for the aerial survey role. The L-410AS was equipped with a Soviet avionics fit. In 1973 the Motorlet M 601 engine became available, and the L-410M entered production with the 410kW (550shp) M 601A, soon superseded by the L-410MA with the more powerful M 601B. The L-410MU included equipment specified by Aeroflot, and production of all 'M' variants totalled 110. To overcome Soviet criticism of handling characteristics, the L-410UVP, first flown on 1 November 1977, introduced increased

LOCKHEED L100 HERCULES USA

Above: US charter company Southern Air Transport operates the largest commercial Hercules fleet in the world, using the type's excellent short-field performance to carry cargo to remote areas with little or no surface access.

The commercial L100 originated as a 'civilianised' version of the C-130 Hercules military tactical transport, and was first flown in the form of a Model 382 company demonstrator on 21 April 1964. FAA type approval was obtained on 16 February 1965. The origin of the Hercules goes back to an US Air Force specification of 1951 for a tactical transport and multi-mission aircraft capable of carrying up to 128 troops. More than 2,100 Hercules have been delivered, in more than 70 different variants.

VARIANTS
Small numbers of Model 382B Hercules (some also known as L100s) were built for commercial use from 1965 onwards. These early models had the same 29.79m (97ft 9in) overall length as the basic C-130B. The projected L100-10, with D22A engines replacing the 3,022kW (4,050shp) 501-D22s, was followed by the L100-20 with the same uprated engines and a 2.54m (8ft 4in) lengthening of the fuselage.

SPECIFICATION
(Lockheed L100-30)

Dimensions: Wingspan 40.41m (132ft 7in);
length overall 34.37m (112ft 9in); height overall
11.66m (38ft 3in), wing area 162.12m²
(1,745ft²).
Power Plant: Four 3,490kW (4,680shp) Allison
501-D22A turboprops, driving four-blade
Hamilton Standard constant-speed feathering and
reversing propellers.
Weights: Operating weight empty 35,325kg
(77,680lb); max take-off 70,308kg
(155,000lb); max landing 61,235kg
(135,000lb); max payload 23,183kg
(51,110lb).
Performance: Max cruising speed 315kts
(583km/h); initial rate of climb 8.64m/s
(1,700ft/min); take-off field length 1,890m
(6,200ft); landing field length 1,480m (4,850ft);
range with max payload 1,363nm (2,526km).
Accommodation: Flight crew of four. Seating for
up to 128 passengers.

The original demonstrator was converted to Model 382E (L100-20) form and first flew on 19 April 1968, gaining type approval on 4 October that year. The L100-30 had another 2.03m (6ft 8in) fuselage stretch and first flew on 14 August 1970, type approval being gained on 7 October.

SERVICE USE
Around 110 civil Hercules have been delivered, just over half being L100-30s. Almost all were for cargo transport by airlines and government agencies, although Indonesia's oil company Pelita Air Services has used the aircraft in passenger configuration, seating 128 passengers. Others have been fitted with modules to enable the carrying of passengers.

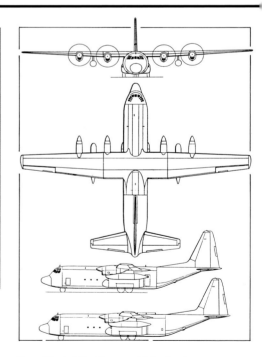

Above: The L-100-20 version of the Hercules is shown in this three-view drawing, with the side-view of the L-100-30 added below for comparison. This model, the most numerous in commercial service, has a 2.03m (6ft 8in) fuselage stretch.

Right: Outsize cargo specialist HeavyLift uses the Lockheed Hercules to supplement its larger Russian and Ukrainian aircraft on worldwide ad hoc and contract charter flights.

wing span and vertical tail area, dihedral on the tailplane, spoilers, automatic bank control flaps and numerous other systems and equipment changes. Soviet certification of the L-410UVP was obtained in 1980. Generally similar to this variant, the L-410UVP-E first flew on 30 December 1984 and introduced five-blade propellers, tip tanks and more powerful engines. It replaced the UVP from early 1985 onwards. Other suffixes were used for specialised versions. The L-420 was proposed as an export version fitted with new M-601F engines.

SERVICE USE

The L-410A entered service on Czech domestic routes operated by Slov-Air in late 1971. The L-410M began deliveries in 1976, followed by the L-410 UVP after certification in 1979. Aeroflot took delivery of its 500th L-410 in March 1985. A total of 1001 were produced, of which 872 were delivered to the then Soviet Union.

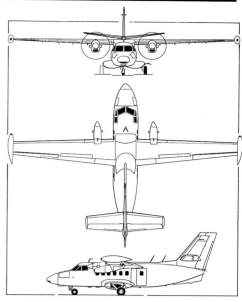

Left: This L-410UVP-E20 aircraft registered in Finland is the executive version, normally seating a maximum of 13 passengers and first certificated in 1990. It introduced emergency exits, separate baggage hold and Bendix/King avionics including autopilot.

Above: From 1986, the production version was the L-410UVP-E. The most obvious external feature of this variant was the provision of the wingtip tanks, but a number of internal changes were also made in order to improve comfort and economy.

LOCKHEED L1011 TRISTAR USA

SPECIFICATION
(Lockheed L1011-500)

Dimensions: Wingspan 50.09m (164ft 4in); length overall 50.05m (164ft 2½in); height overall 16.87m (55ft 4in), wing area 329.0m² (3,541ft²).
Power Plant: Three 222.4kN (50,000lb) Rolls-Royce RB211-524B4 turbofans.
Weights: Operating weight empty 111,312kg (245,400lb); max take-off 231,330kg (510,000lb); max landing 166,920kg (368,000lb); max payload 42,003kg (92,600lb).
Performance: Max cruising speed 525kts (973km/h); max rate of climb 14.3m/s (2,820ft/min); service ceiling 13,100m (43,000ft); take-off field length 2,800m (9,200ft); landing field length 2,065m (6,770ft); range with max payload 5,345nm (9,905km).
Accommodation: Flight crew of three. Seating for up to 330 passengers, nine-abreast with twin aisles. Total baggage/cargo volume 118.9m³ (4,200ft³).

Like the Electra, Lockheed's TriStar owes its origins to an American Airlines specification – but contrary to the case of the Electra, this airline did not in the end become a launch customer for the Lockheed jetliner. The 1966 specification was for a short/medium-range large-capacity transport, and to meet it Lockheed and Douglas produced very similar project designs, the most notable feature of which was the combination of podded engines on the wing with a third at the rear of the aircraft. Lockheed obtained launch orders for its L1011 design on 29 March 1968, from TWA and Eastern Airlines, after American had opted for the Douglas competitor. From the big new turbofan engines offered by Pratt & Whitney, General Electric and Rolls-Royce, Lockheed chose – with the full approval of its initial customers – the RB.211, a decision that committed Rolls-Royce to a programme of development and production that led it into bankruptcy in February 1971, placing not only the TriStar but the whole of the Lockheed company in jeopardy. The first L1011 had flown, meanwhile, on 17 November 1970, with four more required for the certification programme following by 2 December 1971. With the future of Rolls-Royce assured through its nationalisation, Lockheed was able to proceed with the TriStar, using the RB.211-22 at its initial rating of 186.9kN (42,000lb), the first flight with engines of this standard being made on 8 September 1971. Production and development proceeded throughout the 1970s, but sales of the Lockheed TriStar failed to match market projections and production was ended by Lockheed in 1984, leaving the company without a commercial jet transport programme.

VARIANTS

The original TriStar, with a fuselage length of 54.17m (177ft 8½in) and up to 400 seats, was the L1011-1, with a gross weight of 195,045kg (430,000lb). This was followed in 1974 by the L1011-200 with RB.211-524 engines rated at 213.6kN-222.4kN (48,000-50,000lb) and maximum take-off weight of up to 216,363kg (477,000lb) depending on fuel capacity. With the same higher operating weights and increased fuel capacities but the lower-rated -22B engines the aircraft was designated L1011-100. The first flight of a TriStar with -524 engines was made on 12 August 1976. In 1976 Lockheed launched the L1011-500, which combined higher weights and enlarged fuel capacity with a shorter fuselage to achieve very long ranges. Advanced aerodynamic features were also introduced in the L1011-500, including active controls, resulting in a 2.74m (9ft) increase in wing span and a reduction in tailplane area. The first L1011-500 flew in October 1978, with 222.4kN (50,000lb) 524B engines but without the extended wingtips, which were first flown in November 1979. The designation L1011-250 applies to conversions of the L1011-1 to have the same 524B4 engines as used in the L1011-500, allowing maximum take-off weight to be increased to 224,985kg (496,000lb). Fuel capacity is also increased. Conversion of six L1011-1s to -250 standard for Delta Air Lines began in 1986. Other L1011-1 conversions included the L1011-50, increasing maximum weight from 195,047kg (430,000lb) to 204,119kg (450,000lb), and the L1011-150, with a 10 per cent increase in range.

SERVICE USE

The L1011-1 was certificated on 14 April 1972, and Eastern Airlines flew the first revenue service on 26 April, with TWA flying its first service on 25 June 1972. The L1011-200 was certificated on 26 April 1977 and entered service with Saudia. The L1011-500 entered service with British Airways on 7 May 1979 and, with extended wings and active controls, was introduced by Pan American in 1980. Production of the TriStar totalled 250 of all versions of which some 180 remained in active service in 1998. The vast majority are now flown by charter airlines in Europe and North America, with the type remaining in front-line scheduled service only with Delta Air Lines, TransWorld Airlines, Royal Jordanian and AirLanka.

Lockheed TriStar 500 Cutaway Drawing Key

1 Radome
2 VOR localiser aerial
3 Radar scanner dish
4 ILS glideslope aerial
5 Front pressure bulkhead
6 Curved windscreen panels
7 Windscreen wipers
8 Instrument panel shroud
9 Rudder pedals
10 Cockpit floor level
11 Ventral access door
12 Forward underfloor radio and electronics bay
13 Pitot tubes
14 Observer's seat
15 Captain's seat
16 First officer's seat
17 Overhead panel
18 Flight engineer's station
19 Cockpit roof escape hatch
20 Air conditioning ducting
21 Forward galley units
22 Starboard service door
23 Forward toilet compartments
24 Curtained cabin divider
25 Wardrobe
26 Forward passenger door
27 Cabin attendant's folding seat
28 Nose undercarriage wheel bay
29 Ram air intake
30 Heat exchanger
31 Nose undercarriage leg strut
32 Twin nosewheels
33 Steering jacks
34 Nosewheel doors
35 Air conditioning plant, port and starboard
36 Cabin window panel
37 Six-abreast first class seating, 24 seats
38 Forward underfloor freight hold
39 Forward freight door
40 VHF aerial
41 Curtained cabin divider
42 Overhead stowage bins
43 Nine-abreast tourist class seating, 222 seats
44 Baggage/freight containers, twelve LD3 containers forward
45 Fuselage frame and stringer construction
46 Wing root fillet
47 Taxying lamp
48 Bleed air system ducting
49 Escape chute and life raft stowage
50 Mid-section entry door
51 Centre section galley units
52 Fuselage centre section construction
53 Wing centre section carry-through structure
54 Dry bay
55 Centre section fuel tanks, capacity 6,711 Imp gal (30,510l)
56 Floor beam construction
57 Fuselage/front spar attachment main frame
58 Anti-collision lights
59 Starboard inboard fuel tank bay, capacity 6,649 Imp gal (30,226l)
60 Thrust reverser cascade, open
61 Starboard engine nacelle
62 Nacelle pylon
63 Fixed portion of leading edge
64 Fuel surge box and boost pump reservoir
65 Fuel system piping
66 Outboard fuel tank bay, capacity 3,169 Imp gal (14,407l)
67 Pressure refuelling connections
68 Screw jack drive shaft
69 Slat screw jacks
70 Leading-edge slat segments, open
71 Extended wing tip fairing
72 Starboard navigation light
73 Wing tip strobe light
74 Static dischargers
75 Starboard 'active control' aileron
76 Aileron hydraulic jacks
77 Fuel jettison pipe
78 Outboard spoilers
79 Outboard spoilers/speedbrakes
80 Flap screw jacks
81 Flap track fairings
82 Outboard double slotted flap, down
83 Inboard aileron

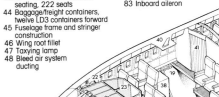

Far Right: Bahrain-based four-nations airline Gulf Air bought four TriStar 1s in 1976, later supplemented by eight more. They entered service on its prestige routes, linking Bahrain, Doha, Abu Dhabi, Dubai and Muscat to London, Cairo, Karachi and Bombay.

Right: Delta Air Lines is the largest airline still operating the TriStar on mainline services. It was one of the first to order the type when it contracted to buy 24 in April 1968 and eventually operated 54 of all variants. The first entered Delta service in December 1973.

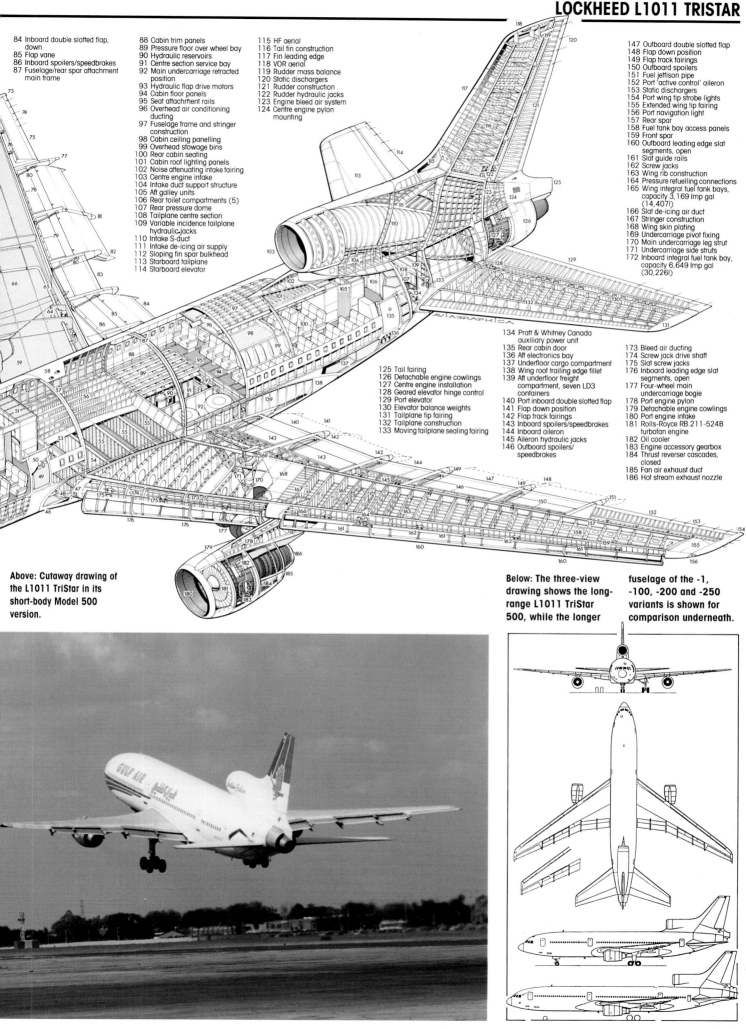

84 Inboard double slotted flap, down
85 Flap vane
86 Inboard spoilers/speedbrakes
87 Fuselage/rear spar attachment main frame

88 Cabin trim panels
89 Pressure floor over wheel bay
90 Hydraulic reservoirs
91 Centre section service bay
92 Main undercarriage retracted position
93 Hydraulic flap drive motors
94 Cabin floor panels
95 Seat attachment rails
96 Overhead air conditioning ducting
97 Fuselage frame and stringer construction
98 Cabin ceiling panelling
99 Overhead stowage bins
100 Rear cabin seating
101 Cabin roof lighting panels
102 Noise attenuating intake fairing
103 Centre engine intake
104 Intake duct support structure
105 Aft galley units
106 Rear toilet compartments (5)
107 Rear pressure dome
108 Tailplane centre section
109 Variable incidence tailplane hydraulic jacks
110 Intake S-duct
111 Intake de-icing air supply
112 Sloping fin spar bulkhead
113 Starboard tailplane
114 Starboard elevator

115 HF aerial
116 Tail fin construction
117 Fin leading edge
118 VOR aerial
119 Rudder mass balance
120 Static dischargers
121 Rudder construction
122 Rudder hydraulic jacks
123 Engine bleed air system
124 Centre engine pylon mounting

125 Tail fairing
126 Detachable engine cowlings
127 Centre engine installation
128 Geared elevator hinge control
129 Port elevator
130 Elevator balance weights
131 Tailplane tip fairing
132 Tailplane construction
133 Moving tailplane sealing fairing

134 Pratt & Whitney Canada auxiliary power unit
135 Rear cabin door
136 Aft electronics bay
137 Underfloor cargo compartment
138 Wing root trailing edge fillet
139 Aft underfloor freight compartment, seven LD3 containers
140 Port inboard double slotted flap
141 Flap down position
142 Flap track fairings
143 Inboard spoilers/speedbrakes
144 Inboard aileron
145 Aileron hydraulic jacks
146 Outboard spoilers/ speedbrakes

147 Outboard double slotted flap
148 Flap down position
149 Flap track fairings
150 Outboard spoilers
151 Fuel jettison pipe
152 Port 'active control' aileron
153 Static dischargers
154 Port wing tip strobe lights
155 Extended wing tip fairing
156 Port navigation light
157 Rear spar
158 Fuel tank bay access panels
159 Front spar
160 Outboard leading edge slat segments, open
161 Slat guide rails
162 Screw jacks
163 Wing rib construction
164 Pressure refuelling connections
165 Wing integral fuel tank bays, capacity 3,169 Imp gal (14,407l)
166 Slat de-icing air duct
167 Stringer construction
168 Wing skin plating
169 Undercarriage pivot fixing
170 Main undercarriage leg strut
171 Undercarriage side struts
172 Inboard integral fuel tank bay, capacity 6,649 Imp gal (30,226l)

173 Bleed air ducting
174 Screw jack drive shaft
175 Slat screw jacks
176 Inboard leading edge slat segments, open
177 Four-wheel main undercarriage bogie
178 Port engine pylon
179 Detachable engine cowlings
180 Port engine intake
181 Rolls-Royce RB.211-524B turbofan engine
182 Oil cooler
183 Engine accessory gearbox
184 Thrust reverser cascades, closed
185 Fan air exhaust duct
186 Hot stream exhaust nozzle

Above: Cutaway drawing of the L1011 TriStar in its short-body Model 500 version.

Below: The three-view drawing shows the long-range L1011 TriStar 500, while the longer fuselage of the -1, -100, -200 and -250 variants is shown for comparison underneath.

McDONNELL DOUGLAS DC-9 USA

Douglas project studies in the early 1950s for an aircraft to complement the then recently-launched DC-8 concentrated upon a scaled-down version of that type to operate over medium ranges. Intensive market studies over a period of several years led the company to extend the timescale for the launch of this new type, and to initiate a wholly original design rather than attempt to use DC-8 components. As the DC-9, the new jetliner was firmed up in 1963 and was formally launched on 8 April of that year as a short/medium range aircraft with about 75 seats in typical mixed-class arrangement. In configuration the DC-9 closely resembled the BAC One-Eleven, with rear-mounted engines and a T-tail. Delta Air Lines became the launch airline with an order for 15, and the first of five aircraft for the certification programme flew on 25 February 1965. From the outset, Douglas planned to offer a variety of fuselage lengths and fuel capacities, with appropriate engine powers and operating weights, and this policy has helped to keep the DC-9 in production for a long period, with the very latest variants designated as the MD-80 series and yet more derivatives in the MD-90 series, both described separately.

VARIANTS
With 53.4kN (12,000lb) Pratt & Whitney JT8D-5 engines, the DC-9 Srs 10 had an overall length of 31.82m (104ft 4¾in) and up to 90 seats. More powerful 63.3kN (14,000lb) JT8D-7 engines were also available. The DC-9 Srs 20 was similar with more powerful JT8D-9 or -11 engines and the increased wing span of the Srs 30 with full-span leading-edge slats, for hot-and-high performance. It first flew on 18 September 1968, preceded by the first DC-9 Srs 30 on 1 August 1966, with fuselage lengthened by 4.6m (14ft 11in) to seat up to 115 passengers. The DC-9-30 was available in several sub-variants with differing weights and engine combinations, and was also produced for the United States Air Force (USAF) as the C-9A Nightingale, and for the US Navy as the C-9B Skytrain II. The C-9A was produced for aeromedical duties, while the C-9B was used as a logistic transport. To meet the needs of SAS, the Srs 30 was further evolved in the mid-1960s to produce the DC-9 Srs 40 with another stretch of 1.87m (6ft 4in) and up to 125 seats. This version first flew on 28 November 1967. Yet another fuselage stretch was announced in July 1973 when Swissair ordered the DC-9 Srs 50, longer than the Srs 40 by 1.87m (6ft 4in) at an overall length of 40.72m (133ft 7½in). The Srs 50 introduced the uprated -15 or -17 versions of the JT8D engine and several other engineering improvements, these engines later becoming options for the Srs 30 and 40. With a forward port-side freight loading door and

appropriate cabin arrangements, convertible (C) or all-freight (F) versions of the DC-9 Srs 10 and Srs 30 have also been delivered. These included the DC-9-15MC (multiple-change) and DC-9-15RC (rapid change) which had a roller floor for quick changes in configuration, and the DC-9-30CF (convertible freighter) with no cargo door for small package use, and the all-freight DC-9-30AF, later DC-9-30F, with no windows. The final DC-9 variant emerged in 1979 as the Super 80 but was subsequently redesignated McDonnell Douglas MD-80 and is separately described as such.

SERVICE USE
The DC-9 Srs 10 was approved by the FAA on 23 November 1965 and entered service with Delta Air Lines on 8 December. The DC-9 Srs 30 was certificated on 19 December 1966 and entered service with Eastern Airlines in early 1967. The DC-9 Srs 20 was bought only by SAS, entering service on 27 January 1969, and SAS was also first to use the DC-9 Srs 40, starting on 12 March 1968 after certification on 27 February. The DC-9 Srs 50 gained FAA approval in 1975, to enter service with Swissair on 24 August of that year. Continental Airlines was the first to receive the convertible DC-9C Srs 10 on 7 March 1966; Overseas National received the first convertible Srs 30 in October 1967 and Alitalia accepted the first all-cargo DC-9 Srs 30F on 13 May 1968. Production of all DC-9 variants totalled 976, including 137 Series 10, 10 Series 20, 662 Series 30 (including 24 C-9A and 17 C-9B), 71 Series 40 and 96 Series 50. Some 750 remained in service in 1998, several equipped with hushkits.

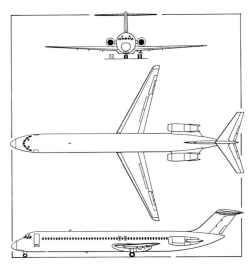

Below: The three-view drawing depicts the DC-9 in its final Series 50 form from 1976. This version was the result of the progressive development from 1965 of the basic aircraft.

Below: US low-fare, no-frills airline Valujet operated close on 50 DC-9s from a hub at Atlanta, before a much-publicised crash in Florida led to a temporary grounding of the airline.

Right: Scandinavian Airlines System (SAS) was the first and one of only two airlines (with Toa Domestic of Japan) to order the 125-seat DC-9-41. It traded range requirements for more seating and payload.

SPECIFICATION
(McDonnell Douglas DC-10-30ER)

Dimensions: Wingspan 50.41m (165ft 4in); length overall 55.50m (182ft 1in); height overall 17.70m (58ft 1in), wing area 367.7m² (3,958ft²). Power Plant: Three 240.2kN (54,000lb) General Electric CF6-50C2B turbofans.
Weights: Operating weight empty 121,198kg (267,197lb); max take-off 263,085kg (580,000lb); max landing 182,978kg (403,000lb); max payload 48,330kg (106,550lb).
Performance: Max cruising speed 530kts (982km/h); max rate of climb 14.7m/s (2,900ft/min); service ceiling 10,180m (33,400ft); take-off field length 3,170m (10,400ft); landing field length 1,630m (5,350ft); range with max payload 5,730nm (10,620km).
Accommodation: Flight crew of three. Seating for up to 380 passengers, nine-abreast with twin aisles. Total baggage/cargo bulk volume 155.4m³ (5,489ft³).

Right: Cutaway drawing of the DC-10 series 30CF, which is the convertible passenger/freighter variant of the basic aircraft, with the freight-loading door in the forward fuselage port side. The dividing bulkhead between freight and passenger compartments can be moved to vary the 'mix'. More freight is carried underfloor.

With the DC-8 in production and the DC-9 recently entering service, the Douglas Aircraft Company (not then merged with McDonnell), turned its attention in March 1966 to the so-called 'Jumbo Twin' specification prepared by American Airlines. Subsequent discussions between the company and the airline, and an assessment of broader market needs, led to the final proposal becoming a three-engined wide-body type of larger capacity than first planned, and in this form, the type became the DC-10 as ordered by American Airlines on 19 February 1968. A full production launch was achieved in April, when United Airlines also placed a large order. The configuration and size closely matched that of the TriStar which Lockheed launched in March 1968, the most significant difference being that the rear engine of the DC-10 was located in an individual nacelle above the fuselage, on a short pylon, with the fin and rudder carried above this nacelle. The DC-10 had a 35 deg swept wing including full-span leading-edge slats and large-chord double-slotted trailing-edge flaps for high lift and low approach speeds. Capacity was for up to 380 passengers in all-economy seating. All early versions of the DC-10 were powered by General Electric CF6-50 turbofan engines, the Pratt & Whitney JT9D being offered as an option at a later time, and the flight test programme began on 29 August 1970, with the second and third aircraft, in American Airlines and United Airlines colours respectively, following on 24 October and 23 December 1970. In the early 1980s, McDonnell Douglas introduced a common performance improvement package (CPIP), aimed at reducing drag and consequently bettering cruise performance. The CPIP incorporated the elimination of spoiler steps, improved slat rigging, the addition of stabiliser fillets and revised contouring of the horizontal stabiliser fairing. Additional drag improvements changes were applied on an individual model basis.

VARIANTS

The launch version of the DC-10 was aimed at providing non-stop US transcontinental range and, after the subsequent introduction of longer-range versions, this initial model became known as the DC-10 Series 10. This had CF6-6D or 6D1 engines of 178kN or 182.45kN (40,000lb or 41,000lb) respectively and 185,976kg (410,000lb) or, later, 206,388kg

Above: The ORBIS International DC-10-10 is fitted out as a flying eye hospital and teaching facility. Over a period of 15 years, the ORBIS team has made 250 flights to 71 countries around the world, enabling them to save the eyesight of more than 20,000 people. The team has taught sight-saving skills to 32,000 doctors and nurses.

(455,000lb) gross weight. The DC-10 Srs 15 introduced CF6-50C2F engines at 206.9kN (46,500lb) for high-temperature, high-altitude operations by Mexican airlines, and first flew on 8 January 1981. Both these variants had the original DC-10 wing with a span of 47.35m (155ft 4in). For long-range operations, Douglas developed centre-section and fuselage (underfloor) fuel tanks, and a 3.05m (10ft) increase in wing span to allow for higher weights; a third main landing gear leg was also introduced, on the fuselage centreline. With CF6-50 engines, this variant was the DC-10 Srs 30, first flown on 21 June 1972. With JT9D-20 engines, it was at first the DC-10 Srs 20, later changed to DC-10 Srs 40, first flown on 28 February 1972; the first Srs 40 with JT9D-59 engines flew on 25 July 1975. Progressive increases in certificated weights and fuel capacities were made once the Srs 30 and 40 were in production, and in 1980 the designation DC-10 Srs 30ER was adopted for the extended-range variants. A convertible freighter version with a forward side cargo door was introduced as the DC-10 Srs 30CF, first flown on 28 February 1973, and a maximum take-off weight of 267,620kg (590,000lb) was certificated for this variant. Some DC-10 Srs 10CFs were also built. A windowless pure freighter, the DC-10 Srs 30F, appeared in 1985 to meet the requirements of Federal Express and could accommodate up to 36 standard containers. The KC-10A Extender tanker/cargo transport for the USAF was based on the DC-10-30CF and first flew on 12 July 1980. Several improvements including a remote operator's station and advanced boom were introduced in the KDC-10 for the Royal Netherlands Air Force. A number of fuselage-stretched variants of the DC-10 was studied under the Srs 50 and 60 designations and as the MD-100, leading eventually to the McDonnell Douglas MD-11. A two-man cockpit upgrade, taking the DC-10 even beyond MD-11 sophistication, will commence in 1998 for Federal Express. The upgraded aircraft will be known as the MD-10.

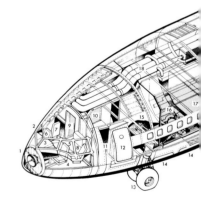

SERVICE USE

The DC-10 Srs 10 was certificated on 29 July 1971, and entered service on 5 August 1971 with American Airlines. The Srs 15 was certificated on 12 June 1981 for service with Mexicana and Aeromexico. The Srs 30 was certificated 21 November 1972, with first deliveries to KLM and Swissair. The first Srs 30ER deliveries were made to Swissair, and the first Srs 30ER with maximum supplementary tankage was delivered to Finnair. The Srs 40 was certificated on 20 October 1972, with the first delivery following to Northwest Orient Airlines. The Srs 30CF was first delivered to TIA and ONA on 19 April and 21 April 1973 respectively. The first Srs 30F was delivered to Federal Express on 24 January 1986. DC-10 sales totalled 446 when production finished in December 1988, including 60 KC-10A tanker transports for the USAF. Some 360 were in commercial service in 1998.

McDonnell Douglas DC-10 Series 30 CF Cutaway Drawing Key

1 Weather radar
2 Windshield
3 Instrument console
4 Flight deck
5 Captain's seat (Aircraft Mechanics Inc)
6 First officer's seat (ditto)
7 Flight engineer's position
8 Supernumary crew seat
9 Flight deck door
10 Forward starboard toilet
11 Forward port toilet
12 Crew passenger forward entry door
13 Twin wheel nose gear (Abex or Dowty Rotol; Goodyear tyres)
14 Air conditioning access doors
15 Forward cargo bulkhead
16 Air conditioning bay (Garrett AiResearch equipment)
17 Forward lower galley area (used for containerized cargo)
18 Air conditioning trunking
19 Cargo deck lateral transfer area (omni-caster rollers)
20 Cargo deck pallet channels (rollers)
21 Main cargo door (fully open position)
22 VHF antenna
23 Frame-and-stringer fuselage construction
24 Main deck cargo (ten 88 x 125in, 2.23 x 3.17m (pallets), capacity 4,958 cu ft (140.4m³)
25 Passenger door
26 Forward lower compartment (five 88 x 125in, 2.23 x 3.17m (pallets), capacity 1,890 cu ft 53.5m³)
27 Centre-section fuselage main frame
28 Centre-section front beam
29 Sheer-web floor support over centre-section fuel tank
30 Cargo/passenger compartment dividing bulkhead
31 Starboard engine pod (Rhor subcontract)
32 Engine intake
33 Nacelle pylon
34 Leading-edge slats
35 Integral wing fuel tank
36 Starboard navigation lights
37 Low-speed outboard aileron
38 Fuel ventpipe
39 Wing spoilers/lift dumpers
40 Double-slotted flaps
41 All-speed inboard drooping aileron
42 Passenger doors
43 Centre-section fuselage mainframe
44 Cabin air ducts
45 Centre undercarriage bay
46 Keel box structure
47 Fuselage/wing attachment points
48 Wing torsion-box construction
49 Leading-edge structure
50 Nacelle pylon
51 Engine intake
52 General Electric CF6-50 turbofan
53 Exhaust outlet
54 Four-wheel main undercarriage (Menasco Manufacturing; Goodyear tyres and brakes)
55 Leading-edge slats
56 Outboard slat extended
57 Port navigation lights
58 Low-speed outboard aileron
59 Fuel vent pipe
60 Outboard flap hinge fairings
61 Fuel pipes
62 All-speed inboard drooping aileron
63 Inboard flap hinge actuator and fairing
64 Undercarriage support structure
65 Flap construction
66 Wing root fairing
67 Fuselage-attached flap track
68 Centre cargo compartment, capacity 1,280 cu ft (36.25m³)
69 Cabin floor support
70 Overhead luggage lockers
71 Eight-abreast coach-class seating (147 passengers)
72 Baggage containers
73 Bulk cargo hold door
74 Rear passenger door (port and starboard)
75 Rear toilet (port and starboard)
76 Three toilets/washrooms
77 Underfloor bulk cargo hold capacity 805 cu ft (22.79m³)
78 Rear pressure bulkhead
79 Tailplane centre-section
80 Tailplane leading-edge
81 Tailplane construction (LTV subcontract)
82 Elevator actuators
83 Dual elevators (LTV subcontract)
84 Tail cone (Mitsubishi subcontract)
85 Exhaust outlet
86 General Electric CF6-50 turbofan
87 Intake trunking
88 Intake hot-air duct
89 Engine intake
90 Starboard tailplane
91 Dual elevators
92 Tailfin leading-edge
93 Rudder actuator
94 Tailfin torsion box construction
95 VOR
96 Upper rudder sections (Aerfer subcontract)
97 Lower rudder sections
98 Tail pylon

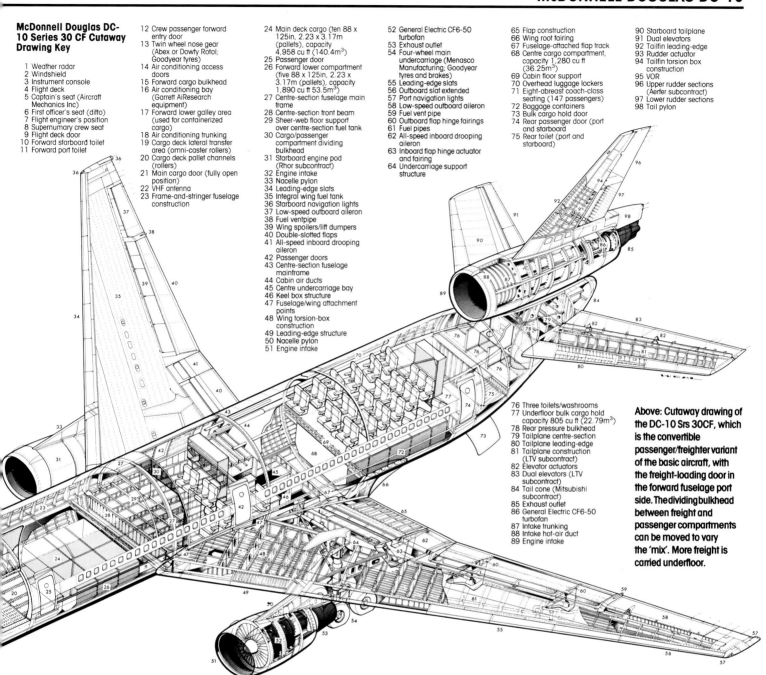

Above: Cutaway drawing of the DC-10 Srs 30CF, which is the convertible passenger/freighter variant of the basic aircraft, with the freight-loading door in the forward fuselage port side. The dividing bulkhead between freight and passenger compartments can be moved to vary the 'mix'. More freight is carried underfloor.

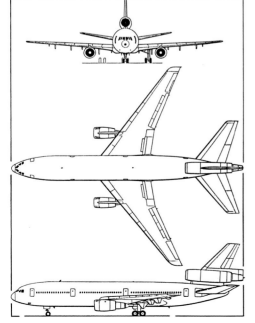

Left: The three-view drawing shows the Series 30 version of the McDonnell Douglas DC-10, which proved the most numerous variant of the 446 aircraft sold. The Series 30CF and Series 40 are externally similar giving good grounds to confuse them with one another.

Right: The DC-10 has carved itself a buoyant second-hand market and many are chartered to provide additional capacity. This DC-10-30 belonging to Mexican airline TAESA was leased to Dominicana and photographed on a charter flight at Leipzig. (Lothar Müller)

McDONNELL DOUGLAS (BOEING) MD-11 USA

SPECIFICATION
(McDonnell Douglas MD-11)

Dimensions: Wingspan 51.66m (169ft 6in); length overall 61.37m (201ft 4in); height overall 17.60m (57ft 9in), wing area 338.9m² (3,648ft²).
Power Plant: Three 276kN (62,000lb) Pratt & Whitney PW4462, or 267kN (60,000lb) PW4460, or 274kN (61,500lb) General Electric CF6-80C2D1F turbofans.
Weights: Operating weight empty 129,680kg (285,900lb); max take-off 285,990kg (630,500lb); max landing 195,040kg (430,000lb); max payload 51,755kg (114.100lb).
Performance: Max cruising speed 511kts (945km/h); take-off field length 3,185m (10,450ft); landing field length 2,118m (6,950ft); range with typical payload 6,840nm (12,667km).
Accommodation: Flight crew of two. Seating for up to 410 passengers, nine-abreast with twin aisles. Underfloor baggage/cargo volume 194.0m³ (6,850ft³).

For many years, stretched (and in some cases 'shrunk') versions of the DC-10 were studied by the Douglas Aircraft Company under a number of different designations, while production of the DC-10 itself continued in a form little changed from that in which it was launched. As noted in its own entry, the DC-10 was produced in only four principal series, all having fundamentally the same fuselage length and differing primarily in weights, fuel capacities and engine type and power. Almost from the start of the design, however, possible stretched-fuselage versions were being considered and in the early 1970s, for example, a 12.8m (42ft) lengthening

was considered a possibility, to allow the DC-10 to carry 365 passengers for 3,600nm (6,680km). Stretched versions of the Srs 10, Srs 30 and Srs 40 continued under study throughout the 1970s but no market was found for these projects. New power plants, such as the RB.211-535 and PW2037, were then being considered, and two-crew cockpits with digital instruments and CRT displays were under review. When McDonnell Douglas decided, in late 1982, to replace the famous 'DC' series of designations with a new 'MD' series, this project became the MD-100, but was discontinued in November 1983 when all work on projected new commercial aircraft was temporarily suspended by the parent company. In 1984, work resumed, with a high priority, on a stretched derivative of the DC-10 with the designation MD-11, and on 29 December 1986 this was formally launched into production. Based on a close study of the prospective market, the MD-11 evolved between 1984 and 1986 as a very-long-range large-capacity transport, using the basic DC-10 fuselage cross section, with a 5.66m (18ft 7in) stretch. The wing has a 3.05m (10ft) increase in span and outward-canted winglets that add another 1.32m (4ft 4in), plus other new features such as a smaller tailplane containing fuel that can be used to assist aircraft trimming, carbon brakes, revised tail cone, greater use of composites and advanced metals, a two-man cockpit and digital FMS and EFIS on the flight deck. First flight took place on 10 January 1990, powered by three General Electric CF6-80C2 turbofan engines, while the Pratt & Whitney PW4460-powered model made its first flight on 26 April 1990. A total of five aircraft (four with GE engines and one with P&W engines) was used in the flight test programme which culminated in FAA certification on 8 November 1990.

VARIANTS

The standard passenger MD-11 failed to meet its design guarantees and from the outset has been undergoing a Performance Improvement Programme (PIP) aimed at weight and drag reductions and range extension. Maximum take-off weight for all versions is 273,289kg (602,500lb), but an optional 285,990kg (630,500lb) is also available. The MD-11 Combi, certificated in April 1992, is a mixed passenger/cargo version, capable of carrying four to 10 cargo pallets on the main deck, in addition to between 168 and 240 passengers. It has a main cargo door at the rear. A convertible model, the MD-11CF convertible freighter, was launched in August 1991 with an order from Martinair Holland, and features a main deck port side cargo door at the front. A windowless all-freighter MD-11F is also in production, as is an extended-range version, the MD-11ER, launched in February 1994. The MD-11ER carries up to 11,356 litres (3,000 US gallons) in an auxiliary tank in the lower cargo compartment, increasing range by up to 480nm (889km). All models can be fitted with a choice of three engines, including the 267kN (60,000lb) thrust PW4460, the 274kN (61,500lb) CF6-80C2D1F, and the 276kN (62,000lb) PW4462.

SERVICE USE

The MD-11 was committed to full-scale development on 29 December 1986, at which time 12 companies had placed orders for 52 aircraft with 40 more on option. The MD-11 obtained its FAA certification on 8 November 1990. First delivery was made to Finnair on 29 November, entering service on 20 December. The first MD-11F freighter went to Federal Express on 11 September 1991, followed by the MD-11 Combi, delivered to Alitalia on 27 November 1991. Martinair Holland took delivery of the first MD-11CF convertible freighter on 2 December 1994. Launch customer World Airways accepted the first MD-11ER in March 1996. At 1 January 1998, 174 MD-11s had been delivered, with 12 remaining on order. Total orders of 188 include 136 passenger MD-11, 47 MD-11F and five MD-11CF.

Left: Swissair was an early operator of the passenger MD-11 and now has the largest number of them on its fleet with a total of 15 aircraft.

McDonnell Douglas MD-11 Cutaway Drawing Key

1 Radome
2 Weather radar scanner
3 ILS glidescope aerials
4 Pitot heads
5 Front pressure bulkhead
6 Radome hinge points
7 Windscreen wipers
8 Electrically heated windscreen panels
9 Overhead systems switch panel
10 Maintenance engineering panel
11 Observer's seat
12 First Officer's seat
13 Instrument panel shroud
14 Captain's seat
15 Electronic flight instrumentation system (EFIS), six colour CRT displays
16 Underfloor avionics equipment bay
17 Floor hatch access to avionics bay
18 Optional second observer's seat
19 Crew wardrobe
20 Cockpit bulkhead doorway
21 Conditioned air delivery ducting
22 Sidewall galley units, port and starboard
23 Curtained entry lobby
24 Forward cabin doorway, port and starboard
25 Cabin attendant's folding seat
26 Nose undercarriage wheel bay
27 Air conditioning system intake ducts

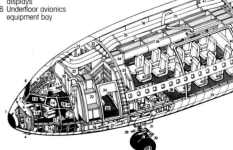

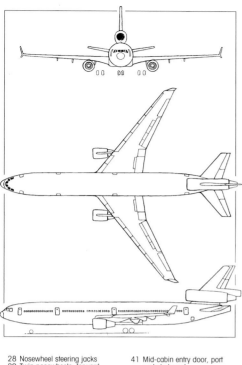

Left: Three-view of the MD-11 reveal the main differences from the DC-10, from which it is derived, as a longer fuselage and distinctive winglets.

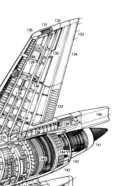

Right: Federal Express took delivery of the first MD-11F in 1991 and is its largest operator.

59 Central section skin panels
60 Floor beam construction
61 Centre section cabin door way, port and starboard
62 Centre fuselage frame and stringer construction
63 Anti-collision light
64 Starboard wing integral fuel tank, total fuel capacity 34,893 Imp gal (41,800 US gal, 158,662 l)
65 Fuel system piping
66 Inboard leading-edge slat segment
67 Thrust reverser cascades, open
68 Starboard engine nacelle
69 Intake duct acoustic lining
70 Nacelle strakes
71 Nacelle pylon
72 Outboard slats hydraulically actuated cable drive
73 Pressure refuelling connections
74 Wing skin panelling
75 Wing stringers
76 Outboard integral fuel tankage
77 Slat guide rails
78 Outboard leading-edge slat segments
79 Starboard navigation light
80 Starboard upper winglet
81 Tail navigation and strobe lights
82 Fixed portion of trailing edge
83 Outboard, low-speed aileron
84 Aileron hydraulic actuator
85 Fuel jettison pipe
86 Outboard double-slotted flap segment
87 Articulated flap vane and guide rails
88 Outboard spoiler panels
89 Spoiler hydraulic actuators
90 Flap hydraulic jacks
91 External flap hinges
92 Inboard, high-speed aileron
93 Hydraulic actuator
94 Inboard spoiler
95 Inboard double-slotted flap segment
96 VHF aerial
97 Pressure floor above wheel bay
98 Starboard main undercarriage wheel bay
99 Mainwheel door hydraulic jack

100 Hydraulic reservoir, tripe system
101 Seat mounting rails
102 Dual ADF aerials
103 Rear cabin air ducting
104 Cabin roof trim and lighting panels
105 Overhead baggage lockers
106 Passenger service units
107 Rear cabin passenger seating
108 LD3 baggage containers, 14 in rear hold
109 Rear freight hold door and actuator
110 Rear under floor freight hold 2,212 cu ft (62.6m³)
111 Freight hold bulkhead
112 Cabin wall trim panelling
113 Rear seat rows
114 Central toilet compartments, two
115 Central galley unit
116 Rear galley units, port and starboard
117 Rear pressure bulkhead
118 Slopping fin spar attachment frames
119 HF aerial
120 Central engine intake ducting
121 Intake lip hot air de-icing
122 Starboard trimming tailplane
123 Fin roof fillet
124 Intake duct ring frames
125 Fin attachment joint
126 Starboard elevator
127 Ruder actuator cable drive
128 Fin spar and rib construction
129 VOR localiser No 1 aerial
130 Fin tip aerial fairing
131 VOR localiser No 2 aerial
132 Rudder horn balance 3

143 Translating cowl thrust reverser
144 Thrust reverser cascades
145 Centre General Electric CF6-80C2-D1F turbofan engine
146 Engine nacelle pylon structure
147 Extending maintenance access ladder
148 Hinged tailcone fairing, carbon reinforced plastic
149 Two-segment port elevator
150 Carbon reinforced plastic elevator construction
151 Static discharges
152 Port trimming tailplane rib construction
153 Leading-edge hot air de-icing
154 Leading-edge nose ribs
155 Tailplane integral fuel tank
156 Elevator hydraulic actuators
157 Tailplane hinge point
158 Hydraulic reservoir
159 Fire extinguisher bottles
160 Tailplane centre section carry through
161 Auxiliary Power Unit (APU)
162 Tailplane trim screw jack, port and starboard
163 Rear sidewall toilet compartment, port and starboard

178 Undercarriage bay keel member
179 Twin-wheel centre main undercarriage
180 Wing mounted mainwheel leg struct pivot fixing
181 Port inboard spoiler panel
182 Inboard double slotted flap segment
183 Aileron hydraulic actuator
184 Port high-speed aileron
185 Flap down position
186 Outboard double-slotted flap, segment
187 Carbon reinforced plastic flap construction
188 Carbon reinforced plastic spoiler panels
189 Outboard roll control spoiler/lift dumpers
190 Fuel jettison
191 Port low-speed aileron
192 Carbon reinforced plastic aileron construction
193 Fixed trailing-edge rib construction
194 Static dischargers
195 Port upper winglet
196 Tail navigation and strobe lights
197 Lower winglet segment
198 Port navigation light
199 Outboard leading-edge slat segment
200 Port outer wing panel integral duel tank
201 Rear spar
202 Wing rib construction
203 Lower wing skin/stringer panel
204 Front spar
205 Leading-edge slat rib construction
206 Slat guide rails
207 Port pressure refuelling connections
208 Leading-edge slat de-icing air duct
209 Rolls-Royce RB211-524L Trent alternative power plant
210 Four wheel main undercarriage bogie
211 Main engine mounting rib
212 Pylon attachment joint
213 Inboard wing panel integral fuel tank
214 Inboard wing ribs
215 Wing root joint crib

28 Nosewheel steering jacks
29 Twin nosewheels, forward retracting
30 Torque scissor links
31 Noosewheel leg doors
32 Air conditioning packs (two port and one starboard)
33 Sidewall toilet compartment, port and starboard
34 Central galley unit
35 Conditioned air distribution ducting
36 Overhead baggage lockers
37 First-class passenger cabin, 34 seats, 6-abreast
38 Cabin window panels
39 Fuselage lower lobe skin panelling
40 Outline of cargo door on windowless all-freight version

41 Mid-cabin entry door, port and starboard
42 Mid-cabin galley unit
43 ATC aerial
44 Sidewall toilet compartments, port and starboard
45 Forward freight hold door
46 Door actuating motor
47 Forward underfloor freight hold, capacity 2,844 cu ft (80.5m³)
48 LD3 baggage containers, 18 in forward hold
49 Cabin air outflow valve
50 Freight hold conditioned air ducting
51 Glassfibre/Kevlar wing root fillet fairing
52 Tourist-class passenger cabin, 289 seats, nine-abreast
53 Cabin wall insulating blankets
54 Engine bleed air ducting to air conditioning plant
55 Main electrical distribution panels
56 Hydraulically actuated slat cable drive unit
57 Wing centre-section carry through
58 Centre section integral fuel tank, with bag tank beneath

133 Static dischargers
134 Double-acting rudder upper segment
135 Rudder mass balance
136 Rudder hydraulic actuators
137 Lower rudder segment rib construction

164 Cabin attendants' folding seat and interphone
165 Rear cabin doorway, port and starboard
166 Bulk cargo door
167 Underfloor bulk cargo hold, 510 cu ft (14.4m³)
168 Cargo hold air distribution ducting
169 Powered roller cargo handling floor
170 Rear fuselage frame and stringer construction
171 Glassfibre/Kevlar trailing edge fillet construction
172 Inboard flap guide rail
173 Main undercarriage wheel bay
174 Hydraulic reservoir

216 Slat guide rails and roller tracks
217 Engine bleed air ducting
218 Port inboard leading-edge slat segment
219 Slat de-icing air duct
220 Bleed air pre-cooler
221 Engine pylon construction
222 Port engine
223 Translating cowl thrust reverser
224 Main engine mounting
225 Engine accessory equipment gearbox
226 Fan casing
227 Hinged cowling access panels

138 Central engine mounting beam
139 Bleed air pre-cooler
140 Pylon tail fairing
141 Core engine, hot steam, exhaust nozzle
142 Fan air, cold stream, exhaust duct

175 Hydraulic retraction jack
176 Centre main undercarriage wheel bay
177 Centre main undercarriage leg and pivot fixing

228 Intake duct acoustic lining
229 Intake lip de-icing air duct
230 Nacelle strake
231 Pratt & Whitney PW4000 alternative power plant

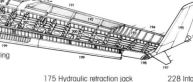

McDONNELL DOUGLAS (BOEING) MD-80 USA

SPECIFICATION
(McDonnell Douglas MD-88)

Dimensions: Wingspan 32.87m (107ft 10¼in); length overall 45.06m (147ft 10in); height overall 9.19m (30ft 2in), wing area 115.1m² (1,239ft²).
Power Plant: Two 93.4kN (21,000lb) Pratt & Whitney JT8D-219 turbofans.
Weights: Operating weight empty 35,369kg (77,976lb); max take-off 67,810kg (149,500lb); max landing 58,965kg (130,000lb); max payload 19,969kg (44,024lb).
Performance: Max cruising speed 499kts (924km/h); take-off field length 2,552m (8,375ft); landing field length 1,585m (5,200ft); range with max payload 2,502nm (4,635km).
Accommodation: Flight crew of two. Seating for up to 172 passengers, five-abreast with single aisle. Underfloor baggage/cargo volume 35.48m³ (1,253ft³).

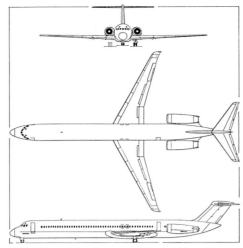

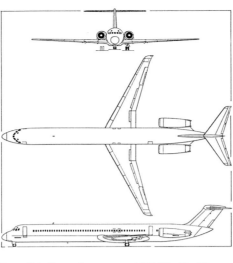

From 1975 onwards, Douglas Aircraft Company (a division of McDonnell Douglas) studied a number of possible derivatives of the DC-9 that would take advantage of the refanned versions of the Pratt & Whitney JT8D engine. An early example of this engine, the JT8D-109, was flown on a DC-9 starting on 9 January 1975, to gain data on the new engine, which went into production as the JT8D-209. DC-9 variants identified as the Srs 50RS, Srs 60, Srs 50-17R and DC-9SC were among those studied with this or other engines and with such innovations as a supercritical wing and/or fuselage extensions. Market surveys eventually led to the launch, in October 1977, of what was then known as the DC-9 Super 80, with a fuselage 4.34m (14ft 3in) longer than that of the Srs 50, JT8D-209 engines and other new features. Swissair, Austrian Airlines and Southern Airways became the launch customers for what would prove to be the most successful of all DC-9 variants. Three Super 80s required for certification made their first flights on 18 October 1979, 6 December 1979 and 29 February 1980.

VARIANTS

Three subvariants of the Super 80 were offered, all with the same overall dimensions but with different engine powers, fuel capacities and operating weights. These were the DC-9 Series 81 as initially deployed; the DC-9 Srs 82 with 89kN (20,000lb) JT8D-217s (plus emergency thrust reserve) and the same fuel as the Srs 81; and the DC-9 Srs 83 with 93.45kN (21,000lb) JT8D-219s and an extra 4,390l (966 Imp gal) of fuel in cargo compartments tanks. First flights were made of the series 82 on 8 January 1981 and of the MD-83 on 17 December 1984. In 1984, the designation of the DC-9 Super 80 was changed to MD-80 and the three production variants became the MD-81, MD-82 and MD-83. In 1985, the MD-87 was announced, featuring a fuselage reduced in length by 5.0m (16ft 5in), 89kN (20,000lb) JT8D-217B engines and a standard fuel capacity of 22,101l (4,863 Imp gal), plus optional auxiliary tanks. The MD-87 was ordered first by Finnair and Austrian Airlines, and made its first flight on 4 December 1986. A 25.4cm (10in) extension of the fin above the tailplane was introduced on the MD-87 to balance the shorter moment arm. A fifth member of the family was launched early in 1986 when Delta Air Lines ordered the MD-88, a close relative of the MD-82 with JT8D-217C engines, a 72,575kg (160,000lb) gross weight and a number of systems and equipment refinements including electronic flight instrument system (EFIS) in the cockpit, combined with a flight-management system and an inertial reference system. The MD-88 made its first flight on 15 August 1987. Executive versions were also produced. MD-82s were also built in China.

Above: This three-view drawing is representative of the basic members of the McDonnell Douglas (now Boeing) MD-80 family, comprising the MD-81, MD-82, MD-83 and MD-88. All of these have the same overall dimensions and external configuration, and differ primarily in their fuel capacities, weights, power plants and flight deck equipment.

Above: First flown at Long Beach, California, in December 1986, the MD-87 is the only member of the MD-80 family to differ in size. Designed to meet the needs of some airlines for a smaller capacity aircraft, it has a fuselage of the same length as the DC-9-50, a taller tailfin and a blunt tail cone, later also adopted on the other models.

SERVICE USE

The MD-81 gained FAA certification on 26 August 1980 and entered service with Swissair on 5 October 1980. Certificated on 30 July 1981, the MD-82 entered service with Republic Airlines in August, followed in 1982 by the higher gross weight option at 67,812kg (149,500lb) with JT8D-217A engines to provide a significant increase in range with maximum payload. The MD-83 received FAA certification in 1985 and went into service with Alaska Airlines and Finnair in early 1986. Finnair, together with Austrian Airlines, also became the first operator of the MD-87, which was certificated on 21 October 1987. The final MD-88 version was granted FAA certification on 9 December 1987 and entered service with launch customer Delta on 5 January 1988. Production continues and by 1 January 1998, a total of 1,167 had been ordered of all versions. Of these, 1,157 had been delivered. Orders have slowed down and production is unlikely to continue beyond 1998, now that the aircraft is part of the Boeing stable and competes directly with the 737 series.

Above: The acquisition of MD-81/82 aircraft enabled Adria Airways, now independent Slovenia's national carrier, to expand internationally.

McDonnell Douglas MD-81 Cutaway Drawing Key

1 Radome
2 Weather radar scanner
3 Front pressure bulkhead
4 Pitot tube
5 Radio and electronics bay
6 Nosewheel well
7 Twin nosewheels
8 Rudder pedals
9 Instrument panel
10 Instrument panel shroud
11 Windscreen wipers
12 Windscreen panels
13 Cockpit eyebrow windows
14 First officer's seat
15 Overhead switch panel
16 Captain's seat
17 Nosewheel steering control
18 Underfloor electrical and electronics bay
19 Nose strake
20 Retractable airstairs
21 Door mounted escape chute
22 Forward passenger door, open
23 Entry lobby
24 Starboard service door
25 Forward galley
26 Toilet compartment
27 Wash hand basin
28 First class seating compartment, 12 passengers four-abreast
29 D/F loop aerials
30 VHF aerial
31 Curtained cabin divider
32 Cabin window panel
33 Pressurization valves
34 Fuselage lower lobe frame construction
35 Wardrobe
36 Tourist class seating, 125 passengers five-abreast
37 Overhead stowage bins
38 Cabin roof frames
39 Air conditioning ducting
40 Cabin roof trim panels
41 Floor beam construction
42 Forward freight hold, capacity 849cu ft (24.04m³)

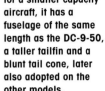

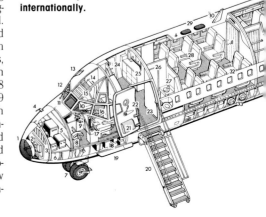

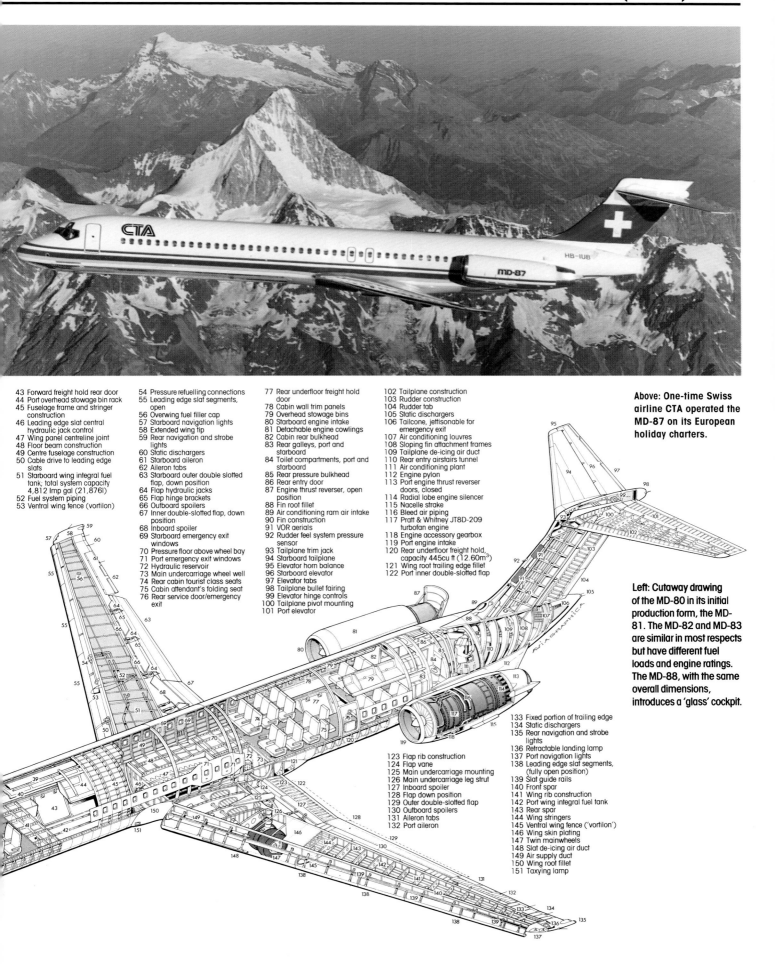

Above: One-time Swiss airline CTA operated the MD-87 on its European holiday charters.

Left: Cutaway drawing of the MD-80 in its initial production form, the MD-81. The MD-82 and MD-83 are similar in most respects but have different fuel loads and engine ratings. The MD-88, with the same overall dimensions, introduces a 'glass' cockpit.

43 Forward freight hold rear door
44 Port overhead stowage bin rack
45 Fuselage frame and stringer construction
46 Leading edge slat central hydraulic jack control
47 Wing panel centreline joint
48 Floor beam construction
49 Centre fuselage construction
50 Cable drive to leading edge slats
51 Starboard wing integral fuel tank; total system capacity 4,812 Imp gal (21,876l)
52 Fuel system piping
53 Ventral wing fence (vortilon)

54 Pressure refuelling connections
55 Leading edge slat segments, open
56 Overwing fuel filler cap
57 Starboard navigation lights
58 Extended wing tip
59 Rear navigation and strobe lights
60 Static dischargers
61 Starboard aileron
62 Aileron tabs
63 Starboard outer double slotted flap, down position
64 Flap hydraulic jacks
65 Flap hinge brackets
66 Outboard spoilers
67 Inner double-slotted flap, down position
68 Inboard spoiler
69 Starboard emergency exit windows
70 Pressure floor above wheel bay
71 Port emergency exit windows
72 Hydraulic reservoir
73 Main undercarriage wheel well
74 Rear cabin tourist class seats
75 Cabin attendant's folding seat
76 Rear service door/emergency exit

77 Rear underfloor freight hold door
78 Cabin wall trim panels
79 Overhead stowage bins
80 Starboard engine intake
81 Detachable engine cowlings
82 Cabin rear bulkhead
83 Rear galleys, port and starboard
84 Toilet compartments, port and starboard
85 Rear pressure bulkhead
86 Rear entry door
87 Engine thrust reverser, open position
88 Fin root fillet
89 Air conditioning ram air intake
90 Fin construction
91 VOR aerials
92 Rudder feel system pressure sensor
93 Tailplane trim jack
94 Starboard tailplane
95 Elevator horn balance
96 Starboard elevator
97 Elevator tabs
98 Tailplane bullet fairing
99 Elevator hinge controls
100 Tailplane pivot mounting
101 Port elevator

102 Tailplane construction
103 Rudder construction
104 Rudder tab
105 Static dischargers
106 Tailcone, jettisonable for emergency exit
107 Air conditioning louvres
108 Sloping fin attachment frames
109 Tailplane de-icing air duct
110 Rear entry airstairs tunnel
111 Air conditioning plant
112 Engine pylon
113 Port engine thrust reverser doors, closed
114 Radial lobe engine silencer
115 Nacelle strake
116 Bleed air piping
117 Pratt & Whitney JT8D-209 turbofan engine
118 Engine accessory gearbox
119 Port engine intake
120 Rear underfloor freight hold, capacity 445cu ft (12.60m³)
121 Wing root trailing edge fillet
122 Port inner double-slotted flap

123 Flap rib construction
124 Flap vane
125 Main undercarriage mounting
126 Main undercarriage leg strut
127 Inboard spoiler
128 Flap down position
129 Outer double-slotted flap
130 Outboard spoilers
131 Aileron tabs
132 Port aileron

133 Fixed portion of trailing edge
134 Static dischargers
135 Rear navigation and strobe lights
136 Retractable landing lamp
137 Port navigation lights
138 Leading edge slat segments, (fully open position)
139 Slat guide rails
140 Front spar
141 Wing rib construction
142 Port wing integral fuel tank
143 Rear spar
144 Wing stringers
145 Ventral wing fence ('vortilon')
146 Wing skin plating
147 Twin mainwheels
148 Slat de-icing air duct
149 Air supply duct
150 Wing root fillet
151 Taxying lamp

McDONNELL DOUGLAS (BOEING) MD-90 USA

The MD-90 has been designed as a stretched, high-technology follow-on to the successful MD-80 series. The most notable external difference, apart from the 1.45m (4ft 9in) lengthening of the fuselage forward of the wing to provide accommodation for another 10 passengers to a maximum of 172, is the replacement of the Pratt & Whitney JT8D engines by the International Aero Engines (IAE) V2500 turbofans with electronic control. Another external feature is the enlarged tailfin of the MD-87. New characteristics include an improved cabin interior with larger overhead bins, better lighting, handrail at bin level, digital environmental control system and vacuum toilets; Bendix variable-speed constant frequency electrical generation; 421kW (565shp) AlliedSignal GTCP131-9D auxiliary power unit (APU); carbon wheel brakes with digital anti-skid system saving 181kg (400lb) in weight; and powered flight controls to cope with increased pitch-axis inertia caused by heavier engines and longer forward fuselage. The flight deck is similar to the MD-88, but an optional Advanced Common Flightdeck (ACF) with six flat-panel colour displays will be offered. The MD-90 programme was launched on 14 November 1989, with an order from Delta Air Lines for 50 firm and 115 options, later revised downwards. The first aircraft flew on 22 February 1993, followed by a second on 27 August. Both were used in the test programme leading to FAA certification on 15 November 1994, two months after the first production aircraft took to the air on 20 September. The MD-90 is built on the same production line as the MD-80, with major subassemblies provided by Alenia of Italy, AeroSpace Technologies in Australia, Aerospatiale of France, Spain's CASA, and several plants in China.

VARIANTS

The baseline model, and the only one in service by 1998, is the MD-90-30, powered by two 111.2kN (25,000lb) thrust IAE V2525-D5 turbofans. A 2,200nm (4,000km) range is possible with the MD-90-30ER, which also features increased take-off weight of 76,270kg (168,145lb) and additional fuel. The MD-90-50 is a heavier gross weight version and has provision for up to 6,738 litres (1,780 US gallons) extra fuel to add 700nm (1,296km) to the range, compared to the MD-90-30. Maximum take-off weight is increased from 70,760kg (156,000lb) to 78,245kg (171,500lb), necessitating reinforcing of the wing, fuselage, tail surfaces, landing gear, wheels and brakes. More powerful 124.5kN (28,000lb) IAE V2528-D5 engines also distinguish this variant from the MD-90-30. The MD-90-55 is similar to the -50, but has additional emergency doors on each side of the forward fuselage to allow the carriage of up to 187 tourist-class passengers. The MD-90-30T is being built in China to meet a Trunkliner requirement for the local market, under an agreement signed on 4 November 1994. The first of 20 aircraft is due to fly in April 1998. Shanghai Aviation Industrial Corporation (SAIC) is the prime contractor, with Shanghai Aircraft Manufacturing Factory (SAMF) responsible for the tailplane and elevators, to be assembled by Shenyang Aircraft Corporation (SAC). Xi'an Aircraft Company (XAC) will build the forward fuselage and wings, while Chengdu Aircraft Industrial Corporation will make the nose section, passenger and crew doors and airstairs. Offset work on the V2500 engines is also part of the agreement.

SERVICE USE

The first MD-90-30 was delivered to Delta Air Lines on 24 February 1995 and entered service between Dallas/Fort Worth and Newark, New Jersey, on 1 April. Orders totalled 132 aircraft at 1 January 1998, with 64 delivered to 10 airlines.

SPECIFICATION
(McDonnell Douglas MD-90-30)

Dimensions: Wingspan 32.87m (107ft 10in); length overall 46.51m (152ft 7in); height overall 9.33m (30ft 7¼in), wing area 112.3m² (1,209ft²).
Power Plant: Two 111.2kN (25,000lb) IAE V2525-D5 turbofans.
Weights: Operating weight empty 39,916kg (88,000lb); max take-off 70,760kg (156,000lb); max landing 64,410kg (142,000lb); max payload 17,350kg (38,250lb).
Performance: Max cruising speed 437kts (809km/h); take-off field length 2,166m (7,105ft); landing field length 1,600m (5,250ft); range with typical payload 2,275nm (4,216km).
Accommodation: Flight crew of two. Seating for up to 172 passengers, five-abreast with single aisle. Total baggage volume 36.8m³ (1,300ft³).

Left: Launch customer of the MD-90 in 1995, Delta Air Lines had taken delivery of 20 of its MD-90s by January 1998.

Right: US carrier Reno Air operates a large fleet of MD aircraft from its hub at Reno, including two MD-90s.

Below: Japan's third-largest airline uses the MD-90 on domestic services, fitted out in a single-class arrangement for 166 passengers.

PILATUS BRITTEN-NORMAN ISLANDER UK

The Islander was conceived in the early 1960s by the original Britten-Norman company founded by John Britten and Desmond Norman, in an effort to produce a very simple, light twin-engined transport for third-level and commuter airlines. The company had a 25 per cent interest in Cameroon Air Transport and the BN-2, as the new twin was designated, was designed specifically to meet the needs of that company, which was regarded as typical of many throughout the world which needed an aircraft with 6-10 seats, good take-off performance, low purchase cost, low operating costs and easy maintenance. Featuring a high-mounted, untapered and strutted wing, fixed land-

ing gear and unusual 'wall-to wall' seating in the fuselage, with three access doors (two to port and one to starboard), the BN-2 prototype was powered by a pair of 157kW (210hp) Continental IO-360-B engines and flew on 13 June 1965. With a span of 13.7m (45ft) and gross weight of 2,155kg (4,750lb), it was later fitted with 194kW (260hp) Lycoming O-540-E engines, with which it flew on 17 December 1965, the span then being increased to 14.9m (49ft) and gross weight to 2,585kg (5,700lb). A production prototype to similar specification flew on 20 August 1966. After it had encountered financial difficulties in 1972, the Britten-Norman company was acquired by the Fairey Group, but the latter also went into receivership in 1977, whereafter the Britten-Norman designs and facilities at Bembridge in the Isle of Wight were acquired by Pilatus, part of the Swiss Oerlikon-Bührle manufacturing group.

VARIANTS

The first production standard of the Islander, as the BN-2, was similar to the prototype in its modified form, the first aircraft flying on 24 April 1967. In June 1969, the production standard became the BN-2A, with a number of product improvements, a further change to BN-2B being made in 1978 with higher landing weight and improved interior design. Both the BN-2A and BN-2B were made available in a number of subvariants, the most significant options being 224kW (300hp) Lycoming IO-540-K1B5 engines in place of the original standard O-540-E4C5s (first flown on 30 April 1970); Riley-Rajay superchargers on standard O-540 engines; extended-span wing tips containing extra fuel tankage; and a long-nosed BN-2S with two more seats in the cabin, replacing baggage stowage space that was pro-

SPECIFICATION

(Pilatus Britten-Norman BN-2T)

Dimensions: Wingspan 16.15m (53ft 0in) with extended wingtips; length overall 10.87m (35ft 7¾in); height overall 4.18m (13ft 8½in), wing area 31.31m² (337ft²).
Power Plant: Two 298kW (400shp) Allison 250-B17 turboprops with Hartzell three-blade constant-speed fully-feathering propellers.
Weights: Operating weight empty 1,832kg (4,040lb); max take-off 3,175kg (7,000lb); max landing 3,084kg (6,800lb); max payload 1,113kg (2,454lb).
Performance: Max cruising speed 170kts (315km/h); initial rate of climb 5.3m/s (1,050ft/min); service ceiling 7,620m (25,000ft); take-off field length 380m (1,250ft); landing field length 340m (1,115ft); range with max payload 141nm (261km).
Accommodation: Flight crew of one and seating for up to 9 passengers on individual side-by-side and bench seats with no aisle. Baggage compartment volume 1.39m³ (49ft³).

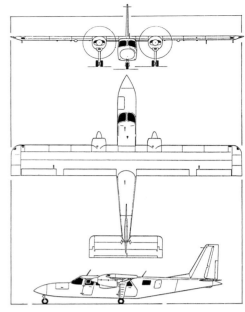

Above: A three-view drawing of the Islander in BN-2B piston-engined form, with the optional long-nose to provide extra baggage space, and standard wingtips without the fuel tank extensions. The latest Defender version is longer.

Right: The piston-engined BN-2A-26 Islander was flown by Police Aviation Services on behalf of the Hampshire police on aerial surveillance and EMS work. Islanders remain in service with several UK police forces.

PIPER PA-31 NAVAJO USA

A number of related light twins produced by Piper in the PA-31 family can be traced back to the original Navajo, which first flew on 30 September 1964 as a six/eight seater with a pair of 224kW (300hp) Lycoming IO-540-MIA5 engines. Progressive variants over the next decade included a turbocharged version, the Turbo Navajo, with 231kW (310hp) TIO-540-A engines; the PA-31P Pressurized Navajo with 317kW (425hp) TGO-540-E1A engines, and the PA-31-325 Turbo Navajo CR with 243kW (325hp) TIO-540-F2BD engines and handed propellers. All these variants had applications in the air taxi and small third-level airline markets, but of more specific interest was the PA-31-350 Navajo Chieftain, which was announced in September 1972 as a lengthened version of the Navajo C/R powered by 261kW (350hp) handed TIO-540-J2BD engines. A 610mm (2ft) lengthening of the fuselage allowed the Chieftain (as it is now usually known) to seat up to 10 occupants including the pilot, and all-cargo versions were also developed. The success of this type in the commercial air transport market led Piper to set up an Airline Division in 1981 to support Chieftain operations and to evolve

vided, instead, in the nose (first flown 22 August 1972). A series of suffix numbers added to the BN-2A and BN-2B designations indicated these and other options, such as revised wing leading-edge camber to meet US certification requirements, drooped flaps for better single-engined climb, and (the -20 series) a higher gross weight. On 6 April 1977, the BN-2A-40 prototype flew with 448kW (600shp) Lycoming LTP 101 turboprops, but a switch was made to Allison 250 engines for the production BN-

2T Turbine Islander. The BN-2T prototype first flew on 2 August 1950 and many of the previously described options are also available on this model. Military derivatives include the BN-2T Defender, BN2T-4R Westinghouse MSSA, and the latest model, the BN-2T-4S Defender.

SERVICE USE

The BN-2 Islander received British certification on 10 August 1967 and first deliveries were made on 13

and 15 August respectively, to Glosair and Loganair. FAA approval on 19 December 1967 was followed by first deliveries to the USA in January 1968. The BN-2T Turbine Islander obtained UK certification in May 1981 and US approval (to FAR Pt 23) on 15 July 1982. A milestone was reached on 7 May 1982 when the 1,000th Islander was delivered, and at 1 January 1998 the production total of all models exceeded 1,200, including those built in Romania and the Philippines.

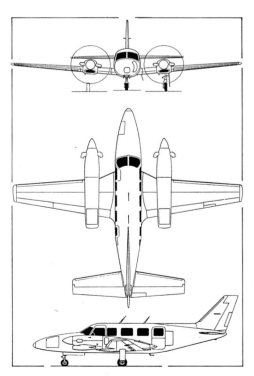

Left: Adelaide, South Australia-based Williams Airlines was one of many small operators using the PA-31-350 Navajo Chieftain on commuter services.

Above: The Piper T-1040 was the final derivative of the PA-31 design. It can be distinguished from the Chieftain and earlier versions by its Pratt & Whitney turboprop engines.

PA-31 derivatives more specifically intended for airline use, as described below.

VARIANTS

The PA-31-350, first flown on 25 September 1981, is known as the T-1020 and is a Chieftain with special interior and structural modifications to suit short-haul commuter airline operation, with a high rate of landings to flight hours. Up to 10 passengers can be accommodated in addition to the pilot, and the T-1020 has a maximum take-off weight of 3,175kg (7,000lb). In parallel with the T-1020, Piper evolved the T-1040 as an aircraft of similar capacity but offering the advantages of turboprop power. For speed of

> ### SPECIFICATION
> (Piper T-1040)
>
> **Dimensions:** Wingspan 12.52m (41ft 1in); length overall 11.18m (36ft 8in); height overall 3.96m (13ft 0in), wing area 21.27m² (229ft²).
> **Power Plant:** Two 373kW (500shp) Pratt & Whitney Canada PT6A-11 turboprops with Hartzell three-blade constant-speed fully-feathering propellers.
> **Weights:** Operating weight empty 2,097kg (4,624lb); max take-off 4,082kg (9,000lb); max landing 4,082kg (9,000lb); max payload 1,350kg (2,976lb).
> **Performance:** Max cruising speed 236kts (437km/h); initial rate of climb 8.2m/s (1,610ft/min); service ceiling 7,315m (24,000ft); take-off field length 810m (2,650ft); landing field length 640m (2,100ft); range with max payload 590nm (1,093km).
> **Accommodation:** Flight crew of one or two and seating for up to 9 passengers on individual side-by-side seats with no aisle. Baggage compartments front and rear volume 0.96m³ (34ft³).

development and minimum cost, the T-1040 made use, so far as possible, of existing Piper components, by combining the fuselage of the T-1020 and Chieftain with the PT6A-11 engines of the Cheyenne I (itself a Navajo derivative, as indicated by the PA-31T-1 designation), the wings and landing gear of the Cheyenne IIXL (PA-31T-2) and the engine nacelles with baggage lockers of the larger Cheyenne IIIA (PA-42). Small improvements were made, especially to the design of the air inlets, and the first of three pre-production T-1040 airframes flew on 17 July 1981. The designation for this member of the Navajo/Cheyenne family is PA-31T-3. After deliveries had begun, Piper obtained certification of a wingtip tank installation, giving the T-1040 an extension of some 300nm (555km) in range, and another option is a cargo pod which, fitted under the fuselage, has a volume of 0.85m³ (30cu ft). In all-cargo configuration, the T-1040's cabin offers a volume of 7m³ (246cu ft) and the cargo payload is nearly 1,315kg (2,900lb). Access to the cabin is facilitated by the 'Dutch' door, the top half of which hinges up and the bottom half (incorporating steps) down. Adjacent and to the rear of this door is a second, upward-hinged hatch giving access to the rear baggage compartment.

SERVICE USE

Some 500 Chieftains have been delivered specifically for commuter airline use since production of this PA-31 variant began. The T-1020 was certificated to FAR Pt 23 during 1982 and 22 were built. The T-1040 obtained FAA Type Approval, to CAR Pt 3, FAR Pt 23, FAR Pt 36 and SFAR Pt 27 as appropriate, on 25 February 1982 and first deliveries were made in May 1982. Piper built 23 T-1040s before ending production of both it and the T-1020.

SAAB 340 SWEDEN

After studying project designs for a number of possible civil aircraft, including all-cargo types, Saab-Scania of Sweden concluded an agreement with Fairchild Industries of the USA to proceed with project definition of a regional airliner. Known as the SF-340, it was to be a fully collaborative venture – the first of its kind between a European and an American company – in which each company would be responsible for the design and production of a portion of the airframe, and marketing and sales activities would be shared. All aircraft were to be assembled in Sweden, but those for the North American customers were to be finished and furnished by Fairchild in the USA. Project definition was completed during 1980 and in September of that year the two companies agreed to a full go-ahead for the SF-340, which had evolved as a twin-engined, low-wing monoplane with 34 passenger seats – hence the designation. Features of the design included a circular-section pressurised fuselage, a high aspect ratio wing with long-span single-slotted flaps, extensive use of composite materials and adhesive bonding in the structure, and a design fatigue life of 45,000 flight hours and 90,000 landings. Three aircraft were used for flight development and certification, these being first flown on 25 January, 11 May and 25 August 1983 respectively. The first full production standard aircraft flew on 5 March 1984. Saab-Scania assumed control of the SF-340 programme on 1 November 1985, after Fairchild indicated that it wished to relinquish its participation, and the aircraft was re-designated the Saab 340.

VARIANTS

Early deliveries of the initial production 340A had 1,215kW (1,630shp) General Electric CT7-5A turboprops and a gross weight of 11,794kg (26,000lb), but from mid-1985, engine power was increased to 1,294kW (1,735shp) and propellers enlarged. Aircraft built before then were subsequently retrofitted. The 340A was replaced from the 160th aircraft by the 340B, first flown in April 1989. The 340B introduced CT7-9B engines with automatic power reserve, higher weights and increased tailspan, providing better payload/range performance and hot-and-high capability. The 340BPlus was launched in

SPECIFICATION
(Saab 340B)

Dimensions: Wingspan 22.75m (74ft 7¾in) with optional extensions; length overall 19.73m (64ft 8¾in); height overall 6.97m (22ft 10½in), wing area 41.81m² (450ft²).
Power Plant: Two 1,305kW (1,750shp) General Electric CT7-9B turboprops with Dowty four-blade slow-turning constant-speed reversible-pitch auto-feathering propellers.
Weights: Operating weight empty 8,225kg (18,133lb); max take-off 13,155kg (29,000lb); max landing 12,930kg (28,505lb); max payload 3,795kg (8,366lb).
Performance: Max cruising speed 282kts (522km/h); max rate of climb 10.2m/s (2,000ft/min); service ceiling 9,450m (31,000ft); take-off field length 1,135m (3,710ft); landing field length 995m (3,265ft); range with typical payload 870nm (1,611km).
Accommodation: Flight crew of two and seating for up to 37 passengers in three rows with aisle. Baggage compartment volume 8.30m³ (293.1ft³).

February 1994, adding considerably to passenger comfort and performance. Main changes include a 'Generation III' interior with 15 per cent increase in overhead bin volume, improved lighting, redesigned seats and toilet, and an optional active noise control system. Further improvements to hot-and-high performance were achieved with 610mm (2ft) wingtip extensions, permitting up to 680kg (1,500lb) increase in take-off weight and reduction in field length of 122m (400ft). Optional low pressure tyres and gravel runway protection kit are available. Corporate, QC (Quick-change) and Combi versions have also been produced, as have two militarised versions, the 340AEW&C reconnaissance aircraft for the Swedish Air Force, and the 340BPlus SAR-200 rescue version for the Japan Maritime Safety Agency.

SERVICE USE

Type certification was obtained in Sweden on 30 May 1984 and ratified by FAA in US and by nine other European authorities (members of the JAR – Joint Airworthiness Requirements group) on 29 June 1984. Australian approval was gained on

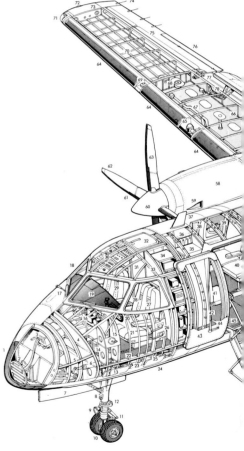

October 1984. Revenue passenger service began with the 340A on 15 June 1984 in the hands of Crossair of Switzerland. Other early operators were Comair of Cincinnati in the US, in October 1984, and Kendall Airlines of Australia in March 1985. Finnaviation began operating the 340QC in September 1986. The 340B was certificated on 3 July 1989 and joined launch customer Crossair on 15 September 1989. At 1 March 1998, orders totalled 454 aircraft, with 432 delivered.

Left: More than half of the Saab 340s produced are operated in the Americas, including this 340A operated by Argentine airline TAN on regional services from its hub at Neuquen.

Above: American Eagle is the largest operator of the Saab 340, totalling 116 aircraft, including 26 of the 340Bplus, shown here.

Above: The SF-340 was designed specifically for short-haul low-density routes, and this cutaway emphasises the compactness and neatness of the design. Cabin accommodation is for up to 35 passengers. The wing area and planform were chosen for low operating costs over short stages.

Saab SF-340 Cutaway Drawing Key

1 Radome
2 Weather radar scanner
3 Radar transmitter/receiver
4 Front pressure bulkhead
5 Nose undercarriage wheel bay
6 Hydraulic retraction jack
7 Nosewheel doors
8 Nose undercarriage leg strut
9 Taxying lamp
10 Twin nosewheels
11 Torque scissor link
12 Steering control link
13 Nosewheel leg pivot fixing
14 Rudder pedals
15 Angle of attack transmitter
16 Instrument panel
17 Windscreen wipers
18 Windscreen panels
19 Instrument panel shroud
20 Control column handwheel
21 Pilot's seat
22 Flight deck floor level
23 Underfloor control linkages
24 External hydraulic pipe duct
25 Control mechanism access panels
26 Pitot tubes
27 Safety harness
28 Centre control pedestal
29 Co-pilot's seat
30 Overhead systems switch panel
31 Starboard side toilet compartment
32 Cockpit roof escape hatch
33 Cockpit rear bulkhead
34 Radio and electronics rack
35 Galley/closet unit
36 Wardrobe
37 VHF aerial
38 Starboard side emergency exit
39 'Pull-down' window blinds

40 Front seat row, total 34 passengers
41 Cabin attendant's folding seat
42 Airstairs stowage
43 Entry door, open position
44 Door latch
45 Entry lobby
46 Airstairs
47 Folding handrail
48 Cabin window panel
49 Sidewall seat mounting rail
50 Cabin air vent duct
51 Landing lamp
52 Floor beam construction
53 Seat mounting rails
54 Glassfibre floor panels
55 Fuselage frame and stringer construction
56 Bonded fuselage skin/stringer panel
57 ADF aerial
58 Starboard engine cowling panels
59 NACA-type cooling air intake
60 Propeller spinner
61 Propeller blade de-icing boots
62 Dowty-Rotol four-bladed variable and reversible pitch, fully feathering propeller
63 Composite propeller blades
64 Wing leading-edge de-icing boots
65 Pressure refuelling connection
66 Starboard wing outer integral fuel tank, fuel capacity 733 Imp gal (3,331l)
67 Fuel system piping
68 Overwing filler cap

69 Compass flux valve
70 Bonded wing skin/stringer panel
71 Starboard navigation lights
72 Starboard light
73 Glassfibre wing tip fairing
74 Static dischargers
75 Starboard aileron
76 Aileron geared tab
77 Aileron actuator
78 External flap hinges
79 Starboard single-slotted trailing edge flap, down position
80 Engine exhaust nozzle
81 VLF/Omega aerial (option)
82 Starboard emergency exit window panel
83 Wing spar attachment main frames
84 Wing panel centreline splice
85 Spar attachment links
86 Port emergency exit window panel
87 Cabin wall trim panelling
88 Fuselage skin panelling
89 Overhead hand-baggage lockers (option)
90 Three-abreast seating
91 Overhead conditioned air distribution duct
92 Rear four-abreast seat row
93 Passenger cabin rear bulkhead
94 Anti-collision beacon (option)
95 Fin root fillet construction
96 HF aerial coupler (option)

97 Tailplane leading-edge de-icing boot
98 Starboard tailplane
99 Static dischargers
100 Starboard elevator
101 HF aerial cable (option)
102 Fin leading-edge de-icing boot
103 Leading-edge ribs
104 Aluminium honeycomb tail unit skin panels
105 VOR aerial
106 Fin construction
107 Rudder horn balance
108 Static dischargers
109 Honeycomb rudder construction
110 Rudder tab

111 Vortex generators
112 Rudder hinge control mechanism
113 Tailcone
114 Cabin pressure valves
115 Rear pressure bulkhead
116 Elevator tab
117 Port elevator honeycomb construction
118 Elevator tip fairing
119 Tailplane construction
120 Ventral strake, port and starboard
121 Rear fuselage ventral access hatch
122 Elevator hinge control
123 Fin/tailplane attachment main frames
124 Tail control cables
125 Cockpit voice recorder
126 Air data recorder
127 Baggage compartment bulkhead
128 'Up-and-over' baggage compartment door
129 Baggage restraint net
130 Door guide rails
131 Baggage loading door
132 DME aerial (option)
133 Wing trailing edge root fillet
134 Battery
135 Air conditioning plant, port and starboard
136 Flap inboard section
137 Wing stringers
138 Port inboard integral fuel tank
139 Heat shrouded engine exhaust pipe
140 Exhaust nozzle
141 Flap hydraulic jack
142 Rear spar
143 Composite flap shroud construction
144 Flap honeycomb construction
145 Port single-slotted trailing-edge flap, down position
146 Aileron geared tab
147 Static dischargers
148 Port aileron honeycomb construction
149 Glassfibre wing tip fairing
150 Lighting power supply
151 Strobe light
152 Wing navigation light
153 Wing leading edge de-icing boot
154 Wing rib construction
155 Fuel tank bay end rib
156 Overwing fuel filter cap
157 Port outer integral fuel tank
158 Front spar
159 Leading-edge nose ribs
160 Twin mainwheels
161 Main undercarriage leg strut
162 Torque scissor links
163 Mainwheel doors, closed after cycling of undercarriage leg
164 Hydraulic retraction jack
165 Main undercarriage pivot fixing
166 Engine bay fireproof bulkhead
167 Intake particle separator
168 Accessory gearbox
169 General Electric CT7-5A turboshaft engine
170 Engine nacelle construction
171 Ventral oil cooler
172 Gearbox mounting strut
173 Engine drive shaft
174 Propeller reduction gearbox
175 Propeller hub pitch change mechanism
176 Engine air intake
177 Propeller spinner
178 Port Dowty-Rotol four-bladed composite propeller

SAAB 2000 SWEDEN

The general trend for greater capacity aircraft in the regional market, coupled with the growing success of its 34-seat 340 model, convinced Saab of the viability of producing a 50-seat aircraft as a complement to the 340. In sharp contrast to other manufacturers which were developing regional jets, the Swedish company opted for a turboprop-powered aircraft, although its principal design objective was to combine jet speeds with turboprop economy, aiming at a 370 knots (685km/h) cruising speed, fast climb and high-altitude operation up to 9,450m (31,000ft). On hindsight, its decision appears to have been the wrong one, as sales have been slow, and are down to a trickle, now that the Canadair and Embraer regional jets, both 50-seaters, are in service. Design definition started in the autumn of 1988, and the programme was formally launched on 15 December 1988, on the back of a firm commitment from Crossair (which had also been the launch customer for the 340) for 25 aircraft, plus 25 options. Formal go-ahead was made in May 1989, and the Allison GMA (now AE) 2100 engine, driving six-bladed propellers, was selected in July. Contracts were also signed with other major subcontractors to spread the development risk. These include CASA of Spain which builds the wing, Finland's Valmet, producing the tail unit and elevators, and Westland Engineering in the UK for the rear fuselage. The same fuselage cross-section of the 340 was chosen for the Model 2000, but another 7.55m (24ft 9¼in) was added to the length to provide accommodation for 50 passengers, although an extra eight passengers can be accommodated by moving the rear bulkhead into the baggage space. The span was also stretched by 3.32m (10ft 10¾in) to increase wing area by 33 per cent. External and cabin noise reduction was a major design goal and, apart from choosing the Allison engine and slow-turning Dowty propellers with six swept blades, the engines were moved further outboard and an Ultra Electronics active noise control (ANC) system was fitted in the cabin. The ANC employs 72 microphones and 36 loudspeakers which continually monitor noise levels and generate, via an electronics system controller, an anti-phase sound field to lower interior noise levels. The first Saab 2000 was rolled out on 14 December 1991 and made its first flight on 26 March 1992. Two further aircraft in the certification programme flew on 3 July and 28 August 1992. The certification programme was delayed by problems with the aircraft's high-speed longitudinal stability, but this was overcome by a new Powered Elevator Control System (PECS), first flown on 19 May 1994. European certification to JAR 25 (Amendment 13) was obtained on 31 March 1994, followed by US certification to FAR 25 (Amendment 70) on 29 April. Full PECS certification was granted in December 1994

VARIANTS

Only one basic Saab 2000 passenger model is available at present, delivered to both airlines and corporate customers. First five aircraft delivered with manual elevator controls, but subsequently retrofitted with PECS.

SERVICE USE

First aircraft was delivered to launch customer Crossair, which put the type into service in September 1994. The second airline, Deutsche BA, took delivery on 17 March 1995, and the first corporate customer, General Motors, accepted the 20th aircraft off the production line on 30 October 1995. At 1 March 1998, Saab had received orders for 58 aircraft, of which 48 had been delivered. Production will cease in the year 2000.

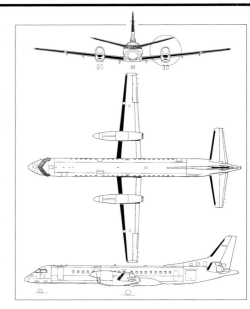

Saab 2000 Cutaway Drawing Key

Structure and general
1 Radome of glass/nomex sandwich – Norton company
2 Nose section of aluminium alloy semi-monocoque construction
3 Canted forward pressure bulkhead
4 Windscreen wipers
5 Crew escape hatch
6 Machined windscreen frame
7 Two crew cockpit
8 Crew seats – Ipeco
9 Main entry door 0.69m x 1.6mm aluminium honeycomb
10 Passenger fold-up airstairs
11 Stowage unit
12 Toilet
13 Flight attendant's seat
14 Wardrobe
15 Carry on baggage stowage unit
16 Passenger cabin 50 seats at a 0.81m pitch
17 Cabin interior furnishing and exterior painting – AIM Aviation
18 Overwing emergency exits, type III 0.51m x 0.91m, aluminium honeycomb
19 Overhead bins 360mm3 per passenger
20 Galley
21 Service door 0.61m x 1.22m, aluminium honeycomb
22 Cargo compartment door 1.35m x 1.3m aluminium honeycomb
23 Cargo bay 10m³
24 Cabin structure of semi-monocoqua bonded aluminium alloy
25 Side fuselage panel – bonded stringers and frames
26 Top fuselage panel – bonded stringers
27 Windows – Swedlow
28 Bottom fuselage panel – bonded stringers
29 Rear fuselage of semi-monocoque aluminium alloy – Westland
30 Rear pressure bulkhead, lower section canted
31 Dorsal fin – composite, Fischer Advanced Composite Components
32 Twin spar fin – Valmet
33 Attachment points fin to fuselage
34 Twin spar tailplane – Valmet
35 Attachment points tailplane to fuselage
36 Elevator/fuselage fairing
37 Fuselage to wing fairing - Kevlar/Nomex sandwich
38 Two spar wing torsion box with machined and built up ribs joined at centreline complete wing manufactured by CASA
39 Front wing spar – machined
40 Rear wing spar – machined
41 One piece upper and lower skins with bonded stringers
42 Flap coving supported by struts – composite
43 Aileron coving – composite
44 Wing leading edge in four sections
45 Forward main frame
46 Aft main frame
47 Four main frame to wing attachment points
48 Four drag links

Air conditioning
A1 Oxygen storage bottle for cockpit oxygen system
A2 Environmental control system cycle pack – Hamilton Standard, pack also on Starboard side
A3 Air risers
A4 Cockpit air ducts
A5 Recirculating air ducts
A6 Mixing unit

Controls
C1 Rudder pedals
C2 Control wheels – Mason Electrik
C3 Twin-spar ailerons hinged at two points – Graphite/Nomex sandwich
C4 Aileron control actuation linkage, rod and cable actuation
C5 Aileron trim tab
C6 Electro-mechanical actuation for aileron trim tab
C7 One piece, twin spar flap – Graphite/Nomex sandwich skins
C8 Flap hinge and support brackets (four)
C9 Hydraulic actuator for flaps, housed at rear of engine nacelle
C10 Twin-spar rudder hinged at two points – Graphite/Nomex sandwich skins
C11 Dual hydraulic servos for rudder actuation, electrically actuated – Dowty Aerospace
C12 Fairing for rudder hydraulic servos
C13 Twin spar elevator hinged at three points – Graphite/Nomex sandwich skins
C14 Elevator control quadrant with interconnect
C15 Elevator spring tab
C16 Elevator trim tab

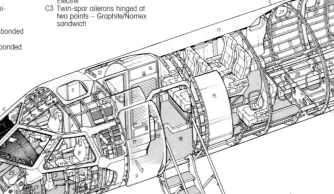

SPECIFICATION
(Saab 2000)

Dimensions: Wingspan 24.76m (81ft 2¾in); length overall 27.28m (89ft 6in); height overall 7.73m (25ft 4in), wing area 55.74m² (600ft²).
Power Plant: Two 3,096kW (4,152shp) Allison AE 2100A turboprops with FADEC. Dowty slow-turning constant-speed propellers with six swept blades, full auto-feathering and revese pitch.
Weights: Operating weight empty 13,800kg (30,423lb); max take-off 22,800kg (50,265lb); max landing 22,000kg (48,501lb); max payload 5,900kg (13,007lb).
Performance: Max cruising speed 368kts (682km/h); max rate of climb 11.4m/s (2,250ft/min); service ceiling 9,450m (31,000ft); take-off field length 1,285m (4,220ft); landing field length 1,245m (4,085ft); range with max payload 1,200nm (2,222km).
Accommodation: Flight crew of two and seating for up to 58 passengers, three-abreast with aisle. Baggage/cargo compartment volume 10.2m³ (360ft³).

SAAB 2000

Left: This three-view of the Saab 2000 shows the external similarities to the 340, the main difference being the longer fuselage to carry 50 passengers

Right: The only customer outside Europe for the Saab 2000 was AirMarshall Islands, which uses the aircraft on inter-island services in the Pacific.

Below: Cutaway drawing of the Saab 2000.

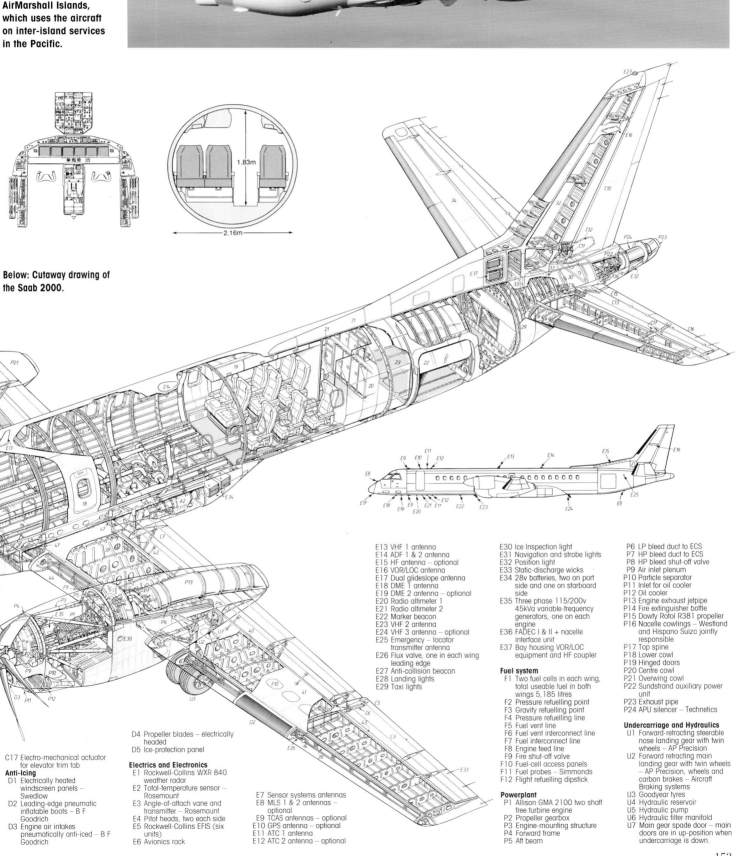

C17 Electro-mechanical actuator for elevator trim tab

Anti-Icing
D1 Electrically heated windscreen panels – Swedlow
D2 Leading-edge pneumatic inflatable boots – B F Goodrich
D3 Engine air intakes pneumatically anti-iced – B F Goodrich
D4 Propeller blades – electrically headed
D5 Ice-protection panel

Electrics and Electronics
E1 Rockwell-Collins WXR 840 weather radar
E2 Total-temperature sensor – Rosemount
E3 Angle-of-attach vane and transmitter – Rosemount
E4 Pitot heads, two each side
E5 Rockwell-Collins EFIS (six units)
E6 Avionics rack
E7 Sensor systems antennas
E8 MLS 1 & 2 antennas – optional
E9 TCAS antennas – optional
E10 GPS antenna – optional
E11 ATC 1 antenna
E12 ATC 2 antenna – optional

E13 VHF 1 antenna
E14 ADF 1 & 2 antenna
E15 HF antenna – optional
E16 VOR/LOC antenna
E17 Dual glideslope antenna
E18 DME 1 antenna
E19 DME 2 antenna – optional
E20 Radio altimeter 1
E21 Radio altimeter 2
E22 Marker beacon
E23 VHF 2 antenna
E24 VHF 3 antenna – optional
E25 Emergency – locator transmitter antenna
E26 Flux valve, one in each wing leading edge
E27 Anti-collision beacon
E28 Landing lights
E29 Taxi lights

E30 Ice Inspection light
E31 Navigation and strobe lights
E32 Position light
E33 Static-discharge wicks
E34 28v batteries, two on port side and one on starboard side
E35 Three phase 115/200v 45kVa variable-frequency generators, one on each engine
E36 FADEC I & II + nacelle interface unit
E37 Bay housing VOR/LOC equipment and HF coupler

Fuel system
F1 Two fuel cells in each wing, total useable fuel in both wings 5,185 litres
F2 Pressure refuelling point
F3 Gravity refuelling point
F4 Pressure refuelling line
F5 Fuel vent line
F6 Fuel vent interconnect line
F7 Fuel interconnect line
F8 Engine feed line
F9 Fire shut-off valve
F10 Fuel-cell access panels
F11 Fuel probes – Simmonds
F12 Flight refuelling dipstick

Powerplant
P1 Allison GMA 2100 two shaft free turbine engine
P2 Propeller gearbox
P3 Engine-mounting structure
P4 Forward frame
P5 Aft beam

P6 LP bleed duct to ECS
P7 HP bleed duct to ECS
P8 HP bleed shut-off valve
P9 Air inlet plenum
P10 Particle separator
P11 Inlet for oil cooler
P12 Oil cooler
P13 Engine exhaust jetpipe
P14 Fire extinguisher bottle
P15 Dowty Rotol R381 propeller
P16 Nacelle cowlings – Westland and Hispano Suiza jointly responsible
P17 Top spine
P18 Lower cowl
P19 Hinged doors
P20 Centre cowl
P21 Overwing cowl
P22 Sundstrand auxiliary power unit
P23 Exhaust pipe
P24 APU silencer – Technetics

Undercarriage and Hydraulics
U1 Forward-retracting steerable nose landing gear with twin wheels – AP Precision
U2 Forward retracting main landing gear with twin wheels – AP Precision, wheels and carbon brakes – Aircraft Braking systems
U3 Goodyear tyres
U4 Hydraulic reservoir
U5 Hydraulic pump
U6 Hydraulic filter manifold
U7 Main gear spade door – main doors are in up-position when undercarriage is down.

153

SHORTS 330 UK

Based on its experience in the design and operation of the Skyvan, Shorts began to study, in the early 1970s, the possibility of developing a larger commuter airliner, in the 30-seat category, for which there then appeared to be an emerging market. To make such an aircraft attractive to a market that was traditionally unlikely to be able to finance expensive new equipment, the company set itself the target of producing an aircraft having a first cost no greater than $1 million (about £400,000) in 1973 values. Such a restraint ruled out any possibility of

starting the design of a new type from scratch. Instead, what became known initially as the SD3-30 evolved as an aircraft sharing several features with the Skyvan: it used the same outer wing panels, on a longer centre wing; had the same, basically square, cross-section for the fuselage, which was 3.78m (12ft 5in) longer; and used a similar, though enlarged, tail unit. Improving the appearance of the SD3-30 (compared with that of its progenitor) was a longer nose and a longer top fuselage fairing, extending from the flight deck to the tail. Other significant changes were

the introduction of retractable landing gear and a switch from the Skyvan's Garrett engines to Pratt & Whitney Canada PT6As, judged to be more acceptable to the regional airline industry and more readily able to meet the power requirements of the enlarged aircraft, since suitably uprated PT6A-45s were already under development for the de Havilland Canada Dash 7. Helped by a UK government grant towards launching costs (to be repaid through a levy on subsequent sales) Shorts was able to announce a formal go-ahead for the SD3-30 on 23

SPECIFICATION
(Shorts 330–200)

Dimensions: Wingspan 22.76m (74ft 8in); length overall 17.69m (58ft 0in); height overall 4.95m (16ft 3in), wing area 42.1m² (453.0ft²).
Power Plant: Two 893kW (1,198shp) Pratt & Whitney Canada PT6A-45R turboprops, with Hartzell five-blade constant-speed fully-feathering and reversing propellers.
Weights: Operating weight empty 6,680kg (14,727lb); max take-off 10,387kg (22,900lb); max payload 2,653kg (5,850lb).
Performance: Max cruising speed 190kts (352km/h); initial rate of climb 6.0m/s (1,180ft/min); take-off field length 1,040m (3,420ft); landing field length 1,030m (3,380ft); range with max payload 473nm (876km).
Accommodation: Flight crew of two. Seating for up to 30 passengers in two plus one arrangement with offset aisle. Total baggage compartment volume 4.10m³ (145.0ft³).

SHORTS 360 UK

For many years, operators of commuter-style services in the USA (where a large proportion of the market for this type of aircraft exists) had been limited by the terms of the CAB Economic Regulation 298 to flying aircraft with no more than 30 passenger seats. To fly larger types required the airline to seek authority under a substantially different set of operating regulations, compliance with which frequently imposed extra costs which were necessarily passed on to the traveller and thus served to diminish the number of passengers carried. The deregulation of the US airline industry in 1978 brought a relaxation of these rules and made it possible for many third-level airlines to contemplate growth of a kind previously thought impossible. One obvious impact of this sea-change in the fortunes of at least some of the commuter specialists was that the aircraft manufacturers found a new opportunity to market aircraft of more than 30-seat capacity. In the late 1970s Shorts had already been studying several ways of improving the basic Shorts 330 without increasing capacity, one such option being to use more powerful PT6A-65 engines in order to achieve higher operating weights. When the limit on capacity became less important, it became possible to combine this new engine installation (with a modified cowling and improved air intake) with a new or modified fuselage. As a first step, it was decided to restrict the 'stretch' to a modest six seats, emphasis being placed upon improvement to the rear fuselage profile to reduce drag and thus improve operating economics. Wind tunnel testing embraced several options, including a T-tail layout, but an entirely conventional low-mounted tailplane and single fin-and-rudder finally met the design objectives, allied to a somewhat lengthened rear fuselage of improved aerodynamic form. This redesign allowed one extra seat row (three passengers) at the rear of the cabin; a 915mm (36in) plug ahead of the wing provided for another seat row. For the most part, the remainder of the airframe was little

SPECIFICATION
(Shorts 360–300)

Dimensions: Wingspan 22.80m (74ft 9½ n); length overall 21.58m (70ft 9½in); height overall 7.27m (23ft 10¼in), wing area 42.18m² (454.0ft²).
Power Plant: Two 1,062kW (1,424shp) Pratt & Whitney Canada PT6A-67R turboprops, with Hartzell six-blade constant-speed fully-feathering propellers.
Weights: Operating weight empty 7,870kg (17,350lb); max take-off 12,292kg (27,100lb); max payload 12,020kg (26,500lb).
Performance: Max cruising speed 216kts (400km/h); max rate of climb 4.8m/s (952ft/min); take-off field length 1,305m (4,280ft); landing field length 1,220m (4,000ft); range with max payload 402nm (745km).
Accommodation: Flight crew of two. Seating for up to 36 passengers in two plus one arrangement with offset aisle. Total baggage compartment volume 6.10m³ (215.0ft³).

changed from that of the Shorts 330, although Dowty landing gear was chosen to replace the earlier Menasco gear, and improved Hartzell propellers were matched to the new power plant, which incorporated an emergency reserve feature to provide a power boost in the event of one engine failing during the critical stages of take-off. Since the Shorts 330 designation was indicative of a 30-seat version of the basic SD-3 design, the new 36-seat project became known as the Shorts 336 in the drawing office, but this was changed to Shorts 360 for marketing purposes. The go-ahead for the Shorts 360 was given in January 1981, and a first flight was achieved on 1 June of the same year, indicating the extent to which standard components of the Shorts 330 were applicable to the new aircraft. In the prototype, this commonality extended to the PT6A-45R engines fitted for the first six months of flight testing, the definitive PT6A-65Rs first being flown in January 1982.

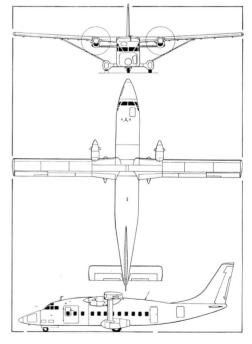

Above: The Shorts 360 has the same wing and front fuselage of the 330, but has been stretched at the rear to provide seating for six more passengers. The 330's twin tail unit is replaced by a more conventional and larger single fin.

Right: Although the Shorts 360 has now been supplanted in front line service by newer and faster types, it can still be seen on many third-level routes. BAC Express Airlines uses its 360s on passenger flights by day and freight flights at night

May 1973, and construction of prototypes and pre-production aircraft was put in hand at the Queen's Island, Belfast, factory in Northern Ireland. The first and second aircraft made their initial flights there on 22 August 1974 and 8 July 1975 respectively. The first production aircraft, flown on 15 December 1975, was also used to complete the final stages of certification.

VARIANTS
The SD3-30, which was re-styled as Shorts 330 soon

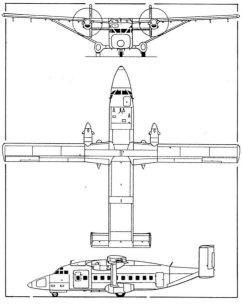

Left: Its simplicity and low cost have made the Shorts 330 attractive for commuter services between smaller towns and cities. Flying Enterprise operates them in southern Sweden.

Above: The Shorts 330 retained the box-like structure of the earlier Skyvan, but was given a more streamlined look with a longer nose and fuselage fairing.

after entering service, was initially powered by 862kW (1,156shp) PT6A-45A engines. After delivering 26 aircraft with these engines, Shorts introduced the slightly modified PT6A-45B, and these were used in the next 40 aircraft. A switch was then made to the PT6A-45R, with slightly higher flat-rated power and a power reserve system and some previously optional items of equipment became standard. The power increase allowed the gross weight to go up by 95.3kg (210lb) from the original certification weight of 10,292kg (22,690lb). Fuel capacity in the Shorts 330 was increased in January 1985 and in this form, the aircraft was known as the Shorts 330-200. Although the Shorts 330 was primarily a regional airliner, it was readily adaptable for all-cargo and military transport roles. Specifically for military use, the Shorts 330-UTT (Utility Tactical Transport) has a strengthened floor, inward-opening rear cabin doors for paradropping, and structural reinforcement for a max take-off weight of 11,158kg (24,600lb). The C-23A Sherpa flew on 23 December 1982 and was sold to the USAF as a military freighter with a full width rear cargo ramp/door.

SERVICE USE
The SD3-30 gained full UK certification in the transport category on 18 February 1976, and won FAA type approval to FAR Pt 25 and FAR Pt 36 on 18 June 1976. Deliveries began in the same month, and revenue service was inaugurated by Time Air in Canada on 24 August 1976. A total of 139 Shorts 330 were built, and some 45 remained in airline use in 1998.

VARIANTS
Between prototype first flight and production definition, some small changes were made in the control system of the Shorts 360, including deletion of one of the two trim tabs from each elevator. The first production batch of aircraft had PT6A-65R engines each rated at 875kW (1,173shp) for maximum continuous operation and at 990kW (1,327shp) with emergency reserve for take-off. During 1986, the more powerful PT6A-65AR engines were introduced in aircraft designated Shorts 360 Advanced. The final variant was the 360-300 in 1987, which featured new PT6A-67ARs, autopilot and substantially enhanced passenger comfort. Earlier models were then re-dubbed 360-100 and 360-200.

SERVICE USE
The first production Shorts 360 flew on 19 August 1982 and UK certification was obtained on 3 September of that year, followed in November by FAA approval to FAR Pts 25 and 36. The first delivery was made to Suburban Airlines at Reading, Pennsylvania on 11 November 1982, and service use began on 1 December. The first Shorts 360 Advanced went to Thai Airways in early 1986. Shorts had built 164 aircraft when production ceased in 1992. Around 100 are still in service.

TUPOLEV TU-134 RUSSIA

The Tupolev design bureau began development of this twin-engined short/medium-range jetliner in the early 1960s, in an effort to provide Aeroflot with an aircraft of better performance than the Tu-124, which had only then recently entered service. The Tu-124 was essentially a scaled-down derivative of the first Soviet jet transport, the Tu-104, which itself was adapted from the Tu-16 jet bomber and therefore lacked some of the refinements that were coming to be taken for granted by airline passengers in the west. The Tu-134, initially designated Tu-124A, emerged in September 1964, by which time a prototype was reputed to have completed more than 100 test flights, to show that its configuration matched quite closely that chosen by BAC and Douglas for, respectively, the One-Eleven and the DC-9, aircraft both in a similar category to the Tu-134. The Soviet aircraft had more wing sweepback, however, combining this with a rugged tricycle landing gear design to allow short-field and rough-field operation, in line with Aeroflot requirements. It also had the characteristic Tupolev fairings at the wing trailing edge to house main units of the landing gear when retracted. Six prototypes or pre-production aircraft are reported to have been used in development of the Tu-134, which is believed to have made its first flight in December 1963. Production was launched in 1964 at Kharkhov.

VARIANTS

The first production batch was followed by the appearance, in the second half of 1970, of the Tu-134A, featuring a 2.10m (6ft 10½in) fuselage 'stretch', providing for eight extra passengers (two seat rows) in the maximum-density one-class layout. All early Tu-134s and some Tu-134As had the Tupolev glazed nose, similar to that of the original Tu-16 bomber, but later aircraft had a 'solid' nose radome containing weather radar. Soloviev D-30 Srs II engines were introduced on the Tu-134A, as was a locally-strengthened wing and improved avionics. Further versions of the aircraft began to appear from the autumn of 1981 onwards, but these were the result of modification programmes rather than new production, which is believed to have ended in 1978. These variants included the Tu-134B with

SPECIFICATION
(Tupolev Tu-134A)

Dimensions: Wingspan 29.00m (95ft 1¾in); length overall 37.05m (121ft 6½in); height overall 9.14m (30ft 0in), wing area 127.3m² (1,370.3ft²).
Power Plant: Two 64.5kN (14,990lb) Soloviev D-30 Series II turbofans.
Weights: Operating weight empty 29,050kg (64,045lb); max take-off 47,000kg (103,600lb); max landing 43,000kg (94,800lb); max payload 8,200kg (18,075lb).
Performance: Max cruising speed 486kts (898km/h); service ceiling 11,900m (39,040ft); take-off field length 2,400m (7,875ft); landing field length 2,200m (7,220ft); range with max payload 1,020nm (1,890km).
Accommodation: Flight crew of three. Seating for up to 84 passengers, four-abreast with central aisle. Total baggage/cargo volume 14.16m³ (500ft³).

TUPOLEV TU-204/214/224/234 RUSSIA

Russia's first truly modern airliner, the twin-engined Tu-204 was announced in 1983 as a replacement for the Tu-154 and Il-62 in Aeroflot service. Dimensionally and in appearance similar to the Boeing 757, noticeable external differences are a slightly greater 28 deg sweepback and winglets. The Tu-204 has a wing of supercritical aerofoil section, with a relatively high aspect ratio, and makes extensive use of composites in wing control surfaces, wingroot fairings, nose radome and the tail unit, making up about 18 per cent of the structural weight. It features a triplex digital fly-by-wire control system with triplex analog back-up, and EFIS cockpit with two-colour CRTs for flight, navigation, engine and systems displays. Sidestick controllers were evaluated on a Tu-154 testbed, but these were rejected in favour of conventional 'Y' control yokes. The first prototype, powered by Aviadvigatel PS-90AT turbofans, made its maiden flight on 2 January 1989, flown by Tupolev's chief test pilot A. Talakine. It was followed by three more prototypes, and the first aircraft with Rolls-Royce RB.211-535E4-B engines flew on 14 August 1992, prior to being introduced at the Farnborough air show three weeks later. Small-scale production of the basic version began at Ulyanovsk in 1990.

VARIANTS

The basic Tu-204 for 214 passengers with twin PS-90A engines and a take-off weight of 94,500kg (208,557lb) was supplemented in 1993 by the extended range Tu-204-100, which differs largely in having additional fuel and a higher weight of 103,000kg (227,070lb). Increased payload, but reduced range is available in the Tu-204-100C. The Tu-204-120 is similar to the -100 but has Rolls-Royce engines and avionics systems from Honeywell and AlliedSignal. Further increase in payload and gross weight produced the Tu-204-200, first flown on 21 March 1996, but now marketed as the Tu-214. The same designation has also been given to the Tu-204-200C with more payload, and the Tu-204C³ (cargo, converted, containerised) proposal. The Tu-204-220 is similar to the -200 but is powered by 191.7kN (43,100lb) Rolls-Royce RB.211-535E4 or 535F5 turbofans and marketed by British Russian Aviation Corporation (BRAVIA). Shorter fuselage versions for up to 166 passengers with RB.211-535E4 and 158.3kN (35,580lb) PS-90P engines respectively are the Tu-224 (formerly Tu-204-320) and Tu-234 (formerly Tu-204-300). Windowless all-cargo versions direct from the factory, suffixed C, are available for all main models, as is a conversion programme undertaken by Oriol-Avia. Production of all Tu-204 models is shared between plants at Kazan and Ulyanovsk.

SERVICE USE

Initially used on freight services following Russian certification for the basic type on 12 January 1995. First revenue passenger flight between Moscow and Mineralnye Vody operated by Vnukovo Airlines on 23 February 1996. First Tu-204-120 with Rolls-Royce engines entered KrasAir service at the end of 1997.

SPECIFICATION
(Tupolev Tu-204-200)

Dimensions: Wingspan 42.00m (137ft 9½in); length overall 46.00m (150ft 11in); height overall 13.90m (45ft ¼in), wing area 182.4m² (1,963ft²).
Power Plant: Two 158.3kN (35,580lb) Aviadvigatel PS-90A turbofans.
Weights: Operating weight empty 59,000kg (130,070lb); max take-off 110,750kg (244,155lb); max landing 89,500kg (197,310lb); max payload 25,200kg (55,555lb).
Performance: Max cruising speed 448kts (830km/h); service ceiling 12,600m (41,340ft); required runway length 2,250m (7,380ft); range with max payload 3,415nm (6,330km).
Accommodation: Flight crew of two or three. Seating for up to 212 passengers, six-abreast with central aisle. Total baggage/cargo volume 30.8m³ (1,088ft³).

Right: Vnukovo Airlines, one of Russia's major trunk airlines, became the first operator of the Tu-204 in 1993, when it received the type for operational trials, before inaugurating offical scheduled passenger services in February 1996. The most likely version to succeed in the market, especially for use on international routes, is the Tu-204-120 with Western engines and avionics being marketed by Sirocco Aerospace International which sold the first 10 to Russia's KrasAir in August 1997.

spoilers for direct lift control, and a forward-facing crew compartment including engine controls and navigation instruments on the centre panel, with a jump seat (between the two pilots' seats) for the navigator/flight engineer. The Tu-134B-1 had interior revisions, including a small reduction in toilet size, to allow an increase in basic capacity to 84 passengers, or a maximum of 90 if galley facilities were removed. The Tu-134A-3 introduced new lightweight seats permitting five-abreast seating for 96 passengers, with full toilet and galley provisions retained; improved D-30-III engines were also introduced.

SERVICE USE

Proving flights with the Tu-134 on Aeroflot routes were made before the first commercial service began in September 1967, between Moscow and Stockholm. The Tu-134A went into service in the second half of 1970. Production of all versions of the Tu-134 is estimated at more than 700, of which up to 100 were exported, for use by most of the East European airlines, and other Soviet satellite countries. More than 400 were still in service in 1998, almost all in Russia and the CIS, although their use is now fast diminishing as many airlines are equipping with Western aircraft.

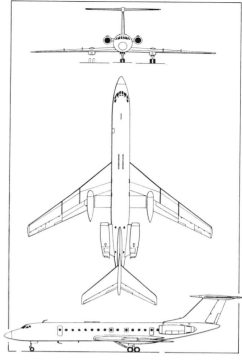

Left: The Tu-134, once standard on the scheduled services networks of Aeroflot, has found its way into the fleets of charter airlines which emerged out of its shadows. This Tu-134B of Latcharter was fitted out by British Aerospace with a VIP interior.

Above: The Tupolev Tu-134A is shown in this three-view drawing with the lengthened radar-carrying nose featured in most production aircraft. Several modifications were produced in the 1980s, although these were largely carried out to the interior.

TUPOLEV TU-204/214/224/234

TUPOLEV TU-154/155/156 RUSSIA

Intended to take the modernisation of Aeroflot a step further following the introduction of the first generation of turbojet and turboprop transports, the Tu-154 had the same overall configuration as its two Western contemporaries, the Boeing 727 and Hawker Siddeley Trident, but also some significant differences to meet the operational requirements of Soviet air transport. In particular, the power-to-weight ratio is considerably higher than that of the Model 727, giving the aircraft a lively airfield performance and allowing it to operate from the relatively short and poorly-surfaced Class 2 airfields at many Russian cities. The wing pods for landing gear stowage are also a distinctive feature of the Tupolev design. Flight development involved six prototypes and pre-production aircraft, and the first prototype took to the air on 4 October 1968, powered by three 93.2kN (20,950lb) Kuznetsov NK-8-2 turbofans, similar to those being developed for the Ilyushin IL-62.

VARIANTS

The initial production version, identified simply as Tu-154, had 93.2kN (20,950lb) Kuznetsov NK-8-2 engines, and a number of possible interior layouts, ranging from 128 to 167 seats. The standard all-economy layout had 160 seats, and a typical mixed-class arrangement provided 24 first-class seats in the forward cabin in place of 54 economy-class. Soviet sources indicated the availability of an all-cargo version, but this may not have appeared in definitive form until the Tu-154C was developed as a Tu-154B derivative, as noted below. The Tu-154A was the first improved version to appear, in 1973, with its uprated NK-8-2U engines, and maximum take-off weight increased from 90,000kg (198,416lb) to 94,000kg (207,235lb). This allowed an increase in fuel capacity, from the original 33,150kg (73,082lb), with provision for 6,600kg (14,550lb) in a centre-section tank that was not connected to the aircraft's main fuel system but the contents of which could be transferred to the main tanks at destination airports where refuelling facilities were restricted or expensive. Numerous changes and improvements were made in the avionics and other systems and the cabin interior. The Tu-154B superseded the Tu-154A in 1977, and was followed by the slightly refined Tu-154B-2. This introduced a Thomson-CSF/SFIM automatic flight control and navigation system for Cat II landings and had higher operating weights, matched to a rearranged cabin layout that increased maximum seating to 180. The supplementary tank of the Tu-154A was also fully integrated into the aircraft's fuel system. As a conversion of the Tu-154B, the Tu-154C is an all-cargo carrier with a side-loading door ahead of the wing and a 1,565nm (2,900km) range with 20,000kg (44,100lb) payload. The latest development is the Tu-154M (sometimes described as the Tu-164 in early references), which appeared in 1982 with Soloviev D-30KU-154-II engines derived from those of the Il-62M and each rated at 104kN (23,380lb). Overall dimensions were unchanged but the tailplane was redesigned, and wing slats and spoilers modified. A modernised Tu-154M2 with more fuel efficient 156.9kN (35,274lb) Aviadvigatel/Perm PS-90A turbofans and area navigation system is under development and may have flown. A special version for 'Open Skies' treaty observations flights, with side-looking synthetic aperture radar, is being developed under a co-operative agreement between Russia and Germany. Known as the Tu-154M/OS, the aircraft is being used to trial the new radar, for incorporation into the Tu-154M by 1999. The Tu-155 was a development aircraft with Kuznetsov NK-88 turbofans operating on liquid hydrogen and liquefied natural gas (LNG), flown on 15 April 1988. This is now being proposed to be replaced by the Tu-156, several versions of

which are to be made available from 1998, although the timetable looks optimistic. These are the 130-seat Tu-156S with NK-89 turbofans, a kerosene/LNG-powered conversion of the Tu-154B; the Tu-156M, a similar conversion from the Tu-154M; and the Tu-156M2 with NK-94 turbofans operating on LNG only.

SERVICE USE

Aeroflot conducted Tu-154 proving flights early in 1971 and began services in mid-year on an *ad hoc* basis, with full commercial exploitation starting on 9 February 1972 on the Moscow-Mineralnye Vody route. First international services were on the Moscow-Prague route, starting on 1 August 1972. The Tu-154A entered service in April 1974, the Tu-154B in 1977 and the Tu-154M at the beginning of 1985. The Tu-154M remains in production and continues to find export customers, being in service with many airlines in Europe, Asia and with Cubana in Central America. Production is approaching 950 units of all models, with some 750 in active service.

SPECIFICATION
(Tupolev Tu-154M)

Dimensions: Wingspan 37.55m (123ft 2½in); length overall 47.90m (157ft 1¾in); height overall 11.40m (37ft 4¾in), wing area 201.45m² (2,168ft²).
Power Plant: Three 104kN (23,380lb) Aviadvigatel D-30KU-154-II turbofans.
Weights: Operating weight empty 55,300kg (121,915lb); max take-off 100,000kg (220,460lb); max landing 80,000kg (176,365lb); max payload 18,000kg (39,680lb).
Performance: Max cruising speed 504kts (935km/h); service ceiling 12,100m (39,700ft); take-off field length 2,500m (8,200ft); landing field length 2,500m (8,200ft); range with max payload 1,997nm (3,700km).
Accommodation: Flight crew of three. Seating for up to 166 passengers, six-abreast with central aisle. Total baggage/cargo volume 43.0m³ (1,517ft³).

Tupolev Tu-154B-2 and 154M Cutaway Drawing Key

1 Upward hinging radome
2 Weather radar scanner
3 Scanner mounting and tracking mechanism
4 Front pressure bulkhead
5 Ventral Doppler antenna
6 Rudder pedals
7 Control column hand wheel
8 Instrument panel
9 Electrically-heated windscreen panels
10 Windscreen wipers
11 Cockpit eyebrow windows
12 Overhead systems switch panel
13 VHF antenna
14 Flight Engineer's station
15 First Officer's seat
16 Captain's seat
17 Navigator's station
18 Underfloor avionics equipment bay
19 Dual pitot heads
20 Twin nosewheels, aft retracting

21 Nose undercarriage leg strut
22 Escape chute stowage (all door positions)
23 Crew wardrobe
24 Starboard side toilet compartment
25 Galley/buffet unit
26 Curtained cabin bulkhead
27 Forward entry door
28 Cabin attendant's folding seats (3)
29 Nose undercarriage wheel bay
30 Fuselage lower lobe frame and stringer structure
31 Fuselage skin panelling
32 Six-abreast passenger seating, 166-seat tourist-class layout shown
33 Forward emergency exit/service door

34 Cabin wall trim panelling
35 Floor beam structure
36 Baggage hold door
37 Forward underfloor baggage hold, 21.5m³ (758ft³)
38 Cabin window panels
39 Mid-cabin emergency exit/service door
40 Mid-cabin toilet compartment
41 Wardrobe
42 Cabin attendant's folding seats (3)
43 Mid-cabin entry door
44 Central slat drive electric motor and gearbox

45 Cabin insulation blankets
46 Centre fuselage frame and stringer structure
47 Front spar attachment fuselage main frame
48 Wing centre-section fuel tank
49 Wing centre-section carry-through structure
50 Emergency exit hatches, port and starboard

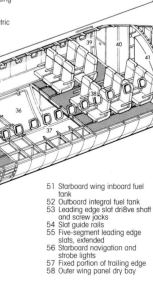

51 Starboard wing inboard fuel tank
52 Outboard integral fuel tank
53 Leading edge slat dri8ve shaft and screw jacks
54 Slat guide rails
55 Five-segment leading edge slats, extended
56 Starboard navigation and strobe lights
57 Fixed portion of trailing edge
58 Outer wing panel dry bay

Left: Among the large fleet of government-owned Air Ukraine are more than 20 Tupolev Tu-154Bs.

70 Baggage hold door
71 Rear underfloor baggage hold 16.5m³ (582ft³)
72 Overhead baggage racks
73 Passenger service units
74 Starboard engine nacelle
75 Intake suction relief louvers
76 Centre engine intake, intake 1 ips thermally de-iced
77 Intake S-duct
78 Bleed air pre-cooler
79 Rudder and elevator hydraulic actuators
80 Three-spar fin torsion box structure
81 Extended tailplane fairing/HP antenna
82 Trimming tailplane electrically operated screw jack
83 Anti-collision beacon
84 Tailplane pivot mounting
85 Starboard trimming tailplane
86 Starboard elevator
87 Fin/tailplane trailing edge fairing
88 Port elevator rib structure
89 Elevator hinge control linkage
90 Trimming tailplane three-spar torsion box structure
91 Leading edge thermal de-icing
92 Rudder
93 Rudder rib structure
94 Auxiliary Power Unit (APU) intake

103 Clamshell-type thrust reverser
104 Cascade-type thrust reverser
105 Reverser blocker door actuators
106 Kuznetsov NK-8-2U turbofan engine (Tu-154B-2)
107 Unpressurised rear cargo hold, 5m[3] (176ft[3])
108 Rear pressure bulkhead
109 Rear toilet compartments
110 Rear emergency exit/service doors, port and starboard
111 Cabin side wall conditioned air ducting
112 Wing root trailing edge fairing
113 Port inboard tripe-slotted flap segment
114 Flap rib structure
115 Inboard spoiler/lift dumper
116 Flap screw jack and drive shaft
117 Wing root attachment multi-bolt joint
118 Three-spar inboard wing panel torsion box structure
119 Port wing inboard integral fuel tank

127 Ventral flap track fairings
128 Spoiler/airbrake panel
129 Outer roll-control spoilers
130 Outboard wing fence
131 Port aileron
132 Aileron dual hydraulic actuators
133 Fixed trailing edge ribs
134 Static discharger
135 Port navigation and strobe lights
136 Wingtip panel two-spar and rib structure
137 Port leading edge slat segments
138 Slat guide rails
139 Slat operating torque shaft and screw jacks
140 Three-spar outer wing panel structure
141 Port outboard integral fuel tank
142 Six-wheel main undercarriage bogie
143 Mainwheel leg strut
144 Hydraulic retraction jack
145 Inboard slat segment
146 Slat rib structure
147 Position of pressure refuelling/defuelling connections in starboard wing leading edge
148 Heat exchanger exhaust
149 Air conditioning pack, port and starboard
150 Heat exchanger ram-air intake

59 Aileron hydraulic actuators
60 Starboard aileron
61 Flap screw jacks, electrically-operated via torque shaft
62 Flap tracks and carriages
63 Roll control spoiler panels (2)
64 Spoiler/airbrake panel
65 Outboard triple-slotted flap segment
66 Starboard main undercarriage, stowed position
67 Wing root spoiler/lift dumper
68 Rear spar attachment fuselage main frame
69 Rear cabin passenger seating

95 TA-92 APU, relocated to starboard side of centre engine bay in Tu-154M
96 APU exhaust
97 Centre engine exhaust
98 Engine bay ventral access hatches
99 Centre engine installation
100 Fin spar attachment rear fuselage main frames
101 Port engine pylon
102 Avidvigatel D-30KU-154-II turbofan engine (Tu-154M)

120 Main undercarriage leg pivot mounting
121 Outer wing panel multi-bolt joint
122 Inboard wing fence
123 Port main undercarriage nacelle
124 Nacelle rib structure
125 Outboard triple-slotted flap segment
126 Flap extended position

YAKOVLEV YAK-40 RUSSIA

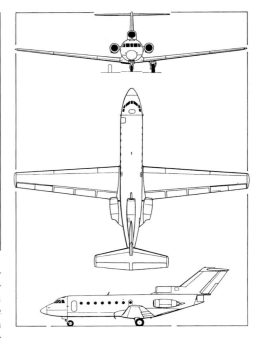

Best-known for its long series of piston-engined fighters and later for jet fighters including the first Soviet VTOL types, the Yakovlev design bureau turned its attention to the small airliner class of aircraft in the early 1960s. Its interest in this category of aircraft had been shown during the 1940s with the design of several light transports, but as a replacement for the many Lisunov Li-2 (licence-built DC-3) aircraft still then in service in the Soviet Union, the Yak-40 broke new ground both for the design bureau and for Aeroflot, its principal operator. A major requirement, in this context, was that the new aircraft should be able to operate from Class 5 airfields, having no paved runways – a requirement reflecting the special needs of the Soviet Union and one which was unmatched in any contemporary jet aircraft of Western origin. With the emphasis upon good field performance, the Yakovlev design team chose a three-engined configuration for the new transport. This meant that take-off weights and runway lengths could be calculated for the 'engine out' case with the loss of only one third, rather than one half (as in a twin-engined design) of available engine power. The rear engine location also has advantages over podded engines beneath the wings in terms of possible ingestion of debris when operating on grass and gravel strips. In common with most other Soviet jet transports, the Yak-40 was designed to have a relatively high thrust-to-weight ratio, again with benefit to airfield performance (including operation at high altitude airfields), albeit with some sacrifice in operating economy. To power the aircraft as planned by Yakovlev, turbofans of about 13.35kN-15.60kN (3,000-3,500lb) were required, and the Ivchenko bureau undertook the development of a suitable engine specifically for

SPECIFICATION
(Yakovlev Yak-40)

Dimensions: Wingspan 25.00m (82ft 01/4in); length overall 20.36m (66ft 91/2in); height overall 6.50m (21ft 4in), wing area 70.0m^2 (753.5ft^2).
Power Plant: Three 14.7kN (3,300lb) Ivchenko AI-25 turbofans.
Weights: Operating weight empty 9,400kg (20,725lb); max take-off 16,000kg (35,275lb); max payload 2,720kg (6,000lb).
Performance: Max cruising speed 297kts (550km/h); initial rate of climb 8.0m/s (1,575ft/min); take-off field length 700m (2,295ft); landing field length 360m (1,180ft); range with max payload 950nm (1,758km).
Accommodation: Flight crew of two. Seating for up to 32 passengers, four-abreast with central aisle.

this purpose, the AI-25 two-shaft turbofan. To minimise the requirement for ground equipment to support operation of the Yak-40 at smaller airfields, an APU was fitted as standard, primarily for engine starting, and access to the cabin was by way of a ventral airstair/door in the rear fuselage. Five prototypes were used to develop the Yak-40, whose first flight was made on 21 October 1966. The type was assigned the NATO reporting name 'Codling'.

VARIANTS
Modifications to the basic Yak-40 in the course of the production run included the introduction of a clam-shell thrust reverser on the centre engine, and deletion of an acorn fairing at the fin/tailplane leading-edge junction. Other than these, all production

Yak-40s were externally similar, although several alternative interior layouts were available. Freight-carrying and ambulance versions also were produced. In 1970, a Yak-40M was projected, with a lengthened fuselage, to carry 40 passengers. This may have reached prototype testing, but in any case did not proceed to production. The Yak-40V designation was used to identify an export variant, powered by AI-25T engines rated at 17.2kN (3,858lb) each and with the maximum take-off weight

YAKOVLEV YAK-42 RUSSIA

The Yak-42 was developed as a short-haul, medium-capacity jetliner for Aeroflot, to replace the Tu-134, Il-18 and An-24 primarily on the shorter domestic routes within the Soviet Union. Design began in the early 1970s, with a mock-up displayed in Moscow in mid-1973, showing that the overall configuration closely resembled that of the Yak-40, including the three-engined layout and rear-fuselage ventral stairway for access to the cabin. A key design requirement for the Yak-42 was the ability to operate reliably in the more remote regions of the USSR, in a wide range of climates, with the minimum of ground support and maintenance facilities. At the project stage, the design bureau apparently had difficulty assessing

the relative merits, particularly in terms of operating economy and performance, of alternative designs with different degrees of wing sweepback. The unusual step was taken of building prototypes for comparative testing with 11 deg and 23 deg of sweepback, the first of these making its maiden flight on 7 March 1975. The 23-deg version was found to be superior and the third prototype was completed to the same standard while production plans were made and a first batch of 200 was put in hand at the Smolensk factory. Initial production aircraft were similar to the third prototype, but a switch was made from twin main wheels to four-wheel bogie units on the main undercarriage.

VARIANTS
The first production Yak-42s had a wing span of 34.02m (111ft 71/2in) and gross weight of 53,500kg (117,950lb). The bogie main landing gear was standard, and alternative interiors were for 120 passengers in a one-class layout or 104 two-class in a local-service configuration with carry-on baggage

SPECIFICATION
(Yakovlev Yak-42D)

Dimensions: Wingspan 34.88m (114ft 51/4in); length overall 36.38m (119ft 41/4in); height overall 9.83m (32ft 3in), wing area 150.0m^2 (1,614.6ft^2).
Power Plant: Three 63.74kN (14,330lb) ZMKB Progress D-36 three-shaft turbofans.
Weights: Operating weight empty 34,515kg (76,092lb); max take-off 57,000kg (125,660lb); max landing 51,000kg (112,433lb); max payload 13,000kg (28,660lb).
Performance: Max cruising speed 437kts (810km/h); service ceiling 9,600m (31,500ft); take-off field length 2,200m (7,220ft); landing field length 1,100m (3,610ft); range with max payload 1,185nm (2,200km).
Accommodation: Flight crew of two or three. Seating for up to 120 passengers, six-abreast with central aisle. Total baggage volume front and rear 29.3m^3 (1,035ft^3).

Left: Three-view of the Yak-40, the first commercial design of this prolific bureau. The three-engined layout, and the built-in APU and ventral access stairs in the rear fuselage, were chosen to permit operations from smaller airfields and to minimise reliance on ground equipment in remote locations.

Right: The three-engined Yak-40 is now rarely seen outside Russia and the CIS, although small numbers continue to be operated. The Bulgarian airline Hemus Air is one of the largest operators, flying seven aircraft out of its base at Sofia.

increased to 16,500kg (36,376lb). The Yak-40 achieved reasonable export success, including the Yak-40EC with westernised avionics and in the early 1980s plans were made for an 'Americanised' version to be developed and marketed by ICX Aviation in Washington. Known as the X-Avia, this was to have been re-engined with Garrett TFE 731-2 turbofans and was projected in three variants: the 30-seat LC-3A, the 40-seat LC-3B and the all-cargo LC-3C. A conversion programme along similar lines, but

replacing the Ivchenko power plants with 31.14kN (7,000lb) Textron Lycoming LF 507-1N turbofans, was projected in 1991, but neither programme went ahead. The same fate befell the proposed twin-engined Yak-40TL.

SERVICE USE
The Yak-40 entered production at the Saratov factory in 1967 and deliveries to Aeroflot began in 1968, with the first passenger-carrying flight made on 30

September of that year. Production ended in 1978 with approximately 1,000 built; most entered service with Aeroflot but exports were made to Afghanistan, Bulgaria, Czechoslovakia, France, West Germany, Italy, Poland and Yugoslavia for commercial use, and elsewhere for government or military operation in a VIP role. Use of this tri-jet is now diminishing, but around 750 remain in service. The vast majority operate in Russia and the CIS, with some 30 to be found in Africa, the Far East and Central America.

and coat stowage compartments at the front and rear of the cabin. An enlarged loading door in the forward-fuselage port side could be fitted to allow the Yak-42 to operate in the convertible passenger/cargo role. A modification programme was undertaken in 1983 to overcome handling difficulties encountered during early service with Aeroflot, and led to a small increase in wing area. The Yak-42 also had a higher maximum take-off weight than initially approved. The first major development was the Yak-42D, which offers increased fuel capacity

extending range to 2,200km (1,185nm) with 120 passengers. Specialist versions are the Yak-42F with large underwing sensor pods for Earth resources and environmental surveys and the Yak-42E-LL propfan testbed. A stretched Yak-42M development announced in 1987 has now been superseded by the planned Yak-42-200, while work continues on a Yak-42D-100 with Western avionics. Production has started on the Yak-42A, an improved Yak-42D with a more comfortable interior and better performance.

SERVICE USE
First passenger proving flights were made by Yak-42s in late 1980, on the Moscow-Krasnodar route, and about 20-30 aircraft were delivered to Aeroflot by the end-1981. Following an accident in 1982, the Yak-42 was withdrawn until modified aircraft were put back into operation in October 1984, starting with the Saratov-Leningrad and Moscow-Pykovo routes. More than 160 had been built by 1998, and particularly the Yak-42D has found export success in Cuba, Europe, Africa, and the Middle and Far East.

Left: The Yakovlev Yak-42 serves as mainline equipment with some of the smaller, new national carriers such as Lithuanian Airlines which operates nine Yak-42Ds, refurbished to bring the interior up to western standards.

Right: The three-view shows the Yak-42 in its basic production form, with the 23-deg wing sweepback and twin-wheel main undercarriage. Work is proceeding on several developments, one of which, the Yak-42-200, will have a 6.03m (19ft 9in) fuselage stretch to accommodate 150 passengers

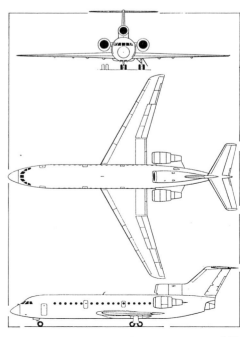

The following pages present details, in a slightly more condensed form than in the main part of the book, of aircraft which continue to play their part in the air transport business, but for various reasons are now used only in small numbers. This includes a mix of types. Some passenger aircraft are now aged, others were not successful or not intended primarily for airline use, and there are those aircraft built in small quantities for specialist applications only.

Aircraft used only or principally to carry freight and outsize cargo items are also included in this section. Almost without exception, these are types originally designed for military use, although examples can be found of elderly passenger transports that are ending their days as freighters.

A few aircraft will invoke nostalgia for the fact that age has relegated them from one-time frontline scheduled passenger service to a passenger or freight charter role. These should in no way be regarded as minor aircraft but, with only a handful remaining in service across the world, cannot be justified to be given the detailed treatment of those types in the main section.

There are many other aircraft that could justify entry in this book. All over the world, small commuter airlines and air taxi operators use light twin-engined aircraft, survivors from earlier eras and other assorted types. However, to include all of them would unacceptably change the size of this volume.

AERO SPACELINES GUPPY 201 USA

The series of Guppy outsize transports originated in an idea by the late John M. Conroy, who formed Aero Spacelines to modify a Boeing Stratocruiser to have a lengthened fuselage with a new upper lobe of increased diameter. Known as the Pregnant Guppy, this prototype first flew on 19 September 1962. Two further developments, intended primarily to carry stages of the Saturn rocket launchers and other space hardware between manufacturing and launch sites in the United States, were the Super Guppy, with piston engines and a swing tail. These two aircraft first flew on 31 August 1965 and 24 May 1967 respectively. A variant of the Mini Guppy with Allison 501 turboprops flew on 13 March 1970 but was lost two months later, before entering service. Finally, Aero Spacelines produced two Super Guppy 201s, which combined Allison power with the same outsize fuselage as the earlier Super Guppy prototype. First flown on 24 August 1970 and 24 August 1971, these two aircraft were acquired by Airbus Industrie and, after certification on 26 August 1971, entered service in October of that year, being used to ferry major fuselage components and wings of the A300/A310 family from their production centres to the final assembly line in Toulouse. Two more aircraft, to similar specification, were then converted for Airbus by UTA in France, making their first flights on 11 June 1982 and 2 August 1983 respectively. The Guppys have now been replaced by the new Airbus Super Transporter.

SPECIFICATION
(Super Guppy 201)

Dimensions: Wingspan 47.62m (156ft 3in); length overall 43.83m (143ft 10in); height overall 14.78m (48ft 6in), wing area 182.5m² (1,964ft²).
Power Plant: Four 3,666kW (4,912shp) Allison 501-D22C turboprops with four-blade constant-speed Hamilton Standar propellers.
Weights: Operating weight empty 45,360kg (100,000lb); max take-off 77,111kg (170,000lb); max landing 72,575kg (160,000lb); max payload 24,494kg (54,000lb).
Performance: Max cruising speed 250kts (463km/h); initial rate of climb 7.6m/s (1,500ft/min); service ceiling 7,620m (25,000ft); take-off field length 2,560m (8,400ft); landing field length 2,055m (6,750ft); range with max payload 440nm (813km).
Accommodation: Flight crew of four. Total usable cabin volume 1,104m³ (39,000ft³). Sideways-hinged nose for straight-in loading.

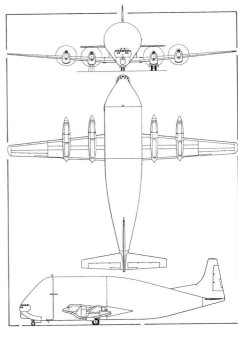

Left: Airbus Industrie operated the Super Guppy for 26 years, between 1971 and 1997.

Above: The three-view shows that little of the original Boeing KC-97 Stratocruiser was retained in the design.

AEROSPATIALE (NORD) 262

This small regional airliner evolved from a design by Max Holste, whose company flew on 20 May 1959 the prototype of a utility transport powered by Pratt & Whitney Wasp radial piston engines and based on a square-section fuselage. Known as the MH-250, this was followed by the MH-260 with Bastan turboprops, flown on 29 July 1960. State-owned Nord (now merged into Aérospatiale) undertook further development of the basic design and produced as a result the Nord 262, which differed from the MH-260 primarily in having a pressurized circular-section cabin large enough for 24-26 passengers. A prototype flew on 24 December 1962.

SPECIFICATION
(Nord 262C)

Dimensions: Wingspan 22.60m (74ft 2in); length overall 19.28m (63ft 3in); height overall 6.21m (20ft 4in), wing area 55.0m² (592.0ft²).
Power Plant: Two 843kW (1,130shp) Turboméca Bastan VIIA turboprops, with Ratier Forest four-blade propellers.
Weights: Operating weight empty 7,225kg (15,929lb); max take-off 10,800kg (23,810lb); max landing 10,450kg (23,040lb); max payload 3,075kg (6,781lb).
Performance: Max cruising speed 224kts (415km/h); initial rate of climb 6.1m/s (1,200ft/min; service ceiling 7,160m (23,500ft); take-off field length 820m (2,690ft); landing field length 630m (2,060ft); range with max payload 550nm (1,020km).
Accommodation: Flight crew of two. Seating for up to 29 passengers, three-abreast with single aisle. Total baggage volume 4.50m³ (159.0ft³).

This and three pre-production aircraft were known as the 262B, with the definitive production being the Nord 262A. After the Nord 262A and 262B with Bastan IVC engines, the models 262C and 262D were evolved with higher-powered Bastan VIIC, which flew in July 1968, although most sales were in military guise as the 262D Frégate to the Armée de l'Air. The designation Mohawk 298 was adopted for a variant developed in the USA and flown on 7 January 1975 with Pratt & Whitney Canada PT6A-45 turboprops, to meet FAR 298 regulations. The modification programmed was managed by Mohawk Air Services and undertaken by Frakes Aviation in Texas, at the instigation of Allegheny Airlines whose associate Ransome Airlines was the initial operator. Apart from the engines and new wingtips, the Mohawk 298 incorporated many new systems. The Nord 262 was certificated on 16 July 1964 and entered service with Air Inter. Total production amounted to 110 aircraft, but only a handful remained in service by 1998.

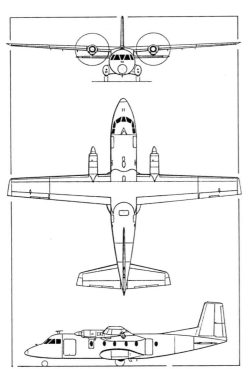

Left: This three-view of the Nord 262 shows the original Bastan-engined version. The Mohawk 298 differed in its engines and nacelles.

Right: British scheduled and charter airline Dan-Air was the only UK airline to operate the high-wing Nord 262. It was in service from July 1970 to February 1972.

AEROSPATIALE (SUD-EST) CARAVELLE FRANCE

At the end of 1952, SNCA Sud-Est (one of the state-owned companies later merged to form Aérospatiale) was selected by the French air ministry to develop a twin-jet civil transport for short/medium-range operations. Designs had been submitted to meet the official specification drawn up in 1951; that by Sud-Est selected for further development featured engines mounted on the rear fuselage – an innovative idea at that time, and one which had a number of attractions. Two prototypes were funded by the French government and made their first flight on 27 May 1955 and 6 May 1956, powered by Rolls-Royce Avon RA.26 Mk 521.

French certification was achieved on 2 April 1959, with US FAA endorsement following on 8 April. The first service was flown by Air France on 6 May that same year. The initial production versions were the Caravelle I and IA with Avon RA.29 Mk 522 and Mk 526 turbojets respectively, later converted to Series III standard, which had Avon Mk 527s and increased weights. A further change of engine to the Mk 531 produced the Srs VI-N, first flown on 10 September 1960 and then, with thrust reversers on Mk 532R or 533R engines, the Srs VI-R. The Caravelle 10B1R, flown on 18 January 1965, was similar, but had Pratt & Whitney JT8D-1 or -7 turbofan engines. The General Electric-powered Srs VII led to the Caravelle 10A, with a 1.0m (3ft 4in) longer fuselage, while the Srs 10B3 (Super B) was identical except for having JT8D-1, -7 or -9 engines. The Caravelle 11R was the 10BR with a forward side cargo door for mixed passenger/cargo operations. The final variant was the still longer Caravelle 12, which first flew on 29 October 1970. Production ended in March 1973 after 282 had been completed. Less than 20 remained in service in 1978.

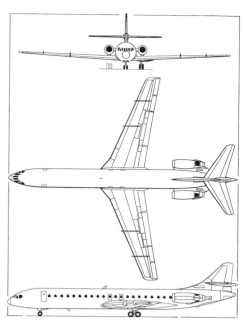

SPECIFICATION
(Caravelle 10B3)

Dimensions: Wingspan 34.30m (112ft 6in); length overall 33.01m (108ft 3½in); height overall 8.72m (28ft 7in), wing area 146.7m² (1,579ft²).
Power Plant: Two 63.2kN (14,000lb) Pratt & Whitney JT8D-1 or -7 or 64.5kN (14,500lb) JT8D-9 turbofans.
Weights: Operating weight empty 30,055kg (66,259lb); max take-off 56,000kg (123,457lb); max landing 49,500kg (109,127lb); max payload 9,100kg (20,062lb).
Performance: Max cruising speed 445kts 825(km/h); take-off field length 2,090m (6,850ft); landing field length 1,580m (5,180ft); range with max payload 1,450nm (2,685km).
Accommodation: Flight crew of three. Seating for up to 100 passengers, five-abreast with single aisle. Aft baggage volume 4.2m³ (148ft³).

Below: The Caravelle was operated by many leading European airlines, including France's Air Inter.

Right: Three-view drawing of the Caravelle 12, the final production version between 1970 and 1973.

AIRBUS (SATIC) A300-600ST BELUGA

On 20 October 1991, Aerospatiale and Deutsche Aérospace Airbus (now Daimler-Benz Aerospace Airbus), two of the partners in Airbus Industrie, set up the Special Air Transport International Company (SATIC), to undertake engineering, production and certification work for a new specialist freighter to replace the four Super Guppys, which have transported Airbus parts between the various manufacturing locations since 1971. Dubbed the A300-600ST Beluga Super Transporter, the aircraft is based on the A300-600R, but almost equals the construction of a new aircraft, since little similarity is retained. The main elements of the work involve the relocation of the cockpit 1.5m (4ft 11in) forward of the main cargo deck and to a lower level, allowing the cargo door - the largest ever - to be positioned in the nose above. A new upper fuselage, which enlarges the diameter to 7.40m (24ft 3¼in), permits a greatly increased cargo volume. The tailplane has been strengthened, and to maintain longitudinal stability during the flight, horizontal stabilisers have been modified and equipped with auxiliary fins. New components for the Beluga are being produced by 12 main subcontractors in five European countries. Final assembly is at Toulouse. The first aircraft made its maiden flight on 13 September 1994 and was delivered to Airbus in September 1995, immediately following certification. Airbus has placed orders for five aircraft, for delivery at yearly intervals to 2000. The new freighter will also be targeted at the general commercial and military market.

SPECIFICATION
(A300-600ST)

Dimensions: Wingspan 44.84m (147ft 1in); length overall 56.16m (184ft 3in); height overall 17.25m (56ft 7¼in).
Power Plant: Two 262.45kN (59,000lb) General Electric CF6-80C2A8 turbofans.
Weights: Max take-off 150,000kg (330,693lb); max zero fuel 130,000kg (286,598lb); max payload 45,500kg (100,310lb).
Performance: Max cruising speed 420kts (778km/h); range with max payload 900nm (1,667km).
Accommodation: Flight crew of two. Main-deck cargo volume 1,400 m³ (49,440ft³).

Below: The Beluga Super Transporter bears little resemblance to the Airbus A300-600R from which it is derived. The giant 'whale-like' aircraft has now taken over from the Super Guppy in carrying Airbus assemblies across Europe. Four are in service and a fifth will be built. Airbus is also examining similar outsize freighter concepts based on its larger A330/A340 models.

ANTONOV AN-12 UKRAINE

he An-12 freighter had its origins in the An-10, which appeared in 1957 as one of the first of Aeroflot's turboprop transports, entering service in 84-seat form and being developed into the 100-seat An-10A. The An-12 appeared in 1959 as a dedicated freighter and became numerically more important than the An-10, entering service both with Aeroflot and with the Soviet military forces. Its military significance was shown by the provision of a twin-gun tail turret, and this feature (less the guns) was usually retained in aircraft operated by Aeroflot on freight services and supply missions outside the Soviet Union, for which the An-12 continues to be widely used. The type has also been exported to several Soviet bloc air forces and to the airlines of some countries in the Soviet sphere of influence, including Bulgaria, China, Cuba, Iraq, Poland and Guinea. A version similar to the Soviet An-12BP production model has been manufactured in China as the Hanzhong Y-8, with Chinese-built Wojiang WJ-6 turboprops. The NATO reporting name for the An-12 variant is 'Cub'.

SPECIFICATION
(Antonov An-12)

Dimensions: Wingspan 38.00m (124ft 8in); length overall 33.10m (108ft 7¼in); height overall 10.53m (34ft 6½in), wing area 121.7m² (1,310ft²).
Power Plant: Four 2,983kW (4,000shp) Ivchenko AI-20K turboprops with four-blade constant-speed feathering and reversing AV-68 propellers.
Weights: Operating weight empty 28,000kg (61,730lb); max take-off 61,000kg (134,480lb); max payload 20,000kg (44,090lb).
Performance: Max cruising speed 361kts (670km/h); initial rate of climb 10.0m/s (1,970ft/min; service ceiling 10,200m (33,500ft); take-off field length 700m (2,300ft); landing field length 500m (1,640ft); range with max payload 1,940nm (3,600km).
Accommodation: Flight crew of five. Seating for up to 100 in troop-carrying version. Total usable cabin volume for freight 97.2m³ (3,433ft³). Rear ramp/door for direct loading.

Above: In this three-view of the An-12, the rear gun turret is faired over, but it can often be seen in commercial service with it still in place

Left: An-12 freighters are often seen in the West, including this version operated by Bulgarian carrier Inter Trans Air, photographed at Manston, UK.

ANTONOV AN-38 UKRAINE

eveloped from the Polish-built Antonov An-28, primarily to replace large numbers of Let L-410 Turbolets and to a lesser extent the Antonov An-24 and the small Yakovlev Yak-40 trijet, the high-wing An-38 is distinguished by a lengthened passenger cabin to provide accommodation for typically 26 passengers seated three-abreast and a high content of western equipment, to make it more attractive on the world market. As its predecessor, it has a high degree of self-sufficiency for operation in outlying areas, in all conditions and from unpaved runways. An initial batch of six aircraft was produced, with the prototype making its first flight at Novosibirsk on 23 June 1994. Four more aircraft were used in the test programme, with the fifth used for static tests at the Antonov Design Bureau in Kiev. Production started by Novosibirsk Aircraft Production Association in 1995. Initial variants include the An-38-100, powered by two 1,227 kW (1,645 shp) AlliedSignal TPE331-14GR-801E turboprops; An-38-200 with alternative 1,029 kW (1,380 shp) Omsk MKB 'Mars' TVD-20 turboprops; and the An-38K, a convertible version of the -100 with a large upward-opening side door at the rear to permit loading of LD-3 cargo containers, and a built-in cargo handling system. Specialised versions are available for a number of different utility and specialist applications, including an ambulance configuration with six stretchers, nine seated casualties and medical attendant. An 8-10 seat executive variant is also projected. Orders claimed for 150 aircraft from various Russian airlines, plus interest from abroad. First delivery to Vostok Airlines.

SPECIFICATION
(Antonov An-38-100)

Dimensions: Wingspan 22.06m (72 t 4½in); overall length 15.54m (51ft 0in); overall height 4.30m (14ft 1¼in); wing area
Power Plant: Two AlliedSignal TPE331-14GR-801E turboprops each rated at 1,227kW (1,645shp) for take-off, with Hartzell HC-B5MA five-bladed propellers.
Weights: Operating weight empty 5,087kg (11,215lb); Max take-off weight 8,800kg (19,400lb); max payload 2,500kg (5,510lb).
Performance: Normal cruising speed around 200kts (370km/h); take-off field length 790m (2,590ft); range with max payload 324nm (600km).
Accommodation: Flight crew of two. Seating for up to 27 passengers, two-abreast with central aisle.

Right: The 26-passenger An-38 was developed mainly to replace large numbers of the smaller Let L-410 Turbojet.

ANTONOV AN-72/AN-74 UKRAINE

The An-72 was developed as much for military duties as for commercial use. It is unique as a production aircraft for its use of upper surface blowing (USB) as a means of increasing lift and thus providing STOL performance. The two high-bypass turbofans are mounted well ahead of the high-positioned wing, which causes the airflow to attach itself to the wing upper surface with the result of enhanced lift and good low-speed performance. Other notable features are the multi-leg main landing gear contained in fuselage side blisters and its rear-loading provisions, indicative of its military applications and the requirement to operate from unprepared airstrips. The first of two prototypes, built at Kiev, flew on 22 December 1977, but after eight pre-series aircraft production was transferred to Kharkov. The first Kharkov-built production aircraft made its maiden flight in 1985. The An-74 Polar version was announced in February 1984. The An-72 (NATO reporting name 'Coaler C') is the standard transport version with ZMKB Progress D-36 Series 2A engines each rated at 63.74kN (14,330lb) thrust, but

many specialised mission aircraft are available. Variants of the An-74 'Coaler B' include the An-74-200 for all-weather Arctic operations; An-74T-200 cargo aircraft with loading winch and roller conveyors; An-74TK-200 convertible for up to 52 passengers or 10,000kg (22,045lb) payload in cargo configuration; and An-74-100, An-74T-100 and An-74TK-100, which vary in having a navigator station, bringing crew level to four. More than 150 An-72/74 have been built, the majority for military use in Russia and the CIS. The only export to the Peruvian Air Force.

Below: The convertible passenger/cargo Antonov An-74TK was demonstrated at the 1997 Paris Air Show. Like many Antonov designs, it has the capability to operate from unprepared airstrips.

Right: A three-view drawing of the An-74, which reveals the substantial differences in detail from the earlier An-72, although both aircraft share the same basic configuration overall.

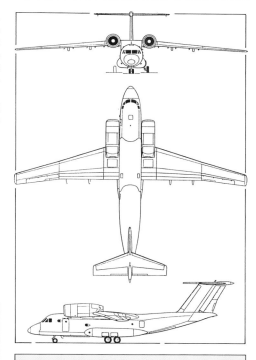

ANTONOV AN-225 MRIYA UKRAINE

The An-225 Mriya (Dream) was the first aircraft to fly at a gross weight exceeding one million pounds and remains the world's largest aircraft by some distance. It was developed principally to carry on its back the Soviet space shuttle orbiter *Buran*, together with Energyia rocket elements, between the Moscow production plant and the Baikanour Cosmodrome. Based on the An-124 heavy freighter, Antonov stretched the wings by adding a new centre section which increased the

overall wingspan by 15.10m (49ft 6½in), and lengthened the fuselage to enlarge the aircraft by about 50% compared to the An-124. The basic fuselage cross-section was unchanged, as were the turbofan engines, although the heavier weight required six Progress/Lotarev D-18T turbofans, each generating 230kN (51,650lb) thrust, instead of four engines. It has an upward-hinged visor-type nose door, identical to the An-124, but no rear ramp/door. The prototype was rolled out at Kiev on 30 November 1988

and first flew on 21 December. It made its first flight with the *Buran* space shuttle on its back on 13 May 1989 and has since also been used on a number of commercial tasks to support the energy sector in Russia, the Ukraine and other CIS countries, ferrying equipment and personnel into remote and inhospitable regions. It has a freight-carrying capacity of 250 tonnes, as well as an upper passenger cabin for 60-70 people. Two aircraft have been built to date. NATO reporting name is Cossack.

Right: The giant An-225 is the largest aircraft in the world. On 22 March 1989, flown by Alexander V Galunenko, it set a total of 106 world and class records during a 3-hour flight from Kiev, taking off at a weight of 508,200kg (1,120,370lb), with a payload of 156,300kg (344,576lb).

BEECHCRAFT 99 AIRLINER USA

Beech entered the commuter airliner market in 1965 using the twin-piston Queen Air as a base for development. Using a wing similar to the Queen Air and a lengthened fuselage to accommodate 15 passengers, the new model was identified as the Beech 99. A standard feature of the design was an airstair incorporated in the main cabin door, but a wide cargo-loading door was offered to facilitate use of the aircraft in a mixed passenger/cargo configuration. Beech flew a development airframe in the shape of a long-fuselage piston-powered Queen Air in December 1965, but in July 1966, this prototype began a new series of trials with Pratt & Whitney Canada PT6A-20 turboprops. It represented the Model 99 in all respects and formed the basis for

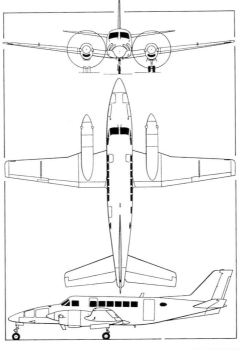

SPECIFICATION
Beech C99 Airliner)

Dimensions: Wingspan 13.98m (45ft 10½in); length overall 13.58m (44ft 6¾in); height overall 4.37m (14ft4¼ in), wing area 25.98m² (279.7ft²).
Power Plant: Two 533kW (715shp) Pratt & Whitney Canada PT6A-36 turboprops, Hartzell three-blade constant-speed fully-feathering reversible-pitch propellers.
Weights: Operating weight empty 2,946kg (6,494lb); max take-off 5,125kg (11,300lb); max landing 5,125kg (11,300lb); max payload 1,474kg (3,250lb).
Performance: Max cruising speed 268kts (497km/h); initial rate of climb 11.1m/s (2,220ft/min); service ceiling 8,560m (28,080ft); range with max payload 578nm (1,072km).
Accommodation: Flight crew of two. Seating for up to 15 passengers, two-abreast with central aisle. Total baggage volume front and rear 1.72m³ (60.9ft³).

FAA certification on 2 May 1968. Deliveries began the same month, the first entering service with Chicago-based Commuter Airlines. The first production aircraft were powered by 410kW (550shp) PT6A-20 engines. When 507kW (680shp) PT6A-27 turboprops were introduced, the designation became A99, although these engines were flat-rated to the same power as the orginal PT6A-20s. The B99 had a higher gross weight, was otherwise identical. Production ended in 1974 after 164 had been built, but a new version, announced as the Commuter C99, was included in Beechcraft's plans to re-enter the commuter airliner market in May 1979. The improved C99 Airliner, as it became officially known, first flew on 20 June 1980 and entered service with Christman Air System on 30 July 1981. A total of 63 were sold, with production ending in 1985. Most aircraft were delivered for airline use, though an executive version was also produced. Some remained in airline service in 1998.

Left: The three-view shows the C99, which was the final production version of this commuter aircraft.

Below: GP Express Airlines was one of many US commuters using the 15-seat Beech C99.

CANADAIR CL-44 CANADA

SPECIFICATION
(Canadair CL-44-D4)

Dimensions: Wingspan 43.37m (142ft 3½in); length overall 41.70m (136ft 10in); height overall 11.80m (38ft 8in), wing area 192.8m² (2,075ft²).
Power Plant: Four 4,276kW (5,730shp) Rolls-Royce Tyne RTy.12 Mk 515/10 turboprops, with four-blade Hamilton Standard Hydromatic constant-speed fully-feathering and reversing propellers.
Weights: Operating weight empty 40,348kg (88,952lb); max take-off 95,250kg 210,000(lb); max landing 74,843kg (165,000lb); max payload 29,959kg (66,048lb)
Performance: Max cruising speed 349kts (647km/h); take-off field length 2,255m (7,400ft); landing field length 1,900m (6,230ft); range with max payload 2,850nm (5,300km).
Accommodation: Flight crew of three or four. Seating for up to 214 passengers, but used primarily for freight, with usable cabin volume 178.2m³ (6,294ft³), plus two underfloor freight holds totalling 31.4m³ (1,109ft³). Rear fuselage, including tail unit, hinged to starboard for straight-in loading.

Above: Cargolux Airlines began flying scheduled and charter services with CL-44 swing-tail freighters in May 1970.

Right: Three-view of the CL-44, mainly differing from the Bristol Britannia in fuselage length and engines.

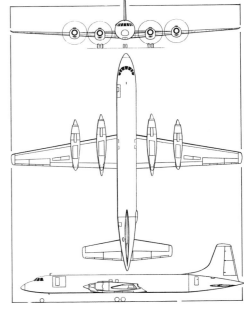

The CL-44 was derived in Canada from the original Bristol Britannia, initially to meet an RCAF requirement for a long-range troop and freight transport. Principal changes were a lengthening of the fuselage, increased wing span and a switch from Bristol Proteus to Rolls-Royce Tyne engines. The first of 12 CL-44D Yukons for the RCAF flew on 15 November 1959. The CL-44D-4, first flown on 16 November 1960, was optimized for commercial

operation as a freighter, with a swing tail (at the time unique) and 27 were produced with first deliveries made to Flying Tiger on 31 May 1961, to Seaboard on 20 June 1961 and to Slick on 17 January 1962. Loftleidir acquired four to use as passenger transports, and for this company, Canadair developed the CL-44J with a 4.6m (15ft) fuselage stretch to increase seating from 178 to 214. Four aircraft were converted to CL-44J standard (first flight 8 November 1965) and were used by Loftleidir as Canadair 400s. A single CL-44D-4 was modified by Conroy Aircraft to 'Guppy' configuration with increased-diameter upper fuselage lobe, and first flying (as the CL-44-O) on 26 November 1969. Most of the CAF Yukons were sold for commercial use when retired in 1973, but lack the swing-tail feature. Just six remained operational in 1998.

CASA C-212 AVIOCAR SPAIN

Development of the C-212 began in the late 1960s to meet the requirements of the Spanish air force for a small tactical transport and multi-role aircraft. Layout and construction followed conventional practice for an aircraft of the type, with a high wing, fixed landing gear with the main units attached on each side of the fuselage with sponson-type fairings over the mountings, and a rear loading ramp providing straight-in loading to the box-section cabin. Prototypes were first flown on 26 March and 23 October 1971, and the Aviocar entered production against Spanish air force orders. The C-212 was subsequently developed for civil use as a 19-seat commuterliner, whose initial sale was made to Pertamina in Indonesia. An agreement was then concluded with P T Nurtanio (now IPTN) for

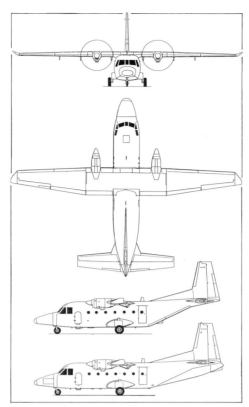

SPECIFICATION
(CASA C-212-300)

Dimensions: Wingspan 19.00m (62ft 4in); length overall 15.16m (49ft 9in); height overall 6.30m (20ft 8in), wing area 40.0m² (430.6ft²).
Power Plant: Two 671kW (900shp) AlliedSignal TPE331-10R-513C turboprops, with Dowty four-blade constant-speed feathering and reversing propellers.
Weights: Operating weight empty 3,780kg (8,333lb); max take-off 7,700kg 16,975(lb); max landing 7,450kg (16,424lb); max payload 2,800kg (6,172lb).
Performance: Max cruising speed 191kts (354km/h); max climb rate 8.3m/s (1,630ft/min); service ceiling 7,925m (26,000ft); take-off field length 895m (2,935ft); landing field length 865m (2,840ft); range with max payload 750nm (1,388km).
Accommodation: Flight crew of two. Seating for up to 26 passengers, four-abreast, two seats each side of central aisle. Total baggage volume 3.5m³ (123.6ft³).

Above: The three-view shows the military model with rear-loading ramp, with the extra side-view of the Srs 300 civil aircraft.

Right: The good short-field performance and ruggedness of the C-212 is ideally suited to inter-island operations of Cape Verde Airlines.

the licence production (also in Indonesia) of the Aviocar as a means, in particular, of providing access to a substantial market for this type of aircraft in that country and the Pacific Basin generally. The initial production aircraft were powered by the 579kW (776shp) TPE331-5'251C engine and had a gross weight of 5,675kg (12,500lb) in the first C-212 CA civil variant, increased to 6,300kg (13,890lb) in the C-212CB. In 1978 CASA introduced the more powerful TPE331-10-501C engine, which allowed the gross weight to be increased again. At this stage, the aircraft with the different engine versions were designated as the C-212-5 and C-212-10 respectively, but this nomenclature was quickly changed to C-212 Srs 100 and C-212 Srs 200. In 1984, CASA announced the availability of the C-212 Srs 300, with 671kW (900shp) TPE331-10R-512C engines and Dowty Rotol propellers of a more recent type than those which had replaced Hartzell propellers in Srs 200 aircraft in July 1983. The Srs 300 has redesigned wing tips, a modified nose with larger baggage compartment, and a gross weight of 16,975lb (7,700kg). It also has, as an option, a rear fuselage fairing in place of the loading ramp, allowing 28 passengers to be carried at the increased seat pitch of 75cm (29.5in). An improved C-212-400 model is projected with 820kW (1,100shp) Allied Signal TPE331-12 engines.

CURTISS C-46 COMMANDO USA

Of the types of aircraft serving the airlines in 1998, the C-46 can claim to be the second oldest, only the Douglas DC-3 having flown earlier. Of similar configuration to the famous Douglas type, the Curtiss transport was conceived in 1937 as the CW-20. Considerably larger than the DC-3, it differed also in having a fuselage of 'double bubble' cross section, to offer the largest possible cabin volume for the smallest drag. First flown on 26 March 1940, the CW-20 appeared too late to capture any part of the pre-war airline market although,

strangely enough, the prototype was impressed for military service with the USAAF and was passed to the UK, where it joined the war time fleet of BOAC. For the USAAF, Curtiss built 3,141 examples of the CW-20 in military guise, designated C-46 and named Commando. After World War II many hundreds of these aircraft were acquired by civilian operators, at first for passenger use but subsequently (and more particularly) as freighters, for which their military style cargo-loading doors made them particularly suitable. As 'aerial tramps', C-46s became much used in the US and Central and South America, and some three dozen could still be found flying in this role, well away from the trunk routes, in 1998.

Below: The C-46 found a ready market in Bolivia, being well suited for freight operations via its cargo loading doors.

Right: The C-46 was designed initially as a passenger transport, but the war and a freighter role intervened.

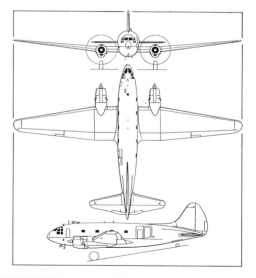

SPECIFICATION
(Curtiss C-46A)

Dimensions: Wingspan 32.92m (108ft 0in); length overall 23.27m (76ft 4in); height overall 6.60m (21ft 8in), wing area 126.15m² (1,358ft²).
Power Plant: Two 1,496kW (2,000shp) Pratt & Whitney R-2800-34 air-cooled 14-cylinder piston engines, with three-blade Hamilton Standard Hydromatic constant-speed fully-feathering propellers.
Weights: Operating weight empty 14,970kg (33,000lb); max take-off 21,772kg (48,000lb); max landing 21,228kg (46,800lb); max payload 5,265kg (11,630lb).
Performance: Normal cruising speed 162kts (301km/h); initial rate of climb 6.6m/s (1,300ft/min); service ceiling 8,410m (27,600ft); range with typical payload 1,000nm (1,850km).
Accommodation: Flight crew of two. Seating for up to 62 passengers, five-abreast with single aisle. Total cabin volume for freight 65.1m3 (2,300ft³), plus additional underfloor holds totalling 12.9m³ (455ft3).

CESSNA TWINS USA

The Cessna company produced a long series of twin-engined light transports over the years, primarily for business use, and these have also gone into use with local service airlines and air taxi operators in various parts of the world. The smaller of the piston-engined twins are in the 300 series, and include the original Model 310 which first flew in 1953 and was Cessna's first business twin; the pressurised Model 340; and the lightweight Model 303 Crusader. Of more specific interest to air transport operators, the Model 402 was launched in the mid-1960s and featured a convertible interior for passengers or cargo, a reinforced cabin floor and optional cargo door. More than 1,500 were produced in Utililiner and Business liner variants. The Model 411, which had appeared in the early 1960s as Cessna's largest twin, was succeeded by the pressurised Model 421 Golden Eagle, production of which exceeded 1,900. Another piston twin with airline application was the Model 404 Titan, with up to 10 seats in the commuter role. Turboprop power was introduced with the Model 441, which first flew on 26 August 1975 and led to production of the Conquest II, with Garrett TPE331 engines and up to 10 seats, and the Conquest I with PT6A-112 engines and up to eight seats. Largest in the range is the unpressurised Reims-Cessna F406 Caravan II, jointly developed with Cessna's European licencee as a light utility transport. First flown on 22 September 1983, the Caravan II is powered by 373kW (500shp) PT6A-112 engines and seats up to 10 in a Model 404-type fuselage, which has been locally strengthened.

SPECIFICATION
(Cessna 402C Utililiner)

Dimensions: Wingspan 13.45m (44ft 1½in); length overall 11.09m (36ft 4½in); height overall 3.49m (11ft 5½in), wing area 20.98m² (225.8ft²).
Power Plant: Two 242kW (325hp) Continental TSIO-520-VB flat-six turbo-supercharged air-cooled piston engines, with McCauley three-blade constant-speed fully-feathering propellers.
Weights: Operating weight empty 1,872kg (4,126lb); max take-off 3,107kg (6,850lb); max landing 3,107kg (6,850lb).
Performance: Max cruising speed 213kts 394(km/h); initial rate of climb 7.4m/s (1,450ft/min); service ceiling 8,200m (26,900ft); take-off field length 670m (2,195ft); landing field length 755m (2,485ft); range with max fuel 1,273nm (2,359km).
Accommodation: Flight crew of one or two. Seating for up to 8 passengers in four individual and two double seats.

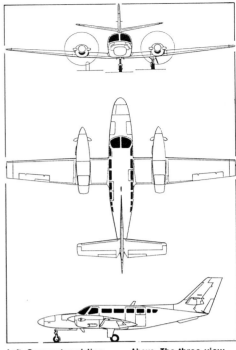

Left: Commuter airline Opal Air was one of many using the 402B on services to outlying towns in Australia.

Above: The three-view drawing depicts the F406 Caravan II, built under licence by Reims Aviation in France.

CONVAIR 540, 580, 600 and 640 USA

During the 1950s and early 1960s the Convair 240, 340 and 440 family of twin-engined transports became the subject of several conversion programmes to fit turboprop engines. In all, about 175 of the original airframes were converted in this way, making the Convair the most successful of several contemporary schemes to apply turboprop power to what had been designed as piston-engined transports. The first programme aimed at airline application was initiated by the Napier engine company in the UK in 1954, and a Convair 340 with 2,288kW (3,060shp) Eland NEI.1 turboprops flew on 9 February 1955 as the model 540. Six more of these conversions were made, and the type entered airline service in July 1959. The second turboprop conversion scheme was set up by the Allison company. Either the Model 340 or Model 440 could be converted in this scheme to produce a new variant known as the Convair 580, or sometimes

the Super Convair, with Allison 501-D13 engines. The first conversion was flown on 19 January 1960, and this proved to be the most successful of the three turboprop Convair programmes with 130 aircraft being converted eventually, the majority for airline use. The added power of the turboprops required increases in the span and area of the tailplane, and in the height and area of the fin, and considerable changes were made internally. Third and last of the turboprop Convairs introduced a pair of Rolls-Royce RDa10 Dart Mk 542-4 engines with Rotol 3.96m (13ft) diameter four-bladed propellers, and was applicable to all models of the piston-engined transport. When modified, Model 240s became Model 600s, while Model 340s and 440s became known as Model 640s with Darts. The first Model 600 flew at San Diego on 20 May 1965, and the first Model 640 later the same year. The Convair 580 was certificated on 21 April 1960 and entered service with Frontier Airlines in June 1964, earlier deliveries having been for corporate customers. Service entry of the 600 with Central Airlines followed on 30 November 1965, and of the 640, with Caribair, on 22 December 1965. In 1998 some 100 turboprop models remained in service.

SPECIFICATION
(Convair 580)

Dimensions: Wingspan 32.12m (105ft 4in); length overall 24.84m (81ft 6in); height overall 8.89m (29ft 2in), wing area 85.5m² (920.0ft²).
Power Plant: Two 2,796kW (3,750shp) Allison 501-D13H turboprops, with Aeroproducts four-blade constant-speed feathering and reversing propellers.
Weights: Operating weight empty 13,732kg (30,275lb); max take-off 26,371kg (58,140lb); max landing 22,985kg (50,670lb); max payload 4,023kg (8,870lb).
Performance: Max cruising speed 297kts (550km/h); initial rate of climb 11.2m/s (2,200ft/min); take-off field length 1,435m (4,700ft); landing field length 1,270m (4,160ft); range with typical payload 1,970nm (3,650km).
Accommodation: Flight crew of two. Seating for up to 56 passengers, four-abreast, two seats each side of central aisle. Total baggage/cargo volume 14.56m³ (514.0ft³).

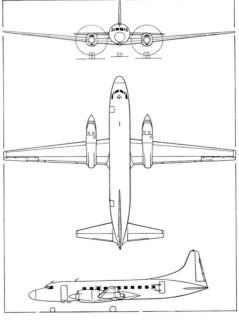

Above: The three-view shows the distinctive nacelles housing the Allison engines. The R-R Dart installation in the 600 and 640 models give a more streamlined appearance.

Right: Many Convair 580s have been converted for freight use, as shown here in service with DHL International.

DOUGLAS DC-6 and DC-7 USA

Prevented by wartime exigencies from exploiting fully the commercial potential of its first four-engined airliner, the DC-4, Douglas embarked in the early 1940s upon the design of an enlarged successor to the DC-4. Future military needs, as well as prospective airline demand, were kept in mind as the DC-6 took shape, and prototype construction was in fact launched on the basis of a USAAF contract for a single example designated XC-112. Using substantially the same wing as the DC-4, the DC-6, as the type became known in civil guise, had a fuselage lengthened by 2.06m (81in) to increase the basic passenger capacity to 52. The

fuselage was pressurised, and more powerful engines and improved systems were introduced. The XC-112 first flew on 15 February 1946. Orders from American Airlines and United Airlines established the DC-6 in production, however, as the Douglas company's first significant post-war commercial aircraft, a total of 174 being built by 1951. Subsequent evolution of the type brought a further lengthening of the fuselage to produce the all-cargo DC-6A (74 built) and passenger-carrying DC-6B (288 built). When another redesign of the fuselage was undertaken, coupled with the introduction of Wright R-3350 Cyclone engines in place of the DC-6B's Pratt & Whitney Double Wasps, the designation was changed to DC-7. The wing of the DC-4 remained little changed in the DC-7 and DC-7B until the DC-7C emerged in December 1955, with wing-root extensions adding 3.05m (10ft) to the span. Production of all DC-7 variants totalled 336 and brought the piston-engined era of the 'Douglas Commercial' series to an end. Deliveries of the DC-6 began in November 1946 with the first service flown on 27 April 1947. The DC-6 became widely used on US trunk routes, while the DC-7 added trans-Atlantic capability.

SPECIFICATION
(Douglas DC-6B)

Dimensions: Wingspan 35.81m (117ft 6in); length overall 32.18m (105ft 7in); height overall 8.92m (29ft 3in), wing area 135.9m² (1,463ft²).
Power Plant: Four 1,864kW (2,500hp) Pratt & Whitney R-2800-CB17 Double Wasp 18-cylinder air-cooled radial piston engines, with Hamilton Standard Hydromatic three-blade constant-speed and feathering propellers.
Weights: Operating weight empty 28,123kg (62,000lb); max take-off 48,534kg (107,000lb); max landing 40,000kg (88,200lb); max payload 11,143kg (24,565lb).
Performance: Max cruising speed 275kts 509(km/h); initial rate of climb 6.2m/s (1,120ft/min); take-off field length 1,875m (6,150ft); landing field length 1,525m (5,000ft); range with max payload 1,650nm (3,058km).
Accommodation: Flight crew of four. Seating for up to 102 passengers. Total baggage volume 25.1m³ (886.0ft³).

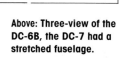

Above: Three-view of the DC-6B, the DC-7 had a stretched fuselage.

Left: Greenlandair operated two Douglas DC-6A/B on charter flights, to Scandinavia and nearby Canada.

GAF NOMAD AUSTRALIA

Development of a small utility transport suitable for military or civil roles began at Australia's Government Aircraft Factories (GAF) during the mid-1960s. As the N2, this project took shape as a strutted high-wing monoplane having a slab-sided fuselage of almost square cross section, large side-loading doors and retractable landing gear with stub wings, carrying nacelles into which the main wheels retracted. Prototypes of this N2 design flew on 23 July and 5 December 1971, respectively. The name Nomad was adopted for the production version, and several variants were developed, starting with the N22, with a gross weight of 3,629kg (8,000lb). This was later increased to 3,855kg (8,500lb) in the N22B, which became the standard short-fuselage variant for commercial use, with up to 12 passengers. Meanwhile, GAF had 'stretched' the Nomad's fuselage by 1.14m (3ft 9in) to produce, in 1976, the N24, with seating increased from 12 to a maximum of 17. With the same power plant as the N22, the N24 was introduced at a gross weight of 3,855kg (8,500lb), but this was increased to 4,263kg (9,400lb) in the definitive N24A. In May 1985, GAF recertificated the N22B at increased gross weight of 4,060kg (8,950lb) as the N22C, this version also featuring a force-feed oil filter system. During 1979, a version of the N22B was certificated as a seaplane, fitted with a pair of Wipaire (of Minnesota) aluminium floats, and in the following year an amphibious variant was also certificated, using Wipaire floats incorporating Cessna wheels and tyres in a retractable installation. Approximately half of the total production of Nomads has been in military versions of the short-fuselage N22 as the Missionmaster, Searchmaster B and Searchmaster L. N22 went into service on 18 December 1975 with Aero Pelican, after certification of the production version on 29 April 1975. The N22B was certificated

in August 1975. The N22C was approved in May 1985. Certification of the N24 was obtained in October 1977 and of the N24A in May 1978, with FAR Pt 135 (Appendix A) approval gained in December 1978. Production ended in late 1984 after the completion of 170 aircraft.

SPECIFICATION
(GAF Nomad N22B)

Dimensions: Wingspan 16.51m (54ft 2in); length overall 12.57m (41ft 3in); height overall 5.54m (18ft 2in), wing area 30.10m² (324.0ft²).
Power Plant: Two 313kW (420shp) Allison 250-B17C turboprops, with Hartzell three-blade
Weights: Operating weight empty 2,446kg (5,432lb); max take-off 3,855kg (8,500lb); max landing 3,855kg (8,500lb); max payload 1,685kg (3,714lb).
Performance: Max cruising speed 169kts (313km/h); initial rate of climb 7.4m/s (1,460ft/min); service ceiling 6,400m (21,000ft); take-off field length 360m (1,180ft); landing field length 410m (1,340ft); max range 580nm (1,074km).
Accommodation: Flight crew of one or two. Seating for up to 12 passengers with central aisle. Total front baggage volume 0.76m³ (27.0ft³).

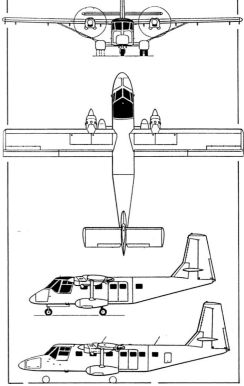

Left: The GAF Nomad saw service with several Australian commuter airlines, including this N24A with ARAS.

Above: Three-view of the basic N22, with the lengthened N24A depicted in the extra side-view below.

GRUMMAN ALBATROSS USA

The G-111 has its origins in the Grumman G-64 Albatross design of the period immediately after World War II, first flown on 24 October 1947 as the XJR2F-1 utility transport amphibian for the US Navy. Later production batches for the USAF as search and rescue amphibians were designated SA-16, and all variants later received HU-16 designations. During the late 1970s, as Albatross amphibians became available upon being retired by the USAF and USN, Grumman developed a conversion programme, in conjunction with Resorts International, for a version of the Albatross to operate in the commuter role. Identified as the G-111 (the original Grumman design number for the HU-16B variant), a prototype of this civil conversion first flew on 13 February 1979 and FAA type approval was obtained on 29 April 1980. The conversion included restoration of the airframe to zero-time standard through a full inspection and repair, removal and overhaul of

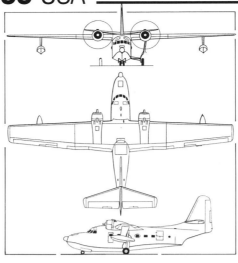

the engines, modernization of the flight deck, installation of passenger seats in the cabin, with provisions of suitable access doors and emergency hatches, and a lightweight, solid-state avionics system throughout. Although Grumman purchased 57 Albatrosses for conversions, only 12 were delivered to Resorts International by 1986, some of these going into service with Resorts subsidiary Chalks International and others being available for sale. A variant with Garrett TPE331-15UAR turboprops and Dowty-Rotol four-blade propellers was also studied by Grumman and Resorts International, but not developed. Plans by Frakes International to re-engine the Albatross with Pratt & Whitney Canada PT6A turboprops also came to nothing.

Above: Three-view drawing of the Grumman G-111 Albatross, which is externally difficult to distinguish from the original military and maritime versions.

Left: A Grumman G-111 Albatross belonging to Chalks International comes in to land at Lakeland's Sun'n Fun festival.

SPECIFICATION
(Grumman G-111 Albatross)

Dimensions: Wingspan 29.46m (96ft 8in); length overall 18.67m (61ft 3in); height overall 7.87m (25ft 10in), wing area 96.2m² (1,035ft²).
Power Plant: Two 1,100kW (1,475hp) Wright R-1820-982C9HE3 air-cooled radial piston engines, with Hamilton Standard three-blade constant-speed feathering and reversing propellers.
Weights: Operating weight empty 10,659kg (23,500lb); max take-off 14,129kg (31,150lb); max landing 14,129kg (31,150lb); max payload 3,630kg (8,000lb).
Performance: Normal cruising speed 206kts (383km/h); initial rate of climb 6.35m/s (1,250ft/min); service ceiling 2,440m (8,000ft); take-off distance on water 1,340m (4,400ft); landing distance on water 965m (3,170ft); range with max payload 405nm (750km).
Accommodation: Flight crew of two. Seating for 28 passengers in single seats with central aisle. Total baggage compartment volume 7.93m³ (280.0ft³).

GRUMMAN GOOSE and TURBO-GOOSE USA

SPECIFICATION
(McKinnon G-21G Turbo Goose)

Dimensions: Wingspan 15.49m (50ft 10in); length overall 12.07m (39ft 7in); height overall 3.71m (12ft 2in), wing area 35.08m² (377.6ft²).
Power Plant: Two 507kW (680shp) Pratt & Whitney Canada PT6A-27 turboprops, with Hartzell three-blade constant-speed feathering and reversing propellers.
Weights: Operating weight empty 3,040kg 6,700(lb); max take-off 5,670kg (12,500lb).
Performance: Max cruising speed 211kts (391km/h); service ceiling 6,095m (20,000ft); range with max fuel 1,390nm (2,575km).
Accommodation: Flight crew of one. Seating for up to 11 passengers in main and rear cabins.

The Goose amphibian, developed as a four/six-seat business amphibian, first flew in June 1937 and obtained US type approval on 29 September of that year in its initial G-21 form and on 5 February 1938 in improved G-21A form. Produced for USAAF and USN service during the war, numbers of Goose amphibians found applications in airline operation, especially in countries with extensive coastlines and lakes, such as Alaska, Canada, New Zealand and Scandinavia. Starting in 1958, the McKinnon company in the USA and later in Canada developed a number of Goose conversions, and some of these were still in small-scale commercial use in 1998. The G-21C and G-21D had four 254kW (340hp) Lycoming engines in place of the original Wasp Junior, the G-21D also featuring a lengthened

bow. The G-21E introduced 432kW (579shp) Pratt & Whitney Canada PT6A-20 turboprops and the G-21G had 534kW (715shp) PT6A-27s, optional retractable wing-tip floats and increased accommodation.

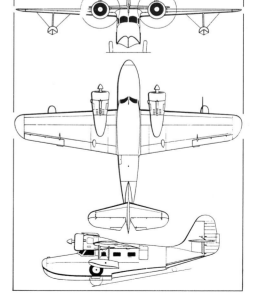

Above: The amphibious Grumman Goose saw extensive service in Canada and with island operators.

Above: The three-view depicts the Goose in its piston-engined version, but most still flying have turboprops.

GRUMMAN GULFSTREAM I and I-C USA

Design of this long-range, large-capacity corporate transport began in 1956 and set the basic circular fuselage cross-section and nose, which has been carried through all subsequent derivatives, including the latest jet-powered models. Grumman opted for the Rolls-Royce Dart turboprop for high-speed cruise, and an auxiliary power unit to permit independent operation from remote airfields. The G-159 Gulfstream I first flew on 14 August 1958, and deliveries began soon after the type received FAA certification on 21 May 1959. While designed primarily as a corporate aircraft with 10-14 executive seats, the Gulfstream I was also used on commuter airline services in Britain and the United States configured for 24 passengers. The US Coast Guard accepted two aircraft, designated VC-4A, for VIP duties in the summer of 1963, and the US Navy ordered nine TC-4s for navigator training in December 1966. Production totalled 200 and ceased in 1969. Ten years later, Gulfstream American Corporation, which had purchased the rights to the

SPECIFICATION
(Gulfstream I-C)

Dimensions: Wingspan 23.88m (78ft 4in); length overall 22.96m (75ft 4in); height overall 7.01m (23ft 0in), wing area 56.7m² (610.3ft²).
Power Plant: Two 1,484kW (1,990shp) Rolls-Royce Dart 529-8X or -8E (RDa.7/2) turboprops, with Rotol four-blade constant-speed propellers.
Weights: Operating weight empty 10,747kg (23,693lb); max take-off 16,329kg (36,000lb); max landing 15,551kg (34,285lb); max payload 3,356kg (7,400lb).
Performance: Max cruising speed 308kts (571km/h); initial rate of climb 9.7m/s (1,900ft/min); service ceiling 9,145m (30,000ft); take-off field length 1,480m (4,850ft); landing field length 845m (2,770ft); range with max payload 434nm (804km).
Accommodation: Flight crew of two. Seating for up to 37 passengers, three-abreast with offset aisle. Total baggage volume front and rear 7.1m³ (251.0ft³).

Gulfstream I, offered a conversion for up to 38 passengers three-abreast, with the fuselage stretched by 3.25m (10ft 8in). Known as the Gulfstream I-C, this model made its first flight on 25 October 1979, and a total of nine were delivered from November 1980. -

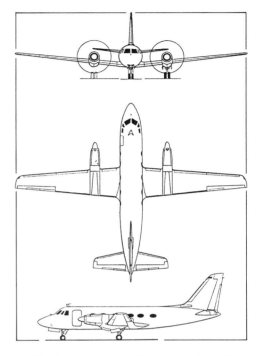

Left: Birmingham Executive used the 24-seat Gulfstream I on scheduled services.

Above: Three-view of the basic Gulfstream I; the I-C conversions have stretched fuselages.

GRUMMAN MALLARD and TURBO-MALLARD USA

The G-73 Mallard was developed as one of Grumman's first commercial ventures after World War II, in continuation of the company's pre-war interest in amphibious transports for the private and business owner. The Mallard first flew on 30 April 1946, powered by a pair of 448kW (600shp) Pratt & Whitney R-1340-8WH1 Wasp air-cooled radial piston engines. With a gross weight of 5,670kg (12,500lb), the Mallard cruised at 257km/h (139kts) at 2,450m (8,000ft) and had a range of 975nm (1,800km). Production totalled 61, and ended in 1951. Most Mallards were purchased by private owners but a few reached airline service, and continued in this role, primarily in Canada, Alaska and the

SPECIFICATION
(Grumman G-73 Turbo Mallard)

Dimensions: Wingspan 20.32m (66ft 8in); length overall 14.73m (48ft 4in); height overall 5.72m (18ft 9in), wing area 41.25m² (444.0ft²).
Power Plant: Two 534kW (715shp) Pratt & Whitney Canada PT6A-27 or -34 turboprops, with three-blade constant-speed propellers with automatic feathering..
Weights: Operating weight empty 3,969kg (8,750lb); max take-off 6,350kg (14,000lb); max landing 6,124kg (13,500lb).
Performance: Max cruising speed 191kts (354km/h); initial rate of climb 6.9m/s (1,350ft/min); service ceiling 7,470m (24,500ft); take-off length on water 1,495m (4,900ft); landing length on water 1,370m (4,500ft); range with max payload 750nm (1,388km).
Accommodation: Flight crew of two. Seating for up to 52 passengers, four-abreast , two seats each side of central aisle. Total baggage volume m³ (ft³).

Caribbean. In 1964, one Mallard operated by Northern Consolidated Airways in Alaska was fitted with a PT6A-9 turboprop on the starboard wing (retaining the R-1340 to port) and used for a 15-hour flight trial. After reverting to standard, this aircraft returned to NCA service but in 1969 was purchased by Frakes Aviation Inc. in Texas and modified to full Turbo-Mallard configuration as the G-73T, considerably boosting performance and operating economy. It first flew in this guise in September 1969 and after FAA type approval in October 1970 several more similar conversions were made by Frakes, for operation by Chalks International Airlines on its services in the Bahamas, alongside standard Mallards already used by that company.

Left: The three-view shows the Grumman Mallard as originally produced. Several have been converted to turbine power.

Below: West Coast Air was one of a number of Canadian airlines to operate the Mallard on its operations in British Columbia.

HANDLEY PAGE HERALD UK

The design of a medium-sized, short-range feeder liner with a pressurised fuselage was begun by the Handley Page company in the early 1950s. As the HPR 3, the new airliner emerged as a high-wing monoplane of conventional design, powered by four Alvis Leonides Major piston radial engines. Two prototypes were built in this configuration, with the first flight made on 25 August 1955, but early commitments for the purchase of some 29 aircraft, mostly for Australian operators, were not made good and it became clear to Handley Page that the HPR 3 could not hold its own in the new era of the turboprop. Consequently, in May 1957, the company announced that a version of the Herald would be offered with two Darts in place of the four piston engines, and the latter variant was subse-

quently dropped. Both prototypes were converted to have Dart RDa.7 engines, flying for the first time in this form on 11 March and 17 December 1958 respectively. The initial production standard was the Herald Srs 100, with a fuselage length of 21.92m (71ft 11in) and a maximum take-off weight of 17,690kg (39,000lb). The Herald Srs 200 featured a 1.09m (3ft 7in) lengthening of the fuselage to give two more seat rows, and higher weights. After the second prototype HPR 7 had flown in Srs 200 configuration on 8 April 1961, the first production example flew on 13 December 1961, and 36 of this variant were delivered. In addition, the company built eight Herald Srs 400s as military transports for the Royal Malaysian Air Force. The Herald Srs 300 designation referred to the Srs 200 with small modifications to meet US certification requirements. Series 500, 600, 700 and 800 were projected but never built, the company collapsing in 1968. The Srs 100 Herald entered service with British European Airways, following certification on 25 November 1959. The Srs 200 was certificated on 1 June 1961 and entered service with Jersey Airlines. A total of 48 were produced plus two prototypes. Only a handful remain in service.

SPECIFICATION
(Handley Page HPR.7 Herald 200

Dimensions: Wingspan 28.88m (94ft 9in); length overall 23.01m (75ft 6in); height overall 7.34m (24ft 1in), wing area 82.3m² (886.0ft²).
Power Plant: Two 1,570kW (2,105shp) Rolls-Royce Dart 527 (RDa.7) turboprops, with Rotol four-blade constant-speed fully-feathering propellers.
Weights: Operating weight empty 11,703kg (25,800lb); max take-off 19,505kg (43,000lb); max landing 17,915kg (39,500lb); max payload 5,307kg (11,700lb).
Performance: Max cruising speed 239kts 443(km/h); initial rate of climb 9.2m/s (1,805ft/min); service ceiling 8,505m (27,900ft); take-off field length 823m (2,700ft); landing field length 580m (1,900ft); range with max payload 608nm (1,127km).
Accommodation: Flight crew of two. Seating for up to 56 passengers, four-abreast , two seats each side of centrl aisle. Total baggage volume 8.1m³ (286ft³).

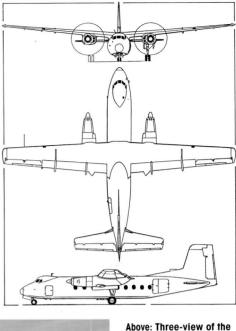

Above: Three-view of the Herald in its basic Series 200 form which, with 36 aircraft, was the most-produced variant of all.

Left: Cargo airline Channel Express is the last UK operator of the Herald, retaining a single Herald 401 at the beginning of 1998.

IAI ARAVA ISRAEL

The first indigenous design by Israel Aircraft Industries (IAI), the B-101C, was for a nine-seat corporate jet transport, and reached the mock-up stage but proceeded no further, whilst a second design, for a six-seat corporate jet, was also abandoned when IAI acquired the design and manufacturing rights for the Rockwell Jet Commander, which it went on to develop and produce as the Westwind. Attention then switched to a light STOL transport, for which there seemed to be a large world-wide market, both military and civil. Design work began in 1965 and led to a project for a high-

wing twin-turboprop transport with STOL performance characteristics. The most unusual feature of the design was the twin-boom layout, combined with a circular-section fuselage having a hinged tail cone for straight-in loading of vehicles or cargo. Like most other aircraft in its class, the new transport, which took the designation IAI-101, was designed to meet the American FAR Pt 23 regulations; which established the maximum take-off weight at 5,670kg (12,500lb) for civil operations. The first prototype of the IAI-101 flew on 27 November 1969. The name Arava was adopted for both civil and military types. The original Arava was designed around a pair of Turboméca Astazou turboprops, but PT6A-27s were adopted instead for the IAI-101 prototypes, switching to the 584kW (783shp) PT6A-34 for the IAI-101 initial production standard, later identified as the IAI-102. This was matched by the IAI-201 military version, which had a maximum weight of 6,804kg (15,000lb). The IAI-101B has PT6A-36 engines and improved performance in hot and high conditions, as well as a better cabin interior. An all-cargo version, with a 2,360kg (5,200lb) payload, was known as the Cargo Commuterliner in the USA. The IAI-202 was a modified version with PT6A-36 engines, winglets and a lengthened fuselage. The IAI-102 was type-approved by the Israeli authorities in April 1976, and was the first commercial version to go into service. FAA certification of the IAI-101B was obtained on 17 November 1980 to SFAR Pt 41 provision, and in October 1982 to the upgraded SFAR Pt 41C. Production ceased in January 1986 after delivery of 91 aircraft. Fewer than 10 of this STOL transport remain in commercial service in Central and South America.

SPECIFICATION
(IAI-101B Arava)

Dimensions: Wingspan 20.96m (68ft 9in); length overall 13.05m (42ft 9in); height overall 5.21m (17ft 1in), wing area 43.7m² (470.0ft²).
Power Plant: Two 559kW (750shp) Pratt & Whitney Canada PT6A-36 turboprops, with Hartzell three-blade variable-pitch fully-feathering and reversing propellers.
Weights: Operating weight empty 4,000kg (8,818lb); max take-off 6,800kg (14,991lb); max landing 6,800kg (14,991lb); max payload 2,350kg (5,182lb).
Performance: Max cruising speed 172kts (308km/h); initial rate of climb 6.5m/s (1,290ft/min); service ceiling 7,620m (25,000ft); take-off field length 745m (2,450ft); landing field length 655m (2,150ft); range with max payload 237nm (440km).
Accommodation: Flight crew of one or two. Seating for up to 19 passengers, four-abreast with central aisle. Total baggage compartment volume 2.60m3 (91.8ft³), plus 3.20m³ (113.0ft³) in tail cone.

Below: The IAI-202 version had unusual winglets and a lengthened fuselage.

Above: The basic IAI-201 Arava has a side-hinged rear fuselage cone to facilitate cargo loading.

ILYUSHIN IL-14 SOVIET UNION

The Il-14 was an improved derivative of the Il-12, which was itself the first product of the Ilyushin design bureau after World War II to achieve large scale production for non-military use, although it was probably designed primarily as a replacement for the Li-2 in the role of a military tactical transport. The Il-14, which flew as a prototype in 1952, differed from the Il-12; but like the Il-12, the Il-14 was built for both military and commercial use, the latter in the hands of Aeroflot and designated Il-14P (*Passazhirskii*) with accommodation for 18-26

passengers. In 1956, a slightly stretched version appeared, with a 1.0m (3ft 4in) section inserted in the forward fuselage, increasing accommodation to a maximum of 36. This was designated Il-14M (*Modifikatsirovanny*). Later, considerable numbers of Il-14Ps and Ms were adapted to serve Aeroflot as freighters under the designation of Il-14T (*Transportny*). Up to 3,500 examples of the Il-14 are reported to have been built in the Soviet Union, and VEB Flugzeugwerke built 80 in East Germany. As the Avia 14, the type was also built in large numbers in Czechoslovakia, in several different versions. These aircraft were used in both civil and military guise by the relevant operators in East Germany and Czechoslovakia and were exported to other countries in the Soviet sphere of influence, including Albania, Poland, Romania, Bulgaria, Cuba and China. Some 100 are still in use in Russia for various passenger and cargo activities.

SPECIFICATION
(Ilyushin Il-14M)

Dimensions: Wingspan 31.69m (104ft 0in); length overall 22.30m (73ft 2in); height overall 7.90m (25ft 11in), wing area 99.7m² (1,075ft²).
Power Plant: Two 1,440kW (1,930hp) Shvetsov ASh-821-7 air-cooled 14-cylinder radial piston engines, with four-blade feathering AV-50 propellers.
Weights: Operating weight empty 12,600kg (27,776lb); max take-off 18,000kg (39,683lb); max landing 17,250kg (38,030lb).
Performance: Max cruising speed 208kts (385km/h); initial rate of climb 6.2m/s (1,220ft/min); service ceiling 6,705m (22,000ft); range with max payload 558nm (1,034km).
Accommodation: Flight crew of three or four. Seating for up to 36 passengers, four-abreast, two seats each side of central aisle.

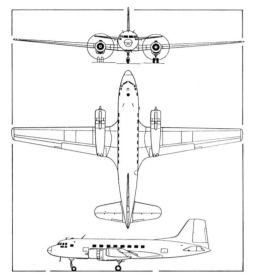

Left: The IL-14 was the standard equipment of the airlines of the Soviet Union and Eastern Europe in the 1950s and 1960s.

Right: The East German airline Interflug started its operations in 1955 with a large fleet of mostly locally-built VEB IL-14s.

ILYUSHIN IL-18 SOVIET UNION

SPECIFICATION
(Ilyushin Il-18D)

Dimensions: Wingspan 37.40m (122ft 8½in); length overall 35.90m (117ft 9in); height overall 10.17m (33ft 4in), wing area 140.0m² (1,507ft²).
Power Plant: Four 3,169kW (4,250shp) Ivchenko AI-20M turboprops, with AV-68I four-blade constant-speed feathering and reversing propellers.
Weights: Operating weight empty 35,000kg (77,160lb); max take-off 64,000kg (141,100lb); max payload 13,500kg (29,750lb).
Performance: Max cruising speed 364kts (675km/h); service ceiling 10,000m (32,820ft); take-off field length 1,300m (4,265ft); landing field length 850m (2,790ft); range with max payload 1,997nm (3,700km).
Accommodation: Flight crew of five. Seating for up to 122 passengers, six-abreast with central aisle.

Above: While no longer used on scheduled services outside Russia, the IL-18 has joined the fleets of charter carriers such as German European Airlines.

Right: This three-view drawing of the Ilyushin IL-18 is representative of all production versions described in the text, which are externally similar.

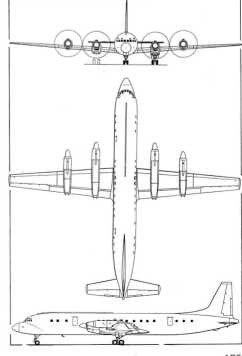

The Il-18 first flew in July 1957 as one of the first of a new generation of airliners developed after World War II to meet the needs of Aeroflot and to take advantage of then new technology including gas turbine engines. Named *Moskva*, the prototype was followed by two pre-production aircraft and a service trials batch of 20, of which some were powered by the Kuznetsov NK-4 engine and others by the AI-20. The latter was adopted as the standard power plant on the basis of early service results and, with maximum take-off weight increased from 57,200kg (126,100lb) to 59,200kg (130,514lb), the Il-18B became the first major production version, with 84 seats. This was followed in production in 1961 by the Il-18V, with AI-20K engines rated at 2,983kW (4,000shp) each, fuel capacity of 23,700l (6,253 US gal) and standard layouts for 90 or 110 passengers. In 1964, the more powerful AI-20M engine was introduced. Some internal

redesign of the cabin, with the deletion of the rear cargo hold and extension aft of the pressurized section, made it possible to increase accommodation to 110 or, by omitting coat stowage space during summer, a maximum of 122. With these changes the designation became Il-18E, but this was swiftly followed by the Il-18D, in which fuel capacity was increased to nearly 27 per cent, with extra bag tanks in the centre section of the aircraft. Some Il-18s were modified as cargo carriers after being retired from passenger service, with a large freight door in the rear fuselage side. The Il-18 entered service with Aeroflot on 20 April 1959, followed by the Il-18V in 1961, and by the Il-18D and Il-18E in 1965. NATO reporting name is 'Cub'. Production is believed to have amounted to around 800 aircraft. Some 100 are still in service, mainly in the CIS and Eastern Europe, with a few operating in the Far East and Central America.

LET L-610 CZECH REPUBLIC

The Let National Corporation, based at Kunovice, began development of the L-610 in the mid-1980s, primarily in response to a Soviet specification for a regional airliner with about 40 seats, to operate over stage lengths of 400-600km. Similar in configuration to the smaller L-410, the L-610 is, nevertheless, an entirely new design, incorporating a two-spar high wing with single-slotted Fowler flaps and spoilers and integrated fuel tanks, fixed-incidence tailplane high on the fin, two 1,358kW (1,822shp) Motorlet Walter M-602 three-shaft turbine engines, auxiliary power unit, and retractable tricycle landing gear. The first prototype

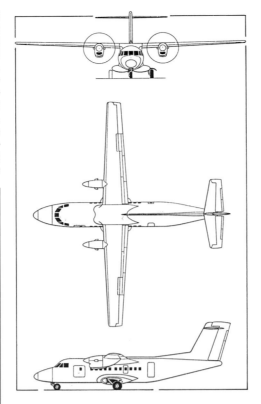

SPECIFICATION
(Let L-610G)

Dimensions: Wingspan 25.60m (84ft 0in); length overall 21.72m (71ft 3in); height overall 8.19m (26ft 10½in), wing area 56.0m^2 (602.8ft^2).
Power Plant: Two 1,305kW (1,750shp) General Electric CT7-9D turboprops, with Hamilton Standard HS-14RF-23 four-blade fully feathering reversible-pitch metal propellers.
Weights: Operating weight empty 9,220kg (20,326lb); max take-off 14,500kg (31,967lb); max landing 14,200kg 31,305(lb); max payload 4,200kg (9,259lb).
Performance: Max cruising speed 237kts (438km/h); max rate of climb 8.5m/s (1,673ft/min); service ceiling 8,400m (27,560ft); take-off field length 1,090m (3,577ft); landing field length 645m (2,117ft); range with max payload 302nm (560km).
Accommodation: Flight crew of two. Seating for 40 passengers, four-abreast, two seats each side of central aisle.

Above: The L-610, in addition to being larger, has the tail plane mounted high on the fin.

Right: The Let L-610, a stretched and modernised L-410, has yet to find a buyer.

flew on 28 December 1988, and was joined by two more flying prototypes and two for static and fatigue testing. With the Soviet market collapsing in 1990 - Aeroflot had a requirement for 600 aircraft, but has yet to take any - Let began making modifications to increase its appeal to other airlines, the principal differences being the introduction of the General Electric CT7-9D turboprops with Hamilton Standard 4-blade propellers, and Rockwell Collins digital avionics including EFIS, weather radar and autopilot. The first flight of this version, designated L-610G, took place on 18 December 1993. The Motorlet-powered L-610M received Czech certification in December 1994, with FAA certification to FAR Pt 25 of the L-610G still awaited. In spite of a strong sales push, the L-610 has yet to find a commercial buyer. and the aircraft's future rests on plans for joint production with Russia's Smolensk plant, either with the Motorlet engine, or a suitable local power plant. If customers are found for the L-610G - CSA Czech Airlines is understood to have secured options – this will be built in the Czech Republic.

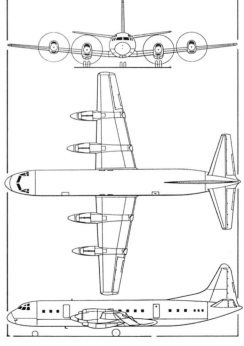

LOCKHEED L-188 ELECTRA USA

The trigger for initial design activity by Lockheed's Burbank, California, company was a 1954 specification produced by American Airlines for a short/medium-range transport to operate on its US domestic routes. Broadly, the design was for a 100-seater with a range of some 2,000nm (3,700km), grossing about 49,900kg (1100,000lb). It was the first US-originating airliner to feature turboprop power, and was destined to be the only such aircraft to achieve production status in the USA. The first of four prototype/flight test Electras flew on 6 December 1957 and the fifth, which was to be the first delivered for airline service, flew on 19 May 1958. After the launch orders by American Airlines and Eastern Air Lines for 75 aircraft, orders quickly accumulated, but evaporated just as rapidly, as the new turbojets proved their ability to compete. Confidence in the Electra was also shaken within the first 15 months of service by two fatal accidents that were traced, after painstaking research, to structural failures occuring in an unforeseen chain reaction after damage to the power plant mounting, for example in a heavy landing. A major structural modification programme was put in hand by Lockheed after the FAA imposed strict flight limitations in March 1960, and a modified aircraft was granted an unrestricted airworthiness certificate on 5 January 1961. The problem has not occurred since. The initial L-188A version, which accounted for most of the production, was followed by the longer-range L-188C, which provided extra fuel and operated at higher weights. From 1967, five years after the end of production, Lockheed converted 41 aircraft to freighters or convertible cargo/passenger aircraft, by fitting a large port cargo door forward of the wing and strengthened floor. Aircraft thus modified have been designated L-188AF and L-188CF respectively. The L-188A obtained FAA certification on 22 August

Above: Hunting Cargo Airlines is one of several operators in the UK using the Lockheed Electra.

Right: All versions of the Electra are similar externally, although all remaining aircraft now have a cargo door.

SPECIFICATION
(Lockheed L-188A Electra)

Dimensions: Wingspan 30.1 8m (9ft 0m); length overall 31.81 m (1 04ft 6in); height overall 10.0m (32ft l0in), wing area 120.8m2 (1,300ft2).
Power Plant: Four 2,800kW (3,750shp) Ailison 501-D13 turboprops, with four-blade reversing and feathering propellers.
Weights: Operating weight empty 27,895kg (61,500lb); max take-off 52,664kg (116,000lb); max landing 43,385kg (95,650lb); max payload 12,020kg (26,500lb).
Performance: Max cruising speed 352kts (652km/h); initial rate of climb 8.5m/s (1,670ft/min); service ceiling 8,230m (27,000ft); take-off field length 1,440m (4,720ft); landing field length 1,310m (4,300ft); range with max payload 1,910nm (3,540km).
Accommodation: Flight crew of three. Seating for up to 98 passengers, six-abreast with central aisle. Underfloor baggage/cargo volume 14.95m3 (528.0ft3).

1958 and entered service with Eastern Air Lines on 12 January 1959, followed by American Airlines 11 days later. The L-188C went into service with KLM that same year. The commercial production run totalled 170, but the Electra was also evolved into the highly successful P-3 Orion, which has passed the 600 mark. Around 50 commercial examples, mostly with cargo operators, remained in service in 1998; the UK alone has three users in Hunting Cargo Airlines, Channel Expresss and Atlantic Airlines.

MARTIN 4-0-4 USA

Turning from its military activities in World War II and seeking to re-establish its pre-war reputation as a manufacturer of commercial aircraft, the Glenn L Martin Co of Baltimore, Maryland, announced in November 1945 its plan to produce a twin-engined 40-seat transport of modern design, offering a substantial performance advance over the pre-war types such as the Douglas DC-3 and Curtiss CW-20 (C-46) on which the world's airlines were heavily dependent. The US domestic airlines made up the market of most immediate interest to Martin and early success in meeting the needs of this market appeared to have been achieved when Martin recorded large orders for its Model 2-0-2 (as the new design was styled) from several other operators. Powered by 2,400hp (1,790kW) Double Wasp R-2800-CA18 engines, the first 2-0-2 flew on 23 November 1946 and was a conventional low-wing monoplane of stressed-skin light-alloy construction, having an unpressurized fuselage and a relatively high aspect ratio (10.0:1) wing that was notable for its considerable dihedral angle and large double-slotted flaps. Featuring tricycle landing gear, the 2-0-2 had several design innovations aimed at the needs of airlines with short stage lengths and quick turn-arounds. In particular, passenger access to the cabin was by way of a ventral airstair under the tail so that engines could remain at ground idle during short stops; and a door in the front fuselage side was intended for galley and cabin servicing, but not for passenger use. An accident which was attributed to structural failure in the wing grounded the aircraft in 1948 and it returned to service only in 1950 after modification to 2-0-2A standard. The second 2-0-2 served as the vehicle for development of the 2-0-2A, and first flew as such in July 1950. On 20 June 1947, a Martin 3-0-3 prototype was flown, this being in effect a pressurized version of the 2-0-2, but the difficulties encountered with the original model led to the cancellation of production plans for the 3-0-3. Instead, Martin proceeded to develop a more extensively modified and improved variant as the 4-0-4, whose first flight was made on 21 October 1950. The Martin 2-0-2 was awarded its US Approved Type Certificate (ATC No. 795) on 13 August 1947, nine months after first flight, and flew its first revenue service in October 1947 with LAN Chile, the first US operator, Northwest, following in November. After modification, the first 2-0-2A entered service with TWA on 1 September 1950, and this same airline put the 4-0-4 into service on 5 October 1951. Martin built 43 of the Model 2-0-2s and 103 of the Model 4-0-4s. A handful remained in active service in 1998.

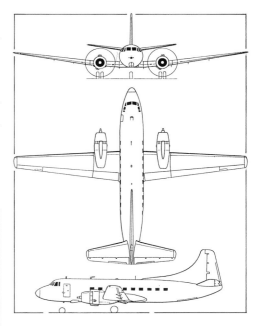

Above: Three-view of the Martin 4-0-4, which is slightly larger than the 2-0-2 it replaced.

Below: Shawnee Airlines was one of several smaller airlines to use the Martin 4-0-4.

NAMC YS-11 JAPAN

Above: Caribbean Airways flies the 60-seat YS-11A-500 on high-frequency shuttles.

Right: Three-view of the YS-11; note the forward freight door feature from the Srs 300 and 600.

Six Japanese companies (Mitsubishi, Kawasaki, Fuji, Shin Meiwa, Showa and Japan Aircraft Manufacturing) began during 1956 to study the design of a short/medium-range civil airliner as a wholly indigenous project, primarily with a view to meeting the requirements of Japanese domestic airlines. The design emerged as a relatively large twin turboprop, for whose construction the six companies set up Nihon Aircraft Manufacturing Co Ltd (NAMC) in May 1957. The development programme embraced four airframes: two flying prototypes and two structural test specimens. The first flights were made on 30 August and 28 December 1962, by

which time plans had been completed to launch production of the aircraft known as the YS-11. After production of 48 YS-11s, the first of which flew on 23 October 1964, NAMC developed the YS-11A with higher operating weights and increased payload. First flown on 27 November 1967, the YS-11A was offered in three versions which became known as the Srs 200, 300 and 400, the original YS-11s then becoming Srs 100 aircraft. The YS-11A-200 was the basic 60-passenger aircraft with a 1,350kg (2,700lb) increase in payload over that of the Srs 100, and 92 were built. With the same overall weights as the Srs 200, the YS-11A-300 was a mixed-traffic version featuring a side-loading cargo door in the forward side of the fuselage and able to carry 46 passengers plus 15.3m³ (540 cu ft) of cargo. The YS-11A-300, which first flew on 17 September 1969, was an all-cargo variant, with the cargo door in the forward fuselage side. The nine YS-11A-400s built were all for military use, as were a few of the earlier models. With an increase in maximum take-off weight of 500kg

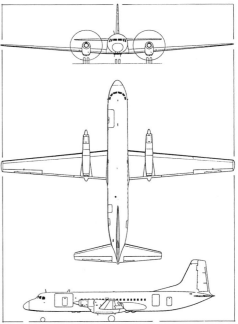

(1,105lb) to 25,000kg (55,115lb), the YS-11A-500, 600 and 700 were otherwise similar, respectively, to the Srs 200, 300 and 400. Production of four Srs 500 and five Srs 600 aircraft brought the YS-11A programme to an end, totalling 182 aircraft. Japanese certification was obtained on 25 August 1964, followed by FAA Type Approval on 7 September 1965. Deliveries of the YS-11 began in March 1965. Around 70 remain in commercial service, mainly in Asia/Pacific.

PILATUS PC-6 TURBO PORTER SWITZERLAND

Design work on a single-engined utility aircraft with STOL capability began in 1957, and developed into a braced high-wing monoplane of all-metal construction with variable incidence tailplane. Its impressive STOL characteristics permit operation from unprepared strips under harsh weather conditions and in inhospitable terrain. The PC-6 can operate from soft ground, snow, glacier and water, and has been used for a multitude of aerial missions across the world, including passenger and cargo transport, and aeromedical roles, for which its box-like fuselage and large loading door are particularly suitable. The first piston-engined PC-6 Porter flew on 4 May 1959 and Swiss certification of the basic version was obtained in August 1959. Several engine and gross weight combinations were produced before the first PC-6/A-H1 Turbo Porter with a 390kW (523shp) Turboméca Astazou IIE made its first flight on 2 May 1961. A number of variants were built, with different Astazou and Pratt & Whitney Canada turboprop engines, before the current production version, the PC-6/B2-H4, entered service in 1985. Compared with previous models, this introduced a 600kg (1,323lb) increase in maximum take-off weight, resulting in a payload increase of 570kg (1,257lb), particularly for commercial passenger operations, achieved by strengthening of the airframe, improved aerodynamic efficiency of the wings with new wingtip fairings, enlarged dorsal fin, and uprated mainwheel shock absorbers. Total production of Porters and Turbo Porters exceeds 500 and the latter remains in limited production.

SPECIFICATION
(Pilatus PC-6/B2-H4 Turbo Porter)

Dimensions: Wingspan 15.87m (51ft 1in); length overall 10.90m (35ft 9in); height overall 3.20m (10ft 6in); wing area 30.15m² (324.5ft²).
Power Plant: One 507kW (680shp) Pratt & Whitney Canada PT6A-27 turboprop, with Hartzell three-blade constant-speed reversing propeller.
Weights: Operating weight empty 1,270kg (2,800lb); max take-off 2,800kg (6,173lb); max landing 2,660kg (5,864lb); max payload 945kg (2,083lb).
Performance: Max cruising speed 125kts (232km/h); max rate of climb 5.2m/s (1,010ft/min); service ceiling 8,840m (29,000ft); take-off field length 197m (646ft); landing field length 127m (417ft); range with typical payload 500nm (926km).
Accommodation: Flight crew of one. Seating for up to 10 passengers.

Below: New Zealand's Mount Cook Line operates the Turbo Porter in the country's South Island. Because it uses mountainous airstrips it has to be equipped with wheels in the summer and with skis in winter.

PILATUS BRITTEN-NORMAN TRISLANDER UK/USA

The uniquely-configured Trislander resulted from the effort that began in 1968 to 'stretch' the Islander to carry more passengers. The first result of this activity was a long-fuselage Islander (converted from the original BN-2 production prototype), which first flew on 14 July 1968. Consideration of the flight test result obtained with this aircraft led the Britten-Norman company to conclude that additional power was needed to match the higher operating weights that were, in their turn, required to allow the full potential of a stretched aircraft to be achieved. Rather than redesign the wing to accept engines of greater power, the designers decided to fit a third engine of the same type as already used in the Islander, and chose to locate this extra power plant in a nacelle at the top of the fin. A redesigned, enlarged tailplane was fitted in line with the propeller of the third engine for maximum effectiveness; the fuselage cross section was unchanged, as was the wing geometry, but a little strengthening was required for the higher weights. Known as the BN-2A Mk III, this three-engined derivative of the Islander was sensibly named the Trislander and made its first flight at Bembridge on 11 September 1970. Production of the Trislander was initiated in 1970 by the original Britten-Norman company and continued under Fairey and then Pilatus ownership. On 5 June 1982, International Aviation Corporation in Florida acquired a licence to produce the Trislander in the USA, under the new name of Tri-Commutair. The BN-2A Mk III entered production with a gross weight of 4,245kg (9,350lb), this being increased in the BN-2A Mk III-1 version to 4,540kg (10,000lb). A further change was then made by adopting as standard the long nose (with extra baggage capacity) that had been developed for the BN-2S version of the Islander. This first flew on a Trislander on 18 August 1974 and resulted in the designation BN-2A Mk III-2. Introduction of an auto feather system, which put the propeller into feather in the event of an engine failure at take-off, without action by the pilot, brought with it the designation BN-2A Mk III-3. The first production Trislander flew on 6 March 1971, followed by UK certification on 14 May and US Type Approval (to FAR Pt 23) on 4 August of the same year. Aurigny Air Services in the Channel Islands took delivery of the first customer aircraft on 29 June 1971 and remains the largest operator with nine in service. Production of the Trislander amounted to 73 aircraft in the UK and 12 in the USA as the TriCommutair. Plans in 1994 to revive production in China with the Shenzhen General Aircraft Company came to nothing.

SPECIFICATION
(BN-2A Mk III Trislander)

Dimensions: Wingspan 16.15m (53ft 0in); length overall 15.01m (49ft 3in); height overall 4.32m (14ft 2in); wing area 31.3m² (337.0ft²).
Power Plant: Three 194kW (260hp) Avco Lycoming O-540-E4C5 flat-six piston engines, with Hartzell two-blade constant-speed fully feathering propellers.
Weights: Operating weight empty 2,650kg (5,843lb); max take-off 4,540kg (10,000lb); max landing 4,540kg (10,000lb); max payload 1,610kg (3,550lb).
Performance: Max cruising speed 143kts 265(km/h); initial rate of climb 5.0m/s (980ft/min); service ceiling 4,010m (13,150ft); take-off field length 595m (1,950ft); landing field length 440m (1,445ft); range with max payload 130nm (241km).
Accommodation: Flight crew of one. Seating for up to 17 passengers on individual side-by-side and bench-type seats. Total baggage voOlume 1.33m³ (47.0ft³).

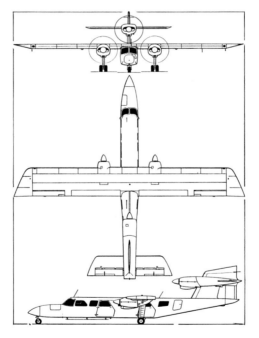

Above: Three-view of the BN-2A Mk.III Trislander, using the wing and fuselage cross-section of the smaller Islander.

Below: Aurigny Air Services flies the Trislander on its bus-stop services in the Channel Islands.

PILATUS PC-12 SWITZERLAND

The single-engined PC-12 (or PC XII) was launched in October 1989 for executive use and to muscle in on the multi-purpose utility market, successfully developed by the Cessna Caravan I. Combining a conventional airframe with a low-wing and T-tail configuration with advanced systems, has produced a fast, comfortable and rugged pressurised aircraft, able to operate from soft unprepared airstrip. Although largely of metal construction, the PC-12 introduces composite winglets,

engine cowling and dorsal and ventral fin fairings. Advanced flight avionics and instrumentation as standard, including EFIS primary displays, 3-axis autopilot, weather radar and global positioning system, allow routine single-pilot operation by day and night. A large cargo door at the rear and flat strengthened cabin floor permit straight-in palletised loading. The PC-12 made its first flight on 31 May 1991 and received certification to FAR Pt 23 Amendment 42 on 30 March 1994. First deliveries

took place in April, at which time 33 orders had been received.. The Pilatus PC-12 Corporate Commuter seats up to nine passengers, while the PC-12 Executive normally offers customised interiors for six people. A PC-12 Combi, typically carrying four passengers and 5.95 m³ (210 cu ft) of cargo, and a PC-12F freighter version with a payload of 1,000kg (3,086lb), are also available. Production at 1 January 1998 had exceeded 100 aircraft with sales accelerating.

Left: The fitting of advanced flight avionics allow single-pilot operation of the Pilatus PC-12 by both day and night.

SPECIFICATION
(Pilatus PC-12)

Dimensions: Wingspan 16.08m (52ft 9in); length overall 14.38m (47ft 2in); height overall 4.26m (14ft 0in), wing area 25.8m² (277.8ft²).
Power Plant: One 1,197kW (1,605shp) Pratt & Whitney Canada PT6A-67B turboprops, with Hartzell four-blade constant-speed propeller.
Weights: Operating weight empty 2,386kg (5,260lb); max take-off 4,000kg (8,818lb); max landing 4,000kg (8,818lb); max payload 1,634kg (3,602lb).
Performance: Max cruising speed 269kts (498km/h); mac climb rate 10.6m/s (2,080ft/min); service ceiling 10,670m (35,000ft); take-off field length 310m (1,020ft); landing field length 425m (1,395ft); range with typical payload 1,790nm (3,311km).
Accommodation: Flight crew of one or two. Seating for up to 9passengers. Total baggage volume 1.12m³ (39.5ft³).

PZL-MIELEC M-28 (ANTONOV AN-28) POLAND

SPECIFICATION
(M-28 Skytruck PT)

Dimensions: Wingspan 22.07m (72ft 5in); length overall 13.10m (43ft 0in); height overall 4.90m (16ft 1in), wing area 39.7m² (427.5ft²).
Power Plant: Two 820kW (1,100shp) Pratt & Whitney Canada PT6A-65B turboprops
Weights: Operating weight empty 3,917kg (8,635lb); max take-off 7,000kg (15,432lb); max landing 6,650kg (14,661lb); max payload 2,000kg (4,409lb).
Performance: Max cruising speed 181kts (335km/h); service ceiling 6,200m (20,340ft); take-off field length 265m (870ft); landing field length 185m (607ft); range with typical payload 765km (1,417km).
Accommodation: Flight crew of two. Seating for up to 18 passengers.

A braced high-wing monoplane, the An-28 made its first flight appearance in September 1969, then known as the An-14M, indicating its relationship with the earlier An-14 piston-engined light transport. Intended to replace the ubiquitous An-2 biplane, offering higher standards of comfort and performance but comparable short take-off and landing capabilities, the An-28 underwent a lengthy period of flight development and proving trials before entering production. Following the first flight of the Antonov-built An-28 prototype on 23 April 1975, production was assigned to PZL-Mielec in Poland in February 1978, where the first of a pilot-batch of 15 (including one for static testing) flew on 22 July 1984. Certification was obtained on 7 February 1986. PZL-Mielec's production planned envisaged a total of 1,200 in the first five years, but less than 100 were delivered to Aeroflot before the

collapse of the Soviet Union. Since then, small quantities have been built for the Polish armed forces in a range of different variants. Commercial variants (now all prefixed M) include the basic M-28 transport model with 705kW (945shp) TVD-10B turboprops; M-28A for polar use with increased fuel capacity; and the M-28 Skytruck PT. PZL-Mielec is now planning to produce two stretched versions of the Skytruck for 30 passengers. The new models are the M28-03 and M28-04, both of which will be stretched by 1.84m (6ft) and have a 0.25m (10in) higher ceiling to allow passengers to stand upright. The M28-03 has rear clamshell doors, while the M28-04 has a side cargo door. Both models have uprated 880kW (1,200shp) PT6A-65B engines. Three prototypes are planned for first flight in mid-1998 and deliveries in 1999. NATO reporting name for the M-28/An-28 is 'Cash'.

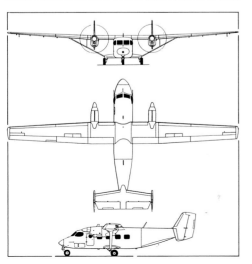

Left: Three-view of the production M-28 (An-28), showing the final arrangement of the landing gear, wings and tail unit, after modification of the prototypes used for initial flight testing.

Right: After having built some 100 18-seat M-28s, PZL-Mielec is now working on a stretched Skytruck to carry up to 30 passengers in a larger, stand-up cabin, or three LD-3 cargo containers.

SHORTS SC.5 BELFAST UK

Left: London Stansted-based HeavyLift Cargo Airlines is the only carrier to operate the ex-RAF strategic Belfast freighter on commercial flights, but its days are now believed to be numbered.

Below: In its day, the Shorts SC.5 Belfast was the largest military freighter in service. The design stemmed from the Bristol Britannia, but as this three-view shows it eventually bore little resemblance to the Bristol design.

The Belfast was developed to meet an RAF requirement for a heavy strategic freighter, and the first of 10 ordered for military use flew on 5 January 1964. Deliveries to the RAF began on 20 January 1966 and all 10 aircraft were operated by No. 53 Squadron until retirement in September 1976. Five of the ex-RAF aircraft were then acquired for conversion for operation in civil guise as all-cargo transports carrying outsize loads. Conversion design, engineering and certification was handled by Marshall of Cambridge (Engineering) and involved changes to the autopilot, avionics, power plant and flight control systems to meet civil certification standard, CAA approval being obtained on 6 March 1980. Commercial operation of the Belfast began later in March 1980, the company at first being known as TAC HeavyLift, subsequently simply as Heavylift after the parent TAC had gone out of business. Two Belfasts remain in full-time service with Heavylift, carrying awkward and outsize loads to many different parts of the world.

SPECIFICATION
(Shorts SC.5 Belfast)

Dimensions: Wingspan 48.41m(158ft 10in); length overall 41.58m (136ft 5in); height overall 14.33m (47ft 0in), wing area 229.1m² (2,465ft²).
Power Plant: Four 4,276kW (5,730shp) Rolls-Royce Tyne RTy.12 turboprops, with four-blade Hawker Siddeley (DH) constant-speed feathering and reversing propellers.
Weights: Operating weight empty 58.967kg (130,000lb); max take-off 104,325kg (230,000lb); max landing 97,520kg (215,000lb); max payload 34,020kg (75,000lb).
Performance: Normal cruising speed 275kts (510km/h); take-off field length 2,500m (8,200ft); landing field length 2,075m (6,800ft); range with max payload 850nm (1,575km).
Accommodation: Flight crew of three or four. Total usable cabin cargo volume 321.4m³ (11,350ft³), with provision for up to 19 passengers on upper deck.

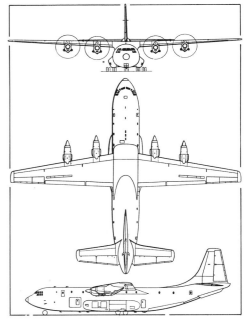

SHORTS SC.7 SKYVAN UK

Plans by Belfast-based Short Brothers for a small multi-role STOL freighter took shape as the PD.36 project design and acquired the engineering number SC.7, when construction of a prototype was launched in 1959. The Skyvan, as it was later dubbed, had a conventional fuselage based on a payload 'box' with a 1.98m (6ft 5in) square cross-section, and also featured a high aspect ratio, untapered, strut-braced high wing, incorporating the results of research by F G Miles, and a fixed landing gear. The prototype first flew on 17 January 1963 with a pair of 291kW (390hp) Continental GTSIO-520 piston engines, but these were replaced with Turbomeca Astazou II turboprops, with which the aircraft flew again on 2 October 1963. An initial production batch of 19 Skyvan Srs IIs was built with 545kW (730shp) Astazou XII engines, the first flight being made on 29 October 1965. The type could carry 19 passengers or 1,815kg (4,000lb) of freight and was used by several commercial operators. To

produce a definitive version of the Skyvan, Shorts then switched to the Garrett TPE331-201 engine to produce the Skyvan Srs 3 which first flew on 15 December 1967. Some Srs 2s were converted to have the Garrett engines, and some aircraft were produced as Skyvan IIIAs with a 6,215kg (13,700lb) gross weight. Furnished to higher standard for airline use, the Skyliner version of the Skyvan Srs 3 could carry up to 22 passengers. Several military variants were also developed, as the Skyvan Srs 3M and Skyvan 3M-200, the latter with clearance to operate at weights up to 6,804kg (15,000lb). Certification of the Astazou-engined Skyvan Srs 2 was obtained early in 1966, and deliveries began at that time. The Skyvan Srs 3 entered service in 1968, and in 1970 it was certificated in accordance with new UK civil airworthiness requirements for short take-off and landing (STOL) operations. The Skyvan's total production was eventually in excess of 150 aircraft.

SPECIFICATION
(Shorts SC.7 Skyvan 3

Dimensions: Wingspan 19.79m (64ft 11in); length overall 12.21m (40ft 1in); height overall 4.60m (15ft 1in), wing area 35.1m² (378.0ft²).
Power Plant: Two 533kW (715shp) Garrett TPE331-2-201A turboprops, with Hartzell three-blade variable-pitch propellers.
Weights: Operating weight empty 3,674kg (8,100lb); max take-off 5,670kg 12,500(lb); max landing 5,670kg (12,500lb); max payload 2,086kg (4,600lb).
Performance: Max cruising speed 175kts (324km/h); initial rate of climb 8.3m/s (1,640ft/min); service ceiling 6,860m (22,500ft); take-off field length 490m (1,600ft); landing field length 450m (1,480ft); range with typical payload 162nm (300km).
Accommodation: Flight crew of one or two. Seating for up to 19 passengers in a two plus one arrangement with offset aisle.

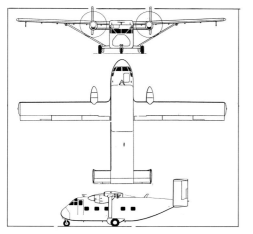

Left: Three-view drawing of the Shorts Skyvan 3, the final production version from 1967. The Skyliner version of the Skyvan Series 3 was similar in appearance, but better furnished.

Right: Del-Air (Delaware Air Freight Company) acquired nine Shorts Skyvans in 1970 and operated them on local scheduled cargo services, before acquiring Convair 580s.

TRANSALL C-160 INTERNATIONAL

The Transall C-160 was developed originally to meet the requirements of the French and German air forces, the AG Transall concern being set up to manage production as a shared activity in France and Germany, with final assembly lines in both countries. The first of three prototypes flew on 25 February 1963, these being followed by six pre-production examples and then 110 C-160Ds for the Luftwaffe, 50 C-160Fs for the Armée de l'Air and nine C-160Zs for the South African Air Force. Production was completed in 1970, and in 1973 four C-160Fs were converted for operation (as C-130Ps) by Air France on the regular night mail services, primarily between Paris and Bastia, Corsica. In 1977 production of a second batch of Transalls began and the first of these improved aircraft flew on 9 April 1981. The Armée de l'Air bought 29 second-series C-160s, and six more were ordered by the Indonesian government. The latter are operated in civil guise by Pelita Air Service on the transmigration services to ferry inhabitants from Java to the less densely populated islands of Indonesia.

SPECIFICATION
(Transall C-160)

Dimensions: Wingspan 40.00m (131ft 3in); length overall 32.40m (106ft 3½in); height overall 11.65m (38ft 2¾in), wing area 160.0m² (1,722ft²).
Power Plant: Two 4,550kW (6,100shp) Rolls-Royce Tyne RTy.20 Mk 22 truboprops, with four-blade BAe Dynamics (Ratier-Forest built) constant-speed fully-feathering and reversing propellers.
Weights: Operating weight empty 29,000kg (63,935lb); max take-off 51,000kg 112,435(lb); max landing 47,000kg (103,615lb); max payload 16,000kg (35,275lb).
Performance: Max cruising speed 277kts (513km/h); initial rate of climb 6.6m/s (1,300ft/min); service ceiling 8,230m (27,000ft); take-off field length 990m (3,250ft); landing field length 870m (2,850ft); range with max payload 1,000nm (1,850km).
Accommodation: Flight crew of three. Max cargo volume, including ramp area, 139.9m³ (4,940ft³), or seating for up to 128 passengers.

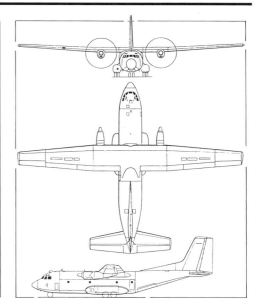

Left: Although designed and produced for military use, a small number also went into commercial service with Air France, and the Indonesian airline Pelita Air Service, which operated the type for its parent Pertamina, the national oil company, ferrying its workers between the islands.

Above: The configuration of the C-160 Transall, shown in this three-view, is classic for a dedicated freighter, with a high-wing and cabin floor line close to the ground for ease of loading through the rear door and ramp. The civil examples which are in use have no external differences.

VICKERS VISCOUNT UK

The result of project design work that began before the end of World War II under the aegis of the Brabazon Committee, the Viscount emerged in 1948 as the world's first airliner with turboprop engines, and went on to become the UK's most successful commercial aircraft production programme. With government backing, Vickers launched construction of two prototypes in March

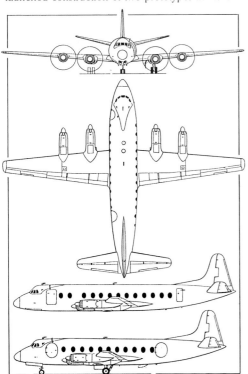

Left: The three-view drawing shows the Viscount 800 series. The additional side-view below clearly illustrates the difference in length of the earlier V.700s.

Above: The last Viscounts in service in the UK were operated by British World Airlines on contract cargo services; such as this V.800 in Parcel Force markings.

SPECIFICATION
(Vickers V.800 Viscount)

Dimensions: Wingspan 28.55m (93ft 8in); length overall 26.11m (85ft 8in); height overall 8.15m (26ft 9in), wing area 89.4m² (963.0ft²).
Power Plant: Four 1,300kW (1,740shp) Rolls-Royce Dart Mk 510 (RDa.6) turboprops, with Rotol four-blade constant-speed fully-feathering propellers.
Weights: Operating weight empty 18,600kg (41,000lb); max take-off 29,260kg (64,500lb); max landing 26,535kg (58,500lb); max payload 6,000kg (13,224lb).
Performance: Max cruising speed 282kts (523km/h); service ceiling 7,620m (25,000ft); take-off field length 1,620m (5,310ft); landing field length 1,510m (4,950ft); range with max payload 565km (1,050km).
Accommodation: Flight crew of three. Seating for up to 71 passengers, five-abreast with offset aisle. Total baggage volume 10.48m³ (370.0ft³).

1946 and the first of these (Vickers 630) flew on 16 July 1948, with Dart RDa.1 engines and accommodation for 32 passengers. The first enlarged production standard was defined as the Viscount 700, with Dart Mk 505 engines (replacing Dart Mk 504s in the prototype), a gross weight of 240,040kg (53,000lb) and 47 seats five-abreast. Individual 700-series type numbers applied to each customer variant, starting with 701 for the BEA aircraft. In the mid-1950s Vickers stretched the Viscount's fuselage by 1.17m (3ft 10in) and moved the rear cabin bulkhead aft to obtain enough space to seat up to 71 passengers. With RDa.6 engines and 29,256kg (64,500lb) gross weight this was the Viscount 800, first flown on 27 July 1956, and with more powerful RDa.7 Mk 520 engines it was the Type 806, a BEA 'special'. The Type 806A prototype first flew on 9 August 1957. Based on the Type 806, the Viscount 810 series combined RDa.7/1 engines with structural modifications to allow the maximum take-off weight to increase to 32,885kg (72,500lb). A prototype of the Viscount 810 flew on 23 December 1957, and most of the final production batches, for several overseas operators, were of this type. Viscount production ended in 1964 with 444 built. The Viscount 700 obtained its UK certificate of airworthiness on 17 April 1953 and BEA put the type into service between London and Cyprus on the following day, which was the world's first revenue airline service by turboprop airliner. In the US, FAA approval of the Type 745 for Capital Airlines was obtained on 7 November 1955. Deliveries of the Type 802 began (to BEA) on 11 January 1957, and of the Type 806 (also to BEA) on 1 January 1958. Continental Airlines received the first of the 810-series (Type 812) in May 1958 and revenue service began on 28 May. Only around 15 are still in service.

This section presents the main types of passenger and cargo aircraft under development in 1998. These present a spread of types from small turboprop and jet aircraft to the New Large Aircraft (NLA), which can carry up to 1,000 passengers and are expected to dominate the principal high-density long-haul routes in the new millennium. Unusually, it also features a new tiltrotor aircraft which, although small, represents the beginning of a new type of passenger transport which combines the speed of a turboprop aircraft with the vertical take-off and landing capability of a helicopter.

Some of the types illustrated have just made their maiden flights and will enter service in 1999, others are more long-term projects, some of which may not make it into production. There are absentees, especially on the Russian front, where designers present many paper projects and models, and it becomes difficult to decide which are the most likely to progress beyond the drawing board. An assessment had, therefore, to be made, and only the future will reveal how accurate this has been.

The most interesting battle has been fought over the New Large Aircraft, which has generated much discussion among manufacturers, airlines and the travelling public. While the sheer size of the double-deck aircraft concerns some, the inexorable rise in air traffic and consequent congestion in the air and at airports, make such an aircraft inevitable. Some new airports are already designing for the NLA and it will be a momentous day in 2004, when the first of the type is expected to begin passenger service. But in the intervening years, several other new aircraft will undoubtedly be added to the list of future aircraft, including perhaps a new supersonic type.

AIRBUS A3XX INTERNATIONAL

In parallel with the eventually inconclusive joint studies between Airbus members and Boeing, the European consortium decided in May 1994 to continue feasibility studies into its own A3XX high-capacity aircraft. In March 1996, Airbus set up a Large Aircraft Division tasked with preparing the launch and to enter into discussions with key airlines to establish a design definition. Airbus currently projects three basic versions of the A3XX, the 550-seat A3XX-100, the same-size but heavier and extended-range A3XX-100R, and the longer, higher-capacity 650-seat A3XX-200. Consideration is also being given to a reduced-capacity 480-seat deriva-

tive, and freighter and combi versions of the A3XX-100, designated A3XX-100F and A3XX-100C respectively. The A3XX-300, which could seat up to 1,000 passengers in a high-density, single-class arrangement, may follow much later. Three new power plants are being offered, although Airbus has indicated that it will give airlines a choice of two engines only. The three engines in contention are the 356kN (80,000lb) Rolls-Royce Trent 900, the GP7200 series of the Pratt & Whitney and GE Aircraft Engines alliance, with thrusts also up to 356kN (80,000lb), and the Pratt & Whitney PW4500, maximum rated at 347kN (78,000lb). The two-deck aircraft will provide four-aisle boarding from dual-lane stairs, typically seating 205 passengers in a 2/4/2 upper deck layout, and 350 passengers in a 3/4/3 main deck economy configuration. All models will have the same 79.00m (259ft 2½in) wingspan, but the A3XX-200 will have a 6.60m (21ft 7¾in) longer fuselage, keeping all models within the 80m x 80m 'box', which requires minimum adaptation of existing airports. Maximum take-off weight has been set at 583,000kg (1,285,280lb). Typical range is 7,675nm (14,200km), with the -200 capable of flying a distance of 8,755nm (16,200km). Launch decision is expected in 1998, to meet a projected in-service date is 2004. Estimates for the potential market for this size aircraft vary from 500 to more than 1,400.

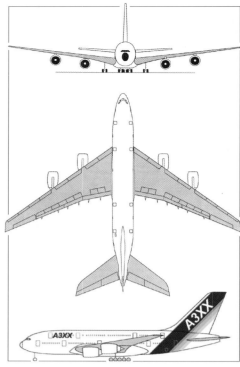

PRELIMINARY SPECIFICATION
(A3XX-100R)

Dimensions: Wingspan 79.00m (259ft 2½in); length overall 70.80m (232ft 3½in); height overall 24.30m (79ft 8¾in).
Power Plant: Two 347-356kN (78,000-80,000lb) turbofans.
Weights: Max take-off 583,000kg (1,285,280lb).
Performance: Max cruise speed Mach 0.85+; take-off field length 3,350m (11,000ft); max range 8,755nm (16,200km).
Accommodation: Flight crew of two. Seating for up to 555 passengers.

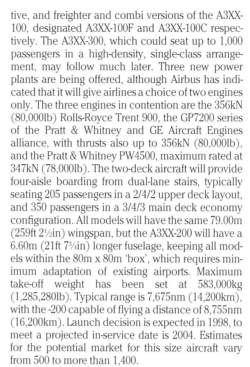

Left: In all-passenger configuration, the A3XX will have 10-abreast seating on the main deck and six-abreast on the upper deck. LD1 and LD3 cargo pallets can still be carried in the lower hold.

Below: Computer generation of the four-engined double deck A3XX, which will challenge Boeing's domination of the large airliner market.

Above: The proposed large A3XX is of conventional layout, with the exception of a double-deck fuselage. The wingspan will be larger than the Boeing 747 – which has dominated this airliner market since the late 1960s – but will be kept within 80m (262ft 6in), to enable it to fit into existing docking arrangements at the main airports it is likely to serve.

AIA/AVIC/STAe AE31X INTERNATIONAL

Aviation Industries of China (AVIC) and Airbus Industrie Asia (AIA) signed a framework agreement in February 1997 for the joint development of the proposed AE31X regional jet airliner family, formerly known as the AE-100 and A318. The new aircraft will be developed by a new joint-venture company, owned 46 per cent by AVIC, 39per cent by AIA, with Singapore Technologies holding the remaining 15 per cent. AIA itself will be owned 62 per cent by Airbus Industrie and 38 per cent by Italy's Alenia. Workshare will be allocated in accordance with the shareholding, and final assembly will take place in China. Launch is planned for early 1999, with first flight in 2002 and service entry a year later. The new family is targeted at the 95-125 seat market, to fill a gap below the A319 and compete more effectively with Boeing's smaller 737s, and will be available in two sizes, both in basic and high gross-weight versions. The standard AE316 will seat 95 or 105 passengers in two-class and single-

class layouts respectively, the latter in five-abreast seating. Maximum range has been set at 1,800nm (3,300km), with the HGW version capable of a range of 2,750nm (5,100km). The larger AE317 will seat 115 or 125 passengers in a fuselage lengthened by 3.80m (12ft 5½in), and will have identical range envelopes. Maximum take-off weight will be limited to 58,200kg (128,300lb). The fuselage cross-section will be smaller than the A320 family, but there will be a high degree of commonality, including common pilot-rating. Controls will be fly-by-wire. Engine choice lies between the BMW Rolls-Royce BR715, CFM International CFM56-9 and Pratt & Whitney PW6000 turbofans. Airbus is predicting a market of 3,000 aircraft over the next 20 years, of which it hopes to capture around 30 per cent. Sales are expected to be led by North America with 43 per cent, followed by Europe (24 per cent), Asia (10per cent), China (9 per cent) and the rest of the world (14 per cent).

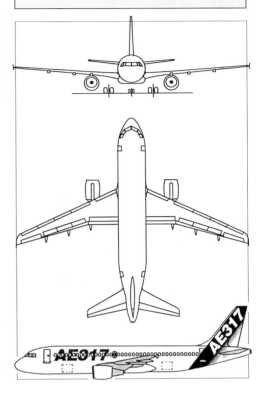

Left: The AE316 will be competing with the Boeing 717, but under the present schedule will not enter service before 2002, three years later. Efforts are being made to speed up design and production.

Right: Three-view drawing of the proposed new multi-national AE317, which is shorter than the existing A319, but is itself 3.80m (12ft 5¾in) longer than the AE316. The fuselage diameter is smaller than the A320 family.

ANTONOV AN-140 UKRAINE

The Antonov An-140 is of traditional high-wing design and closely resembles the An-24 which it is intended to replace, offering twice the fuel efficiency and range, as well as a high cruise speed of 310kt (575km/h). Production of this new aircraft was committed in 1994, following receipt of orders from unnamed Ukrainian and Russian airline companies, and the first prototype was rolled out at the Ukrainian design bureau's Kiev base on 6 June 1997 and made its maiden flight. First deliveries are

expected in late 1998/early 1999. To be built at the Kharkov State Aircraft Manufacturing Company and Kiev State Aviation Plant, Ukraine and by Aviacor in Samara, Russia, the An-140 is a true joint venture programme, with aerodynamic research by TsAGI, the 2,500shp turboprop engines designed by Klimov but assembled by Motor-Sich, wings by KhGAPP, the AB-140 propellers by Aerosila, landing gear by PA South Machine Building Plant, and the AE9-3B auxiliary power unit by ZMBK Progress. Western input is

provided by French companies Auxilec and Eros, providing power supply and oxygen systems respectively, while MAN of Germany supplies the toilet system. The An-140 is initially being offered in a passenger version with a maximum seating capacity of 52, and as a combi, with 3,650kg of cargo in the forward cabin and 20 passenger seats at the rear. To enhance its market opportunities, Antonov is also considering offering the aircraft with western engines and avionics.

Right: The Antonov An-140 is now in its flight test programme, which should be completed **before the end of 1998, with first deliveries in early 1999. It may also be built in Iran.**

FAIRCHILD DORNIER 328 JET GERMANY/USA

Fairchild Dornier completed the critical design review into a new 32-seat regional jet at the company's German plant at Oberpfaffenhofen in June 1997 and a few days later at the Paris air show announced launch orders for six aircraft from French regional, Proteus Airlines, and four from US company Aspen Mountain Air/Lone Star. The 328JET, which started life as an offshoot of feasibility studies into the stretched 328S, is a derivative of the 328 turboprop aircraft and will be the first turbofan aircraft in the new 30-plus seat jet category. It closely resembles the turboprop model, but features the Pratt & Whitney Canada PW306B high by-pass ratio turbofan, each generating a static thrust of 26.9kN (6,050lb). The additional fuel required will be incorporated in a modified wing structure. The only other structural changes are a 20 per cent increase in the length of the rudder trim tab, to maintain minimum speed, and a strengthened undercarriage to handle the heavier weights and landing speeds. The AlliedSignal 36-150(DD) auxiliary power unit, an option on the turboprop, will be a standard item on the 328JET. Fairchild Dornier aims at an 80 per cent commonality with the turboprop aircraft, allowing both types to be built simultaneously, and change between turboprop and jet types, based on customer demand, late in the production run. Aermacchi, in partnership with OGMA of Portugal, will build the fuselage and Messier-Dowty the landing gear. The first 328JET, converted from the second 328 turboprop aircraft, was rolled out in December 1997, with the first flight of the prototype taking place on 20 January 1998. Three further aircraft will be used in the certification programme which is expected to be completed by February 1999, to be followed by the first customer deliveries in March. The 528JET, a 50-seat stretch, could enter service by 2001, provided it is launched later in 1998. Engine choice for the bigger variant lies between the PW308, Allison AE 3007G or AlliedSignal AS 908D. Fairchild Dornier estimates a market for 2,294 aircraft in the 20-39-seat category, of which it hopes to sell 450 jets.

Below: The 328JET is very similar to the turboprop aircraft from which it is derived. It will give customers a choice of a turboprop and/or jet aircraft in the 30-plus seat category.

PRELIMINARY SPECIFICATION
(328JET)

Dimensions: Wingspan 20.98m (68ft 10in); length overall 21.28m (69ft 10in); height overall 7.24m (23ft 7in).
Power Plant: Two 26.9kN (6,050lb) Pratt & Whitney Canada PW306B turbofans.
Weights: Max take-off 14,990kg (33,047lb); max payload 3,410kg (7,518lb).
Performance: Max cruise speed 375kt (694km/h); take-off field length 1,240m (4,070ft); landing field length 1,185m (3,890ft); design range 900nm (1,670km), or 1,200nm (2,220km) for extended range version.
Accommodation: Flight crew of two. Seating for up to 34 three-abreast passengers with single aisle.

IPTN N2130 INDONESIA

The initial NTP study (N2130 Technology Program) into a 100-seat regional jet was started in October 1994, but the decision to proceed has yet to be made. The present timetable projects a first flight by mid-2002, with certification and first deliveries expected in early 2004. The N-2130 is of conventional low-wing design with underwing podded engines, sweptback wings and tail unit. It features an advanced digital fly-by-wire control system, based on the N-250, and integrated avionics computer which provides data processing and distribution functions. Three candidates have been identified for the power plant: the CFM International CFM56-9, BMW Rolls-Royce BR 715-56, and the Pratt & Whitney PW6000. Required static thrust is in the area of 82kN (18,500lb) each. The circular fuselage cross-section incorporates passenger service units (PSU) to permit easy changes in business and economy class arrangements, choice of a normal or wider aisle width, and large capacity overhead luggage bins per passenger. The proposed family comprises the baseline N2130-100 for up to 114 passengers and the stretched N2130-200, which can accommodate 132 passengers in an all-tourist layout. Each version will be available with the option of basic and increased grossweight (IGW). The N2130 will be able to take off and land on 1,750m (5,740ft) runways and cruise at Mach 0.8 up to 39,000ft. Maximum range is 1,850nm (3,420km). IPTN projects a market for 100-130 seat aircraft of more than 3,200 between 2005 and 2025, but will find the competition tough.

PRELIMINARY SPECIFICATION
(N2130-100IGW)

Dimensions: Wingspan 29.90m (98ft 1¼in); length overall 31.25m (102ft 6½iin); wing area 107.4m² (1,150ft²).
Power Plant: Two 85.9kN (19,300lb) turbofans.
Weights: Max take-off 51,500kg (113,537lb); max landing 46,350kg (102,183lb); max payload 11,400kg (25,132lb).
Performance: Max cruise speed Mach 0.80; take-off and landing field length 1,750m (5,740ft); max range 1,850nm (3,420km).
Accommodation: Flight crew of two. Seating for up to 114 passengers.

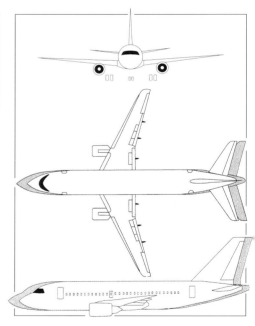

Left: The IPTN 2130 twin-engined jet represents the enormous ambition for Indonesia's aircraft manufacturing industry of its Minister of Technology. If built, the aircraft will enter a well-established market already occupied by the Airbus A319, Boeing 737 and others, and will have to battle hard for market share.

Above: This three-view drawing shows a comparison between the IPTN N2130-100 and stretched N2130-200 models. Although of conventional configuration, the N2130 features an advanced digital fly-by-wire control system.

TUPOLEV TU-330/338 RUSSIA

The Tu-330 was announced in early 1993 as a replacement for the large numbers of Antonov An-12s still flying in Russia and the CIS. The first flight had not been made by the end of 1997, but the designer still hopes to fly the aircraft before the end of 1998, with certification by the end of the year. This was one of the conditions imposed by the Russian Government in a resolution dated 23 April 1994 to finance the aircraft. Design is based on the Tu-204 with a similar, but high-mounted wing and two turbofan engines on pylons, with a large over-fuselage fairing to aerodynamically blend the carry-through structure. A 4.0 x 4.0m (rear-loading ramp facilitates loading and unloading of freight. For the local market, the aircraft will have two Aviadvigatel PS-90A turbofans, but Rolls-Royce RB.211-535 or Pratt & Whitney PW2000 engines are being considered to enhance the new aircraft's appeal in the foreign market. The aircraft has been designed to land on grass runways. No variants have yet been disclosed, although a cryogenic-fuelled version with Samara NK-94 engines and 20,000kg (44,092lb) of liquefied natural gas (LNG) is proposed as the Tu-338. Another possibility is a derivative of the standard Tu-330 for the carriage of LNG, which would be accommodated in three tanks in the cabin with a total capacity of 22,800kg (50,265lb). Production of the Tu-330 will be undertaken at Kazan, where 10 are believed to be in various stages of construction. Tupolev forecasts a market for cargo aircraft of the Tu-330 type of 1,000 aircraft, for both civil and military applications.

PRELIMINARY SPECIFICATION
(Tu-330)

Dimensions: Wingspan 43.50m (142ft 8½in); length overall 42.00m (137ft 9½in); height overall 14.00m (45ft 11¼in); wing area 196.50m² (2,115.2ft²).
Power Plant: Two 158kN (35,500lb) Aviadvigatel PS-90A turbofans.
Weights: Max take-off 103,500kg (228,175lb); max payload 35,000kg (77,160lb).
Performance: Cruising speed 458kt (850km/h); Range with 30t payload 1,620nm (3,000km).

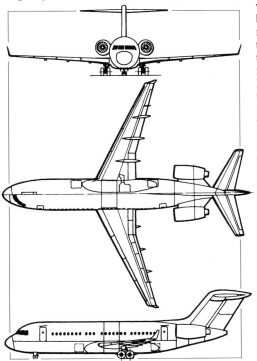

Below: Model of the Tu 330 cargo aircraft, believed to be under construction in Kazan.

Right: The proposed Tu-330 has the classic features of a purposely designed cargo aircraft, with a high anhedral wing, low ground line and rear loading ramp.

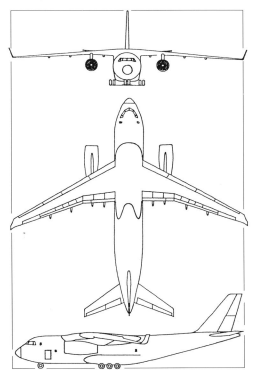

TUPOLEV TU-334/354 RUSSIA

This twin-fan replacement for the Tu-134 on domestic routes in the Russian Federation and the CIS countries, has been under development since the late 1980s. Although the prototype was rolled out at Zhukovsky during the Moscow air show on 25 August 1995, it had not made its maiden flight by the end of 1997, due largely to funding shortages, although several aircraft are believed under construction at Taganrog, Kiev and Samara. Based on the Tu-204, but with a considerably shortened fuselage for up to 102 passengers, the Tu-334 uses many of the Tu-204's systems and has an identical flight deck. Design features include a supercritical dihedral wing with 24-deg sweepback and winglets, rear-mounted engines and a T-tail and fly-by-wire controls. Composites and other lightweight materials make up around 20 per cent of the structural weight. Retractable tricycle landing gear is fitted with a slush and ice deflector grille behind the mainwheels. Several models are available to airlines, apart from the basic 102-seat Tu-334-100 with two Ivchenko Progress D-436T1 turbofans, rated at 73.5kN (16,535lb) static thrust each. These include the Tu-334-100D extended-range version with uprated 80.5kN (18,100lb) D-436T2 turbofans, increased gross weight and fuel; the Tu-334C cargo variant; and the Tu-354, originally designated Tu-334-200. The latter is being offered with either the D-436T2 or 88.95kN (19,995lb) BMW Rolls-Royce BR 715-55, and has an increased wingspan and a lengthened fuselage to accommodate up to 126 passengers. Letters of intent have been received for some 40 aircraft from Rossiya Airlines, Bashkiri Airlines, Tatarstan Airlines and Tyumen Airlines, but the home market in Russia and the CIS is estimated to be at least 500 aircraft.

PRELIMINARY SPECIFICATION
(Tu-334-100D)

Dimensions: Wingspan 32.61m (107ft 0in); length overall 31.80m (104ft 4in); height overall 9.38m (30ft 9¾in); wing area 100.0m² (1,076.4ft²).
Power Plant: Two 80.5kN (18,100lb) Ivchenko Progress D-436T2 turbofans.
Weights: Max take-off 54,420kg (119,975lb); max payload 11,000kg (24,250lb).
Performance: Cruising speed 442kt (820km/h); take-off and landing field length 2,200m (7,220ft); Range with typical payload 2,213nm (4,100km).
Accommodation: Flight crew of two. Seating for up to 102 passengers, six-abreast with central aisle.

Left: The Tu-334 departs from the traditional Tupolev design in having dihedral wings and winglets.

Right: The short-range Tu-334 made its public debut at Zhukovsky in 1995, but has yet to fly.

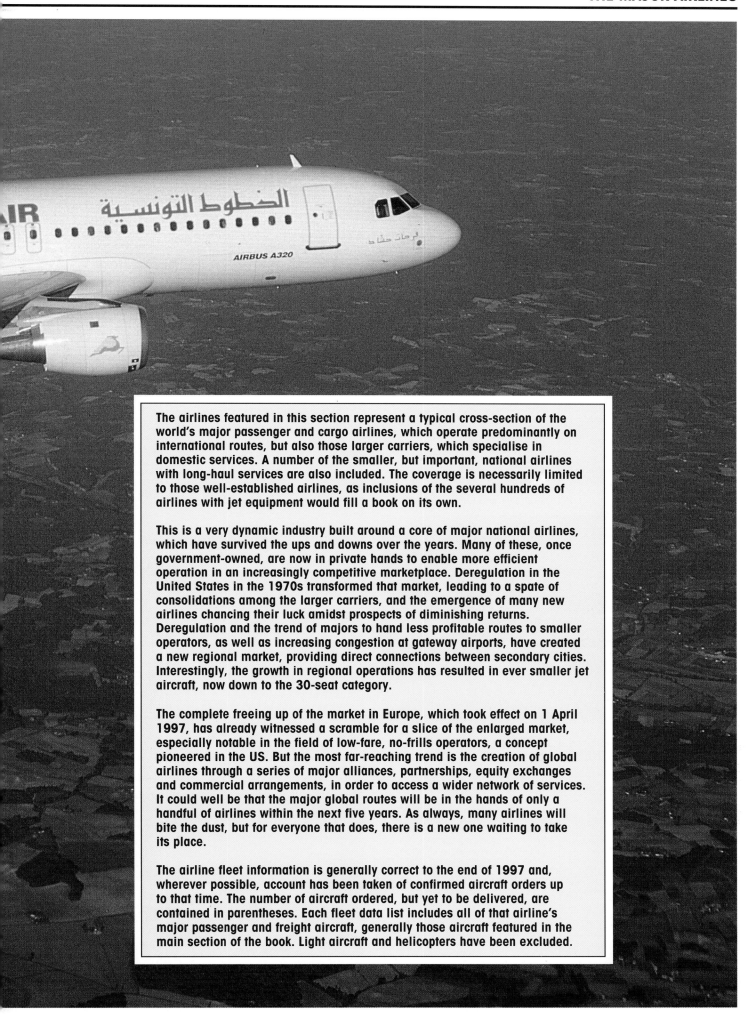

AIRBUS A320

The airlines featured in this section represent a typical cross-section of the world's major passenger and cargo airlines, which operate predominantly on international routes, but also those larger carriers, which specialise in domestic services. A number of the smaller, but important, national airlines with long-haul services are also included. The coverage is necessarily limited to those well-established airlines, as inclusions of the several hundreds of airlines with jet equipment would fill a book on its own.

This is a very dynamic industry built around a core of major national airlines, which have survived the ups and downs over the years. Many of these, once government-owned, are now in private hands to enable more efficient operation in an increasingly competitive marketplace. Deregulation in the United States in the 1970s transformed that market, leading to a spate of consolidations among the larger carriers, and the emergence of many new airlines chancing their luck amidst prospects of diminishing returns. Deregulation and the trend of majors to hand less profitable routes to smaller operators, as well as increasing congestion at gateway airports, have created a new regional market, providing direct connections between secondary cities. Interestingly, the growth in regional operations has resulted in ever smaller jet aircraft, now down to the 30-seat category.

The complete freeing up of the market in Europe, which took effect on 1 April 1997, has already witnessed a scramble for a slice of the enlarged market, especially notable in the field of low-fare, no-frills operators, a concept pioneered in the US. But the most far-reaching trend is the creation of global airlines through a series of major alliances, partnerships, equity exchanges and commercial arrangements, in order to access a wider network of services. It could well be that the major global routes will be in the hands of only a handful of airlines within the next five years. As always, many airlines will bite the dust, but for everyone that does, there is a new one waiting to take its place.

The airline fleet information is generally correct to the end of 1997 and, wherever possible, account has been taken of confirmed aircraft orders up to that time. The number of aircraft ordered, but yet to be delivered, are contained in parentheses. Each fleet data list includes all of that airline's major passenger and freight aircraft, generally those aircraft featured in the main section of the book. Light aircraft and helicopters have been excluded.

AER LINGUS (EI)

Aer Lingus is the trade name under which the combined operations of Aer Lingus Teoranta and Aerlinte Eireann are known. Aer Lingus Teoranta was formed on 22 May 1936 as the national airline of the Irish Republic to operate scheduled services between Ireland and Great Britain. Aer Lingus was the first carrier outside Great Britain to order the Viscount and was the first European operator of the Fokker F27 Friendship. The carrier initiated short haul jet services in May 1965 with BAC One-Elevens.

Aerlinte Eireann was formed on 26 February 1947 to operate transatlantic services, but due to a change in government policy the proposed services (initially to Boston and New York) were shelved. The carrier finally began operations with the inauguration of the Dublin-Shannon-New York service on 28 April 1958, using Super Constellations leased from Seaboard. Jet operations on the route began in December 1960 with the delivery of three Boeing 720-048 aircraft.

The operations of the two carriers are now fully integrated into an international and regional network of passenger and cargo services from Dublin, Shannon and Cork to London and several provincial centres throughout the UK, 14 European cities, and Boston, Chicago, New York and Newark in North America. The carrier's major shareholder is the Ministry of Finance for the Irish government, with management holding a small number of qualifying shares. Aer Lingus currently employs 5,600 personnel. Aer Lingus Commuter is a wholly owned subsidiary formed in 1984.

Fleet Data
5 Airbus A330-300, **(4)** A321-200, **6** Boeing 737-400, **9** × 737-500, **2** BAe 146-200, **5** BAe 146-300, **6** Fokker 50.

Aer Lingus Airbus A330-300.

AEROFLOT RUSSIAN INTERNATIONAL AIRLINES (SU)

Until the break-up of the Soviet Union, state-owned Aeroflot was the world's largest airline undertaking all types of aerial services with a fleet of several thousand aircraft and close to half-a-million employees. Aeroflot Russian International Airlines is the legal successor of Aeroflot-Soviet Airlines, concentrating on international operations and domestic trunk routes. Its former directorates have been spun off into mostly independent operations in Russia and the CIS countries.

The carrier was formed in March 1923 under the name of Dobrolet, and services were operated from Moscow to Odessa, Georgia and into Central Asiatic Russia. Dobrolet merged with the Ukrainian airline Ukvozduchput in 1929 to form Dobroflot, which was subsequently reorganised as Aeroflot in 1932. However, it was not until 1960 that the last remaining separate entity, the Polar Aviation division operating services

Aeroflot Airbus A310-300.

in the Arctic regions, became part of Aeroflot. During the 1930s emphasis was placed on developing the domestic route network; very few international services were operated at this time. On 15 September 1956 Aeroflot initiated jet services, on the Moscow-Irkutsk route, with the Tupolev Tu-104. From 1958 onwards substantial development of international routes was undertaken, initially to West European cities and subsequently to the underdeveloped third world countries in Asia and Africa under the organization of the Directorate of International Routes. The carrier operated its first transatlantic service on 7 January 1963.

Aeroflot serves 135 international point in 100 countries in Europe, Africa, Middle East, Far East, and North, Central and South America. Domestic trunk routes link its base at Moscow's Sheremetyevo Airport with St Petersburg, Khabarovsk, Novosibirsk, Yakutsk and others. In 1996, the airline carried 3.82m passengers and employed 15,000 people.

Fleet Data
10 Airbus A310-300, **2** Boeing 767-200ER, **(10)** 737-400, **28** Ilyushin IL-62M, **14** IL-76TD, **19** IL-86, **5** Il-96-300, **(17)** Il-96M, **(3)** Il-96T, **1** McDonnell Douglas DC-10-30F, **8** Tupolev Tu-134A-3, **25** Tu-154M, **4** Tu-204C.

AEROLINEAS ARGENTINAS (AR)

Aerolineas Argentinas was founded on 14 May 1949 as a state corporation. It superseded four separate operators: Flota Aerea Mercante Argentina (FAMA), Aviacion del Litoral Fluvial Argentina (ALFA), Zonas Oeste y Norte de Aerolineas Argentinas (ZONDA), and Aeroposta Argentina. Of these, Aeroposta Argentina was the oldest, having begun operations in late 1928. ALFA had inaugurated flying-boat services in 1938 as Corporation Sudamericana de Servicios Aereos, while ZONDA was established in February 1946 operating domestic and regional routes with DC-3 aircraft. FAMA, the largest of the four operators was founded on 8 February 1946, and had been established as the Argentine flag carrier. FAMA initiated services to London in September 1946 with DC-4 aircraft. The four companies ceased operations on 31 December 1949, and were merged to form the new carrier. Services from Buenos Aires to New York were initiated

in March 1950 and domestic services were significantly expanded. Jet operations to Europe began in May 1959 following the acquisition of Comet 4 aircraft, and from 1962 Caravelle VI-R aircraft provided domestic and regional jet services.

Aerolineas Argentinas, presently employing 7,000 personnel, operates a network of scheduled passenger and cargo services to North, Central and South America, and to Amsterdam, Frankfurt, London, Madrid, Paris, Rome and Zürich in Europe.

Fleet Data
3 Airbus A310-300, **8** Boeing 727-200, **10** 737-200C, **6** 747-200B, **3** Fokker F.28-1000, **6** McDonnell Douglas MD-88.

Aerolineas Argentinas Boeing 747-200B.

AEROMEXICO (AM)

Aeromexico was formed on 1 September 1934 as Aeronaves de Mexico. Domestic operations were initiated with the opening of services between Mexico City and Acapulco. Between 1952 and 1962 Aeronaves took over Lineas Aereas Mexicanas SA (LAMSA), Aerovias Reforma SA, Aerolineas Mexicanas SA, and Guest Aerovias Mexico (which had been operating transatlantic services). Aeronaves was nationalised in July 1959 and a Pan American holding was acquired by the Mexican government. The first major international route, from Mexico City to New York, was opened up in December 1957 by Britannia 302 aircraft; later, DC-8 aircraft were used. In 1970, as part of a government plan, domestic operators in Mexico were nationalised into an integrated system consisting of eight smaller operators under the control of Aeronaves de Mexico.

The airline changed its name to Aeromexico in February 1972.

The airline collapsed in April 1988, but was re-activated under private ownership the following September. Holding company Cintra, in which the government has a minority stake, took over in June 1996.

Aeromexico operates a large domestic network serving 40 towns and cities, together with international flights to the United States and Europe, serving Atlanta, Dallas/Ft Worth, Houston, Madrid, Miami, Los Angeles, New Orleans, New York, Orlando, Paris, Phoenix, San Diego and Tucson. The airline employs 5,500 staff.

Fleet Data
6 Boeing 757-200, **3** 767-300ER, **18** McDonnell Douglas DC-9, **10** MD-82, **4** MD-83, **2** MD-87, **10** MD-88.

Aeromexico Boeing 757-200.

AIR AFRIQUE (RK)

Air Afrique (Société Aérlenne Africaine Multinationale) was formally constituted on March 28, 1961, with the signing of the Treaty of Yaoundé in Cameroun. The carrier was formed by Air France, the French independent airline UAT and 11 African states comprising Benin (then Dahomey), Cameroun, Central African Republic, Chad, Gabon, Ivory Coast, Mauritania, Niger, Republic of the Congo, Senegal and Burkina Faso (then Upper Volta), which were formerly French colonies. The state of Togo joined the Air Afrique consortium in 1965, but Cameroun withdrew in September 1971 and Gabon in 1977, each to develop its own international carrier. Each of the member states contributes towards Air Afrique's capital, totalling 70.4 per cent, with

Air Afrique Airbus A310-300.

the balance held by Air France, DHL and French and West African development banks. The carrier began services on August 19, 1961, taking over the route structure operated by Air France and UAT in French Africa and using Boeing 707 and DC-8 aircraft leased from the two carriers.

As black Africa's largest carrier, Air Afrique currently operates a route network encompassing 17 African states and linking these with Paris, Bordeaux, Lyon, Marseilles, Rome, Las Palmas, New York and Jeddah. Some 4,900 personnel are employed by Air Afrique.

Fleet Data
3 Airbus A300B4-200, **2** A300-600R, **6** A310-300, **2** Boeing 737-200C.

AIR ALGÉRIE (AH)

The carrier was formed as a result of the merger of Compagniè Générale de Transport Aériens (CGTA) (established in 1947) and the French operator Compagnie Air Transport in June 1953. Air Algérie officially became the country's national carrier in 1963, and was wholly government-owned by 1972.

In 1968, piston-engined aircraft were replaced by four Convair 640s, followed in 1971 by the first Boeing 727s and 737s. A small number of Nord 262s were acquired with the integration of local carrier Société de Travail Aérien (STA) on 1 May 1972. The first long-haul route was established to Havana, after leasing an Airbus A300B4 from Lufthansa in 1981.

Air Algérie (Société Nationale de Transport et de Travail Aérien), employing some 9,000 personnel, currently operates scheduled passenger and cargo services to 31 destinations in West Africa, Europe and the Middle East. An extensive domestic network is also operated.

Fleet Data
4 Airbus A310-200, **11** Boeing 727-200, **15** 737-200, **3** 767-300, **2** Lockheed L100-30, **7** Fokker F27.
(Note: A number of smaller aircraft types are operated including Grumman Ag-Cat and Beechcraft Queen Air aircraft and helicopters.)

Airbus A310-200 in Air Algérie colours.

AIR CANADA (AC)

Air Canada was formed as Trans-Canada Airlines (TCA) by the Canadian government on 10 April 1937 to function as a wholly owned affiliate of Canadian National Railways. The carrier began scheduled operations on 1 September of that year with a passenger and airmail service between Vancouver and Seattle. Transcontinental passenger services on the Vancouver-Montreal routes were inaugurated on 1 April 1939 and transatlantic services in support of the Canadian armed forces overseas began on 22 July 1943 between Montreal and Prestwick. The carrier began operating its North Atlantic services on a commercial basis on 7 May, 1947 with Canadair DC-4M North Stars.

TCA became the first operator of turboprop aircraft in the Americas with the inauguration of Viscount 724 services on 1 April 1955 between Montreal and Winnipeg. A total of 51 Viscounts eventually entered service with the carrier. DC-8-41 aircraft inaugurated jet operation for TCA on 1 April 1960 on the Montreal-Toronto-Vancouver route.

The airline adopted its present title on 1 January 1965 and on 1 November 1966 Air

Air Canada Airbus A319.

Canada became the first North American airline to operate to the Soviet Union.

The flag carrier became a Crown Corporation in its own right in February 1978 and currently operates to 120 destinations from hubs at Calgary, Halifax, Montreal, Toronto and Vancouver. In addition to 90 points in North America, flown by Air Canada and five feeder airlines under the *Air Canada Connector* banner, the airline also serves cities in the Caribbean, Europe and the Far East. Air Canada employs 19,500 people and carries 12m passengers annually.

Fleet Data
27 (8) Airbus A319, **34** A320-200, **(5)** A330-300, **8** A340-300, **3** Boeing 747-100, **3** 747-200B, **3** 747-400, **23** 767-200, **6** 767-300ER, **24** Canadair Regional Jet, **35** McDonnell Douglas DC-9-32.

Air China Boeing 747-200F.

AIR CHINA (CA)

Air China was established on 1 July 1988 following major structural reforms of the country's aviation structure which separated the airline from the administrative and regulatory functions of the Civil Aviation Administration of China (CAAC). The new airline was tasked with taking over all CAAC's international routes and domestic trunk services previously operated by the Beijing Regional Bureau. CAAC was set up in 1952 as a Chinese-Soviet undertaking known as SKOGA, to take over and expand services within China, which until then had been provided by the Central Air Transport Corporation (founded in 1931 with German capital as the Eurasia Aviation Corporation) and China National Aviation Corporation (CNAC). The new airline began operations with Lisunov Li-2s between Beijing and Hangchow, Kunming and Canton, and to Chita, Irkutsk and Alma Ata to link up with Aeroflot services to Moscow. The CAAC title was adopted in 1954 when the Soviet Union's 50 per cent holding reverted to the Chinese Government. The first long-haul route was not introduced until 1973 following the arrival of five Ilyushin Il-62 jets. The carrier operated a mix of Soviet and Western aircraft, the latter including the Vickers Viscount (from 1963), Hawker Siddeley Trident (from 1970) and the Boeing 707-320C from 1973. The fleet later became predominantly Boeing-led. Air China

acquired the status of an independent trade group on 10 December 1993, permitting it to engage in other non-airline activities.

The government-owned flag-carrier today operates passenger and cargo services to 30 cities in 23 countries on all continents except South America. An extensive domestic trunk route system is also scheduled. The airline carries 15 million passengers a year and employs more than 10,000 people.

Fleet Data
(3) Airbus A340-300, **2** Antonov An-12, **4** BAe 146-100, **19** Boeing 737-300, **3** 747-200(SCD), **1** 747-200F, **8** 747-400, **3 (2)** 747-400(SCD), **4** 747SP, **6** 767-200ER, **4** 767-300, **(5)** 777-200, **2** Lockheed L100-30 Hercules, **6** Xi'an Y7, **9** Shijiuazhuang Y5.

AIR FRANCE (AF)

The carrier was founded on 30 August 1933, when Société Centrale pour l'Exploitation de Lignes Aériennes (formed on 17 May 1933, by the merger of four French operators) purchased the bankrupt Compagnie Générale Aérospatiale. The combination resulted in a fleet of 259 aircraft comprising 35 different types. French airlines were nationalised after World War II, Société Nationale Air France being established on 1 January 1946 but succeeded by Compagnie Nationale Air France on 16 June 1948, when the carrier was incorporated by act of parliament. Air France introduced Comet 1A services on 26 August 1953 over its Paris-Rome-Beirut route, and Viscount 708 services initially between Paris and London on 15 September 1953.

The Sud-Aviation Caravelle entered service on 6 May 1959, followed on 31 January 1960 by the four-engined Boeing 707. The next 20 years marked the introduction of the

Air France Airbus A321-100.

Boeing 727 on 15 April 1968, Boeing 747 (the first wide-body aircraft) on 3 June 1970, Airbus A300 on 23 May 1974, and the Concorde supersonic airliner on 21 January 1976. The latter now only operates between Paris and New York. The success of the Airbus consortium was reflected in the acquisition by Air France of a large fleet of most models produced.

On 12 January 1990 the operations of all government-owned airlines were merged into the Air France Group. This included long-haul carrier Union de Transports Aériens (UTA), formed on 1 October 1963 through the merger of Union Aeromaritime de Transport (UAT) and Compagnie de Transports Aeriens Intercontinentaux (TAI). UTA operated mainly to West Africa and the South Pacific.

A state-owned holding company, Groupe Air France, was established in 1994, which has a 75.2 per cent share, with the remainder held by state organisations and employees. The group includes Air France, Air France Europe (formerly Air Inter and Air Inter Europe), and Air Charter.

Worldwide scheduled passenger and cargo services link France with 165 destinations on all continents. An extensive route network within Europe serves 62 cities, plus another 31 within France. Air Charter undertakes short/medium-haul charters. Air France also operates the night mail service with the Post Office under the title of L'Aeropostale.

Fleet Data
6 Concorde, **9** Airbus A300B, **9** A310-200/300, **29** A320, **3** A321-100, **5** A340-200, **7** A340-300, **(10)** A340-300E, **43** Boeing 737, **14** 747 Combi, **11** 747F, **5** B767-300, **(10)** 777-200IGW, **10** Fokker F27. Air France Europe: **13** Airbus A300B, **9** A319, **35** A320-200, **5** A321-100, **2** A330-300.

Airbus A310-300 in Air India colours.

AIR-INDIA (AI)

Air-India was formed as Air-India International on 8 March 1948 by Air-India Limited (51 per cent holding) and the Indian government (49 per cent holding) to operate international services. Air-India had started operations as Tata & Sons Limited on 15 October 1932, providing scheduled air mail services on the Karachi-Ahmedabad-Bombay-Bellary-Madras route with de Havilland Puss Moths, the carrier changing its title to Tata Airlines in January 1938. On 29 July 1946 Tata became a public company and was renamed Air-India.

Air Malta Avro RJ70.

Vickers Viking aircraft were acquired in 1947 and during that year plans were drawn up with the Indian government for the creation of Air-India International which inaugurated service on 8 June 1948 between Bombay and London, via Cairo and Geneva, with Lockheed Constellation aircraft. Following the passage of the Air Corporations Act in March 1953, Air-India International was nationalised in August 1 of that year (Air-India Limited being absorbed into the Indian Airlines Corporation).

Jet operations were inaugurated on the Bombay-London route with Boeing 707-437 aircraft on 19 April 1960. The carrier's title was abbreviated to Air-India on 8 June 1962 by an amendment to the Air Corporations Act.

Air-India currently operates a network of schedules passenger and cargo services from Mumbai (Bombay), Calcutta, Delhi, Hyderabad, Madras and Trivandrum to destinations in the Middle and Far East, Europe, Africa, Australia, the USA and Canada. Air India employs some 17,000 people and carries 2.5m passengers a year.

Fleet Data
3 Airbus A300B4-200, **9** A310-300, **7** Boeing 747-200B, **2** 747-200C, **4 (2)** 747-400.

AirLanka Airbus A340-300.

AIRLANKA (UL)

AirLanka was established on 10 January 1979 as the national carrier of Sri Lanka, replacing Air Ceylon, which ceased operations on 31 March 1978. Scheduled passenger and cargo operations from Colombo utilising Boeing 707 aircraft began on 1 September 1979 with management and technical assistance initially provided by Singapore Airlines under contract.

The government has a 60 per cent shareholding in the carrier with the remaining 40 per cent held by public companies in Sri Lanka.

AirLanka currently provides services linking Sri Lanka with Bangkok, Hong Kong, Kuala Lumpur, Tokyo, Tiruchirapalli, Trivandrum, Madras, Bombay, Male, Karachi, Dubai, Bahrain, Abu Dhabi, Fukuoka, Singapore, Delhi, Muscat, Jeddah, Riyadh, Dhahran, Kuwait, Rome, Vienna, Zürich, Paris, Frankfurt, Amsterdam and London. The carrier employs 4,000 personnel.

Fleet Data
2 Airbus A320-200, **3** A340-300, **2** Lockheed L1011 TriStar 100/50, **2** TriStar 500.

AIR MALTA (KM)

Registered by the Maltese Government with a 51 per cent stake on 30 March 1973, the new national airline began operations on 1 April 1974, using a Boeing 720B leased from Pakistan International Airlines (PIA), which took a 20per cent stake. By November 1980, the government's holding had increased to 96.4 per cent. It purchased its first 720B in 1978 and the fleet eventually reached five of the type. Having concentrated on Europe, the airline then introduced services to Australia, first in association with Singapore Airlines, then with Qantas, but these could not be sustained. The 720Bs were replaced in March 1983 with 737-200s, before a further modernisation brought the 737-300 and Airbus A320 into the fleet in the early 1990s.

Air Malta now operates a good network throughout Europe and to North Africa and the Middle East, taking in 39 cities. A helicopter service is operated between the islands of Malta and Gozo by Malta Air Charter, founded in May 1990 as a wholly-owned subsidiary. The service uses four Russian-built Mil Mi-8s. Air Malta carries 1 million passengers and employs 1,750 people.

Fleet Data
2 Airbus A320-200, **2** Boeing 737-200A, **3** 737-300, **4** Avro RJ70.

AIR NEW ZEALAND (NZ)

Air New Zealand was formed in 1939 as Tasman Empire Airways Ltd (TEAL) by the Governments of New Zealand (50 per cent), Australia (30 per cent) and the United Kingdom (20 per cent). Following delivery of two S30 Empire-class flying boats, operations commenced on 30 April, 1940, between Auckland and Sydney. The decision of the British government to withdraw from participation in the carrier in October 1953 left the New Zealand and Australian governments as sole shareholders, each with a 50 per cent holding. In July 1961 the New Zealand government took over sole ownership of TEAL in return for which Qantas was permitted to commence trans-Tasman services in competition with TEAL.

DC-8-52 aircraft entered service with TEAL on the Christchurch-Sydney route on 3 October, 1965, and the carrier adopted its present title on 1 April 1965

In 1977 the New Zealand Government decided to merge Air New Zealand with the other state owned airline New Zealand National Airways Corporation (NZNAC) and the two were amalgamated on 1 April 1978, as Air New Zealand. NZNAC had been formed as a result of an Act of Parliament in November 1945 to merge three private operators (Union Airways of New Zealand, Cook Strait Airways and Air Travel (NZ) Limited) into one national domestic airline.

Air New Zealand operates a route network encompassing 24 domestic points and international services linking Auckland and Christchurch with 28 destinations in Australasia, the Pacific, the Far East, North America and Europe. Approximately 8,250 personnel are employed by the carrier. Subsidiary companies are Air Nelson, Eagle Airways and The Mount Cook Group, which together operate under the Air New Zealand Link banner. Air New Zealand also holds a 50 per cent stake in Ansett Australia.

Fleet Data
12 Boeing 737-200A, **(5)** 737-300, 747-200B, **5 (1)** 747-400, **5** 767-200ER, **7** 767-300ER.

Air New Zealand Boeing 747-400.

ALITALIA (AZ)

Alitalia (Linee Aeree Italiane) was established in its original form as Alitalia-Aviolinee Italiane Internazionali on 16 September 1946, a joint-capital company in which the Italian government subscribed 47.5 per cent of the capital, BEA subscribed 40 per cent and the remainder came from private interests. The carrier started operations between Turin, Rome and Catonia on 5 May 1947, using Fiat G.12 aircraft leased from the air force. By 1955 Alitalia was one of only two carriers in Italy operating scheduled services, the other operator being LAI (Linee Aeree Italiane) which was formed by the Italian government and TWA in the same year as Alitalia. With the exception of the Rome-Turin route, operated by Alitalia, all domestic services were undertaken by LAI. Both carriers operated European, Mediterranean and transcontinental services. Alitalia changed its corporate designation to Alitalia-Linee Aeree Italiane and absorbed LAI in 1957.

The carrier inaugurated jet services in 1960 with the Caravelle VI-N starting on the Rome-London route on 23 May, and the DC-8-43 commencing operations on the Rome-New York route on 1 June. Alitalia currently operates an extensive worldwide scheduled network covering Europe, Africa, the Near, Middle and Far East, Australia, North and South America. An extensive domestic

Alitalia McDonnell Douglas MD-82.

network is also served.

The airline has equity interests in charter companies Eurofly (owned partly by Olivetti) and Air Europe, and in regional airline Avianova, which now operates under Alitalia Team colours. Alitalia carries more than 23 million passengers. Its staff count is 18,600.

Fleet Data
16 (14) Airbus A321-100, **10** Boeing 747-200B, **6** 767-300ER, **3** McDonnell Douglas MD-11, **5** MD-11F, **90** MD-82, **4** ATR72-210, **9** ATR42-300.

Alaska Airlines McDonnell Douglas MD-83.

ALASKA AIRLINES (AS)

The Alaskan airline has a long history, tracing its foundation to 27 November 1937 and the incorporation of Star Air Lines. On 10 November 1943, Star bought three small airlines and was renamed Star Alaska Airlines, and again on 6 June 1944 to the present title. On 24 May 1951 Alaska Airlines won the coveted Fairbanks-Anchorage-Seattle route, flown with the DC-4, and in December that same year operated the first commercial flights over the North Pole. Alaska Airlines became the first civil operator of the Lockheed Hercules in March 1965 and acquired its first jet aircraft, two Boeing 727-100s, in October and November 1966. Flights across the Bering Strait to Siberia were started in 1970 and remain in the airline's schedules. It became the launch customer of the McDonnell Douglas MD-83 twin-jet with an order for six announced in March 1983. Further orders brought the MD-83 fleet to 44. A re-organisation in 1985 saw the formation of the Alaska Air Group as a holding company, which acquired Horizon Air and Jet America. The latter was merged into Alaska Airlines in October 1987.

Alaska Airlines provides low-cost, high-frequency services over an extensive north/south route network, extending from Barrow in Alaska to Puerto Vallarta in Mexico, and including all major cities on the US Western Corridor and Toronto in Canada. It also offers trans-Bering Strait flights to Russia's Far East. Associate Horizon Air, founded in May 1981, provides scheduled services to 40 destinations on the US West Coast and to Canada, while several smaller airlines operate within Alaska under the *Alaska Airlines Commuter* banner. Annual passenger carryings amount to 9 million, and employees total 6,300.

Fleet Data
8 Boeing 737-200C, **28 (9)** 737-400, **9** McDonnell Douglas MD-82, **35** MD-83.

ALL NIPPON AIRWAYS (NH)

All Nippon Airways (ANA) has grown to become Japan's largest airline in terms of fleet size and passengers carried. ANA was founded in 1952 as the Japan Helicopter and Aeroplane Transport Company and began service between Tokyo and Osaka in December 1953 with de Havilland Dove aircraft. The carrier changed its name to All Nippon Airways in December 1957 and merged in March 1958 with Kyokuto Airlines, a domestic airline that had started operations in March 1953 flying from Osaka to points in southern Japan. In spite of strong competition from Japan Air Lines and railway transportation, ANA experienced vigorous growth and rapid expansion in

All Nippon Airways Boeing 767-300.

America West Boeing 737-300.

domestic travel, and in November 1963 the carrier absorbed Fujita Airlines, followed by Central Japan Airlines in 1965 and Nagasaki Airways in 1967. Jet services with a 727 aircraft leased from Boeing were introduced between Tokyo and Sapporo in May 1964. A number of routes were transferred to Nihon Kinkyori Airways (now Air Nippon), a third-level operator formed in March 1974 by Japan Air Lines, ANA, Toa Domestic and other Japanese airlines to operate government-subsidized feeder services to isolated communities and remote mainland destinations. Another associate is Nippon Cargo Airlines (formerly Nippon Air Cargo), which was formed in September 1978 to operate scheduled cargo services with Boeing 747-200Fs.

ANA currently employs 13,600 personnel and operates a scheduled passenger and cargo network covering 70 domestic and operated to destinations which include Beijing, Hong Kong, Shanghai, Sydney, Dalian, Kuala Lumpur, Brisbane, Manila and Singapore, and in 1986 ANA inaugurated its first intercontinental scheduled operations with services to Los Angeles and Washington, DC. London, Moscow, New York, Paris, Rome and Vienna have since been added. In 1996 ANA carried 39.8 million passengers, nearly 37m on domestic services.

Fleet Data
23 Airbus A320-200, **(7)** A321, **(5)** A340-300, **14** Boeing 747SR, **6** 747-200LR, **18 (2)** 747-400, **25** 767-200, **40** 767-300, **6 (10)** 777-200, **(10)** 777-300.

AMERICAN AIRLINES (AA)

American Airlines was formed in May 1934 as a successor to American Airways, which had been established in 1930 by the Aviation Corporation (AVCO) to unify the operations of the five operators under AVCO's control. These operators in turn had succeeded many pioneer air operators with roots stretching back to 1926. American represented the conglomeration of 85 original companies. The carrier was heavily dependent upon air mail business in the early 1930s, and sponsored development of the DC-3 aircraft in order to develop passenger operations.

Since World War II American has been responsible for sponsoring the design of a number of significant commercial aircraft, including the Convair 240 and 990, Douglas DC-7 and DC-10, and Lockheed Electra. From 1945 American operated a transatlantic division, American Overseas Airlines, to serve a number of European countries, but this division was sold to Pan American in September 1950. American began nonstop transcontinental service with DC-7 aircraft between New York and Los

American Airlines MD-11.

Angeles on 29 November 1953. Jet operations with the first of many 707 aircraft began on the same route on 25 January 1959.

The carrier became the largest customer for the BAC One-Eleven aircraft which entered service on American's short-haul routes in March 1966. The world's first DC-10 service was operated by American between Los Angeles and Chicago, on 5 August 1971. In the same year American absorbed Trans Caribbean Airways and began flying to Caribbean destinations. Aircal was acquired in 1986.

American Airlines is today one of the world's largest airlines, operating an extensive domestic network with hubs at Dallas/Fort Worth, Chicago, Miami and San Juan, together with four subsidiaries operating under the *American Eagle* banner. International schedules are flown to Canada, Mexico, the Caribbean, South America, Japan and Europe. American Airlines carries more than 80m passengers a year and employs 86,000 people.

Fleet Data
35 Airbus A300-600R, **81** Boeing 727-200A, **(75)** 737-600/700/800, **90 (12)** 757-200, **8** 767-200, **22** 767-200ER, **41 (4)** 767-300ER, **(12)** 777-200, **75** Fokker 100, **16** McDonnell Douglas DC-10-10, **4** DC-10-30, **17** MD-11, **250** MD-82, **10** MD-83.

American Trans Air Lockheed L1011 Tristar.

AMERICAN TRANS AIR (TZ)

This leisure airline was established in August 1973, initially to provide contract flying for the Ambassadair Travel Club, first with Boeing 720s, then from 1980 with 707-120Bs. The acquisition of its own charter certificate in March 1981 led to period of rapid expansion, which culminated in 1985 with the purchase of nine Lockheed TriStars, making American Trans Air the biggest charter airline in the United States. The fleet was modernised with new Boeing 757-200s in the early 1990s, which enabled the airline to enter the scheduled passenger market with low-fare leisure routes to Florida, Arizona and Nevada.

The airline today provides scheduled services for leisure travellers from Boston, Chicago, Milwaukee and Philadelphia to several points in Florida, and to Las Vegas, Nevada and Phoenix, Arizona. A strong charter-only business serves leisure destinations in the United States, the Caribbean and across the Atlantic to Europe. The airline is owned by AmTran Corporation and carries 4.5 million passengers a year. It employs 2,750 people.

Fleet Data
24 Boeing 727-200A, **8 (2)** 757-200, **4** Lockheed L1011 TriStar 1, **11** L1011 TriStar 50.

AMERICA WEST AIRLINES (HP)

America West Airlines, a low-fare regional airline with headquarters in Phoenix, Arizona, was incorporated in September 1981 and commenced scheduled operations on 1 August 1983 with three Boeing 737 aircraft and 280 employees. Initially serving Colorado Springs, Kansas City, Los Angeles, Phoenix and Wichita, America West now operates on extensive hub and spoke system centred on Phoenix Sky Harbor International Airport, Las Vegas' McCarran International and a mini-hub at Columbus, Ohio, serving 90 cities and communities in 36 states and the District of Columbia, as well as points in Canada and Mexico. Feeder services are provided by Mountain West Airlines and Desert Sun Airlines under the title of America West Express. The airline carries more than 20m passengers and employs 11,000 staff.

Fleet Data
25 Airbus A320-200, **21** Boeing 737-200, **40** 737-300, **14** 757-200.

ANSETT AUSTRALIA (AN)

The carrier was originally formed in February 1936 as Ansett Airways Limited by R.M. Ansett. Operations commenced between Melbourne and Hamilton using a Fokker Universal. By 1939 Ansett was operating additional routes from Melbourne to Adelaide, Broken Hill and Sydney. In late 1945 Ansett acquired three C-47s and extended its network to Hobart and Brisbane. Barrier Reef Airways, which operated seaplane routes radiating from Brisbane to Sydney, Hayman Island and Townsville, was taken over in 1952, and additional routes from Sydney were acquired from the bankrupt Trans Oceanic Airways during the following year. Convair 340 and 440 aircraft were subsequently introduced to provide low-fare services between state capitals in competition with Trans-Australia Airlines (TAA) and Australian National Airways (ANA).

Then parent company Ansett Transport Industries (ATI) succeeded in 1957 in

Ansett Airbus A320-200.

purchasing ANA to form Ansett-ANA on 4 October that year. ANA's network stretched through Sydney and Melbourne to Tasmania and across West Australia to Perth. ANA name was dropped in June 1969 in favour of Ansett Airlines of Australia. In 1959, Ansett had also purchased South Pacific Airlines and renamed it Ansett of New Zealand.

Ansett inaugurated Lockheed Electra turboprop services between Sydney and Melbourne on 10 March 1959, and Boeing 727-77 aircraft initiated jet services on 2 November 1964.

In 1980, the airline was taken over by Rupert Murdoch's News Limited, with the other shares acquired by TNT, since sold to Air New Zealand. International services were inaugurated on 11 September 1993 with a flight to Bali. Ansett today operates throughout Australia from main hubs at Sydney, Melbourne and Perth. Also flies regional and international services to Bali, Hong Kong, Jakarta, Kuala Lumpur and Osaka. Associate companies are Ansett New Zealand, Skywest Airlines, Kendell Airlines and Aeropelican.

Fleet Data
20 Airbus A320-200, **7** BAe 146-200, **5** 146-300, **1** 727-200F, **22** 737-300, **3** 747-300, **8** 767-200, **7** Fokker 50, **13** F.28.

AUSTRIAN AIRLINES (OS)

Austrian Airlines (Österreichische Luftverkehrs AG) was founded on 30 September 1957, by a merger of Air Austria and Austrian Airways, which had been formed but had not started operations. The nation's previous operator, ÖLAG, had been incorporated into Deutsche Luft Hansa in 1938, and after cessation of hostilities in 1945 the Allies did not permit civil aviation activities until the State Treaty was signed in 1945. Austrian inaugurated services on 31 March 1958 between Vienna and London using chartered Viscount 779 aircraft. Jet services were introduced with Caravelle VI-Rs on 20 February 1963 to cope with the carrier's fast-growing European route system. Austrian operated its first domestic service with DC-3 on May 1 of that year.

DC-9 aircraft were progressively introduced from 19 June 1971, and on 30 October 1977 Austrian become one of the

195

launch customers for the MD-80, which began service with them in October 1980.

Embarked on a fleet renewal which included acquisition of the latest Airbus aircraft starting with the A310-300, which entered service between Vienna and New York on 26 March 1989. The airline now serves 80 cities in 45 countries throughout Europe and to the Middle and Far East, North America and South Africa. Austrian Airlines owns 80 per cent of charter subsidiary Austrian Air Transport (AAT), and has a 42.85 per cent stake in Tyrolean Airways, 35.9 per cent in Lauda Air, and 18.37 per cent in Ukraine International Airlines (UIA).

Fleet Data
4 Airbus A310-300, **(7)** A320-200,
3 (3) A321-100, **(4)** A330-200,
1 (1) A340-300, **2** A340-200,
17 McDonnell Douglas MD-80, **5** Fokker 70.

Austrian Airlines Airbus A321-100.

AVIANCA (AV)

Avianca is the oldest airline in the Americas, and has the longest unbroken record of scheduled operations in the world. The carrier was founded on 5 December 1919, under the name of Sociedad Colombo-Alemana de Transportes Aereos (SCADTA) by a group of German and Colombian businessmen. Scheduled operations began in September 1921 with services between the capital Bogota, and the northerly port of Barranquilla using Junkers F13 seaplanes. Pan American acquired an 80 per cent shareholding in the carrier in 1931 and in June 1940 SCADTA merged with Servicio Aereo Colombiano, a small domestic airline established in 1933, adopting the current name Avianca. Several domestic operators were taken over between 1941 and 1952, including in September 1951 Lineas Aereas Nacionales (LANSA), an operator serving all major points in Colombia and also Caracas.

Boeing 707-121 aircraft leased from Pan American enabled Avianca to initiate jet services to Miami and New York in October 1960 before the carrier took delivery of Boeing 720B aircraft. Pan American's remaining shareholding was purchased by Avianca in 1978.

Employing some 3,400 personnel, Avianca currently operates a large domestic network from Bogota, and international services to London, Madrid, Paris and Frankfurt in Europe; to Miami, New York and Los Angeles in North America; and to major points in Central and South America. Sociedad Aeronautica de Medellin Consolidad SA (SAM), a scheduled operator, and Helicopteros Nacionales de Colombia SA (Helicol) are wholly-owned subsidiaries.

Avianca Boeing 767-200ER.

Fleet Data
2 Boeing 727-200A, **3** 757-200,
2 767-200ER, **1** 767-300ER, **10** Fokker 50,
11 McDonnell Douglas MD-88.

BALKAN BULGARIAN AIRLINES (LZ)

Bulgaria's national carrier was originally formed by the government as Bulgarshe Vazdusne Sobstenie and domestic operations began on 29 July 1947. In 1949, the carrier became a joint Bulgarian-Soviet enterprise known as TABSO (Bulgarian-Soviet Joint Stock Company for Civil Aviation, or Bulgarian Civil Air Transport as it was also known). The Soviet Union's half-interest in TABSO was bought out in 1954 and the carrier became wholly Bulgarian-owned although the title was retained until 1968.

Lisunov Li-2 aircraft were supplemented by Ilyushin Il-14s and a number of international services to European capitals were initiated. The introduction of Ilyushin Il-18 aircraft in 1962 enabled the carrier to develop services to Algiers and Tunis, and charters to Black Sea holiday resorts. Bulair was formed in 1968 as a division of the carrier to undertake passenger and cargo operations with IL-12 and An-12 aircraft leased from BALKAN Bulgarian. Bulair was integrated with the parent carrier in 1972. Jet services were inaugurated with Tupolev Tu-134 aircraft in 1968. Began transition to Western equipment in 1990 with lease of two Boeing 737-500s.

BALKAN Bulgarian currently operates a network of scheduled passenger and cargo services covering 52 destinations in Europe, North America, Africa and Asia as well as three domestic points.

Fleet Data
3 Antonov An-12F, **14** An-24V, **3** Boeing 737-500, **2** 767-200ER, **2** Ilyushin Il-18D, **4** Il-18V, **5** Tupolev Tu-134A-3, **15** Tu-154B-2, **7** Tu-154M.

Balkan Ilyushin Il-18V.

BIMAN BANGLADESH (BG)

Biman Bangladesh was formed on 4 January 1972 as the national airline of the People's Republic of Bangladesh. Scheduled services began on 4 February of that year on domestic routes linking Dhaka, Chittagong, Sythet and Jessore using a DC-3 aircraft. Leased Fokker F27 aircraft were

Biman Airbus A310-300.

subsequently used, and wet-leased Boeing 707 equipment opened up a service to London on January 1, 1973.
First wide-body aircraft, the McDonnell Douglas DC-10-30, was delivered in August 1983, and the latest fleet re-equipment programme was started in 1996 with the delivery of two Airbus A310s. The government-owned flag-carrier now serves 27 international points in 21 countries, regionally and to the Middle East, Europe and the United States. A seven-point domestic network is also flown.

Fleet Data
2 Airbus A310-300, **2** BAe ATP,
2 Fokker F.28-4000, **4** McDonnell Douglas DC-10-30.

BRITANNIA AIRWAYS (BY)

The Luton-based UK charter airline was formed on 1 December 1961 by Universal Sky Tours under the name of Euravia (London) and began flying inclusive tours with two Lockheed Constellations on 5 May 1962. The first flight operated between Manchester and Palma de Mallorca. Six more Constellations were quickly added to the fleet, but the name was changed to the present in 1964 when the airline re-equipped with Bristol Britannia turboprop aircraft, which entered service on 6 December. The airline became part of the Thomson Organisation on 26 April 1965. It achieved a number of European firsts, including becoming the first charter airline to operate the Boeing 737-200, taking delivery of the first aircraft on 8 July 1968, and the first to operate the 767-200 in February 1984. Horizon Travel, and its East Midlands-based airline Orion Airways, were taken over in August 1988. A major fleet review was initiated in the early 1990s, which resulted in the standardisation on the Boeing 757 and 767, with the last 737 leaving the fleet in 1994.

Britannia Airways claims to be the world's largest inclusive-tour charter airline, carrying 8 million passengers a year. It serves over

Britannia Airways Boeing 767-300ER.

100 regular destinations throughout Europe and the Mediterranean Basin, together with long-haul flights to the Maldives, India, South Africa, Australia, New Zealand, Canada, the United States, Mexico and the Caribbean.

Fleet Data
14 Boeing 757-200, **5** 757-200ER,
6 767-200ER, **7** 767-300ER.

BRITISH AIRWAYS (BA)

British Airways was formed on 1 September 1972 through the amalgamation of British Overseas Airways Corporation (BOAC), BOAC Associated Companies, BOAC Engine Overhauls, British European Airways Corporation (BEA), BEA Airtours, BEA Helicopters, Northeast Airlines, Cambrian Airways and International Aeradio which were brought together under the British Airways Group established by the 1971 Civil Aviation Act.

BEA had been formed on 1 August 1946, as a nationalised concern to take over the European routes operated by BOAC's British European Airways division and to absorb a number of British domestic airlines. BEA introduced the world's first turboprop service on April 1953, with Viscount 701 aircraft between London and Nicosia, and began jet operations with Comet 4Bs in April 1960. BOAC was formed as a result of an act of parliament which provided for the acquisition and amalgamation of Imperial Airways (formed on 31 March 1924) and the pre-war British Airways (established in 1935) on 1 April 1940. BOAC took over British South American Airways on 30 July 1949, and became the world's first commercial jet operator when services with the Comet 1 were inaugurated between London and Johannesburg on 2 May 1952.

After problems with the Comet were solved following two catastrophes, the airline inaugurated the first trans-Atlantic jet service between London and New York with the improved Comet 4. Up to the 1970s, both BOAC and BEA operated mostly British aircraft, before switching almost entirely to Boeing types, beginning with the 747 in May 1970. On 21 January 1976, British Airways began supersonic services with Concorde to Bahrain. The year 1987 saw the controversial take-over of British Caledonian Airways (B.Cal) (formed as Caledonian Airways in April 1961), and a highly successful privatisation.

British Airways today operates the world's largest global passenger network linking the UK with 170 cities in 80 countries on all continents. It also operates a comprehensive domestic route system, including 'Super Shuttle' services from London to Manchester, Glasgow, Edinburgh, Belfast and Newcastle. Major equity stakes are held in Brymon European Airways (100 per cent), TAT European Airlines (100 per cent), Air Liberté (67 per cent), Deutsche BA (49 per cent) and Qantas (25 per cent), and the airline

British Airways Boeing 747-400.

also has non-equity franchise agreements with several regional airlines. British Airways carries more than 33 million passengers and employs some 53,000 people.

Fleet Data
7 Concorde, 10 BAe ATP, 39 Boeing 737-200A, 33 737-400, 15 747-100, 16 747-200B, 31 (32) 747-400, 44 (3) 757-200, 25 (3) 767-300ER, 7 (16) 777-200, 8 McDonnell Douglas DC-10-30.

British Midland Fokker 70.

BRITISH MIDLAND AIRWAYS (BD)

British Midland was formed on 16 February 1949 as Derby Aviation, although it can trace its history back still further to Air Schools of 1938. Charters only were flown until 18 July 1953 when it began scheduled services from Derby to Jersey with the de Havilland DH.89A Dragon Rapide. It changed its name to Derby Airways on 12 March 1959, then to British Midland on 1 October 1964. Several British aircraft were introduced into the fleet, including the Handley Page Herald, Vickers Viscount and BAC One-Eleven 500, and the airline also ventured into long-haul inclusive-tour operations with Boeing 707-320s. On 25 October 1982, it inaugurated a low-fare London Heathrow-Glasgow service in competition with British Airways' Shuttle, adding London-Edinburgh in March 1983, before beginning its expansion into Europe with a service to Amsterdam in 1986. In November 1982 it had launched Manx Airlines with Air UK and acquired a controlling interest in Scottish airline Loganair. SAS took a 24.5 per cent stake, later increased to 40 per cent, in newly set up holding company Airlines of Britain.

British Midland, 'The Airline of Europe' as it styles itself, operates a comprehensive domestic network and services to 12 points in Europe. Although based at East Midlands Airport near Derby, many of its services operate out of London Heathrow, where it is now is the second-largest carrier after British Airways. In 1996, it carried 7.7 million passengers and employed 4,200 staff. The operations of subsidiaries Loganair (now part of British Regional Airlines) and Manx Airlines have been restructured and de-merged. Another Scottish airline, Business Air, continues under its own name.

Fleet Data
(12) Airbus A320-200, (8) A321, 7 Boeing 737-300, 6 737-400, 11 737-500, 3 Fokker 70, 6 Fokker 100, 6 Saab 340A, 2 340B.

CANADIAN AIRLINES INTERNATIONAL (CP)

Canada's second airline was formed as Canadian Pacific Airlines (later simply known as CP Air) on 31 January 1942 through the purchase and amalgamation of 10 small independent operators by Canadian Pacific Railways. These had been operating primarily isolated northern routes, but in late 1948, CPAL was awarded its first international route from Vancouver to Sydney, via Honolulu, Fiji and Auckland. Services started on 13 July 1949 with the Canadair DC-4M North Star. In 1959, the airline was finally successful in securing its first transcontinental route, from Vancouver to Winnipeg, Toronto and Montreal in competition with TCA (now Air Canada), and services commenced on 4 May that year with Bristol Britannias. Long-haul jet services were introduced with the DC-8-43 in 1961. On 27 March 1987, CP Air amalgamated with Eastern Provincial Airways, Nordair and Pacific Western Airlines (PWA) to form Canadian Airlines International. PWA had been formed on 1 July 1945 and had become Canada's third-largest airline through a series of acquisitions, operating a large fleet of

Canadian Airlines International 767-300ER.

Boeing 737-200s and three 767-200s at the time of the merger. Eastern Provincial came into being in 1949 and Nordair in 1957. After the merger the fleet was standardised on the 737-200 and McDonnell Douglas DC-10-30, before being modernised with the addition of 767-300s, 747-400s and Airbus A320s. Parent company PWA Corporation acquired Wardair Canada in 1989. AMR Corporation, parent of American Airlines, acquired an equity investment in the airline in April 1994.

Canadian Airlines international today serves over 150 cities in 18 countries on five continents. Together with its *Canadian Partner* associates, it serves another 110 communities within Canada. Total passengers amount to more than 11 million a year. Employees total 15,500.

Fleet Data
12 (10) Airbus A320-200, 46 Boeing 737-200A, 9 737-200C, 4 747-400, 11 767-300ER, 4 McDonnell Douglas DC-10-30, 5 DC-10-30ER.

CATHAY PACIFIC AIRWAYS (CX)

Cathay Pacific was founded on 24 September 1946, and initial operations consisted of freight and passenger services between Asia and Australia and charter flights to the United Kingdom using DC-3 aircraft. In 1948 the Swire Group became the major shareholder and manager of the carrier with Australian National Airways (later absorbed by Ansett Airlines of Australia) as a minority shareholder. By the end of that year Cathay Pacific operated seven DC-3 aircraft and two Catalina flying-boats on scheduled services from Hong Kong to Manila, Bangkok, Singapore and Rangoon. A DC-4 aircraft was introduced in 1949 to operate the Singapore route and open new services to Saigon, Haiphong and North Borneo. In 1959 the carrier acquired Hong Kong Airways giving Cathay access to northern routes including Japan. Jet service was introduced in 1962 when the first of nine Convair 880-22M aircraft was delivered.

The airline became an all-jet operator from February 1967 and added wide-body TriStars on 2 September 1975. A major $9 billion fleet modernisation programme was put in hand in the 1990s. Some ownership changes were effected prior to Hong Kong's handover to China at midnight on 30 June 1997, reducing Swire Pacific's stake to 43.9 per cent. Other major shareholders are CITIC with 25 per cent, and China Travel Service and CNAC, both with 5.01 per cent. Cathay Pacific operates scheduled passenger and cargo services to 44 destinations in 27 countries in the Far East, Australasia, Europe, Africa and North America. Major points in China are served through associate Dragonair. In 1996,

Cathay Pacific Airbus A330-300.

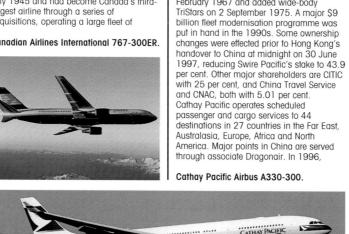

Cathay Pacific carries close to 11 million passengers and 568,000 tonnes of cargo, and employs 13,800 people.

Fleet Data
11 (2) Airbus A330-300, 2 A340-200, 6 (4) A340-300, 7 Boeing 747-200B, 7 747-200F, 6 747-300, 19 747-400, 2 747-400F, 4 777-200, (7) 777-300.

China Airlines Boeing 747-400.

CHINA AIRLINES (CI)

China Airlines Ltd (CAL) was founded by a group of retired Taiwanese air force officers on 19 December 1959, and began charter operations with two PBY Catalina amphibious aircraft. Cargo operations were subsequently initiated and various additional activities undertaken, including fishery patrol, insecticide spraying and aerial photography. Scheduled domestic services were inaugurated in October 1962 between Taipei and Taichung, and subsequently to Hualien, Tainan, Makung and Koohsiung, for which DC-3, DC-4 and C-46 aircraft were acquired. CAL became the national carrier of Taiwan in 1965, and a year later initiated its first international service between Taipei and Saigon (now Ho Chi Minh City). Jet operations were inaugurated following delivery of CAL's first Boeing 727-100 aircraft on 3 March 1967. Following suspension of all domestic operations by Civil Air Transport (CAT) in 1968, CAL took over CAT's traffic rights to enhance its domestic system. NAMC YS-11A turboprop aircraft entered service with the carrier in 1970 on short-haul routes, and in February of that year CAL inaugurated service to San Francisco via Tokyo with a Boeing 707-309C. Direct flights to the USA were initiated in April 1977 using Boeing 747SPs.

China Airlines became the first operator of the Boeing 767 in Asia, introducing the type between Taipei and Bangkok on 1 January 1983, and that same year expanded operations into Europe with a cargo service to Luxembourg, followed by a passenger flight to Amsterdam. Initiated a major fleet re-equipment programme in the late 1980s with orders for Boeing 747-400s, Airbus A300-600Rs and McDonnell Douglas MD-11s, all delivered between 1990 and 1994. China Airlines now provides international flag services to 29 cities, regionally and to Australia, the Middle East, Europe and North America. Domestic flights are scheduled on the main Taipei-Kaohsiung trunk route. In 1996, it carried 7 million passengers and 333,000 tonnes of cargo. Employees totalled 5,900. Mandarin Airlines is a wholly-owned subsidiary, and China Airlines also owns 33 per cent of Formosa Airlines and 10 per cent of Far Eastern Air Transport.

Fleet Data
8 Airbus A300-600R, 6 A300B4-200, 6 737-400, (6) 737-800, 3 747-200B, 8 747-200F, 4 747-400, 3 747SP, 4 McDonnell Douglas MD-11.

CHINA EASTERN AIRLINES (MU)

China Eastern is a product of the re-organisation of China's civil aviation industry and was established on 25 June 1988, based on the Civil Aviation Administration of China's (CAAC) Shanghai Administration. It was authorised to fly on the Japan and US markets and inaugurated a Shanghai-Los Angeles service in May

China Eastern Airbus A300-600R.

1991, followed by expansion into Europe. Fleet modernisation followed with Western aircraft, the airline taking delivery of 10 Airbus A300-600R between 1989 and 1994, six McDonnell Douglas MD-11 (including one MD-11F freighter) between 1991 and 1993, and 10 Fokker 100 between 1992 and 1993. Deliveries of locally-assembled McDonnell Douglas MD-82 twinjets started in late 1987. China Eastern became the first customer for the long-range Airbus A340-300 with an order for five aircraft placed in 1991. The status of the airline was changed to an autonomous aviation enterprise group in October 1993, clearing the way for a planned flotation on the Shanghai, Hong Kong and New York stock exchanges, and eventually complete privatisation.

China's second largest Government-owned airline now operates domestic trunk routes to 43 cities in China, together with fast-expanding regional and international network, extending as far as Brussels and Madrid in Europe, and Chicago, Los Angeles and Seattle in the United States. Munich is the likely next terminus in Europe to access Central Europe and the Commonwealth of Independent States (CIS) countries. The airline is responsible for its share of general aviation activities, including agricultural spraying with locally-built aircraft. Main base is located at Shanghai, with important operating branches at Jinan (Shandong province), Nanchang (Jianxi) and Hefei (Anhui). Annual passenger figures exceed 6 million. Employees total 8,800.

Fleet Data
10 Airbus A300-600R, **5** A310-300,
4 (4) A340-300, **10** Fokker 100, **5** McDonnell Douglas MD-11, **1** MD-11F,
2 MD-82, **(9)** MD-90-30,
11 McDonnell Douglas (SAIC) MD-82,
18 Shijiazhuang Y5, **6** Xi'an Y7-100.

CHINA SOUTHERN AIRLINES (CZ)

The Government-owned airline emerged on 1 February 1991 from the CAAC Guangzhou Regional Administration, completing the regional reform of China's air transport system. China Southern developed a regional network, in addition to extensive domestic flights, with the acquisition of Western aircraft, focusing on the Boeing 737, first delivered in 1991; the 757-200, which had joined the fleet under the CAAC regime during 1987; and six new 767-300ER, delivered between October 1992 and May 1994. It became the only airline in China to order the Boeing 777, with a contract for six 777-200 models signed in December 1992, which replaced an order for the Airbus A340, confirming airline's preference for an all-Boeing fleet. Along with Air China and China Eastern, its status was changed to autonomous aviation enterprise group in October 1993.

Fast-growing China Southern operates an extensive domestic network in southern and eastern China, radiating from its main base at Guangzhou's Baiyun International Airport, and from branch operations in Hubei, Hunan, Guangxi, Guangdong and Hainan provinces. A growing regional network presently takes in Bangkok, Hanoi, Ho Chi Minh City, Hong Kong, Jakarta, Kuala Lumpur, Manila, Penang, Singapore and Vientiane, and long-haul routes are under consideration. The airline is also involved in general aviation work, which forms an important part of its activities. It carries more than 12 million passengers a year and employs some 12,000 people. Associate Xiamen Airlines (MF), 60 per cent owned, provides a domestic network from Xiamen to 28 cities, together with flights to Hong Kong.

Fleet Data
2 (18) Airbus A320-200, **2** Bell 214ST,
23 Boeing 737-300, **11** 737-500,
20 757-200, **3** 767-300ER,
5 (4) 777-200, **2** Eurocopter SA 365N Dauphin II, **4** Saab 340B,
20 Shijiazhuang Y5, **3** Sikorsky S-76A.

China Southern Airlines Airbus A320-200.

CONTINENTAL AIRLINES (CO)

Continental's history can be traced to Varney Speed Lines (South West Division) which inaugurated passenger and air mail service on 15 July 1943 from El Paso to Pueblo with Lockheed Vegas. The carrier adopted its present title on 1 July 1937 and acquired Pioneer Airlines at the end of 1954 which gave Continental access to Pioneer's extensive network in Texas and New Mexico. On 1 May 1957 service was inaugurated between Chicago and Los Angeles via Kansas City and Denver using DC-7B aircraft, marking Continental's full transition to a mainline trunk carrier. Viscount 812 aircraft entered service between Chicago and Los Angeles on 26 May 1958, and Boeing 707-124s began jet operations for Continental on 8 June 1959.

In October 1981 Texas Air Corp, parent company of Texas International Airlines, acquired a controlling interest in Continental and the operations of the two airlines were combined on 31 October 1982 to form a single carrier under the name Continental. Low-cost carrier PeopleExpress was taken over in 1980, together with affiliates Frontier Airlines and Britt Airways. The last-named, plus Bar Harbor Airlines and Rocky

Continental Boeing 737-300.

Mountain Airways, were combined into the Continental Express feeder subsidiary in August 1990. Continental Airways has a 17.7 per cent stake in America West, and is itself owned 27.5 per cent by Air Canada.

After overcoming severe financial difficulties, which resulted in three periods under Chapter 11 bankruptcy protection, Continental Airlines is now back in profit. It is now the fifth-largest airline in the US, serving 137 domestic and 58 international destinations throughout the Americas, the Far East and Europe. Continental Micronesia, owned jointly with the United Micronesia Development Association, links the US Trust Territory of the Pacific, and also flies to Hong Kong and Japan.

Fleet Data
31 Boeing 727-200A, **12** 737-100,
18 737-200, **65** 737-300LR,
37 (18) 737-500, **(30)** 737-600,
(18) 737-700, **(30)** 737-800,
2 747-200B, **(8)** 757-200,
(12) 767-300ER, **5** 777-200,
30 McDonnell Douglas DC-9-30,
7 DC-10-10, **16** DC-10-30, **7** MD-81,
58 MD-82, **2** MD-83.

CSA CZECH AIRLINES (OK)

Ceskoslovenske Aerolinie (CSA), the national airline of the Czech Republic, was originally formed on 29 July 1923 as Ceskoslovenske Statni Aerolinie. The carrier operated in competition with the privately-owned Ceskoslovenske Letecka Spolecnost (CLS) formed in 1927. The two carriers were absorbed into Deutsche Luft Hansa during World War II. The present carrier came into being on 1 March 1946, and began domestic and international operations with DC-3 aircraft. CSA was nationalised by the Communist government in 1949.

Jet operations began in 1957 with the

CSA Czech Airlines Airbus A310-300.

delivery of Tupolev Tu-104A aircraft, which inaugurated the first jet link between Prague and Moscow on 9 December of that year. In 1959 CSA became the first Communist carrier to operate international services outside Europe with the opening of a route to Bombay via Cairo and Bahrain. Ilyushin Il-62 operations were started with the lease of one aircraft from Aeroflot in May 1968 before the delivery of CSA's own Il-62s, and a service to New York via Amsterdam and Montreal with the type was inaugurated on 4 May 1970. In January 1976 CSA took over the third-level domestic operations of Slov-Air, which was originally formed in 1969.

Began process of replacing Soviet aircraft with Western types, starting with Airbus A310s in 1991. This process is almost complete, with only a few Tupolev Tu-134As and Tu-154Ms remaining. The airline changed to the present title on 26 March 1995, following the break-up of the Czechoslovak federation on 1 January 1993. CSA Czech Airlines serves 57 international destinations in Europe, the Middle and Far East and North America, carrying 1.75 million passengers. Employee strength is 3,900.

Fleet Data
2 Airbus A310-300, **2** ATR42-400,
4 ATR72-200, **4 (2)** Boeing 737-400,
7 (3) 737-500, **3** Tupolev Tu-134As,
4 Tu-154M.

CYPRUS AIRWAYS (CY)

Cyprus Airways was jointly formed on 24 September 1947 by BEA (now part of British Airways), with a 40 per cent holding and the Cyprus government (40 per cent), the remaining 20 per cent being held by private interests. The airline commenced operations on 6 October 1947 between Nicosia and Athens, with BEA operating the services until April 1948 when the airline acquired its own equipment, namely three DC-3 aircraft. BOAC acquired a 23 per cent interest in Cyprus Airways in 1950 and BEA took over all the airline's operation in February 1958. BOAC sold its shareholding to the Cyprus government in June 1959.

Jet services were inaugurated with BEA Comet 4B aircraft on 4 July 1961. The airline acquired its own jet aircraft with the delivery of the first two Trident 2E aircraft on 19 September 1969. All operations were suspended following the Turkish invasion of Cyprus in July 1974. Cyprus Airways recommenced operations in 1975 with services between Larnaca and Athens, and Beirut and Tel Aviv, using leased equipment. Fleet was modernised in the 1980s with the acquisition of Airbus A310 and A320 aircraft. In 1992, the airline set up EuroCypria Airlines, to obtain a greater share of holiday charter traffic into the island.

The airline currently serves 26 destinations in Europe and the Middle East, and employs over 1,800 personnel. Cyprus Airways is owned by the Cyprus government and local interests.

Fleet Data
4 Airbus A310-200; 8 A320-200.

Cyprus Airways Airbus A310-200.

DELTA AIR LINES (DL)

Delta was formed in 1925 as Huff Daland Dusters, the world's first crop dusting company. The carrier initially started passenger operations in 1929 between Birmingham (Alabama) and Dallas with a subsequent extension to Atlanta. Delta merged with Chicago and Southern Air Lines (founded in 1933) on 1 May 1953 and inaugurated jet services with DC-8 aircraft on 18 September 1959. In May 1960 Delta became the first airline to operate the Convair 880 and Delta premiered DC-9 service in December 1965. Northeast Airlines was acquired on 1 August 1972.

International growth started on 30 April 1978 with an Atlanta-London Gatwick route, flown with the TriStar 500. In April 1987, it acquired Los Angeles-based Western Airlines, incorporated on 13 July 1925 as Western Air Express, giving Delta valuable access to the US West Coast and completing its national network. New aircraft delivered in the last 10 years, including the McDonnell Douglas MD-11, MD-90 and MD-88, were backed up by new routes acquired from the defunct Eastern Air Lines, and Pan American (since reformed).

Delta operates the world's third-largest airline network, serving 197 cities in 26 countries, including a domestic feeder network operated by four regional airlines under the *Delta Connection* title. Delta carries nearly 90 million passengers a year and employs 59,000 staff.

Fleet Data
132 Boeing 727-200A, 54 737-200A, 13 737-300, (70) 737-600/700/800. 86 (5) 757-200, 15 767-200, 26 767-300, 26 (17) 767-300ER, (21) 767-400ERX, 55 Lockheed L1011 TriStar, 14 (1) McDonnell Douglas MD-11, 120 MD-88, 20 (11) MD-90-30.

Delta Air Lines.

EGYPTAIR (MS)

Egyptair was originally formed as Misr Airwork in May 1932 by the Misr Bank and Airwork Limited, London. The company began domestic operations in July 1933 between Cairo, Alexandria and Mersa Matruh with D.H.84 Dragons. By the end of the year Asyut, Luxor and Aswan were also served and in 1934 the carrier's first international route, to Lydda and Haifa, was opened, followed by services to Baghdad and Cyprus in 1936. After World War II, Misrair entered a period of rapidly expanding operations with the emphasis on new Middle East destinations. In 1949 it became completely Egyptian-owned, and the title was changed to Misrair SAE. On 1 January 1961 the carrier merged with Syrian Airways to form United Arab Airlines (UAA), following the union of Syria and Egypt in 1958. Syria withdrew during 1961, and the two carriers became independent once again, though the Egyptian carrier retained the UAA name.

Jet operations were started on 16 July 1960 with Comet 4C aircraft. The carrier adopted its present title on October 10, 1971, following the country's change of title to the Arab Republic of Egypt.

Since then, the fleet has been progressively modernised, first with Boeing types, including the 737, 747 and 767, then with Airbuses. The airline remains firmly under government control and provides flag services throughout the Middle East, and to the Far East, Africa, Europe and the United States. A domestic network is provided to 11 points, including all the tourist destinations. Egyptair has a 50 per cent stake with Kuwait Airways in charter airline Shorouk Air.

Fleet Data
9 Airbus A300-600R, 3 A300B4-200, 7 A320-200, (4) A321, 3 A340-200, 1 Boeing 707-320C, 5 737-500, 2 747-300(SCD), 3 767-200ER, 2 767-300ER, (3) 777-200.

EgyptAir Airbus A340-200.

EL AL ISRAEL AIRLINES (LY)

EL AL was founded on 15 November 1948 as the country's national carrier. EL AL's inaugural flight took place between Geneva and Tel Aviv in September of that year, and scheduled commercial services started in July 1949 to Paris and Rome using Curtiss C-46 and DC-4 aircraft. Service to Johannesburg was started in 1950 and three Constellations were acquired in that year, initiating a Tel Aviv-London-New York route on 16 May 1951. Jet operations commenced in 1961, initially with leased Boeing 707 equipment, and subsequently with the carrier's own Boeing 707-458 aircraft which began direct New York-Tel Aviv service in June of that year.

The first Boeing 747-200B was put on the New York service from 8 June 1970. Throughout the 1960s and 1970s, the airline suffered badly from terrorist action and the 1973 war, and a four-month strike

El Al Boeing 747-200B.

put EL AL into technical receivership in 1982, a situation which persisted until 1995. Plans for privatisation are being held up by the difficulties in selling an airline which can only operate six days. The question of flying on the Sabbath is being addressed.

Scheduled passenger services are dominated by European connections, but also extend to the United States, Canada, Africa and the Far East, linking Tel Aviv with some 50 points in 31 countries. Wholly-owned subsidiary Sun D'Or International Airlines, established on 1 October 1977, operates charter flights to European resorts. EL AL also has a 24.9 per cent stake in North American Airlines.

Fleet Data
2 Boeing 737-200A, 1 747-100F, 7 747-200B, 2 747-200F, 3 747-400, 7 757-200, 4 767-200.

EMIRATES (EK)

Emirates Airline was founded in May 1985 by the Dubai Emirate in competition with national United Arab Emirates carrier Gulf Air. Dubai wanted its own capacity to match the huge growth in the local economy, and began operations on 25 October that year with two Boeing 727-200s, provided by the Dubai Air Wing, to Bombay, Karachi and Delhi. Frankfurt and London-Gatwick were added to the schedule from 1 July 1987 with the Airbus A310-300. The Far Eastern sector was opened with flights to Bangkok, Manila and Singapore from June 1990. A major fleet modernisation programme was put in hand, first with the Airbus A300-600R, then the Boeing 777-200, and a recent order for 16 Airbus A330-200. The fleet renewal process will be completed by 2002.

Emirates now links its home base with 38 cities throughout the Middle East, Europe and Asia, carrying 2.5 million passenger a year. It employs 4,000 people. Emirates Sykcargo is a separate entity, operating joint freight services with KLM and its own schedule to Hong Kong and Moscow.

Fleet Data
6 Airbus A300-600R, 10 A310-300, (16) A330-200, (6) A340-500, 7 Boeing 777-200.

Emirates Boeing 777-200.

ETHIOPIAN AIRLINES (ET)

The national carrier of Ethiopia was formed on 26 December 1945 by proclamation of Emperor Hailé Selassie. Ethiopian began scheduled services on 8 April 1946, utilising an initial fleet of five DC-3 aircraft. Trans World Airlines provided technical and management assistance under contract until 1970. The carrier developed routes to neighbouring African countries and initiated operations to Western Europe in June 1958 with services to Frankfurt. Ethiopian became the first African carrier to serve the People's Republic of China with the inauguration of scheduled services to Shanghai via Bombay on 23 February 1973.

Jet services began in 1963 between Addis Ababa, Athens and Madrid with two Boeing 720Bs, and all mainline services have been flown with Boeing aircraft ever since. Ethiopian Airlines operates flag services from Addis Ababa to many points throughout Africa, and to destinations in Europe and the Middle and Far East. An extensive and vital domestic network serves more than 40 points on a regular basis. The airline's passenger traffic is edging up to 0.8 million. Staff number 3,300.

Fleet Data
2 ATR42-300, 1 Boeing 707-320C, 1 737-200, 4 757-200, 1 757-200PF, 2 767-200ER, 1 DHC-5A Buffalo, 4 DHC-6 Twin Otter, 5 Fokker 50, 2 Lockheed L100-30 Hercules.

Ethiopian Airlines Boeing 767-200ER.

EVA AIR (BR)

One of the world's fastest-growing airlines, Eva Airways, generally referred to as Eva Air, was formed in March 1989 by Taiwan's massive Evergreen Group, which includes Evergreen Marine, the world's biggest container shipping company. The airline began operations on 1 July 1991, using leased Boeing 767-200ERs from Taipei to Bangkok, Singapore, Kuala Lumpur and Jakarta. It placed a large order for eight Boeing 747-400, four 767-300ERs and four McDonnell Douglas MD-11s on 6 October 1989, later augmented with follow-up orders. The first long-haul service to Vienna, inaugurated on 11 November 1991, was followed by trans-Pacific flights to Los Angeles in December 1992, both flown with the 747-400. First European freighter service (with the MD-11F) to Amsterdam was launched in October 1995, while the Los Angeles passenger service was extended to Panama City two months later to pave the way for access into South America.

Eva Air now serves more than 30 destinations in Asia, New Zealand, Europe, the United States and Central America. Apart from the Taipei-Kaohsiung trunk route, the dense domestic network is served through associate local airlines in which Eva Air has a financial interest. These include Uni Air (formerly Makung Airlines), 42 per cent owned, Great China Airlines (25 per cent) and Taiwan Airlines (30 per cent). In 1996, Eva Air carried 4.25 million passengers and 275,000 tonnes of cargo. It employs 5,000 people.

Fleet Data
12 (3) Boeing 747-400, **4** 767-200, **5** 767-300ER, **3** McDonnell Douglas

Eva Air Boeing 767-200.

MD-11, **3 (2)** MD-11F, **3** MD-90-30.

FEDEX (FM)

Federal Express was founded by Frederick W Smith in 1972 and began overnight express package delivery services on 17 April 1973, flying converted Dassault Falcon business jets to 25 cities from Little Rock, Arkansas. After the deregulation of the US air cargo business in 1977, the carrier began to acquire larger aircraft, first the Boeing 727-100C, followed in March 1980 by ex-Continental McDonnell Douglas DC-10-30s.

Fedex McDonnell Douglas MD-11F.

In 1984, Federal Express moved into the international arena, opening scheduled freight services to Brussels, followed by Tokyo in 1988. This expansion accelerated with the acquisition of The Flying Tiger Line in 1989, and that airline's 21-country route network and aircraft. Incorporated on 25 June 1945, Flying Tigers was at the time of the take-over the world's largest cargo airline. A fleet modernisation programme began in May 1991 with the delivery of the first of 15 MD-11Fs, followed by ex-Lufthansa A310-200Fs, and the new A300-600F, for which Federal Express was the launch customer.

In just 25 years, Federal Express, now trading as FedEx, has grown into the world's biggest express transportation company, providing scheduled and charter services in the United States and to more than 200 countries worldwide. Its turboprop fleet, mostly Cessna Caravans, are contracted out to smaller carriers. FedEx handles more than 750 million shipments a year and employs nearly 120,000 people.

Fleet Data
19 (17) Airbus A300-600F, **30** A310-200F, **75** Boeing 727-100F, **88** 727-200F, **2** 747-100F, **10** Cessna 208A Caravan I, **286** 208B Super Cargomaster, **24** Fokker F27-500F Friendship, **8** F27-600F, **22 (4)** McDonnell Douglas MD-11F, **13 (10)** DC-10-10F, **22** DC-10-30.

FINNAIR (AY)

Finnair, the Finnish national carrier, was founded on 1 November 1923 as Aero O/Y and operations began on 24 November 1924, with a Helsinki-Reval (Tallinn) service using Junkers F13 seaplanes. 1936 saw the end of the seaplane era with the construction of airports at Helsinki and Turku. The ending of hostilities in 1944 resulted in a six-month suspension of operations, after which services recommenced from Hyvinkaa (some 30 miles, 48km, from the capital). Services were resumed from Helsinki in 1947, and the first of nine DC-3 aircraft entered service with the carrier. Düsseldorf and Hamburg were served from April 1951, and the carrier now operated under its present title of Finnair, though this did not become the official name until July 1968. Finnair became the first European airline to purchase the Convair 340, and the type entered service with the carrier in 1953, later initiating a Helsinki-London service on 1 September 1954. An agreement was reached between Finnair and Aeroflot in 1955 as a result of which Finnair became the first non-communist airline to be granted traffic rights to Moscow after the war.

Jet operations with Caravelle III aircraft began on 1 April 1960 with services to Stockholm and Frankfurt. Finnair later became the first operator of the Super Caravelle when the first of eight of the type commenced operations in 1964.

Finnair McDonnel Douglas MD-83.

Transatlantic services began in January 1969 with the inauguration of a Helsinki-Copenhagen-Amsterdam-New York route using DC-8-62CF aircraft.

During the 1970s and '80s the fleet was boosted by large numbers of DC-9s and MD-80s, and the first of four MD-11s arrived in December 1990. Finnair, owned 60.7 per cent by the Finnish Government, provides long-haul services from Helsinki to Toronto, San Francisco, New York, Bangkok, Singapore, Beijing, Osaka and Tokyo, together with an extensive European network, serving a total of 45 destinations. It also operates one of the world's densest domestic route systems, in relation to population, serving 21 towns and cities. In 1996, Finnair carries close to 7 million passengers and 67,000 tonnes of cargo. Employees total 8,200. The activities of subsidiaries, Finnaviation and Karair, were integrated into Finnair in September 1996.

Fleet Data
2 Airbus A300B4-200, **(12)** A320-200, **6** ATR72-200, **(4)** Boeing 757-200, **4** McDonnell Douglas MD-11, **12** DC-9-51, **10** MD-82, **11** MD-83, **3** MD-87, **5** Saab 340A, **2** 340B.

GARUDA INDONESIA (GA)

Garuda was established on 31 March 1950 as the national carrier of Indonesia, with the Indonesian government and KLM as equal shareholders. Garuda succeeded the post-war Inter-Island Division of KLM, which had been operating throughout the East Indies since August 1947, and the pre-war KNILM. The carrier's initial fleet comprised 20 DC-3s and eight Catalinas. The carrier was nationalised in 1954 and began its first international service, to Singapore, in the

Garuda Indonesia Airbus A300-600R.

same year. With the return of Irian Jaya (formerly Dutch New Guinea), the operations of the domestic airline De Kroonduif were absorbed by Garuda on 1 January 1963.

Jet operations were initiated following the introduction of Convair 990A aircraft in September 1963 on routes to Manila and Tokyo. Services to Rome, Prague, Frankfurt and Amsterdam through Bangkok, Bombay and Cairo were started in 1965 in association with KLM. Garuda took delivery of its first DC-8-55 in June 1966 and began services with the type to Sydney from Jakarta via Bali. DC-9-32 aircraft entered service on domestic and regional routes in 1969, followed by F28 Fellowship 1000 aircraft in 1971. In October 1878 Garuda took over Merpati Nusantara Airlines, which had been formed by the Indonesian government on 6 September 1962, and operated services in Borneo, Irian Jaya and a number of regional routes. Merpati continues under its own name.

Initiated massive increase in fleet from 1989, which put the airline into difficulties, but some rationalisation is being implemented, albeit slowly. The Government-owned flag carrier links Jakarta and the main tourist resort of Bali with many regional points, and further afield to Europe, the Middle East, Australia, New Zealand and the United States, serving 32 cities. It also operates an extensive 30-point network throughout the Indonesian archipelago.

Fleet Data
8 Airbus A300B4-200, **9** A300-600R, **6 (3)** A330-300, **12** 737-300, **(12)** 737-300, **6** 747-200B, **5** 747-400, **(6)** 777-200, **5** McDonnell Douglas DC-10-30, **7** MD-11.

GHANA AIRWAYS (GH)

Ghana's national carrier was formed on 4 July 1958 as the airline of the former Gold Coast to take over the Ghana operations of

Gulf Air Boeing 767-300ER.

Iberia McDonnell Douglas MD-87.

West African Airways Corporation. Ghana Airways was a BOAC associate company until February 1961, when the carrier became wholly government-owned. BOAC Boeing Stratocruisers initiated services for the carrier between Accra and London on 16 July 1958. Jet operations were inaugurated with VC10 aircraft in 1965, and DC-9-50 and Fokker F28 aircraft were subsequently introduced on Ghana Airways' regional and domestic routes.

Ghana Airways currently provides regional services to Abidjan, Banjul, Canakry, Cotonou, Dakar, Freetown, Harare, Lagos, Lome, and Johannesburg, and long-haul intercontinental services to Düsseldorf, London, Rome and New York. Approximately 1,100 personnel are employed by the carrier.

Fleet Data
2 McDonnell Douglas DC-10-30,
1 DC-9-50.

Ghana Airways DC-10-30.

GULF AIR (GF)

Gulf Air was formed on 24 March 1950 as Gulf Aviation Company Limited by F. Bosworth, and from modest beginnings the carrier has grown rapidly to become a full international airline and the major carrier for the Gulf states of Bahrain, Qatar, Oman and the United Arab Emirates. Services connecting Bahrain, Doha, Dhahran and Sharjah began with a single Anson. In October 1951 BOAC became a major shareholder; four de Havilland Herons were purchased in the following year, at which time services to Abu Dhabi, Dubai, Kuwait, and Muscat were started. Four DC-3s were acquired to meet increasing traffic demand and also to operate charters on behalf of petroleum companies.

Jet operations started with Trident 1E aircraft chartered from Kuwait Airways before the arrival of Gulf Aviation's first One-Eleven 432 in January 1970. The carrier formally adopted its present title in late 1973, and on 1 April 1974, the Gulf states of Bahrain, Oman, Qatar and the UAE became sole owners of the carrier with equal shareholdings. 'Golden Falcon' services from the Gulf to London were initiated in that year with VC 10 Type 1101s purchased from British Airways. In 1985 Gulf Air ceased operations to Dubai, which set up its own official carrier, Emirates Airline. In 1994, Gulf Air operated its first service to the

Americas, linking the Middle East direct with New York, using its newly-delivered Airbus A340-300. Gulf Air now links the four Gulf States with 50 destinations in 39 countries, extending from the Middle East into Europe, East Africa, the Indian sub-continent, the Far East and Australasia. The airline carries around 5 million passengers a year and has 5,500 employees.

Gulf Air also undertakes charter services and subsidiaries of the carrier include Gulf Helicopters Limited, and hotel and airport handling interests.

Fleet Data
13 Airbus A320-200, **(6)** A330-300,
5 A340-200, **10** Boeing 767-300ER.

IBERIA (IB)

Iberian (Lineas Aéreas de España), Spain's national carrier, was originally formed in 1927, with services starting between Madrid and Barcelona on 14 December of that year. In 1928 Iberia merged with CETA and Union Aéreas España to form CLASSA (Compañia de Linea Aéreas Subvencionadas SA) which initiated operations on 27 May 1929 from Madrid to Seville with Junkers aircraft. International service began on 19 August of that year between Madrid and Biarritz. In 1931 the carrier became Lineas Aéreas Postales Espanolas and by 1933 had opened routes to Bordeaux, Paris, Casablanca and Las Palmas. The carrier adopted its former name of Iberia in 1937. Transatlantic operations commenced with service to Buenos Aires on 22 September 1946 and jet services were introduced with DC-8-52 aircraft on the New York route in July 1961.

Wide-body services were added with the Boeing 747 in October 1970, followed by the DC-10-30 in March 1973 and the Airbus A300B4-200 in the same month in 1981.

As part of a new Latin American strategy in the early 1990s, Iberia embarked on a spree of equity alliances with Aerolineas Argentinas, Ladeco and VIASA, but financial difficulties forced it to sell a substantial part of its holdings.

Today, Iberia, owned 99.99 per cent by the Spanish Government through holding company Teneo, provides scheduled domestic and international services to all continents, serving 68 destinations in 53 countries, carrying 14 million passengers annually. It has a workforce of 21,000. Virtually wholly-owned are regional carriers Binter Canarias and Binter Mediterraneo, as well as charter subsidiary viva Air. Iberia also has a 32.93 per cent holding in domestic airline Aviaco.

Fleet Data
6 Airbus A300B4-200, **22** A320-200,
(8) A321-100, **6 (2)** A340-300, **23** Boeing 727-200A, **5** 757-200, **5** McDonnell Douglas DC-10-30, **24** MD-87.

ICELANDAIR (FI)

The Icelandic flag-carrier can trace its history back to the foundation of Flugfelag Akureyrar on 3 June 1937, beginning operations on 4 May 1938 with a single Waco YKS floatplane. After re-organisation as Flugfelag Islands and a move to the capital Reykjavik, the airline started a scheduled service to Prestwick and Copenhagen with Liberators and DC-3s on 27 May 1946, then to London with DC-4s on 3 May 1949. It adopted the name of Icelandair and in February 1952 took over the domestic service from the other Icelandic airline Loftleidr. The first Boeing 727-100 jet aircraft was introduced on 24 June 1967. The decision to merge the two airlines under the Flugleidr holding company became

Icelandair Boeing 757-200.

effective on 6 October 1973. Loftleidr had been founded on 10 March 1944 and initially concentrated on domestic and European flights, before pioneering low-cost services across the Atlantic in 1953 on a Reykjavik-New York service, with connections to Denmark, Britain and Luxembourg. After the merger, the two airlines continued to use the old names for a time, with Loftleidr Icelandic concentrating on trans-Atlantic flights with Douglas DC-6B, then Canadair CL-44s and stretched DC-8s, and Icelandair maintaining a domestic and European network. A wholesale fleet modernisation programme was completed in May 1992, replacing previous types with Boeing 737 and 757s and Fokker 50s.

The national flag-carrier provides international services to 22 destinations with direct flights, and links 15 European cities to its four US gateways of New York, Baltimore/Washington, Orlando and Fort Lauderdale. It also operates a comprehensive domestic network and flights to Greenland and the Faroe's. Icelandair carries 1.2 million passengers a year.

Fleet Data
4 Boeing 737-400, **3** 757-200ER,
4 Fokker 50.

Indian Airlines Airbus A320-200.

INDIAN AIRLINES (IC)

Indian Airlines came into being as a State corporation on 28 May 1953, as a consequence of India's 1953 Air Corporation Act, which was aimed at rationalizing the fragmented domestic operations within the country. The assets and liabilities of eight major domestic operators were acquired by Indian Airlines, and operations by the new carrier began on 1 August 1953. The fleet comprised 99 piston-engined aircraft, including DC-3s, DC-4s and Vikings, and an equipment modernization plan was formulated. Viscount 768 aircraft joined that fleet in 1957, with service inauguration on 10 October, 1957, and the Fokker F27 Friendship 100 began operations with Indian Airlines in May 1961. The carrier entered the jet era with the introduction of Caravelle VI-Ns on routes from February 1964. These aircraft provided the mainstay of Indian Airlines' fleet until the introduction of the HS 748 (assembled under licence by Hindustan Aeronautics Limited of Kanpur) with deliveries starting in June 1964.

Boeing 737-200s took over on trunk routes from January 1971, and wide-body aircraft in the shape of the Airbus A300B2, were added in December 1976. A low-cost subsidiary, Alliance Air, was established to meet growing competition in the newly-liberated Indian domestic market, and began operations in June 1996.

Fleet Data
10 Airbus A300B2-100, **30** A320-200, **13** Boeing 737-200A.

IRAN AIR (IR)

Iran Air (Iran National Airlines Corporation), also known as Homa (an acronym of its Persian name), was established in February 1962 through the merger of Iranian Airways and Persian Air Services to become the state-owned national carrier. Iranian Airways had been formed as a private airline in December 1944 and began operations on 31 May 1945. The first scheduled service was inaugurated in May 1946 linking Tehran and Meshed, and a domestic network was subsequently developed using DC-3 aircraft. Regional services to Baghdad, Beirut and Cairo were initiated by the end of 1946, and a route to Paris was opened in April 1947. Persian Air Services had been formed in 1954 and commenced operations the following year with a cargo service between Tehran and Geneva using Avro Yorks operated under charter by Trans Mediterranean Airways. Regional and international services were developed, and in 1960 a DC-7C was leased from Sabena, followed by a Boeing 707 from the same source.

Iran Air began jet operations with Boeing 727-86 aircraft on 4 July 1965, and the route network was subsequently expanded to include London, Frankfurt and Moscow. In the meantime the carrier had signed a three-year agreement with Pan American in 1964 covering the provision of management and technical assistance. Wide-bodied operations began with the introduction of Boeing 747SP-86 aircraft in March 1976, and services to New York with the type were subsequently initiated.

After the Islamic revolution in 1979, the airline was hit hard by the eight year war with Iraq and political isolation backed by economic sanctions, but these are now easing. Iran Air Tours was established in 1992, jointly with Tajik Air, to provide tourist charter flights.

Iran's flag-carrier now serves 31 cities in 27 countries in the Middle East, the Asian CIS republics, Europe and the Far East, together with a 20-point domestic network. These routes generate some 5.5 million passengers a year. Employees number 11,800.

Fleet Data
5 Airbus A300B4-200, 2 A300-600R, 4 Boeing 707-320C, 2 727-100, 5 727-200A, 3 737-200A, 1 747-100, 2 747-200B(SCD), 1 747-100F, 4 747SP, 6 Fokker 100.

Iran Air Boeing 747SP.

JAPAN AIRLINES (JL)

JAL-Japan Air Lines (Nihon Koku Kabushiki Kaisha) was established in its original form on 1 August 1951, as a private company. The previous national carrier (Greater Japan Airways) had ceased operations in 1945. JAL began services on the Tokyo-Osaka route with a leased Martin 2-0-2 on 25 October 1951. The carrier took delivery of its own aircraft, DC-4s, in October 1952, and placed an order for five DC-6A/Bs for international services. The financial requirements of such expansion resulted in dissolution of JAL in August 1953, to be replaced by a national carrier of the same name, with 50 per cent government financial participation. The carrier's first DC-6B was delivered on 15 September 1953, and began services between Tokyo and Sapporo on 2 October, the day after the new carrier had been legally established. After flight trials over the Tokyo-San Francisco route via Wake Island and Honolulu had taken place, JAL's first regular international commercial service was inaugurated over the route on 2 February 1954. International services were subsequently expanded to Hong Kong, Bangkok and Singapore. A Tokyo-Paris polar route was flown with Boeing 707-328 equipment in association with Air France from 1 April 1960. Jet operations with the

Japan Airlines Boeing 747-400.

carrier's own equipment were started on the Tokyo-San Francisco route with DC-8-32 aircraft on 12 August 1960. Wide-bodied operations began on JAL's trans-Pacific routes from 1 July 1970, with Boeing 747-146 aircraft, and 747SR-46 (short range) aircraft began serving the Tokyo-Okinawa route in October 1973.

The latest aircraft were added to the fleet in the 1990s, including the Boeing 747-400 (1990), McDonnell Douglas MD-11 (1993) and the Boeing 777 in 1996.

JAL's global passenger and cargo network today serves 62 cities in 26 countries worldwide, except Africa. A domestic trunk-route network serving 20 major cities gives the airline a quarter share of the domestic traffic. It carries 27 million passengers and 750,000 tonnes of cargo. Associate airline companies are Japan Asia Airways (JAA), founded on 8 August and 90.5 per cent owned, Japan Air Charter (JAZ), 82 per cent owned, and Japan TransOcean Air (formerly Southwest Air Lines), formed in June 1967 and 51 per cent owned.

Fleet Data
5 (5) Boeing 737-400, 6 747-100, 29 747-200B/F, 13 747-300, 24 (18) 747-400, 8 747-400D, 3 767-200, 17 767-300, 6 (4) 777-200, (5) 777-300, 14 McDonnell Douglas DC-10-40, 10 MD-11.

JAPAN AIR SYSTEM (JD)

Japan's third-largest carrier was founded on 15 May 1971 as Toa Domestic Airlines (TDA) through merger of two prominent domestic carriers, Japan Domestic Airlines (JDA) and Toa Airways (TAW). JDA itself was established on 15 April 1964 through amalgamation of three feeder airlines whose histories went back to 1952/53. JDA utilised fleet of NAMC YS-11s on a network stretching from Tokyo north to Wakkanai and west to Kagoshima. TAW was founded on 30 November 1953 and provided short-haul flights in the western part of Japan from Osaka to Okinoerabu in the Nansei Islands. The airline inaugurated its first jet service on Tokyo-Oita route with Douglas DC-9-31 on 1 August 1972 and began serving major trunk routes from Tokyo to Sapporo and Fukuoka on 1 March 1975. Fleet was modernised with initial orders for five McDonnell Douglas MD-81 and six Airbus A300B2K, increased considerably with later follow-on orders. From 1986 regular charter flights were added to many regional points beyond its borders. It changed its name to Japan Air System (JAS) on 1 April 1988 and began the first international schedule to Seoul on 1 July 1988, followed by Singapore on 3 February 1990, but since discontinued.

Japan Air System today is responsible for a comprehensive domestic network, serving 38 communities across Japan, together with a single regional route to Seoul in South Korea. Regular charter flights are operated

Japan Air System MD-90.

throughout the region. Associate carrier Japan Air Commuter (JAC), owned 60 per cent, was established on 1 July 1983 and provides scheduled and non-scheduled commuter services in the Nansei Islands region. Japan Air System carries 17 million passengers, giving it a 22 per cent domestic marketshare, and employs 6,000 people. Major shareholders are the Tokyo Group (25.6 per cent), Japan Airlines (8.83 per cent), Kinki Nippon Railway (8.83 per cent) and Fujisash Industries (7.78 per cent).

Fleet Data
7 Airbus A300B4, 10 A300B2K, 17 A300-600R, 3 (4) Boeing 777-200, 26 McDonnell Douglas MD-81, 6 MD-87, 14 (2) MD-90-30, 2 DC-10,30, 12 NAMC YS-11A-500.

Kenya Airways Boeing 737-300.

KENYA AIRWAYS (KQ)

Kenya's national airline was formed on 22 January 1977 by the government, following the demise of East African Airways Corporation (EAAC), the carrier owned jointly by Kenya, Tanzania and Uganda. Kenya Airways began operations over routes linking Nairobi with Mombasa and London on 4 February 1977, using Boeing 707-321 equipment leased from the UK independent,

British Midland Airways. Operations gradually extended to cover a number of domestic and regional services previously operated by EAAC, using former EAAC Fokker F27-500 and DC-9-32 aircraft. Kenya Airways acquired three ex-Northwest Orient Boeing 707-351B aircraft and expanded services to Europe.

Airbus A310s took over long-haul flights in May 1986. Ten years later, Kenya Airways became the first national airline in Africa to be privatised, with strategic partner, KLM Royal Dutch Airlines acquiring a 26 per cent stake in January 1996.

Fleet Data
3 Airbus A310-300, 2 Boeing 737-200, 2 (1) 737-300, 3 Fokker 50.

KLM-ROYAL DUTCH AIRLINES (KL)

KLM (Koninklijke Luchtvaart Maatschappij NV) was founded on 7 October 1919, and is the world's oldest airline still operating under its own name. The first and now oldest air route in the world was opened on 17 May 1920, between Amsterdam and London with a leased de Havilland D.H.16. In the subsequent years a European network was developed and various types of Fokker aircraft introduced into service. Initial services to the East Indies in 1929 led to the opening of a weekly service from Amsterdam to Batavia (now Jakarta) in October 1931. The DC-2 entered KLM service in 1935, and in 1937 the carrier became the first European operator of the DC-3 aircraft. Services in the West Indies based on Curacao were initiated in 1935 and were developed to serve Colombia, Venezuela, Barbados, Trinidad and the Guianas. These services were continued throughout World War II, and subsequently extended to Cuba and Miami. On 21 May 1946, KLM started scheduled services to New York, making the carrier the first European airline to operate scheduled flights between two continents after the war. South America and South Africa were added to the network in 1946 and 1947 respectively, and Australia was included in KLM's route network from 1951. Viscount 803 aircraft entered service on European routes in 1957, and the Electra began serving with the carrier in 1959, primarily on Middle and Far East routes. KLM became the first non-US airline to operate the DC-8 in April 1960.

Wide-body services were introduced with Boeing 747-200B in February 1971. In July 1989, KLM took the first step towards establishing a global airline system through the acquisition of a 20 per cent stake in Northwest Airlines, the fourth-largest carrier in the United States. A 100 per cent stake has since been acquired in Air UK, which provides valuable feed from the UK into its Amsterdam hub. The Dutch national flag-carrier, in whom the Netherlands Government still has a stake, serves 148 cities in 82 countries in Europe, North, Central and South America, Africa, the Middle and Far East and Australia, carrying 12 million passengers a year. Apart from equity stakes in Northwest, Air UK and ALM Antillean Airlines (40 per cent), KLM also

KLM-Royal Dutch Airlines Boeing 737-300.

has substantial holdings in several local carriers, including Transavia (80 per cent) and Martinair Holland (50 per cent). KLM Cityhopper, formed in April 1991 through the merger of NLM CityHopper and Netherlines, is wholly-owned.

Fleet Data
16 Boeing 737-300, **18** 737-400, **(4)** 737-800, **3** 747-300, **10** 747-300 (SCD), **5 (1)** 747-400, **14** 747-400 (SCD), **10** 767-300ER, **6** Fokker 100, **10** McDonnell Douglas MD-11.

KLM UK (UK)

Britain's third-largest airline was formed on 16 January 1980 as Air UK through the amalgamation of British Island Airways, Air Anglia, BIA/Air West and Air Wales. The most prominent of its predecessor companies were Air Anglia itself formed from three smaller operators on 1 August 1970, which operated out of Norwich, serving several domestic points and Paris and Bergen, and British Island Airways (BIA), whose three founder companies were Jersey Airlines, Manx Airlines and Morton Air Services. Air Wales was a third-level airline based at Cardiff, which started operations on 6 December 1977. Air UK inherited a large fleet of diverse types, included Fokker F27s and F28s, Handley Page Heralds, BAC One-Elevens and Embraer Bandeirantes, as well as a 31-point domestic and European network. From 1984, international services were added from many provincial cities, leading eventually to the acquisition of jet aircraft in the shape of the BAe 146 in 1989 and the Fokker 100 from 1992. In 1987, KLM Royal Dutch Airlines acquired a 14.9 per cent holding, since increased to 100 per cent, and the partnership now involves joint marketing of KLM's Amsterdam hub into which the airline feeds lots of passengers.

KLM UK operates extensively with the UK and the Channel Islands, and to 16 cities in continental Europe, operating from all three London airports, including its main base at Stansted. It carries 3.6 million passengers and operates with a staff of 2,000.

Fleet Data
4 ATR72-200, **1** BAe 146-100, **10** 146-300, **9** Fokker 50, **11** Fokker 100, **5** F27-500.

KLM UK ATR72-200.

KOREAN AIR (KE)

Korean Air, known until 1984 as Korean Air Lines, was formed as a government-owned carrier in June 1962 to succeed Korean National Airlines which was organized in 1945 by Captain Yong Wook Shinn, the country's first licensed pilot. Korean National was granted a permit in 1948 to establish scheduled domestic services, and operations from Seoul to Kusan, Kwanju, Puson and Chunmunjin were started with Stinson aircraft. DC-3s were acquired in April 1950 and international services to Tokyo began in 1952, followed by services to Hong Kong in 1954.

Korean Air Lines, as it then was, introduced F27 Friendship 200 aircraft in January 1964. Services to Fukuoka and Osaka were initiated and the Hong Kong route was reopened in 1966. Jet operations began following the delivery of a DC-9-32 aircraft in July 1967, and two former Eastern Air Lines Boeing 720-025s were

Korean Air Boeing 777-300.

added to the fleet in 1969. Wide-bodied operations with Boeing 747-2B5B aircraft began in May 1973, and the first DC-10-30 was delivered in February 1978. Korean became one of the early operators of the Airbus when its first A300 aircraft was delivered on 31 August 1978.

It signed the largest aircraft order in its history in February 1979 for 18 Boeing 747s and has continued the modernisation process ever since.

Today, privately-owned Korean Air is one of the fastest-growing carriers in the world, serving more than 70 cities in 32 countries, together with a dense network. Korean Air carries more than 20 million passengers annually, as well as 750,000 tonnes of freight. It employs 16,500 people.

Fleet Data
27 Airbus A300-600R, **8** A300B4-200, **2** A300F4-200, **1 (12)** A330, **4** Boeing 747-200B/C, **12** 747-200F, **3** 747-300, **23 (11)** 747-400, **2** 747SP, **(14)** 777, **12** Fokker 100, **3** McDonnell Douglas MD-11, **2** MD-11F, **11** MD-82, **3** MD-83.

KUWAIT AIRWAYS (KU)

Kuwait Airways was formed in late 1953 as Kuwait National Airways and began scheduled operations from Kuwait to Basra and Beirut in 1954 with DC-3 aircraft. Services to Bahrain and Cairo were introduced in 1956, and the carrier adopted the title of Kuwait Airways Corporation (KAC) in March of the following year. On 1 June 1958, BOAC took over the management under a five-year contract, and in March 1959 KAC absorbed British International Airlines, a then BOAC subsidiary providing local charter services. Operations with Viscount 754 aircraft leased from MEA were inaugurated in 1958, replacing DC-4 equipment. By 1963 the airline had become wholly-owned by the government of Kuwait and adopted its present title.

Kuwait Airways took delivery of its first Comet 4C on 18 January 1963, and a London service with the type was inaugurated in March 1964. During the following month it acquired Trans Arabia Airways, a major competitor since 1959. The latter operated a fleet of DC-6B aircraft on services throughout the Middle East and to London. Boeing 707-369Cs entered service in 1968, and wide-bodied operations began in 1978 following delivery of the carrier's first Boeing 747-269B on 28 July. Routes to New York and Manila were opened in December 1980.

The airline suffered badly from Iraq's invasion of Kuwait in August 1990, when five aircraft were destroyed by air attacks and some others flown to Baghdad. By mid-1992, Kuwait Airways was back in business with a new Airbus fleet and operations are now back to pre-invasion levels.

Kuwait Airways operates scheduled passenger and cargo services to 42 destinations in the Middle East, Europe,

Africa, North America, and Asia. Kuwait Airways employs some 4,750 people and carries 2 million passengers a year.

Fleet Data
1 Airbus A300C4-600, **5** A300-600R, **4** A310-300, **3** A320-200, **4** A340-200, **2** Boeing 747-200B(SCD), **1** 747-400 Combi, **(2)** 777-200.

Kuwait Airways Airbus A340-200.

LAN CHILE (LA)

LAN-Chile (Linea Aérea Nacional de Chile) is the second oldest airline in South America and was founded on 5 March 1929, as a branch of the Chilean air force. The carrier, originally known as Linea Aeropostal Santiago-Arica, began operations between Santiago and Arica with D.H.60G Gipsy Moths. In 1932, the carrier became independent of the air force and adopted its present title, although LAN-Chile remained a government-owned concern. Following the acquisition of Lodestars, LAN-Chile used the type in 1946 to inaugurate international operations with a service from Santiago to Buenos Aires which was later extended to Montevideo. LAN-Chile began jet operations

LAN Chile Boeing 767-300ER.

following the delivery of the first of three Caravelle VI-R aircraft in March 1964. In April 1967, LAN-Chile initiated service to New York with a Boeing 707-330B acquired from Lufthansa, and subsequently opened a European route with the type. Passenger services to Easter Island were started on 3 April 1967, and these were later extended to Papeete (Tahiti) thereby forming the first regular air link between South America and the South Pacific. In 1974 LAN-Chile operated a Boeing 707 transpolar flight between Punta Arenas and Sydney and thus became the first airline to link South America with Australia via the South Pole.

Fleet was progressively modernised with wide-bodies, including the McDonnell Douglas DC-10-30 and Boeing 767. In July 1985, the name was changed to Linea Area Nacional Chile SA when partially privatised, and full privatisation occurred on 26 May 1994.

LAN-Chile presently operates scheduled domestic services linking 15 points and international services to Buenos Aires, Mendoza, Montevideo, Caracas, Rio de Janeiro, Lima, La Paz, Frankfurt, Mexico City, Bogota, Miami, New York, Madrid, Easter Island and Papeete. LAN-Chile employs approximately 2,700 personnel.

Fleet Data
10 (4) Boeing 767-300ER, **16** 737-200, **8** Douglas DC-8F.

LAUDA AIR (NG)

Lauda Air was founded by former Formula 1 motor racing champion Niki Lauda in April 1979 and began charter operations on 24 May with two Fokker F27s. These were replaced in 1985 with two BAC One-Elevens, before the fleet was modernised with two Boeing 737-300s, and 767-300ERs with which Lauda Air began long-haul flights to Bangkok, Sydney and Hong Kong in 1988. A Vienna-London Gatwick schedule, introduced in December 1990, was followed by further European destinations following an alliance arrangement with Deutsche Lufthansa and the acquisition of Canadair Regional Jets. Lufthansa took an equity stake in January 1993, which was increased to 39.7 per cent in 1994, but reduced to 20 per cent two

years later when Austrian Airlines bought into the airline.

Lauda Air operates long-haul scheduled leisure services from Vienna to Bangkok, Phuket, Hong Kong, Ho Chi Minh City, Singapore and Sydney, and to Miami via Munich. It also operates joint services with Lufthansa to 15 cities in Europe, and provides a large short- and long-haul charter programme. In 1996 Lauda Air carried 1.225 million passengers. Shareholding is divided between Austrian Airlines (35.9 per cent), Niki Lauda (30 per cent), Lufthansa (20 per cent) and private individuals.

Fleet Data

2 Boeing 737-300, 2 737-400,
5 767-300ER, 1 (3) 777-200,
7 Canadair Regional Jet 100ER.

Lauda Air Canadair Regional Jet.

LOT POLISH AIRLINES (LO)

LOT (Polske Linie Lotnicze) was established as the state-owned national carrier of Poland on 1 January 1929, to take over the two existing private operators, Aero and Aerolot. Aero had been formed in May 1925 and operated domestic services from Warsaw with Farman F.70 biplanes. Aerolot was founded as Aerolloyd in 1922 and operated Junkers F.13 aircraft on domestic services and, in 1925, the country's first international routes to Austria and Czechoslovakia. LOT undertook a major expansion programme resulting in a network which covered 13 countries by 1939. The formidable task of re-establishing LOT after the adversities of World War II began early in 1945. Initially domestic services were restarted, and subsequently international routes to Berlin, Paris, Prague, Moscow and Stockholm were opened using Li-2 aircraft (Soviet-built DC-3s).

Jet operations with the Tupolev Tu-134 started in November 1968, and from May 1972 the Ilyushin Il-62 began serving on the London, Paris and Moscow routes. Services to New York and Montreal were subsequently inaugurated, and in September 1977 LOT initiated scheduled operations to Bangkok via Baghdad and Bombay.

The gradual process of changing from Soviet to Western aircraft was started in 1989 with the acquisition of the Boeing 767-200ER, and has now been completed. LOT became a joint-stock company in 1992 in preparation for partial privatisation, which is now expected to take place on a limited scale in 1998.

Government-owned LOT now offers scheduled international services to 46 cities in 33 countries in Europe and the Middle

LOT Boeing 737-500.

East, with some extensions into Africa, North America and the Far East. An 8-point domestic network is also operated. A low-cost operation, Eurolot, began operations in July 1997. LOT carries nearly 2 million passengers and employs 4,000 people.

Fleet Data

(5) ATR42-500, 8 ATR72-200, 7 Boeing 737-400, 6 737-500, (2) 737-800, 2 767-200ER, 3 767-300ER.

LTU INTERNATIONAL AIRWAYS (LT)

Germany's largest holiday airline had modest beginnings, being founded on 20 October 1955 as Lufttransport-Union, initially operating five Vickers Vikings. Its first jet aircraft, the Sud-Aviation Caravelle III joined the fleet in 1965, and by 1969, LTU had become an all-jet operator. Wide-body equipment, in the shape of the Lockheed TriStar, arrived in 1973 and served the airline until replaced by more modern equipment, including Boeing 757 and 767s, and the McDonnell Douglas MD-11. LTU expanded its passenger base by setting up Lufttransport-Süd in Munich in December 1983, and LTE International Airways in Spain in April 1987. The first new Airbus A330-300 was added in December 1994.

LTU now operates extensive scheduled European and international leisure flights, together with charters, carrying some 7 million passengers a year. Wholly-owned subsidiaries are LTU Süd International Airways (LTS), based at Munich, and LTE International Airways, operating out of Palma de Mallorca and the Canary Islands. LTU is owned 60.6 per cent by Conle & Company, 34.2 per cent by the Westdeutsche Landesbank, and 5.1 per cent by Walter Gräber.

Fleet Data

6 Airbus A330-300, 13 Boeing 757-200,
5 767-300ER, 4 McDonnell Douglas MD-11.

LTU Airbus A330-300.

LUFTHANSA (LH)

Lufthansa was formed in 1953 as Luftag to succeed its pre-war forerunner, Deutsche Luft Hansa (DHL), which had been established on 6 January 1926, through a merger of Deutscher Aero Lloyd AG and Junkers AG Luftverkehr and which ceased operations in April 1945 as a result of an Allied ban on German aviation. The origins of DHL go back to February 1919 when Deutsche Luft-Reederei commenced scheduled services between Berlin and Weimar.

Luftag was formed on 6 January 1953,

Lufthansa Airbus A340-200.

and the carrier adopted its present title, Lufthansa (Deutsche Lufthansa AG), in August 1954. Scheduled operations began on 1 April 1955, with domestic services between Hamburg, Düsseldorf, Köln/Bonn, Frankfurt and Munich. Service to London, Paris and Madrid followed shortly afterwards. Substantial development of the domestic and European route system followed the service introduction of Convair 440 aircraft in 1957 and Viscount turboprop aircraft in 1958. Boeing 707-430 services between Frankfurt and New York from March 1960, and to San Francisco in May of that year, marked the beginning of jet operations for Lufthansa. The carrier became the first European customer for the 727 aircraft, and European services with the type commenced in 1964. Lufthansa subsequently launched the 737 airliner with an order for 21 of the type being placed in 1965.

The wide-body era began on 27 April 1970 with the inaugural service of the Boeing 747-100. A privatisation process was initiated in October 1994 and is expected to be completed before the end of 1997 with the sale of the government's remaining 35.68 per cent holding. The year 1997 also marked the formal establishment of the Star Alliance with United Airlines, Air Canada, SAS, Thai International and Varig.

Germany's flag-carrier operates an extensive worldwide network linking Germany with 227 destinations in 88 countries, carrying more than 40 million passengers and 1.5 million tonnes of cargo and mail. Cargo services are flown by autonomous Lufthansa Cargo, charters by Condor and thinner European routes by Lufthansa CityLine. All ware wholly-owned. Lufthansa also has financial interests in Lauda Air and Luxair, and franchise arrangements with Augsburg Airways, and Air Littoral in France.

Fleet Data

13 Airbus A300-600, 10 A310-300,
8 (12) A319, 33 A320-200, 20 A321-100,
6 A340-200, 10 (2) A340-300,
19 Boeing 737-200, 39 737-300,
7 737-300QC, 6 737-400, 30 737-500,
6 747-200B, 4 747-200C, 15 747-400,
7 747-400(SCD).

MALAYSIA AIRLINES (MH)

MAS (Malaysian Airline System) was formed by the government of Malaysia in April 1971 as the national carrier to succeed Malaysia-Singapore Airlines (MSA), following the decision by the respective governments to establish separate operations. The history of the carrier dates from 1937 with the registration of Malayan Airways Limited, a company formed by the Straits Steamship Company, the Ocean Steamship Company and Imperial Airways. During its first year of operation, in 1947, domestic services between Singapore, Kuala Lumpur, Ipoh, Penang, Kuantan and Kota Baru were inaugurated. Later in the year regional services to Jakarta, Palembang and Medan began when the airline took delivery of its first DC-3 aircraft. International services to Saigon were also initiated. In 1963 the carrier was renamed Malaysian Airways Limited and two years later absorbed Borneo Airways. The title of Malaysia-Singapore Airlines was adopted following acquisition of a majority shareholding in the company by the governments of Malaysia and Singapore in 1966.

Following the split-up of MSA, the new airline began operations on 1 October 1972, taking over the former MSA routes in the Malayan peninsula, Sabah and Sarawak.

Long-haul routes to Europe, Australia and the Middle East were developed with the McDonnell Douglas DC-10-30 and the Boeing 747-200B, acquired in 1976 and 1982 respectively. The present operating name was adopted in October 1987.

Malaysia Airlines operates to 57 destinations regionally, and in Australasia, the Middle East, Europe and the Americas, carrying 15 million passengers a year. It employs around 19,000 staff. Local feeder services are flown by associate Pelangi Air.

Fleet Data

1 Airbus A300B4-200, 12 A330-300,
2 Boeing 737-300F, 39 737-400,
9 737-500, 2 747-200B, 1 747-300,
13 (10) 747-400, (11) 777-200,
(4) 777-300, (15) 777-200X, 6 DHC-6
Twin Otter, 10 Fokker 50, 4 McDonnell
Douglas DC-10-30, 2 MD-11, 2 MD-11F.

Malaysia Airlines Boeing 777-200.

MALÉV HUNGARIAN AIRLINES (MA)

Malév (Magyar Légiközlekedési Vállalat) the Hungarian state airline, was formed in March 1946 as a joint Hungarian/Soviet undertaking under the title of Maszoviet (Magyar Szovjet Polgari Legiforgalmi Társaság). Maszoviet commenced operations on 15 October 1946, with domestic services linking Budapest, Debrecen and Nyireghaza, and utilising Lisunov Li-2 and Polokarpov Po-2 aircraft. The airline adopted its present name on 25 November 1954, when it became wholly Hungarian-owned. Several West European destinations were added to Malév's scheduled network between 1958 and 1960, and in May 1960 the airline inaugurated turboprop services with Ilyushin Il-18s. Jet operations commenced following the delivery of Tupolev Tu-134 aircraft in December 1968.

A gradual move towards the West started in 1988 with the acquisition of the Boeing 737, accelerating in September 1993, when Alitalia purchased a 30 per cent stake in Hungary's national airline, since purchased back.

Today, Malév operates an intra-European and Near East network, as well as long-haul routes to the United States and Thailand. It carries close to 2 million passengers and 14,000 tonnes of cargo. Staff totals 3,600.

Fleet Data
6 Boeing 737-200, **4** 737-300, **2** 737-400, **2** 767-300ER, **3** Fokker 70, **2** Tupolev Tu-134A-3, **7** Tu-154B-2.

Malév Hungarian Airlines Boeing 737-200.

MARTINAIR HOLLAND (MA)

This Dutch carrier was founded by Martin Schröder as Martin's Luchvervoermaatschappij (Martin's Air Charter) on 24 May 1958 and began operations with a single de Havilland Dove. Other aircraft types, including the Vickers Viking, de Havilland Heron and Douglas DC-3 were soon added, but expansion began to take shape in 1964, when the carrier entered the inclusive-tour business and acquired Fairways Rotterdam. At the same time, KLM took a 25 per cent stake, since increased to 50 per cent, enabling Martin's Air Charter to upgrade its fleet with Convair 340s and Douglas DC-7Cs. Long-haul flights were added in November 1967 with its first jet aircraft, the Douglas DC-8-33. Wide-body DC-10-30CFs entered service on 30 November 1973, and this was followed by a name change to the present title a few months later.

Martinair Boeing 767-300.

Martinair Holland now provides scheduled and charter passenger and cargo flights, together with sub-services for other airlines. Many destinations are served in Europe, the Middle East, Far East, Africa and the Americas. It has taken a 40 per cent stake in Colombian cargo carrier Tampa Airlines, to strengthen its presence in the Latin American market. In 1996, Martinair carried nearly 2 million passengers and 152,000 tonnes of cargo.

Fleet Data
4 Boeing 747-200C, **1** 747-200F, **6** 767-300ER, **4** McDonnell Douglas MD-11C, **1** MD-11F.

Mexicana Airbus A320-200.

MEXICANA (MX)

Mexicana (Compañia Mexicana de Aviacion) is the fourth oldest airline in the world and the second oldest in Latin America, having been originally founded as Compañia Mexicana de Transportes Aéreos (CTMA) on 12 July 1921. Operations started from Mexico City to Tuxpan and Tampico with Lincoln Standards. The assets of CMTA were acquired in September 1924 by Compañia Mexicana de Aviacion (Mexicana) which was formed on 20 August 1924. Initial operations centred on payroll deliveries to remote oil fields (due to the vulnerability of ground routes to armed robbery). The carrier signed an air mail contract with the Mexican government for the Mexico City-Tampico route on 16 August 1926, and passenger services were subsequently introduced on the route with Fairchild 71 aircraft on 15 April 1928. Pan American purchased Mexicana in January 1929 as part of its ambitious expansion plans in Latin America though Mexicana retained its separate identity. In January 1936 Mexicana began services on its first international trunk route from Mexico City to Los Angeles with Lockheed 10 Electra aircraft.

In 1960 the carrier took delivery of its first Comet 4C jet aircraft which initiated service to Chicago on 4 July of that year. In the same year Mexicana acquired the routes of ATSA and TAMSA which gave access to the route structure in the Yucatan and additional services to Texas. Pan American sold its remaining shares in the carrier in January 1968, and Mexicana gradually expanded its international route structure to include Dallas in 1972, St Louis in 1973, Kansas City in 1974, Costa Rica in 1977, San Francisco in 1978 and Seattle in 1979.

High-capacity DC-10-15s were added to the fleet in 1981. The airline was re-

privatised in September 1989, and since June 1996, comes under the holding company Cintra (along with Aeromexico), in which the Mexican Government has a 21 per cent stake.

Mexicana today operates high-frequency domestic services to 40 destinations, and has regional links to the United States and Latin America. Associate Mexicana Inter, operated by Aerocozumel and Aerocaribe, serves the 'Mayan' routes in the Yucatan peninsula.

Fleet Data
12 (8) Airbus A320-200, **22** Boeing 727-200A, **2** 757-200, **10** Fokker 100.

MIDDLE EAST AIRLINES (MEA) (ME)

MEA (Middle East Airlines-Air Liban) was founded as a private company in May 1945. Middle East Airlines Company SA, as it was then known, began regular commercial services on regional routes from Beirut in January 1946 with three de Havilland Rapides. DC-3 aircraft were acquired and the network was expanded to include Ankara and Istanbul in 1947 and Kuwait, Bahrain and Dhahran in 1948. Following negotiations with Pan American in 1949, MEA became a joint-stock company, Pan American acquiring a 36 per cent shareholding in the Lebanese carrier in return for which MEA received three additional DC-3s. In January 1955 the association with Pan American was terminated and in March of that year BOAC acquired a 38.74 per cent holding as a result of which MEA was able to purchase a fleet of Viscount 754 aircraft, commencing services with the type on 2 October 1955. During the next six years MEA's network was successfully expanded to include London, Rome, Geneva, Athens, Frankfurt and Vienna in Europe, as well as additional destinations in the Middle East. Four Comet 4C aircraft were ordered in 1960 and jet operations began with Comet 4s leased from BOAC before the introduction of MEA's own comet 4Cs on 6 January 1961. The formal association with BOAC was terminated in August of that year and the British carrier sold its MEA stock to Lebanese shareholders.

On 7 June 1963, MEA merged with Air Liban, another major Lebanese carrier, which operated to Paris and to destinations in North and West Africa. Air France acquired a 30 per cent holding in MEA through association with Air Liban. By 1965 the two companies were fully integrated and the new carrier had adopted its current title. The major part of MEA's fleet was destroyed by an armed attack on Beirut International Airport on 28 December 1968, forcing the carrier to lease various aircraft prior to acquiring a fleet of Convair 990A and

Middle East Airlines Airbus A321-100.

subsequently Boeing 720-023B aircraft from America Airlines. MEA absorbed Lebanese International Airways (a scheduled carrier which also served Europe and the Middle East) on 1 July 1969.

Continuing troubles in the area forced several closures of Beirut International Airport, one of which, in June 1976, resulted in MEA moving its operations temporarily to Paris. The political situation had stabilised somewhat, giving MEA the opportunity to renew its fleet, but the outlook again bleakened with further Israeli bombardments in April 1996.

MEA operates scheduled services to destinations throughout the Middle East, North and West Africa, Europe, the Far East, Australia and South America. The airline employs 4,300 people and carries 800,000 passengers a year.

Fleet Data
2 Airbus A310-200, **3** A310-300, **2** A321-100, **6** Boeing 707-320C, **3** 747-200C.

Nigeria Airways Boeing 737-200.

NIGERIA AIRWAYS (WT)

Nigeria Airways began operations on 1 October 1958, as WAAC (Nigeria) Limited, taking over the domestic services of West African Airways Corporation (WAAC) in Nigeria. WAAC had operated in the former British colonies in West Africa. Services to Dakar and London were undertaken for WAAC by BOAC. The Nigerian carrier became wholly government-owned in March 1961, and Fokker F27 Friendship 200 aircraft entered service in early 1963.

A former BOAC VC 10 Type 1101 was acquired in September 1969 and Boeing 707-3F9C aircraft entered service in May 1971. The airline adopted its present title in the same year and introduced the F28 Fellowship 2000 on domestic routes in 1973. Wide-bodied operations were initiated following delivery of Nigeria's first DC-10-30 on 14 October 1976.

The airline suffered long periods of financial instability and political interference, further exacerbated by heavy competition from independent airlines following withdrawal of its domestic monopoly in 1988. Plans to set up Air Nigeria with an equity partner to take over long-haul routes came to nothing and the network was drastically reduced as a result of unserviceability of much of the fleet.

Government-owned Nigeria Airways today operates regional services to destinations in East and West Africa, together with long-haul flights to Jeddah and London. Other European routes, as well as the Lagos-New York service are currently suspended.

Fleet Data
2 Airbus A310-200, **1** Boeing 707-320C, **6** 737-200A, **1** McDonnell Douglas DC-10-30.

NORTHWEST AIRLINES (NW)

Northwest is the second oldest airline in the USA with a continuous identification, and was formed on 1 August 1926 as Northwest Airways. The airline began air mail service on 1 October 1926, between Minneapolis/St. Paul and Chicago, and passenger services in July of the following year. On 16 April 1933 the airline adopted the name Northwest Orient and acquired Northern Air Transport. On 1 June 1945 Northwest became the fourth US transcontinental airline when service was extended eastward from Minneapolis/St Paul to Newark and New York via Milwaukee and Detroit. Northwest expanded its routes through Canada, Alaska and the Aleutian Islands, and on 15 July 1947 a new Great Circle route through Anchorage to Tokyo, Seoul, Shanghai, and Manila was inaugurated with DC-4 aircraft. Jet operations began on 8 July 1960 with DC-8-32 aircraft on the Far East routes.

Northwest adopted its current title when it acquired Republic Airlines on 12 August 1986, making the airline one of the largest operators in the USA.

In 1985 it was re-organised under the NWA holding company, and four years on forged an alliance with KLM Royal Dutch Airlines, which was later developed, through equity participation, into a major strategic alliance.

Northwest now operates an extensive network throughout the United States, supplemented by four feeder airlines operating under the *Northwest Airlink* banner, and to Canada, the Caribbean, Mexico, across the Pacific to the Far East, and trans-Atlantic services to Europe. It serves more than 240 cities in 22 countries, carrying 50 million passengers a year. Employees total 47,000.

Fleet Data
50 (20) Airbus A320-200, **(16)** A330-300, **47** Boeing 727-200, **3** 747-100, **20** 747-200B, **8** 747-200F, **10 (4)** Boeing 747-400, **44 (29)** 757-200, **22** McDonnell Douglas DC-9-10, **106** DC-9-30, **12** DC-9-41, **35** DC-9-51, **11** DC-10-30, **21** DC-10-40.

Northwest Airlines Boeing 727-200.

OLYMPIC AIRWAYS (OA)

Olympic was formed in January 1957 under the ownership of the Greek shipping magnate Aristotle Onassis to succeed the state-owned carrier TAE (Technical and Air Enterprises Company), which was placed into liquidation. TAE in its original form was established in 1935 to provide technical services, pilot training and air taxi charter services. In an attempt to improve the economic performance of air transportation in Greece, TAE merged with two other Greek carriers, Hellas and A.M.E., at the behest of the Greek government, to form the new TAE.

Olympic Airways Airbus A300-600R.

The economic difficulties persisted and in 1955 the carrier was taken over by the government. Subsequent agreement was reached with Onassis as a result of which the latter acquired the assets of the carrier together with a 50-year guarantee of sole designation as national airline and a monopoly of domestic routes. Olympic began operations on 6 April 1957, with a fleet of 14 DC-3s and one DC-4 aircraft. In order to match stiff competition from other foreign operators, DC-6B aircraft were leased from UAT in advance of the carrier's own DC-6B fleet acquisition. The type inaugurated Olympic's first international flights on 2 June 1957, with services from Athens to Rome, Paris and London. Services to Zürich and Frankfurt were added to the network in August of the following year.

Comet jet services began on Middle East routes to Tel Aviv, Nicosia, Beirut and Cairo in May 1960. In December 1974 Onassis relinquished his rights to operate Olympic and the carrier resumed operations in January 1975 under the control of the Greek government. Domestic monopoly was ended in January 1993, but no other carrier has been able to enter the still tightly controlled market.

Olympic Airways serves 35 international destinations, mainly in Europe and the Middle East, but extending also to Australia, the USA and South Africa. Together with wholly-owned subsidiary Olympic Aviation, it also serves 33 domestic points on the mainland and the many Greek islands, transporting 6 million passengers annually.

Fleet Data
6 Airbus A300B4-200, **2** A300-600R, **(2)** A340-300, **3** Boeing 727-200, **11** 737-200, **7** 737-400, **4** 747-200B.

PAKISTAN INTERNATIONAL AIRLINES (PK)

Pakistan International Airlines (PIA) was formally established as a scheduled carrier on 11 March 1955, with the takeover of Orient Airways. PIA had, however, initiated operations with Super Constellations on 7 June 1954, between Karachi and Dacca (now Dhaka) following its formation as a department of the Pakistan Ministry of Defence in 1951. Orient Airways became a registered company in 1947 and took over the routes of the pre-partition Indian operators in East and West Pakistan. On 1 February 1955 PIA inaugurated its first international service on the Karachi-Cairo-London route. The first of an eventual fleet of five Viscount 815 aircraft entered service in January 1959.

Jet services were started on 7 March 1960, to London, with a Boeing 707-121 leased from Pan American and operations were extended to New York on 5 May 1961. PIA then acquired its own Boeing 720-040B aircraft, and the first of these began operation in February 1962. Services to Canton and Shanghai began on 29 April 1964. PIA's operations underwent substantial change following the 1971 war which resulted in East Pakistan becoming the independent state of Bangladesh, and services to and within the latter were terminated. New York services were resumed in 1972 and on 20 January 1973, PIA became the first foreign carrier to operate to Beijing.

Wide-body aircraft, in the shape of the McDonnell Douglas DC-10-30, took over long-haul routes in 1974.

Pakistan's flag-carrier today serves more than 40 destinations in Africa, Europe, the Middle and Far East, and the United States and Canada, together with a 35-point domestic network. Its passenger carryings amount to 5.5 million passengers, and it has a high staff number of 20,000.

Fleet Data
9 Airbus A300-B4-200, **6** A310-300, **2** Boeing 707-320C, **6** 737-300, **8** 747-200B(SCD), **2** DHC-6 Twin Otter, **13** Fokker F27 Friendship.

PIA Airbus A310-300.

PHILIPPINE AIRLINES (PR)

Philippine Airlines (PAL) was formed on 26 February 1941 by a group of industrialists, and inaugurated flights between Manila and Baguio on 15 March of that year with a Beech 18. PAL resumed post-war operations with a Manila-Legaspi service on 14 February 1946, using newly acquired DC-3 aircraft. The carrier was designated the Philippine flag carrier to the US on 14 November 1946, and services to San Francisco with DC-4 aircraft began on 3 December. On 3 May 1947, the carrier purchased its main competitor, Far Eastern Air Transport, Inc. (FEATI). DC-6 aircraft were acquired in May 1948, and in August of that year Commercial Air Lines, Inc., (CALI) sold out to PAL making the latter the

Philippine Airlines Airbus A340-300.

nation's only scheduled domestic airline at that time.

Jet operations were inaugurated on the Hong Kong route with Boeing 707 aircraft chartered from Pan American on 11 December 1961. BAC One-Eleven 402 aircraft entered service on PAL's domestic and regional routes in May 1966. Wide-bodied services were introduced on the Pacific route following delivery of PAL's first DC-10-30 in July 1974.

A lack of cash hampered expansion plans and the airline was sold back to the government, which now retains a one-third stake, with the rest owned by PR Holdings.

The national flag-carrier now links the capital Manila with 34 cities in 23 countries. In addition to a strong focus on its regional market, Philippine Airlines also operates long-haul flights across the Pacific to the US, and westwards to the Middle East and Europe. It carries 7 million passengers and 140,000 tonnes of freight a year, and employs 14,000 people.

Fleet Data
11 Airbus A300B4-100/200, **(12)** A320-200, **(8)** A330-300, **4** A340-200, **1 (3)** A340-300, **12** Boeing 737-300, **11** 747-200B/C, **4 (7)** 747-400, **10** Fokker 50.

QANTAS AIRWAYS (QF)

Qantas was registered by two ex-flying corps Lieutenants, W. Hudson Fysh and P. J. McGinness, as The Queensland and Northern Territory Aerial Services Limited (from which 'Qantas' was derived) on 16 November 1920, with a paid-up capital of £6,037. For the first two years an Avro 504K and a B.E.2E were used to provide air taxi services and pleasure flights. The first scheduled service was inaugurated on 1 November 1922, from Charleville to Cloncurry in Queensland, via Longreach, using an Armstrong Whitworth F.K.8. A 1,475-Mile (2,375-km) route network in Queensland was established over the subsequent 12 years, with flying doctor services forming part of the operations. On 18 January 1934, Qantas and Imperial Airways (forerunner of BOAC) formed Qantas Empire Airways Limited to operate the Brisbane-Singapore portion of the England-Australia route. An order was placed for Constellations in October 1946, and on 3 July 1947, the Australian government purchased the remaining local shareholding in the carrier (having earlier purchased BOAC's holding) and became the sole owner of the airline, designating Qantas Empire Airlines as the operator of Australia's international air services. The carrier began its own Sydney-London Constellation services on 1 December 1947, and subsequent overseas operations were rapidly developed. During this time Qantas participated as a shareholder in Tasman Empire Airways Limited (TEAL) of New Zealand to develop air links between the two countries. The San Francisco route (opened on 15 May 1947) was extended in 1958 to New York and London, making Qantas the first operator to provide regular round the world service by linking London with its

Qantas Boeing 747-400.

South-East Asia route to Sydney.
Jet operations were inaugurated on the North American services on 29 July 1959, following delivery of Boeing 707-138 aircraft. Lockheed Electras were also acquired in the same year and were used to start the carrier's own services to New Zealand in 1961, and on 1 August 1967, the name was changed to Qantas Airways Limited.

First wide-body service (with Boeing 747-200B) was added to Singapore in September 1971, eventually leading to an all-Boeing fleet, although some Airbus aircraft were acquired with the take-over of Australian Airlines (formerly Trans-Australia Airlines-TAA) in September 1992. British Airways purchased a 25 per cent stake in March 1993, and the remaining 75 per cent government holding was floated on the Stock Exchange in July 1995.

Qantas serves 41 international destinations in 27 countries in Europe, Asia/Pacific, Africa and North America. Another 52 towns and cities are served in Australia together with five associate local carriers. Subsidiary Australia-Asia Airlines operates the flights to Taiwan. The airline carries more than 16 million passengers and around 300,000 tonnes of cargo. Employees total 29,500.

Fleet Data
4 Airbus A300B4-200, 16 Boeing 737-300, 22 737-400, 5 747-200B(SCD), 6 747-300(EUD), 18 747-400, 2 747SP, 7 767-200ER, 17 767-300ER.

Royal Air Maroc Boeing 727-200.

ROYAL AIR MAROC (AT)

Royal Air Maroc (Compagnie Nationale de Transports Aériens) is the national carrier of the Kingdom of Morocco, and was formed on 28 June 1953, by the merger of Air Atlas and Air Maroc, brought about largely through the efforts of the Moroccan government. Air Atlas (Compagnie Cherifienne d'Aviation) was formed in 1946 to provide local services plus international links with Algiers and key cities in southern France. Air Maroc (Société Avia Maroc Ligne Aérienne) was established in 1947 as a charter airline. Following the merger, Royal Air Maroc undertook development of both domestic and international services. Routes to Dakar, Gibraltar, Madrid and Frankfurt were opened, and Meknes, Oujda, Tetuan, Fez and Mellila-Nadar were added to the domestic network.

The carrier introduced jet operations in 1960 with Caravelle III aircraft entering service on the Casablanca-Paris route on 20

May. Wide-bodied services were initiated following delivery of a Boeing 747-2B6B aircraft on 29 September 1978.

Royal Air Maroc currently operates scheduled services from Casablanca and Tangier to 13 domestic points and to 50 destinations in North and West Africa, the Middle East, Europe, North and South America. Charter and inclusive-tour operations are also undertaken. The Moroccan government has a 92.7 per cent holding in the carrier. Royal Air Maroc employs approximately 5,300 personnel, and carries more than 2.2 million passengers.

Fleet Data
2 ATR42-300, 4 Boeing 727-200A, 6 737-200A, 7 737-400, 5 737-500, (9) 737-800, 1 747-200B(SCD), 1 747-400, 2 757-200.

Royal Jordanian Boeing 727-200.

ROYAL JORDANIAN (RJ)

ALIA – The Royal Jordanian Airline was founded in December 1963 as the wholly government-owned national carrier of Jordan to supersede the previous national airline, Jordanian Airways. Operations started on 15 December 1963 with services to neighbouring Middle East countries using a leased DC-7 aircraft and subsequently Handley Page Heralds. Jet operations began following delivery of Alia's first Caravelle 10R in July 1965 and services were inaugurated to Paris and Rome. Alia was the first Arab carrier to link the Middle East with North America inaugurating North Atlantic service in July 1977 using 747-2D3B equipment. Four years later, eight Lockheed TriStars were acquired, supplemented between 1987 and 1990 by six Airbus A310-300s used on European routes. The name was changed to Royal Jordanian Airlines (generally referred to as Royal Jordanian) in December 1986.

Royal Jordanian presently operates services from Amman to 28 destinations in Europe, the Middle and Far East, North America and North Africa, and employs 5,000 personnel. Subsidiary interests include wholly-owned Arab Wings, established in 1975 to provide executive charter services, and Royal Wings, formed on 1 January 1996 to offer the first direct service between Jordan and Israel, following the ending of the state of war between the two countries and the signing of a bilateral agreement. Royal Jordanian is wholly government owned, but privatisation is being considered.

Fleet Data
2 Airbus A310-200, 4 A310-300, 3 A320-200, 3 Boeing 707-320C, 2 727-200A, 5 Lockheed L1011 TriStar 500.

SABENA (SN)

Sabena (Société anonyme Belge d'Exploitation de la Navigation Aérienne) was established on 23 May 1923. Principal shareholders were the Syndicat National pour l'Etude des Transports Aériens (SNETA), the Belgian government and the Belgian Congo. SNETA was Sabena's predecessor, and had been formed to develop the necessary infrastructure for the establishment of air services within Europe and to the Belgian Congo (later Zaire and now the Democratic Republic of Congo). Sabena's initial route development focused on air links between the Low Countries and Switzerland, and on 1 April 1924, a cargo service was inaugurated on the Rotterdam-Brussels-Strasbourg route, extended to Basle on 10 June. With the arrival of Handley Page W.8 aircraft, Sabena began passenger services on the route on 14 July 1924. In addition to building up European operations, Sabena proceeded to develop what became an extensive network of services in the Belgian Congo, where the SNETA-formed company LARA had already pioneered air services. Delivery of DC-4 aircraft, ordered during World War II while Sabena was temporarily headquartered in Leopoldville, facilitated the inauguration of services between Brussels and New York on 4 June 1947.

In 1949 Sabena was granted a monopoly of scheduled services in the Congo, and the carrier acquired two small local independent operators, Aeromas and the original Air Congo. Following independence for the Congo, Sabena assisted in the formation in June 1961 of the new Air Congo (later Air Zaire). Sabena introduced jet operations with the Boeing 707 starting Brussels-New York services in January 1960.

The first Boeing 747 wide-body service was inaugurated between Brussels and New York on 8 January 1971. An equity alliance with Air France, which bought a 37.5 per cent stake in April 1992, was not a success and was replaced by an association with Swissair, which bought a 49.5 per cent interest, with the Belgian Government holding the remainder.

Sabena operates a comprehensive European network and has a still expanding African presence. Other long-haul services are flown to the US and the Far East. Regional associate Delta Air Transport (DAT) in which it has a 90 per cent stake, operates

Sabena Boeing 737-200.

thinner European routes, while wholly-owned Sobelair provides charter services. Sabena carries close to 5 million passengers and 90,000 tonnes of cargo. It employs 9,500 people.

Fleet Data
2 Airbus A310-200, 1 A310-300, 3 (1) A330-300, 2 A340-200, 2 A340-300, 13 Boeing 737-200, 6 737-400, 6 737-500, 2 747-300, 9 Embraer EMB-120 Brasilia.

SAS (SK)

Scandinavian Airlines System (SAS) is the national carrier of Denmark, Norway and Sweden, and was originally formed on 1 August 1946 as a consortium of Det Danske Luftfartselskab (DDL), Det Norske Luftfartselskap (DNL) and AB Aerotransport (ABA), the leading pre-war airlines of those three nations respectively, for intercontinental operations. Scheduled services were inaugurated on the Stockholm-Copenhagen-New York route on 17 September 1946, with DC-4 aircraft. On 18 April 1948, the three partner airlines formed the SAS European division and in July of that year Svensk Interkontinental Lufttrafik (SILA), another Swedish airline, merged with ABA. Agreement was reached on 8 February 1951, for unification of the whole SAS consortium under a centralized management, and the three participating carriers became non-operating holding companies. The consortium is owned by 28.5 per cent by DDL, 28.5 per cent by DNL and 43 per cent by ABA, each of the parent airlines being a private company owned 50-50 by private shareholders and the respective governments.

SAS initiated service to Buenos Aires on 29 December 1946, and opened a route to Bangkok in October 1949. The carrier inaugurated the world's first scheduled polar service between Copenhagen and Los Angeles on 15 November 1954, using DC-6B aircraft. Jet operations started with a Copenhagen-Beirut Caravelle service on 26 April 1959, making SAS the first airline to put the type into scheduled operation. DC-8-32 aircraft entered service on the New York

SAS Fokker F28 Fellowship.

route on 1 May 1960. The carrier introduced the DC-9-21 and DC-9-41 aircraft into domestic and European service in 1968 (both models having been developed to the SAS' specifications).

SAS began wide-body services on the New York route in 1971, and added the McDonnell Douglas DC-10-30 in October 1974. The domestic subsidiary Linjeflyg was fully integrated on 1 January 1993. A major restructuring subsequently saw the divestment of its shareholdings in Continental Airlines and Lan Chile, but it retains a 40 per cent holding in Airlines of Britain, parent of British Midland, and a one-third stake in Greenlandair (Grönlandsfly). It also has a 49 per cent stake in Spanish holiday airline Spanair.

The SAS network, centred on three hubs at Oslo, Copenhagen and Stockholm, encompasses more than 100 destinations in 32 countries in Europe, the Middle and Far East and North America. Wholly-owned SAS Commuter operates secondary routes with Scandinavia. The airline carries more than 20 million passengers and has a staff of 22,700 people.

Fleet Data
(41) 737-600, **1** Boeing 747-200C, **14** 767-300ER, **16** Fokker F28 Fellowship, **4** McDonnell Douglas DC-9-21, **23** DC-9-41, **71** MD-80, **8 (2)** MD-90-30.

SAUDI ARABIAN AIRLINES (SV)

Saudi Arabian Airlines was founded in 1945 by the Saudi government as the national carrier, and domestic operations started with three DC-3 aircraft on 14 March 1947. A fleet of Bristol Freighter 21 and DC-4 aircraft was introduced into service from 1949, followed by 10 Convair 340s from 1954. Three DC-6 aircraft were added in 1960 to enhance the route system within the Arab world and improve travel facilities for pilgrims. The acquisition of two Boeing 720-068B aircraft permitted jet services to be inaugurated in April 1962, progressively to cover Amman, Beirut, Cairo, Istanbul, Bombay and Karachi. In 1963 King Faisal decreed the corporate status of Saudia, as the company became known. 1967 marked the opening of Saudia's inaugural route to Europe, serving Geneva, Frankfurt and London, and later that year the carrier initiated services to Tripoli, Tunis and Casablanca. Acquisition of Boeing 707-368Cs enabled non-stop Jeddah-London operations to begin in 1968. Wide-bodied services were inaugurated with Lockheed TriStar 100 aircraft in 1975.

All schedules were suspended between 17 January and 4 March 1991, as Saudi Arabian airports closed during the Gulf War. The airline embarked on a long-overdue fleet modernisation in October 1995, signing a $6 billion contract for 61 aircraft. This was followed by a new corporate identity, unveiled in June 1996, dropping the name of Saudia.

The wholly government-owned flag-carrier operates services to 52 international and 25 domestic destinations. Apart from services throughout the Arab world of the Middle East and North and North East Africa, services also reach the rest of Africa, Europe, the Far

Saudi Arabian Airbus A300-600.

East and North America, carrying 12 million passengers and 225,000 tonnes of cargo. Employees total 24,500 people.

Fleet Data
11 Airbus A300-600, **2** Boeing 707-320C, **20** 737-200A, **10** 747-100, **1** 747-200B, **2** 747-200F, **10** 747-300, **1** 747SP, **(5)** 747-400, **(23)** 777-200, **17** Lockheed L1011 TriStar 200, **(29)** McDonnell Douglas MD-90-30, **(4)** MD-11F.

SINGAPORE AIRLINES (SQ)

Singapore Airlines (SIA) was formed on 24 January 1972, as the state-owned national carried to succeed the jointly operated Malaysia-Singapore Airlines (MSA) following the decision in January of the preceding year by the Malaysian and Singapore governments to set up separate national airlines. SIA began operations on 1 October 1972, serving the total MSA international network with former MSA Boeing 737 and 707 aircraft. On 2 April 1973, SIA began daily services to London, and in September of that year the carrier's first two 747B aircraft were delivered. Boeing 727-212 aircraft entered SIA service on regional routes in September 1977.

Concorde services between Singapore and London via Bahrain in conjunction with British Airways were inaugurated on 10 December 1977, but suspended shortly afterwards due to the Malaysian government decision to ban supersonic operations over Malaysia. Although the service was allowed to resume in January 1979, it was finally terminated in November 1980.

The last decade has been noteworthy for a tremendous growth and record aircraft purchases. A 'Global Excellence' alliance was established with Swissair and Delta Air Lines in November 1990, including a small equity swap.

Singapore Airlines today serves 77 cities in 42 countries in Europe, the Middle East, Asia, South West Pacific, Australia, New Zealand and North America. Wholly-owned subsidiary Silk Air (formerly Tradewinds) links Singapore with 20 destinations in eight Asian countries. The airline carried an

SIA Boeing 777-200.

impressive 12 million passengers and 675,000 tonnes of cargo in 1996. It employs 27,700 people.

Fleet Data
6 Airbus A310-200, **17** A310-300, **7 (10)** A340-300E, **1** Boeing 747-200F, **4** 747-300, **3** 747-300 Combi, **36 (9)** 747-400, **5 (2)** 747-400F, **7 (23)** 777-200, **(4)** 777-300, **1** Douglas DC-8-73CF.

SOUTH AFRICAN AIRWAYS (SA)

SAA is the national for the Republic of South Africa and was formed on 1 February 1934, when the government (through the South African Railways Administration) took control of Union Airways which had been operating since 1929 as a private company providing air mail services from Port Elizabeth to Johannesburg, Cape Town and Durban. On 1 February 1935 SAA acquired South West African Airways which had been operating a Windhoek-Kimberley air mail service since 1932. By the outbreak of World War II SAA had established a regional network of services which encompassed all adjacent territories. Operation between Johannesburg and London, known as the 'Springbok' service, began in co-operation with BOAC on 10 November 1945. By the end of 1947 a network of domestic, regional and international services was being operated with a fleet of 41 aircraft comprising DC-3, DC-4, Viking, Lodestar and Dove aircraft.

Early in the 1950s SAA took delivery of Constellation aircraft for use on the Springbok service, and in 1953 the carrier began jet operations with Comet 1 aircraft leased from BOAC. In 1956 SAA became the first airline outside the United States to operate the DC-7B, which entered service for SAA on the London route. Viscount 813 aircraft entered major domestic and regional service with the carrier in November 1958 and SAA recommenced jet operations on 1 October 1960, following delivery of Boeing 707-344 aircraft.

The first Boeing 747-200B entered service in 1971. On 1 April 1990, the airline became a division of the commercialised state company Transnet, as a first step towards privatisation.

The national airline today operates intercontinental long-haul flights to Europe,

South African Airways Airbus A320-200.

the Far East and North and South America, together with a strong regional network in Africa, serving a total of 34 cities. Domestic trunk services focus on the 'Golden Triangle' routes between Cape Town, Durban and Johannesburg, while secondary routes are flown by associates SA Express and SA Airlink. South African Airways also has a 40 per cent stake in Alliance Air, the long-haul venture with Uganda and Tanzania. Passengers total nearly 5 million, and the airline also handles some 70,000 tonnes of cargo. Employees number 10,000.

Fleet Data
4 Airbus A300B2K-3C, **3** A300B4-200, **7** A320-200, **13** Boeing 737-200A, **5** 747-200B, **1** 747-200F, **4** 747-300, **4 (2)** 747-400, **2** 747SP, **1** 767-300ER, **(4)** 777-200.

Southwest Airlines Boeing 737-200.

SOUTHWEST AIRLINES (WN)

Southwest was formed on 15 March 1967 as Air Southwest to provide scheduled intra-state low-fare passenger services in Texas. The current name was adopted on 29 March 1971 and services were inaugurated on 18 June of that year between Houston, Dallas and San Antonio with three Boeing 737-2H4 aircraft.

Southwest was certificated as an interstate carrier in December 1978. Muse Air was taken over on 25 June 1985.

The airline has undergone tremendous expansion and has become the role model for low-fare, no-frills operations. It now operates high-frequency jet services between 44 airports in 20 US states, and the network continues to grow. The airline carries more than 45 million passengers and employs 24,000 people.

Fleet Data
50 Boeing 737-200, **191** 737-300, **25** 737-500, **4 (46)** 737-600/700/800.

SWISSAIR (SR)

Swissair was founded on 26 March 1931, through the merger of Ad Astra Aero and Balair. In April 1932 Europe's first regular services with the Lockheed Orion single engine monoplane were initiated on the Zürich-Munich-Vienna route, establishing new standards in fast air transportation. Swissair was the first European airline to employ air stewardesses, following the introduction of the 16-seat Curtiss Condor. The airline was designated as the national carrier in February 1947. Swissair's first transatlantic service, from Geneva to New York, was operated by a DC-4 on 2 May of that year, but a regular service did not begin until April 1949. Swissair began Convair 240 services in 1949, and acquired DC-6B aircraft from 1951 for long haul operations. Jet operations began on 30 May 1960, with DC-8 services to New York. Caravelles were introduced on European routes in the same year and Convair 990s entered service in 1962 to the Far East and South America. Wide-bodied services to New York began in April 1971 following delivery of two 747B aircraft, Swissair was the launch customer for the DC-9-51 and also the DC-9-81 (MD-81), the latter entering service on European routes on 5 October 1980.

In November 1990, Swissair established the 'Global Excellence' alliance, including a small cross-equity, with Singapore Airlines and Delta Air Lines. In November 1995, Swissair transferred the short-haul charter operations of subsidiary Balair/CTA, together with eight MD-80s, to Crossair, and has set up a new low-cost, long-haul charter division, Charter-Leisure. Swissair was re-organised into four operating divisions under SAir Holding during 1996. The national carrier, in which government entities retain a 20.5 per cent stake, operates a worldwide network serving 125 destinations in 67 countries, except Australia. It has a 56.1 per cent holding in Crossair, which links 78 destinations in 21 European countries, 49.5 per cent in Belgian flag-carrier Sabena, and 10 per cent in Austrian Airlines.

Fleet Data
8 Airbus A310-300, 5 (3) A319, 15 (3) A320-200, 8 A321-100, (9) A330-200, 5 Boeing 747-300, 15 (1) McDonnell Douglas MD-11, 8 MD-81.

Swissair Airbus A321-100.

TAP-AIR PORTUGAL (TP)

Air Portugal was established by the Portuguese government as a division of the Civil Aeronautics Secretariat in 1944 under the name of Transportes Aereos Portugueses SARL. Regular commercial services were inaugurated between Lisbon and Madrid on 19 September 1946, and later to Luanda (Angola), Laurenco Marques (Mozambique) and Paris, using DC-3s and subsequently DC-4 aircraft. TAP's first domestic route (Lisbon-Oporto) was opened in 1947. In 1953 the government sold its interest in the carrier, principally to a private business consortium, and TAP became a limited liability company. Super Constellations were introduced into service from July 1955 and in 1959 TAP embarked on a policy of route expansion on the African continent. Services to Rio de Janeiro via Ilha do Sal and Recife in association with Panair do Brasil began in 1960 using Panair DC-7C aircraft. Caravelle VI-Rs were delivered from July 1962 although jet operations had started earlier through the operation of Comet 4Bs in association with BEA. North Atlantic services were inaugurated on the Lisbon-New York route in 1969 and to Montreal in 1971. TAP once again came under state ownership when the carrier was nationalised on 15 April 1975. The carrier adopted its present name in 1979.

Air Portugal operates a network of scheduled services covering Europe, the Canary Islands, Africa, and North, Central and South America, as well as domestic services linking Lisbon, Oporto, Faro, Madeira and the Azores. Charter operations are also undertaken. Approximately 8,800 personnel are employed by the carrier.

TAP-Air Portugal Boeing 737-200.

Fleet Data
(18) Airbus A319, 6 A320-200, 5 A310-300, 4 A340-300, 8 Boeing 737-200, 8 Boeing 737-300, 2 Lockheed TriStar 500.

TAROM ROMANIAN AIRLINES (RO)

Tarom (Transporturile Aeriene Române) was originally formed in 1946 as Transporturi Aerlene Romana Sovietica (TARS) by the governments of Romania and the Soviet Union. TARS succeeded the pre-war state airline LARES and provided domestic and international services radiating from Bucharest. Routes to Prague, Budapest and Warsaw were opened with Li-2 aircraft, and in 1954 TARS adopted its present title when Romania took over complete control of the carrier. Ilyushin Il-14 aircraft were acquired, enabling Tarom to expand its international network, including new services to Moscow, Vienna, Zürich, Paris, Brussels and Copenhagen. Ilyushin 18 turboprops entered service in 1962 and further expansion took place with services to Belgrade, Sofia, Athens and Frankfurt.

Jet operations on European routes began after delivery of the first of an initial fleet of six One-Eleven 424 aircraft on 14 June 1968. Ilyushin Il-62s were acquired in 1973, primarily for holiday charter traffic, and the first of three Boeing 707-3K1C aircraft entered service in 1974. In 1975 Tarom formed Liniile Aeriene Romane (LAR), a charter subsidiary which began operating in December of that year with former Tarom One-Eleven 424s. Tarom acquired a number of One-Eleven 560 aircraft built under licence in Romania.

Tarom Romanian Airlines Airbus A310-200.

Tarom acquired the Airbus A310, its first wide-body aircraft in December 1992.

The national airline serves 33 cities in 20 European countries, and another 17 in the Middle and Far East, and the United States, all served from Bucharest-Otopeni Airport. A domestic network is centred on Bucharest-Baneasa. Tarom's annual passenger figure in nearing 1.5 million. Employees total 3,300.

Fleet Data
2 (1) Airbus A310-300, 7 Antonov An-24RV, 2 ATR42-500, 11 BAC/Rombac 1-11, 2 Boeing 707-320C, 5 737-300, 2 Ilyushin Il-18V, 2 Tupolev Tu-154B-2.

THAI AIRWAYS INTERNATIONAL (TG)

Thai Airways International Limited (Thai International) is the designated national flag carrier of Thailand for scheduled international services, and was formed in August 1959 by Scandinavian Airlines System (SAS) with a 30 per cent shareholding, and Thai Airways Company Limited (the government-owned domestic airline of Thailand) with a 70 per cent shareholding. Operations began in May 1960 on regional services within Asia, utilising technical and managerial assistance provided by SAS, and three DC-6B aircraft leased from the airline. Rapid development of international routes led to the opening of 'Royal Orchid' services to Kuala Lumpur, Singapore, Jakarta, Rangoon, Calcutta, Saigon (now Ho Chi Minh City), Hong Kong, Taipei and Tokyo.

Jet services were inaugurated in 1962 with two Convair 990A aircraft on lease from SAS. Wide-bodied operations with DC-10-30 aircraft leased from SAS and UTA were initiated prior to delivery of Thai's own DC-10-30s from March 1977. On 1 April of that year, SAS's residual shareholding in the carrier was acquired by Thai Airways Company Limited.

Growth accelerated on 1 April 1988 as a result of the merger with Thai Airways. This gave Thai International sole domestic and international rights, although the government is in the process of licensing a second international airline. A slow process of

Thai Airways International Boeing 777-200.

privatisation was initiated with the floating of some shares on the Stock Exchange in 1991, but the government still holds 93 per cent of the shares.

Thai International now operates an extensive regional network and flights to Europe, North America, Australia and New Zealand, serving 51 cities in 36 countries. It also operates a 20-point domestic route system. In 1996, Thai International carried 14.6 million passengers. Staff numbers 21,500.

Fleet Data
3 Airbus A300B4, 6 A300-600, 10 (5) A300-600R, 2 A310-300, 8 (4) A330-300, 2 ATR42-300, 2 ATR72-200, 8 (4) Boeing 737-400, 2 747-300, 12 747-400, 8 777-200, (6) 777-300, 3 McDonnell Douglas DC-10-30ER, 4 MD-11.

TWA Boeing 757-200.

TRANS WORLD AIRLINES (TW)

TWA can trace its history back to the formation of Western Air Express (WAE) which initiated mail services between Las Angeles and Salt Lake City in April 1926. In 1929, the carrier absorbed Standard Air Lines and in July 1930 WAE merged with Transcontinental Air Transport, Inc (TAT) to form Transcontinental and Western Air (TWA). Prior to the merger, TAT had acquired Moddux Airlines which gave TAT access to San Francisco and San Diego. In 1934 the former WAE was bought out of TWA and subsequently became Western Airlines.

Constellation services were inaugurated in February 1946 between New York and Paris via Gander and Shannon, representing TWA's first international route and also the first commercial link between the USA and Paris. In 1950 the corporate name was changed to Trans World Airlines, reflecting TWA's international route expansion. On 20 March 1959, TWA operated its first jet service with the introduction of Boeing 707 aircraft. Wide-bodied services with Boeing 747-131 aircraft were initiated in 1979, and the Lockheed TriStar, for which TWA was one of three launch customers, entered service in June 1972.

TWA took over St Louis-based Ozark Airlines on 30 September 1986, but the enlarged operation was mainly responsible for subsequent financial problems which resulted in the controversial sale of its profitable London Heathrow routes in May 1991 and a period under Chapter 11 protection, from which it emerged in August 1995.

TWA now operates extensive trunk services within the United States, and also serves Central America and the Caribbean, together with trans-Atlantic routes to Europe. Together with its Trans World Express feeder partner Trans States Airlines, TWA serves more than 100 destinations. The airline carries more than 21 million passengers and 125,000 tonnes of cargo, and employs 23,000 staff.

Fleet Data
(10) Airbus A330-300, 41 Boeing 727-220A, 9 747-100, 2 747-200B, 5 (17) 757-200, 12 767-200ER, 3 767-300ER, 14 Lockheed L1011 TriStar, 7 McDonnell Douglas DC-9-15, 35 DC-9-30, 1 DC-9-33F, 3 DC-9-41, 12 DC-9-51, 29 MD-82, 19 MD-83.

TUNISAIR (TU)

Tunisair (Société Tunisienne de l'Air) was founded in 1948 as a co-operative venture between the Tunisian government, Air France and various private investors who were later bought out. Operations started in 1949 with DC-3 aircraft serving the traditional markets between Tunisia, France and Algeria. The declaration of independence resulted in the Tunisian government taking a 51 per cent (and later, 85 per cent) controlling interest in the carrier in 1957, with Air France holding the balance. The fleet was then composed of three DC-3s and two DC-4 aircraft and the route network covered international services to Paris, Marseille, Lyon, Rome and Algiers. The introduction of the airline's first Caravelle III in September 1961 represented a major advance for Tunisair, and as additional Caravelles were added to the fleet, the route system was progressively expanded to include services to Amsterdam, Brussels and Frankfurt in 1966, Zürich in 1967, and Casablanca in 1968. The carrier's first Boeing 727-2H3 entered service in 1972, during which year Luxembourg and Jeddah were added to the system. London services were inaugurated in the following year.

Modernisation of the fleet was effected with the arrival of the first Airbus A320-200 in October 1990. The national airline, still owned 42.5 per cent by the government, serves a short/medium-haul network, linking Tunisia with 37 destinations in Europe, the Middle East and North and West Africa. Extensive charters are also flown into the tourist gateways of Jerba and Monastir. Tuninter, set up on 27 July 1991 with a 40 per cent shareholding by Tunisair, operates domestic services and routes to Sicily and Malta. Another associate, Tunisavia, owned jointly with Heli-Union of France, undertakes charter flights. Tunisair carries 2.7 million passengers, and employs 7,200 people.

Fleet Data
1 Airbus A300B4-200, **8** A320-200, **7** Boeing 727-200A, **4** 737-200A, **4** 737-500.

Tunisair Airbus A320-200.

TURKISH AIRLINES-THY (TK)

THY-Türk Hava Yollari , Turkey's national airline, was founded on 20 May 1933, as Devlet Hava Yollari (State Airlines), and was part of the Ministry of National Defence. In 1935 the airline was transferred to the Ministry of Public Works. Operations started between Ankara and Istanbul with aircraft which included the de Havilland D.H.86B

THY Airbus A310-300.

Express and Rapide. On 3 June 1938, the airline became known as the General Directorate of State Airways, and the Ministry of Transportation assumed control. The airline operated only domestic services until 1947, when a route to Athens was opened. DC-3 aircraft were introduced, and the airline took delivery of the first of seven de Havilland Herons in February 1955. In May of that year the Turkish government established a corporation to handle air transportation and on 1 March 1956, the new corporation began operations under the present title of Turk Hava Yollari AO. The Turkish government had a 51 per cent holding in THY, and BOAC held 6.5 per cent of the share capital, through which THY was able to order a fleet of five Viscount 794 aircraft.

Jet services were introduced in August 1967, with a DC-9-15 leased from Douglas, and Boeing 707-321 aircraft were acquired from Pan Am in 1971. Wide-bodied services began in December 1972 with DC-10-10 aircraft.

The first of seven Airbus A310-200s arrived in May 1985 and further fleet expansion in the early 1990s, including the A340-300, permitted the introduction of its first long-haul flights to New York, Bangkok and Singapore.

Turkey's national airline operates international routes to 56 cities, with a strong emphasis on Europe, but also including Central Asia, North Africa, the Middle and Far East and the United States. A dense domestic network includes 26 towns and cities. The airline is owned 98.24 per cent by the government through the Public Participation Administration. It has a half share in Kibris Turkish Airlines (Kibris Türk Hava Yollari), operating from the Turkish part of the island of Cyprus, and jointly owns with Lufthansa the holiday airline SunExpress. More than 7 million passengers and 80,000 tonnes of cargo are carried per annum. Staff numbers 8,500.

Fleet Data
7 Airbus A310-200, **7** A310-300, **5** A340-300, **28** Boeing 737-400, **2** 737-500, **4** Avro RJ70, **10** RJ100, **3** Boeing 727-200F.

UNITED AIRLINES (UA)

United traces its origin to Varney Air Lines which began air mail services between Paso, Washington and Elko, Nevada on 6 April 1926. Varney Air Lines was later

United Airlines Boeing 777-200.

merged with Pacific Air Transport and National Air Transport, both of whom were air mail carriers, into Boeing Air Transport which was part of a combine that included the Boeing Airplane Company and Pratt & Whitney, the engine manufacturer. United was organized on 1 July 1931, as the management company for the airline division. Three years later the combine broke up and the corporate divisions became separate entities. By May 1947 the route network had been expanded to include Boston, Denver, Washington DC and Hawaii. Jet operations with DC-8 aircraft were inaugurated on 18 September 1959.

United's size increased significantly on 1 June 1961, when the carrier took over Capital Airlines, founded in November 1936 as Pennsylvania Central Airlines. As a result of the merger United's route system was increased by 7.200 miles (11,600km) and the carrier became the world's largest privately-owned airline in terms of annual passengers carried and passenger miles flown.

Wide-body services were introduced with the Boeing 747 on 23 July 1970, followed by the McDonnell Douglas DC-10-10 on 14 August 1971. Its international route system was strengthened in February 1986 with the purchase of Pan American's Pacific division, adding 11 cities on the Pacific Rim. Europe was reached on 15 May 1990, and later that year, United became the launch customer for the new Boeing 777. United Airlines is today the world's second-largest carrier, serving 39 international destinations in 30 countries and two US Territories, plus 98 airports in the US. Another 185 local cities are served by its five *United Express* partners. United is part of the new *Star Alliance*, formed with Lufthansa and four other airlines. United carries 75 million passengers and over 500,000 tonnes of cargo. It has a workforce of 82,000 people.

Fleet Data
(28) Airbus A319, **41 (12)** A320-200, **75** Boeing 727-200A, **67** 737-200, **101** 737-300, **57** 737-500, **17** 747-100, **9** 747-200B, **30 (14)** 747-400, **90 (4)** 757-200, **19** 767-200, **23** 767-300ER, **31 (5)** 777-200, **26** McDonnell Douglas DC-10-10, **8** DC-10-30.

UNITED PARCEL SERVICE (UPS) (5X)

After a brief spell in the air express business in the US West Coast between 1929 and 1931, UPS began air operations again in 1981, with a package delivery service from a hub at Louisville, Kentucky. After using its own aircraft, but flown under contract by others, the company decided it would be more cost-effective to form its own airline, which was set up on 1 February 1988. By that time, the fleet had grown to more than 100 aircraft, including the Boeing 727 and 757, Douglas DC-8 and Fairchild Expediters. In October 1995, UPS became the launch customer for the Boeing 767-300F freighter.

UPS now vies with FedEx for the title of the world's largest package delivery service, providing next day and two-day delivery service to more than 200 countries. Major hubs and distribution points include Bergamo, Cologne/Bonn, East Midlands, Gudalajara, Hamilton, Hong Kong, Louisville, Mexico City, Montreal, Monterrey, Nuremberg, Porto, Rome, Seoul, Singapore, Taipei, Tokyo, Vienna and Zaragoza. It carries some 200,000 tonnes of cargo, and employs 1,830 people.

Fleet Data
51 Boeing 727-100F, **7** 727-200F, **15** 747-100F, **60 (15)** 757-200PF, **20 (10)** 767-300F, **24** McDonnell Douglas DC-8-71F, **28** DC-8-73F.

UPS Boeing 767-300F.

US AIRWAYS (US)

US Airways was formed on 5 March 1937, under the name of All-American Aviation. The carrier was the first to be certificated by the former Civil Aeronautics Board following the passage of the Civil Aeronautics Acts in 1938 and began a specialised 'pick-up' air mail service to isolated communities without adequate airport facilities. With the introduction of passenger operations, the carrier changed its name to All-American Airways. The title was changed again in 1953 to Allegheny Airlines Inc. By 1959 Allegheny's system extended from Boston in the east to Cleveland and Detroit in the west. In 1963 Allegheny relocated its principal operations and maintenance base from Washington DC to Pittsburgh.

In July 1968 Allegheny merged with Indianapolis-based Lake Central Airlines. Further rapid growth was enhanced by a merger with Mohawk Airlines of Utica in April 1972. Mohawk operated in the eastern seaboard states, and also to eastern Canada. By mid-1978 the carrier had become an all-jet operator and adopted the name USAir on 30 October 1979. The acquisition of Piedmont Airlines in April 1988 and Pacific Southwest Airlines (PSA) a year later virtually doubled its fleet and operations. It also gave it access to its first international route – Charlotte to London, now flown with Boeing 767s. An equity partnership was established with British Airways, but has now been dissolved. On 27 February 1997, the airlines adopted its present title.

US Airways Boeing 757-200.

US Airways serves a vast domestic network connecting 210 points throughout the US, plus Canada, Central America and the Caribbean. Trans-Atlantic flights serve five capital cities in Europe. A large feeder network is provided under the *US Airways Express* title by 10 local airlines. US Airways carries in excess of 57 million passengers, and employs 42,000 people.

Fleet Data
64 Boeing 737-200A, **85** 737-300, **54** 737-400, **34** 757-200, **12** 767-200ER, **8** Fokker F28-4000 Fellowship, **40** Fokker 100, **64** McDonnell Douglas DC-9-30, **19** MD-81, **12** MD-82.

VARIG (RG)

Varig (Viação Aérea Rio Gradense), the national carrier of Brazil, was founded on 7 May 1927, with technical assistance provided by the German-backed Kondor Syndikat and proceeded to develop domestic services within Rio Grande do Sul. Service to Montevideo began in August 1942, and Lockheed 10A Electras were acquired in 1943 inaugurating service to Rio de Janeiro via Florianopolis, Curitiba and Sao Paulo. The acquisition of Aéro Geral in late 1951 gave Varig access to routes north of Rio de Janeiro for the first time. Buenos Aires was added to the network in the following year, and on 2 August 1955, Varig's first Super Constellation inaugurated services to New York.

Jet services were inaugurated with Caravelle IIIs on the New York route from 19 December 1959. In August 1961 Varig obtained a controlling interest in the REAL Aerovias airline consortium. REAL had been founded in February 1946 and had become the largest operator in South America through a series of mergers and takeovers, operating a very extensive domestic network as well as international services. REAL's route system and aircraft fleet were progressively integrated with those of Varig, and in 1965 the route network and aircraft of the bankrupt Panair do Brasil were also acquired. The Foundation of Employees (the owners of Varig, and nowadays known as the Ruben Berta Foundation) acquired control of Cruzeiro do Sul in May 1975. The two carriers maintained separate identities

VARIG Boeing 747-300.

until fully integrated into Varig in January 1993.

Varig remains Brazil's principal airline, providing extensive regional and domestic services together with long-haul flights to Mexico, the United States, Europe, Africa and the Far East, serving 30 destinations in 23 countries, plus another 90 in Brazil in association with wholly-owned subsidiaries Rio-Sul and Nordeste. In 1996, it carried 9.7 million passengers and 320,000 tonnes of cargo. Employees total 19,000.

Fleet Data
5 Boeing 727-200F, **17** 737-200A, **25 (10)** 737-300, **5** 747-300, **(6)** 747-400, **6** 767-200ER, **4** 767-300ER, **8** McDonnell Douglas DC-10-30, **2** DC-10-30F, **7** MD-11.

VASP BRAZILIAN AIRLINES (VP)

VASP (Viação Aérea Sao Paulo) was founded on 4 November 1933 by the Sao Paulo State Government, City of Sao Paulo and Municipal Bank, and began operations with two small Monospar ST.4 monoplanes on 1 April 1934, initially linking Sao Paulo with Rio Preto, Sao Carlos, Ribeirao Prêto and Uberaba. A de Havilland DH.84 Dragon biplane was added in November 1934 and two three-engined Junkers Ju 52/3m (later increased to four) went into service on 5 August 1936 on new route between Sao Paulo and Rio de Janeiro, which soon became the busiest sector in Brazil. Douglas DC-3s were introduced in January 1946, eventually building up to a fleet of 25 aircraft, joined in 1950 by the first of 15 Saab Scandia, ordered by Aerovias but transferred to VASP after state government acquired Aerovias' shares. Network strengthened during 1950s with important new destinations including the key coastal route between Rio and Natal. It was party to the world's first non-reservation service, established on 6 July 1959 over Rio-Sao Paulo 'Ponte Aérea' air-bridge in pool with Varig and Cruzeiro do Sul. When VASP took over Loide Aéreo Nacional on 4 April 1962 as part of the rationalisation of the airline industry in Brazil, its network served 75 cities in all states. Fleet was modernised with new turboprop and jet aircraft, culminating in November 1982 with the introduction of the wide-body Airbus A300B2-200 for high-density routes. VASP was privatised on 4 September 1990 and

started a gradual programme of international expansion, following removal of Varig's monopoly. International services were started to Los Angeles and San Francisco in October 1991, followed by trans-Atlantic flights to Brussels. Long-haul fleet was then standardised on McDonnell Douglas MD-11, first delivered in February 1992.

Brazil's second-largest airline now provides a comprehensive domestic network to all Brazilian states, together with a growing network of international services, linking Sao Paulo and Rio de Janeiro with other points in the Americas, and across the South Atlantic to Europe. It also operates the 'Ponte Aérea' air-bridge between Rio and Sao Paulo, jointly with Varig and Transbrasil. It carries 3 million passengers and 62,000 tonnes of cargo, and employs 11,000 people. Shareholders are the VOE/Canhedo Group (60 per cent) and the Sao Paulo State Government (40 per cent). It has itself bought a 50.1 per cent controlling interest in Ecuatoriana, founded in July 1974, and a 49 per cent holding in Bolivian flag-carrier LAB Airlines (Lloyd Aéreo Boliviano). Founded on 15 September 1925, LAB serves 13 domestic points and 17 international destinations within the Americas.

Fleet Data
3 Airbus A300B2-100, **1** Boeing 727-200, **2** 727-200F, **20** 737-200, **2** 737-200F, **2** 737-300, **9** McDonnell Douglas MD-11.

VASP McDonnell Douglas MD-11.

VIRGIN ATLANTIC AIRWAYS (VS)

Colourful Virgin Atlantic Airways was initially founded by Randolph Fields as British Atlantic Airways, but was renamed when Richard Branson's Virgin Group took over. Low-cost, high-quality services were started on 22 June 1984 from London Gatwick to Newark, New Jersey with a Boeing 747-100. A Miami service was opened prior to the delivery of two 747-200Bs in 1986. After a long struggle against British Airways and the UK authorities, Virgin Atlantic obtained access to London Heathrow in January 1991, and the New York, Los Angeles and Tokyo services were transferred there from July. The network was further expanded with new Airbus A340-300s, which joined the fleet in December 1993, and the Boeing 747-400 in May 1994.

Today, Virgin Atlantic provides value-for-money passenger services from London Heathrow to Hong Kong, Johannesburg, Los

Virgin Atlantic Airways Boeing 747-400.

Angeles, New York (JFK and Newark), San Francisco, Washington DC, and Tokyo. Services from London Gatwick link Boston, Miami and Orlando, with the last-named also served from Manchester. Athens is served from both London airports. Virgin Express is a subsidiary based at Brussels which was established in May 1996 when the Virgin Group acquired a 90 per cent interest in EuroBelgium Airlines. Virgin Atlantic carries more than 2 million passengers and employs 4,000 people.

Fleet Data
8 Airbus A340-300, **1** A320-200, **8** A340-600, **1** Boeing 747-100, **5** 747-200B, **4 (2)** 747-400.

World Airways McDonnell Douglas MD-11.

WORLD AIRWAYS (WO)

World Airways was founded on 29 March 1948 and, after being taken over by Ed Daly in 1959, World Airways became a leading US supplemental carrier. It started with two leased Curtiss C-46A Commandos, but soon doubled the fleet with purchase of two ex-military Douglas C-54 (DC-4), used on leisure travel and military charter work. From 11 April 1950 it offered a low-fare coast-to-coast service, and in 1956 was awarded military contracts to serve all Far Eastern ports. A further major step forward came in 1959 when the carrier gained worldwide charter rights, except for services from the USA to Canada and Mexico. The first 707 jet entered service in September 1963. After ending of the Vietnam War, its business changed from predominantly military to commercial contracts. The jet fleet was further enlarged with various types, but from March 1978, World standardised on the Douglas DC-10-30CF. It inaugurated scheduled, low-cost coast-to-coast service on 11 April 1979, linking Los Angeles, Oakland, Newark and Baltimore, but these ceased in 1986. Another attempt to re-enter the scheduled market in 1993 also proved short-lived. In 1994 World Airways became the first airline to take delivery of McDonnell Douglas MD-11F freighter, and in spring 1996 of the extended-range MD-11ER.

World Airways now concentrates on worldwide passenger and cargo charter flights, with the emphasis on cargo, as well as leasing services. It is part of a seven-airline 'teaming arrangement' providing contract flight for the US Department of Defense, which accounts for 20 per cent of revenue. Major shareholders are WorldCorp (59 per cent) and MHS of Malaysia (17 per cent).

Fleet Data
3 McDonnell Douglas DC-10-30, **1** DC-10-30F, **4** MD-11, **2** MD-11ER, **3** MD-11F.